Hertfordshire
COUNTY COUNCIL
Community Information

7/12

Please renew/return this item by the last date shown.

So that your telephone call is charged at local rate,
please call the numbers as set out below:

	From Area codes 01923 or 020:	From the rest of Herts:
Renewals:	01923 471373	01438 737373
Enquiries:	01923 471333	01438 737333
Minicom:	01923 471599	01438 737599

L32

D1514586

WINSTON S. CHURCHILL
1874–1965

WINSTON S. CHURCHILL

by

MARTIN GILBERT

VOLUME III
Companion
Part 1
Documents
July 1914 – April 1915

HEINEMANN : LONDON

William Heinemann Ltd
15 Queen St, Mayfair, London W1X 8BE
LONDON   MELBOURNE   TORONTO
JOHANNESBURG   AUCKLAND

434 13012 5
First published 1972

Printed in Great Britain by
Butler & Tanner Ltd, Frome and London

Contents

PART I

INTRODUCTION   vii

ACKNOWLEDGEMENTS   xiii

JULY 1914   1

AUGUST 1914   9

SEPTEMBER 1914   74

OCTOBER 1914   147

NOVEMBER 1914   243

DECEMBER 1914   288

JANUARY 1915   357

FEBRUARY 1915   477

MARCH 1915   593

APRIL 1915   764

PART 2

MAY 1915   839

JUNE 1915   975

JULY 1915   1068

AUGUST 1915   1114

SEPTEMBER 1915   1165

OCTOBER 1915   1190

NOVEMBER 1915   1247

DECEMBER 1915   1298

JANUARY 1916   1350

FEBRUARY 1916   1407

MARCH 1916   1439

APRIL 1916   1476

MAY 1916   1497

JUNE 1916   1509

JULY 1916   1522

AUGUST 1916   1534

SEPTEMBER 1916   1551

OCTOBER 1916   1572

NOVEMBER 1916   1582

DECEMBER 1916   1589

MAPS   1591

INDEX   1613

Introduction

THIS VOLUME OF documents spans Churchill's career
from July 1914 to December 1916. It is in two parts: the
first covers Churchill's wartime months as First Lord of the
Admiralty from August 1914 until April 1915; the second, the
period from the political crisis of May 1915, when Churchill had
to leave the Admiralty, to December 1916, during which time
he was successively Chancellor of the Duchy of Lancaster,
a battalion commander on the western front, and a Member
of Parliament, holding no political office, and in continual
opposition to Government policy.

Many of the documents quoted here were first published, a
few in full, some in part, but most only in brief extract, in
Winston S. Churchill, Volume III. A substantial number are
published here for the first time.

The text of more than half of these documents is taken from
the Churchill papers; the text of the remainder comes from over
seventy different archival sources. Other than the Churchill
papers, the principal archives used for official material are those
of the Admiralty and the Cabinet Office. Among private
archives, those of Baroness Spencer-Churchill and the Hon Mrs
Edwin Montagu both provided substantial material. The
Spencer-Churchill papers include all Churchill's letters to his
wife written from the front between January and May 1916;
and the Montagu papers contain the letters which Asquith
wrote to Venetia Stanley between August 1914 and May 1915.
From these, as from the other archives consulted, I have restricted my selection to those letters and documents which help
to establish the range of Churchill's activities, to show the
development of the policies with which he was involved, and to

delineate the evolution of his ideas and character. Sometimes these documents provide the wider historical perspective in which Churchill's actions must be seen; sometimes they contain detailed accounts of the events with which he was connected.

The selection is not restricted to Churchill's own writings. I have tried wherever possible to indicate the context in which Churchill was putting forward his opinion, and the part played by his colleagues in influencing the policies with which he was associated. I have therefore printed in full not only Churchill's proposals at the end of December 1914 for breaking the stalemate in the western front, but also the suggestions put forward, in the same week, by both Lloyd George (quoted on p 350), and Lieutenant-Colonel Hankey (p 337). Similarly, I have printed substantial extracts from the minutes both of the War Council and the Dardanelles Committee, even when Churchill was not the principal speaker. I have also included several extracts from his brother John's diary, for the period in which John Churchill was serving on Sir Ian Hamilton's staff at the Dardanelles; and I have printed in full Josiah Wedgwood's remarkable letter written before, during and after the 'V' beach landing of 25 April 1915 on the Gallipoli Peninsula (p 825).

Among the material included in this volume for Churchill's ten wartime months as First Lord of the Admiralty are his detailed proposals, drawn up five days after the outbreak of war, for naval action against the north German coast (p 24). I have printed in full the correspondence provoked within the Admiralty by Lord Charles Beresford's attack on the loyalty of Prince Louis of Battenberg (p 66) and also the acrimonious exchange of letters between Churchill and Austen Chamberlain about the Liberal Government's Irish policy (p 109). I have also included Sir John Jellicoe's appeals for secrecy about the sinking of the battleship *Audacious* (p 220) and Valentine Fleming's account of the conditions of trench warfare in November 1914 (p 272). For the first time, Lord Fisher's memorandum on the possibility of an offensive naval policy in the Baltic Sea is printed in full (p 284), together with Churchill's detailed plans, drawn up in the same month, for the capture of the island of Sylt, off the German North Sea coast (p 291).

For the Dardanelles and Gallipoli campaigns I have printed in full many documents bearing on the evolution of the naval and military attacks, including Rear-Admiral Limpus' assessment, on 26 August 1914, of the political situation in Constantinople after the outbreak of the European war (p 56) and Major Cunliffe-Owen's assertion, on the following day, that troops would have to be used if an attack on the Dardanelles were to succeed (p 61). I have also printed Major-General Callwell's memorandum of 3 September 1914, in which he envisaged 60,000 men taking part in the attack (p 81); Balfour's criticisms of an offensive against Turkey (p 363); Sir Henry Jackson's detailed plan of attack on the Dardanelles (p 506); Sir Mark Sykes' letter to Churchill about the morale and psychology of the Turks (p 581); General Birdwood's doubts about the possibility of forcing the Dardanelles by ships alone (p 637) and Kitchener's instructions of 13 March 1915 to Sir Ian Hamilton (p 684).

For the months following the attack I have printed a selection of materials dealing with the naval, military and political aspects of the continuing crisis, including Sir Ian Hamilton's letter to Sir John French describing the tactical situation in June 1915 (p 1028) and a letter from a Liberal MP, Harold Cawley, describing the same situation in less hopeful terms, shortly before he was killed in action (p 1049). Churchill's own views of what should be done can be followed in a series of four memoranda which he wrote on 4 October (p 1193), 5 October (p 1197), 7 October (p 1205) and 15 October 1915 (p 1220), some of his most prolific ten days during the First War, including, as they did, four meetings of the Dardanelles Committee on 6, 7, 11 and 14 October (pp 1200, 1208, 1213, 1216). I have also included a selection of the many letters which he received when he left the Admiralty in May 1915, and a further selection when he resigned from the Cabinet in November 1915.

During Churchill's six months on the western front, between November 1915 and April 1916, the fullest material, both personal and political, is contained in his letters to his wife. For this period there are also several letters of political gossip from his mother, and a charming letter of encouragement from his sister-in-law, Lady Gwendeline Churchill (p 1386). I have also printed in full a long letter sent to him by Lord Curzon, describing Cabinet proceedings in the last week of November 1915, when the decision had to be taken about the future of the Gallipoli campaign (p 1294). Also included are Churchill's detailed proposals for some mechanical means of breaking the stalemate on the western front (p 1303) and Tennyson D'Eyncourt's account of the development of the tank by February 1916 (p 1422). Lord Fisher's seven appeals to Churchill to give up his military duties and take the lead in trying to overthrow the Government are printed in full (beginning on p 1439).

In the second half of 1916 Churchill divided his energies between attacking the Government's conduct of the war and presenting his evidence to the Dardanelles Commission of Enquiry. I have printed in full his criticism of the Somme offensive, a criticism which was circulated to the Cabinet on 1 August 1916 (p 1534), and the final draft of the statement which he read to the Dardanelles Commission on 8 September 1916 (p 1553).

The documents published in this volume form only a small proportion of those available in the Churchill papers, or in the principal archives elsewhere. I have selected them in the hope that they will provide a practical guide to Churchill's life during the first two and a half years of the First World War. In order to make the book as serviceable as possible, I have prepared an itemized index to all the individuals mentioned. The volume is divided into monthly sections, and the documents printed in chronological order. Where possible, telegrams are arranged hour by hour within a single day.

I have standardized the headings of the documents, putting the date on the left of the heading, and the address on the right. The spelling and printing styles of the original documents have been retained. For example, ships' names in an incoming telegram put before Churchill at the Admiralty were usually printed in capitals, but in other documents they were either inside inverted commas, or simply given a capital letter like a surname: in each instance I have used the original style. I have not altered the spellings of place names within the documents; the Gallipoli Peninsula was particularly fertile in variants: thus

Gaba Tepe was sometimes spelt Kaba Tepe, Eren Koi was spelt Arenkeui, and Sedd-el Bahr was spelt Seddul Bahr. All words underlined in the original document have been printed in italics.

I have used footnotes to elaborate the historical background, and to provide relevant material not explicit in the documents themselves. A series of sixteen maps covering the areas mentioned in the volume—the North Sea, the Baltic, the Dardanelles and the Western front—are printed on pages 1590–1608.

Every individual mentioned in the documents is given a short biographical note on the first occasion he or she appears in the text. For a few people I have been unable to find any biographical material. These are: the Commander and Navigator of HMS *Edgar* in November 1915; Flight-Lieutenant Brown and Petty Officer Merchant (Royal Naval Air Service pilots at the Dardanelles); Mrs G. Gillespie of Edinburgh and her sons; J. McMath, a merchant navy Captain; S. H. Phillips, an Admiralty Clerk in July 1914; Lance Corporal Urquhart, of the Machine Gun Corps, and Private H. C. Waterlow, of the Army Service Corps.

I should much welcome any corrections or additions on points of detail, and any new documentation, for subsequent editions.

Martin Gilbert

Merton College
Oxford
30 March 1972

Acknowledgements

THE PREPARATION OF this volume began in October 1962, when Mr Randolph Churchill asked me to devote my principal researches to gathering documentary materials for the years 1914 to 1922. This I did for nearly five years. During those years I was helped by the friendship and guidance of Mr Michael Wolff, who directed the research, and by Randolph Churchill's personal assistant, Mr Andrew Kerr.

Nearly three-quarters of the documents printed here for the years 1914 to 1916 had been selected, and set up in type, by the time of Randolph Churchill's death in June 1968. Since then, while writing Main Volume III, I continued the search for new material both in the Churchill papers and elsewhere. I was assisted in this by Dr Sidney Aster, who worked in the Public Record Office on my behalf, and by Jane K. Cousins, who advised on the selection. I also am grateful to Dr Cameron Hazlehurst for many valuable suggestions, and to Susie Sacher, who read the volume in both galley and page proof, and helped me to compile the index. In preparing the footnotes, I was fortunate to be able to call upon Kate Fleming, whose perseverance led to the discovery of much elusive detail.

Many individuals and institutions sent me material, otherwise unobtainable, which enabled me to complete the biographical notes. Without this help, I could not have carried out my intention to include a note for every person mentioned in the text. In addition to those who provided material which was used in the notes in Main Volume III, and whom I acknowledged there, I should like to thank those who gave me material for the extra notes which appear in this volume alone: Mr. H. Aitken, Secretary, Clydesdale Bank Limited; Mr Walter Annenberg,

Ambassador of the United States of America, London; Mr Hirosuke Arai, Co-ordinating Officer, Japan Information Centre, London; Miss J. Atkinson, Savory and Moore Limited; J. Audouy, Chef du Service Historique de la Marine, Paris; Mr Mark Barrington-Ward, Editor, *Oxford Mail*; Dr Richard Blaas, Direktor des Haus-, Hof- und Staatsarchivs, Öster-reichisches Staatsarchiv, Vienna; M. Jean Bruno, Conservateur, Bibliothèque Nationale, Paris; Major C. W. G. Bullocke, Staff College, Camberley; Miss J. M. R. Campbell, Archivist, National Westminster Bank Limited, London; Lady Carey Evans; Mr A. J. R. Collins, Withers, Solicitors, London; Mr T. G. Downes, Lord Mayor's Secretary, Birmingham; Dr Michael Dunnill, Director of Clinical Studies, University of Oxford; Mustafa Ertürk, Assistant Cultural Attaché, Turkish Embassy, London; D. W. Evans, Rare Book Librarian, The University of Birmingham; Mr J. W. Fawcett, Mayor's Secretary, Scarborough; Mr J. H. Fegarty, Deputy Secretary, Midland Bank Limited, London; Général de Division, Fournier, Chef du Service Historique de l'Armée, Vincennes, France; M. Jean Guéguinou, French Embassy, London; Lord Hartwell; the Director, Heeresgeschichtliches Museum (Militärwissen-schaftliches Institut), Vienna; Mr Michael Hichisson, Managing Director, Debenham & Freebody, London; Mr T. L. Ingram, Archivist, Baring Brothers & Co, Limited, London; D. H. Johnson, Secretary, Barclays Bank Limited, London; Therese J. Lang, Press and Public Relations Officer, Fortnum & Mason Ltd; Mr E. A. McClean, Managing Director, Selfridges, London; His Grace the Duke of Marlborough; E. Menhofer, Press Attaché, Austrian Embassy, London; Dr Elizabeth Monroe, Middle East Centre, St Antony's College, Oxford; Ruggero Moscati, President of the Commission for the Publication of Diplomatic Documents, Ministry of Foreign Affairs, Rome; Sir Leslie O'Brien, Governor of the Bank of England; D. B. Omand, Naval Home Division, Ministry of Defence, London; Dr Sasse, Auswärtiges Amt, Bonn; P. J. Saunders, Secretary, Associated Newspapers Group Limited, London; Mr D. A. Savory; Mr H. E. Scrope, Vickers Limited, London; Miss Ann Sheehy, Central Asian Research Centre; Mr H. J. C. Stevens,

Secretary, *The Daily Telegraph and Morning Post*; Mr W. A. Taylor, City Librarian, Birmingham Public Libraries; Sir Burke Trend, Cabinet Office, London; Mr William Ugeux, General Manager, Institut Belge, Brussels; Dr Wagner, Direktor des Kriegsarchivs, Österreichiches Staatsarchiv, Vienna; Rear-Admiral A. Walbaum, Naval Attaché and Chief of the Naval Mission, Chilean Embassy, London; D. J. van Wijnen, Counsellor for Press Affairs and Information, Royal Netherlands Embassy, London; and Mr S. F. Wise, Director, Directorate of History, Department of National Defence, Ottawa.

For help in providing documentary material and factual information subsequent to the publication of Main Volume III I should like to thank Colonel T. A. Cave; the Dowager Marchioness of Cholmondeley; Dr Christopher Dowling; Miss Anita Leslie; Professor Paul G. Halpern; Commander Norman D. Holbrook, VC; and Wing-Commander H. A. Williamson.

I am grateful to all those who gave permission to publish material in which they hold the copyright, and in particular to Her Majesty's Stationery Office, who gave me permission to reproduce Crown Copyright material.

Most of the typing was done by Miss Sarah Graham, and in the latter stages of the work by Mrs Wendy Lofts, to both of whom my sincerest thanks are due.

It is to Randolph Churchill's guidance and enthusiasm that I owe my understanding of the importance of the publication of documents as a means to historical clarity, and my determination to make this volume as comprehensive as possible.

July 1914

Admiralty to Sir George Callaghan[1]*: telegram*

(*Copy, Admiralty papers: 137/50*)

26 July 1914   Admiralty
4.00 pm

No ships of First Fleet or Flotillas are to leave Portland until further orders. Acknowledge.[2]

Winston S. Churchill to Prince Louis[3] *and Sir Archibald Moore*[4]

(*Admiralty papers: 137/880*)

28 July 1914   Admiralty
Secret

In case it may become necessary to acquire the 2 Turkish battleships[5] that are nearing completion in British yards, please formulate plans in detail

---

[1] George Astley Callaghan, 1852–1920. Entered Navy, 1865. Rear-Admiral, 1905. Knighted, 1909. Admiral commanding the First and Second Fleets, 1911–14. Commander-in-Chief, the Nore, 1915–18. Admiral of the Fleet, 1917.

[2] This telegram, which prevented the fleet being demobilized, was sent from the Admiralty by order of Prince Louis, although it was unsigned. Referring to it, Churchill wrote to him on 19 October 1914: 'The first step which secured the timely concentration of the Fleet was taken by you.' (*Churchill papers: 13/27.*)

[3] Prince Louis Alexander of Battenberg, 1854–1921. Cousin of George V. Naturalized as a British subject in 1868, when he entered the Royal Navy. First Sea Lord, 1912–14. At the King's request he discontinued the title of Prince and assumed the surname of Mountbatten, 1917. Created Marquess of Milford Haven, 1917. Admiral of the Fleet, 1921.

[4] Archibald Gordon Henry Wilson Moore, 1862–1934. Entered Navy, 1875. Naval assistant to Fisher, 1907–8. Director of Naval Ordnance and Torpedoes, 1909–12. Rear-Admiral, 1911. Third Sea Lord, 1912–14. Commander of 2nd Battle Cruiser Squadron, 1914; present at the actions in the Heligoland Bight, 28 August 1914, and Dogger Bank, 23 January 1915, after which relieved of his command on Jellicoe's insistence. Knighted, 1914. Admiral, 1919.

[5] The *Reshadieh* was ordered by the Turkish Government in 1911; the *Sultan Osman I* in 1913. Both ships had been under construction for the Brazilian Government before being purchased by the Turks. They cost Turkey a total of £3,680,650. On being taken over by the British they were renamed *Erin* and *Agincourt* respectively, and served with the Royal Navy throughout the war. After Turkey's surrender to the Allies on 30 October 1918, they remained in British possession.

showing exactly the administrative action involved in their acquisition and
the prospective financial transactions. Also let me know the earliest date
on which by concentrating work upon them they could be made available.

WSC

Sir Archibald Moore to Winston S. Churchill

(*Admiralty papers: 137/880*)

29 July 1914   Admiralty

I have given the D.I.D.[1] a table shewing *all* the vessels building in England for Foreign Governments, the condition & emergency dates of completion being given—We could get the Osman immediately, she is due to
leave England 16 Aug 1914, & crew arrives today. The Reshadieh could
be acquired in a fighting condition by the end of August. The financial
transactions would probably be best made by a direct offer to buy through
the Contractors.

AGHWM

Sir Eyre Crowe[2] to Sir Graham Greene[3]

(*Admiralty papers: 137/880*)

29 July 1914   Foreign Office
Urgent & Confidential

Sir:—
    I am to state, for the information of the Lords Commissioners of the
Admiralty, that Sir E. Grey[4] has learnt from a reliable source that the new

---

[1] Henry Francis Oliver, 1865–1965. Entered Navy, 1878. Naval Assistant to Sir John
Fisher, 1908–10. Rear-Admiral, 1913. Director of the Intelligence Division at the Admiralty,
1913–14. Churchill's Naval Secretary, October 1914. Acting Vice-Admiral and Chief of the
Admiralty War Staff, November 1914 to 1917. Knighted, 1916. Commanded 1st Battle
Cruiser Squadron, 1918. Commanded the Home Fleet, 1919; the Reserve Fleet, 1919–20.
Second Sea Lord, 1920–4. Admiral, 1923. Commander-in-Chief, Atlantic Fleet, 1924–7.
Admiral of the Fleet, 1928.

[2] Eyre Crowe, 1864–1925. Entered Foreign Office as a Clerk, 1885; Senior Clerk, 1906.
Knighted, 1911. Assistant Under-Secretary of State, Foreign Office, 1912–19; Permanent
Under-Secretary of State, 1920–5.

[3] William Graham Greene, 1857–1950. Entered Admiralty, 1881. Private Secretary to
successive First Lords of the Admiralty, 1887–1902. Principal Clerk, Admiralty, 1902–7.
Assistant Secretary, Admiralty, 1907–11. Knighted, 1911. Permanent Secretary, Admiralty,
1911–17. Secretary, Ministry of Munitions, 1917–20.

[4] Edward Grey, 1862–1933. 3rd Baronet, 1882. Liberal MP, 1885–1916. Foreign Secretary,
1905–16. Created Viscount Grey of Fallodon, 1916. Ambassador on a special Mission to the
USA, 1919.

Turkish battleship, built by Messrs Armstrong Whitworth and Co, is being equipped with coal today and is under orders to proceed to Constantinople as soon as possible, though still unfinished.

I am, Sir, Your most obedient humble Servant

Eyre A. Crowe

Sir Archibald Moore to Winston S. Churchill

(*Admiralty papers: 137/880*)

29 July 1914   Admiralty

First L,

I have consulted the second legal adviser to the F.O. (Mr Hurst)[1] as to the international question involved in taking over the two Turkish ships & the position appears to be as follows:—

The ships are the property of the Turkish Govt & though it may be true that the ships are not in commission & flying the national flag yet this would not affect the question of proprietary rights—

There is no precedent for seizing a foreign man of war in time of peace & adding her to the fleet of the state where she may happen to be.

In time of war it is a question of might & not of law & it becomes a question of policy whether to exercise the arbitrary rights of belligerency.

It would seem that at the present time, if action is desired, it should take the form of getting the builders to prevent by some means or other the ships being commissioned—

If it is desired to obtain them at once it should be by negotiation with the Turkish Govt.

If hostilities are imminent, then it would become a question of taking forcible possession of the ships, paying compensation & risking the result of such action.

Winston S. Churchill to Prince Louis and Sir Archibald Moore

(*Admiralty papers: 137/880*)

29 July 1914   Admiralty

The builders shd by every means prevent & delay the departure of these ships while the situation is strained: & in no case shd they be allowed to leave without express permission.

[1] Cecil James Barrington Hurst, 1870–1963. Called to the Bar, 1893. Assistant Legal Adviser, Foreign Office, 1902–18. British Delegate, International Naval Conference, London, 1908. Legal Adviser, Foreign Office, 1918–20. Knighted, 1920. Judge of the Permanent Court of International Justice at the Hague, 1929–46; President, 1934–46. Chairman of the United Nations War Crimes Commission, 1943–4.

If necessary authority will be given to restrain them.

If war comes they can be taken over as shown in your last paragraph. Report to me what is being done.

WSC

Sir Graham Greene to Captain Power[1]

(*Copy, Cabinet papers: 1/34*)

29 July 1914   Admiralty
Secret

Captain Superintendent of Contract-built ships, Tyne,

I am to inform you that in view of present European circumstances, His Majesty's Government have decided that the battleship 'Osman' building at Messrs Armstrong's works cannot be permitted to be handed over into the hands of any foreign purchaser or to be commissioned or manned as a public ship of a foreign navy or to leave the jursidiction of this country.[2]

Their Lordships desire that you will put yourself in communication with Messrs Armstrong, who have been informed confidentially of the above through their representatives in London, Mr Saxton Noble[3] and Sir Percy Girouard,[4] and that you will keep the Admiralty advised of any action that may be taken with regard to this ship and take any necessary steps to prevent her leaving the Tyne for trials or any other purpose, if such should be called for.

In connection with this, you are authorised, if requisite, to communicate with the police or with the officer commanding the troops in the district should it be necessary in any eventuality that force should be employed to give effect to these instructions.

You are particularly enjoined to exercise great discretion in any action

[1] Laurence Eliot Power, 1864–1927. Entered Navy, 1877. Captain, 1905. Captain Superintendent of Contract Work on the Tyne, 1912–15. Director of Dockyards and Repairs, 1915–23. Rear-Admiral, 1916. Vice-Admiral, 1920. Knighted, 1921. Admiral, 1925.

[2] A similar letter was sent on the same day from Sir Graham Greene to Sir Arthur Nicolson informing him that arrangements had been made to take over the Turkish battleship *Reshadieh*, being built by Vickers at Barrow-in-Furness.

[3] Saxton William Armstrong Noble, 1863–1942. Director of the Mond Nickel Company and the Whitehead Torpedo Company. Managing Director, Armstrong, Whitworth and Company. Succeeded his brother as 3rd Baronet, 1937

[4] Edouard Percy Cranwill Girouard, 1867–1932. Entered Royal Engineers, 1888. Major, responsible for the construction of the Sudan railway during the Nile Expedition, 1896–8. Director of Railways in South Africa through the Boer War. Knighted, 1900. Governor and Commander-in-Chief, East Africa Protectorate, 1909–12. A director of Armstrong, Whitworth & Co, 1912. Director-General of Munitions Supply, 1915–17; resigned to return to Armstrong, Whitworth.

that you may take, and to use every means in your power to secure the absolute secrecy of these orders.

By Command of Their Lordships

Sir John Simon[1] to Winston S. Churchill
(Admiralty papers: 137/880)

30 July 1914   Attorney General

The Foreign Enlistment Act 1870 does not apply unless the ship is handed over with the interest of its being employed by a foreign state at war with a friendly state, or with *reasonable cause to believe* this. But 'salus republicae suprema lex' & I think the notice might run thus:

'In view of present circumstances Messrs. Armstrong must understand that the Government cannot permit the ship to be handed over to a foreign buyer, or to be commissioned as a public ship of a foreign navy, or to leave their jurisdiction.'

Sir Eyre Crowe: minute
(Foreign Office papers: 371/2137)

30 July 1914   Foreign Office

I think we must let the Admiralty deal with this question as they consider necessary, and afterwards make such defence of our action to Turkey as we can.

EAC

Sir Archibald Moore to Winston S. Churchill
(Admiralty papers: 137/880)

30 July 1914   Admiralty

The Battleship 'Osman I' built by Elswick for the Turkish Government is now complete. She is a very powerful ship, and her possession by any Nation would be a serious factor in the balance of naval strength. It is

[1] John Allsebrook Simon, 1873–1954. Liberal MP, 1906–18; 1922–31. Solicitor-General, 1910–13. Knighted, 1911. Attorney-General, with a seat in the Cabinet, 1913–15. Home Secretary, May 1915–January 1916, when he resigned in opposition to conscription. Major, Royal Air Force, serving in France, 1917–18. Liberal National MP, 1931–40. Secretary of State for Foreign Affairs, 1931–5. Home Secretary, 1935–7. Chancellor of the Exchequer, 1937–40. Created Viscount, 1940. Lord Chancellor, 1940–5.

therefore contrary to the Public Interest that she should be permitted to leave England at the present moment. Her original arrangements were for the ship to carry out gun trials, dock in a Government dock, embark ammunition, and leave for Turkey late in August. During the past few days the Turkish crew has arrived in the Tyne, and the Turkish authorities are pressing Messrs. Armstrong to hoist the Turkish flag on board the ship. The balance of the purchase money, about £800,000, is due, and Messrs. Armstrong have received cables from their agent which lead them to believe the money will be found today or tomorrow and deposited in a British bank. When that has been done Messrs. Armstrong will be unable to advance reasons for not hoisting the flag, which the Turkish authorities propose should be done on Saturday, the ship leaving on Monday for gun trials, docking being dispensed with, and the ship to leaving English waters as soon as possible. Messrs. Armstrong have been pressed to put all difficulties in the way of hoisting the flag, for it is obvious that once the Turkish ensign is hoisted, the action of detaining the vessel may involve questions of very serious import.

AGHWM

Winston S. Churchill to H. H. Asquith[1]

(*Admiralty papers: 137/452*)

31 July 1914   Admiralty
Most Secret

Prime Minister,

Last year by my directions Admiral Bayly,[2] Colonel Aston[3] & Admiral Leveson[4] made a prolonged examination of all points on the German, Dutch,

---

[1] Herbert Henry Asquith, 1852–1928. Liberal MP, 1886–1918; 1920–4. Home Secretary, 1892–5. Chancellor of the Exchequer, 1905–8. Prime Minister, 1908–16. Secretary of State for War, 30 March–5 August 1914; acting Secretary of State for War, 5–30 November 1915 and 6 June–5 July 1916. Created Earl of Oxford and Asquith, 1925.

[2] Lewis Bayly, 1857–1938. Entered Navy, 1870. Vice-Admiral commanding the 3rd Battle Squadron, 1913–14. Knighted, 1914. Commanded the 1st Battle Squadron, 1914–15. Commander-in-Chief of the Western Approaches, 1915–19. Admiral, 1917.

[3] George Grey Aston, 1861–1938. Entered Royal Marine Artillery, 1879. Naval Intelligence Department, Admiralty, 1887–80. Professor of Fortification, Royal Naval College, Greenwich, 1896–9. Brigadier-General, General Staff, South Africa, 1908–12. Attached to the Admiralty War Staff for special services, 1913–14. Knighted, 1913. Commanded the Marine expeditions to Ostend and Dunkirk, 1914. Retired from active service through ill-health, 1914. Employed in the War Cabinet Secretariat 1918–19. Military historian and biographer.

[4] Arthur Cavenagh Leveson, 1868–1929. Midshipman, 1883. Rear-Admiral, 1913. Director of Operations Division, Admiralty, 1914–15. Served at the Battle of Jutland, 1916. Knighted, 1919. Commanded the Second Battle Squadron, 1919–20. Commander-in-Chief, China Station, 1922–4.

Danish, Swedish & Norwegian coasts, suitable for oversea bases for offensive action against Germany.[1]

Their reports are attached with charts etc.

It is now necessary that the War Office shd study these plans so that military and naval action can be coordinated & concerted in harmony.

Two officers of highest attainments shd therefore be detailed in strictest secrecy for this duty. Reports shd deal with each project separately, and without regard either to (a) questions of violation of neutrality (b) questions of whether the troops could be better employed elsewhere. These are matters of policy wh must be decided later by higher authorities.

From the Admiralty Colonel Aston, & Major Ollivant[2] will be detailed: & Admiral Leveson will be available if naval questions require further elucidation.

No time shd be lost. Reports shd be furnished one by one. I do not now discuss the questions of policy.

The following shd be the order in wh the work shd be undertaken

1. Ameland or Born deep
2. Ekersund
3. Laeso Channel
4. Kungsbacka Fiord
5. Esbjerg ⎫ These last 4 are less
6. Sylt ⎪ urgent on account of
7. Borkum ⎬ the forces required being
8. Heligoland ⎭ probably not available.

WSC

Sir Graham Greene to Sir John Jellicoe[3]
(Jellicoe papers)

31 July 1914　　　　　　　　　　　　　　　　　Admiralty

Sir,

I am commanded by my Lords Commissioners of the Admiralty to inform you that, in the circumstances which will have arisen when the present letter

[1] See map 1 on page 1592.

[2] Alfred Henry Ollivant, 1871–1919. Entered Royal Artillery, 1891. Major, 1911. General Staff Officer attached to the Colonial Office, 1909–11, and to the Admiralty, 1913–14. Lieutenant-Colonel, September 1914. Attached to the Royal Naval Division at Antwerp, October 1914; the Dardanelles, 1915; France, 1916–17.

[3] John Rushworth Jellicoe, 1859–1935. Entered Navy, 1872. Captain, 1897. Knighted, 1907. Vice-Admiral, 1910. Second Sea Lord, 1912–14. Commander-in-Chief of the Grand Fleet, 1914–16. Admiral, 1915. First Sea Lord, 1916–17. Chief of the Naval Staff, 1917. Created Viscount, 1918. Admiral of the Fleet, 1919. Governor-General of New Zealand, 1920–4. Created Earl, 1925.

will have been opened, they have been pleased to select you to be Commander in Chief of the Grand or First Fleet in succession to Admiral Sir George Callaghan. You are therefore forthwith on receipt of orders to open this letter to repair with it on board H.M.S. 'Iron Duke', show it to Sir George Callaghan as your authority for so doing, and arrange with him for whatever immediate steps may be necessary to make your succession to his command effective. Thereafter Sir George Callaghan will come on shore.

I am, Sir, Your obedient servant

W. Graham Greene

Note on envelope:

ONLY to be opened on receipt of telegraphic instructions from the Admiralty to that effect, which will be conveyed in the words:—'Open secret personal envelope taken with you from London'.

August 1914

Sir John Jellicoe to Winston S. Churchill: telegram

(*Copy, Jellicoe papers*)

1 August 1914   Wick
10 pm

Detained Wick by fog. Am firmly convinced after consideration that the step you mentioned to me is fraught with gravest danger at this juncture and might easily be disastrous owing to the extreme difficulty of getting into touch with everything at short notice. The transfer even if carried out cannot be accomplished safely for some time. I beg earnestly that you will give the matter further consideration with First Sea Lord before you take steps.

Winston S. Churchill to Sir Archibald Moore

(*Admiralty papers: 137/880*)

1 August 1914   Admiralty

3rd Sea Lord

Simultaneously with the order to Mobilise you should notify the firms building foreign ships which are almost completed viz. the two Turkish battleships, destroyers at Messrs White, & the 3 Brazilian monitors[1] of our intention in the event of war to enter into negotiations for their purchase, & warn them not to permit them to pass into foreign hands or leave the country.

WSC

---

[1] The three Brazilian monitors were bought by the Royal Navy on the outbreak of the war with Germany. Each of them first saw action off the Belgian coast in October 1914. One, HMS *Humber*, was at the Dardanelles in the autumn of 1915, and the White Sea during the Intervention, 1919. Both her sister ships, HMS *Mersey* and HMS *Severn*, assisted in the destruction of the Königsberg in the Rufiji River in July 1915. HMS *Severn* later formed part of the British squadron and went to Constantinople and the Black Sea in November 1918, after the armistice.

Sir Arthur Nicolson[1] to Sir Edward Grey

(Foreign Office papers: 371/2137)

1 August 1914   Foreign Office

Sir Edward Grey,

The Turkish Ambad[2] called to enquire why the Turkish battleship had been 'embargoed' by the Admiralty. I told him that in view of the serious situation abroad it was not possible to allow a battleship to leave these waters and pass into the hands of a foreign buyer. Of course had she been here on a visit it would have been different, but it was considered that in the present tension it was not right to hand over to the buyer a newly built battleship. The Admiralty had, I believed, taken possession temporarily of her—as it would have been discourteous to have taken any steps once the Turkish flag had been hoisted and a Turkish crew placed on board. The Ambad seemed puzzled—and said three million pounds had been paid for the ship. I told him he would not lose the money. He asked for how long the ship would be detained. I told him we were before the unknown—& it was impossible to say.

                                                                        AN

Sir John Jellicoe to Winston S. Churchill and Prince Louis: telegram

(Copy, Jellicoe papers)

2 August 1914   Scapa

To First Lord and First Sea Lord

Reference my personal telegram last night, am more than ever convinced of vital importance of making no change. Personal feelings are entirely ignored in reaching this conclusion.

Winston S. Churchill to Sir John Jellicoe: telegram

(Jellicoe papers)

2 August 1914   Admiralty
received 8.30 pm

I can give you 48 hours after joining you must be ready then.

[1] Arthur Nicolson, 1849–1928. Entered Foreign Office, 1870. Knighted, 1888. 11th Baronet, 1899. Ambassador, St Petersburg, 1906–10. Permanent Under-Secretary for Foreign Affairs, 1910–16. Created Baron Carnock, 1916.

[2] Ahmed Tewfik Pasha, 1845–1936. Turkish Ambassador to Berlin, 1885–95. Foreign Minister, 1895 and 1908–9. Grand Vizier, 1909. Ambassador to London, 1909–14. Grand Vizier, 1921–22.

Winston S. Churchill: précis of a conversation

(*Copy, Admiralty papers: 137/988*)

2 August 1914   Admiralty

The First Lord in the presence of the First Sea Lord and Chief of the War Staff,[1] informed the French Naval Attaché[2] of the Cabinet's decision and the note on naval matters handed to M. Cambon[3] at 2.30 p.m., August 2nd.

But without prejudging this question, in order to prepare for the possibility of an alliance being concluded between the Governments, the following preliminary steps are to be taken:—

The package containing the secret signal books to be distributed and opened but not used.

Mutual regulations for the entry of allied ships into each other's ports to be issued now.

The officers in command of the Mediterranean and China Stations will be given permission to enter into communication with the French Senior Officers in command on their stations.

Certain staff questions were discussed, but the First Lord clearly pointed out that these involved no question of policy which would have to be decided by Parliament.

The general direction of the naval war to rest with the British Admiralty.

In the event of the neutrality of Italy being assured, France would undertake to deal with Austria assisted only by such British ships as would be required to cover German ships in that sea, and secure a satisfactory composition of the allied fleet. The direction of the allied fleets in the Mediterranean to rest with the French, the British Admiral being junior.

The arrangement come to locally on the China Station would be carried out under the general direction of the British Admiral.

British naval bases would be at the disposal of the French.

Should any portion of the German main fleet make its way South towards the Mediterranean, it would be followed by a superior British force.

[1] Frederick Charles Doveton Sturdee, 1859–1925. Entered Navy, 1871. Assistant Director of Naval Intelligence, 1900-2. Rear-Admiral, Home Fleet, 1909-10. Knighted, 1913. Chief of the Admiralty War Staff, 1914. Commander-in-Chief at the Battle of the Falkland Islands, December 1914. Commander of the Fourth Battle Squadron, 1915-18. Created Baronet, 1916. Admiral, 1917. Commander-in-Chief, the Nore, 1918-21.

[2] Jean Charles Just Benigne de Saint-Seine, 1865–1954. French Naval Attaché in London, 1911-16. Commanded the battleship *Démocratie* in the eastern Mediterranean, 1916.

[3] Paul Cambon, 1843–1924. French Ambassador in London, 1898-1920. Honorary knighthood, 1903. One of the most active promoters of the Anglo-French Entente of 1904.

The Attaché was asked to communicate the above at once to his Government by telegraph and obtain full knowledge and authority for a further discussion on details to-night.

WSC

Winston S. Churchill and Prince Louis to Sir Berkeley Milne:[1] telegram
(Copy, Churchill papers: 13/31)

2 August 1914   Admiralty

Goeben[2] must be shadowed by two Battle Cruisers. Approaches to Adriatic must be watched by Cruisers and Destroyers. Remain near Malta yourself.[3] It is believed that Italy will remain neutral but you cannot yet count absolutely on this.

Winston S. Churchill to Sir Berkeley Milne: telegram
(Milne papers)

2 August 1914   Admiralty
Sent 7.6 pm

You can enter into communication with the French Senior Officer on your station for combined action in case Great Britain should decide to become ally of France against Germany. Situation very critical. Be prepared to meet surprise attacks.

Winston S. Churchill to Sir Edward Grey and H. H. Asquith
(Copy, Churchill papers: 13/27)

3 August 1914   Admiralty
Urgent & Secret

We regard the part to be played in a naval war with Germany by the three small states bordering on the North Sea, viz Norway, Holland & Belgium, as of serious importance. The advantages wh their alliance wd offer us

---

[1] Archibald Berkeley Milne, 1855–1938. Entered Navy, 1869. Rear-Admiral, 1903. Knighted, 1904. Admiral, 1911. Commander-in-Chief of the Mediterranean Fleet, 1912–14.

[2] At the end of July the *Goeben*, a German battle cruiser, had been undergoing repairs in the Austro-Hungarian port of Pola, in the Adriatic. She had ten 11-inch guns, and a speed of 24 knots. On 1 August 1914 she was reported to be about to leave the Adriatic, having put in that day to the Italian port of Brindisi to coal, but having been refused permission to do so. She entered the Mediterranean on 2 August. The ship was commanded by Admiral Souchon, commander of the German Mediterranean Squadron.

[3] See map 2 on page 1593.

in blockading Germany & in controlling her naval movements cannot be over-estimated. Their decision appears now to be trembling in the balance, & strong action by England may rally them to our cause. Belgium is already resisting Germany, Holland evinces the strongest hostility to her, & Norway, if relieved of Russian fears, appears thoroughly friendly to us.

It is not our province to do more than place the naval aspects of the international situation strongly before you: & it is only as an indication of the sort of thing we think necessary that we suggest and press, in this or some other form, the following proposals:

Ask simultaneously, telling each that you have done so, these three countries whether they are willing to join an Anglo-French-Russian alliance, provided that the three Powers guarantee to maintain their independence & integrity by every means in our power, & not to withdraw from the war until these are upheld.

We do not refer to Denmark, not because we do not regard her inclusion as desirable, but because we feel the risk is a greater one than she should be asked to bear. We feel that any time lost in addressing these small states may result in losing great advantages; & that a firm initiative by England might secure them.

The Br attitude towards Portugal in naval matters requires special attention.

The Admy War Staff have recorded their opinion that if we had to choose between the friendship of Portugal & the friendship of Spain, that of Spain is of the greater value. The King of Spain[1] is strongly attached to England & France, and Spain might easily be made to range herself against the Germanic Powers. On the other hand, it is more than likely that Spain will take this opportunity of annexing Portugal.

Portugal also has minor useful services to render us, tho' not equal to those wh cd be derived from a Spanish alliance. The Portuguese Govt is not one with wh it wd be easy to act. We certainly do not want to get so involved with them that if Spain attempts to annex them we are expected to make exertions on their behalf, or to consider ourselves offended by what Spain has done. The Admy have asked that the Portuguese declaration of neutrality shd be delayed; & of course we shd prevent any Portuguese island or Colonies from being made use of by Germany.

The Portuguese Govt, if they have reason to apprehend a Spanish attack,

[1] Leon Fernando Maria Jaime Isidoro Pascual Antonio, 1886–1941. Posthumous son of King Alfonso XII of Spain, he was proclaimed King at birth (as Alfonso XIII). He married Victoria Eugénie, a granddaughter of Queen Victoria, in 1906. He was outlawed, and fled the country, following the Republican majority in the 1931 elections. He died in exile in Rome.

may be vy anxious to proffer their services, such as they are under the alliance, in the hope of obtaining protection against Spain. It is suggested therefore that our attitude towards Portugal shd be a cool one, & that we shd take as little service from them as possible. And if unfortunately Spain shd swallow them we shd be in a position to avail ourselves of the cooperation of Spain, in case it is available, & so get any facilities wh we may require, not only in the islands belonging to Spain, but also in those wh now belong to Portugal.

WSC
Battenberg
Sturdee

Winston S. Churchill to Sir Berkeley Milne: telegram
(Milne papers)

3 August 1914   Admiralty
Sent 12.50 am

Watch on mouth of Adriatic should be maintained but Goeben is your objective. Follow her and shadow her wherever she goes and be ready to act on declaration of war which appears probable and imminent.

Admiralty to Sir Berkeley Milne: telegram
(Copy, Churchill papers: 13/31)

3 August 1914   Admiralty

The two battle cruisers must proceed to Straits of Gibraltar at high speed ready to prevent 'Goeben' leaving Mediterranean.

Winston S. Churchill to Sir Edward Grey
(Grey papers)

3 August 1914   Admiralty

In connection with our minute attached, Mr Clerk[1] of the Foreign Office has asked how Norway is to be protected from Sweden. Our argument is

[1] George Russell Clerk, 1874–1951. Entered Diplomatic Service, 1898. 1st Secretary, Constantinople, 1910. Senior Clerk, Foreign Office, 1912. Knighted, 1917. Minister to the Czecho-Slovak Republic, 1919–26. Ambassador to Turkey, 1926–33; to Brussels, 1933–34; to Paris, 1934–7.

as follows: the Triple Entente possess substantial preponderance of the sea. Therefore, the invasion of Sweden by Russia is a practicable operation from the moment when it becomes convenient to establish the naval control of the Baltic. Let Russia tell Sweden she will not be attacked or molested in any way, so long as she observes a strict neutrality; but that if she attacks Norway this assurance must be completely withdrawn.

WSC

Winston S. Churchill to H. H. Asquith and Sir Edward Grey

(*Admiralty papers: 137/988*)

3 August 1914   Admiralty
for immediate action

Prime Minister
Sir Edward Grey

In consequence of declarations in the House this afternoon, I must request authorisation immediately to put into force the combined Anglo-French dispositions for the defence of the channel. The French have already taken station & this partial disposition does not ensure security.

My naval colleagues & advisers desire me to press for this; & unless I am forbidden I shall act accordingly. This of course implies no offensive action & no warlike action unless we are attacked.

WSC

Sir William Tyrrell:[1] *note*
5 pm
The Prime Minister & Sir E. Grey approve.   WT

Sir John Jellicoe to Winston S. Churchill and Prince Louis: telegram

(*Copy, Jellicoe papers*)

3 August 1914   Scapa
Personal

Yours of Second. Can only reply am certain step contemplated is most dangerous. Beg that it may not be carried out. Am perfectly willing to act on board Fleet Flagship as assistant if required to be in direct communication.

[1] William George Tyrrell, 1866–1947. Entered the Foreign Service, 1889. Private Secretary to Sir Edward Grey, 1907–15. Knighted, 1913. Assistant Under-Secretary of State at the Foreign Office, 1919–25; Permanent Under-Secretary, 1925–8. Ambassador in Paris, 1928–1934. Created Baron, 1929. President of the British Board of Film Censors, 1935–47.

Hard to believe it is realised what grave difficulties change Commander-in-Chief involves at this moment. Do not forget long experience of Commander-in-Chief.

Prince Louis: minute
(Admiralty papers: 137/880)

3 August 1914   Admiralty

The British Gov't are going to take over 'Osman I' forthwith.

Inform Elswick to make all arrangements. Negotiations as regards payment will follow.

Foreign Office to Henry Beaumont:[1] telegram
(Copy, Foreign Office papers: 371/2137)

3 August 1914   Foreign Office
8.10 pm

Please inform Turkish Govt that H.M.G. desire that the Contracts for the Turkish Battleship 'Osman I' now building by Armstrong Whitworth and Co should be transferred to H.M.G. Arrangements are being made with that firm for taking over the ship.

Sir John Jellicoe to Winston S. Churchill and Prince Louis: telegram
(Copy, Jellicoe papers)

4 August 1914   Scapa
9.15 am
Personal

Quite impossible to be ready at such notice. Feel it my duty to warn you emphatically you court disaster if you carry out intention of changing before I have thorough grip of fleet and situation. Am sure Hamilton,[2] Madden[3] or an admiral recently Home Fleet will be of my opinion.

---

[1] Henry Hamond Dawson Beaumont, 1867–1949. Entered Diplomatic Service, 1892. Counsellor, Constantinople, 1914; Rome, 1915–16. Minister to Venezuela, 1916–23. Knighted, 1926.

[2] Frederick Tower Hamilton, 1856–1917. Entered Navy, 1869. Vice-Admiral commanding the Second and Third Fleets, 1911–13. Knighted, 1913. Second Sea Lord, 1914–16. Commander-in-Chief, Rosyth, 1916–17.

[3] Charles Edward Madden, 1862–1935. Entered Navy, 1875. Jellicoe's wife's brother-in-law. Fourth Sea Lord, 1910–11. Rear-Admiral in the Home Fleet, 1911–12. Commanded the 3rd and 2nd Cruiser Squadrons in Home Fleet, 1912–14. Chief of Staff to Sir John Jellicoe, 1914–16. Knighted, 1916. 2nd in Command, Grand Fleet, 1917–19. Commander-in-Chief, Atlantic Fleet, 1919–22. Admiral of the Fleet, 1924. First Sea Lord and Chief of the Naval Staff, 1927–30.

Sir John Jellicoe to Winston S. Churchill and Prince Louis: telegram
(*Copy, Jellicoe papers*)

4 August 1914   Scapa
11.15 am

Add to my last message. Fleet is imbued with feelings of extreme admiration and loyalty for C-in-C. This is a very strong factor.

Winston S. Churchill to Sir John Jellicoe: telegram
(*Jellicoe papers*)

4 August 1914   Admiralty

Expeditionary force will not leave at present and therefore fleet movements with it will not be immediately required. I am sending Madden tonight to be at your side. I am telegraphing Commander-in-Chief directing him to transfer command to you at earliest moment suitable to the interests of the Service. I rely on him and you to effect this change quickly and smoothly, personal feelings cannot count now only what is best for us all. You should consult him frankly.

Winston S. Churchill to H. H. Asquith and Sir Edward Grey
(*Copy, Churchill papers: 13/45*)

4 August 1914   Admiralty
Most Urgent

German Battle Cruiser Goeben and fast Light Cruiser Breslau[1] have been found west of Sicily and are being shadowed by British Battle Cruisers Indomitable and Indefatigable. It would be a great misfortune to lose these vessels as is possible in the dark hours. She is evidently going to interfere with the French transports which are crossing today.
The following telegram has already been sent:—

'Good. Hold her. War imminent.'

We wish to add this:—

'If Goeben attacks French transports you should at once engage her.'

An immediate decision is required.

                                                                  WSC

[1] The *Breslau*, a German light cruiser, had joined the *Goeben* at Messina on 2 August 1914. She had bombarded the French north-african port of Bône on the morning of 4 August.

Admiralty to all ships: telegram
(*Milne papers*)

4 August 1914   Admiralty
Sent 2.5 pm

The British ultimatum to Germany will expire at midnight GMT August 4th. No act of war should be committed before that hour at which time the telegram to commence hostilities against Germany will be despatched from the Admiralty.

Special addition to Mediterranean, Indomitable, Indefatigable sent at 2.5 pm

This cancels the authorisation to Indomitable and Indefatigable to engage Goeben if she attacks French transports.

Admiralty to Sir Berkeley Milne: telegram
(*Copy, Churchill papers: 13/31*)

4 August 1914   Admiralty

The Italian Government have declared neutrality. You are to respect this neutrality rigidly and should not allow any of HM Ships to come within six miles of the Italian coast.

Walter Long[1] to Winston S. Churchill
(*Spencer-Churchill papers*)

4 August 1914
Private

Dear Winston Churchill,
Let me say that I feel you have placed us all under a debt which we cannot easily repay. This is no time for sentiment but it is right you should know that we realise and appreciate the work you have done in this supreme crisis.

Sincerely yours
Walter H Long

[1] Walter Hume Long, 1854–1924. Conservative MP, 1880–1921. President of the Local Government Board, 1900–5. Chief Secretary, Ireland, 1905. Created the Union Defence League, the leading anti-Home Rule organization, 1907–14. President of the Local Government Board, May 1915–December 1916. Under-Secretary of State for the Colonies, 1916–19. First Lord of the Admiralty, 1919–21. Created Viscount, 1921.

Sir Edward Grey to Henry Beaumont: telegram

(*Draft, Foreign Office papers: 371/2137*)

4 August 1914   Foreign Office
7.00 pm

I am sure Turkish Govt. will understand necessity for H.M. Govt. to keep all war ships available in England for their own needs in this crisis.

But financial & other loss to Turkey will receive all due consideration & is subject of sincere regret to H.M. Govt. You should inform Grand Vizier.[1]

EG

Winston S. Churchill to Sir Edward Grey

(*Grey Papers*)

5 August 1914   Admiralty

Sir Edward Grey,
    If Holland:—
        a. condones the violation of her territory by Germany
        b. closes the Scheldt to the supplies for Antwerp
        c. allows free importation of supplies to Germany through Rotterdam,
we shall be at grave disadvantage if we are forced to respect her neutrality.

She ought to accept our offer of alliance. Failing this we must insist on absolute equality with Germany in the use made by either belligerent of Dutch territory or ports.

WSC

Winston S. Churchill to Sir Edward Grey

(*Grey Papers*)

5 August 1914   Admiralty

We should be much obliged if you would send the following to the Belgian Government:—

'British Admiralty intend to keep open the mouths of the Scheldt for the supply of Antwerp, and they need have no fear on that score.'

---

[1] Mehmed Said Halim, 1863–1921. Grandson of Mehmet Ali of Egypt. Appointed to the Ottoman Council of State, 1888. President of the Council of State, 1912. Grand Vizier, 1913–17. Assassinated by Rumanians in Rome.

Sir Edward Carson[1] to Winston S. Churchill

(*Churchill papers: 2/64*)

5 August 1914

Dear Churchill,

I know too well what a strain you are going through & at such a moment a friendly line from an opponent may be a little help. Whatever bitterness has existed in the past[2] believe me I desire to shew to you my appreciation of the patriotic & courageous way you have acted in the present grave crisis for our country's best interests & the honour of the Empire. Whatever be the result you may rest assured that for whatever it is worth my present admiration of what you have done will not be transitory & I wish you every comfort & assurance in yr present anxieties that yr most devoted friends cd desire for you & I remain

Yrs sincerely
Edward Carson

John Gretton[3] to Winston S. Churchill

(*Spencer-Churchill papers*)

7 August 1914

Dear Churchill,

I have often as one of the Opposition written you controversial letters. I would like, at this time, to write something to give you pleasure. It is known that you have done well for the Admiralty and when the troops and Reservists marched down through Belfast to embark two nights ago your name was cheered enthusiastically. This comes from a reliable source a strong Orange man and relation of mine who is delighted differences are sunk to defend the country.

Yours sincerely
John Gretton

---

[1] Edward Henry Carson, 1854–1935. Conservative MP, 1892–1921. Knighted, 1900. Solicitor-General, 1900–6. Leader of the Ulster Unionists in the House of Commons, 1910–21. Attorney-General, May–October 1915. First Lord of the Admiralty, December 1916–July 1917. Minister without Portfolio in the War Cabinet, July 1917–January 1918. Created Baron, 1921.

[2] On 14 March 1914, speaking at Bradford during the Ulster crisis, Churchill had accused Carson of a 'treasonable conspiracy' against Home Rule. On 4 April 1914, at a rally in Hyde Park, Carson had described Churchill as 'the Belfast butcher'.

[3] John Gretton, 1867–1949. Director and Chairman of Bass, Ratcliffe and Gretton Limited, brewers. Conservative MP, 1895–1943. Created Baron, 1944.

Winston S. Churchill to Lord Kitchener[1]

(*Kitchener Papers*)

7 August 1914   Admiralty

My dear Kitchener,

I find on enquiry from our Transport Department that if the ships go only by night, the passage may take nearly twice as long. In these circumstances, after consultation with the First Sea Lord, I think the risk from submarines must be faced. Otherwise it will throw out all your railway arrangements as well as those for embarkation and transport, and cause a delay which I expect you would regard as fatal.

I send you herewith a copy of the scheme worked out between the Naval and Military Wings for the patrol of the East Coast. I think that the part assigned to the Naval Wing is more than we have machines enough to do. A better arrangement would be for the Military to take everything North of the Humber as well as the neighbourhood of Dover, and leave us the section from the Thames to the Humber. We would, however, put three or four seaplanes in the neighbourhood of the Firth of Forth and the Tyne. Experience shows that unless numbers are available, no regular patrol can be maintained by aeroplanes day after day.

Yours sincerely
Winston S. Churchill

Winston S. Churchill to Rear-Admiral Hood[2]

(*Admiralty papers: 1/8388*)

8 August 1914   Admiralty

Circulate the following:

For the present departments shd proceed on the general assumption that the war will last one year of wh the greatest effort shd be concentrated on

---

[1] Horatio Herbert Kitchener, 1850–1916. Entered Army, 1868. 2nd Lieutenant, Royal Engineers, 1871. Attached to the Palestine Exploration Fund, 1874–8. Surveyed Cyprus, 1878–82; the Sinai Peninsula, 1883. Governor-General, Eastern Sudan, 1886–8. Commander-in-Chief of the Egyptian Army, 1892–8. Knighted, 1894. Defeated the Dervishes at Omdurman, 1898. Created Baron Kitchener of Khartoum, 1898. Commander-in-Chief, South Africa, 1900–2. Created Viscount, 1902. Commander-in-Chief, India, 1902–9. Field-Marshal, 1909. A Member of the Committee of Imperial Defence, 1910. British Agent and Consul-General in Egypt, 1911–14. Created Earl, 27 July 1914. Secretary of State for War, 5 August 1914 until drowned at sea, 5 June 1916.

[2] Horace Lambert Alexander Hood, 1870–1916. Entered Navy, 1883. Rear-Admiral, 1913. Churchill's Naval Secretary, 1914. Accompanied Churchill to Antwerp, October 1914. Commanded the Dover Patrol, 1914–15. Commanded the 3rd Battle Cruiser Squadron, 1915–16. Knighted, 1916. Killed at the Battle of Jutland.

the first 6 months: and all arrangements for construction of works vessels supplies, etc shd be made with this period in view. Later on it may be necessary to extend the war period in wh case the arrangements made now cd be modified to include work wh is too far from completion now to stand in the way of more urgent services & to provide for the permanent supply and maintenance of the fleet.

2. Although the transition from peace to war conditions must be attended with a certain amount of emergency action, that period is passing, and the adoption of regular & careful methods is enjoined on all departments. In particular thrift & scrupulous attention to details are the mark of efficient administration in war. After all these years the Admiralty is now on its trial as an organisation, & the First Lord is vy anxious that vigorous action shd be combined with strict economy—so that the work of the department may subsequently become a model.

The work done by all in the last ten days is admirable.

WSC

Notes of a Conversation between Winston S. Churchill and Captain Henderson[1]

(Churchill papers: 13/29)

8 August 1914   Admiralty

Feeling in Germany

Buoyant before England's declaration of war: markedly depressed afterwards. When first inkling reached the populace news was received with frenzied yells in Unter den Linden and the crowd surged towards the British Embassy, where they demonstrated for about a couple of hours, and about 9 o'clock attacked the Embassy with stones, sticks, umbrellas, and any missile they could lay their hands on. Police did nothing to clear the streets until assistance was telephoned for to the German Foreign Office. That night, at between 1 and 2 a.m., when members of the Embassy were returning to their homes, they were followed by the crowds and insulted and attacked with sticks by men who got hold of the motor cabs in which members of the Embassy were driving and some even mounted on to the steps of the cars.

A telephone message of apology was received from the German Foreign

---

[1] Wilfred Henderson, 1873–1930. Entered Navy, 1888. Commander, Admiralty, under Sir John Fisher, 1905–9. Commanded Destroyer Flotillas, 1909–13. Naval Attaché, Berlin, 1913–14. Commodore, commanding the 1st Naval Brigade, 1914. Interned in Holland after the siege of Antwerp. Rear-Admiral, 1920. Vice-Admiral, 1925.

Office, and next day the Emperor[1] sent one of his most unpleasant ADC's to the Ambassador[2] to convey a message which was curtly given more or less in the following words:—

'His Majesty the Emperor commands me to express his regret for the 'demonstration last night against the British Embassy, *but* bids me to add 'that it is an indication of the general feeling through Germany at Eng- 'land's faithless conduct.'

'His Majesty begs you to inform King George[3] that although he has 'in the past been proud to wear the uniform of the British Navy and 'Army, that is all now at an end.'[4]

That same afternoon the officers and men of Queen Victoria's Regiment at Potsdam tore their shoulder straps with Queen Victoria's royal cipher off their coats.

Treatment of British nationals in Germany

Every Englishman recognised as such was arrested. Many of those arrested in Berlin are now interned at Spandau. Naval Instructor Holland,[5] lent to the Turkish Navy and travelling to England on leave, arrived in Berlin the day after the British Ambassador asked for his passports. The American Ambassador[6] personally took this officer to the German Foreign Office to explain that he was a non-combatant and to ask for a passport for him to go to England. The German Government, on hearing that this officer was entitled to wear a sword, refused passport and made him a prisoner of war. He is also at Spandau.

Departure of the Embassy

At first it was intended to send the Embassy to Denmark, but presumably as compensation for the demonstration against the Embassy the route was

---

[1] Wilhelm, 1859–1941. First cousin of George V. Succeeded his father as German Emperor, 1888. Abdicated, November 1918. In exile in Holland from 1918 until his death.

[2] William Edward Goschen, 1847–1924. Entered Diplomatic Service, 1869. Minister, Belgrade, 1898–1900; Copenhagen, 1900–5. Knighted, 1901. Ambassador, Vienna, 1905–8; Berlin, 1908–14. Created Baronet, 1916.

[3] George Frederick Ernest Albert, 1865–1936. Succeeded his father as King George V, 1910.

[4] The Kaiser had been appointed an honorary Admiral of the Fleet in 1889 and a Field-Marshal in 1908. He was also a Knight of the Garter and a Knight Grand Cross of the Victorian Order.

[5] Horace Herbert Holland, 1865–1952. Entered Navy, 1891. Lent to Turkish Government as Director of Studies at Imperial Ottoman Naval College, Constantinople, 1911–14. Interned in Germany, 1914. Deputy Inspector of Naval Schools, 1918–22. Instructor Captain, 1919.

[6] James Watson Gerard, 1867–1951. Lawyer, Supreme Court Judge, State of New York, 1907. United States Ambassador to Berlin, 1913–17; acted as an intermediary between the British and German Governments on all matters concerning British prisoners of war in Germany, 1914–17. Honorary knighthood, 1917. Returned to Law in the United States, 1917.

subsequently changed to Holland, but only between 30 and 35 passports were offered although the Ambassador asked for 100. The Embassy left Berlin in the early morning, the train starting at 8.15 a.m. Police were on duty and were lined up a road leading away from the station of departure so as to deceive the crowd. There was therefore no demonstration when the Ambassador left with a few of his staff, the rest of the staff having gone separately to the station. During the 24 hours' trip to the Dutch frontier there were demonstrations at nearly every station at which the train stopped.

Arrival in England

The Ambassador was cheered by the ships and by the populace on the shore on arrival at Harwich.

Remark made by Captain of 'Petersburg'[1] about an hour out from the Hook of Holland:—

'I have never seen this part of the North Sea so empty of ships before in my life.'

Naval Attaché's impression is that the Dutch are friendly to England but afraid of their German neighbour.

It was rumoured in Holland that inundations had already been started and that 150,000 Dutch troops were on the South-East frontier to prevent violation of Dutch neutrality. This rumour wants confirmation.

Two opinions in Germany as to use of German Fleet:—

(1) Not to risk it against Britain's overwhelming preponderance, but to keep it intact during this war and increase it afterwards at any sacrifice with a view to meeting England on equal terms and crushing her.

(2) To use it offensively at once, to seek a decisive engagement with the British Fleet, and see what the result is.

Winston S. Churchill to Prince Louis and Sir Doveton Sturdee
(Admiralty papers: 137/452)

9 August 1914   Admiralty
Very Secret

1. It is necessary to sustain and relieve our general strategic defensive by active minor operations. The objective shd be to establish for a time a

[1] The Captain of the *Petersburg* was Francis Hastie. The ship itself, after being renamed the *Petrograd* in 1915, was employed by the Admiralty as a collier, 1916–19. She was struck by two torpedoes in the Bristol Channel in February 1918, but both failed to explode. In 1924 she was sold to an Italian company, and renamed *Nautilus*; in 1928 to a French company, and renamed *Berbere*; in 1936 to a Mexican company, and renamed *Jalisco*; in 1937 to a French company, and renamed *Yolande*. In January 1938 she was sunk after an air attack on Barcelona harbour during the Spanish Civil War.

close observation and control of the Southern approaches to the Elbe.
For this purpose an advanced flotilla base is necessary. Born Deep between
the islands of Ameland & Terschelling is suitable.[1] The following plan
shd be worked out & examined in detail:—

2. First—a strongly supported destroyer reconnaissance along the Dutch
coast towards Heligoland.

> 3 Flotillas of the 1st Fleet⎫
> 1 Patrol Flotilla   ⎬ 80 boats
> 4 Minelayers   ⎭

> supported by { 5 Bacchantes & 4 Didos.
>   { 6 E class submarines.

in reserve support. Burney's[2] battle Fleet.

3. While this is in progress and under its cover

> 4 Depot ships of the above flotillas
> 1 Submarine depot ship
> 12 C Class submarines
> 8 small colliers & tankers
> 2 transports carrying *each* 1,500 marines & 8 4·7″ guns
> & { 8 seaplanes } with tents and stores
>   { 8 aeroplanes }

escorted by 3 Brazilian monitors.

To go to Born Deep: occupy & take possession of Ameland island: construct defences at the northern or causeway end to prevent an attack across
the sands. The causeway can of course be swept easily by fire. The sandy
tongue across wh it runs is only 3600 yards broad. Only a division at the
most cd deploy, & the attack wd have to be made over 4 miles of bare
sand. Probably (but this can be ascertained) the sand is itself quaggy &
impassable.

4. Bombardment from the shore. 60 miles about from the German frontier.
An attack by Germans therefore involves a much more tangible violation
of Dutch territory & on their mainland. The coast on the mainland is
flat and bare. To transport guns sufficiently heavy to fire with effect at
6 or 7 miles range & construct batteries there wd take time. This operation cd be rendered very difficult & costly by the 3 Brazilian Monitors

---

[1] See map 13 on pages 1606–1607.

[2] Cecil Burney, 1858–1929. Lieutenant, 1882. Rear-Admiral commanding 5th Cruiser
Squadron, 1911. Vice-Admiral commanding 3rd Squadron, 1912–13. Knighted, 1913. Com-
manded 2nd and 3rd Fleets, 1913–14. Commanded Channel Fleet, August-December 1914.
Second-in-Command, Grand Fleet, 1914–16. 2nd Sea Lord, 1916–17. Commander-in-Chief,
Coast of Scotland, 1917–19. Admiral of the Fleet, 1920.

whose shallow draft (4'6") wd enable them to lie inshore in the creeks and fire on the working parties from 6 6" guns & 6 4·7 howitzers.

5. Bombardment from the sea. If our position at Born Deep leads the enemy to send heavy ships along the coast to attack it, that is the best thing for us. The objective presented to the C class boats will be superior to any they are likely to get off our own coasts. Mines can also be laid to entrap the enemy, without hampering our movements. If modern ships are sent we may inflict losses 1 of wh wd compensate for the whole risks of the enterprise. If old ships are sent Burney can tackle them. If destroyers are sent that is what we want—close & continuous destroyer actions. If cruisers are sent there are the Didos & Bacchantes retiring if pressed through their own minefields. The more they send to attack Born Deep from the sea, the better our plan will have succeeded.

If their main Fleet comes out to attack Burney, ours must intervene to cut their retreat. Otherwise all our modern vessels will be out of direct contact.

6. Use to be made of advanced base.

To maintain an active surveillance & control of the southern approaches of the Elbe.

To give the destroyer flotillas a chance of fighting German destroyers by gunfire in their own waters, & thus utilising their great superiority as gunboats.

To give the C class submarines a part in the oversea warfare from wh they are now excluded, & thus compensate to some extent for our deficiences in numbers of big boats.

To give the aeroplanes & seaplanes a base from wh they can report all movements in the Heligoland Bight, & later attack with explosives the locks of the Kiel canal or vessels in the canal.

And above all to maintain in lively vigour the spirit of enterprise & attack wh when excluded from warlike operations, means that you are only waiting wondering where you will be hit.

WSC

H. H. Asquith to Venetia Stanley[1]

(Montagu papers)

9 August 1914   10 Downing Street

. . . Winston has been very tiresome about Ivor Guest[2] whom he wishes to have at the Admiralty as Civil Lord in place of Lambert.[3] L. is not very competent but to boot him out at this moment wd be cruel, & the place is one wh no peer has ever held: let alone the fact that Ivor Guest is very unpopular, & the whole thing wd be denounced as a Churchill job. I thought & still think it inconsiderate of Winston to raise & press such a point at such a time. . . .

Lord Haldane[4] to Winston S. Churchill

(Churchill papers: 28/152)

9 August 1914   28 Queen Anne's Gate

My dear Winston,

You know how much I appreciate the great things you have done for the nation, & how we should like to meet your wishes in any point.

But I want you to let me say frankly, as one who is attached to you, that you ought not to press this point at this time.

Lambert does not want to go. It would be a humiliation for him at such a period. In the Lords there is not much Admiralty work, &, with all his excellent qualities, Wimborne would not add strength. I am sure that there would be much adverse comment on yourself if you pressed the change.

Let me again appeal to you to let this go. Have a room for Wimborne in

[1] Beatrice Venetia Stanley, 1887–1948. Clementine Churchill's cousin. On 26 July 1915 she married Edwin Montagu. Of some of Asquith's letters, Churchill wrote in *Great Contemporaries*: 'They were addressed to brighter eyes than peer through politicians' spectacles'; Venetia Stanley's were the eyes to which Churchill was referring.

[2] Ivor Churchill Guest, 1873–1939. Conservative MP, 1900–6. Liberal MP, 1906–10. Created Baron Ashby St Ledgers, 1910. Paymaster-General 1910–12. Lord in Waiting, 1913–15. 2nd Baron Wimborne, 1914. Lord Lieutenant of Ireland, 1915–18. Created Viscount Wimborne, 1918.

[3] George Lambert, 1866–1958. Liberal MP, 1891–1924; 1929–31. Civil Lord of Admiralty, 1905–15. Chairman of the Liberal Parliamentary Party, 1919–21. Liberal National MP, 1931–45. Created Viscount, 1945.

[4] Richard Burdon Haldane, 1856–1928. Liberal MP, 1885–1911. Secretary of State for War, 1905–12. Created Viscount, 1911. Lord Chancellor, first under Asquith, 1912–15; then under Ramsay MacDonald, 1924.

the Admiralty by all means: that he represents you in the Lords would be a
justification. But don't let it be said that you expelled Lambert.[1]

Yours always most sincerely

Haldane

Winston S. Churchill to Clementine Churchill[2]
(Spencer-Churchill papers)

9 August 1914   Admiralty

My darling one,

The enclosed[3] will tell you what is known officially. It is a good summary.
You must *not* fail to burn it at once.

I am over head & ears in work & am much behindhand.

It makes me a little anxious that you shd be on the coast. It is 100 to 1
agst a raid—but still there is the chance: & Cromer has a good landing
place near.

I wish you wd get the motor repaired & keep it so that you can whisk
away, at the first sign of trouble. I am really in doubt whether I ought not
to recall you at once a la Callaghan—'Strike your flag & come ashore'.

Kiss the Kittens[4] for me.

Tender love to you all.

Your fondest & devoted

W

Sir Edward Grey to Sir Conyngham Greene:[5] telegram
(Copy, Churchill papers: 13/43)

11 August 1914   Foreign Office

On August 3rd Japanese Government made statement contained in your
telegram No 58 'leaving it entirely to His Majesty's Government to formulate
the reason for and nature of the assistance required'.

---

[1] Lambert remained Civil Lord throughout Churchill's wartime tenure of the Admiralty.
Lord Wimborne received no political appointment until January 1915, when Asquith
appointed him Lord Lieutenant of Ireland, a post which he held until 1918.

[2] Clementine Ogilvy Hozier, 1885–   . Daughter of Lady Blanche and Sir Henry
Hozier. She married Winston Churchill in 1908. Created Baroness Spencer-Churchill, 1965.

[3] A secret War Office summary, giving details of British troop movements, and the
relative positions of the French, Belgian and German forces.

[4] Diana Churchill, 1909–63. Churchill's eldest child.

Randolph Frederick Edward Spencer Churchill, 1911–68. Churchill's only son. His
godfathers were F. E. Smith and Sir Edward Grey. Conservative MP, 1940–5. Major,
British mission to Yugoslav Army of National Liberation, 1943–4. Journalist and historian;
author of the first two volumes of this biography.

[5] Conyngham Greene, 1854–1934. Entered Foreign Office, 1877. Knighted, 1900. Ambassador to Japan, 1912–19.

Subsequently I made request limited to hunting down armed merchant vessels preying upon our commerce.

Japanese Government replied as in Aide Memoire given me by Japanese Ambassador[1] yesterday that Japan could not limit action to this.

I deprecated unlimited action which might give rise to serious disturbances in China and said that under the circumstances I would not at present invoke action by Japan under the Treaty.

Under these circumstances and in the absence of any present danger apparent to Hongkong or British concessions *I cannot say the special interests of Great Britain in Eastern Asia are so seriously menaced as to make it essential to appeal to the Alliance on that ground alone.*

But I recognize that Japan has interests also to be considered as is apparent in your telegram No 72, and what action the menacing language used by German Ambassador[2] to Japanese Government requires is something which Japan alone has the right to judge.

I agree therefore to a statement that the two Governments having been in communication with each other are of opinion that it is necessary for each to take action to protect the general interests contemplated by the Anglo-Japanese Alliance. It should also be stated that the action of Japan will not extend to the Pacific Ocean beyond the China Seas nor extend beyond Asiatic waters westward of the China Seas, or to any foreign territory except territory in German occupation on the continent in Eastern Asia. This is important to prevent unfounded misapprehension abroad.

Japanese Ambassador observed that Minister for Foreign Affairs[3] had already implied that they did not desire to go beyond these limits, but that they might have to protect Japanese shipping lines in Pacific from German cruisers. I assume this would be action on high seas only, but I leave it to Minister for Foreign Affairs to express his own views....

[1] Katsunosuke Inoue, 1861–1929 Japanese Minister, Berlin, 1906–8; Chile, 1910–13. Ambassador in London, 1913–16. Succeeded his uncle as Marquess, 1915. A Director of the South Manchurian Railway.

[2] In August 1914 the German Ambassador to Japan was Graf von Rex.

[3] Taka-Akira Kato, 1859–1926. Japanese Ambassador in London, 1894–99. Foreign Minister, 1900–1; 1906. Ambassador in London, 1908–13. Created Baron, 1912. Foreign Minister, 1913; 1914–15. Member of the House of Peers, 1915. Created Viscount, 1916. Prime Minister, 1924–5. Created Count while on his death-bed.

Winston S. Churchill to Sir Edward Grey
(*Copy, Churchill papers: 13/43*)

11 August 1914   Admiralty

My dear Grey,

Your last telegram to Japan:

Statement at X[1] is not borne out by our information, see attd telegram from Tokio.

I must say I think you are chilling indeed to these people. I can't see any half-way house myself between having them in and keeping them out. If they are to come in, they may as well be welcomed as comrades. This last telegram is almost hostile. I am afraid I do not understand what is in yr mind on this aspect—tho I followed it so clearly till today.

The Balkan position is even more hopeful & critical. But if you do not agree with the line urged by L.G.[2] & myself—do tell us why & wherefore.[3]

This telegram gives me a shiver. We are all in this together & I only wish to give the fullest effect & support to your main policy. But I am altogether perplexed by the line opened up by these Japanese interchanges.

You may easily give mortal offence—wh will not be forgotten—we are not safe yet—by a long chalk. The storm has yet to burst.

Don't bother to answer.

Yours ever
W

Winston S. Churchill to Clementine Churchill
(*Spencer-Churchill papers*)

11 August 1914   Admiralty

My dear one,

This is only a line from a vy tired Winston. The Expedy Force about wh you are so inquisitive is on its road & will be all on the spot in time.[4] I wish

[1] The italicized sentence in the previous document.

[2] David Lloyd George, 1863–1945. Liberal MP, 1890–1931. Chancellor of the Exchequer, 1908–15. Minister of Munitions, May 1915–July 1916. Secretary of State for War, July–December 1916. Prime Minister, December 1916–October 1922. Independent Liberal MP, 1931–45. Created Earl Lloyd-George of Dwyfor, 1945.

[3] Churchill and Lloyd George both wanted Britain to persuade the neutral Balkan States (Greece, Bulgaria, and Rumania) to join the war against Austria–Hungary by promising them territory and offering liberal monetary inducements. Britain declared war on Austria–Hungary on 16 August 1914.

[4] On 14 August 1914 Sir John French landed at Boulogne, at the head of the British Expeditionary Force, consisting of one cavalry and four infantry divisions. The BEF moved at once into Belgium where, on 23 August, it was attacked by the German First Army at Mons. From 24 August to 6 September the BEF was in retreat. On 6 September it joined the French troops in driving the Germans northwards across the Marne, which it crossed on 9 September.

I cd whisk down to you & dig a little on the beach. My work here is vy heavy
& so interesting that I cannot leave it.

Now I am really going to knock off.

Ever your loving
W

Lord Esher:[1] *diary*

(*Esher papers*)

11 August 1914

The naval position is still very obscure. It is very difficult to understand
how the 'Goeben' has managed to escape the watching cruisers; she is very
fast, and obviously very ably commanded. In the North Sea, the 'Monarch'
had a very narrow escape; the submarine that attacked her fired a torpedo
that only missed her by a few feet. This was not the submarine that was
ultimately sunk; the latter came up to breathe, and was destroyed by gunfire from the 'Birmingham'.

The idea seems to be that the 'Imperator' is lying full of troops, about
5,000, ready for a raid; this may be a scare, or it may be part of the original
plan for preventing our army leaving these shores. So far, all has gone well,
and three of our transports got across in perfect security on Sunday.

It is not likely that the French reconnaissance towards Mulhouse will
succeed in doing more than ascertaining what the Germans are doing in that
quarter. If the Germans are in any force, they will obviously have to come
back.

The general situation has been rather complicated by the action of Japan.
The Japanese say, very naturally, that they will come into the war on the
understanding that they are free to fight all over the world. This means, of
course, that they will not limit their operations to seizing German territory
in China, but that they will take anything else that they can get hold of.
This would mean Samoa, and possibly other islands, that have already been
offered to the Dominions. If Japan were to seize these places, it would
probably lead to very serious trouble with the Colonies. So, for the present,
the Japanese are being asked to stand fast until we have been able to communicate with the Dominions.

[1] Reginald Baliol Brett, 1852–1930. Liberal MP, 1880–5. Secretary to the Office of Works,
1895–1902. 2nd Viscount Esher, 1899. A permanent member of the Committee of Imperial
Defence, 1905–18. In 1914 he established himself in Paris at the head of a British Mission,
and remained there for the rest of the war.

H. H. Asquith to Venetia Stanley
(Montagu papers)

11 August 1914   10 Downing Street

. . . We had a long Cabinet, in which a huge part of the talking was done by Winston & Kitchener: the former posing as an expert on strategy, and the latter as an expert on Irish politics! The Japs are coming into action, and Venizelos,[1] the Greek Prime Minister, who is much the most capable man in Eastern Europe, has a great scheme on foot for a federation of Balkan States against Germany & Austria: to be rewarded by slices of Austrian territory. If they can get this on to its legs we will help them with any amount of money. . . .

Winston S. Churchill to Sir Berkeley Milne: telegram
(Copy, Milne papers)

11 August 1914   Admiralty
4.00 pm

Information received Dardanelles that 'Goeben' and 'Breslau' arrived there 8.30 p.m. 10th August. You should establish a blockade of Dardanelles for the present but be on the lookout for mines.

Sir Berkeley Milne to Admiralty: telegram
(Copy, Milne papers)

11 August 1914
5.20 pm

Am I to understand that all vessels are to be denied egress and ingress to Dardanelles or German vessels only. If a formal blockade is to be established will declaration be issued by home government.

Admiralty to Sir Berkeley Milne: telegram
(Copy, Milne papers)

11 August 1914

In reply to your telegram mistake in wording no blockade intended only to carefully watch the entrance in case enemy's cruisers come out.

---

[1] Eleutherios Venizelos, 1864–1936. Prime Minister of Greece, 1910–15. Forced to resign by King Constantine, May 1915. Prime Minister for the second time, August to October 1915. Subsequently Prime Minister 1917–20, 1924, 1928–32 and 1933.

George Russell Clerk: minute

(*Foreign Office papers: 371/2137*)

11 August 1914   Foreign Office

. . . . I think we should wait to hear how the 'Goeben' incident develops and if the Porte abide by their obligations as neutrals, we should at once undertake to pay the *full* cost to Turkey of both vessels and guarantee their immediate delivery after the war.

GRC

H. H. Asquith to Venetia Stanley

(*Montagu papers*)

12 August 1914   10 Downing Street

. . . We had a Cabinet this morning as usual. The only interesting thing is the arrival of the Goeben in the Dardanelles & her sale to Turkey! The Turks are very angry—not unnaturally—at Winston's seizure of their battleship here. As we shall insist that the Goeben shall be manned by a Turkish instead of a German crew, it doesn't much matter: as the Turkish sailors cannot navigate her—except on to rocks or mines. . . .

Sir Berkeley Milne to Admiralty: telegram

(*Copy, Milne papers*)

12 August 1914
2.25 pm

French vessel reports 'Goeben' left Chanak 2 p.m. 11th August under German colours and sale to Turkey was reported Chanak same afternoon 'Goeben' compelled steamer to disconnect wireless instruments. . . .

Winston S. Churchill to Count Albert Mensdorff[1]

(*Copy, Churchill papers: 13/5*)

13 August 1914   Admiralty

My dear Mensdorff,

My naval sec Adl Hood, who brings this letter, is instructed to put himself at yr disposal in arranging for the comfort & contrivance of yr journey by

[1] Albert Victor Jules Joseph Michael Mensdorff-Pouilly-Dietrichstein, 1861–1945. His grandmother was an aunt of Queen Victoria. Entered the Austro-Hungarian Foreign Office, 1884. Attaché, London, 1889; 1st Secretary, 1896–1904; Ambassador, 1904–14. A friend of Edward VII and George V. In 1917 he met General Smuts in Switzerland to discuss the possibilities of a negotiated peace between Britain and Austria-Hungary. Austrian representative at the League of Nations, 1920.

sea. If there is any way in wh I can be of service to you at this time you
will not I hope fail to command me.

Altho' the terrible march of events has swept aside the ancient friendship
between our countries, the respect & regard wh spring from so many years of
personal association cannot pass from the hearts of yr English friends.

Yours vy sincerely
WSC

Count Albert Mensdorff to Winston S. Churchill

(*Churchill papers: 13/44*)

13 August 1914   Austro-Hungarian Embassy
                                                Belgrave Square

My dear Churchill,

Please accept my sincerest thanks for the great courtesy with which
you placed a boat at our disposal to get home and for all the trouble the
Admiralty is taking about the arrangements. I have just seen Admiral Hood.

I shall never forget the happy years I spent in this country and all the
kindness shown to me by my English friends.

Hoping that in future happier quieter days we may meet again.[1]

Yrs very sincerely
Albert Mensdorff

Winston S. Churchill to Clementine Churchill

(*Spencer-Churchill papers*)

13 August 1914   Admiralty
Blenheim Day

My dear one,

How right you were not to hesitate to send back the ring,[2] & what a good
thing it is to have high & inflexible principles! You are a dear & splendid
Kat. I am vy proud of you. What you have done for me no one can measure.

---

[1] In an early version of *The World Crisis*, drafted in 1923, but not published, Churchill
wrote, after this letter: 'I felt the greatest sympathy for Count Mensdorff, and indeed for two
other charming and distinguished Austrian gentlemen, Count Kinsky and Sir Rudolph
Slatin, for all these, and many others of their fellow countrymen were deep lovers of England,
had never dreamed of war between the two nations, and though they did their duty as
honourable men must do to their own country, it was not done without broken hearts.'
(*Churchill papers: 8/64*)

[2] The shipowner and Conservative MP, Robert Houston (1853–1926), had sent Clementine
Churchill an emerald and diamond ring, together with a letter praising her husband's work
as First Lord. She had returned the ring at once, on her own initiative.

This is only a salutation with many kisses & fondest love from your devoted

W

Lord Fisher[1] *to Edward Marsh*[2]

(*Marsh papers*)

14 August 1914   Langham House
                                                 Ham Common

My dear Eddie,

Thanks for your letter! Dei Gratiâ I'll be at Admiralty in my own motor from here at 1.30 *tomorrow Saturday* to lunch with Winston, unless you telephone to the contrary (848 Kingston). I am APPALLED at the Goeben incident! I looked up the 'Naval Gazeteer' of the Old War yesterday for precedents! I see the wording of the telegram to Sir B. Milne should be 'Haul down your Flag and Come on Shore'
(He never ought to have left the shore!!) *What a vista if he remains!* another mess with the Austrian Fleet! (as the French Admiral[3] is too old though brave.)

The telegram you will get at the Admiralty after the coming Naval Battle off Cattaro will be—

'The French Admiral shot himself'

'The English Admiral "shit" himself'

Yours

F

Kindly submit to Winston that in my humble opinion it's the SERPENT not the *Lion* in dealing with the German Fleet—just at the PRESENT time!
'*Our strength is to sit still*'!
(That comes out of the Bible!)
Yesterday came to see me a very dear friend (He was a Colleague of

---

[1] John Arbuthnot Fisher, 1841–1920. Known both as 'Jackie' and, because of his somewhat oriental appearance, 'the old Malay'. Entered Navy, 1854. First Sea Lord, 1904–10. Admiral of the Fleet, 1905. Created Baron, 1909. Retired, 1911. Head of the Royal Commission on Fuel and Engines, 1912–14. Re-appointed First Sea Lord, October 1914; resigned, May 1915. Chairman of the Admiralty Inventions Board, 1915–16.

[2] Edward Howard Marsh, 1872–1953. Known as 'Eddie'. Entered Colonial Office as a 2nd Class Clerk, 1896. Private Secretary to Churchill, December 1905–November 1915. Assistant Private Secretary to Asquith, November 1915–December 1916. Private Secretary to Churchill, 1917–22; 1924–9. Private Secretary to successive Secretaries of State for the Colonies, 1929–36. Knighted, 1937.

[3] Auguste Emmanuel Hubert Gaston Marie Boué de Lapeyrère, 1852–1924. Minister of Marine, 1909–11. Vice-Admiral Commanding the French naval forces, Mediterranean, 1914–15.

mine at the Hague Peace Conference).[1] He had just been at Strassbourg his
daughter married to a German Baron commanding a Regiment of Uhlans,
their son (my friend's grandson) is now serving in the German High Sea
Fleet who writes that the German Fleet was greatly upset by
I   Jellicoe's totally unexpected appointment
II   By our concealed mobilization and Precautions
III By the buying of the Battleships who had orders to pass through the
North Sea.

My friend heard that Germany had supplied Turkey with the whole of
the money for building of the Battleships—

Winston S. Churchill to Sir Edward Grey
(Grey papers)

14 August 1914   Admiralty

Sir Edward Grey,

If you shd find it convenient to accept Portugal as a formally allied state,
the Admiralty wd be convenienced to some extent, & wd find no difficulty
in affording general protection to the Portuguese islands or to Portugal itself
from overseas attack.[2]

It is presumed however that no obligation to defend Portugal against a
land attack wd be incurred.

                                                              WSC

Francis Grenfell[3] to Winston S. Churchill
(Churchill papers: 13/45)

15 August 1914   Ninth Lancers
                                                         Moultan Barracks
                                                              Tidworth

My dear Winston,

When you get this we will have gone forth, quietly and calmly to War.
We have mobilized very comfortably & leave here with great enthusiasm.

---

[1] In 1899 Fisher had attended the Hague Peace Conference as Britain's Naval Representative. The Conference sought to establish certain rules of war, but Fisher expressed the
view privately that: 'Moderation in war is imbecility . . . the essence of war is violence';
and again, 'The humanity of war! You might as well talk of humanizing Hell!'

[2] On 24 August 1914, German troops attacked the Portuguese in Mozambique. Three
months later, on 23 November 1914, Portugal agreed to participate in military operations
against Germany. The fighting was confined to Africa until 1917, when a Portuguese
Expeditionary Force of 40,000 men was sent to the western front.

[3] Francis Octavius Grenfell, 1880–1914. Lieutenant, 9th Lancers, 1914. He and his twin
brother Riversdale embarked for France together on 15 August 1914. Won the Victoria
Cross at Messines, 31 October 1914. Killed at Ypres on 13 May 1915. An elder brother,
Robert, fell in the charge of the 9th Lancers at Omdurman, 1898, in which Churchill also
rode.

No regiment ever left England better prepared. We are splendidly mounted, have the best Colonel in the army,[1] a very good, & not too old lot of Reservists. With great traditions in the past, we are determined to uphold them in the future.

I was 2 hrs in London on Thurs: & had intended to come & see you, which I looked forward to very much—but I was detained at the dentist & when I arrived at the admiralty it was too late to see you & catch my train— a great disappointment. I have thought so much of you during this crisis, & know what you must be going through. Lord K's appointment worked wonders for the army. It has filled us with confidence. With him & you in charge of the services, we leave ready to go anywhere, & do anything—as there will now be no half measures.

I am in Command of a squadron, & can hardly believe my good fortune of being in the prime of Life—a soldier at this time—

Rivy[2] comes with me in my squadron & sends you his love. Please give Mrs Winston my love—Goodbye my dear Winston. We must teach these foreigners again—what a Great nation we are—& what 'England' means.

My kindest and best wishes.

Yours ever
Francis

After the war we must get Bendor[3] to give a Dinner for all the warriors, & ministers—Luck for Bendor, this war. He cld well fight most comfortably, & have no need for excuses for being in France!

---

[1] David Graham Muschet Campbell, 1869–1936. Entered Army, 1889. Commanded 9th Lancers, 1914–15. Commanded a Cavalry Brigade in the 21st Division, 1916–19. Knighted, 1919.

[2] Riversdale Grenfell, 1880–1914. Known as 'Rivy'. A financier, he lost his fortune early in 1914 when his family firm went bankrupt. Lieutenant, 9th Lancers. Killed in action, 11 September 1914.

[3] Hugh Richard Arthur Grosvenor, 1879–1953. Known as 'Bendor'. 2nd Duke of Westminster, 1899. ADC to Lord Roberts, South Africa, 1900–2. Commanded an armoured car detachment, Royal Naval Division, 1914–15. Personal Assistant to the Controller, Mechanical Department, Ministry of Munitions, 1917. His brother, Lord Hugh Grosvenor, a Captain in the Household Cavalry was killed in action in November 1914.

Winston S. Churchill to Sir Edward Grey

(*Copy, Churchill papers*)

15 August 1914   Admiralty

My dear Grey,

Don't jump: but do you mind my sending this personal message to
Enver.[1] I have answered this man & am sure it will do good. But of course
your 'NO' is final.

Yours ever
WSC

Winston S. Churchill to Enver Pasha: telegram

(*Draft, Churchill papers: 21/36*)

15 August 1914   Admiralty

I hope you are not going to make a mistake wh will undo all the services
you have rendered Turkey & cast away the successes of the second Balkan
War. By a strict & honest neutrality these can be kept secure. But siding
with Germany openly or secretly now must mean the greatest disaster to
you, your comrades & your country.[2] The overwhelming superiority at sea
possessed by the navies of England, France, Russia & Japan over those of
Austria & Germany renders it easy for the 4 allies to transport troops in
almost unlimited numbers from any quarter of the globe & if they were
forced into a quarrel by Turkey their blow could be delivered at the heart.

On the other hand I know that Sir Edward Grey who has already been
approached as to possible terms of peace if Germany & Austria are beaten,
has stated that if Turkey remains loyal to her neutrality, a solemn agreement
to respect the integrity of the Turkish Empire must be a condition of any
terms of peace that affect the near East.[3]

[1] Enver Pasha, 1881–1922. A member of the Young Turk Triumvirate, 1908. Military
Attaché, Berlin, 1909–11. Returned to Turkey and deposed Abdul Hamid, 1909. Served in
the Italo-Turkish war at Benghazi, 1912. Lieutenant-Colonel, 1913. Forced the Sultan to
transfer power to the Young Turks, June 1913. Appointed himself Major-General and
Minister of War, 3 January 1914. Commanded the Turkish Army in the Caucasus, 1914–15.
Fled, via Odessa, to Germany, 1918. Helped the Russian General Denikin in the Caucasus
against the Bolsheviks, 1919. Supported the Bolsheviks as director of the Asiatic Bureau,
Moscow, 1920. Turned against the Bolsheviks, and killed fighting at the head of an anti-
Bolshevik force in Turkestan, as the champion of 'Pan-Turanianism'.

[2] Turkey had already signed a secret alliance with Germany, on 2 August 1914. At the
end of October the *Goeben* and *Breslau*, flying the Turkish flag but commanded by a German
admiral, bombarded several Russian ports in the Black Sea. Britain declared war on Turkey
on 5 November 1914.

[3] The whole of this paragraph was drafted in longhand by Sir Edward Grey, and incorporated without alteration by Churchill into the telegram as finally sent.

The personal regard I have for you, Talaat[1] & Djavid[2] and the admiration with which I have followed your career from our first meeting at Wurzburg[3] alone leads me to speak these words of friendship before it is too late.

Winston S. Churchill

Winston S. Churchill to Sir William Tyrrell

(*Grey Papers*)

15 August 1914   Admiralty

Sir William Tyrrell,

I suggest this shd be ciphered to the Embassy at C'ple & then taken by Admiral Limpus[4] direct to Enver thus making it a personal message from me & different from the regular diplomatic communications.

Winston S. Churchill to Prince Louis and Sir Frederick Hamilton

(*Copy, Churchill papers: 13/31*)

16 August 1914   Admiralty

In order to make the best possible use of the surplus naval reservists of different classes, it is proposed to constitute permanent cadres of one marine and two naval brigades. The marine brigade has already been partially formed in four battalions, aggregating 1,880 active service men. To this will be added an approximately equal number of reservists, making the total strength of the brigade 3,900, organized in four battalions of four double companies of approximately 250 men. The two naval brigades will also consist of four battalions, each, if possible, of 880 men, organized in sixteen double companies of 220. . . .

The formation of these brigades should be completed so far as resources allow in the present week. The officers commanding the companies and battalions must be appointed forthwith. The first essential is to get the men drilling together in brigades; and the deficiencies of various ranks in the battalions can be filled up later. It may ultimately be found possible in the

---

[1] Mehmed Talaat, 1874–1921. Member of the Young Turk Triumvirate, 1908. Minister of the Interior, 1913–17. Grand Vizier, 1917–18. Fled to Europe, 1918. Assassinated in Berlin.

[2] Mehmed Djavid, 1875–1926. Teacher of political economy. Minister of Finance and Public Works, 1914. Hanged for conspiring to assassinate Mustafa Kemal.

[3] Churchill had met Enver at German Military manœuvres in Wurzburg in 1909. They met again in London in 1910. In 1911 Churchill had met Talaat and Djavid in Constantinople. He described his first meeting with Enver in *Thoughts and Adventures* (1929).

[4] Arthur Henry Limpus, 1863–1931. Entered Navy, 1876. Rear-Admiral, 1910. Naval Adviser to the Turkish Government, 1912–14. Admiral-Superintendent, Malta Dockyard, 1914–16. Knighted, 1916.

course of the war to build up all battalions of the marine and naval brigades
to the army strength of 1,070, and the organization will readily adapt itself
to this. All the men, whether sailors or marines, while training in the three
brigades will be available if required for service afloat, and it must be distinctly understood that this is the paramount claim upon them; but in the
meanwhile they will be left to be organized for land service.[1]

H. H. Asquith to Venetia Stanley
(*Montagu papers*)

17 August 1914   10 Downing Street

. . . We had a Cabinet at noon: Ll George has got neuralgia & could not
come. Turkey has come into the foreground, threatens vaguely enterprises
against Egypt, and seems disposed to play a double game about the Goeben
and the Breslau. Winston, in his most bellicose mood, is all for sending a
torpedo flotilla thro' the Dardanelles—to threaten & if necessary to sink the
Goeben & her consort. Crewe[2] & Kitchener very much against (in the
interest of the Moslems in India & Egypt) our doing anything wh could be
interpreted as meaning that we were taking the initiative agst Turkey. She
ought to be compelled to strike the first blow. I agreed to this. But the
Turks must be obliged to come out & tell us whether they are going at once
to dismiss the German crews. . . . .

Sir Louis Mallet[3] to Sir Edward Grey: telegram
(*Copy, Churchill papers: 21/36*)

18 August 1914   Constantinople

As reported in my telegram No 557[4] Minister of War was very much
pleased with First Lord's message. He said revulsion of public feeling here

[1] This document marked the origin of the Royal Naval Division, which fought at Antwerp
(October 1914), the Dardanelles (April 1915–January 1916) and on the western front (1916–
1918). Churchill wrote an introduction to Douglas Jerrold's official history of the Division,
The Royal Naval Division, published in 1923.

[2] Robert Offley Ashburton Crewe-Milnes, 1858–1945. Lord-Lieutenant of Ireland, 1892–
1895. Secretary of State for India, 1910–15. Created Marquess of Crewe, 1911. Lord President
of the Council, 1915–16. President of the Board of Education, 1916. Ambassador to Paris,
1922–8. Secretary of State for War, 1931.

[3] Louis du Pan Mallet, 1864–1936. Entered Foreign Office, 1888. Private Secretary to Sir
Edward Grey, 1905–7. Under-Secretary of State for Foreign Affairs, 1907–13. Knighted,
1912. Ambassador at Constantinople, 1913–14.

[4] On 18 August 1914, in his previous telegram, Mallet had informed Grey: 'Minister of
War is delighted with Mr Churchill's message, and told Admiral Limpus that he realised
force of his arguments, and would answer it.' (*Foreign Office Papers: 371/2138*) But Enver did
not reply to Churchill.

would be effected immediately if His Majesty's Government would authorise me to make an announcement at once that seizure of Turkish ships was not permanent, that it had been a much regretted necessity of war, that full value and some indemnity would be lodged for the ships and that public promise would be given that they would be restored in good order as soon as possible and seen safely into Turkish waters.

Sir Edward Grey to Winston S. Churchill
(Copy, Churchill papers: 13/45)

18 August 1914   28 Queen Anne's Gate

Dear Churchill,

Ex abundante cautelâ, (if necessary Marsh will explain)[1] I send a line to say that no doubt you will instruct Troubridge[2] not to take hostile action against Turkey, unless etc.

Troubridge may get a too exciting report of the situation from the British commander now on the spot.

It would be well if Troubridge could keep in touch with Mallet at the Embassy at Constantinople.

Yours sincerely
E. Grey

Winston S. Churchill to Vice-Admiral Troubridge: telegram
(Copy, Churchill papers: 13/45)

18 August 1914   Admiralty

Most important to show no hostile intentions to Turkey. Your duty is to prevent the Goeben or Breslau leaving the Dardanelles. Use no threats. Watch events. Keep in touch with Ambassador at Constantinople.

---

[1] 'Out of excess of caution.'

[2] Ernest Charles Thomas Troubridge, 1860–1926. Entered Navy, 1875. Naval Attaché, Tokyo, 1901–4. Chief of the Admiralty War Staff, 1912. Vice-Admiral commanding the Mediterranean Cruiser Squadron, 1912–14. Admiral commanding on the Danube, 1918. President, International Danube Commission, 1919–24. Knighted, 1919. Admiral, 1919.

Sir Louis Mallet to Sir Edward Grey: telegram

(*Copy, Churchill papers: 13/45*)

18 August 1914   Constantinople

I have seen Minister of Marine[1] who is heart-broken at the loss of his ships.

He said you could not understand what an effect our action had had throughout Mussulman world and to what an extent situation was being exploited by Germany. I explained to Minister of Marine that HMG had been actuated solely by exigencies of the naval situation perhaps without sufficient regard for susceptibilities of Turkey, but that he might rest assured that HMG was animated by none but most friendly sentiments towards Turkey. Maintenance of our supremacy at sea was as vital for Turkey as for other countries.

He begged that HMG would let him have the Sultan Osman at least, at once, but I said that I feared it would be impossible to go as far as that at present, although I could assure him that if ships were not wanted during the war they would be restored to Turkey. He asked me whether we could not go further than this and begged me most urgently to try and obtain [this] for him.

I said that I would represent to you his wishes and I hope that it may be possible to do something more but I told him that I feared that serious breach of neutrality committed by Turkey would [lead] HMG to think they had now thrown in their lot with Germany and would seem to justify seizure of ships. He solemnly assured me that Turkey had not thrown in her lot with Germany and that she would never make war on England, that he would get rid of the German crews as soon as he possibly could and that he was impatiently awaiting the arrival of the Turkish transports with Turkish crews who were to replace the Germans. I am convinced that he is absolutely sincere and hope that transports will not be molested by our ships, unless of course fresh circumstances arose here.

He said that he was glad that I had come as he was alone and would work with me for restoration of good relations with Great Britain, if we could only meet him a little. He admitted that the declaration respecting integrity of Turkey had had a good effect already.

He then said that he had been thrown into despair yesterday by the visit

---

[1] Ahmed Djemal, 1861–1922. Lieutenant-Colonel, 1908. Member of the Young Turk triumvirate, 1908. Governor-General of Bagdad, 1911–12. Military Governor of Constantinople, 1913. Minister of Marine, 1914. Commanded the 4th Army in Syria, November 1914–17. Minister of Marine, 1917–18. Fled Turkey, October 1918. In exile in Germany, Switzerland, Russia and Afghanistan. Stimulated Mohammedan nationalism throughout Central Asia, 1920–2. Assassinated by Russians in Georgia. His *Memoirs of a Turkish Statesman 1913–19* were published in 1922, after his death, in English and German.

of the Russian Agent who had told him that the British Government had bought Turkish ships in order to pass them on to Russia and who had proposed bargain by which Russians should have Sultan Osman, Turkey retaining other ships. I said that this was, I was convinced, grotesque invention and I succeeded in reassuring him.

If the First Lord could send sympathetic and friendly message to Minister of Marine it would be well received but it would be as well to avoid in such a message any mention of money payment.

Minister of Marine is entirely French in [sympathy]. He and Dr Nazim,[1] Secretary of the Committee of Union and Progress, both attended ceremony at departure of the French reservists. Rahmi Bey,[2] Vali of Smyrna, has arrived to inform Government on behalf of Smyrna notables that they will not go in with Germany.

Sir Louis Mallet to Sir Edward Grey

(*Copy, Churchill papers: 13/45*)

18 August 1914   Constantinople
12.30 am

I was informed by British Commander at Dardanelles that Admiral Troubridge was arriving to-morrow with rest of fleet.

It is stated to-night by Minister of Marine that British Commander has informed forts at Dardanelles in writing that if German ships come out, forts will be bombarded. I cannot believe that this is true, for such an action however justifiable, would seem to be impolitic as in (? reality) (group undecypherable) would be to improve situation in our favour.

These two circumstances taken in connection with warning to British merchantmen to leave Turkish waters at once will, I fear, cause something like panic and be construed as intention on the part of H.M.G. to attack Turkey at once. It will certainly be used by Germany in this sense.

My French colleague[3] has implored me not to act on my instructions

---

[1] Nazim Bey, 1870–1926. Born in Salonika. A founder member of the Committee of Union and Progress, 1889. Brought together the Salonika and Paris branches of the Committee, 1907. Secretary-General of the Committee, 1909–17. Minister of Education, 1918. Hanged for his part in the conspiracy to assassinate Mustafa Kemal.

[2] Mustafa Rahmi Evranos. Landowner. Joined the Committee of Union and Progress, 1906. Deputy for Salonika, 1908 and 1912. Vali of Smyrna, 1914. Virtually independent of Constantinople, he established good relations with the nationals of enemy powers.

[3] Louis Maurice Bompard, 1854–1935. French Ambassador at St Petersburg, 1902–8; at Constantinople, 1909–14.

respecting warning to British ships, of which he has heard, and reasons for
which he has asked me to communicate to him.

I have replied that I have already acted, but that I have no definite
information.

I should be glad to learn as soon as possible what I should say to the
Turkish Government if they also ask for explanations.

Winston S. Churchill to Prince Louis and Sir Frederick Sturdee
(Admiralty papers 116/3491)

18 August 1914   Admiralty

First Sea Lord
COS

In case of trouble with Turkey we ought to have some means of clearing
mines away from the entrance. Can destroyers do this with a sweep? Have
they got the appliances? Can you suggest any way of meeting this difficulty?

WSC

Prince Louis to Winston S. Churchill
(Admiralty papers 116/3491)

19 August 1914   Admiralty

A pair of destroyers or a pair of picket boats can easily rig up a sweep at any
time. It has often been practised in fleets.

LB

Winston S. Churchill to Enver Pasha: telegram
(Foreign Office papers: 371/2137)

19 August 1914

I deeply regretted necessity for detaining Turkish ships because I knew
the patriotism with which the money had been raised all over Turkey. As a
soldier you know what military necessity compels in war. I am willing to
propose to His Majesty's Government the following arrangement:—

(1) both ships to be delivered to Turkey at the end of the war after being
thoroughly repaired at our expense in British Dockyards; (2) if either is sunk
we will pay the full value to Turkey immediately on the declaration of peace;
(3) we will also pay at once the actual extra expense caused to Turkey by

sending out crews and other incidentals as determined by an arbitrator; (4) as a compensation to Turkey for the delay in getting the ships we will pay £1000 a day in weekly instalments for every day we keep them, dating retrospectively from when we took them over.

This arrangement will come into force on the day when the last German officer and man belonging to the Goeben and Breslau shall have left Turkish territory definitely and finally, and will continue binding so long as Turkey maintains a loyal and impartial neutrality in this war and favours neither one side nor the other.

Do you agree?

Winston S. Churchill to Rear-Admiral Limpus: telegram

(*Copy, Foreign Office papers: 371/2137*)

19 August 1914   Admiralty

Will you please take an opportunity of showing Minister of Marine the telegram I have sent to Enver Pasha & telling HE that had I had the pleasure of his acquaintance I shd have addressed myself directly to him.

Winston S. Churchill: memorandum

(*Churchill papers: 13/27*)

19 August 1914   Admiralty

The Kiel Canal gives the Germans the power of putting their whole naval force either in the North Sea or the Baltic. The British naval strength is not sufficient to provide two Fleets each individually superior to the German Fleet.

The British Admiralty cannot therefore obtain the naval command of the Baltic until either (A) a decisive general battle has been won at sea or (B) the Kiel Canal has been effectively blocked. (A) depends on the enemy's movements, but might happen any day. (B) is a difficult enterprise which might be attempted either by aerial or destroyer attack, or both, on the Brunsbuttel lock-gates [*at the Western end of the canal*]. At the right moment (B) may be tried.

But it is important that plans should be prepared *now* to make the best use of our getting the command of the Baltic through either (A) or (B): & we desire the Russian General Staff to tell us what military use they would think it worth while to make of that command assuming we were able to get it.

The operation of sending a British Fleet through the Bælts [*the passage through the Danish islands*] to enter the Baltic is feasible, &, if the main strategic situation were satisfactory, cd be achieved.

Transports to carry a large invading army cd be supplied at any time from England.

It would be possible if we had the command of the Baltic to land a Russian army in order:—

1) to turn the flank & rear of German armies holding the Dantzig-Thorn line, or which were elsewhere resisting the main Russian attack;

2) to attack Berlin from the North—only 90 miles in the direct line;

3) to attack Kiel & the Canal in force and to drive the German fleet to sea.

All or any of these operations would have to be carried out by the Russian Army; but if either (A) or (B) condition were fulfilled, the British Admiralty cd carry convoy, & land the necessary force.

We desire a full statement of Russian views on these alternative operations, which wd be of course contingent on (A) or (B) being satisfied.

Sir Francis Villiers[1] to Sir Edward Grey: telegram
(*Copy, Churchill papers: 13/43*)

19 August 1914   Antwerp

French Minister[2] has received information that Netherlands authorities are permitting large importation of food-stuffs for Germany via Rotterdam while they refuse admission to Belgium via Antwerp.

Winston S. Churchill to Sir Edward Grey
(*Copy, Churchill papers: 13/43*)

20 August 1914   Admiralty

If this were true it would be serious. I have always felt that if Holland were to try to strangle her small neighbour who is fighting for her life, she wd

---

[1] Francis Hyde Villiers, 1852–1925. Entered Foreign Office, 1870. Minister to Portugal, 1906–11. Knighted, 1909. Minister to Belgium, 1911–19. Ambassador to Belgium, 1919–20.

[2] Antony Wladislaw Klobukowski, 1855–1934. A French citizen of Polish emigré descent. Chef du Cabinet, Government of Cochin China, and Director du Cabinet, Anam and Tonkin, 1887. Minister in Bankok, 1901–3; Lima, 1903–6; Cairo, 1906–7; Addis Ababa, 1907–8. Governor-General, Indo-China, 1908–11. Minister in Brussels, 1911–14. Director of the Information and Propaganda Commissariate, Paris, 1918. He wrote about his three years in Belgium in *Souvenirs de Belgique*, published in 1928.

commit an offence wh wd deprive her of all claims to our sympathy. The Scheldt *must* be kept open to merchant vessels.

Admy are capable of doing this at any time you think it necessary.

Rear-Admiral Sir Charles Ottley[1] to Winston S. Churchill

(*Churchill papers: 28/153*)

21 August 1914   Admiralty

Dear Mr Churchill,

Sir Francis Hopwood[2] has just telephoned to tell me that the Turkish Cabinet are complaining to our Ambassador at Constantinople that—not withstanding that the Sultan Osman (now HMS Agincourt) was seized by the British Government half an hour after the Turkish Government had paid over the sum of £648,000 (odd) being the instalment due on the vessels delivery, and not withdrawn that our Agent (Mr Vere)[3] had given his assurance that Messrs Armstrongs would immediately refund the money; as a matter of fact they (the Turkish Govt) have not yet received a single piastre of it.

This statement is of course fantastically untrue. Messrs Armstrongs took immediate steps to refund the money; and did so, as soon as the Banks in England re-opened, (on August 7th).

On that day the sum of £648,000 (odd) was paid by the Bank of England to the Imperial Ottoman Bank.

I have just seen the Turkish Embassy authorities and have been informed by Captain Riza (Naval Attaché)[4] that the fact that this money had been repaid to the Ottoman Government was telegraphed to Constantinople by the Turkish Ambassador, and he (Captain Riza) regards the whole incident as a regettable mistake, due to the inefficiency of the telegraphic communications.

[1] Charles Langdale Ottley, 1858–1932. Entered Navy, 1871. Present at the bombardment of Alexandria, 1882. Senior Naval Officer at Constantinople, 1898. Captain, 1899. Director of Naval Intelligence, 1905–7. Knighted, 1907. Secretary to the Committee of Imperial Defence, 1907–12. Retired from Navy with rank of Rear-Admiral, 1912. Director of Armstrong Whitworth, 1912–19.

[2] Francis John Stephens Hopwood, 1860–1947. Entered Board of Trade as Assistant Solicitor, 1885. Knighted, 1901. Permanent Under-Secretary of State for the Colonies, 1907–11. Additional Civil Lord, Admiralty, 1912–17. Created Baron Southborough, 1917. Honorary Secretary, Irish Convention, 1917–18. President, Commission to India on Reform, 1918–19.

[3] Arthur de Vere Vere, 1852–1916. A British resident in Constantinople; he returned to London after the outbreak of war between Britain and Turkey in October 1914. His daughter Aimee married, in 1897, Francis Barker, a director of Vickers.

[4] Ali Riza Bey, 1877– . Lecturer at the Naval War Academy, Constantinople, 1897. Naval Attaché, London, 1913–14. Commanded the Cruiser *Turgut Reis*, 1914–16. Aide de Camp to the Sultan, 1918. Director of the 1st Department, Ministry of the Navy, 1921. Harbour Master, Constantinople (Istanbul), 1922. Member of Parliament, 1924.

I will put these facts on paper officially as soon as I get back to my office, for your information.

Yours sincerely
C. L. Ottley

Winston S. Churchill to Sir Edward Grey
(*Grey Papers*)

21 August 1914   Admiralty
Very secret

My dear Grey,

It is necessary for me to discuss with the French Minister of Marine[1] certain questions connected with the general policy of the naval war, & more particularly to open up the possibility of ultimate action in the Baltic. I therefore propose to take advantage of a momentary lull, while the Fleet is resting in a safe position, to go to Paris—starting tomorrow morning & returning here on Monday. I am taking Admiral Oliver, of the Intelligence Department, with me, but am keeping my visit absolutely secret. I hope you approve. I mentioned the project to the Prime Minister today after the Cabinet, & he gave me his permission.

I am asking Tyrrell to get me passports for myself, Admiral Oliver, the Duke of Marlborough,[2] & Eddie Marsh.

Yours ever
Winston S. Churchill

Winston S. Churchill to Sir Edward Grey
(*Grey Papers*)

21 August 1914   Admiralty

My dear Grey,

I am sure it would have been all right, but in view of your letter[3] I will abandon my project & try to find some other means of arranging the Conference.

Yours ever
Winston S. Churchill

[1] Victor Augagneur, 1855–1931. A distinguished French pathologist and colonial administrator. Minister of Marine, 1914–18.

[2] Charles Richard John Spencer-Churchill, 1871–1934. Known as 'Sunny'. 9th Duke of Marlborough, 1892. Paymaster General of the Forces, 1899–1902. Staff Captain and ADC to General Hamilton during the South African War, 1900. Under-Secretary of State for the Colonies, 1903–5. Lieutenant-Colonel, Queen's Own Oxfordshire Hussars, 1910. Employed at the War Office as a Special Messenger, 1914–15. Joint Parliamentary Secretary, Board of Agriculture and Fisheries, 1917–18.

[3] Not found.

H. H. Asquith to Venetia Stanley

(*Montagu papers*)

21 August 1914   10 Downing Street

. . . We had a long Cabinet this morning, mostly about rather boring details connected with the war. The real centre of interest (political, not military) at the moment is Turkey—& the two darkest horses in the European stable, Italy & Roumania. The different points of view of different people are rather amusing—Winston violently anti-Turk, Kitchener strong that Roumania is the real pivot of the situation, Masterman[1] eagerly pro-Bulgarian, I very much against any aggressive action vis a vis of Turkey wh wd excite our Mussulmans in India & Egypt,[2] Ll George keen for Balkan confederation, Grey judicious & critical all round, Haldane misty and unprecise, Simon precise & uninspiring, Hobhouse[3] assertive & irrelevant, Runciman[4] instructive & juiceless, and the Beagles & Bobtails silent & bewildered. There's a picture for you of a united & *most* efficient Cabinet! . . .

Winston S. Churchill to Sir Edward Grey

(*Foreign Office papers: 371/2137*)

22 August 1914   Admiralty

Sir Edward Grey,

We must stick to our point about all German ratings from Goeben & Breslau going home at once. If necessary to a friendly Turkey we wd provide the skilled ratings wh are indispensable ourselves. We must extirpate the Germans from the Turkish Fleet, & above all from German ships transferred illegally to the Turkish flag.

This is of course only the Admiralty view.

[1] Charles Frederick Gurney Masterman, 1874–1927. Liberal MP, 1906–14. Under-Secretary to Churchill, Home Office, 1909–12. Financial Secretary to the Treasury, 1912–14. Chancellor of the Duchy of Lancaster, 1914–15. Forced to leave the Government after nine months of being unable to find a parliamentary constituency after being defeated at a by-election in February 1914. Liberal MP, 1923–4.

[2] There were an estimated 20 million Muslims in Turkey in 1910. In British India there were 62 million Muslims (census of 1901); there were a further 10 million Muslims in Egypt (census of 1907).

[3] Charles Edward Henry Hobhouse, 1862–1941. Liberal MP, 1892–5, 1900–18. Chancellor of the Duchy of Lancaster, 1911–14. Postmaster-General, 1914–15. 4th Baronet, 1916.

[4] Walter Runciman, 1870–1949. Liberal MP, 1899–1900; 1902–18. Shipowner. President of the Board of Education, 1908–11. President of the Board of Agriculture and Fisheries, 1911–14. President of the Board of Trade, 1914–16. Liberal MP, 1924–9; 1929–31. Liberal National MP, 1931–7. President of the Board of Trade, 1931–7. 2nd Baron, 1937. Created Viscount Runciman of Doxford, 1937. Head of Mission to Czechoslovakia, 1938.

Winston S. Churchill to Lord Kitchener

(*Copy, Churchill papers: 8/65*)

22 August 1914   Admiralty

My dear Kitchener,

The Admiralty are confident of their ability to secure this country against invasion or any serious raid. If you wish to send the 6th Division abroad at once we should not raise any objection from the naval standpoint. The situation, now that both the Navy and the Territorials are mobilised and organised, is entirely different from those which have been discussed in the Invasion Committee of the C.I.D., and if you want to send the last Regular division, the First Sea Lord and I are quite ready to agree, and so far as possible to accept responsibility.

Yours very sincerely
Winston S. Churchill

Winston S. Churchill to the Press Bureau

(*Draft, Churchill papers: 13/27*)

23 August 1914   Admiralty

Admiralty wish to draw attention to their previous warning to neutrals of the dangers of traversing the North Sea. The Germans are continuing their practice of laying mines indiscriminately upon the ordinary trade routes. These mines are not laid in connection with any definite military scheme such as the closing of a military port, or as a district operation against a fighting fleet, but appear to be scattered on the chance of catching individual British war or Merchant vessels. In consequence of this policy, no matter what their destination neutral ships are exposed to the gravest dangers. Two Danish vessels, the S.S. Maryland & the S.S. Broberg, have within the last 24 hours been destroyed by these deadly engines, in the North Sea while travelling on the ordinary trade routes at a considerable distance from the British Coast. In addition to this it is reported that two Dutch steamers clearing from Swedish ports were yesterday blown up by mines in the Baltic. In these circumstances the Admiralty desire to impress not only on British but on neutral shipping the vital importance of touching at British ports before entering the North Sea, in order to ascertain according to the latest information the routes & channels which the Admy are keeping swept, & along which these dangers to neutrals, and merchantmen are reduced as far as possible.

The Admy, while reserving to themselves the utmost liberty of retaliatory action against this new form of warfare, announce that they have not so far laid any mines during the present war, & that they are endeavouring to keep the sea routes open for peaceful commerce.

WSC

Winston S. Churchill to Sir John Jellicoe: telegram
(Draft, Churchill papers: 13/44)

24 August 1914   Admiralty
Secret & Personal

First Lord to C in C

News from France is disappointing[1] & serious results of battle cannot yet be measured as it still continues over enormous front. I have had the telegrams about it repeated to you. We have not entered this business without resolve to see it through and you may rest assured that our action will be proportioned to the gravity of the need.

I have absolute confidence in final results.

No special action is required from you at present but you shd address your mind to a naval situation which may arise where Germans control Calais & French coasts, & what ought to be the position of Grand Fleet in that event.

WSC

Winston S. Churchill to John Churchill[2]
(John Churchill papers)

24 August 1914   Admiralty

My dear Jack,

The news from Belgium is disappointing & may be serious. Our men seem to have stood up well to them & no doubt exacted a heavy forfeit. No one can tell how far this great adventure may carry us all. Unless we win, I do not want to live any more. But win we will.

[1] On the morning of 24 August the news reached London that the Germans had captured the Belgian fortress of Namur. That morning Kitchener received a telegram from the Commander-in-Chief of the British Expeditionary Force, Sir John French, implying that the British forces then in Belgium might soon be driven back across northern France, and asking the War Office to take immediate steps to fortify Le Havre.

[2] John Strange Spencer Churchill, 1880–1947. Churchill's younger brother, known as Jack. A stockbroker. Major, Queen's Own Oxfordshire Hussars, 1914–18. Served at Dunkirk, 1914; on Sir John French's staff, 1914–15; on Sir Ian Hamilton's staff, 1915; on General Birdwood's staff, 1916–18.

I have talked to Lord K about the Yeomanry and have showed him yr letters—I am sure the right steps will be taken. It will make me vy anxious if you go to the front, & me tied here. But I shall find my way there before the end.

I am so glad you had a pleasant Sunday with dear Goonie.[1] After all this is a gt moment in the history of the world & of our small country & we must all try to act so as to make them like to read about it in the years that will follow.

I will try one day to make a dart down to see you.

My division [the Royal Naval Division] is forming up well. I shall have over 10,000 trained men this week.

God bless you—& all of them.

Your loving brother
W

Sir Mark Sykes[2] to Winston S. Churchill

(*Churchill papers: 13/45*)

24 August 1914   5/A P W O Yorkshire Regt
                                                  Hammersknot Camp
                                                  Darlington

Dear Winston Churchill,

It would seem criminal of me to write to you at such a time—Yet I venture to do so—because, from various suggestive scraps I have seen in the Times, I infer that the Germans are straining every nerve to involve Turkey and so cause if possible a Pan-Islamic diversion against us, and a Caucasian complication for Russia on the Armenian frontier. If this is so, we shall I presume counter in Syria and S. Mesopotamia.

I know you won't think me self-seeking if I say all the knowledge I have of local tendencies and possibilities, are at your disposal—and you will forgive me for troubling you. If operations are to take place in those parts I might be of more use on the spot, than anywhere else. My Battn is practically willing for foreign service i.e. 85% and with my personal knowledge of its

---

[1] Lady Gwendeline Bertie, 1885–1941. Known as 'Goonie'. Daughter of the 7th Earl of Abingdon. She married Churchill's brother Jack in 1908.

[2] Mark Sykes, 1879–1919. Travelled widely through Turkey at different times between 1898 and 1904. Honorary attaché at Constantinople, 1905–7. Conservative MP, 1910–19. Raised a reserve battalion, Yorkshire Regiment, 1913–14. 6th Baronet, 1913. Lieutenant-Colonel, on special duties in Serbia, Bulgaria, Egypt and India, 1915–16. British negotiator of an inter-Allied territorial settlement for the Near East, known as the Sykes–Picot agreement, 1916. Member of the British Delegation at the Paris Peace Conference, 1919.

possible antagonist in the regions I mention, I could make it serve a turn, raise native scallywag corps, win over notables or any other oddment.

May good prosper your operations.

Yours

Mark Sykes

Grand Duke Nicholas[1] to Winston S. Churchill: telegram

(*Copy, Churchill papers: 13/27*)

24 August 1914

We appreciate in the highest degree the First Lord's offer to cooperate with us in the execution by our land forces of a landing operation on the North German Coast, should the British Fleet gain command of the Baltic Sea. The attainment of the aforesaid command would, in our opinion, in itself prove a most valuable and desirable factor towards the development of our offensive operations against Germany. We consider that the suggested landing operation, under favorable circumstances, would be quite feasible and fully expedient. We therefore gratefully accept in principal the First Lord's offer but we add, that we could avail ourselves thereof, only should the general military situation lend itself to its application.

Winston S. Churchill to H. H. Asquith, Sir Edward Grey and Lord Kitchener

(*Copy, Churchill papers: 13/27*)

25 August 1914   Admiralty

Most Secret

In addition to the contingencies noted in my memorandum,[2] it should be observed that either the destruction of the Austrian naval power, or the accession to our side of Italy and Greece or Italy alone, would enable two Fleets each superior to Germany to be maintained, and one of these could be placed in the Baltic.

This phase of naval operations must be held in view as an event to be sought for during October or later.

WSC

---

[1] Nicholas Nicolaevitch, 1856–1929. Uncle of Tsar Nicholas II. Supreme Commander of the Russian Armies, 1914–15. Viceroy of the Caucasus, 1916–17. He died in exile in Paris.

[2] Churchill's memorandum of 19 August 1914, quoted on page 45.

J. A. Pease:[1] *diary*

(Gainford papers)

25 August 1914

Churchill haranged us for half an hour on the necessity of compulsory service. Pointing out the importance of young unmarried men going to the front rather than the Territorial, a married man who had trained with a limited obligation, & now his patriotism was exploited by being pressed into going abroad & almost compelled to agree to do so, whilst others were loafing & cheering & doing nothing for their country etc. etc. etc.

We all sat and listened, much bored. The P.M. took it with impatience— the matter he said was not urgent. George said we need not be in a panic —the people would not listen to such proposals. The P.M. asked how many of our own men in the H of C would now assent, such a proposal would divide the country from one end to the other . . .

K said it might come to this later on. He made no appeal for compulsion yet, he had got his 120,000 men & recruiting was still going on although he had only asked for 100,000—he could not arm more before April.

Winston S. Churchill to Sir George Aston: telegram

(Copy, Churchill papers: 8/67)

25 August 1914   Admiralty

1. At daylight to-morrow, if circumstances allow, you will disembark such portions of your brigade as have arrived at Ostend and occupy the town. You will push out reconnaissances of cyclists to Bruges, Thourout, and Dixmude. You will establish yourself at Ostend, forming an entrenched picket line around the town in such a way as to enable you to cover the debarkation of a Division of the Army. A squadron of aeroplanes will reach you before noon, having previously made an aerial reconnaissance of the country within 30 miles of Ostend. The aeroplanes will be placed under your orders.

2. The object of this movement is to create a diversion, favourable to the Belgians, who are advancing from Antwerp, and to threaten the western flank of the German southward advance. It should therefore be ostentatious. You should not advance inland from Ostend without further orders, but

---

[1] Joseph Albert Pease, 1860-1943. Liberal MP, 1892–1917. Chancellor of the Duchy of Lancaster, 1910-11. President of the Board of Education, 1911–15. Postmaster-General, 1916. Created Baron Gainford, 1917. Chairman of the British Broadcasting Company, 1922–6. President of the Federation of British Industries, 1927–8.

some enterprise may be permitted to the patrols. Information about the enemy will be supplied you personally at the Admiralty.

The object in view would be fully attained if a considerable force of the enemy were attracted to the coast. You will be re-embarked as soon as this is accomplished.

Winston S. Churchill to Lord Kitchener

(*Kitchener papers*)

26 August 1914   Admiralty

My Dear Kitchener,

We cannot spare these 4 Lewis guns. They belong to us & are needed for the Naval air service.

We have already given the Belgians 24 machine guns & $\frac{1}{2}$ a million rounds out of stores none too plentiful.

Yours sincerely
Winston S. Churchill

H. H. Asquith to George V

(*Royal Archives*)

26 August 1914   10 Downing Street

... The occupation of Ostend by a brigade of Marines supported by 4 battleships of the Majestic class was approved as an operation involving little loss and calculated to give both material and moral support to Belgium. ...

Winston S. Churchill to John Churchill

(*John Churchill papers*)

26 August 1914   Admiralty
Secret

My dear Jack,

I understand you are required to provide 2 Squadrons for Divisional cavalry for some of the regular divisions. This is a gt honour for the regiment. I shd expect there was still a few weeks before sailing.

I am trying to get the 3rd Sqn (yours I hope) for the Infantry division I am forming from Marines & Naval reservists. This force will go out early in the new year & will compare very favourably with any of the new divisions.

I think a great deal of you all.

As soon as the decisive battle has been fought at sea—I shall try to come out too, if there is any use for me.

All good wishes—Clemmie sends love.

Your loving brother
W

The result of the big battle governs the future. We must wait.

Sir Louis Mallet to Winston S. Churchill: telegram

(Admiralty papers: 116/1336)

26 August 1914   Constantinople

In reply to your enquiry 90 German sailors passed through Sofia yesterday on their way to Constantinople. I have protested strongly, but Grand Vizier is unable to control the situation which is dominated by the German Ambassador[1] and Generals.[2]

Rear-Admiral Limpus to Winston S. Churchill

(Churchill papers: 13/45)

26 August 1914   c/o British Embassy
                                        Constantinople

Dear Mr Churchill,

On going to sea on July 22nd. my programme was an exercise cruise, including meeting and bringing back the new ship, which was to have been delivered, and to have started from England, about August 1st.

However, events changed all plans, and after learning about the spread of hostilities the remnant of my Fleet (more than half the Flotilla had already been detached when Turkey mobilised) was called up to Princes' Islands.

First, Lieutenant Boothby (Commodore of the Flotilla)[3] was called ashore (August 10) on the plea that in existing circumstances a man so recently arrived could not know his Turkish Officers, and, a few days later,

---

[1] Hans Freiherr von Wangenheim, 1859-1915. German diplomat. Attaché, St Petersburg, 1887-8. Served at Copenhagen, Madrid, Luxemburg and Lisbon. 1st Secretary, Constantinople, 1899-1904. Councillor, Mexico, 1904-8; Athens, 1908-12. Ambassador in Constantinople from May 1912 until his death in October 1915.

[2] In 1913 a German Military Mission led by the Prussian General of Cavalry, Liman von Sanders, arrived in Turkey. There were five hundred German officers on the mission by August 1914. In March 1915 von Sanders was appointed Commander of the Turkish Fifth Army, whose command included the Gallipoli Peninsula.

[3] Evelyn Leonard Beridge Boothby, 1876-1937. Entered Navy, 1890; retired as a Lieutenant, Royal Marines, 1912. Lieutenant, Turkish Mission, 1914. Lieutenant-Commander, in command of an Armed Yacht, 1914-16. Commander, in command of a Light Cruiser, 1916-18. Captain, 1918.

on Saturday August 15th., I myself was called to the Admiralty by Wireless Telegraphy, and replaced by a Turkish Frégate Captain.

I was given no explanation; but I feel sure that my recall was due to the fact that, the British and Germans being at War, the British mission could not have been expected to work together with Germans for Turkey in taking over the 'Goeben' and 'Breslau'.

For a similar reason, I believe, I and my Staff are now requested not to go on board any of the ships.

The manning difficulty has been lessened by the arrival here in the Golden Horn of the Transport 'Rechid Pasha' at daybreak on Saturday August 22nd. with the Officers and men of the embargoed vessels.

Most of these people are still, August 26th., in barracks.

On August 17th., Monday, as already reported, I delivered your message which was very well received; at any rate it appeared so. But the recipient [Enver Pasha] 'went sick' that evening, and so far as I know has not been seen by any British person since, though several, including myself, have tried to see him.

On Monday 24th. I called and received a message that the Doctor was actually with him, and that he had been operated upon on Sunday 23rd.

On Tuesday 25th. I saw the United States Ambassador,[1] who told me that he had recently seen Enver, who had had a small operation on his foot. Whether he is really laid up, or whether he is avoiding unwelcome advice I do not know. My evidence, poor though it is, favours the former view. But I do know that General Liman von Sanders[2] entered Enver's house 1 minute before me on Monday 24th. and apparently remained.

I also know that in addition to about 70 German Military Officers who were already here in the German Mission, 28 more arrived via Sofia before Sunday 23rd. of August.

Also the bulk, if not all, of the complements of the 'Goeben' and 'Breslau' are somewhere here i.e. either on board their old ships, or in the Flotilla, or in German Merchantmen that have sheltered here.

[1] Henry Morgenthau, 1856–1946. Born in Germany. Emigrated to the United States, 1865. President, Central Realty Bond & Trust Company, 1899–1905. President, Henry Morgenthau Company, 1905–13. Chairman, Finance Committee of the Democratic National Committee, 1912 and 1916. United States Ambassador, Constantinople, 1913–16; in charge of the interests of Britain, France, Russia, Belgium, Serbia and other belligerents, 1914–16. Honorary knighthood, 1920. Chairman, League of Nations Commission for the Settlement of Greek Refugees, 1923.

[2] Liman von Sanders, 1855–1929. Prussian General of Cavalry. Appointed head of the German Military Mission to Turkey, December 1913. Invited by Enver Pasha to command the Turkish 5th Army on the Gallipoli Peninsula, March 1915; remained in command throughout the campaign, April 1915–January 1916. Appointed to command the Turkish forces on the Syrian front, March 1918, with the rank of Field-Marshal. Surrendered to the Allies, November 1918, and interned in Malta during 1919.

A law has been passed forbidding any but Turkish Wireless installations to exist in Turkish territory or waters. Yet three German Steamships, the 'Korkovado' at the north end of the Bosphorus near the German Embassy, the 'General' near Constantinople, and another, name and position unknown, have their aerials still up; and the first-named is in hourly communication with the German Embassy by Motor boat. She may be receiving from Norddeich in Germany direct.

In fact I consider that Constantinople is almost completely in German hands at this moment.

It appears to me that Enver and the Army wish and intend this. That Djavid knows that anything but neutrality means ruin; that Talaat *probably* understands this; that the Grand Vizier certainly does; and that Djemal is—a little uncertain—but has French leanings.

The lesser Ministers and the bulk of the people are on the whole adverse to the Germanophile policy of the few: but so long as the Army remains German they cannot do much.

The Commissariat and Transport of the Army appear at least as, if not more, faulty than in 1912. The place is getting stripped of men: it is doubtful if they can clothe or arm them. The very cabs in Constantinople are stripped of harness—to make up army deficiencies.

The troops as far as Adrianople are fed principally from here.

The mobilisation alternately waxes and wanes. Some days men over 32 who are untrained are released—to be called out again 48 hrs later, and again released.

Foodstuffs here threaten to run short. Transport in the interior is practically non-existent, owing to the requisitions of horses, cattle, and vehicles.

It is clear to me, and it seems to be patent to Sir Adam Block[1] and Sir Richard Crawford,[2] and to all men that I speak to that seem to know Turkey, including the United States Ambassador Mr. Morgenthau (whose personal sympathy and leaning appear to be German) that if Turkey now joins *either* group of Powers Turkey will certainly disappear as a separate state. Her only chance of existence is to remain absolutely neutral. I am doing all that I can to put this view before Ministers and others.

[1] Adam Samuel James Block, 1856–1941. Entered Diplomatic Service as a Student Interpreter, Constantinople, 1877. Consul, Constantinople, 1890. 1st Dragoman, 1894. Represented British Bondholders on the Council of Administration of the Ottoman Public Debt, 1903–29. Knighted, 1907. President of British Chamber of Commerce, Constantinople, 1907–14. Chairman of the Admiralty Sub-Committee at the War Trade Department, and Head of Finance Section of Foreign Trade Department, 1914–16. Controller, Finance Section, Ministry of Blockade, 1916–18.

[2] Richard Frederick Crawford, 1863–1919. A Commissioner of Customs, 1904–11. Customs Adviser to the Egyptian Government. Knighted, 1911. Adviser to Turkish Minister of Finance, 1911–14.

Through Lieutenant Hallifax,[1] who helped me to select the Turkish Electrical officers for the 'Goeben', I have just been informed that many of the officers and men of that ship speak Turkish, or English, or both. It is possible, as she has been in Eastern Waters for about 2 years, and has spent some time here.

I feel that Turkey is at the parting of the ways, and will very shortly decide whether to throw in her lot with Germany or not.

As we—the Triple Entente—are now in the first phase of destroying all chance of a German hegemony for the next 50 years, and will be the arbiters who decide the fate of the straits, it does not really matter very much to England what Turkey decides. But it does matter to Turkey.

I continue to work in order to help Turkey. That is to say I continue to use what influence I can wield to keep Turkey from finally committing suicide.

I feel that now that Sir Richard Crawford is back here we may be successful; but the issue will be a very close one.

It may even be quickly decided by any early appearance of a big German success on land.

Sir Adam Block speaks extremely pessimistically of the financial situation. He says that both the workers who create, and the machinery that collects, the revenues of the Public Debt have been so disorganised and crushed by the latest mobilisation that he anticipates a drop of 25% in the revenues of the Debt for the year, and, making allowances for all that he can think of, including the recent War Credit of $3\frac{1}{2}$ millions, that the total shortage for this year will probably mount up to 15 millions instead of 2 millions, by which sum the Chamber of Deputies recognised that expenditure for 1914–1915 would exceed revenue.

The pity is the greater because, up to the time of mobilising, business was increasing and the revenues were expanding.

In giving my reasons to the authorities here why Turkey should not join the German Group I have studiously omitted all talk of action that England might take, such as keeping the requisitioned ships without payment, and fomenting Arabian and Persian Gulf troubles against Turkey: or might encourage Greece to take, such as a landing between Smyrna and the Dardanelles, taking the forts on the south side of the Straits, admitting Torpedo Craft to the Marmara, cutting off and starving first the Gallipoli

[1] Guy Waterhouse Hallifax, 1884–1941. Entered Navy, 1899; Lieutenant, 1905. Lent for duty to the Turkish Government, 1912–14. Lieutenant-Commander, 1913. Served in HMS *Ajax*, 1914–18; Commander, 1917. Captain, 1924. Naval Representative, League of Nations Disarmament Conference, Geneva, 1925. Naval Attaché, Paris, 1928–31. Director, Signal Division, Admiralty, 1935. Secretary to the Governor General of South Africa, 1936–7. Director of Seaward Defence, South Africa, 1939. Killed in an air accident.

Peninsula, and soon after cutting all communications between Constantinople and the South. But they are each and all things which, methodically undertaken and persistently carried out, would succeed, and would annihilate the remaining power of Turkey.

No doubt there might be disturbances in Constantinople, but whether directed against the local Greeks and the British French and Russians, or whether directed against the Military Dictatorship of Enver and the Germans, they would not have any real effect on the result of the War.

It would be an unpleasant, probably a final and unpleasant, episode for the few thousands of people concerned, and would add perhaps to the completeness of Turkey's subsequent downfall.

The ideas which are probably being fostered by the Germans in the faint hope of hurting England *a little* and seemingly aggrandizing Turkey have no real probability of materialising.

Such are—the recovery of the Islands, perhaps even of Macedonia: the recovery of Egypt: a slice of the Caucasus:[1] a recovery of the Military power and importance of the Turkish Empire: the starvation of England by cessation of Black Sea grain and carrying trade.

As regards the last item, grain etc. can be obtained elsewhere: as regards the others, if the Entente triumphs they vanish with Turkey; if Germany triumphs, then Germany and certainly not Turkey rules the Straits and the Aegean, and if Turkey continues in any shape it will be as a Khedivate in the occupation of Germany.

I believe now, as always, that Turkey is worth saving.

I believe still that it is possible to save Turkey; but now only if she remains absolutely neutral, and relaxes her mobilisation to an extent to permit trade and work to continue.

This, as I see it, is the situation here to-day, Wednesday, August 26th. 1914.

Since this was typed I learn that 90 more German sailors are on their way here via Sophia.

This indicates even more clearly the attitude that Turkey is expected by Germany to take up.

I had very great difficulty getting even a few petty officers for Turkey from England.

Sincerely yours
Arthur Limpus

[1] In February 1914 the Great Powers had assigned to Greece all the Aegean Islands, except Tenedos and Imbros. Bulgaria and Serbia had partitioned the Turkish Province of Macedonia in November 1912. Great Britain had occupied Egypt in 1882, Russia had annexed the Caucasian provinces of Batum and Kars in 1878.

Major Cunliffe-Owen[1] to the Foreign Office: telegram

(*Admiralty papers: 116/1336*)

27 August 1914   Therapia[2]

In the event of Turkey being driven by German element into war with Russia naval position for latter in the Black Sea may be serious and may have also some moral weight towards determining attitude of Bulgaria and Roumania.

Russia has no fear whatever of purely Turkish military movement in any direction but when 'Goeben' is ready this ship together with others disposable may completely control the Black Sea. 'Goeben' is expected to be ready for sea on September 2nd and there is little practical chance of German personnel being removed. On the contrary Turkish flotilla is, it is believed, now being manœuvred by German officers and several German merchant vessels here are now being prepared as armed cruisers.

Therefore, in the event of matters coming to a head in this direction, it may be advisable to consider question of our fleet entering the Straits.

In respect of this, if mines can be negotiated, there should be little apprehension of difficulty in running past the shore defences and once off Stamboul, position would be a commanding one, completely paralysing all military movements between European and Asiatic shores.

On the other hand reconstructed Turkish fleet would have also to be dealt with, and a mere fleet entry is not calculated to have any permanent effect nor might fleet be able to remain without simultaneous action on the part of Russian fleet at Bosphorus and Russian military occupation of adjoining country. Personally, except for giving Russia immediate assistance and possibly casting a balance in Balkans on our side, I should be against a fleet enterprise only. Probability is that it might succeed, but to command situation properly at Dardanelles, requires also use of military force and point arises whether substantial enterprise should be attempted in quite a subsidiary theatre of war.

Moreover military operations against Turks would be far easier in Persian Gulf or Syria where Turkish forces are almost negligible.

---

[1] Frederick Cunliffe-Owen, 1868–1946. Entered Army, 1888. Major, 1903. Attached to the Greek Army during the Balkan Wars, 1912–13. Military Attaché to Turkey, 1913–14. Lieutenant-Colonel, October 1914. He left Constantinople on 2 December 1914. Brigadier-General commanding the Royal Artillery of the Australian and New Zealand Army Corps, Gallipoli, 1915. Served with the British forces in Iraq, 1920. Member of the Refugee Settlement Commission, Greece, 1923–6.

[2] Therapia, a village on the European shore of the Bosphorus, half-way between Constantinople and the Black Sea. The British Embassy, and several others, moved there during the summer months to escape the heat of the capital.

Should decision be eventually taken for a fleet movement I need hardly impress that for local reasons there should be no mistake as to rapidity of execution and minimum risk of failure.

Prince Louis to Winston S. Churchill

(*Copy, Churchill papers: 13/29*)

27 August 1914   Admiralty

Admiral Milne's report and supplementary explanations have been carefully studied. They show that he fully grasped the spirit of his instructions and took the best measures with the force at his disposal during the successive phases of strained relations and actual hostilities, in which this Country, France, Germany, Austria and Italy were involved.

Up to the time that the 2 Germans left Messina Eastward, Admiral Milne's dispositions were the proper ones, and they were successful, in as much as they prevented the Germans from carrying out their primary role of interrupting French troops crossing from Africa.

On leaving Messina to the South and East, the Germans made, as was expected, for the Adriatic, their only friendly locality, where their Allies were in force,—why they went East after a while is beside the point.

Admiral Troubridge with 4 powerful armoured Cruisers and a flotilla was in such a position that he could bar the passage to the Adriatic as well as to the Aegean to the 2 Germans.

Admiral Milne placed his 3, slower Battle-Cruisers in the best position for baring the passage West.

The Enemy being prevented from going North (into Adriatic) East, (into Aegean) or West (at the French transports) could only go South (Egypt) where a superior force could follow him.

There was therefore no particular objection to detaching one of the 3 Battle Cruisers (*Indomitable*) to the Eastward.

Admiral Troubridge signally failed in carrying out the task assigned to him by his C in C. The road to the East was open to the Enemy and he took it, closely shadowed by a determined light Cruiser of inferior speed to both Ships she was following and actually engaging.

As soon as Admiral Milne had received (on the following evening) his subordinate's amazing telegram, which left no doubt that the armoured cruisers had been steering away from the Enemy all day, he recalled *Gloucester* on two grounds as explained by him (1) shortage of coal (2) risk of capture.

This action cannot be found fault with in itself. Both reasons are in themselves quite sound. They were, however not singly or collectively, sufficiently

strong to make the recall imperative. The *Gloucester* could well have continued and trusted to finding coal at Syra or elsewhere. As to risk of capture:
Goeben of superior speed and overwhelming strength could at any moment
turn and destroy *Gloucester* not to mention *Breslau's* assistance. The reason
she never did so, but once, when she turned on her pursuer, was no doubt
her fear that heavier ships (Troubridge's) were in support, if not actually
in sight—That they were really many miles away steering north *Goeben* could
not know, so that the risk was no greater off Matapan than at any time during
the long chase.

Once the Germans had been seen rounding the South point of Greece—
the Gate to the Aegean—they entered Waters where their presence was of
less consequence to us, while the need for light Cruisers off Adriatic was still
great.

The recall of *Gloucester* can therefore be passed over.

It is to be noted that once the C in C knew the Enemy had gone round
Matapan, all his dispositions and movements were perfectly correct and
would certainly have resulted in his finding the Enemy if they had not
sheltered in the Dardanalles.

The outstanding feature of this interesting operation, in which the Enemy
played the part of a harmless fugitive, is the marked superiority in speed of
Goeben over our battle cruisers, as well as *Breslau* over our light Cruisers. This
could only be met by chasing them each with superior numbers which by
spreading wide, could at a given moment hope to cut off by working on
inner and hence shorter lines. It was thus quite correct for Admiral Milne
to keep the Enemy between two groups of ships each superior in numbers,
and had his Second-in-Command done his duty the Enemy was bound to
be brought into action.

LB

The explanation is satisfactory; the result unsatisfactory.

WSC

Prince Louis to Sir Berkeley Milne
(*Copy, Churchill papers: 13/29*)

27 August 1914   Admiralty

My Lords Commissioners of the Admiralty having further considered your
report of proceedings in the Mediterranean, and subsequent explanations
called for, direct me to inform you as follows:—

1. Your general dispositions and the measures taken by you from July 27th

until you handed over the Command in the Mediterranean to the French Admiralissimo are fully approved by Their Lordships.

2. That the two German Cruisers were not brought to action and disposed of is of course to be regretted, but Their Lordships note that this was primarily due to the failure of Rear-Admiral Troubridge to carry out your instructions. Their Lordships intend dealing with this matter independently.

3. Their Lordships request that you will now strike your flag and report yourself at the Admiralty on the termination of your command.[1]

LB

Winston S. Churchill to Lord Kitchener

(*Copy, Churchill papers: 26/1*)

28 August 1914   Admiralty

My dear Kitchener,

Here is an idea which deserves examination. The Siberian troops would, if used against Germany and Austria, have to come South at an awkward moment and derange the communications (so I am told). On the other hand, it would probably be easy to send them to Archangel, and it is (roughly) only 6 days from Archangel to Ostend.

If a couple of Russian Corps d'Armee were transported round this route, it would be possible to strike at the German communications in a very effective manner.

It is an interesting idea, though I dare say it would not greatly commend itself to the Russians. Don't trouble to answer.

Lord Haldane to Winston S. Churchill

(*Churchill papers: 13/45*)

29 August 1914   28 Queen Anne's Gate

My dear Winston,

Your telegram has just come & I have read it to Grey.

Warmest congratulations on this splendid piece of work done by the fleet [2] It is worthy of the inspiring spirit of their First Lord. The British public

---

[1] Milne received no further command. He asked Margot Asquith to influence Churchill on his behalf, but she was unsuccessful. He retired from the Navy in 1919. Two years later he published a detailed defence of his actions, entitled *The Flight of the Goeben and Breslau*.

[2] On 28 August 1914 Commodore Tyrwhitt's Harwich force and Commodore Keyes' submarines engaged a superior German force in the Heligoland Bight. Sir David Beatty arrived in time with his battle cruisers to decide the action in Britain's favour. Thirty-five British sailors died, but no ships were lost. The Germans were impressed by the British boldness in daring so deep a penetration of German waters.

& our allies will grow a cubit in confidence when they read the news to-morrow.

> Ever yours
> Haldane

Winston S. Churchill to John Churchill

(John Churchill papers)

29 August 1914
Secret

Admiralty

My dear Jack,

Kitchener tells me you are to form part of a (regular) Division to be sent shortly to the continent.

When have you got to decide? I wd like to have a talk with you first.

> Your loving brother
> W

Winston S. Churchill to Sir Edward Grey

(Churchill papers: 13/29)

29 August 1914

Admiralty

Sir Edward Grey,

Now that Austria has declared war on Japan, & in view of the general situation including the attitude of Turkey, it would seem only fitting that the Japanese Govt should be sounded as to their readiness to send a battle-squadron to co-operate with the allied powers in the Meditn or elsewhere. The influence & value of this powerful aid could not be over-rated. It would steady & encourage Italy, & would bring nearer the situation so greatly desired of our being able to obtain command of the Baltic.

There is reason to believe that the Japanese would take such an invitation as a compliment.[1]

> WSC

---

[1] During Churchill's period as First Lord the only Japanese naval help outside the Pacific was provided in February 1915, when they sent marines (some were also sent by France and Russia) to help suppress a mutiny of Indian labourers in the Singapore dockyard.

Winston S. Churchill to Lord Charles Beresford[1]

(Copy, Churchill papers: 13/43)

29 August 1914   Admiralty

Dear Lord Charles Beresford,

I learnt with surprise and regret from Mr Arthur Lee[2] that you have been guilty of making statements to the effect that the First Sea Lord cannot be trusted to maintain the interests of this country because of his German descent, and that you have frequently uttered these calumnies in clubs and other semi-public places.

In time of war the spreading of reports likely to cause mistrust or despondency is certainly a military offence. Your name is still borne on the retired list of the Navy. It is not possible that this matter should be passed over. The interests of the country do not permit the spreading of such wicked allegations by an officer of your rank, even tho' retired. And unless I receive from you an absolute retraction and a written undertaking not to repeat the offence during the course of the day, I shall be compelled with great regret to take official notice of the facts vouched for by Mr Lee. The action which would follow would then be necessarily serious.

Of the personal aspects of this incident I do not speak.

Yours faithfully
Winston S Churchill

Arthur Lee to Winston S. Churchill

(Churchill papers: 13/43)

29 August 1914   Chequers Court
Private   Butlers Cross
                                                                     Bucks

Dear Churchill

I have just been called up over the telephone by Beresford, who has assailed me with a torrent of violent abuse, in consequence of a letter which he says he has received from you. He also threatens to 'raise the matter in

[1] Charles William de la Poer Beresford, 1846–1919. Entered Navy, 1859. Conservative MP, 1874–80; 1885–9; 1897–1900; 1902; 1910–16. Knighted, 1903. Commanded the Mediterranean Fleet, 1905–7; the Channel Fleet, 1907–9. Retired from the Navy, 1911. Created Baron, 1916.

[2] Arthur Hamilton Lee, 1868–1947. Entered Army, 1888. Conservative MP, 1900–18. Civil Lord of Admiralty, 1903–5. Colonel, BEF, 1914. Personal Military Secretary to Lloyd George, 1916. Knighted, 1916. Director-General of Food Production, 1917–18. Created Baron Lee of Fareham, 1918. Minister of Agriculture and Fisheries, 1919–21. First Lord of the Admiralty, 1921–2. In 1921 he gave his home, Chequers, to the nation as a residence for successive Prime Ministers. Created Viscount, 1922.

the House of Commons, or otherwise publicly', & might attempt to make some kind of scene on Monday. This would of course be deplorable from a National point of view, & might injure Prince Louis in the very way that I feared & was anxious to avoid. But I can do nothing about it until I know exactly what you have said to Beresford.

I wish now that I had known that you were going to take this action, in order to have consulted with you about it beforehand, but as that is now impossible I must ask if you could manage to see me tomorrow (Sunday) if I returned to town. Any hour between 12.30 and 4 would suit me and I would come either to the Admiralty or anywhere else that suited you better.

Will you kindly have a reply telephoned to me to *Wendover 32*.

Yours sincerely
Arthur Lee

Lord Charles Beresford to Winston S. Churchill
(*Churchill papers: 13/43*)

29 August 1914   1 Great Cumberland Place

Dear Mr Churchill,

The statements made to you by Mr Arthur Lee are absolutely untrue. I have never stated in a club or anywhere else that 'The First Sea Lord cannot be trusted to maintain the interests of this country because of his German descent'. Mr Lee also states an untruth when saying that I have ever spoken of the First Sea Lord in clubs and other semi-public places in any other terms but those of respect for his ability as a Naval Officer. On the contrary I have frequently been a violent supporter of Prince Louis when I have heard his trustworthyness impugned. In the Carlton Club when I believe Mr Arthur Lee was present I remarked on Prince Louis' ability and expressed regret that he was German born. My remarks about German spies were certainly strong but that had nothing whatever to do with Prince Louis. I have never in my life said anything derogatory of Prince Louis, either as to his ability or his loyalty and trustworthyness as a Naval Officer. If what Mr Arthur Lee related to you was true, your letter is not couched in words one bit too strong. It is inconceiveable to me how Mr Arthur Lee could have made so atrocious and untrue a statement to you, and I shall immediately ask him to account for an explanation.

Yours sincerely
Charles Beresford

Rear-Admiral Hood to Lord Charles Beresford
(Draft, Churchill papers: 13/43)

30 August 1914   Admiralty
Copy

Dear Lord Charles Beresford,

The First Lord desired me to tell you[1] that he has now received a written statement from Mr Lee setting forth textually according to his recollection what you said. The First Lord is glad to learn from your letter that it was not your intention to cast aspersions upon the First Sea Lord's character & loyalty.

He has no doubt, however, from the evidence submitted to him, not from one quarter only, that you are in the habit of talking in a rash and loose way about Prince Louis of Battenberg and his German origin, and that persons who hear you are liable to put the worst construction on your language, with the result that alarm and mistrust is created. The First Lord had hoped from your attitude to him since the declaration of war, that you wished to help the Admiralty and the country with you on that basis & it is therefore with great regret that he learns of the kind of language you have been holding. No officer of the active or retired lists, unless wholly insignificant, can be permitted in a war of this vital character to express opinions which are calculated to undermine the confidence of the Service and the public in the Board of Admiralty; and the First Lord would not hesitate, if satisfied that this was being done, to act to the full extent of the powers with which he is entrusted.

In view of the emphatic disclaimer of intention to do injury contained in your letter the First Lord is willing on this occasion to consider the incident closed.

Arthur Lee to Winston S. Churchill
(Churchill papers: 13/43)

30 August 1914   10 Chesterfield Street

Dear Mr Churchill,

In accordance with your request I forward herewith a memorandum of those portions of Lord Charles Beresford's reflections upon the First Sea Lord, which were made openly in the Hall of the Carlton Club on Thursday evening last—in the hearing of several members—and to which I took strong exception at the time.

---

[1] Although this letter was sent as if from Rear-Admiral Hood, the draft was written by Churchill himself.

I deeply regret the necessity of having had to give you this information, but in view of the fact that the country is engaged in a life and death struggle (for the successful conclusion of which we are mainly dependent upon the Navy) I felt it my duty to warn you of the criticisms that were being directed against the First Sea Lord, in order that you might be prepared if necessary to protect him, and the Naval Administration, from a loss of public confidence at this supreme moment.

I do not regret my action, much as I deplore the necessity for it, and I only send the enclosed memorandum in accordance with your special request and because I understand from you that Lord Charles Beresford totally denies having made any such criticisms. He has indeed stigmatised my report to you as a 'Malicious libel' and a 'foul untruth' which he intends to expose in the Law Courts.

As you know, I was not aware that you had decided to write to him officially on the subject, and of course I cannot accept responsibility for any version of his criticisms except that contained in the enclosed memorandum, which you will recognise as accurately summarising the report which I made to you on Friday. Nor do I know any statements of a similar character which Lord Charles Beresford may, or may not, have made at other times and not in my hearing. My knowledge is confined to what I heard, most unwillingly, on the occasion referred to, and I can only repeat that whatever Lord Charles Beresford's *intentions* may have been the effect of his criticisms, in my opinion, could only be to foster a feeling of distrust towards the First Sea Lord and a loss of confidence in his administration.

Yours sincerely
Arthur Lee

Memorandum by Arthur Lee
(*Churchill papers: 13/43*)

30 August 1914

Memorandum of certain criticisms of the First Sea Lord, made by Lord Charles Beresford in the Hall of the Carlton Club on August 28th, 1914, in the presence of several members.

This is a summary only of a record, made immediately afterwards, which formed the basis of my report to Mr Churchill.

The conversation having turned upon German spies, Lord Charles Beresford expressed the opinion that *all* Germans, including highly placed ones, ought to leave the country as they were in close touch with Germans abroad.

Prince Louis' name was not mentioned specifically as a case in point, but Lord C.B. went on to say that his 'good taste' should lead him to voluntarily resign the position of First Sea Lord. He did not advocate his *removal*—but he should resign. He went on to praise Prince Louis as 'an exceedingly able officer' but 'nothing could alter the fact that he is a *German*, and as such should not be occupying his present position.' Lord C.B. added that Prince Louis 'keeps German servants and has his property in Germany.'

I protested against these criticisms and expressed the opinion that Prince Louis was in all respects as loyal, straight, and patriotic as Lord C.B. himself, and that his long record in the Navy entitled him to enjoy our completest confidence. To this Lord C.B. replied 'I admit all that, but none the less he is a *German* and he entered the Navy for his own advantage not for ours.' He added that 'Feeling is very strong in the Service about his being First Sea Lord—it is strongly resented.' On my expressing surprise at this statement, he added: 'I am entitled to speak for the Service—I know the opinion of my brother officers on the subject. It is very strong.'

He added 'If things went badly at sea, as they well may, there would be a howl in the country and the mob would attack Prince Louis' house and break his windows.' Whereupon I asked him 'what do you suggest should be done? Prince Louis *is* the First Sea Lord—Do you suggest that he should be removed?' To this Lord C.B. replied again: 'No, his good taste should tell him to resign. I said all this to the King and asked him to send for Prince Louis in order that I might say it in his presence.'

I once more expressed my total disagreement with these criticisms and the conversation came to an end.

A. Lee

Lord Curzon[1] *to Winston S. Churchill*

(*Churchill papers: 13/45*)

30 August 1914   Hackwood
Confidential   Basingstoke

My dear Winston,

I have a horrid idea that dreadful things are happening in France, and that we may wake up any morning and hear of an appalling disaster. Per-

---

[1] George Nathaniel Curzon, 1859–1925. Conservative MP, 1886–98. Under-Secretary of State for India, 1891–2; for Foreign Affairs, 1892–8. Viceroy of India, 1898–1905. Created Earl, 1911. Lord Privy Seal, May 1915–December 1916. President of the Air Board, 1916. Lord President of the Council and Member of the War Cabinet, 1916–19. Secretary of State for Foreign Affairs, 1919–22. Created Marquess, 1921. Lord President of the Council, 1924–5.

haps that is all the greater reason for pursuing the campaign in the country which I ventured to suggest in the Times 2 days ago, and which the Prime Minister has endorsed on his own responsibility. Since writing I have been inundated with telegrams and letters from all parts of the country asking for meetings.

I am coming up to town first thing to-morrow morning and shall be at 1 Carlton House Terrace at 10.30 a.m. (Regent 1628). I do not wish to trouble the P.M. or the W.O. Can you in the course of the morning spare me a few minutes to answer a few questions?

(1) We must have co-ordination and co-operation between the two parties and organize these meetings, select speakers, and arrange dates. There will be no good in sending two big speakers to one place—waste of force. But the two parties must everywhere co-operate, and the Chairman be the Mayor, Lord Mayor, or Lord Lieutenant. There ought to be a central office in London; yours or ours, or some new one with a staff. No individual can do it, and it must be non-party. Probably there ought to be a Joint Committee.

(2) Where ought the speakers to go? Through the big places where the recruiting is slackest—probably in the North. It is no good attempting work which the local people can do as well. The speakers must go where a dramatic appeal to great numbers is required.

(3) Now the Central London organization ought probably to be supplemented by local organizations started and controlled by local M.Ps., Lord Lieuts., etc., who will map out the country.

But here arises a vital point. What are we to appeal for? Men? Yes; but for what force? Do the Govt. want men for K's new 3-year army? (Will they, if obtained, be any good for 6 months or longer?) Or for his Special Reserve; or for the Regular Army? All these questions will be asked. Can the Govt. cope with large numbers? Have you the officers or the rifles or the ammunition or the uniforms? Do you want in fact to go slow or to go quick?

(4) What are we to say in reply to the question: 'What will become of the new recruits when the war is over? Will they be given a new start? Will the public revenues be used to give them a fair chance with those who have stayed at home?' Can any undertaking be given to that effect?

(5) As important as the question of speakers is that of literature and leaflets. Is there any organization taking this in hand? If not, ought we to create it?

I shall be quite prepared after seeing you (if you will so oblige me) to go to your party headquarters, or to ours, or to the W.O., or to all of these places, and endeavour to get things into shape. Or if there is an existing or contemplated organization, I will gladly accept it.

But 15 minutes with you, if you will have this letter with you, will save

hours of talk and help to put matters on a practical basis, or I will run round
to the Admiralty upon arrival or do whatever you suggest.[1]

Yours sincerely,
Curzon

Winston S. Churchill to Noel Buxton[2]
(*Copy, Churchill papers: 26/1*)

31 August 1914   Admiralty

My dear Buxton,

It is of the utmost importance to the future prosperity of the Balkan States
that they should act together. This is the hour when the metal can be cast
into the mould. It is only by reclaiming from Austria territories which belong
naturally to the Balkan races that the means can be provided to satisfy the
legitimate needs and aspirations of all the Balkan States. Without taking
Austrian territory, there is no way by which any Balkan State can expand
except by internecine war. But the application of the principle of nationality
to the Southern Provinces of Austria will produce results so advantageous to
the Balkan States that the memory and the consequences of former quarrels
could be assuaged for ever.

The creation of a Balkan Confederation comprising Bulgaria, Servia,
Roumania, Montenegro, and Greece, strong enough to play an effective part
in the destinies of Europe, must be the common dream of all their peoples.
The result of this war is not doubtful. Sooner or later, Germany will be
starved and beaten. Austria will be resolved into its component parts. England has always won in the end; and Russia is unconquerable. England has
been the friend of every Christian State in the Balkans during all their years
of struggle and suffering. She has no interests of her own to seek in the Balkan
Peninsula. But with her wealth and power she will promote and aid every step
which is taken to build up a strong union of the Christian peoples, like that
which triumphed in the first Balkan War. By acting together in unity and
good faith the Balkan States can now play a decisive part, and gain advantages which may never again be offered. By disunion they will simply
condemn themselves to tear each other's throats without profit or reward,
and left to themselves will play an utterly futile part in the destinies of the
world.

[1] All-Party recruiting rallies soon became standard practice. Thus Churchill, F. E. Smith
and the Labour, MP, Will Crooks, spoke at a 'Call to Arms' meeting at the London Opera
House on 11 September 1914.
[2] Noel Edward Buxton, 1869–1948. Liberal MP, 1905–6; 1910–18. Labour MP, 1922–30.
Minister of Agriculture and Fisheries, 1924; 1929–30. Created Baron Noel-Buxton, 1930.

I want you to make your friends in Greece and in Bulgaria realize the brilliant but fleeting opportunity which now presents itself, and to assure them that England's might and perseverance will not be withheld from any righteous effort to secure the strength and union of the Balkan peoples.[1]

Yours very sincerely
Winston S. Churchill

[1] Churchill sent this letter to Grey for his comments. Grey noted: 'I am afraid I dont much like a letter of this kind being given to be shown in the Balkans—words wont influence them.' But Churchill gave Buxton the letter nevertheless. (*Churchill papers: 13/44*)

September 1914

Winston S. Churchill to Captain Sueter[1] and Sir Frederick Sturdee

(Copy, Churchill papers: 28/153)

1 September 1914   Admiralty

Director of Air Division
Chief of Staff

The largest possible force of naval aeroplanes should be stationed in Calais or Dunkirk. Reports have been received, and it is also extremely probable, that the Germans will attempt to attack London and other places by Zeppelin airships, of which it is said a considerable number exist.[2] The close proximity of the French coast to England renders such an attack thoroughly feasible. The proper defence is a thorough and continual search of the country for 70 to 100 miles inland with a view to marking down any temporary airship bases, or airships replenishing before starting to attack. Should such airships be located they should be immediately attacked. Commander Samson,[3] with Major Gerrard[4] as second in command, will be entrusted with this duty; and the Director of Air Division will take all steps to supply them with the necessary pilots, aeroplanes and equipment.

[1] Murray Fraser Sueter, 1872–1960. Entered Navy, 1886. Assistant Director of Naval Ordnance at the Admiralty, 1903–5. Member, Advisory Committee in Aeronautics, 1908–17. Captain, 1909. Director of the Air Department at the Admiralty, 1911–15. Commodore, 1915. Superintendent of Aircraft Construction, 1915–17. Commanded Royal Naval Air Service units, Southern Italy, 1917–18. Rear-Admiral, 1920. Conservative MP, 1921–45. Knighted, 1934.

[2] On 25 August 1914 the first Zeppelin attack of the war had taken place on Antwerp, when 12 people were killed. There were no Zeppelin raids on England until January 1915 (see p. 359). Between 1915 and 1918 over 500 British civilians were killed and over 1,300 injured in Zeppelin raids over the Home Counties and the Midlands.

[3] Charles Rumney Samson, 1883–1931. Entered Navy, 1898. A pioneer aviator who carried out some of the earliest experiments with seaplanes and night flights. Commander, Royal Naval Air Service, 1913–15. Commanded the air forces at the siege of Antwerp, October 1914; the Dardanelles, 1915. Wing-Captain RNAS, 1918. Group Captain, RAF, 1919. Air Commodore, 1922.

[4] Eugene Louis Gerrard, 1881–1963. 2nd Lieutenant, Royal Marine Light Infantry, 1901. Squadron Commander, Royal Flying Corps (Naval Wing), 1912. Commander, December 1914. Group Captain, Royal Air Force, 1919. Air Commodore, commanding the forces in Palestine, 1929.

Admiralty to French Ministry of Marine: telegram
(*Copy, Admiralty papers: 116/1352*)

1 September 1914   Admiralty

The Admiralty considers it extremely important to deny the use of territory within 100 miles radius of Dunkirk to German Zeppelins, and to attack by aeroplane all airships found replenishing there. With your permission the Admiralty wish to take necessary measures to maintain aerial command of this region.

The Admiralty proposes therefore to place 30 or 40 naval aeroplanes at Dunkirk or other convenient coast points. In order that these may have good radius of action they must be able to establish mobile temporary bases 40 or 50 miles inland.

The Admiralty desires to reinforce Officer Commanding aeroplanes with 50 or 60 armed motor-cars and 200 or 300 men. This small force will operate in conformity with the wishes of the French military authorities, but we hope it may be accorded a free initiative. The immunity of Portsmouth, Chatham, and London from dangerous aerial attack is closely involved.

Winston S. Churchill to Sir Charles Douglas[1]
(*Copy, Churchill papers: 26/1*)

1 September 1914   Admiralty
Secret

Dear General Douglas,

I arranged with Lord Kitchener yesterday that 2 officers from Admiralty should meet 2 officers from the Director of Military Operations Department of the War Office today to examine and work out a plan for the seizure by means of a Greek Army of adequate strength of the Gallipoli Peninsula, with a view to admitting a British Fleet to the Sea of Marmora.

In his absence I would ask you to give the necessary directions, as the matter is urgent, and Turkey may make war on us at any moment.

The meeting can take place either here or at the War Office as soon as you can arrange with our Chief of the Staff.[2]

Yours sincerely
WSC

[1] Charles Wittingham Horsley Douglas, 1850–1914. Entered Army, 1869. Major-General, 1900. Knighted, 1907. General, commanding Southern Command, 1909–11. Inspector-General, Home Forces, 1911–14. Chief of the Imperial General Staff, 4 August 1914. He died on 25 October 1914.
[2] For the meetings that followed, see pages 91–2.

H. H. Asquith to George V

(Cabinet Office papers: 41/35)

1 September 1914   10 Downing Street

Mr Asquith with his humble duty has the honour to inform Your Majesty that after midnight he had a consultation with Lord Kitchener, Mr Churchill, & Mr McKenna.[1]

In consequence of the unsatisfactory nature of Sir J. French's[2] latest telegrams,[3] and the vital importance of avoiding at this moment a false move at the front, it was determined that Lord Kitchener should himself go over & confer with Sir J. French. Lord Kitchener accordingly left at 1 a.m. via Dover, Havre & Paris, where he ought to be soon after noon.

H. H. Asquith to Venetia Stanley

(Montagu papers)

2 September 1914   10 Downing Street

... We had our regular Cabinet in his [Kitchener's] absence this morning, and you can judge of the kind of thing that comes up day by day by this short synopsis of topics (1) Naval air reconnoitring at Dunkirk (2) protection of London against bomb throwing from Zeppelins (3) Greece & Turkey (on the verge of war)—we to sink Turkish ships if they issue from the Dardanelles (4) Proposed offer of financial help to Roumania & Servia (5) Japan —can she help with her fleet, or army, or both in the European theatre. ...

[1] Reginald McKenna, 1863–1943. Liberal MP, 1895–1918. President of the Board of Education, 1907–8. First Lord of the Admiralty, 1908–11. Home Secretary, 1911–15. Chancellor of the Exchequer, May 1915–December 1916. Chairman, Midland Bank, 1919–43.

[2] John Denton Pinkstone French, 1852–1925. Entered Navy, 1866. Transferred to Army, 1874. Lieutenant-General, commanding the Cavalry in South Africa, 1899–1902. Knighted, 1900. Chief of the Imperial General Staff, 1912–14. Field-Marshal, 1913. Commander-in-Chief of the British Expeditionary Force in France, August 1914–December 1915. Commander-in-Chief, Home Forces, 1915–18. Created Viscount 1916. Lord Lieutenant of Ireland, 1918–21. Created Earl of Ypres, 1922.

[3] On 31 August 1914 Sir John French had telegraphed to Kitchener that he was unwilling to co-operate further with the French Army, and that the British Expeditionary Force would fall back behind Paris. Kitchener had replied that same day, ordering Sir John French to 'conform to the plans' of General Joffre. But in his reply Sir John French had insisted on the need for an independent and immediate British withdrawl, as his troops were, he declared, 'shattered'. This second telegram reached London just before midnight on 31 August. Asquith at once summoned Kitchener Churchill and McKenna to 10 Downing Street.

Captain Guest[1] to Winston S. Churchill

(*Churchill papers: 26/1*)

2 September 1914   France
Secret

Dear Winston,

I am writing this letter with Sir John's knowledge though *not* at his request. He has had a talk with me this morning and has left me to draw my own conclusions and to convey them *privately* to whomsoever in the Government I may think fit. As you are the only soldier I write therefore to you. The intimation that Lord K. was coming to Paris to consult was a great surprise to Sir John (partly because his absence from the War Office at this moment seemed doubtful policy), but of course he took no exception to the visit. When in Paris yesterday Lord K. proposed that he should visit the troops, but as you know now that proposal was happily abandoned.

The reasons for its abandonment are of course clear to you, viz., the French would immediately think that Sir John was either superseded or that *our* Govt. had lost confidence in his judgment. Of course Sir John has felt this frightfully and has been very much upset.

Let me tell you quite simply. He has first of all with his troops between Aug. 23–26 saved the whole French line of armies from being rolled up from West to East. He has with astonishing skill extricated his army, one broken and one damaged corps, from a villainous position tampered rather than assisted by unreliable allies. We were rushed up to Mons by forced marches to be left high and dry; and have now retired, or retreated, in continued contact with the enemy for over 100 miles.

I don't believe that the men would have blindly retreated in that fashion day and night for anyone else. Sir John's reputation as a thruster and a fighter is so well known that they have felt that his reasons for retreat *must* be good enough.

This hastily written rigmarole is to convey to you that we depend upon his personality and skill out here perhaps more than is appreciated at home, and that *anything* which makes his position as C-in-C. out here difficult should be most carefully avoided. I feel sure that you will see his point and understand his frame of mind and take care that he is not hurt again.

Yours,
Freddie

---

[1] Frederick Edward Guest, 1875–1937. The third son of 1st Baron Wimborne; Churchill's cousin. Liberal MP, 1910–29. ADC to Sir John French, 1914–16. Secretary of State for Air, 1921–2. Conservative MP, 1931–7.

James Masterton-Smith[1] to Charles Montgomery[2]

(*Foreign Office papers: 371/2174*)

2 September 1914   Admiralty

My dear Montgomery,

At the request of the Belgian Minister,[3] Mr Churchill has given directions for a battery of 6—4·7″ naval guns, with ammunition, to be despatched for the use of the Belgians in Antwerp. As they are not familiar with our naval guns, a few naval gunnery ratings are being sent at the same time to give instruction.

The Belgian military attaché[4] has been supplied with the necessary information as to weights and measurements, and he is arranging the transport.

As there is no time to spare, we have dealt with the Belgian Legation direct; and I send you this letter so that the Department concerned may note what we are doing.

Yours sincerely
J. E. Masterton Smith

H. H. Asquith to Venetia Stanley

(*Montagu papers*)

3 September 1914   10 Downing Street

. . . . We had a Cabinet this morning—a mass of details, but nothing really interesting, except that Winston has sent 4 of his aeroplanes to Antwerp to scuttle the Zeppelin that has been throwing bombs there. . . .

[1] James Edward Masterton-Smith, 1878–1938. Entered Admiralty, 1901. Private Secretary to five First Lords: McKenna, 1910–11; Churchill, 1911–15; Balfour, 1915–16; Carson, 1916–17; Sir E. Geddes, 1917. Assistant Secretary to Churchill, Ministry of Munitions, 1917–19; War Office, 1919–20. Knighted, 1919. Permanent Under-Secretary of State, Colonial Office, 1921–4.

[2] Charles Hubert Montgomery, 1876–1942. Entered Foreign Office, 1900. Assistant Clerk, 1910–18. Chief Clerk, 1919. Knighted, 1927. Deputy Under-Secretary of State, Foreign Office, 1930. British Minister, The Hague, 1933–8.

[3] Count Charles Maximilien Jacques de Lalaing, 1856–1919. Entered Belgian diplomatic Corps, 1880. Minister, Rio de Janeiro, 1893–6; Bucharest, 1896–9; Berne, 1899–1903; London, 1903–15.

[4] Rodolphe Maton, 1872–1959. Entered Belgian Army, 1892. Captain, General Staff, 1906. Military Attaché, London, 1913–16 and 1919–24. Major, Grenadiers Regiment, 1916–17. Chief of Staff, 8th Infantry Division, 1918. Colonel General Staff, 1921. Military Commander, East Flanders, 1928. Lieutenant General, 1932. Permanent Under-Secretary, Ministry of Defence, 1932. Inspector-General of the Army, 1932–3.

Lord Haldane to Winston S. Churchill

(*Spencer-Churchill papers*)

3 September 1914 28 Queen Anne's Gate

My dear Winston,

I have tonight read your remarkable military appreciation written in 1911.[1] It is extraordinarily accurate as a forecast of events up to now, & shows great insight—a memorable document in full.

Asquith said to me this afternoon that you were the equivalent of a large force in the field & this is true.

You inspire us all by your courage & resolution.

Yrs vy sincerely
Haldane

Sir John French to Winston S. Churchill

(*Churchill papers: 26/1*)

3 September 1914

My dear Churchill,

Thank you very much for your kind & encouraging letter.[2] It was a keen pleasure to hear from you & to read your words.

I have had a terribly anxious time & the troops have suffered severely but they are simply *glorious*! I have 2½ Army Corps here now & a Cavalry Division; multiply the former by 6 & the latter by 4 and I would get to Berlin in 6 weeks without any French help at all.

I think you have heard me say at Penn[3] that I would be ready to take on any enemy in Europe ½ as strong again. I say that more than ever *now*!

I can't find words to say all I think of them.

There has been some outstanding misunderstanding at home as to my

[1] On 13 August 1911, during the Agadir crisis, Churchill had written a memorandum entitled 'Military Aspects of the Continental Problem'. In it he assumed that Britain, France and Russia were in alliance against the combined forces of Germany and Austria-Hungary. He envisaged an initial German attack on France which would drive the French back, in twenty days, to Paris. But he forecast that by the fortieth day, 'Germany should be extended at full strain. . . . If the French Army has not been squandered by precipitate or desperate action, the balance of forces should be favourable. . . . Opportunities for the decisive trial of strength may then occur.' Churchill added that the French ability to take the initiative after the fortieth day 'may depend upon the military support which Great Britain can give'. (*Churchill papers: 24/7*)

[2] Not found.

[3] Penn in Buckinghamshire; army manœuvres were held there every year, and on several occasions before the war Churchill had attended them as Sir John French's guest.

relations with Gen Joffre,[1] the French C in C. We have been on the very best terms all thro' & he has spoken most kindly of the help he has received from us. I can't understand what brought Kitchener to Paris. I am writing to you as one of my greatest friends & I'm sure you'll let me write freely & privately.

K's visit was really most unfortunate—He took me away from the front to visit him in Paris on a very critical day when I should have been directing the operations most carefully and I tell you betweeen ourselves *strictly* that when I returned to my Head Quarters I found a very critical situation existing (8 p.m.!!) and authoritative orders & directions badly needed. It was the day that the Guards & Cavalry Brigades were so heavily engaged.

I do beg of you, my dear Friend, to add one more to all the many & great kindnesses you have done me & *stop this interference* with field operatives. Kitchener *knows nothing* about European warfare. Of course he's a fine organiser but he never was & never will be a Commander in the field.

I was delighted to hear it is likely we may have a Naval & Marine Division in the field.

It pleases me so much to read your broad, far-seeing conception of the strategy of this great campaign. We are as you say, at this moment a holding force. I should like to have seen greater boldness shewn in counter attack but I think it very likely to be good military policy to delay.

You say in your postscript 'You ought to tell more'—I assure you Kitchener has been told almost everything. In spite of sleepless nights I have written him long private accounts of the whole affair and my telegrams have been very full—as *to casualties*, in the continual fighting we have had it has been absolutely impossible to get at them a moment sooner.

My warmest thanks for your kindness & friendship which I value immensely. I am hoping to see you with us. Come whenever you can & everything shall be arranged for your comfort & safety.

Yrs always, my dear Churchill

John French

PS Sept 4, 6 a.m.

On reading over what I wrote at 12 last night I think it may be rather strong—for I have to remember you are a Cabinet Minister as well as a Great Friend of mine. If I have erred in this way forgive me please!

I have opened my heart to you! What I feel is that I have been quite enough tried now between South Africa & this Campaign & I have not given the Gov any reason to distrust me.

---

[1] Joseph Jacques Césaire Joffre, 1852–1931. As a 2nd Lieutenant, he took part in the defence of Paris in 1870. Appointed Commander-in-Chief of the French Army, 5 August 1914. In December 1916 he was deprived of all real authority. The British Government awarded him an honorary GCB in 1914 and an honorary OM in 1919.

To send another FM out here to lecture me (he came in FM's uniform!) seems to me a sign of distrust & it *hurts* me. Remember this if you think I should not have written like this & burn this letter PLEASE.

Winston S. Churchill to Lord Kitchener

(Kitchener papers)

3 September 1914   Admiralty

My dear Kitchener,

Captain Hankey[1] of the C.I.D. has been to me with what seems rather a good idea. He suggests that Girouard should be put at the head of an emergency armament multiplication committee or department to set on foot and develop the maximum possible output of guns, rifles, ammunition, etc. I am sure myself that more could be done by the firms than is being done at present. For instance, after you told me of the pressure you had put upon them and that their complete limits had been reached, our people went round and obtained undertakings from the trade to produce 700 rifles a week more, additional to all that had been ordered by you.

This is only a half-formed idea and I pass it on to you not as a recommendation but simply for what it is worth.

Yours vy sincerely
Winston S. Churchill

Major-General Callwell:[2] memorandum

(Churchill papers: 13/27)

3 September 1914   War Office

It ought to be clearly understood that an attack upon the Gallipoli Peninsula from the sea side (outside the Straits) is likely to prove an extremely

---

[1] Maurice Pascal Alers Hankey, 1877–1963. Entered Royal Marine Artillery, 1895. Captain, 1899. Retired, 1912. Secretary to the Committee of Imperial Defence, 1912–38. Lieutenant-Colonel, Royal Marines, October 1914. Secretary to the War Council, November 1914–May 1915; to the Dardanelles Committee, May–November 1915; to the Cabinet War Committee, December 1915–December 1916. Knighted, February 1916. Secretary to the War Cabinet, 1916–18; to the Cabinet, 1919–38. Created Baron, 1939. Minister without Portfolio, September 1939–May 1940. Chancellor of the Duchy of Lancaster, 1940–1. Paymaster-General, 1941–2.

[2] Charles Edward Callwell, 1859–1928. Entered Army, 1878. Intelligence Branch, War Office, 1887–92. Attached to the Greek Army during the Graeco-Turkish War, 1897. Colonel, 1904. Angered because several of his contemporaries were appointed to General Officer over his head, he retired from the Army in 1909. Satirized Army procedure and War Office routine in *Service Yarns and Memories*, published in 1912. Recalled to the active list, 1914. Acting Major-General, August 1914. Director of Military Operations and Intelligence at the War Office, 1914–16. Special Mission to Russia, 1916. Adviser on ammunition supply, Ministry of Munitions, 1916–18. Major-General, 1917. Knighted, 1917. Military historian.

difficult operation of war. The subject has often been considered before by the General Staff, and it was examined into by the Committee of Imperial Defence in 1906; it was then decided that such an operation could not be regarded as feasible with the British troops that might at short notice have been collected for the purpose at that time. Since then the garrison has been greatly augmented, and, as a consequence of threats on the part of Greeks and Bulgarians during the first Balkan War, and of the attack made upon the Lines of Bulair, the protection of the rear of the various batteries and works dominating the Straits was taken in hand. It is understood that what was then done renders them secure against anything in the nature of a surprise attack.

The garrison of the Peninsula now normally consists of an Army Corps, which may be taken at 27,000 men with 136 guns; but, under existing conditions, this garrison will almost certainly have been strengthened considerably, and it would be unsafe to assume that the attacking side would only have the above number to deal with. In any case, it would not seem justifiable to undertake an operation of this kind with an army of less than 60,000 men against the Ottoman forces likely to be encountered. These 60,000 might, however, cross the sea in two echelons, admitting of the transports returning to Greece after disembarking the first echelon. The Expeditionary Force could dispense almost entirely, if not entirely, with cavalry, and its mobile artillery might well be composed mainly of mountain batteries. It ought, however, to be accompanied by a strong contingent of siege pieces, especially howitzers, for attacking the batteries and forts bearing on the Straits, which are the real objective, but, unfortunately, the Greeks do not seem to have any howitzers, and they have very few siege guns.

It has to be remembered that there is nothing to prevent the Turks bringing strong reinforcements to the Gallipoli Peninsula from Constantinople, Panderma, and elsewhere across the Sea of Marmora until such time as it becomes impracticable for them to disembark such troops within the Peninsula. There is a division—say, 6,000 men—normally stationed on the Asiatic side of the Straits which could get across at the very start if there were a few steamers and launches available to Chanak. Moreover, a report just to hand says that there is now an Army Corps assembled on the Asiatic side, but this seems doubtful.

As a rough outline of the plan of attack, it is suggested that, in the first instance, 30,000 men should be landed, should gain as much ground as possible, and should prepare landing stages, while the transports return for the other 30,000 and the siege ordnance. The first 30,000 would have to be prepared to hold their own for about a week, allowing for the time taken on the voyage and in getting the transports loaded up afresh at the port of embarkation; but the actual details would, of course, have to be worked out by the General appointed to command the Expeditionary Force. It is not unlikely that the Greek War Office and Admiralty are in possession of later information as to the conditions of the land defences and as to the Garrison of the Gallipoli Peninsula than we are.

Charles Callwell

Winston S. Churchill to Rear-Admiral Kerr:[1] *telegram*

(*Grey papers*)

4 September 1914
Most Secret

Admiralty

Without entering into the political probabilities which must be settled by Governments, Admiralty think it necessary now to discuss with Greek General and Naval Staff as a staff precaution the question of the right war policy to be pursued if Great Britain and Greece are Allies in a war against Turkey.

If addressed by the Greek Government, you are authorized to enter into these discussions on behalf of the Admiralty. The following are our general views: In principle, Admiralty would propose to reinforce the Greek Fleet by a squadron and a flotilla strong enough to give decisive and unquestionable superiority over the Turkish and German vessels. They would propose that the whole command of the combined Fleets should be vested in you, and that you should hoist your flag in the British battle-cruiser 'Indomitable'. They will reinforce you to any extent and with any class of vessel that circumstances may render necessary. The right and obvious method of attacking Turkey is to strike immediately at the heart. To do this, it would be necessary for a Greek army to seize the Gallipoli Peninsula under superiority of sea predominance, and thus to open the Dardanelles, admitting the Anglo-Greek Fleet to the Sea of Marmora,[2] whence the Turco-German ships can be fought and sunk, and where in combination with the Russian Black Sea Fleet and Russian military forces the whole situation can be dominated.

Admiralty wish that these conceptions should be immediately examined by the Greek naval and military experts in consultation with you. They wish to know at once the general views of the Greek Government upon this

[1] Mark Edward Frederic Kerr, 1864–1944. Entered Navy, 1877. Naval Attaché, Athens and Constantinople, 1903–4. Rear-Admiral, 1913. Commander-in-Chief of the Greek Navy, 1913–1915. Commander-in-Chief of the British Squadron in the Adriatic, 1916–17. Major-General, Royal Air Force, 1918. Deputy Chief of the Air Staff, 1918. Poet and naval historian.

[2] See map 12 on pages 1604–5.

enterprise, and what force they think would be necessary on the assumption that safe transportation is assured. To what extent and in what time could Greece provide the necessary transports, or should we do so? Or what are their alternative suggestions? You should then report fully to Admiralty by telegraph.

Winston S. Churchill: memorandum

(Churchill papers: 13/29)

4 September 1914   Admiralty

Defence of Calais

There appears to be no immediate danger of an attack on Calais, and the German movement at present is to the east rather than to the west.

It is of great importance not to interrupt the training and formation of the Marine Brigade, which will now have to absorb a larger proportion of the recruits who have poured into Lord Kitchener's Army. In an emergency, if no other means were available, we no doubt should have to help the Governor,[1] but I propose for the present to refuse his request.

The second request can be granted, and arrangements should be made to that end. There is no need to bring the refugees to England. We should say that on notice being given we will supply suitable transports and take them to Havre, La Rochelle, or Bordeaux direct, as may be found necessary. We should ask for an estimate of numbers.

WSC

Sir Francis Villiers to Sir Edward Grey: telegram

(Copy, Churchill papers: 28/153)

4 September 1914   Antwerp

Major Gerrard arrived here this morning to arrange operations with Belgian Authorities who promise all assistance.

He proposes to make Antwerp base.

Attacks by German Airships have been by night and there is not much prospect of repelling them successfully by aeroplanes. Plan is to make counter-attack on German base at Cologne, Dusseldorf or elsewhere. Belgian authorities have been consulted and concur; their own aeroplanes have not sufficient range of action.

[1] Edouard Berard, died 1918. Général de Brigade. Governor of Calais, April–November 1914.

Major Gerrard will bring about six aeroplanes with bombs and also some repairing equipment. Petrol and ordinary repairing necessities can be obtained here. He is returning to Ostend at once. Please ask Admiralty to notify approval of plan to him through Commander Samson and also by message 'Carry on' through Vice-Consul at Ostend.[1]

Captain Sueter: note

4 September 1914   Admiralty

There should be no great difficulty in attacking the airship sheds at Cologne & Dusseldorff. They are no great distance from the Belgian frontier.

Murray F. Sueter

R. D. Blumenfeld[2] to Winston S. Churchill
(Churchill papers: 13/45)

4 September 1914   The Daily Express
                                              St Bride St
                                             London EC

Dear Mr Churchill,

Every day for a month I have been wanting to write you a few lines. But always I have been prevented by the great crush of work.

But even at this late day, a month behind the time, I shall still be discharging my duty to you by sending you my best wishes and conveying to you a sense of my unbounded admiration for having played your part so nobly.

When you took over the Navy I wrote that you now had the opportunity to soar above party and that I believed you would; as I am glad for 'more reasons than many' that you are where you are.

Yours sincerely
R. D. Blumenfeld

---

[1] The Foreign Office have no record of a British Vice-Consul at Ostend on 4 September 1914. The regular Vice-Consul, Captain G. C. Bowen, had returned to England on 21 August 1914 without being officially replaced.

[2] Ralph David Blumenfeld, 1864–1948. Born in the United States, the son of a German immigrant. London Correspondent, *New York Herald*, 1887–93. News Editor, *Daily Mail*, 1900–2. Foreign Editor, *Daily Express*, 1902–4; Editor, 1904–32. He became a British subject in 1907. President, Institute of Journalists, 1928. He declined a knighthood offered by the Conservatives for political services.

H. H. Asquith to George V

(*Royal Archives*)

4 September 1914   10 Downing Street

Mr Asquith, with his humble duty to Your Majesty, has the honour to report that the Cabinet met yesterday & to-day.

The subjects chiefly considered were as follows:

(1) the importance of establishing without delay a Naval air reconnoitring station at Dunkirk;

(2) the precautions to be taken in London against bomb-throwing by Zeppelins. It was agreed that the measures to be taken should be concerted between the Army & Navy, & communicated to the Home Office;

(3) In view of the probable necessity of shifting our base from Havre to La Rochelle, the laying of a Cable to the latter port. This is already in hand.

(4) The possibility of the outbreak of a war between Turkey & Bulgaria on the one side and Greece on the other. We could assure Greece that in such a contingency we should prevent any Turkish ships from coming out of the Dardanelles.

(5) The expediency (agreed to) of offering financial assistance to Servia, and if she agreed to join the allies to Roumania.

(6) The desirability (agreed to) of inviting Japan to send her battle fleet to the Mediterranean. The question of a Japanese land contingent was discussed but not decided.[1]

(7) The proposal of France & Russia that we should join with them in a declaration not to make a 'separate peace'. The terms of the suggested formula were much discussed and criticised, and it was arranged that Sir E. Grey should have a preliminary consultation with the Russian Ambassador.[2]

(8) Mr Lloyd George described at length the various proposals which he has been considering, in consultation with the Bankers & Traders, for the re-establishment of the Foreign Exchanges. . . .

[1] It was only in 1917 that a Japanese naval squadron under Vice-Admiral Kozo Sato undertook convoy duties in the Mediterranean, escorting in the last two years of the war nearly 800 allied troopships and merchant vessels. The Japanese also undertook, in 1917, all allied convoy duties in the Indian Ocean.

[2] Alexander Count de Benckendorff, 1849–1917. Entered Imperial Russian diplomatic service, 1869. Ambassador to London, 1903–17.

Lord Esher to Winston S. Churchill

(*Churchill papers: 13/45*)

5 September 1914   Duke of Yorks HQ
                                                   London

My dear Winston,

. . . I met Bonar Law[1] yesterday who told me that you had *by far* the greatest reception at the Guildhall. He said that this in the City of London with A. J. B.[2] present was a most remarkable tribute.[3]

                                              Yours ever affectionately
                                                        Esher

H. H. Asquith to George V

(*Royal Archives*)

5 September 1914   10 Downing Street

. . . (7) Chilian battleship under construction at Elswick. The Chilian Government are willing to sell it, & it can be completed by the end of April. It has a speed of 23 knots, and is armed with 14-in guns. The Admiralty were authorised to proceed with the matter.

(8) It appears that the Japanese would object to their troops being used in Europe; but this does not seem to apply to their fleet.

(9) The formula proposed by France & Russia—that the three Allies should not separate when it comes to a question of making peace—was approved, with the addition (after much discussion) that no one of the Allies will demand or propose terms of peace without the consent of each of the others.

(10) Zeppelin airships: the Admiralty are taking over the aerial defence of the Country, and in consultation with the War Office & Office of Works will at once make plans for London by night.

---

[1] Andrew Bonar Law, 1858–1923. Conservative MP, 1900–10; 1911–23. Parliamentary Secretary at the Board of Trade, 1902–5. Leader of the Conservatives in the House of Commons, 1911. Secretary of State for the Colonies, May 1915–December 1916. Chancellor of the Exchequer, 1916–19. Lord Privy Seal, 1919–21. Prime Minister, 1922–3.

[2] Arthur James Balfour, 1848–1930. Conservative MP, 1874–85; 1885–1906; 1906–22. Prime Minister, 1902–5. First Lord of the Admiralty, 1915–16. Foreign Secretary, 1916–19. Lord President to the Council, 1919–22; 1925–9. Created Earl, 1922.

[3] The Guildhall was situated in Balfour's constituency; many of those present would have been his constituents. During his speech Churchill declared: 'Sure I am of this, you have only to conquer. You have only to persevere to save yourselves, and to save all those who rely on you. You have only to go right on, and at the end of the road, be it short or long, victory and honour will be found.'

Winston S. Churchill to Prince Louis and Captain Sueter

(*Copy, Churchill papers: 8/67*)

5 September 1914   Admiralty

First Sea Lord

Director of Air Division

In order to discharge adequately the responsibilities which we have assumed for the aerial defence of England, it is necessary that we should maintain an aerial control over the area approximately 100 miles radius from Dunkirk. To do this, we must support the aeroplanes which are stationed on the French coast with sufficient armed motor cars and personnel to enable advanced subsidiary aeroplane bases to be established 30, 40 and 50 miles inland.

According to all accounts received, the Germans, in so far as they have penetrated this region, have done it simply by bluff. Small parties of Uhlans, taking advantage of the terror inspired by their atrocities in Belgium, have made their way freely about the country, and have imposed themselves upon the population. We require, in the first instance, 200 or 300 men with 50 or 60 motor-cars, who can support and defend our advanced aerial bases. I should propose to draw these by suitable volunteers from the Marine Brigade. They should be placed under the orders of Commander Samson, and should operate from Dunkirk. It will be necessary first to obtain permission from the French authorities. This, after consultation with Lord Kitchener, I am taking steps to do. We ought to be able to make it quite impossible for parties of 15 or 20 Uhlans to make their way with safety through this area. During the next week the Germans will presume on their immunity, and will be found in occupation of numbers of places where they cannot possibly maintain any effective force. The advantage of an aeroplane reconnaissance is that the approach of any serious body of troops can be discovered while it is still at least two days' march away. There ought, therefore, to be no difficulty in chopping these small parties of the enemy without our force getting into any trouble.

Propose me plans for immediate action on these lines in detail.

Winston S. Churchill to H. H. Asquith, Sir Edward Grey and Lord Kitchener

(*Copy, Churchill papers: 26/1*)

5 September 1914   Admiralty

I hear from many sources of the keen and widespread desire of individual Americans to take part in the war on our side.[1] It has been stated that 50,000 or 60,000 Americans have volunteered, including a number of Virginians. I also hear that wealthy Americans are anxious to subscribe to the equipment of a force. There is no doubt that a large number of American citizens of quality and character are anxious to fight on our side. The value and advantage of such aid cannot be overrated from any point of view. I am ignorant of the law on these subjects: but Foreign Legions have played their part in many wars. It ought to be possible to organise in Canada an American volunteer force amounting to at least a Division, which could go into action as such. Nothing will bring American sympathy along with us so much as American blood shed in the field. What is wanted now is that there should be an announcement made that we will accept the services of Americans who come to Canada or England and volunteer; that they will be formed into units in which they can serve together with their friends and comrades; that they will be able to choose their own regimental officers; and that the British Government will bear the whole expense of equipment and transportation; and that they shall share in every way the perils and fortunes of our troops.

I believe there is a source of fighting manhood here of the highest possible quality, whose very employment would produce beneficial reactions in every direction. The problem is how to set up the rallying flag in Canada, and so indicate where those who wish to help us can go to join.

                                                                        WSC

H. H. Asquith to Venetia Stanley

(*Montagu papers*)

5 September 1914   10 Downing Street

. . . The papers I see are crying out (not without reason) for news, of which they have had precious little all this week. I am just going to tell Winston to repeat his feat of last Sunday, and to dish up for them with all

---

[1] On 18 August 1914 President Wilson had advised the American people to remain neutral, 'not only in act but in word and in thought'; but individual Americans frequently crossed the Atlantic to serve in the British army (for two such, see pp. 846, 1490). The United States declared war on Germany on 6 April 1917; the first contact between German and US troops took place on the western front on 5 November 1917. By Armistice Day, 11 November 1918, there were over two million US soldiers in Europe.

his best journalistic condiments the military history of the week. K is absolutely no use for this kind of thing, and has an undisguised contempt for the 'public' in all its moods & manifestations. . . .

H. H. Asquith to Winston S. Churchill
(Churchill papers: 2/64)

5 September 1914   10 Downing Street
Private

My dear Winston,

The papers are complaining, not without reason, that we keep them on starvation diet.

I think the time has come for you to repeat last Sunday's feat, & let them have thro' the Bureau an 'appreciation' of the events of the week; with such a seasoning of condiments as your well-skilled hand can supply.

For all that the public know, they might as well be living in the days of the prophet Isaiah, whose idea of a battle was 'confused noise & garments rolled in blood.'

Yrs always
HHA

Winston S. Churchill to Lord Northcliffe[1]
(Copy, Churchill papers: 28/117)

5 September 1914

My dear Northcliffe,

I think you ought to realise the harm that has been done by Sunday's publication in The Times.[2] I do not think you can possibly shelter yourself behind the Press Bureau, although their mistake was obvious. I never saw

---

[1] Alfred Charles William Harmsworth, 1865–1922. Newspaper proprietor. Bought the *Evening News* (1894), *Daily Mail* (1896), *Daily Mirror* (1903), *The Times* (1908). Created Baronet, 1903. Created Baron Northcliffe, 1905. Chairman, British War Mission to the United States, 1917. Director of Propaganda in Enemy Countries, 1918. Created Viscount, 1918.

[2] On Sunday, 30 August 1914, *The Times* front page second column was headed BROKEN BRITISH REGIMENTS. The article which followed was dated Amiens, 29 August, From our Special Correspondent. It began with a plea to the English censor 'to let my message pass'. The despatch dealt with the withdrawal of the British Army from Mons and contained the sentence: 'Our losses are very great. I have seen the broken bits of many regiments.' On Monday, 31 August. Asquith referred in the House of Commons to the despatch as a 'very regrettable exception' to the patriotic reticence of the Press. On Tuesday, 1 September, *The Times* revealed that F. E. Smith, the Head of the Press Bureau, had not only approved of the despatch, but had even added fresh sentences summarizing the effect of the news.

such panicstricken stuff written by any war correspondent before; and this served up on the authority of The Times can be made, and has been made, a weapon against us in every doubtful state.

I send you paraphrases of the telegrams we are receiving, not in reproach, but to prevent things going wrong again. Pray let me have the telegrams back.

Colonel Talbot:[1] *minute*

(*War Office Papers 106/1463*)

5 September 1914   War Office

GALLIPOLI PENINSULA

... On the 1st Sept the D.M.O. [Major-General Callwell] & Col. Talbot attended a meeting at the Admiralty at 6 p.m. present Captain C. F. Lambert,[2] The Director of Transport[3] & Captain H. W. Richmond.[4] The representatives of the Admiralty stated that with 6 weeks warning they could collect sufficient transport to convey 40000, or 50000 men to the selected landing places. Ships of war could also be provided to cover the landing with their fire. The D.M.O. stated that, considering the strength of the Turkish Garrison & the large force already mobilised in European Turkey, he did not regard it as a feasible military operation & that he believed this to be the War Office view.

On the 2nd or 3rd Sept. the D.M.O. attended a meeting at the Admiralty. Present First Lord, First Sea Lord, Capt. Lambert, Capt Richmond. The

[1] Milo George Talbot, 1854–1931. Entered Royal Engineers, 1873. On Kitchener's Headquarters Staff during the Sudan campaign, 1897–9. Director of Sudan surveys, 1900. Retired with rank of Colonel, 1905. Recalled to the War Office for special duties, August 1914.

[2] Cecil Foley Lambert, 1864–1928. Entered Navy, 1877. Captain, 1905. 4th Sea Lord, 1913–16. Rear-Admiral, 1916. Knighted, 1920.

[3] Graeme Thomson, 1875–1933. Entered Admiralty, 1900. Director of Transports, 1914–1917. Director of Shipping at the Admiralty and Ministry of Shipping, 1917–19. Knighted, 1919. Colonial Secretary of Ceylon, 1919–22. Governor of British Guiana, 1922–5. Governor of Nigeria, 1925–31. Governor of Ceylon, 1931–3.

[4] Herbert William Richmond, 1871–1946. Entered Navy, 1885. Captain, 1908. Commanded HMS *Dreadnought*, 1909–11, Assistant Director of Operations, Admiralty, 1913–15. British Liaison officer, Italian Fleet, 1915. Commanded HMS *Commonwealth*, 1915–16; HMS *Conqueror*, 1917; HMS *Erin*, 1918, Commander-in-Chief, East Indies, 1923–5. Knighted, 1926. Commandant, Imperial Defence College, 1926–8. Admiral, 1929. Professor of Naval and Imperial History, Cambridge, 1934–6. Master of Downing College, Cambridge, 1936–1946. Naval historian.

matter was thrashed out again, with the result that the D.M.O. put his
views on D.[1]

M. G. Talbot

Winston S. Churchill to R. D. Blumenfeld
(Copy, Churchill papers: 13/45)

6 September 1914   Admiralty

My dear Mr Blumenfeld,

I was very glad to get your letter, the more so because I heard from F.E.[2]
that you felt some compunction about the attacks which the 'Daily Express'
has made on me during the last year. But really there is no need for this. I
am a regular reader of your paper and have never seen any criticism which
I did not think perfectly fair politics. Above all, there has never been anything so far as I am concerned reflecting on private and personal conduct.
That after all is the line which politicians and political journalists ought to
draw. Also I have been greatly amused by many of your cartoons. Therefore
pray banish from your mind any idea that there has been any breach between us.

Lord Fisher to Cecil Fisher[3]
(Fisher papers)

6 September 1914   Richmond, Surrey

Dearest Cis,

Winston Churchill got me on the telephone this morning and wants me
to be the head of something—some sort of Naval Brigade, I think, and
A. K. Wilson[4] and Beresford, etc., but the telephone not very clear. He said

---

[1] Major-General Callwell's memorandum of 3 September 1914 (printed in full, pp 81–3).

[2] Frederick Edwin Smith, 1872–1930. Known as 'F.E.'. Conservative MP, 1906–19. Head
of the Press Bureau, August 1914; resigned, October 1914. Lieutenant-Colonel, attached
to the Indian Corps in France, 1914–15. Solicitor-General, May 1915. Knighted, 1915.
Attorney-General, November 1915–19. Created Baron Birkenhead, 1919. Lord Chancellor,
1920–2. Created Viscount, 1921. Created Earl, 1922. Secretary of State for India, 1924–8.

[3] Cecil Fisher, 1868–1955. Indian Civil Service, 1890–1906; retired on medical grounds.
2nd Baron, 1920.

[4] Arthur Knyvet Wilson, 1842–1921. Entered Navy, 1855. Fought in the Crimean War.
Awarded the VC in 1884 during the Sudan Campaign. Commander-in-Chief of the Home
and Channel Fleets, 1901–7. Knighted, 1902. Admiral of the Fleet, 1907. First Sea Lord,
1910–11. Worked at the Admiralty, without any formal post, October 1914–June 1918. He
declined a peerage on his retirement.

he had written, but I had never got the letter. Probably some German spy postman has sent it to Berlin! I've promised to have a tête-à-tête lunch with him at the Admiralty on Tuesday to see plans, etc. . . .

Of course, I told Winston Churchill I am ready to do any mortal thing, *even to co-operating with Beresford!* if any good for the War.

Your loving father,
F

Sir Francis Elliot[1] *to Winston S. Churchill*

(*Churchill papers: 26/1*)

6 September 1914   Athens

I have read to Monsieur Venezelos Constantinople telegram No. 707.[2]

He is not afraid of single-handed attack by Turkey by land as General Staff is confident of being able to deal with it. Greek Government have received from Sofia positive assurances of definite neutrality but do not trust them. They would however be satisfied with a formal protest by Bulgarian Government against violation of Bulgarian territory by Turkish troops proceeding to Greece. If however Bulgaria joined Turkey while Servia was occupied with Austria situation would be critical.

It is in my opinion highly desirable to let Turkey know that if she attacks Greece we shall support latter. This would do more than anything to keep Turkey quiet. As regards concessions by Greece see my telegram No. 191.[3] Offer of sovereignty over islands in return for fifty years lease is an immense concession which it will (? require) all Monsieur Venizelos' influence to force upon public opinion should Turkey accept it. . . .

[1] Francis Edmund Hugh Elliot, 1851–1940. Entered Diplomatic Service and appointed Attaché at Constantinople, 1874. Consul-General at Sofia, 1895–1903. Minister at Athens, 1903–17. Knighted, 1904. Employed in the Foreign Trade Department of the Foreign Office, 1917–19.

[2] On 5 September Sir Louis Mallet telegraphed to Sir Edward Grey from Constantinople that the Turkish Ministers had assured him that the Turkish fleet would not try to enter the Aegean, but that 'Danger point is an attack on Greece by land'. (*Foreign Office papers: 71/2138*)

[3] In his telegram 191, sent from Athens on 2 September 1914, and received in London that same day, Elliot stated that, in his opinion, 'Greece will positively decline to make any territorial concessions to Bulgaria, not because she believes that latter will in any case keep quiet in her own interests or under pressure, but because neither King of Greece nor public opinion would consent to such concessions'. (*Foreign Office papers: 371/1901*)

Sir George Buchanan[1] to Sir Edward Grey: telegram

(*Copy, Churchill papers: 26/1*)

6 September 1914   Petrograd

From a telegram received from the Russian Ambassador at Constantinople[2] of which contents will be communicated to you by the Russian Ambassador in London it appears that Turkey will declare war on Greece if the
latter refuses to make concessions about the islands. In that case Bulgaria is,
in the opinion of Minister for Foreign Affairs,[3] almost certain to join her
unless Greece purchases her neutrality or support by territorial concessions.

His Excellency said that he had all along been pressing the necessity of
this on Greece as in present critical stage of the war Russia had no wish to
face a war with Turkey as well. A Turco-Greek war would also paralyse
Servia at a moment when we needed her army for an attack on Austria. He
was not he said going to allow Greece to drag Russia into a war with Turkey
and unless she listened to our advice he would disinterest himself in her altogether. In view of the large number of German troops which are being transferred from western to eastern theatre Russia is calling up every available
man from Asia and the Caucasus and is only leaving one army corps in the
latter. She would not therefore be in a position to give any support nor
would France or England be able to do so if war as seems probable be restricted to land.

Greece will therefore have to bear the brunt of the war single-handed
unless she can square Bulgaria.

Sir Edward Grey to Winston S. Churchill

(*Churchill papers: 26/1*)

6 September 1914   Foreign Office

You will see from the telegram from St Petersburg that Russia can give no
help against Turkey. If things go very badly in France, Italy may come out

[1] George William Buchanan, 1854–1924. Entered Diplomatic Service, 1882. Knighted,
1905. Ambassador in Petrograd, 1910–18; in Rome, 1919–21.
[2] Michael Nikolaevich Giers, 1856–1924. Russian Minister at Rio de Janeiro, 1895;
Peking, 1898; Munich 1901; Bucharest, 1902. Russian Ambassador, Constantinople,
1912–14; Rome, 1915–17. Member of the Russian Political Conference, Paris, 1919. Chief
Diplomatic Representative of the Wrangel Government abroad, 1920.
[3] Sergei Dmitrievich Sazonov, 1866–1927. Russian Minister of Foreign Affairs, 1910–15.
Dismissed by the Tsar in November 1915 following his advocacy of Home Rule for Poland.
Chief Representative Abroad of Admiral Kolchak, 1919–20. In exile in France from 1919
until his death.

on the wrong side & the French fleet may be paralyzed by the way things go in France. I dont like the prospect in the Mediterranean at all, unless there is some turn of the tide in France.

Winston S. Churchill to Sir Edward Grey

(*Copy, Churchill papers: 26/1*)

6 September 1914   Admiralty
Secret

There is no need: or British or Russian anxiety abt a war with Turkey. Even if the Greek army were paralyzed by Bulgarian & Turkish attack, a Russian Army Corps cd easily be brought from Archangel, from Vladivostok, or, with Japanese consent, from Port Arthur, round to attack the Gallipoli position. No other military operations are necessary. The price to be paid in taking Gallipoli wd no doubt be heavy, but there wd be no more war with Turkey. A good army of 50,000 men & sea-power—that is the end of Turkish menace.

WSC

Lord Robert Cecil[1] to Winston S. Churchill

(*Churchill papers: 13/44*)

6 September 1914   Gale
Confidential   Chelwood Gate
                                                                  Uckfield

My dear Churchill,

I have been away stumping etc and have not seen my political friends. Consequently I do not know the present position of the Irish Question. Would it help at all if we as a party were to give an undertaking to keep the present Govt. in office till after the war was over? If you think there is anything in this suggestion let me know. Otherwise no reply is wanted.[2]

Yours very truly
Robert Cecil

---

[1] Lord Edgar Algernon Robert Cecil, 1864–1958. Third son of the 3rd Marquess of Salisbury. Independent Conservative MP, 1911–23. Under-Secretary of State for Foreign Affairs, 1915–16. Minister of Blockade, 1916–18. Created Viscount Cecil of Chelwood, 1923. Lord Privy Seal, 1923–4. President of the League of Nations Union, 1923–45. Chancellor of the Duchy of Lancaster, 1924–7. Nobel Peace Prize, 1937.

[2] Churchill took Cecil's letter to Asquith before replying. His reply is printed on page 100.

Lord Northcliffe to Winston S. Churchill

(*Copy, Churchill papers: 28/117*)

7 September 1914

My dear Churchill,

This is not a time for Englishmen to quarrel, so I will not say all that I might about the publication of the Amiens message in the Times. Nor will I discuss the facts and tone of the message, beyond saying that it came from one of the most experienced correspondents in the service of the paper.[1] I understand that not a single member of the staff on duty last Saturday night expected to see it passed by the Press Bureau. But when it was *not merely passed, but carefully edited, and accompanied by a definite appeal to publish it,* there was no other possible conclusion except that this was the Government's deliberate wish.

Yours very sincerely

Sir Edward Grey to Lord Kitchener and Winston S. Churchill

(*Grey papers*)

7 September 1914   10 Downing Street

Please let me know as soon as possible what answer I can send to the Belgian Minister.

Time presses for the Belgians. I am afraid we can do very little if anything, but if we can do nothing the Belgians may surrender Antwerp very soon.

---

[1] Arthur Moore, 1880–1962. Special Correspondent of *The Times*, in Constantinople, during Young Turk rebellion, 1908; Persia, 1909, 1910–12; St Petersburg, 1913; Albania, 1914; France, August 1914. Captured by German cavalry patrol, 2 September 1914, but released. Joined Rifle Brigade, 1915; served at Dardanelles and Salonika. Lieutenant-Colonel, 1917. Entered Royal Flying Corps, 1917. Assistant Editor, Calcutta *Statesman*, 1924–34. Member, Legislative Assembly, Delhi, 1932–3. Managing Editor, Calcutta *Statesman*, 1934–42. Public Relations Adviser to Lord Mountbatten in South-East Asia 1944–5.

Lord Kitchener to Sir Edward Grey

(Grey papers)

7 September 1914   War Office

My dear Grey,

I am afraid enclosed answers to the Belgian requests will not be very satisfactory to them, but it is all we can do.

I expect they will hang on to Antwerp, the requests they make are only for articles to defend themselves from aircraft—which though annoying will not take Antwerp.

Yours very truly
Kitchener

Winston S. Churchill to Sir Edward Grey

(Grey papers)

7 September 1914   10 Downing Street

6 naval aeroplanes are now at Antwerp and will be supported so far as is necessary to deal with Zeppelins.

I am awaiting their report.

I will find them a few aerial guns.

I will send you a fuller answer later.

WE MUST HOLD ANTWERP

Winston S. Churchill to H. H. Asquith, Sir Edward Grey and Lord Kitchener

(Grey papers)

7 September 1914   Admiralty

The Admiralty regard the sustained and effective defence of Antwerp as a matter of high consequence. It preserves the life of the Belgian nation: it safeguards a strategic point which, if captured, would be of the utmost menace.

In order to save Antwerp, two things are necessary; first, effective defence of the fortress line, and, second, free uninterrupted communication with the sea.

The first is tolerably well provided for by the Belgian army, which could easily be reinforced by British territorial troops. Fortress guns of moderate size with ammunition (6″ and 4·7″) can be provided by the Admiralty. We

W.C.3—H

will immediately provide also two 3″ aerial guns and six aerial pompoms. We have already stationed six aeroplanes with superior pilots at Antwerp, and propose to increase their numbers to 15 or 20 as rapidly as possible. The duty of these aeroplanes will be to attack Zeppelins which approach the city (or, better still, in their homes on the Rhine).

But the second essential, the free communication with the sea, is a larger matter, and in it are involved our whole relations with the Dutch. From a purely naval point of view, war with Holland would be better for us than neutrality. Their reinforcement of German naval forces would be puny, and the closing of the Rhine which we could accomplish without the slightest additional effort, is almost vital to the efficiency of the naval blockade. I attach a letter written three years ago when these problems were studied n cold blood.[1]

But we must also consider the proper treatment of small nations who are neutrals; and I agree that for our own purposes and our own interests we cannot deal roughly with the Dutch, however unfairly their neutrality is interpreted. When, however, Belgium, a small people fighting for its last breath of life, is considered, a different set of standards come into force. The obstruction of the Scheldt by Holland to any supplies, military or non military, troops or cannon, needed for the defence of Antwerp, is a base and hostile act which should be strenuously and fiercely challenged. The Belgians are now asking us to send 25,000 troops to co-operate with an equal number of Belgians to keep open the line Antwerp–St Nicholas–Ghent–Bruges–Ostende. This is a most costly and dangerous operation. It involves practically a flank position for a line of supply protected by forces large enough to be hit hard and perfectly powerless against any determined German attack which it is thought worth while to deliver. At any moment a punch up from Brussels by a German Division or larger force would rupture the line and drive the troops trying to hold it to be disarmed on neutral Dutch territory or into the sea. Such a line could only be maintained on sufferance of the enemy, i.e. if it paid them to smash it, they could do it at any moment; and unless we are prepared to dominate North Belgium with military force, the more troops we put there, the greater our loss.

The Belgians in their weakness, in their fear of Holland playing them false, are forced to beg us to help them keep this line open. This is futile. And why should we lend ourselves to it? Another course much more direct, simple, forceful, and certainly effective, is open as follows:—

Tell the Dutch now bluntly that we insist upon the Scheldt being kept open permanently for supplies and reinforcements of all kinds for Antwerp under siege, and that any attempt to close or obstruct those waters must be

[1] Not traced.

regarded by us as a disloyal act to a small neighbour, and as an unfriendly act to Great Britain; that we propose now and henceforward to send in and bring out all traffic necessary for the support of Antwerp under the white ensign, and that if any ship flying that flag miscarries, is fired on, or is mined, we shall immediately take the necessary naval steps to keep the Scheldt open by force, and we shall also make an effective blockade of the Rhine.

The Dutch, who are simply responding to German pressure, and who, if free agents, would be relieved of the odious function of strangling Belgium, will be all the better off for our taking a strong line. Anything short of this is simply chucking up the Belgian sponge and playing the German game. Why forsooth do they respect the neutrality of Holland? Simply because it pays them.

For the sake of keeping at peace with Holland, we are giving up all the advantages of blockading the Rhine; all the facilities by seizing Dutch islands of controlling the Elbe; and if on top of this we are to allow Antwerp to be choked and murdered and fall into German hands, we shall find it difficult to prove that we have taken the necessary measures to secure the success of the war.

You have only to look at the map to see the folly of trying to feed Antwerp by Ostend and Ghent.[1] And the fact that the Belgians propose this is the measure of their despair. I advocate this course on the assumption that the battle in France does not go against us.

WSC

Winston S. Churchill to Sir Edward Grey

(*Grey papers*)

7 September 1914   Admiralty

S.of S.

There is a military reason for relieving the fortress of Antwerp of refugees (bouches inutiles) and we ought to help this in every way as part of our policy for the sustained defence of Antwerp. But we ought not to concern ourselves with merely helping Belgians from the unpleasant consequences of residing in Ghent & Bruges under German occupation. They ought to stay there & eat up continental food, & occupy German policy attention. There is no reason why the civil population of Belgium, not concerned in the

---

[1] See map 3 on page 1594.

defence of Antwerp, shd come & live in England. The point is important. Everything must be done to help Belgium's military resistance—but this is no time for charity.

WSC

Winston S. Churchill to Sir Edward Grey
(Grey papers)

7 September 1914   Admiralty

S.of S.

This idea of the French Fleet being handed over to Germany is absurd. It passes human reason to suppose that French Officers wd hand over French ships to Germany to enable Germany to destroy their ally England. They wd not do this even if every man woman & child on the soil of France were going to be put to the sword. Of this there is no chance. But even if this monstrous event occurred and the Fleet were handed over, the Germans wd not have within a year crews or skilled ratings to man the ships, & within the year we cd almost certainly destroy them, & probably very early within the year. And even if this failed, & the whole French Fleet, so manned, were added to the German, & the Austrian Fleet released, we shd still have a fighting chance after abandoning the Medit & concentrating in Home Waters. The fact that the Germans think it worth while to coin these lies for international circulation is a measure of their anxieties.

WSC

Winston S. Churchill to Lord Robert Cecil
(Chelwood papers)

8 September 1914   Admiralty

My dear Cecil

I mentioned yr suggestion to the Prime Minister, & we appreciate the spirit in wh: it is made.

I do not think myself that such a guarantee is practicable or desirable. No one can tell from week to week what the course of the War will be, or what political combinations may be necessary to secure its effective conclusion. No one can foresee the shape in which the political parties will emerge from the struggle.

On the other hand I do beg you to consider, as a military measure, the importance of giving the Irish their Bill, & so bringing them round in

England & America to our side. The denial of this will certainly be repaid with disloyalty & rancour, & an element of weakness & discord introduced into our affairs. It is well worth while giving them their trophy, subject to proper conditions as to postponement of operation, and amendment.

Yours very sincerely
Winston S. Churchill

Winston S. Churchill to Admiral Troubridge: telegram
(Copy, Churchill papers, 13/29)

8 September 1914   Admiralty

Your sole duty is to sink the Goeben and Breslau, under whatever flag, if they come out of the Dardanelles.

The safety of important convoys of troops from Egypt and other issues of the highest importance depend on your doing this.

For this purpose you should use and dispose your whole force including the submarines, when they arrive, and the destroyers.

Enemy must be destroyed at all costs by night or day.

Acknowledge.

H. H. Asquith to George V
(Royal Archives)

8 September 1914   10 Downing Street

. . . Strong appeals are coming from the Belgians for assistance in the defence of Antwerp. The suggestion that we should send 20,000 or 30,000 on to help to hold the road from Ostend to Antwerp was, of course, rejected by the Cabinet on military grounds. Mr Churchill is sending to Antwerp guns, both vertical and others, and is ready to undertake its aerial defence. . . .

Winston S. Churchill to Sir Edward Grey
(Copy, Admiralty papers: 137/880)

8 September 1914   Admiralty

Sir Edward Grey,

If Turkey adheres to a strict neutrality (which she certainly has not), we will at the end of the war give her the two ships *plus* £1,000 a day for their use, *minus* that portion of the original cost which we have paid ourselves.

We cannot pay her any lump sum of money during the war for the ships which we do not intend to buy but to lease. That money would only go to Germany or be used to buy other ships for Germany.

WSC

Rear-Admiral Limpus to Winston S. Churchill

(*Churchill papers: 13/45*)

8 September 1914   c/o British Embassy
                                                   Constantinople

Dear Mr Churchill,

My last letter informed you that Constantinople might be said to be in German hands.

Almost daily I acquire further evidence to confirm this view. e.g. I now know that Admiral Souchon[1] is flying the Turkish Commander in Chief Flag in the 'Goeben'; that every Turkish ship has at least one German Officer on board; and that some have Petty Officers as well in the rôle of instructors.

The number of German workmen, sailors and coast defence gunners imported since the 'Goeben's' arrival has now risen to about 800. Many are in the forts of the two straits.

In my last letter I indicated the anger of Djemal Pacha, Minister of Marine, against England. He is an impulsive and passionate man, and I quite believe that he said what was reported.

I have seen nothing of him this past week, but I now consider that his sympathies are much more French than German, and that he is beginning to resent his present position—that of being almost a nonentity—with the Navy under the real control of Enver Pacha (as C. in C. of all Naval and Military forces) and the Germans.

There is evidence that a considerable part of the Army, the Ministry and the people strongly resents this German control of Turkey and is against any War. I enclose a letter from Lieutenant Hallifax to me which indicates that a similar feeling is abroad in the Navy.

It may be that the Germans have gone too quickly. This is a people that will not tolerate being driven beyond a certain point, though they may be led almost anywhere.

[1] Wilhelm Souchon, 1864–1933. Rear-Admiral, commanding the German Mediterranean Squadron, October 1913–August 1914. Appointed Commander-in-Chief of the Turkish Navy, September 1914.

A revolt against the German domination may come at any moment. The only question is—have the Germans got too firm a grip to be ousted.

Personally I think not.

Patience, and events unfavourable to Germany, coupled with resentment against German presumption, may yet cause the Turks to discuss with Great Britain, or France, the means of ridding themselves of their present masters.

But I still think that any marked German success, or the sight of Roumania joining the Germans, would determine the Turks to give way and join the Germans too.

The German effort now seems to be directed towards making Turkey attack Greece. Troops are afloat in Transports in the Marmora, not many I think. Turkish ships are being hurriedly forced out of Dockyard hands. The last three will be out as follows:—

Torpedo Gunboat 'Peik-i-Shevket'	8 days
Light Cruiser 'Hamidieh'	15 days
Light Cruiser 'Mejidieh'	28 days.

By themselves, even with the 'Goeben' and 'Breslau', the Turks would be beaten at sea.

With Germans manning their own ships, and German Officers and Gunlayers etc. in the Turkish ships, the result would be different.

But it seems to me clear that without a guarantee that there are no Germans on board them the 'Goeben' and 'Breslau' would be treated by the Entente as enemy ships if they emerged from the Dardanelles, even if they flew a Flag other than German.

If this were made clear to the Turks it would be a strong deterrent.

I do not know, but I do believe, that the British Ambassador here is impressing this strong probability on the Turks.

I believe still that, even without menaces, patience and the logic of events will make it difficult for the Germans to persuade the Turks to make an irretrievable false step.

The Peace Party in the Committee appears to be gaining ground.

Sincerely yours
Arthur Limpus

H. H. Asquith to Venetia Stanley
(*Montagu papers*)

9 September 1914   10 Downing Street

. . . Entre nous, the adventurous Winston is just off to Dunkirk to superintend his new flying base: he will be back by lunch time to-morrow. Don't

say anything of this, as he doesn't want the colleagues to know. He has
shown me a *very private* letter to himself from French, who keenly resented
K's visit. . . .

Winston S. Churchill: minute
(*Admiralty papers: 137/1010*)

9 September 1914   Admiralty
Secret

I have promised the Belgians, for the defence of Antwerp, six 6″ or 4·7″
guns with six gunners to teach them how to use them; three new 3″ high
angle guns; and six of the 38 converted anti-aircraft pom-poms, together
with the necessary ammunition. Ascertain when these guns will be ready
for despatch. They are urgently needed at Antwerp.

The President of the Local Government Board[1] states that the Great
Eastern Railway boat goes everyday from Tilbury to Antwerp to fetch
refugees. These sailings began yesterday. The war material for Antwerp
should go in one of these boats at the earliest moment. If possible, all should
go in one boat so as to give no time for questions to be raised about subsequent voyages.

In order to conform to the conditions of the Scheldt Convention, the war
material must be sent as from a private British firm. Either Vickers or
Armstrongs should be asked to handle it, and all indents and bills of lading
should sustain this impression.

I leave the conduct of this matter in the hands of the A.C.L.,[2] who will
report progress to me after discussing the details with the parties concerned.

WSC

Rear-Admiral Kerr to Winston S. Churchill: telegram
(*Grey papers*)

9 September 1914   Athens

I have consulted with Greek General Staff on the subject of your telegram.

They are of opinion, and I agree, that force at disposal of Greece is
sufficient to take Gallipoli if Bulgaria does not attack Greece. It is not sufficient guarantee for Bulgaria to undertake to remain neutral. They will not

[1] Herbert Louis Samuel, 1870–1963. Liberal MP, 1902–18; 1929–35. Chancellor of the
Duchy of Lancaster, 1909–10. Postmaster-General, 1910–14. President of the Local Govern-
ment Board, 1914–15. Postmaster-General, May 1915–January 1916. Chancellor of the
Duchy of Lancaster, November–December 1915. Home Secretary, January–December 1916.
High Commissioner for Palestine, 1920–5. Home Secretary, 1931–2. Created Viscount, 1937.

[2] The Additional Civil Lord of Admiralty, Sir Francis Hopwood (see p. 47).

trust her unless she also attacks Turkey at the same time with all her force.

The plan for taking the Straits of the Dardanelles is ready if above conditions obtain.

Greece has sufficient transports to convey troops. Assistance of a British squadron of two battle-cruisers, one armoured cruiser, three light cruisers and flotilla of destroyers and mine-sweepers will be needed. This plan was originally made out by General Staff and myself without outside assistance, but since Turkey has mobilised and obtained German ships operation has become greater.

General Staff has alternative plan ready, but it would require money from England to carry through. Enormous import trade of cereals are sent to Germany by Bagdad Railway from Mesopotamia. This railway can be seized at Alexandretta and position maintained by a very large force.

Winston S. Churchill to Rear-Admiral Limpus: telegram

(*Copy, Churchill papers: 13/35*)

9 September 1914   Admiralty
Secret and urgent

Now that the Turkish Navy is paralysed by German intrigues Admiralty consider your mission at an end.[1] You and your Officers have laboured faithfully and well to raise the efficiency of the Turkish Navy to a level which would make it an effective weapon of war. It is not your fault that these efforts have not been crowned with success. You have borne with patience and loyalty the continued disappointments of your task, and I am glad now to be able to release you from a position which was ceasing to be in accordance with what is due to the Royal Navy.

H. H. Asquith to Venetia Stanley

(*Montagu papers*)

10 September 1914   10 Downing Street

. . . Winston had not returned from his secret visit to Calais and Dunkirk, but was expected at 3.30 this afternoon. He is engaged in another

---

[1] On 15 August the Turkish Government had removed Admiral Limpus from the executive command of the Turkish Navy and appointed the German Admiral Souchon in his place. The Turks told Limpus that if he wished to remain in Constantinople he could continue to work at the Ministry of Marine. Admiral Souchon, continued to fly his flag in his former flagship, the *Goeben*, which had been renamed the *Jawuz Sultan Selim* on being sold to Turkey by Germany on 12 August.

little 'scoop' (almost as bad a word as 'stunt') in the Heligoland bight, but Masterton informed me with an air of mystery that, as yet, there were 'no fish in the pool'. . . .

Sir John French to Winston S. Churchill
(Churchill papers: 26/1)

10 September 1914   General Headquarters BEF

Thank you my dear Friend with all my heart for your truly kind reply to my letter and also for your previous letter of the 4th. I fear I was a little unreasonable about K & his visit but we have been thro' a hard time & perhaps my temper isn't made any better by it! However, as usual, you have poured balm into my wounds—although they may have been only imaginary—and I am deeply grateful.

Freddie Guest & I concocted a telegram to you begging you to come to us but as you haven't said you would I fear it is impossible just now.

Since I wrote last to you the whole atmosphere has changed and for 5 solid days we have been pursuing instead of pursued & the Germans have had simple Hell.

This very day we have captured several hundred, cut off a whole lot of Transport and got 10 or 12 Guns—and the ground is strewn with dead & wounded Germans. Something like this happened yesterday & the day before. But that is nothing to what they have lost in front of the 5 & 6 French Armies which have been much more strongly opposed. They are indeed fairly on the run & we are following hard.

What a wonderful forecast you made in 1911. I don't remember the paper but it has turned out almost as you said. I have shewn it to a few of my Staff.

I was afraid of Joffre's strategy at first & thought he ought to have taken the offensive much sooner—but he was just right.

Each day the German resistance has slackened—I was up with the Cavalry till almost dark last night and noticed a great change.

Our Artillery have got to understand their opponents much better—They have far more confidence in their own guns and the Melinite Explosive[1] isn't such a bugbear. Yesterday the German shells were bursting absurdly high. Our Infantry still 'bunch up' too much & I've written a strong Memo to troop Commanders to-day about it.

---

[1] A French high explosive, containing picric acid, similar to the British high explosive Lyddite. Both were superseded later in the war by Trinitrotoluene (TNT) which was easier both to manufacture and to use.

This is only a hasty scrawl written in haste. I hope to get an opportunity to send you a proper letter quite soon.

Yours alys
JF

Winston S. Churchill to David Lloyd George

(*Lloyd George papers*)

10 September 1914   10 Downing Street

My dear David,

Please look at this.

The 5/– pension is a scandal. No soldier's wife shd be dependent on charity. Your large outlook shd be turned on this.[1]

Yours ever
W

Sir Max Aitken[2] to Winston S. Churchill

(*Churchill papers: 13/45*)

10 September 1914

Dear Mr Churchill,

The Commission you have given my brother[3] I regard as a personal kindness to me.

The debt of gratitude that I owe you in common with every other British subject far outstrips any liability the Empire has ever contracted.

[1] This note was written across a covering letter from H. W. Massingham to Churchill which accompanied the proof of a leading article in *The Nation*. The article complained that the state's present arrangements for soldiers' wives (7s. 7d. a week separation allowance), widows (5s. a week) and war disabled (10s. 6d. to 17s. 6d. a week) were 'a very bitter disgrace and a great obstacle to recruiting'. In November 1914 the widows' pension was raised to 7s 6d. (see p. 251)

[2] William Maxwell Aitken, 1879–1964. A Canadian financier. Conservative MP, 1910–16. Knighted, 1911. Canadian Eye-Witness in France, May–August 1915. Canadian Representative at the Front, September 1915–16. Newspaper proprietor: bought the *Daily Express*, his largest circulation newspaper, in December 1916. Created Baron Beaverbrook, 1917. Chancellor of the Duchy of Lancaster and Minister of Information, 1918. Minister for Aircraft Production, 1940–1. Minister of State, 1941. Minister of Supply, 1941–2. Lord Privy Seal, 1943–5.

[3] Allan Anderson Aitken, 1887–1959. Sub-Lieutenant, Royal Naval Division, 24 September 1914. Served at Antwerp, October 1914. Wounded at Gallipoli, 26 May 1915. Lieutenant, June 1915. Captain, Headquarters Staff Canadian Expeditionary Force, October 1915; Brigade Major, 1918. Member of the Montreal Stock Exchange, 1923–8. Managed Lord Beaverbrook's Canadian interests. Vice-President, Federal Aircraft Company, 1940–6.

I am proud of my slight connection with you in the days before the War.

I said to you then that I hoped sincerely to follow you & my friends in a reorganized party.

Now I am determined that it is my duty to support you in any party & under any circumstances.

Please don't answer.

Yours faithfully
W. M. Aitken

Winston S. Churchill to Sir Edward Grey

(*Grey papers*)

11 September 1914   Admiralty

Sir Edward Grey

The First Sea Lord independently informed me that he regarded Limpus' position as an insult to the British Navy. Mallet said that this was the right time of all others for the withdrawal of the mission. Orders have been given accordingly with yr full approval. Now it appears that Turkey not only can injure our whole naval position by a flagrant breach of neutrality about the Goeben, but also is to have a veto on Admiralty appointments; & the squadron wh occupies so critical a station at the present time is to go without a Commander. Mallet's telegram[1] is a tangle of contradictions. He must indeed be hard up for arguments against us when he complains of our 'letting the Goeben escape'. I do not myself believe that the withdrawal of the mission, the delivery of my message & the appearance of the Admiral in command of the Meditn Sqn, wd have any other effect than to cow and embarrass the Turks. If Mallet thinks he is dealing with a Govt amenable to argument, persuasion, & proof of good faith, he is dreaming. Factions are struggling for ascendancy, & are only actuated by considerations of force & fear, & only restrained by their great doubt as to who is going to win in Europe. The right course wd be to have presented my message to the Minister of Marine as I originally intended, when I believed, and still believe they wd have implored Adl Limpus to remain. Nothing appeals to the Turkish Govt but force; & they will continue to kick those who they think are unable or unwilling to use it against them. You must decide. There

---

[1] On 8 September 1914 Mallet telegraphed to Grey advising that Limpus' Naval Mission 'might now very reasonably be withdrawn'. Later in the same telegram he said that Britain's position at Constantinople was 'in many respects defining itself more favourably'. But he still concluded that the Naval Mission should be withdrawn 'unless His Majesty's Government desire the mission to remain here indefinitely'. (*Foreign Office papers: 371/2141*)

is no question of any other appt for Limpus. He never wd have got this chance but for the fact that he was the only man on the spot, & that it was urgently necessary to fill the place. If he is to be vetoed, another Admiral must go from home at once. In case you take Mallet's view, the mission had better remain until the Germans decide to make it prisoner of war.

I shall not say any more.

WSC

Winston S. Churchill to Austen Chamberlain[1]

(*Copy, Churchill papers: 13/44*)

12 September 1914   Admiralty

My dear Austen,

The Irish policy to which you and your friends would condemn us means the alienation of Irish Nationalism all over the world, combined with serious disaffection in Liberal and Labour ranks. This would amount to a grave weakening in the forces that can now be gathered together for the prosecution of the war. It is not on party grounds that I say 'we cannot afford it'. No question of Parliamentary support is involved; but we must not squander forces which are vitally necessary to the success of our arms and to the national safety.

There is in my opinion no practical difference between the course we propose and the one you ask for, except this: that your course involves a quarrel with the Irish nation, and ours does not. Both policies begin by putting the Home Rule Bill on the Statute Book. Thereafter, you propose that the 6 counties shall be excluded for the time being, and that their final settlement shall stand over for 3 years, i.e. till after a General Election. We propose that there shall be a moratorium for 12 months or till the war is over, whichever is the longer period, before the Bill becomes operative; and even then a further period of at least 8 months must intervene—i.e., a general Election must ensue—before any effective step is taken. We couple this with a declaration of our intention to proceed with the Amending Bill so that it can come into law in time to overtake the Home Rule Bill; and further with a declaration that after what has happened, whatever the fate of the Amending Bill, we shall in no circumstances use force against the Ulstermen. We believe that

[1] Joseph Austen Chamberlain, 1863–1937. Conservative MP, 1892–1937. Chancellor of the Exchequer, 1903–5. Unsuccessful candidate for the leadership of the Conservative Party, 1911. Secretary of State for India, May 1915. Resigned, July 1917. Minister without Portfolio, 1918–19. Chancellor of the Exchequer, 1919–21. Lord Privy Seal, 1921–2. Foreign Secretary, 1924–9. Knighted, 1925. First Lord of the Admiralty, 1931.

in the interval events will occur which will cause the party differences of boundaries now outstanding to fade into insignificance.

Greatly as I should deplore the renewal of party controversy, I am sure that the nation and the Empire will regard you as wanting in judgment and in sense of proportion if on the difference between our policy and yours you either weaken the unity which prevails in Great Britain or seek to force us into a quarrel with the Irish nation.

The Government had a right to claim the absolute support of the Opposition in the measures necessary to carry on the war, and Conservatives throughout the country would not have tolerated any other attitude. Recognizing as we do the advantages which have flowed from that support, and the high motives which evoke it, I am bound to point out in view of your letter that we command, for the purposes of the war and for all measures connected with it, an intact and independent majority of our own of about 100.

In these circumstances I cannot feel that the support which you and your friends were bound in honour to give to the prosecution of the war ought to be made a lever to force us into a breach of faith with our own supporters or into a fatally unwise policy towards the Irish nation.

I cannot take any responsibility for the postponement of the meeting to stimulate recruiting in Birmingham, though I shall certainly conform to your wishes in regard to it. I have therefore telegraphed to the Lord Mayor[1] expressing my regret that as you are unable to be present I must ask to be excused.

It will be for you to justify a public action which cannot but be detrimental to our military strength.

Yours very sincerely
Winston S. Churchill

H. H. Asquith to Venetia Stanley

(*Montagu papers*)

12 September 1914

Munstead House[2]
Godalming

. . . Violet & I lunched at the Admiralty with the Winstons and E. Grey. The two latter were in high spirits at the latest news (did you like French's

[1] William Henry Bowater, 1855–1932. Five times Lord Mayor of Birmingham between 1909 and 1915. Knighted, 1916.
[2] The country home of Reginald McKenna's father-in-law, Sir Herbert Jekyll.

letter?) and Winston showed me an excellent letter wh. he was written to
Austen Ch^m & Hugh Cecil,[1] in reply to violent complaints of [? theirs] of
our breach of faith, chicanery &c, about the Bills. . . .

Austen Chamberlain to Winston S. Churchill
(*Churchill papers: 13/44*)

12 September 1914   9, Egerton Place

Dear Winston,

I have received your letter with infinite regret. To the last I cherished the
hope that after seeing the Prime Minister you might have a different message
to give to me.

What the future now has in store for us I do not know. I shall of course
do nothing to embarrass the national defence, and my services are at the
disposal of H.M. Government, as they have been since the war began, for
as long as the war lasts. But it is impossible that I should appear upon a
public platform with a member of the Government at the very moment
which the Prime Minister chooses, in defiance of all that he has said, to
break the political truce and reopen political controversy in the House of
Commons, and, trading on the patriotism of his opponents, to carry a most
controversial bill in its most controversial form. Your knowledge that in this
crisis we can have recourse to none of the means for resisting and defeating
your action which, but for the war, were open to us should have shown you
what passionate resentment this action must stir in our hearts. Amidst all
the suspicions which have been engendered by the Government's delay in
announcing a decision, I have confidently affirmed that this at least was a
course which as men of honour you could not and would not adopt. I have,
it appears, been mistaken and I am almost as much grieved on personal as
on public grounds.

Yours very truly
Austen Chamberlain

P.S. I have telegraphed to the Lord Mayor of B'ham as follows—'Mr
Churchill and I much regret that we are unavoidably prevented from leaving
London on Monday. Meeting must be indefinitely postponed. Austen
Chamberlain.' I hope that this form of announcement meets your wishes.

[1] Lord Hugh Richard Heathcote Gascoyne Cecil, 1869–1956. Known as 'Linky'. Fifth
son of the 3rd Marquess of Salisbury. Conservative MP, 1895–1906; 1910–37. Provost of
Eton, 1936–44. Created Baron Quickswood, 1941.

Winston S. Churchill to Lord Kitchener

(*Kitchener papers*)

13 September 1914   Admiralty

My dear Kitchener,

I am touched by the promptness with wh you have looked after Marlborough.[1] It is a gt pleasure to work with you, & the two Departments pull well together. As you say—they are only one Department really.

Yours vy sincerely
Winston S. Churchill

Austen Chamberlain to Winston S. Churchill

(*Churchill papers: 13/44*)

13 September 1914   9, Egerton Place

Dear Winston,

I regret that the form of my telegram to the Lord Mayor does not meet with your concurrence. You will remember that when I saw you early on Friday afternoon I told you that this was the only method which I could devise to avoid anticipating the statement which the Prime Minister is to make tomorrow. You took no objections to its terms then, only asking me to delay sending it till after you had spoken to the Prime Minister. For the rest, I accept full responsibility for my action. I have no doubt that it is my duty to be in the House of Commons tomorrow afternoon.

The rest of your letter calls for one or two observations and a correction.

You speak of a certain proposal as the course we 'ask for' and elsewhere as what we 'propose'. You are mistaken. Our proposal was that all controversial legislation should be postponed till the war was ended and that you should then resume its consideration at the stage it had reached when war broke out, the full benefit of the Parliament Act being assured to you by special legislation which we would help to pass. This you refused, though it is the only means of carrying out the Prime Minister's expressed intention that all parties should retain their position uninjured by the support which they feel bound to give to the Government during the war.

[1] As a Conservative, the Duke of Marlborough could not obtain any political appointment. At Churchill's request, Kitchener made him a special War Office messenger; he was employed mostly in carrying special despatches from Kitchener to Sir John French. From 1899 to 1902 Marlborough had been Paymaster-General of the Forces, a political appointment. He was a Lieutenant-Colonel in the Oxfordshire Hussars. In 1917 Lloyd George appointed him Joint Parliamentary Secretary to the Board of Agriculture and Fisheries.

The proposal which you describe as ours is in fact one of two suggestions made to us by the Prime Minister. The first we declared to be wholly inadmissible. To the second we reluctantly agreed to submit in view of the urgent need for complete unity in the prosecution of the war. No sooner were our views made known to you than the Prime Minister's colleagues rejected the suggestion to which he had obtained our assent and insisted on the one to which we had expressed our decided objection.

This is the more remarkable as you say that in your opinion there is 'no practical difference' between them. Why then insist upon the one which you knew was not acceptable to us? It would almost seem as if in the view of the Cabinet that was its chief merit.

I note that you now say that in no circumstances will force be used against the Ulstermen. I am glad to hear it, for the Prime Minister forgot to mention this important condition in his communication to Bonar Law.

One further observation and I have done. You are right in saying that the Government had a right to claim the absolute support of the Opposition in the measures necessary to carry on the war, and that our party in the country would not have tolerated any other attitude. Your calculation is a sound one. Whatever happens we shall do all we can to support the national defence and nothing to embarrass the Government in the conduct of the war. You must wish that the party with which you now act could show an equally good record for the last great war in which our country was engaged.[1]

Yours very truly
Austen Chamberlain

Winston S. Churchill to Austen Chamberlain

(*Copy, Churchill papers: 13/44*)

13 September 1914   Admiralty
Private

My dear Austen,

I beseech you to realise what an act of recklessness and unwisdom it wd be for us—either party—to start a quarrel with Irish nationalism here, in the Colonies, and above all in America, at this time of crisis. Really we ought not to be forced to choose between a scandalous row here, and open Irish disloyalty. Why should the State be impoverished by either catastrophe?

---

[1] A reference to Liberal criticisms of the Boer War. Between 1899 and 1901 Lloyd George had come to national prominence as a leading Parliamentary critic of Conservative policy in South Africa. Churchill's maiden speech had been in answer to some of Lloyd George's strictures.

Our plan prevents anything being done—except the sentimental satisfaction of having an inoperative bill on the Statute book—till the war and the election are both over. And even then—how nearly the differences were adjusted—one poor Irish county—At the end of all the delays, that is all that will be left to fight about.

And why shd we want to fight at all? No one can tell how parties will emerge from this war. And once the old party flags of the Victorian era have been hung up, new principles of action must prevail.

I am sure if you think about it all, you will see that the concession to the Irish of the sentimental point, while reserving every safeguard for the subsequent treatment of outstanding differences—is a prudent and necessary measure wh all parties shd take in common. It will rally to the Empire forces wh otherwise are utterly estranged. It will remove from party warfare the principal obstacle to a real unity of political action.

Never can the Ulstermen who have put aside their weapons to aid the Belgians, and have gone to the front to serve the country be the subject of coercion to put them under Home Rule. Never can Englishmen look upon Irishmen as traitors and rebels, if in this struggle they bear a loyal part and shed their blood willingly and generously with our own men.

It will be a new world. Don't bar it out.

I am quite content about the way the meeting has been put off

Yours very
WSC

P.S. The P.M. saw and approved my letter of yesterday.

Winston S. Churchill: minute
(*Admiralty papers: 137/880*)

13 September 1914   Admiralty

The gross and repeated violations of neutrality by Turkey, the naval disadvantages caused to us thereby, the dominance of the Turkish govt. by German officers make it contrary to the public interest to pay her any lump sum of money during the war.

Afterwards if she behaves herself she can have her ships in the terms already stated by me to F.O. i.e. cost price + £1000 a day for use *minus* any instalments paid by us.

WSC

Austen Chamberlain to Winston S. Churchill

(*Churchill papers: 13/44*)

14 September 1914   9, Egerton Place
Private

Dear Winston,

Your private letter reached me yesterday afternoon. As your last letters were not marked private and appeared to be written with a view to publication I had supposed that you meant to send them to the press. I have not done so and it is not my intention to do so unless I am obliged by events.

I utterly dissent from your reading of the situation. I believe, and I have the best American authority for thinking, that if you had done the obvious thing and announced at the beginning of the war that all domestic controversy must cease till the war was over, you would have had the unanimous approval of America and even the Irish themselves would have recognised the justice and the wisdom of your action. As it is, you deliberately sacrifice the Ulstermen who have shown an unconditional and splendid loyalty in order to pay blackmail to the National Volunteers who have held aloof and forbidden their members to give you any assistance and to their American paymasters whom I see no more reason to trust now than at any time during the last twenty years.

Neither I nor my colleagues want 'a scandalous row' or any row here and we are doing our utmost to prevent it. Nor do I wish to add to the bitterness of controversy, but you have utterly failed to understand the effect produced by your action on opponents who since the crisis began have spared no effort individually or collectively to support the Government of their country, who have buried all ancient feuds, personal and political, and have unreservedly placed themselves, their party and its organisation at your service. The fact is that, as you said to me on Friday, you 'do not care a damn about Home Rule', and you are utterly incapable of appreciating the feelings of those to whom opposition to Home Rule is a deep-rooted and sincere conviction. You have destroyed our belief in the honour of public men and have shattered the hopes that some of us entertained that union in the present crisis might produce a better feeling and a greater agreement than would have seemed possible a few weeks ago. I see no gleam of light in the course that you have chosen. I would have staked my own honour that you would never do this thing and I am heart-broken to find that I am mistaken.

Yours very truly
Austen Chamberlain

Winston S. Churchill to Austen Chamberlain
(*Copy, Churchill papers: 13/44*)

14 September 1914   Admiralty
Private

Dear Austen,

Compared to winning the war I do not care about Home Rule; but that does not mean that apart from this comparison I do not care about it or think it a wise and hopeful policy. Crudely quoted as in your letter, I cannot recognise the sentiment.

Don't bother to answer. With deep regret I must realise that we cannot understand each other's point of view; and it remains for us to confront you with successful results at home as well as abroad.

I have no wish to publish the letters wh were not marked *private*. But in such a matter I shd await an expression of your wishes.

Yrs sincerely
WSC

Winston S. Churchill to Sir Edward Grey and Walter Runciman
(*Copy, Churchill papers: 13/29*)

14 September 1914   Admiralty

We do not consider the provision of convoys on the South American trade route necessary or desirable. The route has been strongly reinforced, and is considered safe. If a convoy was started, it would cause all the non-convoyed trade, now proceeding regularly, to become alarmed, and they would clamour for convoys which it would be impossible to provide. The Dresden has interfered altogether with seven ships, of which two were sunk, the last on the 26th August. When all except one of these incidents took place, the Glasgow was the only British ship on the route, and it was wonderful she did so much to safe-guard British trade. From the 20th August to the 4th September the Glasgow, Monmouth, and Otranto were available. From the 4th to the 11th September the cruisers Good Hope, Glasgow, Cornwall, Bristol, and Monmouth, and the auxiliary Otranto and Macedonia, have been on the route. In view of the possibility that the Scharnhorst and Gneisenau will come to the Straits of Magellan after being driven from the China Station, these are being further reinforced with the battleship Canopus and the very powerful armoured cruiser Defence. The British force in these waters is therefore overwhelming. Nothing has been heard of the enemy since the 26th August. The composition of the force should be kept strictly secret;

but every assurance may be given to trade with confidence, the very remote chance of capture being fully met by insurance.

WSC

Winston S. Churchill to John Churchill

(*John Churchill papers*)

14 September 1914   Admiralty

My dear,

I have explained to Goonie.[1] I am hopeful that this business will not be serious. It is intended only as a demonstration on the enemy's flank: & I expected that the armed motor cars wd do the work: you being merely a support & to enable the infantry to move. But now it seems that German cavalry in gt force has come all over this area. You will be kept in close relation to the perimeter of the fortress wh is extensive & well fortified—as I know from personal inspection.

I beseech you not to be worried about money. Your own credit wd enable you to raise 5 or 6 thousand pounds as easily as I did. But anyhow I can lend you a thousand or two quite easily. I shall make myself absolutely responsible in case things go wrong—that all yr affairs are made good and sure. Trust in me.

It will all come right.

I hope to come over in a day or two to see that things are well started. You know how much I care about you—but it is a gt honour for the regiment—& I am glad to have you in my hands.

Your ever loving
W

Winston S. Churchill to Sir Edward Grey

(*Grey papers*)

15 September 1914   Admiralty

Sir Edward Grey,

I have already written to you about aeroplanes at Antwerp.

24 naval maxims and 500,000 rounds of ammunition were supplied to

[1] John Churchill had been ordered to France with the Queens Own Oxfordshire Hussars, as part of the force under Admiralty control which was to operate, at the request of the French High Command, in the region of Dunkirk, Ostend, Cassel and Douai (see Asquith's letter to Venetia Stanley of 19 September 1914, quoted on p. 124).

them on the 18th of August. 6 4·7″ naval guns and ammunition, with an officer in charge and 6 gunners, were delivered 3 days ago.

3 high-angle 3″ guns and 6 converted anti-aircraft pom-poms have been sent today.

No more maxims or rifles are available.

WSC

Winston S. Churchill to Sir Edward Grey
(Grey papers)

15 September 1914   Admiralty

Sir E. Grey,

I must repeat that grave injury has been done to our naval position by the flagrant violations of neutrality committed by the Turks. The British naval mission was ordered off the ships entrusted to them & has now after many humiliations resigned.

The appointment of a German C in C of the Turkish Fleet as well as of the Turkish Army may not lead directly to war; but the whole attitude of Turkey has been & is still to look for a chance of striking at us if she dares.

We ought to have absolute freedom to deal with her at the peace as the general convenience & interests of the allies require. I earnestly trust that freedom will not be compromised.

WSC

Lord Fisher to Winston S. Churchill
(Churchill papers: 13/43)

15 September 1914

Dear Winston,

I was in a hurry yesterday to see a soldier in hospital (*such tales at first hand I am preparing for you on the war!*) so I did not mention the two following points but it is more than probable they have been very full considered:—

I The movements of the German Fleet will be dictated from the Army Head Quarters (just as Villeneuve was sent to sea by Napoleon from Cadiz). It will in no wise be naval conditions that will actuate the movements of the German Fleet. *Therefore* totally unlikely naval conditions may see it emerge to fight.

II Why is standard of recruits raised 3 inches to 5 feet 6? It's criminal folly! I think Nelson was only 5 feet 4, and the Ghurkas less! What d——d folly to discard supreme enthusiasm because it's under 5 feet 6. *We are a wonderful nation!* astounding how we muddle through!—There's only one explanation:—We are the lost 10 Tribes!

> 'Time and the Ocean and some Guiding Star
> In high Cabal have made us What we are'[1]

Yours

F

What a '*Tria juncta in uno*' we now have to board the Iron Duke! *Jellicoe, Madden* and *Backhouse!*[2] *Trust them implicitly! Lean on them entirely!*

Winston S. Churchill to Prince Louis

(*Copy, Churchill papers: 28/153*)

16 September 1914   Admiralty

Sir Edward Grey reminded me this morning of the Japanese offer to lend warships to relieve any of ours in China waters wanted elsewhere. The hunting down of Scharnhorst, Gneisenau, and also of Emden is so important that we should now ask them to employ a larger force. I suggest we ask for another couple of armoured cruisers capable of hunting in Marshall Islands and thereabouts, and also for two or three light cruisers to hunt Emden or Konigsberg in the Indian Ocean. Sir Edward Grey expressed his readiness to send any request of this kind to Tokyo.

WSC

Lord Kitchener and Winston S. Churchill: Cabinet notes

(*Grey papers*)

16 September 1914   10 Downing Street

LORD KITCHENER:

I agree that Turkey is behaving so disgracefully that she ought to be informed we shall not forget it after the war is over—I am doubtful whether we should tell Bulgaria that she shall have Adrianople after the war—This would definitely tie us down to action that might be unpleasant to carry out

---

[1] From Sir William Watson, *Ode on the Coronation of Edward VII* (published 1902). Watson had written 'fostering' not 'guiding'.

[2] Roger Roland Charles Backhouse, 1878-1939. Brother of Oliver Backhouse. Entered Navy, 1892. Commander, 1909. Gunnery expert. Flag Commander to Admiral Bridgeman on HMS *Iron Duke*, March 1914; to Sir John Jellicoe, August 1914. Captain, *Iron Duke*, on special service, 1914-15. Flag Captain, HMS *Lion*, 1916-18. Rear-Admiral, 1925. Admiral of the Fleet, 1939.

—I quite agree Turkey should be punished but I would not say definitely how this is to be done—

WINSTON S. CHURCHILL:

I don't want vengeance after the show is over—but aid of a Balkan confedn. now—

LORD KITCHENER:

I do not think the Adrianople offer would be very tempting, they want Servian land & Greek.

WINSTON S. CHURCHILL:

Well——all I ask for is no more consideration for Turkish interests if we can get any advantage with Bulgaria.

LORD KITCHENER:

I agree.

H. H. Asquith to George V
(Royal Archives)

16 September 1914   10 Downing Street

. . . Mr Churchill is taking steps to counteract the increased activity of the Germans in the pursuit and capture of British merchant ships in the South Atlantic. There are now 10 British warships in those waters. . . .

Winston S. Churchill to Captain Murray Sueter
(Copy, Churchill papers: 13/29)

16 September 1914   Admiralty

(1) Draft letters to all firms requesting them to accelerate the delivery of machines now on order and furnish a time-table of forthcoming deliveries weekly.

(2) Each firm is to submit proposals for the most rapid rate of delivery of aeroplanes compatible with efficiency and economy within the next six months.

(3) With the exception of Avro machines, new orders will be for B.E.-II.C's., but if a gap in the production of any firm is caused by the adoption of this new pattern, the question of interim orders for any useful type the firm is now producing may be considered as an individual case.

(4) As a number of parts of B.E. aeroplanes are difficult to manufacture, arrangements should be made by conference and co-operation between the Admiralty and the firms given the new orders, so that these parts may be produced at one centre and on the largest scale necessary, the War Office being asked to give all aid and information possible from the Royal Aircraft Factory.

(5) The Royal Aircraft Factory would be asked to supply drawings of B.E.II.C machines without delay. Let me have the past history of this question. Also let me have a report by Monday next as to when the drawings will be supplied. If there is any difficulty I will apply direct to Lord Kitchener.

(6) Messrs Short Brothers, Messrs White and Co, and the Sopwith Aviation Company should be left employed chiefly on seaplane construction.

(7) Firms are to be asked to attend the Admiralty fourteen days from to-day's date to report progress.

(8) A table of the maximum possible deliveries week by week for the next six months should be prepared by the Air Department, together with a programme of distribution of orders which it is thought should reasonably be given.

WSC

Commander Samson to Captain Sueter

(*Copy, Admiralty papers: 116/1352*)

17 September 1914   Dunkirk

Aeroplane squadrons have been formed as follows:

No. 1 Squadron at Antwerp

No. 2 Squadron proceeds to St. Omer (France) in two days.

No. 3 Squadron at Dunkirk.

Headquarters with some staff and machines proceed to Morbecque near Hazebrouck.

Machines sent out from England should be ordered to Dunkirk, and orders will be given for their disposal on arrival.

Hope to be able to get a squadron to Douai soon, and anticipate good work will result. Can get other squadrons quickly as my position is central.

Winston S. Churchill to Sir Edward Grey

(*Grey papers*)

17 September 1914   Admiralty

Sir Edward Grey,

I have ascertained that the telegram about the aeroplanes for Antwerp was sent by the Foreign Office yesterday as requested by us. 9 machines will go there as soon as the Belgians are ready to receive them.

WSC

Lord Esher: diary

(*Esher papers*)

17 September 1914

. . . I lunched with Callwell to-day, and we talked a great deal about the advisability of landing, as soon as possible, Churchill's Sea-dogs, a Territorial Division, and the Canadians at Dunkirk, or on the coast. If this move were not delayed, it would be most effective. I think that he is now most strongly in favour of it, and it all turns upon whether the idea can be insinuated into Lord K's mind. . . . .

George Pratt[1] to Winston S. Churchill: telegram

(*Churchill papers: 2/64*)

17 September 1914   Town Hall Acton

Will you kindly favour us with inspiring message for monster demonstration and great mass meeting to encourage recruiting Acton Park Saturday next.

Chairman Acton Council

Winston S. Churchill: message

(*Draft, Churchill papers: 2/64*)

17 September 1914   Admiralty

We must win this war, but the only sure way is to send Sir John French an army of at least a million men, and to maintain it at full strength in spite of losses. That army will be invincible, for every soldier in it will have gone of his own free will because he knows what is at stake not only for Britain but

[1] George Percy Pratt, 1871–1936. Architect; a pioneer of cinema design: designer of the Globe, the first luxury cinema in London. Councillor, Acton Town Council, 1910–18; Chairman, 1914–16. Hon. Treasurer, Acton Conservative Party, 1924–32.

for civilisation. With that army, but only with that army, we can make certain that splendid achievements from men at the front will not be thrown away.[1]

Nothing less than one million British soldiers in the line together will finish this war as it has got to be finished. Prussian military tyranny must be broken for ever. The cause is worthy of the effort; & the effort is well within our strength. Victory is certain if we act & organise resolutely we must act & organise now. This is the time for sacrifice & daring.[2]

Winston S. Churchill to Prince Louis

(*Copy, Churchill papers: 13/29*)

18 September 1914   Admiralty

The force available for operations in the narrow seas should be capable of minor action without the need of bringing down the Grand Fleet. To this end it should have effective support either by 2 or 3 battle-cruisers or battleships of the Second Fleet working from Sheerness. This is the most efficiently air and destroyer patrolled anchorage we possess. They can lie behind the boom, and can always be at sea when we intend a raid. Battle-cruisers are much to be preferred.

The Bacchantes ought not to continue on this beat.[2] The risk to such ships is not justified by any services they can render. The narrow seas, being the nearest point to the enemy, should be kept by a small number of good modern ships.

The Bacchantes should go to the western entrance of the Channel and set Bethell's[3] battleships—and later Wemyss's[4] cruisers—free for convoy and other duties.

The first four Arethusas should join the flotillas of the narrow seas.

[1] This first paragraph was omitted in the message as finally sent.

[2] The ships did not leave their dangerous beat in time (see Asquith's letter to Venetia Stanley of 22 September 1914, quoted on p. 127–8).

[3] Alexander Edward Bethell, 1855–1932. Entered Navy, 1869. Director of Naval Intelligence, 1909–12. Knighted, 1912. Vice-Admiral Commanding battleships of Third Fleet, 1914. Commanded Channel Fleet, 1915. Admiral, 1916. Commander-in-Chief Plymouth, 1916–18.

[4] Rosslyn Erskine Wemyss, 1864–1933. Entered Navy, 1877. Commodore, Royal Naval Barracks Devonport, 1909–11. Rear-Admiral in command of the 12th Cruiser Squadron, August 1914, charged with escorting the British Expeditionary Force to France. Convoyed the first Canadian troops to France, September 1914. Governor of Mudros, February–April 1915. Commanded the naval squadron at Cape Helles, April 1915. Acting Vice-Admiral at the Dardanelles, November–December 1915; directed the naval aspects of the evacuation of the Gallipoli Peninsula. Knighted, 1916. Second Sea Lord, 1917. First Sea Lord, 1917–19. Created Baron Wester Wemyss, 1919. Admiral of the Fleet, 1919.

H. H. Asquith to Venetia Stanley
(*Montagu papers*)

19 September 1914

. . . Joffre is very anxious that we should make a diversion on the N. coast of France to frighten the Germans as to their lines of communication. (This is *very secret*): so Winston has sent there to reinforce his aeroplanes & armed motor-cars his Marine Brigade (about 3000 men). As he mentioned 'cavalry', I thinking of old jokes about 'horse-marines', began to chaff him as to the composition of his force. And what do you think I discovered? That he had (with K's consent, who is heartily glad to get rid of them) despatched the Oxfordshire Yeomanry! his own corps, with brother Jack (who is a Major in it) &c. I am afraid poor Sonnie [Duke of Marlborough] will be in a state of terrible anxiety, and not without reason. There are about 450 of them, all told, and if they encounter the Germans in any force, I fear we shall see very few of them back again. I hope, however, that like that other little jaunt to Ostend, of wh. I told you some weeks ago, they will follow the example of the 'good old Duke of York', who 'led his men to the top of the hill', and 'led them down again'.

I gather from what W. said that the Admiral & his colleagues (with their 40 Dreadnoughts) are a good deal perturbed by the fear of submarines. (They are all against any attack on Heligoland). In the Scapa flow where they have been of late, there are some small whales, or big porpoises, which in their playful flounderings with all manner of fins & tails, often give the impression of a 'periscope', & have been fired at as such. . . .

Winston S. Churchill to Colonel Seely[1]
(*Mottistone papers*)

20 September 1914   Admiralty

My dear Jack

The days pass in an unbroken succession of events & decisions; & I have hardly had time to write the letters of sympathy wh our severe losses among cherished friends demand.

---

[1] John Edward Bernard Seely, 1868–1947. Liberal MP, 1900–22; 1923–4. Under-Secretary of State for the Colonies, 1908–11. Under-Secretary of State for War, 1912–14. Resigned in March 1914, following the Curragh incident. Commanded the Canadian Cavalry Brigade, 1915–18. Gassed, 1918, and retired from Army with rank of Major-General. Under-Secretary of State to Churchill, Ministry of Munitions and Deputy Minister of Munitions, 1918. Under-Secretary of State for Air, 1919. Created Baron Mottistone, 1933.

I was glad to hear from Captain Hankey some account of yr exploits.[1] I hope you will not expose yourself unnecessarily to danger.

Here the feeling is absolutely united; & running breast high for a prolonged & relentless struggle. There will I think be no difficulty in putting a million men in the field in the spring of 1915. But we must keep the necessary minimum of officers to train them.

I rejoice more than I can say at the splendid deeds of the army and the military repute wh our army has by a few weeks of their achievements altogether revived.

The Navy has been thrilled by all their prowess & valour.

We sit still in the steady cold blooded game & can I think keep it up indefinitely.

Doom has fallen upon Prussian military arrogance. Time & determination are all that is needed.

Yours ever
W

Sir George Aston to Winston S. Churchill: telegram
(*Admiralty papers: 116/1348*)

21 September 1914   Dunkirk

Governor[2] has transmitted to me telegram from French Headquarters to the effect that he must make every effort to cut the German lines of communications passing through Cambrai Valenciennes.

He asks for Commander Samson, his colleagues and five cars to be put under his orders to work tomorrow from Douai where he promises to send 1,000 territorial infantry in support.

Samson with five armed cars and explosives and French Engineers proceeding thence to blow up railway bridge over river between Cambrai and Valenciennes.

In view of strength in which these important bridges must be held considerable risk project.

Shall I place Samson at disposal and under the orders of the Governor as the Governor desires reply by telegraph. Urgent.

[1] Between August 1914 and mid-1915 Seely served on Sir John French's Staff, as a roving intelligence officer, and in liaison duties with the French and Belgian armies. He was often under fire; in October 1914 he was present in Antwerp during the final days of the siege.

[2] Charles Bidon, 1855–1920. Artillery officer. Commanded the 1st Regiment, Foot Artillery, 1912. Governor of Dunkirk and Commander of the Forces for the defence of the Dunkirk region, 1914–15.

Winston S. Churchill to Sir George Aston: telegram
(*Copy: Admiralty papers: 116/1348*)

21 September 1914   Admiralty
Secret

Tell Governor that my views harmonise with his.

In order to concert arrangements thoroughly I will arrive Dunkirk eight a.m. tomorrow 22nd.

Tell Colonel Ollivant to await my arrival.

Explain to him your requirements about supply bases and let him telegraph me full details.

Am endeavouring to procure you 100 motor omnibuses to ensure mobility.

I hope to see Commander Samson on arrival.

We can send you your tents if you want them.

Our reports indicate large forces of enemy in North Belgium and Brussels including 7th. German Cavalry division at Tournai. Churchill.

H. H. Asquith to Venetia Stanley
(*Montagu papers*)

21 September 1914   10 Downing Street

. . . I have been talking seriously to Winston to-day about his 'little army': I am not at all comfortable as to its prospects, having little faith in the fighting or staying powers of the Oxfordsh. Yeomanry. In addition to his 600 or so of armoured motor cars, he has now chartered & is despatching some 200 or 300 motor busses! Their immediate objective is Douai, wh. you will see on the map, but as the Germans have now brought some 60,000 men to Brussels & the neighbourhood, who will be on their flank, it is clear that they must be very cautious. Happily we have a large reconnoitring force of the best aeroplanes. . . .

Winston is a good deal exercised by the activity of the German cruisers— especially the Königsberg, which must have been directed by a wireless spy to come upon the Pegasus,[1] just when it was helpless & refitting at Zanzibar. He hopes to encircle another of their pernicious gad-flies—the 'Emden' wh. is now in Indian waters.[2] The 'Goeben' also is beginning to show signs of new

[1] The British light cruiser *Pegasus* was sunk off Zanzibar on 20 September 1914 by the German light cruiser *Königsberg*.

[2] The German light cruiser *Emden* left the German port of Kiaochow (Tsingtau) in China on 6 August 1914. In seven weeks, from September, with her funnel disguised to look like that of a British cruiser, she sunk 70,000 tons of allied shipping in the Indian Ocean, captured eight ships which she took with her in convoy, destroyed a Russian cruiser and a French destroyer in Penang harbour, and bombarded the oil depot at Madras, setting fire to 50,000 tons of petroleum. On 9 November 1914 she was reduced to a wreck by the Australian light cruiser *Sydney*, and beached on a reef.

life, and if it leaves the Dardanelles will (or aught to be) sunk by our fleet
in that part of the world. . . .

Winston S. Churchill to Vice-Admiral Carden:[1] *telegram*
(*Copy, Admiralty Papers 137/96*)

21 September 1914   Admiralty

Assume command of the squadron off Dardanelles. Your sole duty is to
sink Goeben & Breslau, no matter what flag they fly, if they come out of
Dardanelles. We are not at war with Turkey but German Admiral Souchon
is now C in C Turkish Navy and Germans are controlling and largely
manning it. Turks have been told that any Turkish ships which come out
with Goeben & Breslau will equally be attacked by us. You are authorized
to act accordingly without further declaration or parley. You must deal at
yr discretion with any minor Turkish War vessel which may come out alone
from Dardanelles, either ordering her back or allowing her to proceed as
you may think fit, remembering that we do not want to pick quarrel with
Turkey unless her hostile intention is clear.

Indomitable will be diverted from convoy off Crete, & ordered to join
yr squadron. French C in C has been requested to send 2 battleships of
Patrie class to reinforce yr flag.

H. H. Asquith to Venetia Stanley
(*Montagu papers*)

22 September 1914   10 Downing Street

. . . We have just had some very bad news: the worst, I think, since the war
began. Three good & powerful cruisers of an old but not obsolete type—
the Cressy & 2 of her sisters—were sunk this morning in the North Sea.
They were of 12000 tons & had a complement each of I suppose 500 men.
It is said to be the work of submarines, but I am rather sceptical, as in all
the history of modern naval warfare no submarine or combination of submarines has been successful in torpedoing, almost at one blow, 3 big ships.

[1] Sackville Hamilton Carden, 1857–1930. Entered Navy, 1870. Rear-Admiral, 1908.
Admiral Superintendent, Malta Dockyard, 1912–13. Vice-Admiral in command of the
Anglo-French Squadrons in the Eastern Mediterranean, and at the Dardanelles, 20 September 1914 to 16 March 1915, when ill-health forced him to retire. Knighted, 1916. Admiral,
1917.

I am inclined to suspect that mines had at any rate a share in the catastrophe. It is a blow, particularly as the navy is not doing very well just now: there are nearly ½ a dozen German cruisers, Emden, Dresden, Karlsruhe[1] &c, which are at large on the high seas & in all parts of the world are sinking or capturing British merchantmen. Things came almost to a climax at the Cabinet to-day, when we learnt that the New Zealanders absolutely decline to despatch their expeditionary force—all in transports & ready to sail to-morrow or next day—unless we can provide them with a sufficiently powerful escort to convoy them in safety from Wellington [to] Adelaide, where they were to join up with the Australian contingent. The Admiralty think there is no real risk, but I am inclined to agree with the New Zealanders, and as there are no available ships at hand of the requisite strength, we have been obliged to tell them to wait for what may be as long as another 6 weeks. This will probably excite a good deal of resentment & indignation in N.Z. Unfortunately, on this day, when of all others he was most needed, Winston is away, on one of his furtive missions,—this time again to Dunkirk: and is not expected back till evening. I think (between you & me) that the Admiralty have not been clever in their outlying strategy. . . .

Lord Stamfordham[2] to Maurice Bonham Carter[3]

(*Asquith papers*)

22 September 1914   Buckingham Palace

. . . His Majesty did not quite like the tone of Winston Churchill's speech[4] especially the reference to 'Rats in a Hole'! Indeed seeing what alas! happened today when the rats came out of their own accord and to our cost, the threat was unfortunate and the King feels it was hardly dignified for a Cabinet Minister.

[1] The German light cruiser *Karlsruhe* sank sixteen British merchant ships in the Caribbean between August and October 1914. She was destroyed by an accidental internal explosion on 4 November 1914. News of the loss, which only reached Germany in December, was kept secret by the German Admiralty for several more months.

[2] Arthur John Bigge, 1849–1931. Entered Army, 1869. Entered the Royal Household, 1880. Private Secretary to Queen Victoria, 1895–1901. Private Secretary to George V, 1910–31. Created Baron Stamfordham, 1911. His only son was killed in action, 15 May 1915.

[3] Maurice Bonham Carter, 1880–1960. Called to the Bar, 1909. Private Secretary to H. H. Asquith, 1910–16. Married Asquith's daughter Violet, November 1915. Knighted, 1916. Assistant Secretary, Ministry of Reconstruction, 1917; Air Ministry, 1918.

[4] Churchill spoke at the Tournament Hall in Liverpool to some 15,000 people on 21 September 1914. He was supported by F. E. Smith and T. P. O'Connor; Alderman Salvidge presiding. Churchill said that 'Although we hoped the Navy would have a chance of settling the question with the German fleet, yet if it did not come out and fight in time of war they would be dug out like rats in a hole.'

H. H. Asquith to Venetia Stanley

(*Montagu papers*)

23 September 1914   10 Downing Street

. . . Winston got back last evening from his second expedition to Dunkirk, where he inspected his mixed lot, & colloqued with the French Governor & General.[1] He was lunching in a café there, when who should step in but the Arch-Colonel! the veritable & only Seely. As I said at the Cabinet, it must have been like the meeting of Livingstone & Stanley in the central wilds of Africa 'Mr Churchill, I presume?'. I will tell you to-morrow what Seely reported of things at the front; he characteristically repelled Winston's invitation to cross over in his destroyer, & have 24 hours with his old colleagues, on the ground that he had sworn not to leave France (alive) until the profaning foot of the last of the invaders had withdrawn from her soil. Three of Winston's airmen penetrated far into Germany, & one of them threw down 3 bombs over the air-sheds at Dusseldorff. Unluckily none of them exploded, but altho' much fired at he escaped. . . .

Major Gerrard: report

(*Copy, Admiralty papers: 116/1352*)

23 September 1914   Antwerp

Sir,
    I have the honour to report that an attack was made on the airship sheds at Düsseldorf and Cologne yesterday. Aeroplanes No. 50 (Major Gerrard) and 906 (Lieut. Collet[2]) to Düsseldorf, and Nos. 149 (Lieut.-Commander S. Grey[3] with Lieut. Newton Clare[4]) and 168 (Lieut. Marix[5]) to Cologne. . . .

[1] *Probably* General Plantey, who was Deputy to General Bidon, the Governor and Commanding General.
[2] Charles Herbert Collett, 1888–1915. Entered Royal Naval Air Service, 1913. Killed in action at the Dardanelles.
[3] Spenser Douglas Adair Grey, 1889–1937. Lieutenant, Royal Naval Air Service, 1913. One of Churchill's flying instructors, 1914. Lieutenant-Commander, August 1914. Sent on Admiralty mission to United States to purchase six flying boats, December 1914. Commander, flying boat experimental flying tests, Hendon, March 1915
[4] Edward Thomas Newton-Clare, 1881–1944. Flying Officer, Royal Flying Corps (Naval Wing), May 1914. For his part in the attack on the airship sheds at Cologne he was mentioned in despatches. On 12 October 1914 he flew low over the German lines at Antwerp and dropped his bombs under heavy shell fire at close range. Squadron-Commander, December 1916. Having led his squadron in several air attacks on German controlled aerodromes in Belgium, he was awarded the Distinguished Service Order in May 1917.
[5] Reginald Lennox George Marix, 1889–1966. Lieutenant, Royal Naval Air Service, 1912–15. Served in Belgium, France and the Dardanelles, 1914–16. Lost a leg after a crash while testing an aeroplane near Paris, 1916. Served in Coastal Command and Transport Command, Royal Air Force, 1939–45. Retired as Air Vice-Marshal, 1945.

Only Lieut. Collet succeeded in locating his objective and dropped his three bombs from a height of 400 feet. The first fell a little short and exploded, the others probably hit the shed but failed to explode. The surprise was complete, and the numerous Germans in the vicinity ran in all directions.

Although the material damage was small—possibly the first bomb accounted for a few men—the moral effect must have been considerable. A great many people must have been disturbed by the sound of our engines close over their heads. Lieut. Marix seemed to have penetrated some distance beyond the Rhine.

Lieut. Collet's feat is notable:—Gliding down from 6,000 feet, the last 1,500 feet through the mist, and finally coming in sight of the shed at 400 feet only a quarter of a mile from it. It is discouraging when officers take such considerable risks that their weapons should fail them.

The return journey was safely carried out.

No. 906 got back to Antwerp without a stop, No. 149 refilled at the advanced base, No. 168 landed about 6 miles from the advanced base, No. 50's petrol pressure system failed near the River Meuse, but succeeded in reaching Belgian territory. All the machines were back at Antwerp by 1 p.m.

M. le Baron de Caters,[1] in charge of the armoured cars and supplies at the advanced base, rendered very valuable service. Everything went without a hitch, and the coup was as nearly as possible completely successful.

The Germans are undoubtedly good soldiers, and I think that another attack on these lines, i.e., simultaneous approach from a great height and silent glide right down to the shed, is bound to fail. It would be easy to arrange a zone of fire over the sheds such that every attacking machine must pass through it. Something of the sort will probably now be done.

I would submit that further attacks on these sheds should not be attempted until a properly organised flight of very fast machines with practised pilots is ready.

The Gordon-Bennett machine being built in England would be a very suitable type: they should be sent out in boxes.

I will endeavour to arrange that the existing aerodrome here be improved; it would cost about 2,000*l*.; or that we should move out to Brasscheat, which is now clear of enemy and is a very good ground. I will forward to-morrow a list of material and spares required for the machines.

Lieut-Commander S. Grey reported that a bomb accidentally dropped

---

[1] Baron Pierre de Caters, 1875–1945. Joined the Belgian Air Force, 1 August 1914. 2nd Lieutenant. Commanded a light armoured car assigned to the air force, September–October 1914. Formed and commanded the Belgian Armed Armoured Car Corps, October 1914–June 1915. Returned to aviation, June 1915.

from his machine—he does not know where. I have reported the matter to the British Minister. All our machines passed over a portion of Holland yesterday—mostly at a great height. Submitted that I may be informed of any international ruling there might be on the subject of the neutrality of the air.

There was a Zeppelin scare here last night. I am inclined to think that the comet was the reason of the scarce. I got the machines ready but nothing eventuated.

C. L. Gerrard

Note.—It is reported that all the windows of the shed at Dusseldorf were smashed.

Winston S. Churchill to Sir Edward Grey

(Grey papers)

23 September 1914   Admiralty

My dear Grey,

I must write you a line about Turkey. Poor Mallet's telegrams are in the main mere repetitions of the paragraph attached.[1] We are suffering very seriously from Turkish hostility. Our whole Mediterranean Fleet is tied to the Dardanelles. We are daily trying to buy Turkish neutrality by promises and concessions. Meanwhile the German grip on Turkey tightens and all preparations for war go steadily forward. But all this would in itself be of minor consequence but for the fact that in our attempt to placate Turkey we are crippling our policy in the Balkans.

I am not suggesting that we should take aggressive action against Turkey or declare war on her ourselves, but we ought from now to make our arrangements with the Balkan States, particularly Bulgaria, without regard to the interests or integrity of Turkey. The Bulgarians ought to regain the Turkish territory they lost in the second Balkan War, and we ought to tell them that if they join with Roumania, Greece and Servia in the attack upon Austria and Germany, the allied powers will see that they get this territory at the peace. We always said that Adrianople should never fall back into Turkish hands and the strongest possible remonstrances were addressed to the Porte by you at the time. There is therefore nothing wrong or inconsistent in our adopting this position. If we win the war we shall be quite strong enough

[1] In a telegram to Grey sent from Constantinople on 22 September 1914, Sir Louis Mallet had asserted that 'a majority is against war, and that peace party is gaining strength.' (Grey papers)

to secure this territory for Bulgaria, and Turkey's conduct to us with repeated breaches of neutrality would release us from any need of considering her European interests.

Like you, I sympathise deeply with Mallet in the futile and thankless task on which he is engaged. I do not know what the result will be but I am sure it is not worth while sacrificing the bold and decisive alternative of throwing in our lot frankly with the Christian States of the Balkans to get the kind of neutrality which the Turks have been giving us, and for which we are even asked to pay and be grateful. The whole tone of the telegrams from Roumania and Bulgaria are hopeful. I do most earnestly beg you not to be diverted from the highway of sound policy in this part of the world, both during the war and at the settlement, by wanderings into the labyrinth of Turkish duplicity and intrigue. All I am asking is that the interests and integrity of Turkey shall no longer be considered by you in any efforts which are made to secure common action among the Christian Balkan States.

Yours sincerely
Winston S. Churchill

Winston S. Churchill to Colonel Ollivant and Captain Sueter
(Copy, Churchill papers: 13/45)

23 September 1914   Admiralty

It is most important that the motor transport and armed motor-cars should be provided to a certain extent with cars carrying the means of bridging small cuts in the road, and an arrangement of planks capable of bridging a ten- or twelve-feet span quickly and easily should be carried with every ten or twelve machines. A proportion of tools should also be supplied.

Let me have proposals at once.

J. L. Garvin[1] to Winston S. Churchill
(Churchill papers: 13/45)

23 September 1914   9 Grenville Place

My dear Churchill,

My son[2] is gazetted and though I should never have taxed your good offices could the trouble have been foreseen I shall never forget your friendship.

---

[1] James Louis Garvin, 1868–1947. Editor, the *Observer*, 1908–42. Editor, *Pall Mall Gazette*, 1912–15. Editor-in-Chief, *Encyclopædia Britannica*, 1926–9.

[2] Roland Gerard Garvin, 1896–1916. J. L. Garvin's only son. Killed in action during the battle of the Somme.

Your proofs have been so strong that every body almost is your friend now, in a sense, but whether it is all fair weather or there comes a bit of the foul, you find me to be always

yours faithfully,
J. L. Garvin

H. H. Asquith to George V

(*Royal Archives*)

23 September 1914   10 Downing Street

Mr Asquith, with his humble duty to Your Majesty, has the honour to report that the Cabinet met this morning.

Sir J. French's latest telegram stated that his army had been fully reinforced & re-fitted, and took a sanguine view of the military situation.

Mr Churchill gave a full report of the disaster yesterday to the three 'Cressy' cruisers. Ships will now be ordered not to stand by a disabled consort under conditions which may be dangerous to themselves. The use of mines in the North Sea was sanctioned (in principle): the combination of mines & submarines presents a number of difficulties, which the Admiralty will carefully consider. Mr Churchill also reported the intrepid tho' unsuccessful attempt of his airmen to destroy the German sheds at Dusseldorff, and gave an account of his visit yesterday to Dunkirk, where he accidentally met Colonel Seely. The French General there is planning a raid with French Territorials & artillery in the direction of Douai, to which Commander Sampson will render such assistance as is safe & practicable with his armoured motor-cars.

The dispatch of the New Zealand contingent was again discussed, and it was decided to order the [   ] (now at or near Singapore) & the promised Japanese battle-ship to proceed at once to Wellington as escort to the convoy.

It was agreed to aid Russia in financing a loan here of £20 millions, the proceeds of which are to be applied in discharging the Debts of Russian trade to Great Britain, in the purchase of war material in this country by Russia, and in meeting the interest payable here on pre-existing Russian loans. The Russian Government is prepared to deposit £8 millions in gold in the bank of England. It was considered that the remaining 12 millions might be raised by British Treasury Bills, thus giving Russia the benefit of the credit of the United Kingdom.

A long conversation took place on the unsatisfactory situation in Turkey,

Mr Churchill, Mr Masterman & others expressing a strong opinion that as Turkey was behaving so badly, we ought at once to free ourselves from any obligation as to her future, and make common cause with the Balkan States. Lord Kitchener repeated his opinion that the important thing is to win over Roumania, and with that object induce Russia to offer her the restoration of Bessarabia. In the end a proposal of Sir E. Grey was adopted that he should instruct Sir L. Mallet to inform the Porte, that while not contemplating for the moment hostile measures, we are grievously dissatisfied with the recent action of the Turkish Government, which has resulted in placing Constantinople under German, and no longer under Turkish, control. Unless the 'peace party' soon succeeds in getting the upperhand we shall be compelled to adopt an attitude of hostility & to take measures accordingly.

Colonel Seely to Winston S. Churchill
(*Churchill papers: 26/1*)

24 September 1914   Fere-en-Tardenois

My dear Winston,

I gave your letter to the C in C last night, and your messages this morning. He is writing to you to say that he hopes you may be able to come out here to discuss matters with him—I am quite certain that it is really important that you should do this if you can possibly get away. I motored through from Dunkirk yesterday in my car in a little over nine hours actual travelling, that is a little over 7 from Boulogne. I would suggest that you should be met at Boulogne with two Rolls Royces, and you would do the journey in about six hours. It is a mistake to go too fast on these roads we have found—partly because no car and no tyres will stand the bumping over paved roads, still more because the French civil guards are apt to shoot you if you are going so fast that you cannot stop before you reach them. So much for the detail of the business from 'one who has travelled six thousand miles by motor during the war'. The only other thing that falls to be said is that the sooner you can come the better for every reason.

It was good to see you yesterday—I rejoice that you are so fit and well, and that you are where you are—when you have envisaged the situation here everything will be just right.

I hear the booming of the big guns as I write, and must now go off on my particular job, taking every military precaution.

Please remember me to the Prime Minister and all my friends, not forgetting Ll. G. and Grey.

Good luck to you my dear Winston, and come soon.

Yours ever
Jack

Winston S. Churchill to Sir George Aston
(Copy, Admiralty papers: 116/1348)

24 September 1914   Admiralty

General Aston,

Before you move in force you should get sure information on the whereabouts of the enemy, and make your ground good on both flanks by motor car patrols and observation posts pushed out at least 20 miles if possible and communicating with you by telephones and trustworthy officers or agents.

Until you have the necessary motor cars armoured and otherwise for this service you should not advance (except the battalion mentioned in your No. 182, and this should be avoided if honourably possible).

Every effort is being made to supply you with cars and aeroplanes. When you are properly equipped you should move by rail or road as convenient keeping your motor transport handy until you are within effective striking distance. Then select your point and hit hard. Your object will be either to destroy an important bridge on the enemy's communications or to overwhelm some detached force which is exposed. It is hoped that by Monday the necessary cars etc. will have arrived.

These instructions are to be taken as a guide in making your plans and used at your discretion.

I hope to come over Sunday.

WSC

Winston S. Churchill to Sir Francis Villiers: telegram
(Grey papers)

24 September 1914   Admiralty

Six 6″ guns on central pivot mountings with ammunition are at the immediate disposal of Belgian military authorities. Telegraph when and how they would like delivery made. It is under consideration to offer two 9·2″ guns possibly to be worked from railway trucks if desired.

Sir Percy Scott[1] to Winston S. Churchill
(*Kitchener papers*)

24 September 1914   52 South Audley Street

Dear Mr Winston Churchill,

I venture to lay before you a way in which the Army you are raising could render more service to General French than giving him 50,000 men.

Twenty naval 6-inch or 7·5-inch guns which would outrange every gun that the Allies or the Germans have now in the Field would, in my opinion, be of more value to General French than 50,000 Infantry.

A few days ago I explained my ideas to Lord Roberts,[2] and he quite agreed with me as to the value of the scheme that I now propose to you.

My proposal is that part of your Army in less than a month should be in France with twenty 7·5 or 6-inch (of the most modern pattern) guns, fully equipped in every way.

The mountings for them which I have designed are of such a simple nature that they need not be made by any Arsenal or Gun-making Firm; I could get the parts made by various Firms, and I will guarantee that in three weeks or less I will have these guns ready to go to France.

As regards the crew for these guns, I have taken into consideration their training and will guarantee that they are efficient in three weeks and ready to go to France.

These twenty guns I propose should take up a position behind General French's lines, firing on the enemy at a range of 14,000 to 16,000 yards; this would be out of range of any of the German guns; they would all be electrically connected and fire broadsides, as in Director firing, an aeroplane would easily detect their fall and correct the aim.

There would be no necessity for them to see what they were firing at, as they would be layed by clinometer and piquets.

50 or 60 Lyddite shell per minute falling from them on a hard-pressed or retreating Army would have a terrible effect, and would, in my opinion, do much towards conquering our enemy.

It would treble the offensive power of General French's Army. The Navy

---

[1] Percy Moreton Scott, 1853–1924. Entered Navy, 1866. Captain, 1893. Devised land-mountings and carriages for the heavy naval guns used both in the defence of Ladysmith in South Africa, and in the defeat of the Boxer Rebellion in China, 1900. Knighted, 1906. Admiral, 1913. Retired from the Navy, 1913. Created Baronet, 1913. Appointed to the Admiralty for Special Service, September 1914–May 1918. In charge of gunnery defences of London against aircraft attack, 1915–16.

[2] Frederick Sleigh Roberts, 1832–1914. 2nd Lieutenant, Bengal Artillery, 1851. Wounded during the siege of Delhi, 1857. Commanded the Kabul Field Force, 1874–1880 and the march to Kandakar Field Force, 1880. Commander-in-Chief, India, 1885–93; Ireland, 1895–9; South Africa, 1899–1900; Great Britain, 1901–4. Created Baron 1892; Field-Marshal, 1895; Earl, 1901. Colonel-in-Chief of the Indian Forces in Europe, 1914.

have always come to the front in assisting the Army with heavy guns. Why should they not do so now? At any rate, they could do so, as we have plenty of reserve guns and plenty of ammunition.

If you think my suggestion worth considering, I have a model and drawings that you could see, and from them realise that the mountings could be made in the time that I suggest.

I am, Yours sincerely
Percy Scott

Winston S. Churchill to Lord Kitchener

(Kitchener papers)

24 September 1914   Admiralty

My dear Kitchener,

This has reached me today, & emphasizes what I said on Thursday night. It will be a great mistake not to supply the Army with heavy guns as soon as possible. The sense of inferiority imposed upon the troops by heavier metal is vy far-reaching. All my friends at the front tell me the same thing. The gun with its range is in spite of its weight the true answer to the heavy Howitzer. Percy Scott is right on gunnery questions, & can do what he says. I do not think the argument about the difficulty of transporting them to the front is conclusive, having regard to the number of roads & railways available.

It is surely wrong that we shd continuously have to oppose flesh and blood to German cannon, when we can so easily match them with naval artillery.[1]

Yours vy sincerely
Winston S. Churchill

Edward, Prince of Wales[2] to Winston S. Churchill

(Churchill papers: 13/27)

25 September 1914   Buckingham Palace

Dear Mr Churchill,

I must ask you to forgive my troubling you just now, when you must have more work than you can comfortably attend to, on a subject that I feel very strongly about. But first let me tell you how terribly distressed I was on hear-

---

[1] Someone at the War Office noted on this letter: 'Seen. Sir J. French has told us he does not want us to send out any 6 inch guns which we have already offered'.

[2] Edward Albert Christian George Andrew Patrick David, 1894–1972. Entered Royal Navy as a Cadet, 1907. Prince of Wales, 1910–36. 2nd Lieutenant, Grenadier Guards, August 1914. Attached to Sir John French's Staff, November 1914. Served in France and Italy, 1914–18. Major, 1918. Succeeded his father as King, January 1936. Abdicated, December 1936. Duke of Windsor, 1936.

ing the news of the ghastly disaster which took place on Tues morning in the North Sea. I went at once to the Admiralty & Sir Frederick Sturdee gave me the latest news as to the no saved etc. It is indeed a calamity to lose 3 such good & useful ships, (tho, not *now* of any gt fighting value) & so many officers & men. But I fear that as long as this terrible war lasts we must be prepared for such severe blows.

Now let me come to the point to which I want to call your attention. Commander (Ret) G. L. Saurin[1] who is a gt friend of mine (I knew him at R.N.C. Osborne & in the *V. & A*) wrote to me yesterday to sympathise on not being allowed out to the front yet, & at the end of his letter mentioned the fact that he was without a job & naturally very anxious for employment. He told me had been appointed to a command in the new 'Naval Brigade', but had only held it for 10 days, as he had been very suddenly relieved by a soldier. This was of course a great disappointment to him, as he was anxious to see service, & does not relish the idea of a job at Osborne much, which has been offered him.

I know Saurin is a very good & capable officer having served with him, & was practically forced to retire on account of being a terribly bad sailor. So bad was he in this respect, that in weather he was frequently very seriously ill, & of course consequently unable to do duty. Had his letter been the only way in which my attention had been called to the matter I wouldn't have written, but yesterday I heard about it from another source.

We have 2 retired naval officers (lieuts) attached to my batt & they came out to Richmond with us yesterday to watch a field day. *Of course* I got into conversation with them at once!!

They both command companies in the 'Naval Brigade' & while telling me something about it, its organisation, composition, etc, said how very sorry they were to loose Saurin in this unceremonious manner. Mind you, I never mentioned that I had heard from him; it came from them straight. They said how the men all loved him & how popular he was, & that he was just the man for the job. I could have told them that there is no one better suited to have a command in this new brigade. In fact they told me there was almost a slight mutiny, for a lot of the men wanted to know why he had gone, & clamoured for his return. So after hearing that I simply had to write to you, hoping you wouldn't mind. I expect you will think I am interfering in a matter which does not concern me; so I am really, so I must apologise. But I do feel so strongly that he should return to his command in the Naval

[1] Gerald Louis Saurin, 1880–1954. Entered Navy, 1894. Lieutenant, Osborne College, 1906–8. Commander, 1912. Retired, 1913. Returned to service, 19 August 1914. At Osborne College, September 1914–April 1915. Took part in the bombardment of the Belgian Coast, August–November 1915. Promoted to the rank of Captain (retired), 1918, in recognition of his war service; this promotion was cancelled at his own request, 1919.

Brigade, that I write to you, as *you* have the power to enquire into this, & to find out who, & why he was relieved of this command in favour of a soldier. If the Brigade is called 'Naval', why make military appointments in it? Doesn't that strike you too? Of course it is necessary that there should be soldiers or marine officers attached as instructors, but the commands should be given to N.O.'s. An excellent scheme is the sending of the N.O.'s to infantry battns in order that they may see the drill & general principles of an attack, as the 2 lieuts I met are.

Now to finish up, let me tell you that Saurin *never* asked *me* to help him in any way; I do it all on my own. Then may I ask you to destroy this letter, & not to let Saurin know I wrote, should you find it advisable & possible to reappoint him to the 'Naval Brigade'? I do hope you will, for I know what a *really good* man is being shelved.

Again, with sincere apologies for troubling you & taking up so much of yr time, I remain   Yrs very sincerely
                                                                              Edward

Edward, Prince of Wales to Winston S. Churchill
(*Churchill papers: 13/27*)

25 September 1914   St James's Palace

Dear Mr Churchill,

Thank you so much for your letter just received; it is very good of you to answer so soon.

Of course I absolutely understand about the matter I wrote to you about. I am afraid I was speaking too much from the personal side, & did not give the service point of view enough consideration. Your word is final, therefore will say no more.

It is kind of you to sympathize with me on not being allowed to go to the front: it was a bitter disappointment to be left behind by my battalion last week, & I now have to resign myself to another 3 weeks at home, at the end of which time I may get some staff job. But that is'nt the firing line is it? However I suppose the staff is my proper place, alas!![1]

Again with sincere apologies for having interfered in a matter that I know nothing about, & thanking you for your very prompt reply, I remain,
                                                                  Yours very sincerely
                                                                              Edward

[1] The Prince of Wales had been commissioned as a 2nd Lieutenant, Grenadier Guards, on 6 August 1914. After training in England with the 1st and 3rd Battalions he crossed to France on 16 November 1914, and was attached to Sir John French's staff at GHQ. He was never permitted to take up Regimental duties. In May 1915 he was attached as a General Staff Officer to the 1st Army Corps. Subsequently he served in the Staff of the Guards Division, the 14th Army Corps, and the Canadian Corps.

Winston S. Churchill to Sir Edward Grey

(Grey papers)

25 September 1914   Admiralty

My dear Grey,

It is reported that yesterday the German airship dropped two bombs into Ostend, wh is an open town of no military significance. It is most important to teach the Germans the uselessness of such warfares. After discussing the matter with Kitchener, who agrees, I should propose to instruct the Naval airmen at Antwerp to drop an equal number (or shd we observe the ratio of 16 to 10[1]?) into Aix-la-Chapelle, or some other convenient German town. After this had been done, I shd explain the reason & announce that this course will be invariably followed in the future.

This is the only effective way of protecting civilians & non-combatants. Care will of course be taken to aim at barracks & military property, & to avoid ancient monuments.

Yours vy sincerely
W

Sir Edward Grey: note

25 September 1914

I think it is too soon to begin retaliating in kind. Let us go on with protests a bit more.

Retribution in kind won't stop it: they have more aircraft than we have: & it will only put us on the same plane morally as they are.

E G

Winston S. Churchill: note

26 September 1914

All right. You will have to come to it soon.

WSC

Winston S. Churchill to Lord Kitchener

(Churchill papers: 26/1)

26 September 1914   Admiralty

My dear Kitchener,

French has telegraphed & written that he wd like me to visit him. I can now get away for 24 hours and Westminster is returning in his car this

1 The ratio of British to German capital ships on which Admiralty shipbuilding policy had been based in the twelve months before the outbreak of war.

morning. There wd I am sure be advantage in my having a talk with French not only on the general situation but on the Dunkirk business.

Also I shd vy much like to go.

I hope you can see no objection from your point of view.

Yours vy sincerely
Winston S. Churchill

Kitchener note:

No objection—I hope you will counteract any wild **talk**.

Winston S. Churchill to Clementine Churchill

(*Spencer-Churchill papers*)

26 September 1914   H.M.S. Adventure

at full speed

My darling one,

You were vy good to let me go, & I am vy grateful to you. The courage & good sense you have shown all through these strange times in view of yr own intense preoccupation (to whit—the kitten[1]) are wonderful. Bill[2] will come up today to see you. I am so sorry I cannot see him. Lend him my guns to shoot with.

How right you were about telling K.[3]

Tender love my dearest

Your ever loving
W

Lord Stamfordham to Lord Esher

(*Esher papers*)

27 September 1914   Royal Pavilion

Aldershot camp

. . . HM is not at all keen about honours being conferred until after the War. Winston has, however, persuaded HM to promote & decorate officers,

---

[1] Clementine Churchill was expecting her third child.

[2] William Ogilvy Hozier, 1888–1921. Clementine Churchill's brother. Entered Navy, 1904. Lieutenant, 1909. Commanded the Torpedo Boat Destroyers *Thorn*, 1914–15, and *Nubian*, 1915. 1st Lieutenant on board the Cruiser *Edgar*, 1915–16. Commanded the *Clematis*, 1916–18. Lieutenant-Commander, 1917.

[3] In an undated letter, Clementine Churchill had warned her husband not to go to France without telling Asquith and Kitchener. 'Otherwise,' she wrote, 'the journey will savour of a week-end escapade and not of a mission. You would be surprised & incensed if K slipped off to visit Jellicoe on his own.' (*Spencer-Churchill papers*)

Petty Officers & men for e.g. the Heligoland 'affair' and this is to be done shortly. . . .

Winston argues that a man may be killed during the interval between his act of Gallantry & the end of the War: & of course that is true. I expect H.M. will have to change his views tho' I confess I heartily shared them. I see that I am probably *wrong*!

Winston S. Churchill to Sir George Aston: telegram

(*Copy, Admiralty papers: 116/1348*)

29 September 1914   Admiralty
4.45 am

1. General Aston is placed on the sick list from tonight the 28th instant and to return at once to London for a period of rest before resuming his duties[1] General Aston should hand over his command to General Paris.

2. General Paris[2] will temporarily assume command of the mixed forces now operating from Dunkirk. Colonel Ollivant will for the time being act as Chief Staff Officer.

3. Major Micklem[3] will discharge Colonel Ollivant's duties in London at the Royal Naval Division during his absence. He will make proposals to the First Lord for his own relief in his present duties.

4. The Battalion which has been sent to Lille at the request of the French should maintain itself there if possible until the result of the present battle round Peronne is known, when further orders will be sent by the Admiralty.

5. The proposal of General Aston to move the force into cantounments at Cassel is approved, and the G.O.C. is invited to make proposals for a further advance in the next few days should circumstances and conditions be favourable.

6. A complete system of intelligence will be arranged under the Chief

[1] Aston was unable to resume active military duties. He served as Colonel Commandant of the Royal Marine Artillery until 1917, when he retired at his own request, and devoted himself to writing on military topics.

[2] Archibald Paris, 1861–1937. Entered Royal Marine Artillery, 1879. Commanded a column of troops in South Africa, 1900–2; forced to surrender owing to the flight of most of his troops and promoted Lieutenant-Colonel for distinguished service in the field, 1902. Commanded Royal Marine Brigade, September 1914. Major-General, commanding Royal Naval Division, Antwerp, October 1914; Dardanelles, 1915; France, 1916. Severely wounded, 1916, losing a leg. Knighted, 1916.

[3] Henry Andrew Micklem, 1872–1963. Joined Royal Engineers, 1891. Wounded in the Sudan Campaign, 1898. Severely wounded in South Africa, 1900. Major, 1902. Retired, 1909. Recalled, August 1914. Attached to the Royal Naval Division Headquarters, September 1914. A Deputy Assistant-Director at the War Office, with the rank of Lieutenant-Colonel, 1915; an Assistant Director, 1916. Colonel, 1916. Deputy Director of Railways, 1917–19.

Staff Officer. All information collected by aeroplane reconnaissance and motor car patrols must be digested each night in the form of a short telegraphic report to the Admiralty and duplicated to the British Army Headquarters.

The Chief Staff Officer will formulate his requirements of clerical staff and will as soon as possible submit a full field statement showing the strength, composition, and organisation of the Dunkirk force in all branches and departments. Meanwhile a general statement of the staff and organisation should be submitted. The Force will include the Oxfordshire Yeomanry, The Marine Brigade, Royal Engineer Detachment, all the motor car units, and all forces detached from the Naval Wing whether motor cars or aeroplanes.

WSC

H. H. Asquith to Venetia Stanley

(*Montagu papers*)

29 September 1914   10 Downing Street

. . . Winston turned up this morning and gave me a full & vivid narrative of his journey to the front. He left here on Sat morning & spent Sunday with French & his troops, returning after a visit to his own little army at Dunkirk on Monday night. He went all along the English lines—about 15 miles, and saw everything that was to be seen, tho' no actual fighting, except the reconnaissance of some of our aeroplanes, which flew about over the Germans in fleecy clouds of bursting shells sustaining no damage, and always ready with their revolvers and little machine guns to disable & kill their aerial competitors. The army was in the best possible condition & in a perfectly impregnable position, for the most part lining the N. bank of the Aisne, and protected from the other bank by the best part of 1000 guns of well-placed artillery. There is not much more than 300 yards between the German & English trenches, and every night there is a fierce little mêlée in which our men with their rifles & bayonets kill 3 Germans to every 1 of ours. The Colonel of the Scots Greys[1] told W. that he had not lived in vain, as he had seen a sight he never expected—officers & men of the Prussian Guard, their most famous corps, kneeling on the ground & begging for mercy. . . .

---

[1] Charles Bulkeley Bulkeley-Johnson, 1869–1917. 2nd Lieutenant, 1887. Lieutenant-Colonel commanding the Scots Greys, 1911–14. Brigadier-General, October 1914. Commanded a special reserve Brigade during a decisive phase of the 1st Battle of Ypres, 30 October 1914. Commanded the 8th Cavalry Brigade at the Battle of Arras, April 1917; killed in action, 11 April 1917.

The unhappy Troubridge has come back & has been before a Court of Inquiry of 2 Senior Admirals—Hedworth Meux[1] & Sir G. Callaghan. They have reported (this also is only for you) that this conduct was 'deplorable, & unworthy of the traditions of the Service'. Winston thinks & I agree that he must now be court-martialled. The result is I am afraid inevitable; vain & in many ways futile as he was I can't help feeling sorry; but when small men are saddled with great responsibilities only the chapter of accidents can avert a tragedy. . . .

H. H. Asquith to Winston S. Churchill
(*Churchill papers: 13/44*)

29 September 1914   10 Downing Street
Secret

My dear Winston,

I have been thinking over our conversation this morning, and what you said about *mining* has been reinforced by the conference a few of us had later as to the American attitude in regard to the Declaration of London &c.

I am strongly of opinion that the time has come for you to start mining, and to do it without stinting, and if necessary on a Napoleonic scale. I don't know what supply you have in hand of the infernal machinery, but I feel sure you can't do better than make the most ample provision, and use it freely & even lavishly.

Always
HHA

H. H. Asquith to George V
(*Royal Archives*)

30 September 1914   10 Downing Street

. . . In view of the appearance of German submarines in the channel and the other conditions the Cabinet approved in principle of the laying of mines in the North Sea.

Major-General Paris to Winston S. Churchill: telegram
(*Admiralty papers: 116/1348*)

30 September 1914   Dunkirk

R.N.D. field force Newhaven yesterday moved morning September 29th to Hazebrouck. The Marine battalion still at Lille.

[1] Hedworth Lambton, 1856–1929. Entered Navy, 1870. Rear-Admiral, 1902. Knighted, 1906. Vice-Admiral and Commander-in-Chief, China, 1908–10. Changed his name to Meux, 1911. Admiral, 1911. Commander-in-Chief, Portsmouth, 1912–16. Admiral of the Fleet, 1915. Conservative MP for Portsmouth, 1916–18.

Remainder of field force move to Cassel today, Wednesday; organization base and transport proceeding satisfactorily. Whole motor transport landed as usual and arrived Dunkirk, motor transport at Dunkirk consists approximately 120 lorries and busses and 15 motor cars, exclusive of airship.

Department shortage of mechanics still about 40. Daimler Company have been communicated by telegraph.

Following intelligence collected by Fiennes,[1] this being sent to King's Messenger, Boulogne for transmission to our Army Headquarters.

Intelligence report from R.N.D field force Dunkirk 10 p.m 29th September 1914. Lille news received telephone states 80 Germans seen at Gramont 6 p.m September 28th. Patrol 20 German Cyclists seen at Ligne, train service between Lessine and Gramont stopped. Germans have destroyed bridge over River Dendre.

Douai. Road between this place and Lille is reported clear, Germans are occupying St. Amand and Condé, south Tournai, with two regiments, one squadron cavalry and artillery, exact strength latter unknown. Germans have made considerable entrenchments round Denain near Valenciennes, road from Lille to Tournai quite clear. Germans hold Gramont lines Enghien Braleconte.

German Headquarters Staff now at Mons where there are two regiments infantry. At Valenciennes there is considerable force and at Cambrai and Denain. Between latter place and Helesimes road is entrenched. Force at Brussels varies and it is impossible give any estimate because troops constantly move between Brussels and Louvain. German Headquarters is at Thildonck, North West Louvain, between Mechlin and Louvain. . . . Antwerp outer line of defences has been heavily attacked until night.

Winston S. Churchill to Rear-Admiral Oliver
(*Oliver papers*)

30 September 1914   Admiralty

Proceed at once to Antwerp in company with the military officers detailed. Report on the general situation by telegraph and what measures shd be adopted with the German prizes before the place capitulates.

---

[1] Eustace Edward Twisleton-Wykeham-Fiennes, 1864–1943. 2nd son of the 4th Baron Saye and Sele. Liberal MP, 1906–10 and 1910–18. Parliamentary Public Secretary to Churchill at the Admiralty, 1912–14. Major, Oxfordshire Hussars, 1914. Served with the Royal Naval Division at Antwerp and the Dardanelles, 1914–15. Created Baronet, 1916. Governor of the Seychelles, 1918–21. Governor and Commander-in-Chief Leeward Islands, 1921–9.

Make such arrangements as will ensure their timely destruction.[1]

Communicate with the British Minister and the Belgian military authorities.

Return as soon as possible.

---

[1] Between 30 September and 4 October 1914 Oliver inserted explosive charges in the engines of thirty-eight merchant ships lying in the Scheldt. They were all rendered useless to the Germans, and remained immobile in the Scheldt throughout the war.

October 1914

Edward Marsh to Lord Fisher

(*Fisher papers*)

1 October 1914   Admiralty

My dear Lord Fisher,

Winston says 'War is hell, but one has at any rate the pleasure of muzzling most of the criticism & despising the rest.'

He wants to see you, will you be in London any afternoon early next week?

Yours ever
Eddie M

Lord Crewe to Winston S. Churchill

(*Copy, Crewe papers*)

1 October 1914   India Office
Private

My dear Winston,

A question has occurred to me which I mention to you with much diffidence, in connexion with the recent naval casualty lists. I mean the necessity in the new conditions of warfare at sea of employing so many young midshipmen on the bigger ships of the fleet. One understands how the practice obtained in old days; the perpetual work aloft, and in boats, made it imperative to begin quite young. At that time, too, lads joined the Army at fourteen or so. But now that a man-of-war is a great town full of mechanical devices of all kinds, I do not see why a schoolboy should be an officer in it any more than in the artillery or engineers. Why cannot they learn their job on training-brigs etc. until they can join as sub-lieutenants and look forward to the junior independent commands?

There is another aspect of the business that strikes one. In the old days, if a ship went into action a midshipman took his chance of being hit by a round shot, or being piked in a boarding attack. But that was the chance which the individual had to take; whereas in these days of mines and submarines, when a number of ships may go down with their whole complement, it seems not only sentimentally painful, but also a waste of good and costly material, if the poor lads are not actually necessary for the efficient working of the fleet. As I said, I speak very doubtfully, for I really do not know what midshipmen do nowadays on a big cruiser or battleship, beyond of course improving their own knowledge of guns, torpedoes or whatever it may be. So it may be that no change is possible; but I cannot help feeling that the system may have developed, like so many other systems, in a groove, from which it may be reasonable to escape.

Don't trouble to answer this, but tell me some time what you think.

Yours sincerely
C

Winston S. Churchill to Lord Crewe
(*Crewe papers*)

1 October 1914   Admiralty

My dear Crewe,

It wd be a vy harsh measure to deprive these young boys of an experience wh they will always look back to, & from wh their professional value is sensibly increased. We have had piteous appeals from the parents of the Osborne cadets to allow their boys to go.

I am assured they render useful services. It has always been the custom of the Navy; & for myself I cannot see much difference in the tragedy of a young life cut short at 16 or at 17.[1]

I have satisfied myself that naval opinion supports the present Admiralty practice. I asked that it shd be carefully re-considered; but we were found united in keeping the lads at sea to take their chance. I trust all days will not be so fatal as the 22nd Septr.

Yours vy sincerely
Winston S. Churchill

[1] Some naval cadets went to sea at fourteen. Thus Eric Bush, born on 12 August 1899, had his fifteenth birthday at sea on board the *Bacchante*, was present at the Battle of the Heligoland Bight sixteen days later, and served as a Midshipman in charge of a picket boat during the Gallipoli landings of 25 April 1915. (Promoted Captain, 1939, he commanded an assault group at the Normandy landings, 1944.)

Winston S. Churchill to Lord Kitchener

(*Kitchener papers*)

1 October 1914   Admiralty

My dear Kitchener,

Referring to our conversation in Cabinet this morning, I think the best arrangement for the artillery of the Royal Naval Division will be that you should provide, in the general scope of your arrangements for equipping the new armies, the complete artillery of one more division than you are providing infantry and other units for. I note from your scheme that you propose to include the Royal Naval Division in the organisation of the 8th Army. I expect, therefore, that they will not be required by the War Office until May next. This is quite satisfactory to the Admiralty. In the interval brigades from the division may be used in emergencies and wd play a part in Home defence of Naval ports as has been and is now the case. I can provide without any inconvenience, and without competing with your arrangements, the division complete in April or May of next year, with every detail except the 13 batteries of divisional artillery, and I shall work on those lines. In view of the demands you are making upon the trade, it would only be injurious and cause confusion if the Admiralty were to come in with a whole set of separate orders for field artillery, and if we got them earlier it would only be by using our special influence with the firms to get deliveries in advance and at the expense of yourself.

I have never had any other wish than to help you in these matters, and add to your resources by any means in our power—limited & small though these may be.

I enclose a copy of a letter I have sent to von Donop.[1]

Yours vy sincerely
Winston S. Churchill

H. H. Asquith to Venetia Stanley

(*Montagu papers*)

1 October 1914   10 Downing Street

. . . The Germans are pounding away with their big guns at Antwerp, and tho' the Belgians are in large numerical superiority they seem to have lost

[1] Stanley Brenton von Donop, 1860–1941. Entered Royal Artillery, 1880. Colonel, 1906. Director of Artillery, War Office, 1911–13. Master-General of Ordnance, 1913–16. Major-General, 1914. Knighted, 1914. Commanded the Humber Garrison, 1917–20. Colonel Commandant, Royal Artillery, 1925–41.

morale & nerve, and are making the most piteous appeals for help. One cannot be surprised, or blame them, for the Germans have been unusually active these last few days in burning their villages & shooting the inhabitants. It is now clear that the German soldiers were equipped each man with a supply of small discs of compressed benzine (not much bigger in diameter than a lead pencil) and that with these wh. flare up into a big explosive flame, first breaking the windows & then throwing in the disc, they destroyed the interior of the houses in places like Louvain & Termonde. Whitehouse M.P.[1] who has just come back from Belgium told me this morning that in Termonde there is not a stick of furniture left in many of the houses, all having been blown up in this fashion from the inside. The fall of Antwerp would be a great moral blow to the Allies, for it would leave the whole of Belgium for the moment at the mercy of the Germans; the Minister telegraphs that he does not think they can hold out for more than another 3 days. Of course it would be idle butchery to send a force like Winston's little Army there: if anything is to be done it must be by regulars in sufficient numbers. We had a conference here last night & sent over in the night 3 good officers[2] to report, and to urge upon the Belgians to disregard their forts and to entrench themselves. The French telegraph that they are willing to send a division (of 15000 to 20,000) & to put it under a British general—but they do not say what is the quality of the soldiers, who may be very likely are only Territorials. However, we resolved at the Cabinet to-day that, if the French cooperation is satisfactory, we would divert our 7th Division (of the finest troops) wh. was just going to join Sir J. French, and not throw it into Antwerp but endeavour to raise the siege & capture the German big guns. In the meantime Winston is going in for a big mining operation in the North Sea, which ought to make things easier. All the same I can't help being anxious about Antwerp, & the course of events in the next few days . . .

---

[1] John Howard Whitehouse, 1873–1955. Educationalist; author of over fifty books. Liberal MP, 1910–18. Parliamentary Private Secretary to Lloyd George, 1913–15. Commissioner for Belgian Refugees, 1914; in Belgium during the German occupation for the assistance of the civilian population, 1914. Founded Bembridge School, 1919; Headmaster, 1919–54.

[2] The officers were Rear-Admiral Oliver, from the Admiralty (see p. 145), and Colonels Dallas (see p. 153) and Yarvey (see p. 156) from the War Office.

G. Marconi[1] to Winston S. Churchill

(*Churchill papers: 13/44*)

1 October 1914
Personal

Le Grand Hotel
Rome

Dear Mr Winston Churchill,

I just wish to express to you how very much Italians appreciated the remarks you made[2] to a representative of the Giornale d'Italia,[3] re Italy and the international situation.

I have been here for a few days and have been able to appreciate fully the depth and sincerity of friendly feeling which exists all over Italy towards England and France. Whatever Germany may have done to square part of the Press, the result has been quite ineffectual. No German or Austrian flag can now be safely shown in any part of Italy.

I enclose a newspaper cutting showing an interview which may interest you. In the Navy we are all hoping for the day in which we shall be doing our part. I expect to be back in England about the 12 of this month.

Yours very truly,
G. Marconi

Rear-Admiral Oliver to Major-General Paris: telegram

(*Copy, Admiralty papers: 116/1348*)

2 October 1914
Admiralty

1. Belgian Minister of War[4] stated Wednesday night that in his opinion Germans are seriously undertaking siege of Antwerp and that their operations are not intended as a demonstration to keep Belgian troops occupied or to protect line of communications. Information had come from Brussels to effect that Emperor had ordered capture of the town that this might cost thousands of lives but that order must be obeyed.

---

[1] Guglielmo Marconi, 1874–1937. Pioneer of wireless telegraphy. Established wireless communication across the English Channel, 1899; and between England and Canada, 1902. Received the Nobel Prize for Physics, 1909. Honorary knighthood, 1914. His first wife, whom he married in 1905, was the Hon Beatrice O'Brien, daughter of the 14th Baron Inchiquin (the marriage was dissolved in 1924).

[2] On 22 September 1914, in an interview with the London correspondent of the *Giornale d'Italia*, Churchill said: 'We want this war to reform the geography of Europe according to national principles; we want liberty of the races, the integrity of nations and the diminution of armaments.' The interview was published in *The Times* on 24 September.

[3] Gino Calza Bedolo, 1890–1925. London correspondent, *Il Giornale D'Italia*, 1914. Correspondent on the Belgian Front, October 1914. Reserve Infantry Officer (Lieutenant). After the war, Editor *Il Giornale D'Italia*; Editor-in-Chief, *Epoca*.

[4] Charles Marie Pierre Albert de Broqueville, Comte de Broqueville, 1860–1940. Prime Minister of Belgium, 1911–18. Introduced compulsory military service bill, 1913. Minister of War, 1914–15. In charge of Belgian Government in exile at Le Havre, 1915–17. Prime Minister, 1932–4.

2. Reported large numbers of Germans moved Northwards from direction of Mons then suddenly returned. Seeking confirmation.

3. Large bodies of German reserve troops assembling near Liege to occupy Meuse positions. Local rumours (Holland) prevalent of expected general retirement of Germans in France.

Lord Stamfordham to Winston S. Churchill

(*Copy, Royal Archives*)

2 October 1914   Buckingham Palace

Dear Churchill,

The King has now come to the conclusion that the names of the German Emperor and Prince Henry of Prussia[1] should be removed from the Navy List.

His Majesty, however, does not wish any order promulgated to this effect, and nothing to be done beyond omitting these names.[2]

Yours very truly
Stamfordham

Winston S. Churchill to Captain D'Eyncourt[3] and Captain Sueter

(*Admiralty papers: 116/1339*)

2 October 1914   Admiralty

Director of Naval Ordnance.
Director of the Air Division.

The experiments with regard to projectiles for use against aircraft must be worked out on the most generous scale, eight or ten different lines being pursued simultaneously, the necessary funds being provided. It is perfectly useless in time of war to go through successively the whole series of experiments appropriate to peace-time administration. Let me have a report on the projectiles available. We must have means of attacking Zeppelins, not

---

[1] Prince Henry of Prussia, 1862–1929. A brother of the Kaiser and grandson of Queen Victoria.

[2] The Kaiser had been an Admiral of the Fleet since 1889, Prince Henry since 1910: both appear in the Navy List for October 1914 but not in the November–December List. The only other foreign Admiral of the Fleet was the Tsar, since 1908. King Haakon of Norway and King Gustav of Sweden were both Admirals.

[3] Eustace Henry William Tennyson-d'Eyncourt, 1868–1951. A naval architect, 1898–1912. Director of Naval Construction and Chief Technical Adviser at the Admiralty, 1912–23. Knighted, 1917. Vice-President of the Tank Board, 1918. Managing Director of Armstrong Whitworth's shipyards at Newcastle, 1924–8. Director of the Parsons Marine Steam Turbine Company, 1928–48. Created Baronet, 1930.

only with shells from guns, but with incendiary bullets or grenades from aeroplanes.

H. H. Asquith to Venetia Stanley
(Montagu papers)

2 October 1914   10 Downing Street

... The news from Antwerp this morning is far from good & gives me some anxiety. The Germans battered down 2 of the forts, and what is worse got in between them & drove a lot of Belgians out of their entrenchments. Meanwhile the only relieving force that the French offer is a mass of Territorials & the like, who would be no use for hard fighting and are quite unfit to co-operate with a trained division of ours like the 7th. On the other hand to send the 7th alone is to court almost certain disaster. It is a very difficult situation—particularly as our officer[1] reports that it is the moral of the Belgian Commanders rather than of the men wh. shows signs of collapse. He says (early this morning) that 'any definite statement of assistance that could be given to Belgian Government would have immediate & excellent effect'. But it is no good to lure them with false hopes. ...

Lord Kitchener to Colonel Dallas: telegram
(Copy, Churchill papers: 8/181)

2 October 1914   Foreign Office
1.30 pm
Private and Secret

Be very careful not to raise hopes of British and French forces arriving quickly to relieve Antwerp. The matter has not been decided, as the territorial division offered by France in ten days' time would, in my opinion, be quite incapable of doing anything towards changing the situation at Antwerp. I have represented this. Unless a change is made, I consider it would be useless to put in our little force against the very superior German forces in the field round Antwerp. I hope the following guns and gunners that we are sending will be a valuable assistance:—

Six 4·7-inch, now there.
Six 6-inch, now there.
Two 9·2-inch, left last night.

[1] Alister Grant Dallas, 1866–1931. Entered Army, 1886. Colonel, 1911. General Staff Officer, War Office, 1911–14. Brigadier-General, General Staff, 1915. Commanded 32nd Brigade, Gallipoli, 1915. Major-General, commanding 53rd Division, Egypt and Palestine, 1916–17.

From army—
> One 9·2-inch, on railway truck.
> One 9·2-inch howitzer, departure delayed.
> Two 6-inch, on travelling carriage.

Sir Percy Girouard will go with the 9·2-inch on railway truck, which, if properly handled, might be a very useful weapon. You might select first firing site for this gun and get railway line constructed, ranges computed, so as to be ready to bring the gun into action at the earliest moment. Aeroplane reconnaissance would be most useful for direction. Range of 9·2-inch gun, 12,000 yards as a maximum. Be careful after firing gun to remove it to a second firing position before enemy can bring his fire to bear upon it.

Have Belgians sufficient ammunition for their guns, and cannot they from their inner line of forts shell Germans out of trenches between the outer forts?

Sir Francis Villiers to Sir Edward Grey: telegram
(*Copy, Churchill papers: 8/181*)

2 October 1914   Antwerp
8.20 pm
Private and Secret

Acting on advice unanimously given by Superior Council of War in presence of the King,[1] the Government have decided to leave to-morrow for Ostend. The Queen[2] will also leave. The King with field army will withdraw, commencing with advance guard to-morrow in the direction of Ghent to protect coast-line, and eventually it is hoped to co-operate with the Allied armies.

It is said that town will hold out for five or six days, but it seems most unlikely that when the Court and Government are gone resistance will be so much prolonged.

Decision taken very suddenly this afternoon is result of increasingly critical situation. I have seen both Prime Minister and Minister for Foreign Affairs,[3]

---

[1] Albert, 1875–1934. King of the Belgians, 1909–34. Said to have fired the last shot before Antwerp surrendered, October 1914. Order of the Garter, December 1914.

[3] Elizabeth, 1876–1965. Daughter of Charles Theodore, Duke of Bavaria. She married Albert, later King of the Belgians, in 1900.

[2] Henri François Julien Claude Davignon, 1858–1916. Belgian lawyer and landowner. A leading advocate of the abolition of slavery in the Congo State in the 1880's and 1890's. Minister of Foreign Affairs, 1907–16. On the day before his death King Albert conferred on him and his descendants the title of Viscount.

who maintain that no other course was possible, in view of danger that the King's Government and field army will be caught here.

Corps diplomatique will be conveyed by Belgian packet. I shall take cyphers and archives. I will report arrival giving address.

I will telegraph later respecting military situation.

Colonel Dallas to Lord Kitchener: telegram

(*Copy, Churchill papers: 8/181*)

2 October 1914   Antwerp
Midnight
Private and Secret

With reference to query in your telegram No. 172, situation is undoubtedly critical, and I am of opinion that to save fall of Antwerp encouragement of prompt action by combined French and British force is necessary.

If it is decided to despatch British force, what would be composition, and how soon could it be landed? Any definite statement of assistance that could be given to Belgian Government would have immediate and excellent effect.

Admiral[1] concurs. Please inform First Lord of the Admiralty.

Rear-Admiral Oliver to Admiralty

(*Oliver papers*)

2 October 1914   Antwerp

As the Belgian Field Army is being withdrawn from the defence of Antwerp and it is impossible that the place can hold out, the R.N. forces will be withdrawn as soon as possible.

I. The Air Detachment are to start for Ostend as early as possible. . . .

II. Lt Comdr Littlejohns[2] to be ready to leave Gare des Dames at 4-0 A.M. . . .

---

[1] Rear-Admiral Oliver, who had gone to Antwerp on 30 September 1914 to disable merchant ships in the Scheldt (see page 146).

[2] Astle Scott Littlejohns, 1875–1939. Entered Navy, 1886. Commanded the British armoured trains at Antwerp, October 1914, and in Flanders, 1914–16. Staff, High Commissioner for Australia, 1918–22. Captain, 1921. Served on the Non-Intervention Committee, Spanish Civil War, 1937.

Sir Edward Grey to Sir Francis Villiers: telegram
(*Copy, Churchill papers: 8/181*)

3 October 1914   Foreign Office
12.45 am
Very urgent
Private and Secret

We feel that the importance of Antwerp being held till the course of the main battle in France is determined justifies a further effort. We are trying to send you help from the main army, and, if this were possible, would add reinforcements from here. Meanwhile a brigade of marines will reach you tomorrow to sustain the defence. We urge you to make one further struggle to hold out. Even a few days may make the difference. We hope Government will find it possible to remain and field army to continue operations.

Colonel Dallas to Lord Kitchener: telegram
(*Copy, Churchill papers: 8/181*)

3 October 1914   Antwerp
12.48 am
Private and Secret

Defence of Antwerp by fortress troops only is in my opinion impossible, and I have therefore ordered withdrawal of army guns to Ostend while there is yet time. Admiral has done likewise as regards naval personnel, guns, and aeroplanes. I was with the Belgian troops near Duffel till 8 P.M., and as far as my information goes, I consider action of Belgian Government precipitate.

As you cannot telegraph orders owing to removal of cyphers, I shall observe events with Colonel Harvey[1] and withdraw to Ostend if necessary, keeping you informed when possible.

Owing to railway conditions it is impossible to remove naval 6-inch guns without great delay, and they are being disabled. Admiral Oliver is bringing away naval detachments with a view to their being useful to field army. Please inform First Lord.

[1] Robert Napier Harvey, 1868–1937. 2nd Lieutenant, Royal Engineers, 1888; Lieutenant-Colonel, 1913. Instructor, School of Military Engineering, Chatham, 1914. Sent to Antwerp with Colonel Dallas and Rear-Admiral Oliver, 29 September 1914. Assistant to the Engineer-in-Chief, British Expeditionary Force, France, January 1915; Inspector of Mines, 1916; Chief Engineer, 1918. Major-General, 1919. Engineer-in-Chief, India Command, 1924–8. Colonel Commandant, Royal Engineers, 1935–7.

Sir Edward Grey to Sir Francis Villiers: telegram

(*Copy, Churchill papers: 8/181*)

3 October 1914   Foreign Office
1.15 am
Urgent. Private and Secret

First Lord of the Admiralty will be at Antwerp between 9 and 10 to-morrow. He is fully acquainted with our views, and it is hoped he may have the honour of an audience with the King before a final decision as to the departure of the Government is taken. If any military change takes place which renders the Ostend–Antwerp route insecure, please telegraph to Hotel Chapeau Rouge, Dunkirk, up to 6 and Town Hall, Bruges, up to 8 a.m. tomorrow (3rd October).

Admiralty to Major-General Paris

(*Copy, Churchill papers: 13/40*)

3 October 1914   Admiralty
Bring back the battalion from LILLE at once & concentrate your brigade.
Be ready to move into ANTWERP by the coast road during this morning.
First Lord will arrive at DUNKIRK about 5 am. Meet him there yourself or send Colonel Ollivant.

Tell Commdr: Samson to provide 5 armoured cars to escort First Lord into ANTWERP starting between 6 & 7 from DUNKIRK.

Have as many armoured cars & aeroplanes ready for service to-morrow as possible, subject to the necessary outpost & reconnaissance service.

Take plenty of ammunition with you for ANTWERP.

Let the Officer who meets First Lord be ready to report fully on all these matters.

Acknowledge.

Sir Francis Villiers to Sir Edward Grey: telegram

(*Copy, Churchill papers: 8/181*)

3 October 1914   Antwerp
6.37 am
Private and Secret

I communicated at once with Minister of War. He summoned a meeting of Ministers, who, after deliberation, informed me that they had decided to postpone departure, awaiting arrival of First Lord. Audience of King for Mr Churchill will be arranged for at as early an hour as possible.

Lord Kitchener to Sir Francis Bertie:[1] *telegram*

(Copy, Churchill papers: 8/181)

3 October 1914   [via] Foreign Office
9.40 am
Private and Secret

Please ask [French] Minister of War[2] to make all preparations to send the proposed two divisions of territorials with cavalry and artillery complete as soon as possible, and let us know how soon they can be despatched.

Colonel Dallas to Lord Kitchener: telegram

(Copy, Churchill papers: 8/181)

3 October 1914   Antwerp
11.00 am
Private and Secret

Sir P. Girouard arrived this morning and gave me your instructions, which I understand. Military situation unchanged since last night. Belgian Minister of War much encouraged by news of coming of marines, but such a small force will in no way suffice. I will report again later.

H. H. Asquith to Venetia Stanley

(Montagu papers)

3 October 1914   10 Downing Street

. . . I found on my return[3] that strange things had been going on here. The Belgian Government notwithstanding that we were sending them heavy guns, and trying to get together troops to raise the siege of Antwerp, resolved yesterday to throw up the sponge & to leave to-day for Ostend, the King with his field army withdrawing in the direction of Ghent—They calculated that after their departure Antwerp might hold out for 5 or 6 days—wh. seems very doubtful. This is a *mad* decision, quite unwarranted by the

---

[1] Francis Leveson Bertie, 1844–1919. Second son of 6th Earl of Abingdon; uncle of Lady Gwendeline Churchill. Entered the Foreign Office, 1863. Knighted, 1902. British Ambassador, Rome, 1903–5; Paris, 1905–18. Created Baron Bertie of Thame, 1915. Created Viscount, 1918.

[2] Alexandre Millerand, 1859–1943. Elected to the French Chamber of Deputies as a Radical Socialist, 1885. Minister of War, January 1912–January 1913; and again from January 1914 to October 1915. He resigned following accusations that he had failed to find sufficient heavy artillery. Prime Minister, 1920. President of the Republic, 1920–4.

[3] Asquith had been in Cardiff, making a recruiting speech.

situation, for the German besieging army is only a scratch force, and one way or another a diversion is certain in the course of a few days. So we at once replied urging them to hold out, & promising Winston's marines to-morrow, with the hope of help from the main army & reinforcements from here. I was of course away, but Grey Kitchener & Winston held a late meeting, and (I fancy with Grey's rather reluctant assent) the intrepid Winston set off at midnight & ought to have reached Antwerp by about 9 this morning. He will go straightway & beard the King & his Ministers, and try to infuse into their backbones the necessary quantity of starch. Mean-while Sir J. French is making preparations to send assistance by way of Lille. I have had a long talk with K this morning, & we are now both rather anxiously awaiting Winston's report. I don't know how fluent he is in French, but if he was able to do himself justice in a foreign tongue, the Belges will have listened to a discourse the like of which they have never heard before. I cannot but think that he will stiffen them up to the sticking point. Don't say anything of Winston's mission, at any rate at present; it is one of the many unconventional incidents of the war.

Later. I have just got a telegram which says that W. will not arrive at Ant-werp until 1. I suppose his destroyer was late, or perhaps he burst a tyre. . . .

Lord Kitchener to Colonel Dallas: telegram
(*Copy, Churchill papers: 8/181*)

3 October 1914   via Foreign Office
2.15 pm
Private and Secret

Your last telegram. What force, in your opinion, would suffice? Give full details of what troops are most required to deal with the situation in co-operation with the Belgian field army.

The French Government say they will send two divisions, with full com-plement of cavalry and artillery, but I do not yet know when they will be available. If a corps of our troops, under Sir John French, together with the 7th division and cavalry division from here, concentrated at Lille in order to attack the right flank of the main German army and drive it back, would this action, if accomplished in about four or five days, in your opinion, relieve the situation at Antwerp quickly enough to prevent the fall of the place, or must any troops employed to relieve Antwerp be sent there via Zeebrugge, and, if so, can you give me approximately the longest time we can have to get troops there, so that I can inform French Government?

Lord Kitchener to Sir Francis Bertie: telegram

(*Copy, Churchill papers: 8/181*)

3 October 1914   via Foreign Office
4.30 pm
Private and Secret

We prefer the two divisions complete. The question of time when they will be able to move is of the greatest importance and urgency. I presume they could go by train. Please report as soon as possible time when they could reach neighbourhood of Ostend.

Winston S. Churchill to Sir Edward Grey and Lord Kitchener: telegram

(*Copy, Churchill papers: 13/58*)

3 October 1914   Antwerp
4.55 pm
Private and Secret

Dallas thinks force you mention would be formidable if applied directly to Antwerp besiegers, but that action from Lille east or south-east against German right flank would not relieve imminent situation here. He thinks Lille operation would be ineffective compromise in so far as Antwerp is concerned.

Winston S. Churchill to Sir Edward Grey and Lord Kitchener: telegram

(*Copy, Churchill papers: 13/58*)

3 October 1914   Antwerp
6.53 pm
Private and Secret
Very Urgent

I have made following arrangement with M. Broqueville, Prime Minister, subject to confirmation on both sides:—

Every preparation to be made by Belgian Government now for a resistance of at least ten days, and every step taken with utmost energy. Within three days we are to state definitely whether we can launch big field operations for their relief or not, and when it will probably take effect. If we cannot give them a satisfactory assurance of substantial assistance within three days, they are to be quite free to abandon defence if they think fit. In this case, should they wish to clear out with field army, we (although not able to launch the big operation) are to help their field army to get away by sending covering troops to Ghent or other points on line of retreat. Thus, anything they will have lost in time by going on defending Antwerp with all their strength will be made up to them as far as possible by help on their way out.

Further, we will help their local defence meanwhile in all minor ways, such as guns, marines, naval brigades, &c.

I have put the terms high to avoid at all costs our undertaking anything we could not perform, and also to avoid hurry in our saying what troops we can spare for big operations. You may be able, as your telegram No 7 indicates, to do much better than this, and to give decided promise within three days, but the vital thing is that Belgian Government and army should forwith hurl themselves with revived courage and energy into the defence.

Attack is being harshly pressed at this moment, and half measures would be useless, but Prime Minister informs me that they are confident they can hold out for three days, pretty sure they can hold out for six, and will try ten.

Your telegram No 7 will be answered later, and this arrangement, if adopted, will give time necessary for problem to be solved calmly.

Two thousand marines are arriving this evening.

I am remaining here till tomorrow.

I have read this telegram to Belgian Prime Minister, who says that we are in full agreement, subject to ratification by Council of Ministers which is now being held.

I must impress on you the necessity of making these worn and weary men throw their souls into it, or the whole thing will go with a run.

The Prime Minister asked me if Ministers remain in Antwerp and were made prisoners of war, would England continue to regard them as true Government of Belgium to be consulted in terms of peace?

I expect you will do this, though chance of their capture very remote.

If you clinch these propositions, pray give the following order to the Admiralty: Send at once both naval brigades, minus recruits, via Dunkirk, into Antwerp, without tents or much impedimenta, but with five days' rations and 2,000,000 rounds of ammunition.

When can they arrive?

Prince Louis to Winston S. Churchill: telegram

(*Copy, Churchill papers: 8/181*)

4 October 1914   via Foreign Office
10.30 am
Private and Secret

The naval brigades will embark at Dover at 4 p.m. for Dunkirk, where they should arrive between 7 or 8 o'clock. Provisions and ammunition as indicated in your telegram.

W.C. 3 — M

Winston S. Churchill to Sir Edward Grey: telegram
(*Copy, Churchill papers: 8/181*)

4 October 1914   Antwerp
12.45 pm
Private and Secret

Entrenching tools are to be sent after naval brigade. Also send 2,000,000 extra rounds of rifle ammunition, making 4,000,000 in all.

Sir Edward Grey to Sir Francis Bertie: telegram
(*Copy, Churchill papers: 8/181*)

4 October 1914   Foreign Office
10.30 pm
Private and Secret

Please let Minister of War know that, owing to his cordial co-operation, Lord Kitchener has been able to arrange for the following force to assist in the relief of Antwerp:—

French Force—Territorial division, General Roy[1] 15,000 men, proper complement of guns, and two squadrons, to arrive Ostend 6th to 9th October. Fusiliers marine brigade, under Rear-Admiral Ronarch[2] 8,000 men.

British Force—7th division, under General Capper[3] 18,000 men, 63 guns; cavalry division, under General Byng[4] 4,000 men, 12 guns, to arrive at Zeebrugge 6th and 7th October. Naval detachment, under General Paris 8,000 men, already there, also naval and military heavy guns and detachments already sent. Headquarter Staff will be subsequently notified. Grand total, 53,000 men. (Numbers are approximately correct.)

[1] Eugene Jules Victor Roy, 1850–1916. Commanded the 55th Infantry Brigade, 1905. Commanded the French Territorial Division, 1914.

[2] Pierre Alexis Marie Antoine Ronarch, 1865–1940. Entered the French Navy, 1880. Rear-Admiral, June 1914. Commanded the Marine Fusilier Brigade, 1914–15. Vice-Admiral, 1915. Commander-in-Chief of the Marines in the zone of the Northern Armies, 1916–19. Commander-in-Chief of the Marines, 1919–20.

[3] John Edward Capper, 1861–1955. Lieutenant, Royal Engineers, 1880. Lieutenant-Colonel, 1900. Commandant, Balloon School, 1903–10. Colonel, 1910. Commandant, School of Military Engineering, 1910–14. Deputy Inspector-General of Communications, 1914–15. Chief Engineer, 1915. Major-General, 1915. General Officer Commanding 24th Division, 1915–17. Knighted, 1917. Director-General of the Tank Corps, 1917. Lieutenant-Governor of Guernsey, 1920–25. Commandant, Royal Tank Corps, 1923–24.

[4] Julian Hedworth George Byng, 1862–1935. Entered Army, 1883. Major-General, 1909. Commanded 3rd Cavalry Division, October 1914–May 1915. Knighted, 1915. Commanded Cavalry Corps, May–August 1915. Commanded IXth Corps, Gallipoli, August 1915–January 1916. Lieutenant-General, 1916. Commanded the Canadian Corps, 1916–17. General, 1917. Commanded 3rd Army, 1917–19. Created Baron, 1919. Governor-General of Canada, 1921–6. Created Viscount, 1926. Commissioner Metropolitan Police, 1928–31. Field-Marshal, 1932.

Winston S. Churchill to Prince Louis: telegram

(*Copy, Churchill papers: 8/181*)

4 October 1914   Antwerp
11.50 pm

Following required at once for attacking enemy's fire control balloons: Two of the latest long 4-inch guns, battleship pattern, with pedestal mounting complete, with 500 round of shrapnel and 500 rounds of high-explosive shells. The very longest range time fuses required for shrapnel.

Following required for 4.7 guns: 500 rounds of shrapnel with very long range time fuses. Present time fuses too short.

Fuse scales.

100 fathoms of $2\frac{1}{2}''$ flexible steel wire rope.

150 Duffle suits for crews of armoured trains.

Entrenching tools, required for marine brigade.

30 Maxim guns on tripod mountings, with establishment of proportionate ammunition.

Sufficient material for twelve field telephone sets.

Winston S. Churchill to H. H. Asquith: telegram[1]

(*Beaverbrook papers*)

5 October 1914   Antwerp
8.00 am

If it is thought by HM Government that I can be of service here, I am willing to resign my office and undertake command of relieving and defensive forces assigned to Antwerp in conjunction with Belgian Army, provided that I am given necessary military rank and authority, and full powers of a commander of a detached force in the field. I feel it my duty to offer my services, because I am sure this arrangement will afford the best prospects of a victorious result to an enterprise in which I am deeply involved. I should require complete staff proportionate to the force employed, as I have had to use all the officers now here in positions of urgency. I wait your reply. Runciman would do Admiralty well.[2]

[1] That same day, 5 October, Asquith sent this telegram to Venetia Stanley as a souvenir. After the war she gave it—or sold it—to Lord Beaverbrook; it is now a part of the Beaverbrook archive.

[2] Asquith refused to accept Churchill's offer of resignation, and in his reply asked him to return to the Admiralty as soon as possible. In 1968 Field-Marshal Earl Alexander of Tunis recalled, in a conversation with the author, that Churchill said to him during the Second World War: 'I do envy you, you've done what I've always wanted to do—to command great victorious armies in battle. I thought I got very near to it once, in the First World War, when I commanded those forces at Antwerp. I thought it was going to be my great opportunity.' (*Author's Records, 28 December 1968*)

Lord Kitchener to Sir Francis Bertie: telegram

(*Copy, Churchill papers: 8/181*)

5 October 1914   via Foreign Office
9.12 am
Private and Secret

Please inform [French] Minister of War that Lieutenant-General Sir Henry Rawlinson[1] has been appointed to command the forces advancing to the relief of Antwerp, and ask him to kindly communicate this to General Roy and Rear-Admiral Ronarch.

General Sir H. Rawlinson has left for Antwerp and will be there today. He will get into communication with French forces immediately on their arrival Ostend.

All movements to be kept very secret.

Cecil Hertslet[2] to Admiralty: telegram

(*Copy, Churchill papers: 8/181*)

5 October 1914   Antwerp
9.48 am
Urgent

First Lord has authorised me to wire for 2,000,000 rounds mark VI ·303 rifle ammunition and 30 Maxim guns on tripod mountings.

These can be obtained from Sheerness.

Twenty sets officers' saddlery and 15 motor cars, 20 telephones suitable for the field, and 20 miles of cable.

Above sent request of General Paris.

---

[1] Henry Seymour Rawlinson, 1864–1925. Entered Army, 1884. On Kitchener's staff in the Sudan, 1898. Brigadier-General, 1903. Major-General commanding the 4th Division, September 1914; the 7th Division & 3rd Cavalry Division, October 1914; the IV Corps, December 1914–December 1915. Knighted, 1914. Lieutenant-General commanding the Fourth Army, 1916–18. General, 1917. Created Baron, 1919. Commanded the forces in North Russia, 1919. Commander-in-Chief, India, 1920–5.

[2] Cecil Hertslet, 1850–1934. Entered Foreign Office, 1868. Consul-General, Le Havre, 1896–1903; Antwerp, 1903–15. Knighted, 1905. Consul-General, Zürich, 1915–17; Antwerp, 1918–19.

Winston S. Churchill to Lord Kitchener: telegram

(*Copy, Churchill papers: 1/181*)

5 October 1914   Antwerp
10.18 am
Private and Secret

Line of the Nethe is intact. Marine Brigade is holding important sector
north-west of Lierre, and has been briskly engaged during the night, with
about seventy casualties so far. It seems not unlikely that the German attack
will be directed on this (?) point, as passage of river is easier there. I am
making sure that they are properly supported by detachment of artillery.
General Paris is doing very well.

Later. Infantry attack indicated now appears to be developing.

Colonel Dallas to Lord Kitchener: telegram

(*Copy, Churchill papers: 8/181*)

5 October 1914   Antwerp
11.56 am
Private and Secret

Situation this morning causes anxiety. Germans occupying Lierre with
infantry and have been preparing rafts for bridging the Nethe. They are
concentrating artillery fire on this sector of defences. Naval brigades are due
to arrive during afternoon, and, at special request of Belgian staff, will be
by brigades, with Belgian divisions to keep up morale. Reported German
attack also on Termonde. I am sending British officer there to report
personally, and will telegraph later.

H. H. Asquith to Venetia Stanley

(*Montagu papers*)

5 October 1914   10 Downing Street

. . . Winston succeeded in bucking up the Belges, who gave up their
panicky idea of retreating to Ostend, and are now going to hold Antwerp
for as long as they can, trusting upon our coming to their final deliverance.
Winston had already moved up his Marines from Dunkirk, and they are
now in the Antwerp trenches, where we hear to-day they are doing well but
have already had 70 casualties. He had also sent for the rest of his Naval

Brigade from Betteshanger, and I have a telegram from Oc[1] sent off from Dover pier on Sunday: 'Embarking to-night: love.' I suppose most of the territorials & recruits envy him, being sent off *after 3 days* to the front! I am sure he will do well, but it is a hazardous adventure.

We are doing our best for the Belgians, for tho' we are dangerously short of regulars in this country, K. is sending off to-day to their help an Expeditionary Force, consisting of the 7th division (18,000 of our best infantry) and a Cavalry Division (also of the best) running to 4000. These with 8000 Winstons make 30,000 men & 87 good guns. The French force wh. is to co-operate with them—mainly Territorials & 'Fusilier Marines'—will amount to 23,500 men & 40 guns; wh. gives a total of over 53,500 men, & 127 guns: quite a big army. They ought all to be in Belgium by Wednesday or Thursday at the latest, and it is to be hoped that Antwerp can last as long as that. K. has appointed one of the best of our younger generals—Sir Henry Rawlinson—to command the whole[2]

Then comes a real bit of tragi-comedy. I found when I arrived here this morning the enclosed telegram from Winston, who, as you will see, proposes to resign his Office, in order to take the command in the field of this great military force! Of course without consulting anybody, I at once telegraphed to him warm appreciation of his mission & his offer, with a *most decided* negative, saying that we could not spare him at the Admiralty &c. I had not meant to read it to the Cabinet, but as everybody including K, began to ask how soon he was going to return, I was at last obliged to do so, carefully suppressing the last sentence, in wh. he nominates *Runciman* as his successor!

I regret to say that it was received with a Homeric laugh. W. is an ex-Lieutenant of Hussars, and would if his proposal had been accepted, have been in command of 2 distinguished Major Generals, not to mention Brigadiers, Colonels &c: while the Navy were only contributing its little brigades. I send you the original, which I know you won't show to anybody, to add to your collection of 'memoires pour servir', with K's marginal pencil connotation.[3] Even now, I don't know how or how soon, we shall get him back. . . .

[1] Arthur Melland Asquith, 1883–1939. Known as 'Oc'. Sudan Civil Service, 1906–11. In business, 1911–14. Enlisted in the Royal Naval Volunteer Reserve, 1914. Served in the Royal Naval Division at Antwerp, Dardanelles and western front, 1914–16. Four times wounded. Served in the Ministry of Munitions, 1918; in the Ministry of Labour, 1919. Company director.

[2] Rawlinson was fifty, Churchill thirty-nine.

[3] In a marginal note, Kitchener wrote: 'I am quite prepared to give rank of Lt General.' (*Beaverbrook papers*)

Winston S. Churchill to Lord Kitchener: telegram

(*Copy, Churchill papers: 8/181*)

5 October 1914   Antwerp
12.22 pm
Private and Secret

In view of the situation and developing German attack, it is my duty to remain here and continue my direction of affairs unless relieved by some person of consequence.

If we can hold out for next three days, prospects will not be unfavourable. But Belgians require to be braced to their task, and my presence is necessary. Collapse on their part would be fatal. We have a good deal of ground to sell, if it is well disputed, even if Nethe River is forced.

H. H. Asquith to George V

(*Royal Archives*)

5 October 1914   10 Downing Street

Mr Asquith, with his humble duty to Your Majesty, has the honour to report that the Cabinet met to-day.

Lord Kitchener informed the Cabinet that Sir J. French's new movement began to be executed yesterday, and will be continued day by day, and that he hopes to concentrate his whole force, including the Indian Division, at St Omer not later than the 20th.

Lord Kitchener & Sir E. Grey described the steps which have been taken to encourage the defence & relieve the siege of Antwerp. The German besieging force is believed not much to exceed 60,000 men, of whom a considerable proportion belong to Ersatz & Landwehr corps.

The Belgians have a nominal force of about 105,000, but a considerable part of this is not really effective, and the whole is weary & somewhat demoralised. Mr Churchill has been in Antwerp since Saturday afternoon & has successfully dissuaded the King & his Ministers from retiring to Ostend. He reports that the town can hold out certainly for 3, & perhaps for as long as 10 days, if the resistance is backed up. The Brigade of Marines from Dunkirk are already there, and the two Naval Reserve Brigades left England last night, and should be there to-day—a total of 8,000 men, with two 9.2, six 6 in, and six 4.7 guns.

The French are prepared to send a supporting force of 23,500 men (15,000 Territorials, and 8000 Fusilier Marines, with a few Cavalry & gunners) and 40 guns. Lord Kitchener is ready to despatch the 7th Division (18,000 men)

& the 3rd Cavalry Division (4000 men) with 69 guns, together with one 9.2, one 9.2 Howitzer, & two 6 in heavy guns. The whole force, English & French would be under the command of Lt Gen Sir H. Rawlinson.

The Cabinet, after careful consideration, sanctioned these proposals. The English force will land at Zeebrugge to-morrow & Wednesday, and the French at Ostend between to-morrow & Thursday.

The Prime Minister informed the Cabinet that he had this morning received from Mr Churchill a patriotic offer to resign his office & take command of the forces at Antwerp, but that, while expressing warm appreciation of the zeal & skill with which Mr Churchill had conducted his mission, he had felt it right to inform him that his services could not be dispensed with at home.

Sir John French to Winston S. Churchill

(*Churchill papers: 26/1*)

5 October 1914   General Headquarters
Private

My dear Churchill,

Thank you so much for writing so fully & clearly to me from Antwerp.[1] If the place is to be saved you have saved it by your prompt action. As a matter of principle I hate putting mobile troops *inside* a fortress—but in this case it is very likely that the *appearance* of a large force *inside* the place may have a great moral effect. But the situation ought to be most carefully watched & I am very sorry (this is one of confidential 'growls' for your ear alone) to have received a wire to-day from the S of S saying 'These Troops will not for the present, form part of your forces'. It annoys me, because *all troops* anywhere in the fighting line should be under my command. I am constantly subjected to these pinpricks by the S of S and it makes my very hard & difficult task much harder. I suppose it will all pan out somehow, in case of a successful Sortie from Antwerp or in the event of an evacuation? If the plan by the Mobile Troops—my force—comes into touch with this 'other expedition' what is to happen? Is anyone concerned or no-one or what? I am not even told the instructions that are to be given to Rawlinson.

I shall do the best I can to bring relief to the place at the earliest possible moment and am arranging to concentrate in the North as quickly as circumstances will allow. The Germans are pushing out their flank Defence towards the West and & SW.

[1] Not found.

I was so delighted to have you here. I love a good talk with you. In a few days I shall be in a much more accessible place & shall look forward to another flying visit.

You delighted us all by coming.

Yrs alys

JF

Winston S. Churchill to Lord Kitchener: telegram

(*Copy, Churchill papers: 8/181*)

5 October 1914   Antwerp
4.45 pm
Private and Secret

Attack has been pressed. Marines have stood well, with some loss, but 7th Belgian Regiment, on their right, has fallen back under shell fire, and some German Infantry are across Nethe to west of Lierre. General Paris has ordered his reserve battalion and four Belgian battalions to join another Belgian brigade to drive them back and reoccupy positions. This is now in progress. Every effort is being made to gain time. I am to attend Council of Ministers at 9 p.m. tonight, and shall exert myself to prevent an exodus. I can get no news of time of arrival of naval brigades. They will be wanted tomorrow for certain.

Surely Belgian Ministers in plain clothes and unarmed would have right to pass down Schedlt in a merchant vessel at any time. Please telegraph on this.

They are very downcast.

Lord Kitchener to Winston S. Churchill: telegram

(*Churchill papers: 8/181*)

5 October 1914   Foreign Office
4.45 pm
Private and Secret

It is most necessary that Belgians should not give way before the forces now on the sea arrive for their support. I expect Rawlinson will reach Antwerp today. You know date of arrival of troops at Ostend and Zeebrugge. I cannot accelerate anything owing to difficulties of navigation. Prince Louis is doing all he can. Are any of the guns we sent in action? Our 9·2 on line to Lierre ought to be useful.

I hope Belgians realise the importance of holding Termonde so that relieving force may act promptly on the German left flank. The arrival of our troops should be kept very secret; by moving at night a surprise might be possible in the early morning.

Winston S. Churchill to Lord Kitchener: telegram
(*Copy, Churchill papers: 8/181*)

5 October 1914   Antwerp
6.46 pm
Private and Secret

Our counter-attack has been successful, and we now hold all our positions along the Nethe. Germans will probably throw bridges in night at Lierre. We are in contact with Germans on outskirts of Lierre. I have just returned from advanced trenches and find marines cheereful and well dug in.

General Paris does not think that he has lost more than 150 men killed and wounded.

I presume you keep Sir John French informed.

Lord Kitchener to Winston S. Churchill: telegram
(*Copy, Churchill papers: 8/181*)

5 October 1914   Foreign Office
7.00 pm
Private and Secret

I hear the Marine Fusilier Brigade are expected at Dunkirk today by train, but had not arrived. I have in consequence sent following telegram to French Government:—

As the Fusilier Marine Brigade is training, and their arrival at Antwerp is urgently required, please ask Minister of War to continue their journey by train to Antwerp.

You might, I think, inform Belgian authorities, so as to have facilities for this force of 8,000 to proceed without stopping at Ostend to wherever you think they would be most usefully employed, and if they have not passed Dunkirk they might be warned of their destination.

Edward Marsh to Winston S. Churchill: telegram

(*Churchill papers: 8/181*)

5 October 1914   Admiralty
7.15 pm
Private and Secret

Dunkirk reports naval brigades arrive Antwerp 1 a.m. Tuesday. Sir H. Rawlinson just leaving Dunkirk for Antwerp via Bruges, where he stays tonight. First six transports, containing 10,000 troops, 2,000 horses, should arrive Zeebrugge from 4 a.m. onwards; 9,000 troops, 2,500 horses, arrive mainly at Zeebrugge, partly at Ostend, Wednesday morning; 2,500 cavalry, 2,500 horses, arrive, partly Zeebrugge, partly Ostend, Thursday morning.

Sir Henry Rawlinson's war journal

(*Rawlinson papers*)

5 October 1914   Dunkirk

Two Brigades of Naval Service & Marines left Dunkirk at 8 pm for Antwerp but the line of railway is directly threatened by the Germans who are attacking Termond with some violence today. There is an alternative route further north by which they can get through and if they do this they may save the situation.

The naval heavy guns that were to come have not yet arrived and we do not know where the ships have gone. If there are many mines about and the channels have not been swept we may lose some transport. The situation is complicated—I cannot move forward with my divn for at least 3 or 4 days by which time it is quite possible Antwerp may have fallen.

Sir Edward Grey to Winston S. Churchill: telegram

(*Copy, Churchill papers: 8/181*)

5 October 1914   Foreign Office
10.15 pm
Private and Secret

I do not suppose the Dutch will stop the Belgian Ministers going down Scheldt in a merchant vessel if nothing is said about their departure.

The right may be a matter of argument. On no account should any force be used, however, if the Dutch do make objections. The Dutch Minister[1]

---

[1] Jonkheer R. de Marees van Swinderen, 1860–1955. Entered the Netherlands Diplomatic Service, 1890. Minister in Bucharest, 1902–4; in Washington, 1904–8. Foreign Minister, 1908–13. Minister in London, 1913–20.

has spontaneously informed us that, if Antwerp falls, Netherlands Government will deny all passage through Scheldt to Germans, and resist them by force if necessary, and we must not be the first to violate Scheldt by force.

This is very confidential.

Probability is that if Belgian Ministers go unobtrusively in merchant vessel the Dutch will take no notice.

Edward Marsh to Winston S. Churchill: telegram

(*Churchill papers: 8/181*)

6 October 1914   Admiralty
1 am
Private and Secret

Only three of the six transports mentioned in my former telegram can reach Zeebrugge this morning, 6th October.

Winston S. Churchill to Lord Kitchener and Sir Edward Grey: telegram

(*Copy, Churchill papers: 8/181*)

6 October 1914   Antwerp
1 am
Private and Secret

All well. I have met Ministers in Council, who resolved to fight it out here, whatever happens.

All positions are held along the Nethe. I hope you will not decide finally on plan of operations till I can give you my views.

No 9·2's have arrived yet, even at Ostend.

H. H. Asquith to Venetia Stanley

(*Montagu papers*)

6 October 1914   10 Downing Street

Our immediate pre-occupations are still with Antwerp, where under Winston's stimulus the Belgians are making a resolute stand. I have just seen a telegram sent off at 2 this afternoon, which shews that this morning both the Belgians & our Marines were pushed back. The inner forts (it says) are being held by our naval brigade—which shows that Oc & his companions in arms have arrived, & are already within range. Gen. Rawlinson was 'expected shortly'. Meanwhile the 7th Division & the Cavalry & the French Marines must be well on in their march. It is to be hoped that they will arrive in time, but it is an anxious situation. Winston persists in remaining there, which leaves the Admiralty here without a head, and I have had to tell them (not being, entre nous, very trustful of the capacity of Prince Louis & his Board) to submit all decisions to me. He (i.e. Prince Louis) is coming here directly (5 p.m) to see me. I think that Winston ought to return now that a capable General is arriving. He has done good service in the way of starching & ironing the Belges. . . .

Later. I have just had ½ an hour's talk with 'gallant Prince Louis'. Getting the transports to Belgium thro' the new mine-fields is an anxious job, which I can see keeps him awake at night. I indulged in some mild chaff on the exploits of the still uncaptured 'Emden', but I could see that was rather a sore subject. He had no more idea than I have of when we might look for the return of the First Lord. . . .

Winston S. Churchill to Lord Kitchener: telegram
(*Copy, Churchill papers: 8/181*)

6 October 1914   Antwerp
10.37 pm
Very Urgent. Private and Secret.

Early this morning Germans attacked our position along the Nethe. Marine brigade stood firm, but Belgian troops on their right gave way entirely. General retirement with some loss was effected to a lightly entrenched position on the line Contich–Vremde, where enemy are not for the moment pressing. Ground lost will enable Germans to bombard city tomorrow. In view of this and of complete exhaustion and imminent demoralisation of Belgian army, Rawlinson, who has arrived, has, with my full agreement and that of Belgian General Staff, ordered a general retirement to inner line of forts. The three naval brigades will hold intervals between forts and be supported by about a dozen Belgian battalions. On this line, which is very strong against infantry attack, our troops can certainly hold out as long as the city will endure bombardment. Had naval brigades arrived 24 hours earlier we could probably have held line of the Nethe. They have not been engaged, and marines have not lost more than 200 men.

Rawlinson and I attended a council of war this evening presided over by the King. We suggested an attempt to re-establish Anglo-Belgian forces on line of the Nethe by employing 7th division in a counter-attack in 48 hours time, but they had all clearly made up their minds that their army was not in a fit condition to co-operate in any offensive movement.

Accordingly we have arranged with them:—

(1) That General Paris with naval division and Belgian support will defend inner line forts to the utmost while the town endures bombardment.

(2) That the rest of the Belgian field army shall be immediately withdrawn across the Scheldt to what they call the entrenched camp of the left bank. This area is protected by the Scheldt large inundations and various forts and entrenchments, and here they hope to find time to re-form and recover. From this position they will aid to the best of their ability any relieving movement from the west which may be possible.

(3) Rawlinson will organise relieving force at Ghent and Bruges and prepare to move forward as soon as possible.

But I shall hope to convince you tomorrow that it should be strengthened for operation.

We are all agreed that there is no other course open in the circumstances.

I return with Rawlinson tonight to Bruges, and shall be in London early tomorrow morning.

Heavy guns and aviation park will be moved from Antwerp.

Sir Francis Hopwood to Lord Stamfordham

(Royal Archives)

6 October 1914
Confidential

My dear Stamfordham,

With the aid of talks today I know more of the Churchill business—Mostly from Crewe & Prince Louis—On Friday evening Churchill started about 10.30 in a car for his usual weekend visit to Dunkirk—'ewe lamb' hunting as our soldiers describe the useless game. Somewhere on the way he heard that the Belgian Govt intended to evacuate Antwerp. He rushed back to London & saw K. & E. Grey in the small hours of the morning. Then in spite of their remonstrances he left for Antwerp. He summoned some people including Admiral Oliver over & since then has been telegraphing for supplies of all kinds. Oliver came back today & says that the Germans are well aware that Churchill has bucked up the Belgian Govt & is in charge— 20,000 marks & the Iron cross have been put on his head. He would be very wrath at the sum for it buys him at only one years salary!

The Cabinet gave him peremptory orders to return & H. Samuel & Crewe said he would arrive at Charing X 1.45 this afternoon. Only his messenger turned up! Now the Naval brigade, our other troops & the French are trying to get to the scene of action and attack the Germans on the Flank.

If they succeed Winston will have saved Antwerp! & then the troops are to go south to help in the turning movement on the Aisne.

The Prime Minister is seeing Prince Louis about Admiralty affairs but the Cabinet is both distressed & helpless. One of our transports roamed about in our own mine-field in horrible fashion but escaped by a miracle. I dont think Winston can come away now with credit even if he would & however much the Cabinet may squeal—Crewe today forgetting some of things said to me 'You recollect how Churchill & Seely made the plot to coerce Ulster by military force & Paget[1] went over & gave it away—this is the same kind of thing' . . . He added 'I was ill and could only protest'. It entertained me vastly for the admission was worth its weight in gold—& oh! what was said in the debates!—No reply

Ever yrs
Francis J. S. Hopwood

Lord Stamfordham to Sir Francis Hopwood
(Southborough papers)

6 October 1914   Buckingham Palace

My dear Hopwood,

Your letter of this evening almost took my breath away. Our friend must be quite off his head! and I cannot help being anxious at his being allowed to 'carry on' in Antwerp!

We are sending rather a scratch pack including French territorials, French marines, Winston's Naval Brigade, the 3rd Division of Cavalry that has not had time to work together & some of their horses only came in on Sunday—yesterday—

Can you imagine that until I went to see 'K' yesterday at 1. pm. the King was absolutely ignorant of what had occurred at Antwerp or that W. had gone off there Friday night—Really too bad—

It strikes me that W. & K. are running the show.

Yours ever
Stamfordham

---

[1] Arthur Henry Fitzroy Paget, 1851–1928. Entered Army, 1869. Knighted, 1906. Commanded the Forces in Ireland, 1911–14: played prominent part in the Curragh incident, March 1914. General, 1913. On special missions to the Balkans, 1914–15.

Sir Francis Villiers to Sir Edward Grey: telegram

(*Copy, Churchill papers: 8/181*)

7 October 1914   Antwerp
12.35 am
Private and Secret

King and Belgian Headquarters Staff have moved from Antwerp, Government including Minister of War, have left, or are just about to leave for Ostend.

All the Corps Diplomatique have already left for that place, except my French colleague and myself. We go tomorrow morning on a steamer especially placed at our disposal. First Secretary[1] and honorary attaché[2] accompany me. Military attaché[3] will go to headquarters. I take my cyphers and archives, and will telegraph arrival and address.

Colonel Seely asks me to add that he remains here with naval brigade.

He suggests that it would be of great advantage if a War Office official could be sent out at once for cypher purposes.

H. H. Asquith to Venetia Stanley

(*Montagu papers*)

7 October 1914   10 Downing Street

. . . the Oxfordshire Yeomen are back at or near Dunkirk, while Oc & his naval men at arms are lining the entrenchments of Antwerp & sustaining the full force of the German bombardment. The Court & Ministers have retreated to Ostend, and the Belgian army is completely worn out & demoralised. The trenches are good & strongly protected, and our men could I believe hold them against any assault that the second or third rate German

[1] George Jardine Kidston, 1873–1954. Entered Foreign Office, 1897. 1st Secretary, Constantinople, 1912–14. Transferred to Brussels, 4 August 1914; accompanied the Belgian Government to Antwerp, 19 August; to Ostend, 7 October, and to Le Havre, 13 October. Chargé d'Affaires to the Belgian Government at Le Havre, 1914–15. Served at the Foreign Office, London, 1916–20. Minister to Finland, 1920–1.

[2] Charles Kingston Webber, 1872–1957. Honorary Attaché, British Legation at Brussels, 1907–14. Accompanied the Belgian Government to Antwerp, 19 August; to Ostend, 7 October; and to Le Havre, 13 October. Secretary to the British Minister to Belgium, 1918–20.

[3] William Ernest Fairholme, 1860–1920. Joined Royal Artillery, 1879. Major, 1897. Military Attaché, Vienna, Bucharest, Belgrade and Cettinje, 1902–4. Colonel, 1907. Military Attaché, Paris, Madrid and Lisbon, 1909–12. Brigadier-General, 1912. Military Attaché, Brussels, the Hague, Copenhagen and Christiania, March 1914–August 1915. Employed at Dunkirk by GHQ, France, January 1915. Chief Liaison Officer, British Salonica Force, 1915–16.

besiegers could deliver for an indefinite time: certainly until relief comes. But when the bombardment of the open town once begins the inhabitants (some 300 or 400,000) are sure to get into a panic & to demand a capitulation. Our force will in no case surrender, but if the worst comes will retire on the road to Bruges & Ghent where they will find Rawlinson's Corps entrenched & waiting for reinforcements. But one fears there may be a lot of casualties, from these hellish shells which every one agrees are the German's really formidable weapon.

Much of this I got from Winston who returned from the front early this morning to find himself the father of a new daughter[1] who arrived with the minimum of fuss & pain in the middle of the night. I had a talk with him & Kitchener over the situation, and we telegraphed to French asking him to spare some troops for the relief of the siege, if Joffre & he think it possible. Time is, of course, all important if anything effective is to be done. Winston is in great form & I think has thoroughly enjoyed his adventure. He is certainly one of the people one would choose to go tiger-hunting with, tho' as you very truly say he ought to have [been] born in the centuries before specialism. He was quite ready to take over in Belgium, and did so in fact for a couple of days, the army, the navy & the civil government. The King remains at Antwerp: Winston says he is curiously cool & detached.

We spent the rest of the morning at the Committee of Imperial Defence, where there were amongst others A. J. Balfour, Fisher, Sir A. Wilson, Esher, Lord Nicholson,[2] besides the regular team. We had a very interesting discussion on the possibilities of a German invasion or raid—the conditions being, of course, totally different from any we had ever imagined in our long hypothetical inquiries last year & six years ago. Everybody agreed that nothing of the kind could occur at present; wh. is just as well, as during this next fortnight we shall have less regular troops in the country than has happened for years or is likely to happen again during the war. . . .

Later . . . Since I came back I have had a long call from Winston, who, after dilating in great detail on the actual situation, became suddenly very confidential, and implored me not to take a 'conventional' view of his future. Having, as he says, 'tasted blood' these last few days, he is beginning like a tiger to raven for more, and begs that sooner or later, & the sooner the better, he may be relieved of his present office & put in some kind of military command. I told him that he could not be spared from the Admiralty, but he

---

[1] Sarah Millicent Hermione Churchill, 1914–   . Edward Marsh was her godfather. Actress. Author of *The Empty Spaces* (poems) and *A Thread in the Tapestry* (recollections).

[2] William Gustavus Nicholson, 1845–1918. Lieutenant, Royal Engineers, 1865. Major-General, 1899. Chief of the Imperial General Staff, 1908–12. Field-Marshal, 1911. Chairman of the Commission on Indian Army Expenditure, 1912–13. Created Baron, 1912. A member of the Dardanelles Commission, 1916–17.

scoffs at that, alleging that the naval part of the business is practically over, as our superiority will grow greater & greater every month. His mouth waters at the sight & thought of K's new armies. Are these 'glittering commands' to be entrusted to 'dug-out trash', bred on the obsolete tactics of 25 years ago—'mediocrities, who have led a sheltered life mouldering in military routine &c &c. For about ¼ of an hour he poured forth a ceaseless cataract of invective and appeal, & I much regretted that there was no short-hand writer within hearing—as some of his unpremeditated phrases were quite priceless. He was, however, quite three parts serious, and declared that a political career was nothing to him in comparison with military glory. He has now left to have a talk with Arthur Balfour, but will be back here at dinner. He is a wonderful creature, with a curious dash of schoolboy simplicity (quite unlike Edward Grey's), and what someone said of genius—'a zigzag streak of lightning in the brain'. . . .

David Lloyd George to Winston S. Churchill: note
(*Spencer-Churchill papers*)

7 October 1914   10 Downing Street

Congratulations on your brilliant effort to rescue Antwerp. What are the prospects?

Lord Haldane to Winston S. Churchill: note
(*Spencer-Churchill papers*)

7 October 1914   10 Downing Street

A great and heroic episode—you are a figure for history.

H

Sir Edward Grey to Clementine Churchill

7 October 1914   10 Downing Street

I am sitting next Winston . . . having just welcomed his return from Antwerp. And I feel a glow imparted by the thought that I am sitting next a Hero. I cant tell you how much I admire his courage & gallant spirit & genius for war. It inspires us all.

Major-General Paris to Winston S. Churchill: telegram

(*Copy, Churchill papers: 8/181*)

8 October 1914   Antwerp

The situation here is difficult. Forts 1 and 2 are being attacked. If either fall my flank is turned, and I must act as prearranged. Regret cannot obtain cypher. Referring to your proposal that the British Admiralty should, on General Deguise's[1] demand, block the Scheldt between Fort Philippe and Fort Ste Marie, I have agreed with him that this should be done at once. The Belgians are sinking store-laden ships in the river.

H. H. Asquith to Venetia Stanley

(*Montagu papers*)

8 October 1914   10 Downing Street

. . . The news this morning from Antwerp was distinctly bad. The Germans had been bombarding away all night, and General Paris, who commands Winston's Naval Division, talked of evacuating the trenches, while Gen. Rawlinson who is at Bruges sent a panicky report that the Germans had advanced through Termonde, & were threatening to cut through the line of retirement on Ghent both of the Belgian field army and of our Naval force. The Arch-Colonel [Colonel Seely] on the other hand who has turned up at Antwerp, full of fight & hope, gave a much more optimistic view of the situation.

When the Cabinet met, Kitchener being away inspecting on Salisbury plain, E. Grey (as usual) was most dolorous & despondent. The French have played a poor part as they have diverted the relief forces wh. they had promised to send. Winston was furious (and I quite share his anger) at his General, who is [in] an almost impregnable entrenched position & ought to hold on even by his eye-brows, until either the situation becomes really desperate, or succour is at hand. Rawlinson with his 7th Division (unsupported by the French) is not quite strong enough to keep the road of retirement open. Winston got on the telephone with Gen. Paris & put the

[1] Victor Deguise, 1855–1925. Entered Belgian Army, 1874. Lieutenant-General, July 1914. Appointed Governor of the Fortress of Antwerp, 6 September 1914. Taken prisoner of war by the Germans, 10 October 1914.

fear of God into him,[1] and the reports both as to the effects of the bombardment & as to the German flank movement now seem to have been grossly
exaggerated. Kitchener has just been with me, & is coming again in an
hour's time to confer with me & Winston. I have still some hope that things
may come out right, but both at Antwerp and on the extreme left in France,
the next 48 hours are a critical time. . . .

Later. Just had conference with K & Winston. The French having failed us,
& the Belgian field army being quite untrustworthy, there is alas! nothing
to be done but to order our naval men to evacuate the trenches to-night &
Rawlinson will meet them & the remains of the Belgians at Ghent, after
which point they are safe. Antwerp is I am afraid now in flames, but if the
naval men get safely away, Sir J. French's army will be well reinforced, and
ought to be able to make what Winston calls a 'punch' of an effective kind
on the German right. Poor Winston is very depressed, as he feels that his
mission has been in vain. . . .

Winston S. Churchill to Sir John Jellicoe

(*Copy, Churchill papers: 13/27*)

8 October 1914   Admiralty
My dear Jellicoe,

I am in full agreement with your letter.[2] No change in principle is required
in the naval policy to which we have steadily adhered since 1911. The main
point is to secure the safety of the British Fleet during the long and indefinite period of waiting for a general action. The phase in which raids up
to 10,000 or 20,000 men were dangerous or would have had an object has
passed. A very considerable, though no doubt incomplete, watch over the
Heligoland debouches is being maintained by our oversea submarines. It is
not necessary, as manœuvre experience had suggested, to traverse the waters
of the North Sea with the Battle Fleet with any degree of frequency. Such

---

[1] No record survives of this telephone conversation, but in a telegram to Major-General
Paris sent from the Admiralty at 2.39 that afternoon, Churchill wrote: 'It is not understood
how shelling of individual forts can affect the security of your lines so long as the intervals
between the forts are obstinately defended and the ruins of the forts themselves occupied and
entrenched after dark. You are expected to make good your defence of the position and not
to abandon it for any artillery attack however severe. It is your duty unless you receive further
orders to hold your position at all costs and to stand and repulse an Infantry assault if one
is delivered.' (*Copy, Churchill papers: 13/40*)

[2] On 30 September 1914 Jellicoe had written to Churchill about the danger of risking his
ships 'in waters infested by submarines'. He added that the defences of Scapa Flow against
submarines was inadequate. On 4 October 1914 the Second Sea Lord, Sir Frederick Hamilton,
minuted on Jellicoe's letter: 'we must keep the Battle fleet intact at all costs.' If Scapa Flow
was unsafe, he added, the Battle fleet 'must go to the Atlantic—they are just as valuable there
as in the Heligoland Bight'. (*Churchill papers: 13/27*)

movements should only be undertaken for some definite, grave and primary purpose. Occasional sweeps by cruisers in different directions, and avoiding anything like routine patrolling, are all that is necessary in present circumstances. In order to secure the greatest amount of rest and security for the Fleet, and the maintenance of the highest efficiency both of the steaming and fighting of its ships, you are justified in using occasional anchorages even more remote than Scapa and Loch Ewe; but on this you should make proposals officially. You need not fear that by these withdrawals you will miss a chance of bringing the German Battle Fleet to action. If that ever comes out it will be with some definite tactical object—for instance, to cover the landing of an invading force, to break the line of blockade to the northward in order to let loose battle-cruisers on to the trade routes, or simply for the purpose of obtaining a naval decision by fighting a battle. In the first two of these cases you would have the time to come round and meet or intercept them before their operation was completed; in the third instance, their wishes would be the same as yours.

The Committee of Imperial Defence have again considered the question of invasion in the light of the experience of the first two months of the war. The War Office have pointed out that although no troops can be spared by Germany in the present active state of the land war on all frontiers, it is possible that in the winter a deadlock may arise in both the Eastern and Western theatres, when the Germans might find it possible or useful to create a diversion by attempting to throw a regular invading army across the North Sea. In the Admiralty opinion the difficulties of such a task have been in no wise diminished by anything we have learnt since the war began. We think it is useless to discuss such matters in general terms, and we are sure that a detailed study of a concrete plan of landing, say, 150,000 men will prove fatal to such ideas. In this connection it must be remembered that the war has shown the absolute reliance of the Germans upon their artillery, without which they would cease to be formidable. The landing of great quantities of artillery and the maintenance of an ammunition supply, are operations which, even if every other part of the enemy's plan had succeeded, could not be maintained without giving ample time for the intervention of your Fleet in decisive force. Further, if the Germans could spare 150,000 of their best troops for the invasion of England during a deadlock, a similar number would be released from our side, and it is obvious that even pushing this argument to its most extreme conclusion, we could transport our men back across the Channel with the command of the sea much more swiftly and surely than the Germans could bring theirs across the much wider distances of the North Sea in the face of a greatly superior naval force. All that would have resulted from the success of this most perilous operation on the part of Germany, would be to transfer the fighting of a certain number of Army Corps from the Continent to the British islands, under circumstances unfavourable in the extreme to the Germans, and favourable in every way to our troops; with the certainty that the Germans could not be reinforced, while we could be reinforced to almost any extent, and that unless the Germans were immediately successful before their ammunition was expended, the whole force to the last man must be killed or made prisoners of war. I therefore see no reason why this contingency, any more than that of raids, should force the Battle Fleet to keep a station of danger during the winter months. The power of the superior Fleet is exerted with equal effect over the longer distances, and in fact pervades all the waters of the world.

With regard to anchorages you have only to make your proposals and we will do our best to equip with anti-submarine nets, lights, and guns the places which you may wish to use. It is of importance that these should be varied, absolute safety lying much more in the uncertainty attending the movements of the Grand Fleet than in any passive or fixed defence of any particular place. We must not be led into frittering away resources by keeping half a dozen anchorages in a state of semi-defence, and so far as possible we must organize a movable defence of guardships, trawlers, patrolling yachts, minesweepers, destroyers with towing charges, and seaplanes, which can move while the Fleet is at sea and prepare the new resting-place for its reception.

The employment of a portion or occasionally of the whole of the Battle Fleet, to supplement the Northern Blockade from time to time is a matter on which you must be the judge. A large part of your time must necessarily be spent cruising at sea, and this being so the cruising should be made as useful as possible. Here, again, anything in the nature of routine or regular stations would be dangerous, and would, after a while, draw upon you, even in remote northern waters, the danger of submarine attack.

The enemy in my judgment pursues a wise policy in declining battle. By remaining in harbour he secures for Germany the command of the Baltic, with all that that implies, both in threatening the Russian flank and protecting the German Coast, and in drawing supplies from Sweden and Norway. This is an immense advantage to the Germans, and is the best use to which in present circumstances they can turn their Fleet. It is to secure the eventual command of the Baltic that British naval operations must tend. I have already pointed out, in the papers which I showed you, the three alternative conditions under which this would be possible, and I hope that proceeding on the assumption that one of these conditions exist you will make a study of the actual method by which the entrance to the Baltic could be effected when the time arrives.

Major-General Paris to Winston S. Churchill

(*Copy, Churchill papers: 8/181*)

9 October 1914   Bruges

Royal Naval Division evacuated Antwerp yesterday evening. Position had become untenable. Division now concentrating at Ostend. Troops behaved magnificently, but are very fatigued. Losses slight.[1]

H. H. Asquith to George V

(*Royal Archives*)

9 October 1914   10 Downing Street

Mr Asquith, with his humble duty to Your Majesty, has the honour to report that the Cabinet met yesterday & to-day.

Their main preoccupation was the position at Antwerp. The failure of French co-operation made it impossible to despatch Gen Rawlinson's division as a relieving force; and as the Belgian army has become tired and dispirited, and the German bombardment of the town was being steadily pressed, no useful object would have been served by a continued defence of the entrenchments by our unsupported Naval Division. Its withdrawal was accordingly ordered yesterday afternoon, and careful instructions were given to Sir H. Rawlinson for the carrying out of the movement. He telegraphs this morning that 2000 of the Naval Division have already passed through Selzeate on the way to Ostend, and that the remainder are expected to be at or through Selzeate before dark. There is apparently no German force in this area, and the railway line is guarded by Belgian cavalry. This is very satisfactory news (so far as it goes), but no account has yet come in of the casualties of the Naval Division, and the fall of Antwerp, though in the circumstances not to be avoided, is a deplorable event.

Sir H. Rawlinson's force, after it has accomplished its present task of extricating the Naval Division, who will be sent home, will join Sir John French's command. Sir J. French is now at Abbeville, & hopes to complete the concentration of his 3 Corps at or near St. Omer by about the 12th inst.

The Cabinet, while satisfied that adequate steps have been taken for the equipment of the 14 Divisions which will be in or ready for the field next January, are somewhat uneasy as to the supply of guns, ammunition, & other necessaries for the New Armies, which ought to be fit for action service in the spring & summer. The supply of field guns, in particular, is a cause for

---

[1] Churchill, avid for news, was dissatisfied by the brevity of Major-General Paris's telegrams. Shortly after midnight he replied from the Admiralty, asking for further details of the evacuation, and adding: 'In telegraphing you should not hesitate to express yourself fully, 30 or 40 words being frequently used.' (*Churchill papers: 13/40*). Fifty-seven British soldiers were killed during the siege of Antwerp.

anxiety. It was therefore resolved to appoint a Cabinet Committee to consider by what steps the best provision for all these purposes can be assured. Lord Kitchener is the Chairman, & the other members are the Lord Chancellor, the Chancellor of the Exchequer, Mr Churchill, Mr McKenna, Lord Lucas,[1] & Mr Runciman. The Committee will meet on Monday.

Other subjects of minor importance were discussed, including the definition of Contraband, the seizure of German reservists in neutral vessels on the high seas, the use of Courts Martial in cases of suspected espionage, and the conditions to be imposed on the purchasers of Prize Ships.

H. H. Asquith to Venetia Stanley

(Montagu papers)

10 October 1914   10 Downing Street

... The news of our Naval Division is still rather patchy & not wholly good. The bulk of them—including I hope & believe Oc's brigade—got through yesterday to Blankenbergh (just by Ostend), but the last lot of about 2000 find[ing] the railway cut took refuge in Holland. It is better than being killed or captured by the Germans, but I am afraid it involves their being 'interned' by the Dutch for the rest of the war. As they are presumably good Naval Reserve men, this is a serious loss & I am afraid will be a sore affliction to Winston, who was taking complacency in Spencer Grey's daring & successful raid on the Zeppelins at Düsseldorf. ...

Winston has just been in to talk over the situation. We both agree with Hankey (who is a good opinion) that this last week—which has delayed the fall of Antwerp by at least 7 days, and has prevented the Germans from linking up their forces—has not been thrown away, and may with Sir J. French all the time coming round have been even of vital value. Seely sends word that Oc has got through & is all right—also Violet's[2] (& your?) friend Rupert Brooke[3]—one of Winston's variegated gang of officers.

[1] Auberon Thomas Herbert, 1876–1916. War Correspondent of *The Times*, South African war, 1899–1901; wounded in the leg, which had to be amputated below the knee. Succeeded his uncle as 8th Baron Lucas and 11th Baron Dingwall, 1905. Under-Secretary of State for War, 1908–11; for the Colonies, 1911. Parliamentary Secretary to the Board of Agriculture, 1911–14. President of the Board of Agriculture (without a seat in the Cabinet), 1914–15. Joined the Royal Flying Corps, 1915. On 4 November 1916 he flew over the German lines and did not return.

[2] Violet Asquith, 1887–1969. Asquith's eldest daughter, by his first wife. In November 1915 she married Asquith's Private Secretary, Maurice Bonham Carter. Active in Liberal politics throughout her life. Created Baroness Asquith of Yarnbury, 1964.

[3] Rupert Brooke, 1887–1915. Poet. 2nd Lieutenant Royal Naval Division, September 1914. Served at Antwerp. Died of blood poisoning on his way to the Dardanelles, 23 April 1915. Churchill's obituary of Brooke was published in *The Times*, 26 April 1915.

Winston S. Churchill to Lord Kitchener

(*Kitchener papers*)

10 October 1914   Admiralty

1. Between 5,000 and 6,000 men of the R.N. Division are assembling at Ostend. They will not be ready to embark until to-morrow, the 11th. The whole of these, including Marines, should sail after dark on the 11th for Dover and proceed to camp at Deal, all previous orders to the contrary being cancelled. A.G., R.M.[1] will make arrangements for their reception in the camps and in connection with Admiralty departments concerned will provide for the immediate replacement of all deficiencies in kit and equipment.

2. 1,500 Belgian recruits and volunteers are at Ostend and are to be embarked at once for Cherbourg, the French authorities being informed by telegram.

3. The transportation of the 11,000 Belgian recruits and reservists at Dunkirk to Cherbourg is to continue without intermission as rapidly as possible. The Belgians will be rationed by the Admiralty while on board ship and the Belgians at Dunkirk will be rationed from the supplies of the R.N. Division until embarked.

4. All transports are to leave Zeebrugge at once, and all transports other than those employed above which are not accommodated in safe shelter at Ostend are to leave for convenient British ports.

5. Enough transports to embark the 7th Division and the 3rd Cavalry Division are to be kept in immediate readiness with steam up for the next 48 hours in Ostend, Dunkirk, Dover, and the Thames. It is unlikely, having regard to the military situation, that any re-embarkation will be required, but we must be continually prepared for it and should an emergency arise both Zeebrugge and Ostend must be used notwithstanding any risks. Flotilla dispositions to be arranged accordingly. General Rawlinson to be informed that we are holding these ships in readiness and that he should communicate direct with the Admiralty by telephone if at any moment the situation renders his re-embarkation likely. We are assuming that he could give us 12 hours' notice, within which time the transports could be counted upon.

6. All Marines and R.N. Division details at Dunkirk are to be re-embarked and brought back via Dover to Deal.

---

[1] William Charles Nicholls, 1854–1935. Entered Royal Marine Artillery, 1872. Major-General, 1908. Adjutant-General, Royal Marines, 1911–16. Knighted, 1912. General, 1914.

7. Colonel Osmaston's[1] marine artillery are to remain at Dunkirk for the present.

8. The armoured trains and naval ratings working them and all available aeroplanes and armed motor-cars, except those now at Dunkirk under the command of Commander Samson, are placed under the orders of General Rawlinson.

9. The 3 Monitors are to be held in readiness with steam up to cover a re-embarkation at Ostend or Zeebrugge should it become necessary. General Rawlinson is to be told to telephone or telegraph if at any time he thinks such naval protection will be required.

10. The Transport Department will provide whatever ships are necessary to carry the stores, ammunition, and matériel of the Belgian Field Army. The transports standing by for the 7th Division and the 3rd Cavalry Division are a prior claim on our resources. But as there is no doubt that we can meet the two, the Transport Department is to get into direct telephonic communication with the Belgian authorities and arrange forthwith for the beginning of the embarkation of these stores. For the embarkation of stores, as apart from troops, Zeebrugge may be used equally with Ostend.

11. 8,000 to 10,000 Belgian wounded are to be evacuated from Ostend to England as speedily as possible. The Transport Department is to make proposals and preparations for their movement while at the same time the necessary arrangements for their reception in this country are being concerted by the medical authorities.

12. All motor transports of the R.N. Division, excluding armed and other motor-cars under Commander Samson actually employed, are to be collected at Dunkirk under Colonel Dumble,[2] who is to re-organise them as quickly as possible and will receive further instructions on that subject.

WSC

[1] Cecil Alvend FitzHerbert Osmaston, 1866–1949. Lieutenant, Royal Marine Artillery, 1844; Adjutant, 1894–99. Instructor of Gunnery, Royal Marine Artillery, 1908–10. Member of Ordnance Board, 1910–13. Lieutenant-Colonel, 1912. Commanded the Royal Marine Artillery Brigade, 1914–15. Member of Ordnance Committee, 1916–17. Assistant-Controller, Munitions Inventions Department, 1917–19.

[2] Wilfred Chatterton Dumble, 1871–1963. Born in Canada, of English parents. Entered the Royal Engineers as a 2nd Lieutenant, 1892; retired, with the rank of Captain, 1907. Re-employed, with the rank of Lieutenant-Colonel, September 1914–September 1919. Attached to the Royal Naval Division, 1914; and to the Naval Construction Department of the Admiralty, 1915.

Winston S. Churchill to Austen Chamberlain
(*Austen Chamberlain papers*)

11 October 1914   Admiralty

My dear Austen,

Many thanks for the useful and interesting memorandum about the employment of merchants, which you sent me on 22nd September. I should like to forward it to Runciman for the information of his Anglo-French Commission. There is a great deal of truth in the points made, and as a matter of fact we have, since the war began, followed the plan you recommend in several instances with marked success. We have sent agents scouring the country for sea boots, and specially warm clothing which is urgently wanted for the winter, and we have put the French Government in touch with British Merchants for similar purposes.

This does not imply that we surrender our general principles:—that in ordinary times it is best to go direct to the manufacturers, thus encouraging the widest competition among suitable makers, eliminating middlemen's profits, and avoiding all suspicion of favouritism; but in times of emergency we shall aim at a judicious combination of the two systems.

Yours vy sincerely
Winston S. Churchill

All is well—but the outlook is grim.

WSC

Sir Edward Grey to Sir Francis Bertie: telegram
(*Copy, Churchill papers: 13/58*)

11 October 1914   Foreign Office
10 pm
Private and Secret

His Majesty's Government must have the right to send troops for separate operations against the Germans under whatever command seems to them most desirable. Developments might occur that would render possible and desirable operations that could not be directly combined with operations of Anglo-French army.

The attempt to relieve Antwerp was initiated by His Majesty's Government as a separate operation, in which British forces took much risk and incurred some losses; and it was impossible to subordinate the separate forces sent from England expressly for this purpose to the operations of Field-Marshal French without sacrificing ab initio the object for which the new forces were sent.

The object was not achieved partly because General Joffre did not fulfil the expectation of sending a sufficient French force in time to co-operate with the British force for the relief of Antwerp.[1]

As soon as it was clear that the relief of Antwerp could not be achieved, and General Rawlinson had effected the withdrawl of the Belgian and British forces in Antwerp under cover of his troops, it was decided to place the 7th Division and cavalry under Field-Marshal Sir John French, and this was done on the 9th instant.

Sir Stanley Buckmaster[2] to Winston S. Churchill
(*Churchill papers: 13/45*)

13 October 1914   Press Bureau

My dear Churchill,

. . . I have written to the Editor[3] of The Morning Post pointing out the unfairness of criticism to which in the public interest no answer can be made. To go further would I believe be to court defiance and defeat. I hope I am not wrong and I am glad that you understand my position.

Yours sincerely
Stanley Buckmaster

H. H. Asquith to Venetia Stanley
(*Montagu papers*)

13 October 1914   10 Downing Street

. . . Oc came to London yesterday & I had a long talk with him after midnight, in the course of which he gave me a full & vivid account of the expedition to Antwerp & the retirement. Strictly between ourselves, I can't tell you what I feel of the *wicked* folly of it all. The Marines of course are splendid troops & can go anywhere & do anything: but nothing can excuse Winston (who knew all the facts) from sending in the two other Naval Brigades. I was assured that all the recruits were being left behind, and that the main body at any rate consisted of seasoned Naval Reserve men. As a

---

[1] This was also Kitchener's opinion. On 11 October 1914 he wrote to Sir John French that Joffre, by his orders changing the directions of the French Territorial Division, 'failed to carry out an engagement made by his Government after reference to him and became therefore to a considerable extent responsible for the fall of Antwerp and moreover placed 8000 British marines and Bluejackets who were in Antwerp in considerable peril'. (*Kitchener papers*)

[2] Stanley Owen Buckmaster, 1861–1934. Liberal MP, 1906–14. Solicitor-General, 1913–1915. Knighted, 1913. Director of the Press Bureau, 1914–15. Lord Chancellor, 1915–16. Created Baron, 1915. Created Viscount, 1933.

[3] Howell Arthur Gwynne, 1865–1950. Reuter's chief war correspondent in South Africa, 1899–1902. Editor of the *Standard*, 1904–11. Editor of the *Morning Post*, 1911–37.

matter of fact only about ¼ were Reservists, and the rest were a callow crowd of the rawest tiros, most of whom had never fired off a rifle, while none of them had ever handled an entrenching tool. Oc's battalion was commanded by George West[1]—an ex (very-ex) Subaltern in the Guards who was incompetent & overbearing & hated impartially by both officers and men. Among its principal officers were R. Brooke (the poet) Oc himself & one Dennis Brown[2] (a pianist), who had respectively served 1 week, 3 days, & 1 day. It was like sending sheep to the shambles. Of course when they got into the trenches they behaved most gallantly—but what could they do? The Belges ran away & had to be forced back at the point of the bayonet into the forts, while the Germans at a safe distance of 5 or 6 miles thundered away with their colossal howitzers. When at last (most unwillingly) our men obeyed the order to retire, they found the bridge across the Scheldt & most of the lighters & boats in flames: they just got across on a pontoon, but Oc says that if the wind had blown the other way they cd never have crossed & would have been left in the burning town. Then for 7 or 8 hours they marched (the one thing sailors can't do) for more than 20 miles over cobbled roads, with a ceaseless stream of Belgian refugees & soldiers blocking the way; and at last, more dead than alive, got into trains at St Gilles, wh. gradually took them to Ostend. If the Germans had had any initiative, they might with a couple of squadrons of cavalry have cut them into mincemeat at any state of their retreat. No doubt it is a wonderful experience to look back upon, but what cruel & terrible risks! Thank God they are all now back in England, except the 1500 who, when dead beat, crossed the Dutch frontier in despair, & are now interned in Holland.

I trust that Winston will learn by experience, and now hand over to the military authorities the little circus which he is still running 'on his own' at Dunkirk—Oxfordshire Yeomen, motor-busses (more or less organised by Geoffrey[3]) armoured cars &c &c. They have really nothing to do with the Admiralty, which ought to confine its activities to the sea & the air. . . .

[1] George Frederick Myddelton Cornwallis-West, 1874–1951. Lieutenant, Scots Guards, 1895–1900. Married Lady Randolph Churchill, 1900; the marriage was dissolved, 1913. Married the actress Mrs Patrick Campbell, April 1914. Lieutenant-Colonel, commanding a battalion of the Royal Naval Division at Antwerp, October 1914. Married Georgette, widow of Adolph Hirsch, 1940.

[2] William Denis Browne, 1888–1915. Between 1908 and 1914 Organist at Guy's Hospital; Conductor at the Working Man's College; musical critic of the New Statesman. Composer of Latin church music, several songs and a short ballet. Sub-Lieutenant, Royal Naval Volunteer Reserve, 15 September 1914. Served at Antwerp, October 1914. Wounded on Gallipoli Peninsula, 8 May 1915; returned to action, and killed, 4 June 1915.

[3] Geoffrey William Algernon Howard, 1877–1935. Son of the 9th Earl of Carlisle. Liberal MP, 1906–10; 1911–18; 1923–4. Parliamentary Private Secretary to H. H. Asquith, 1910. Temporary Captain, Royal Marines, Flanders, 1914. Junior Lord of the Treasury, 1915–16.

Winston S. Churchill to Lord Kitchener

(*Kitchener papers*)

14 October 1914   Admiralty

My dear Kitchener,

War Office are asking us to set aside orders for 1000 tons of naval cordite to facilitate your requirements. This is a serious inroad upon the long foreseen & carefully prepared arrangements we have made, wh were judged as more than sufficient for the needs of war.

I am prepared to take the responsibility for this. But I think it shd be mentioned to the cabinet as it is really a question of policy. I shall support you if you bring it forward.

Yours vy sincerely
Winston S. Churchill

Winston S. Churchill to Lord Kitchener

(*Copy, Churchill papers: 2/88*)

14 October 1914   Admiralty

My dear Kitchener,

If the Germans can establish submarine bases at Ostende and Zeebrugge protected by heavy guns (to say nothing of Antwerp), their attempts to harass our cross-channel communications will become much more effective. Stores and small parties may run the risk. But large bodies of troops from England ought in the absence of some extreme need to go to St. Nazaire.

Secondly, is it wise to bring troops to England and incur extra Channel passages needlessly? No doubt the Canadian and Australian troops require training here. But surely the British divisions from India could, like the Anglo-Indian divisions, disembark at Marseilles and fit it out there. Will you turn this over in your mind and talk to me about it?

The War Office ought to consult us before they shift a sea-base.

Yours very sincerely
Winston S. Churchill

Bonar Law to Sir Joseph Larmor[1]
(*Copy, Bonar Law papers*)

14 October 1914

... I agree with the estimate you have formed of Churchill. I think he has very unusual intellectual ability, but at the same time he seems to have an entirely unbalanced mind, which is a real danger at a time like this ...

Winston S. Churchill to J. L. Garvin
(*Garvin papers*)

14 October 1914   Admiralty

. . . That was a very kind and shrewd column I saw tonight in the Pall Mall.

But you must one day let me show you the good military reasons upon which—apart from sentiment—the action was taken.

In war there is only one maxim about executive people. viz Back or Sack.

Above all a man must not be put off his stroke. I am too much in contact with events and consequences to fret at such attacks. But I will profit by them so far as possible.

When are we going to meet? . . .

J. L. Garvin to Winston S. Churchill
(*Churchill papers*)

14 October 1914   9 Greville Place

My dear Churchill,

Just back & sorry to have missed a meeting. When I saw the scandalous column in the Morning Post reproduced yesterday I phoned instructions. The resulting article was fair but might have been better.[2] I agree absolutely

---

[1] Joseph Larmor, 1857–1942. Lucasian Professor of Mathematics, Cambridge, 1903–32. Knighted, 1909. Conservative MP for Cambridge University, 1911–22. President of the Royal Society, 1914–15.

[2] On October 13 the *Morning Post* accused Churchill of recklessness and irresponsibility in going to Antwerp, and in committing British troops to the siege. The *Pall Mall Gazette*'s 'Warnotes' for 14 October, entitled 'Mr Churchill and Antwerp', declared: 'The country owes Mr Churchill a great debt of gratitude for things of which it, as yet, knows but little. He has resolution, energy, driving power, and fearlessness of responsibility.' Troops were sent to Antwerp, the article went on, 'at the call of duty and honour. . . . Rather than cast the blame of failure on a Minister who has worked his working day and night in his country's cause, we should rejoice that he and his colleagues were able to see the path of duty and honour and dared to take it.'

with your spirit. Fight to the Last is the only word for places of importance the proof of nerve and determination being next to victory. What would have been the 'moral effect' had Antwerp been more tamely surrendered— even though one knows now that defence by a sufficient force in the open field is the only defence short of outranging guns?

I sometimes think considering the importance now, and the national reach, of The Observer's big page, that if we met every Thursday if only for five or ten minutes, we might concert decisive lines of comment helpful to the Country.

The censorship is now intensely irritating and the papers 'not mine' will become more likely to be vicious if things go wrong but the origin of the sharp attack is unmistakable—and personal not patriotic.

Yours ever
J. L. Garvin

Lord Stamfordham to Lord Esher

(*Esher papers*)

15 October 1914   Buckingham Palace

. . . What a fiasco at Antwerp! Just as well for the Govt. that Parliament is not sitting! . . .

Lord Sydenham[1] to Lord Esher

(*Esher papers*)

15 October 1914

. . . The Antwerp performance was appalling. I cannot believe any thinking soldier would have agreed to a plan which violated all principles of war. This, following the loss of 3 cruisers given away to the submarine does make me fear the possibilities of the future. . . .

---

[1] George Sydenham Clarke, 1848–1933. Joined Royal Engineers, 1868. On Staff of Royal Indian Engineering College, 1871–80. Secretary to the Colonial Defence Committee, 1885–92; and to the Royal Commission on Navy and Army Administration, 1892–1900. Knighted, 1893. Governor of Victoria, Australia, 1901–4. Secretary to the Committee of Imperial Defence, 1904–7. Governor of Bombay, 1907–13. Created Baron Sydenham of Combe, 1913. Chairman of Central Appeal Tribunal, 1915–16. President, National Council for Combating Venereal Disease, 1915–20. Member of the Air Board, 1916–17.

Winston S. Churchill to Colonel Repington[1]
(*Copy, Churchill papers: 2/64*)

15 October 1914   Admiralty
Private

My dear Repington,

We have been so absorbed in the press of events, that I for one have not given a thought to opinion. After all in war results are the only things that matter. Success carries all before it, & no explanation of non-success is worth making.

I wd gladly do anything in my power to improve the arrangements abt the press. I can well understand from my own past experiences the vexation caused by clumsy fingers. But the difficulty of real guidance except from the top is almost insuperable, & those at the top have many prior claims to meet.

Come & see me & talk things over.

The loss of Antwerp was a bitter pang to me. But you must not suppose that sentiment dictated our movements. The sudden & total collapse of the Belgian resistance, & the diversion of the promised French aid, were factors that destroyed a good & reasonable chance of saving the place—even at the last moment. I take the fullest responsibility for my share, but of course I only acted with & within the fullest authority.

The hand of war will I expect be heavy upon us in the Western Theatre during the next four weeks. The Russian is very slow. We shall require all our tenacity to endure the storm. It has not yet reached its height.

Yrs sincerely
WSC

Winston S. Churchill to Sir John Jellicoe: telegram
(*Copy, Churchill papers: 13/40*)

15 October 1914   Admiralty
Personal

You are invited to give your opinion secretly on every aspect of the Naval situation at home and abroad and we welcome warmly any scheme you may put forward.

Your proposals about mining are being attentively considered.

[1] Charles à Court Repington, 1858–1925. Entered Army, 1878. Lieutenant-Colonel on Kitchener's staff at Omdurman, 1898. Forced to resign his commission because of a personal indiscretion involving another officer's wife. Military Correspondent of *The Times*, 1904–18. Military Correspondent of the *Daily Telegraph*, 1918–25.

The general aspect of the war is grim.

The Russian pressure is not what we expected, and another avalanche of [German] reinforcements is approaching the western theatre.

Winston S. Churchill to John Churchill

(John Churchill papers)

16 October 1914   Admiralty

My dearest Jack,

My heart marched with you down the road from Dunkirk. God guard you and bring you safe home. I feel about this war that it will devour us all—& for my part I am willing when the time comes to pay the price. I know you will do just what is right—not forgetting the responsibilities of a squadron leader, & not failing to discern the real opportunities which flash up here & there in war & lead to glory.

I sent some armed cars etc for you all & hope you are well fitted out as the result of yr sojourn under the Admiralty.

I heard the crack of their shells for 4 days at Antwerp, & I cd be quite content, I can assure you, to ride along in my place with you all.

Write to me and send letters to Goonie by Freddie [Guest] or through HQrs. I have told French you are with the regiment: & have warned him of the limitation of yr training in field work. That all honour & good fortune may go with you is the sincere & profound wish, of your loving brother.

W

PS I have just given S. Grey & Marix the DSO for their wonderful attack on the Zeppelin Sheds at Dusseldorf & Cologne.[1]

En avant. How long is it since John Churchill fought at Lille![2]

H. A. Gwynne to H. H. Asquith

(Copy, Gwynne papers)

16 October 1914   Morning Post
345 Strand

Sir,

. . . Everybody is prepared for errors and even disasters in the field. They are the usual concomitants of warfare, especially of a campaign such as the

[1] For Spencer-Grey's account of the raid, see page 197.

[2] Churchill's ancestor, John Churchill 1st Duke of Marlborough, opened the siege of Lille—then the capital of French Flanders—on 13 August 1708. The city surrendered on 22 October; over 5,000 allied troops, and 5,000 Frenchmen were killed.

present; but the facts set forth in the enclosed[1] are such as to force the belief that Mr Churchill is unfitted for the office which he now holds, and I am firmly convinced that the country will be in a state of considerable disquietude, if not panic, unless a change is made at the Admiralty.

. . . It is my intention to publish the enclosed in the 'Morning Post' with comments asking for the removal of the First Lord of the Admiralty and his replacement by a sailor. . . . I would gladly and willingly suppress all further mention of the Antwerp expedition if some assurances were given that this change would be made. I hope you will not look upon this in any way as a threat. I feel I have a duty as Editor of a paper to protest against the continuance in office of a man who has shown most signally his incompetence to hold this office at least in time of war. . . .

I am yours truly
H. A. Gwynne

General Joffre to Lord Kitchener: telegram

(*Kitchener papers*)

16 October 1914

Now that the operations extend up to the coast of the North Sea between Ostend and the advanced defences of Dunkirk,[2] it would be important for the two Allied Navies to participate in these operations by supporting our left wing and acting with long-range guns on the German right wing. The Commander of the Naval Forces would then act in concert with General Foch[3] through the Governor of Dunkirk.

[1] Details of the activities of the Royal Naval Division, similar to those which Asquith himself had already reported to Venetia Stanley on 13 October (see pp. 188–9)

[2] At the beginning of October Churchill had appointed his Naval Secretary, Rear-Admiral Hood, to command the Dover patrol, and all British naval action along the Belgian coast.

[3] Ferdinand Foch, 1851–1929. Lieutenant, French Army, 1873. Professor, Ecole Supérieure de Guerre, 1894–1900; General Commanding the Ecole, 1907–11. Commanded the XXth Corps, based on Nancy, 1913–14. Commanded the 9th Army, at the battle of the Marne, September 1914. Deputy to the Commander-in-Chief, during the 'race to the sea', October 1914. Honorary knighthood, 1914. Commanded the Group of Armies of the North, 1915–16. Deprived of his command after the battle of the Somme. Recalled, Generalissimo of the Allied Forces, France, April–November 1918. Marshal of France, August 1918. Appointed British Field-Marshal, 1919.

Admiralty to Rear-Admiral Hood: telegram

(*Hood papers*)

17 October 1914
1.02 pm

Most important to send the scouts at once and some destroyers to Dunkirk to work along the coast to Neiuport to support the Belgian left, now being attacked by the Germans; also monitors as soon as weather permits. Acknowledge.

Winston S. Churchill to Sir John French: telegram

(*Copy, Churchill papers: 13/27*)

17 October 1914   Admiralty

Monitors were delayed by weather, but will be in position from daylight 18th; meanwhile eight destroyers should have arrived on the flank between 4 and 5 p.m. 17th, and two scout cruisers an hour later. They have been told to communicate with Colonel Bridges[1] on the quays of Nieuport.

We are sending two battleships mounting eight 12-inch guns to Dunkirk roadstead to-morrow to cover the fortress and its coast approaches.

Admiralty to Rear-Admiral Hood: telegram

(*Hood papers*)

17 October 1914
7.20 pm

Belgian Army is on line River Yser left bank, from Nieuport to Dixmude, with advanced posts on E. bank at Lombartzyde Rattevalle and Mannekensvere.

King is at La Panne, the last village on French coast.

The rôle of ships is as follows:—

Firstly, to prevent any disembarkation of German troops between Nieuport and La Panne and to South-West.

Secondly, to fire against enemy, which are advancing on Nieuport.

---

[1] George Tom Molesworth Bridges, 1871–1939. Entered Royal Artillery, 1892. Lieutenant-Colonel 4th Hussars, 1914. Head of British Military Mission, Belgian Field Army, 1914–16. Major-General, commanding the 19th Division, 1916–17. Wounded five times. Lost a leg at Passchendaele. Head of British War Mission, USA, 1918. Head of British Mission, Allied Armies of the Orient, 1918–20. Knighted, 1919. Governor of South Australia, 1922–7.

Squadron Commander Spencer Grey: report of an air raid on 9 October 1914

(*Copy, Admiralty papers: 116/1352*)

17 October 1914

. . . On arriving at Cologne I found a thick mist. I had been given two different positions for the airship sheds, one to the north-west and one to the south of the town. I came down to 600 feet, but, after searching for 10 to 12 minutes under a heavy fire, I failed to locate them. I now hear they are on the east side of the Rhine, but do not know if this is correct. Failing to locate the sheds, I considered the best point to attack would be the main station in the middle of the town where I saw many trains drawn up, so let fall my two bombs in this. I arrived back at Antwerp at 4.45 pm and landed. . . .

Lieutenant Marix was under a heavy rifle and shell fire during this period, and his machine suffered considerable damage. In spite of this he managed to fly back to within 20 miles of Antwerp, at which point his petrol ran out. From here he succeeded in returning to Antwerp by a bicycle which he borrowed from a peasant and a car which he got later. It was hoped to take out more petrol in an armed car at daylight and recover the machine, but the order to evacuate prevented this. . . .

Sir David Beatty[1] to Winston S. Churchill

(*Churchill papers: 13/43*)

17 October 1914   *HMS Lion*
Private

My dear First Lord,

I take the opportunity of an officer[2] going to London in charge of signal books, to write you of what goes on. I have written you before, or rather to Hood for you. I think it is right that you should know how things generally affect the Fleet. I trust that you will take this as it is written, in fact I know you will, as being written with only one idea of service to the country. I write as I do because I know that the plain truth at times such as these is

[1] David Beatty, 1871–1936. Entered Navy, 1884. Rear-Admiral, 1910. Churchill's Naval Secretary, 1912. Commander of the 1st Battle Cruiser Squadron, 1913–16. Knighted, 1914. Vice-Admiral, 1915. Commander-in-Chief of the Grand Fleet, 1916–18. First Sea Lord, 1919–27. Created Earl, 1919. Admiral of the Fleet, 1919.

[2] Reginald Aylmer Ranfurly Plunkett, 1880–1967. 2nd son of the 17th Baron Dunsany. Lieutenant, Royal Navy, 1901. Commander, 1912. Served with Grand Fleet on board HMS *Lion*, 1914–18. Present at the battles of the Heligoland Bight, the Dogger Bank and Jutland. Assumed the surname Plunkett-Ernle-Erle-Drax, 1916. Director, Royal Naval Staff College, Greenwich, 1919–22. Knighted, 1934. Commander-in-Chief, the Nore, 1939–1941. Commodore of Ocean Convoys, 1943–5.

the only thing worth hearing, and because you are the one and only man who can save the situation. Even at such times, official documents, requisitions and demands, are of little value; they are met at once I admit, but without understanding the true value of all that lies behind them.

At present we feel that we are working up for a catastrophe of a very large character. The feeling is gradually possessing the fleet that all is not right somewhere. The menace of mines and submarines is proving larger every day, and that adequate means to meet or combat them are not forthcoming, and we are gradually being pushed out of the North Sea, and off our own particular perch. How does this arise? By the very apparent fact that we have no Base where we can with *any* degree of safety lie for coaling, re-plenishing, and refitting and repairing, after two and a half months of war. This spells trouble. It is a perfectly simple and easy matter to so equip Scapa Flow, Cromarty, and Rosyth, so that vessels can lie there undisturbed to do all they want, and for as long as they want, provided material and men are forthcoming. The one place that has put up any kind of defence against the submarine is Cromarty, and that is because at Cromarty there happens to be a *man* who grapples with things as they are, i.e. Commander Munro,[1] and because they have trained artillerymen to man their guns. That was one of the best day's work you ever did when you insisted on taking the defences there in hand. At Rosyth it appeared to me in Sept. when there that to deny access to submarines and destroyers was a fairly simple task; it was an awkward place to get into, but when once in it, ought to be, and could be, very easily made a safe asylum for vessels in need of rest, repair, fuel, etc. At Scapa, something has been done towards blocking the many entrances, but that is all. I am sure that all the brain and intellect at the Admiralty could devise a scheme or method of defence which would make the anchorage practically safe, and which could be done in a fortnight. No *seaman* can dispute that these three bases could have been made *absolutely* safe from sub-marine attack during the $2\frac{1}{2}$ months that the war has been in progress. As it is, we have been lulled into a sense of false security, because we have not been attacked before, but I can assure you that it has literally been recog-nized by all that it was only a question of time when we should have this sense rudely shattered. That time has come, and it is only a Divine Providence that has saved us from an appalling disaster. I maintain stoutly that each one

[1] Donald John Munro, 1868–1952. Went to sea, as a merchant seaman, 1880. Entered the Royal Navy, 1895. Inventor of various anti-submarine devices. King's Harbour Master, Rosyth, 1911–12; Cromarty, 1912–14. Acting Captain, 1914–20. At Cromarty he devised a system of submarine obstruction by which, Jellicoe later wrote in *The Grand Fleet 1914–16*, 'the entrance to Cromarty was rendered fairly secure by October 26th, 1914'. In charge of the anti-submarine net defence system at Mudros, during the Dardanelles operations, 1915. Commander RN, 1920.

of our three bases could have been made capable of resisting attack by submarines and destroyers, by means of obstruction gates, etc., and by strengthened patrol (local). At Portsmouth, Devonport, Clyde, Pembroke, and Queenstown, we have local defence flotillas; if others are not forth-coming these should be robbed to supply the same at Cromarty, Rosyth, and Scapa, where they are more urgently needed. These, with the aid of submarine nets, torpedo nets, piles or concrete blocks, sunken ships, wire hawsers, booms, and mines as passive defences, supported by well-placed guns manned by *trained* artillerymen, *not territorials,* who cannot be expected to handle efficiently the modern quick-firing gun against a fast moving target in an uncertain light, to do which requires years of training. These harbours defended thus would free the coastal patrol forces to be *out* in positions where they can cut off minelayers and locate submarines at a distance from, instead of being tied to, to protect a base which should be quite capable of protecting itself.

Having protected these bases, the point at issue is the question of getting there, as far as cruisers and battle cruisers are concerned, by utilising the [?][1] to arrive and depart and proceeding at speed, Scapa has no terrors neither should it have any for the battleships if it is thought necessary to have some stationed or based on it. Cromarty also during hours of darkness is fairly or comparatively safe, but requires taking more care than Scapa. Rosyth is difficult and practically impossible with any degree of safety *except for* a very small number of ships moving very fast; these latter should not in dark hours run great risk. Given freedom from danger of mines in the approach, I can assure you I would have no fear of taking the BCS into any one of the three Ports.

The situation as it is, we have no place to lay our heads. We are at Loch na Keal, Isle of Mull. My picket boats are at the entrance, the nets are out and the men are at the guns waiting for coal which has run low, but ready to move at a moment's notice. Other squadrons are in the same plight. We have been running now hard since the 28th July; small defects are creeping up which we haven't time to take in hand. 48 hours is our spell in harbour with steam ready to move at 4 hours notice, coaling on an average 1400 tons a time; night defence stations. The men can stand it, but the machine can't, and we must have a place where we can stop for from four or five days every now and then to give the engineers a chance. Such a place does not exist, so the question arises, how long can we go on, for I fear very much, not for long, as the need for small repairs is becoming insistent.

The remedy is to fix upon a base and make it impervious to submarine attack; as I have pointed out I am firmly convinced this can be done.

Can I sum up the situation as it appears to me? We are driven out of the

---

[1] Unable to read Beatty's handwriting, Churchill had this letter typed out. The two gaps marked by square brackets were left as gaps in the letter as typed.

North Sea because of the menace of enemy submarines and mines. Presumably the North Sea is denied the enemy ships by our submarines; but is it? All the control we require to exercise over the mercantile traffic in the North Sea can be produced just as well outside the North Sea as in it, if we revert to the methods of the Napoleonic wars, and see that it is carried out by patrols off the coast of Ireland, Cape Wrath and Shetlands, and the Faroe Is. if necessary, but aren't we giving up too much by evacuating the North Sea and permitting their fast craft to lay mines and cut up our patrols ad lib, and if they think desirable, cause a panic by rushing 100,000 men across, which under these circumstances would be quite possible, they would command it, not us, which surely would be detrimental. Therefore, or rather anyhow, it is as well to examine the menace as it really is, and I think it can be summed up by saying that—

The menace is one of submarines and mines only.

Region of menace, our coast lines and entrances to naval and commercial bases and arsenals extending to 60 miles from the coast, and in the case of mines possibly even up to 100 miles from the coast.

To meet this menace, we have a very large force and we are on the right tack. But up to the present this force has accomplished very little, if anything. It presumably consists of the patrol flotillas with a large number of submarines working with them. The 1st & 3rd flotillas are also enlisted practically in this work, and it is supplemented by a vast number of trawlers, etc. On the proper handling of this large force very much depends. What is essential is that whoever runs them should be somebody of great determination who can instil them with a great zeal and imbue them with the spirit of men knowing when they are [   ] and skilful enterprise; a man whom they will trust absolutely and follow anywhere. Such a man you had in John De Robeck.[1] He might not have been a genius, but with guidance from you at the Admiralty, he is a born leader of men, of great energy and determination; in fact with those qualities which come to the front only in war. I am sure that if he had been there he would have curtailed the depredations of the mine-layer and the submarine.

Judging from what I have seen and heard of the force of trawlers in northern latitudes in Orkneys and Shetlands, they are practically valueless

[1] John Michael de Robeck, 1862–1928. Entered Navy, 1875. Rear-Admiral, 1911. Commanded the 9th Cruiser Squadron, charged with protecting British merchant ships in the mid-Atlantic, 1914–15. 2nd in command of the Allied naval forces at the Dardanelles, February–March 1915. Vice-Admiral commanding the Allied naval forces at the Dardanelles, March 1915–January 1916. Knighted, 1916. Commanded the 2nd Battle Squadron in the North Sea, 1916–18. Created Baronet, 1919. Commander-in-Chief of the Mediterranean Fleet, 1919–22. Admiral, 1920. High Commissioner at Constantinople, 1921. Commander-in-Chief of the Atlantic Fleet, 1922–4. Admiral of the Fleet, 1925.

because they are undisciplined and uncontrollable. They receive high wages and are always drunk. To be of value they must be manned by men who understand discipline, who will do exactly what they are told, and who can be depended upon. Such a force manned efficiently, and half at least equipped with a short wireless (which should not be impossible) would be invaluable as an adjunct of the coastal patrols. I would suggest their being manned by R.F.R., R.N.R., or R.N.V.R., equipped with wireless and a gun (hidden). Let them increase their activity by keeping more at sea, rushing numbers to the spot when a submarine has been sighted or reported, gradually pushing out further from the coast as their skill and efficiency increases, until they can hold a line 50 or 60 miles from it. Enemy minelayers laden with high explosives will not risk an encounter with any vessel armed with a gun. Submarines appear to work always with a trawler in the vicinity. In each case of 'Pathfinder', 'Aboukir' and 'Hawke', a trawler was there, being or about to be examined. With all our resources and all our reserves of trained and disciplined men, we ought to ensure that minelayers and submarines are not permitted to act with impunity undetected along our coasts. The *centre* of the North Sea can be swept by vessels at *high speed* from time to time without running any great risk from submarines. Permanent patrol areas must be avoided. The submarine cannot act except from a floating base or in the vicinity of the coastline; navigational difficulties prevent it. Destroy his floating base and you control his action in the centre of the sea. Strong coastal patrol should be able to limit his activities near the coast.

In the case of creating extempore defences against submarine attack or destroyers, it is not sufficient to supply a quantity of material as asked for without also supplying a sufficient number of men to place and work them and to keep them constantly efficient and with experience gained to steadily improve. This again calls for disciplined men to be permanently stationed at each base for this purpose alone, which would entail a large amount of heavy work, particularly in winter months.

You might be told that this idea of making the entrances secure is chimerical. This is not so; and I will guarantee that if the fleet was instructed to defend the entrances to the ports named, and was provided with the material, they could and would devise not one but several methods which would satisfy most requirements, and which would keep out submarines. If the fleet cannot spare the time and labour, turn it over to Commander Munro and give him a free hand and what labour he requires, and he will do it in a fortnight.

I trust, First Lord, you will forgive this long bleat. I think you know me well enough to know that I do not shout without cause. The fleet's tail is still well over the back. We hate running away from our base and the effect is appreciable. We are not enjoying ourselves. But the morale is high and confidence higher. I would not write thus if I did not know that you with your quick grasp of detail and imagination would make something out of it.

Commander Plunkett takes this with him and is perfectly aware of all that I have in my head, so if there is anything in it that requires explanation, he can supply it. He is sound and clear-headed, and you can trust him to give you all information.

Yours ever
David Beatty

If we ever use Scapa anchorage again, I trust that some steps be taken to deal with the spies that exist there, which are a very serious danger. Martial Law of a fortress is the best and only real method.

Winston S. Churchill to Sir Edward Grey
(Grey papers)

18 October 1914   Admiralty

My dear Grey,

Mr Hurd,[1] Naval Correspondent of the D.T., has just been to see me. He tells me that the order about not interfering with enemy reservists in neutral ships has caused wide-spread bewilderment & disapproval. He believes that Beresford got to hear of this from some naval source, & immediately sent it to the Morning Post. He heard from one who was present that a discussion took place on whether it shd be published or not, & that it was decided to publish it as part of a campaign for raising suspicion against Prince Louis. It appears that Beresford & Gwynne are engaged in endeavouring to undermine his position & to sow distrust. Whether a newspaper shd be permitted to pursue such a course in the present state of our affairs is to my mind doubtful. Certainly no other belligerent Govt in Europe wd expose itself to such embarrassments. But if this condition is to be accepted, it seems clear to me that there shd be some full statement of our position; & while I am fully prepared to take all responsibility for the order, it might be easier & more helpful if the F.O. drew up & issued the statement, & not the Admiralty.

I looked in upon you this evening to tell you that our Monitors have been in action all day between Nieuport & Ostend, firing on the German right flank, & that some movements are taking place in what we call the narrow seas, on both sides, which may possibly produce some contacts tomorrow.

Yours always
Winston S. Churchill

[1] Archibald Hurd, 1869–1959. Author and journalist. Contributor of naval articles to English and American publications. On the editorial staff of the *Daily Telegraph*, 1899–1928. Knighted, 1928. Author of the Official History of the Merchant Navy in the War of 1914–18.

Winston S. Churchill to Lewis Harcourt[1]

(*Copy, Churchill papers: 13/27*)

18 October 1914   Admiralty

My dear Harcourt,

We have no cruiser available for Yap at the present time and much inconvenience would be caused by changing existing arrangements.[2] There appear to be no military reasons which require us to eject the Japanese at this juncture. I do not gather that the Australasian Governments are pressing us to act. On the contrary it would seem that you were pressing them. The Admiralty would strongly deprecate any action towards Japan which would appear suspicious or ungracious. We are deriving the greatest benefit from their powerful and generous aid. They have intimated that their occupation is purely military and devoid of political significance and there I trust we may leave the matter for the present.

Yours very sincerely
Winston S. Churchill

Lord Haldane to Winston S. Churchill

(*Spencer-Churchill papers*)

19 October 1914   28 Queen Anne's Gate
Westminster

My dear Winston,

I have been thinking over our talk.

You must not ever consider leaving the Admiralty at this period of course. You are unique & invaluable to the nation—full of courage and resource. Do not pay the least attention to the fools who write & talk in the press. It is this real thing that counts, & the nation thoroughly believes in you.

I should like to see Fisher & Wilson brought in, & Prince Louis kept with them as Second Sea Lord.

The advent of the first two would make our country feel that our old spirit of the navy was alive and come back.

Believe me, with sincere regard,

Ever yours
Haldane

[1] Lewis Harcourt, 1863–1922. Liberal MP, 1904–17. Secretary of State for the Colonies, 1910–15. First Commissioner of Works, May 1915–December 1916. Created Viscount, 1917.

[2] Japanese forces had occupied the German island of Yap, in the Marshall Islands, on 6 October. So little was known of the geography of that part of the Pacific that the British believed Yap to be the administrative centre of the Marshalls, which it was not. But it possessed an important wireless station. The British Government asked the Australians to occupy it before the Japanese could do so, but they were too late.

Lord Kitchener to Winston S. Churchill

(*Asquith papers*)

19 October 1914

My dear Churchill

If it is not thought advisable to lay mines, would it not be a good thing to have some of the more powerful modern ships from the grand fleet in the Eastern ports, so that they could act quickly in case of emergency in the North Sea or Channel.[1]

Yours very truly

Kitchener

Winston S. Churchill to Lord Kitchener

(*Asquith papers*)

19 October 1914   Admiralty

My dear Kitchener,

The foundation of our policy is to keep intact & united under Jellicoe a fleet able to beat the whole German Navy. As long as such a fleet exists, it will dominate the naval situation. There can be no question of dividing it or dispersing it.

The problem of invasion must be studied in detail. You have at yr disposal probably the best experts in the world. Let them make a plan for the landing of 150,000 men (a) on a beach, (b) at a port, anywhere on the East Coast, with the necessary artillery, vehicles & ammunition columns of a German Army on that scale. Let them work out the number of transports, the number of men in each, the number of horses, the number of waggons, the tonnage of supplies and ammunition etc etc. Let them select their beach, or say which harbour they can get into, making sure that the ships are the right draught to get into it. Choose any day in the past month. Assume (a large assumption) that yr Armada has reached the English coast without being detected. Calculate exactly the time taken to land the men, guns, vehicles, horses, stores, under all the limitations of actual physical conditions. Leave out the chance of weather. Assume it all goes perfectly, & that we only get notice when your ships are sighted from the shore. Assume that the whole German

---

[1] On 18 October Churchill circulated a memorandum entitled 'Notes on Mining' to the Cabinet. In it he stressed 'the partial and limited reliance' which the Admiralty placed on mining 'as a method of warfare'. '. . . your own minefield,' he pointed out, 'is a greater deterrent on your operations than on those of the enemy. You have put it down yourself, so you do not want to sweep it up. You know where it is, though not very accurately. You instinctively try to avoid the waters you have yourself fouled.' (*Cabinet papers: 37/121*)

Fleet supports this operation. Make any dispositions you like for them, & keep them secret.

The Admiralty will then say what force we can bring to bear, or could have brought to bear, on a particular day at 3, 6, 12, 24 hours respectively, & what our positions wd be at the end of that time. You will be able to see whether any, & if so what changes are required in our arrangements.

It really is no use dealing with the subject in general terms. All the same, you ought to have the military force to deal with 70,000 men in this country. This is the deterrent on which we rely to give us a proper target or immunity.

Yours sincerely
Winston S. Churchill

Winston S. Churchill to Lord Kitchener
(Kitchener papers)

19 October 1914   Admiralty

My dear Kitchener,

We must not let Dunkirk go the way of Antwerp. Of course if we win the main battle the danger will recede. If we wait till we lose it, it will be too late to act effectively. We ought to act *now*.

Admiral Oliver makes the attd suggestions some of wh have already been carried out.

What do you say?

Yours vy truly
Winston S. Churchill

William Allardyce[1] to Lewis Harcourt: telegram
(Copy, Churchill papers: 13/39)

19 October 1914   Falkland Islands

It is possible that the German squadron now on the west coast of South America[2] may evade Cradock's[3] squadron, and appear in the waters of

[1] William Lamond Allardyce, 1861–1930. Entered Colonial Service, 1879. Served in Fiji and the Western Pacific, 1880–1904. Governor of the Falkland Islands, 1904–14; of the Bahamas, 1915–20; of Tasmania, 1920–22; of Newfoundland, 1922–28. Knighted, 1916.

[2] The German Pacific Squadron, commanded by Admiral von Spee, was based at the German port of Kiaochow (Tsingtau) on the Chinese coast. It left Kiaochow on 6 August 1914, narrowly avoiding the Anglo-Japanese forces which captured the town. On 10 September von Spee reached a British island in the mid-Pacific, Fanning Island, destroying the wireless cable station. On 12 October he reached Easter Island (Chilean), and was supplied with fresh meat by an English overseer, news of the outbreak of war not having yet reached the island. On 18 October von Spee left Easter Island, and headed towards the Chilean coast of South America, 3,000 miles further east.

[3] Christopher Cradock, 1862–1914. Entered Navy, 1875. Rear-Admiral, 1910. Knighted, 1912. Commanded the North American and West Indies station, 1913: his command extended from the St Laurence river to Brazil. Drowned at the Battle of Coronel, 1 November 1914.

the colony. In that case the wireless telegraph installation will probably be destroyed and an indemnity demanded from the Colony, and British Trade through the Straits of Magellan and round Cape Horn will suffer accordingly. Government will withdraw to the hills if forced to do so. My council have advised and I concur that women and children should go to the camps.

Allardyce

Sir David Beatty to Ethel Beatty[1]

(*Beatty papers*)

20 October 1914

. . . If we only had a Kitchener at the Admiralty we could have done so much and the present state of chaos in naval affairs would never have existed. It is inconceivable the mistakes and blunders we have made and are making. . . .

H. H. Asquith to Venetia Stanley

(*Montagu papers*)

20 October 1914   10 Downing Street

. . . Winston has been pouring out his woes into my ears: I think Battenberg will have soon to make as graceful a bow as he can to the British public. Winston has a grandiose scheme (entre nous) for bringing in both Fisher & Sir A Wilson! . . .

Lord Kitchener: memorandum

(*Copy, Cabinet papers: 37/121*)

20 October 1914   War Office

With reference to the notes on mining issued by the Admiralty:—

It was, I believe, always considered in the Committee of Defence that the British Fleet would form the 1st line of defence to protect the shores of this country from invasion, and that that defence would be available at short notice and absolutely secure us against anything greater than a raid of a small body of armed men being landed on our shores. It was considered that if the Army could deal with 70,000 men an ample margin of safety was

---

[1] Ethel Newcomb Field, 1873–1932. Only daughter of the Chicago department store owner and millionaire, Marshall Field. She married Beatty (her second husband) in 1901.

provided. As in so many other points the war has shown us that the premisses on which we based our calculations can no longer be relied upon. We are now aware that, owing to the activity of the German offensive by submarines at sea, our first line of defence, with the exception of small craft, cannot be available in the North Sea for 30 hours from the time of a landing of a German force on our shores or the bombardment by heavy guns of our coast defences, and this period of time may be further extended as the activity and unrestrained enterprise of German submarines become further developed. There is nothing to lead us to think that they have reached the limit of their operations.

The paper that has been circulated by the Admiralty shows that it is not thought advisable to attempt mining in the North Sea. I am not a sufficient expert in naval matters to be able to criticise the decision come to, but I think the situation thereby created is a very grave one as regards the defence of this country from invasion. We have been buoyed up with the hope that a serious invasion of these shores was impossible, but we must remember that that has never been the opinion of German army and navy experts. An expedition carefully planned and arranged with all necessary means of quick disembarkation and ample transport is, we know, in an advanced state of preparation for the purpose on the German coast. As soon, therefore, as men are available the German project of invasion of these shores will, in all probability, be tested. Their information of our military defences through spies may be considered to be absolutely complete, and the German opinion is that, once a considerable force is landed in England, they would have a fair chance of defeating the defensive forces still kept in this country. The one deterrent that they have always felt would have made an invasion impossible—our fleet—has now been removed to such a distance by their action that the opportunity is probably now considered by them a favourable one.

Modern artillery has rendered forts and fortifications no longer a serious obstruction, if vigorously attacked, and I do not know which of our defended ports would hold out against a 30 hours' bombardment by the big guns of the German Fleet. If we consider that a sufficiently large force with all its concomitants necessary for the invasion of this country could not be landed in 30 hours, I can only imagine that the German calculations on this subject are very different from ours, and I must say that, in my opinion and that of my military advisers, there are several places on our coast where such a project would be feasible if undertaken by a determined and active enemy.

We are, therefore, faced with the position that the active offensive defence by our first line may admit of the Germans testing their project by practical demonstration.

The military defence on shore is, I think, fully understood by the Members of the Cabinet. We have denuded this country—and we were forced to do so to maintain the struggle on the Continent—of practically all Regular troops. We have relied upon the Territorial Forces, untrained though they were, badly armed both in rifles and guns, and badly found with ammunition. In the first phase of the war our reserves of officers and men formed a considerable Regular support to the Territorial Forces; these have been rapidly depleted by supplying the wastage of the campaign and can no longer be counted on to the same extent. In order to maintain and increase our forces in the field we have also seriously reduced our Territorial Forces themselves; Territorial Divisions have been sent to Egypt and India, and garrisons to Malta and Gibraltar. At the same time the area of our coast liable to attack has been constantly increasing until now we may say that the coast line from Plymouth to the North of Scotland must be considered within the area available for German enterprise. Numerical superiority with such a long line to defend against a sudden unforeseen attack—for the Navy can give us no assured information of an attempt on our coast—is not of itself sufficient. Once a German force is landed it would take us some time to concentrate any adequate force to give battle, to an enterprising enemy, with a good chance of success. A difficulty with regard to this concentration will undoubtedly be that we can never know, owing to want of information, that the first landing announced is to be the only one, and we shall always have grave doubts as to the numbers landed at any given spot.

These are the principal reasons why I consider that until our forces are trained in this country, a more offensive defensive action on the part of our first line is necessary. What that action entails I am unable to advise, but I would point out that though this campaign can never be won by any general fleet action in the North Sea, it can and may be certainly lost as far as we are concerned.

K

Charles Buxton[1] and Noel Buxton to Sir Edward Grey: telegram

(*Copy, Admiralty papers: 116/1336*)

21 October 1914   Bucharest

We find opinion in responsible circles is that in order to secure military action by Roumania and, in the event of war with Turkey, by Bulgaria it is

---

[1] Charles Roden Buxton, 1875–1942. Liberal MP, 1910. Labour MP, 1922–3; 1929–31. In October 1914, while in Bulgaria, he was shot through the lung by a Turkish would-be assassin. Treasurer of the Independent Labour Party, 1924–7.

not desirable to negotiate with small States, but that Entente Powers should make a Declaration such as follows:—

(1) They support claim of Servia to Bosnia.

(2) In the event of Bulgaria forthwith showing friendly neutrality towards Roumania and Servia and undertaking to (group omitted) ? Turkey in case of war between Turkey and Entente Powers, they will support claim of Bulgaria to parts of Macedonia indicated by Serbo-Bulgarian Treaty of 1912 and in case of war with Turkey they will support Bulgaria's claim to Enos–Midia line.

In the event of Bulgaria receiving these (group omitted ?) they will (? listen to) claim of Servia to Dalmatian ports.

It is thought very important that Declaration should be formal and made by the Three Powers jointly.

Promise to support territorial claims is understood not to be absolute guarantee. Please compare with my letter which expands above suggestions.

Above Declaration would remove menace of Bulgarian attack which hampers Roumania. Please repeat to Lloyd George and Churchill.

Noel Buxton to Winston S. Churchill: telegram

(*Copy, Admiralty papers: 116/1336*)

21 October 1914 Bucharest

With reference to idea of military scheme for Balkan States which you asked me to work for, situation ? is (groups omitted) Roumanian action hitherto obstructed by late King's[1] wishes now being possible. Only remaining difficulties are fear of Bulgaria and uncertainty of European military situation. Powers can obviate this without danger of commitments and with justice to Servia. Small Powers cannot be expected to settle all questions among themselves. Public opinion would be most powerfully affected by a lead from outside especially from England. I beg to suggest utterance by yourself expanding your recent speech would greatly help to secure co-operation and it would be reported verbatim. All steps in support of your policy at Sofia are believed to be deprecated by our Government even when

[1] Prince Charles of Hohenzollern-Sigmaringen, 1839–1914. Elected Prince of Rumania, 1866. Became King, as Carol I, when Rumania was created a kingdom in 1881. He was related both to Napoleon III and to the King of Prussia, and was a personal friend of the Emperor of Austria. Visited by Tsar Nicholas II and Sazonov in June 1914, Sazonov reported that 'Rumania will work with the side that turns out the stronger and offers her the greatest gains'. On 2 August 1914 Carol requested the Crown Council to declare war *against* Russia, but his request was rejected. Died, 10 October 1914. His successor, his nephew Ferdinand, was married to a granddaughter of Queen Victoria.

desired by France and Russia. If it is abandoned please inform me. I can supply further details regarding public opinion if required.

H. H. Asquith to Venetia Stanley

(*Montagu papers*)

21 October 1914   10 Downing Street

. . . We had a long Cabinet this morning. Poor Winston is in rather bad luck just now; that infernally elusive craft the 'Emden' has mopped up 6 or 7 British merchant ships (including what she most needs—2 colliers) somewhere off the West coast of India south of Bombay, despite the fact that she is being assiduously hunted night & day by the Yarmouth & the Hampshire and a very quick unpronounceable Japanese cruiser.[1] Also a submarine of the best class—E3—is reported to have been sunk by the Germans in one of their bags.

We have (but this is secret) succeeded in sending 3 submarines all the way into the Baltic to deal havoc among the German war-ships there. Unluckily they began their proceedings, & advertised their presence by attacking a *Danish* vessel! It is rather an adventurous démarche in any case, as they have no parent ship with them, like the man in the hymn are 'far from home': but in case of need they will put into Libau, which is a Russian port.

We had a rather interesting discussion on home defence & the possibility of German invasion, which pre-occupies & alarms the mind of Kitchener. His view is that the Army is doing all it can both at home & abroad, and that some of the big ships ought to be brought into the home ports. Winston made a very good defence of his policy, which is (in a word, or at least a few words) that the function of the Great Fleet is not to prevent the landing of an invading force (which is the business of the torpedo flotillas & submarines) but to strike at & destroy the enemy's covering fleet. All the same it is agreed to be desirable to have a lot of sheltered or protected harbours wh. no submarine can penetrate, & in which some battleships & cruisers can lie in safety. This is being done, & (tho' I have never shared K's fears) in a very short time we ought to be absolutely secure even in the judgment of the most doubting pessimist.

Ll. George, who generally has a point of view of his own, is very down on the Russians for not taking us more into their confidence both as to the actual & potential strength of their armies, & as to their real plan of campaign.

---

[1] In early October 1914 the Japanese light cruiser *Chikuma* joined the nine other vessels searching for the *Emden* in the Indian Ocean.

He says quite truly that for aught we know the Germans may be holding them back by a mere screen of troops, while they are massing their real attack upon the allies in Belgium & France. It is difficult, but we must try to get them to be less secretive, and to throw more of their designs into the common stock. There is the greatest difference of opinion as to the actual quality & equipment of their troops.

Another urgent matter (upon wh. there threatens to be acute difference of opinion among us) is whether or not we should supply the starving civil population in Belgium with food. E Grey & I are rather *pro*, Ll. George, McKenna, Kitchener & others strenuously *contra*. We shall have to decide this tomorrow.

Winston S. Churchill to Lord Kitchener

(*Kitchener papers*)

21 October 1914   Admiralty

My dear Kitchener,

Repeated evidence comes in about Germans using boys of 17 in the war. Would it not be wise in the near future to recruit special corps or companies of boys of 17 or 18 here, which cd train on without rifles for the first 8 months, & next year be ready to undergo final training before filling gaps in yr army? If you cd get a couple of hundred thousand of these, you wd have a fine fund for drafts from the end of 1915 onwards.

Napoleon's young soldiers did him very well at Lutzen & Bautzen;[1] & surely you ought to get them into training as soon as the pressure becomes less severe.

Yours vy truly
Winston S. Churchill

Lord Fisher to Winston S. Churchill

(*Churchill papers: 13/28*)

21 October 1914   Admiralty

Dear Winston,

Something interesting! After leaving you I had an appointment with an American lady returned last night from Germany. I have employed her on

---

[1] Having lost half a million men in Russia in 1812, Napoleon recruited 300,000 men in 1813; 150,000 of them were under twenty years of age, and would not normally have been recruited until 1815 and 1816. Special mobile columns had to be set up to obtain these recruits, especially in Brittany, the Netherlands and the annexed lands of north Germany. These 'young soldiers', some aged 17, 18 and 19, fought at the battles of Lützen (2 May 1813) and Bautzen (20 May), when Napoleon temporarily checked the Russians and Prussians.

secret service to communicate with my daughter who with her husband are prisoners at Bad-Nauheim near Frankfurt. (He has been in a convict's cell! but now well treated.[1])

(1) This American lady tells me there is *real panic* caused by our heroes who burnt the Zeppelin at Dusseldorf—and people are clearing out of Dusseldorf because expecting another English raid. *The military also are scared!*

(2) The Commander-in-Chief of the Frankfurt Military District (Major-General de Graaf,[2] who has anAmerican wife) asked her if she knew anything of Russian soldiers having passed through England to France!

(3) She also heard the Germans were feeling uncomfortable about the fighting in the neighbourhood of Metz.

(4) Major-General de Graaf said to her that I was thought to be of consequence in Germany! . . .

Yours till death

F

Trafalgar Day

Sir John French to Winston S. Churchill

(*Churchill papers: 26/1*)

21 October 1914   General Headquarters

My dear Churchill,

I haven't written to you because I hoped every day to see you. I don't understand the attitude of the French in this Antwerp affair—at least I should say I *do* understand it—but am necessarily so much accustomed to their vagaries that I have ceased hoping to probe the causes!

I began this letter 2 days ago! I had to stop in the middle of a sentence & had not a single minute since to go on with it. We have been hard pressed the last 2 days—the Enemy has received considerable reinforcement and a big battle has been raging all along our front from a point about 10 miles north of Ypres to La Basse which is W.S.W. of Lille. We have given way now &

---

[1] On 3 December *The Times* reported that on President Wilson's personal initiative (through the American Ambassador in Berlin, James W. Gerard) the Germans had agreed to release Fisher's daughter Beatrix and her husband, Rear-Admiral Reginald Rundell Neeld (1850–1939), without asking for any equivalent concession from Britain. They returned home in mid-December, and for four years Mrs Neeld wrote personally and sent clothing to British merchant seamen imprisoned in Germany.

[2] Heinrich (Hendrik) de Graaff, 1857–1924. Born in The Hague. Military Cadet, Berlin, 1873. Lieutenant-General Commanding Frankfurt Military District, August 1914–April 1915. Chief of Staff, 3rd Army Corps, 1915–18. His wife, Elizabeth Virginia Kremelberg, was born in Baltimore, USA.

then in places and recovered the ground again—and on the whole have lost nothing (except unfortunately *men* & *Officers*!!)—altho' the Enemy has attacked with the utmost vigour.

I have been all along the line but the ground is so flat & the buildings so numerous that it is impossible to see much of the Infantry work. I have this moment got a wire from the 1st Corps that they captured 350 prisoners this afternoon.

Do forgive me, my dear old friend, for worrying you with my petty troubles. Dear old K is all that I could wish but I suppose this tension makes me irritable sometimes—and you are always so sympathetic. You did splendid work at Antwerp. When are you coming to me again? For God's sake don't pay attention to what those rotten papers say.

Thank you my dear friend, Yrs always

JF

This is a hurried & disjointed letter but messages & wires are coming in every minute!

Winston S. Churchill to David Lloyd George

(*Lloyd George papers*)

22 October 1914 Admiralty

My dear David,

Wd you let me invite yr daughter[1] to launch Carysfort[2] from Pembroke. She is a light cruiser, & her sister ship was launched by Miss Violet Asquith.

I have not had a minute to congratulate you on your baptism of fire.[3] The taste forms if not cloyed by surfeit.

Yours vy sincerely

Winston S. Churchill

[1] Olwen Elizabeth Lloyd George, 1892–   . She married, in 1917, Major Thomas John Carey Evans (1884–1947) of the Indian Medical Service, who was knighted in 1924.

[2] The *Carysfort*, a Light Cruiser, served with the Grand Fleet from June 1915 to April 1916, with the Harwich force from April 1916 to March 1918, and with the Grand Fleet from March to November 1918. In June 1917 she fired on and shot down a Zeppelin. In 1922 she was part of the British Occupation Flotilla off Constantinople.

[3] Lloyd George had gone to Paris to find out at first hand what was being done to increase the supply of munitions. On his way home he took the opportunity to visit the front. In his *War Memoirs* he described how on October 19, at Montdidier, 'I heard, for the first time in my life the crack of shells fired with murderous intent against human beings, and my first experience of it gave me a shudder'.

Winston S. Churchill: note

(*Admiralty papers: 116/1351*)

22 October 1914   Admiralty

A precise order shd be given that all transports believed to be conveying German troops to England are to be sunk at once by torpedo or gunfire. No parley with or surrender by a transport on the high seas is possible. Transports enclosed in a bay which surrender wholesale & immediately may be dealt with as mercifully as circumstances allow. British Officers will be held responsible that the enemy gains no advantage by any exercise of humanity.

On the other hand when the fighting has altogether stopped men swimming in the water may be made prisoners of war in the regular way provided the fighting efficiency of the ships is not affected.

WSC

H. H. Asquith to Venetia Stanley

(*Montagu papers*)

23 October 1914   10 Downing Street

. . . the Turks seem to be seriously meditating an invasion of Egypt, where the fellaheen are rather disappointed that they cannot get money for their cotton crop. We have suggested to Italy that this is a 'nouveau fait' which might affect her.

Grey & Haldane were very fussy & jumpy lest the Germans should establish a base at Ostend and keep there a new nest of submarines. Winston (I think with perfectly good reason) derides this, and declares that to-morrow (if necessary) he will shell Ostend into ruins & make it uninhabitable. I wish some people (E.G. for instance) had more sense of proportion and perspective. . . .

Winston S. Churchill to Sir Edward Grey

(*Admiralty papers: 116/1336*)

23 October 1914   Admiralty

My dear Grey,

. . . I am vy unhappy about our getting into war with Turkey without having Greece as our ally. This was the least to be hoped for. Surely it is not too late.

Yours ever

W

Winston S. Churchill to Rear-Admiral Hood: telegram

(Hood papers)

23 October 1914   Admiralty
1.05 am

Vital to sustain Belgian Army with effective Naval Artillery support
to-morrow.

Arrange details with Bridges.

Am sending Gunnery School tenders to Dunkirk; draw upon them as you
need.

Recognize importance to Navy of dominating Belgian Coast; make the
most of your opportunity.

Rear-Admiral Hood to Winston S. Churchill: telegram

(Churchill papers: 13/40)

23 October 1914

Thanks for message. All going well.

Will bombard Ostend. Belgian Headquarters granted permission.

Am quite satisfied that our firing has done good.

Winston S. Churchill to Sir John Jellicoe: telegram

(Copy, Churchill papers: 13/40)

23 October 1914   Admiralty
2.00 am
Private and Personal

Every effort will be made to secure you rest and safety in Scapa and
adjacent anchorages. Net defence hastened utmost, will be strengthened by
successive lines earliest. If you desire, Cabinet will I think agree declare area
30 miles east Kinnaird Head to 30 miles north Shetlands and down to 30
miles South of Hebrides prohibited to all ships not specially licensed by
Admiralty or you.

All vessels whatever Flag should be dealt with in this area as you desire.

I wish to make absolute sanctuary for you there. I also propose proclaim-
ing all Scotland north of Caledonian Canal including all Islands and Inverness prohibited area; you can do what you think necessary for safety of
Fleet.

Use your powers under Defence of Realm Act and ask for anything you want in men, money or material. You must have a safe resting place: tell me how I can help you.

Captain Richmond: diary

(*Richmond papers*)

24 October 1914

Last night, at 8 o'clock, when I was on my way upstairs to dress for dinner, a telephone message came from Churchill asking me to dine. So I took a cab & got there in time. He was in low spirits . . . oppressed with the impossibility of *doing* anything. The attitude of waiting, threatened all the time by submarines, unable to strike back at their Fleet, which lies behind the dockgates of the Canal, Emden or Wilhelmshaven, and the inability of the Staff to make any suggestions seem to bother him. I have not seen him so despondent before. . . . He wanted to send battleships—old ones—up the Elbe, but for what purpose except to be sunk I did not understand, & as I did not wish to oppose & be counted among the do-nothings, I let it alone. . . .

Winston S. Churchill to Prince Louis, Rear-Admiral Tudor,[1]
Captain Lambert and Masterton Smith

(*Copy, Churchill papers: 13/40*)

24 October 1914   Admiralty

Every nerve must be strained to reconcile the Fleet to Scapa. Successive lines of submarine defences should be prepared, reinforced by Electric Contact mines as proposed by the Commander-in-Chief. Nothing should stand in the way of the equipment of this anchorage with every possible means of security. The First Lord and the First Sea Lord will receive a report of progress every third day until the work is completed and the Commander-in-Chief satisfied.

WSC

[1] Frederick Charles Jones, 1863–1946. Entered Navy, 1876. Assumed surname of Tudor, 1891. Director of Naval Ordnance and Torpedoes, 1912–14. Rear-Admiral, 1913. Third Sea Lord, 1914–17. Commander-in-Chief, China Station, 1917–19. Knighted, 1918. Admiral, 1921. President, Royal Naval College, 1920–2.

H. H. Asquith to Venetia Stanley

(*Montagu papers*)

24 October 1914   10 Downing Street

. . . There was no Cabinet to-day, but I attended a very boring Committee at the Foreign Office on the subject of contraband &c. Winston was there & came on here with me afterwards to talk about things in general. It was really interesting, and as I always tell you everything, you will I know say nothing of what follows. (Most secret)

The first & most important thing is that the plan I have long been urging is about to come off. That is to say that to-day a certain number of old & specially prepared ships go to within about 30 miles of Heligoland, protected by destroyers & cruisers. From there, as from a spring board, a detachment of sea planes will fly straight for Cuxhaven: spy out all the German preparations there & in the Kiel Canal; make havoc if they can of the Zeppelins & their sheds; and return (if they can) to their ships. As Winston grimly says, a lot of them will never be able to use the second half of their return tickets. But this is far the most romantic & adventurous side of modern war. *Nobody* knows of this—except W & myself. It may or may not come off—but it is worth trying.

Then he unfolded to me his schemes for cheating and baffling the submarine. Some of the ships are to be clad in enveloping & protecting 'shoes', others to be provided around their keels & lower parts with safe-guarding 'saddle-bags'. And beyond all this, he is going to establish by means of a huge net-work of wire & nets a 'hen-coop'—somewhere off the East coast—with a couple of doors, in which from time to time our big ships can refuge & nestle, without any fear of torpedo attack. A little later we hope we may have a still larger 'bird cage' of the same character further North. I like this: it is inventive & resourceful, & shows both originality and dash. I laugh at our idiotic outside critics who long for an expert instead of a civilian at the head of the Admiralty. Nothing truer was ever said than that 'experts are good servants but bad masters'. I am not sure that we are not really suffering from a neglect of this sound maxim at the War Office. The lunatic who edits the 'Morning Post' writes me a long private letter this morning, urging the supersession of Winston by Jellicoe! . . .[1]

[1] On 23 October 1914 H. A. Gwynne wrote to Asquith that 'that there is grave uneasiness in the country on account of the vast power which Mr. Winston Churchill wields in the Board of Admiralty' and declaring that the public 'profoundly mistrust the exuberant energy of the First Lord'. (*Copy, Gwynne papers.*)

Winston S. Churchill to Leonie Leslie[1]
(Leslie papers)

24 October 1914   Admiralty

My dear Leonie,

I am so sorry for you and grieve more than I can say for your bitter sorrow.

The ever widening conflagration of this war devours all that is precious; and the end is far away. It is a big enough war about a big enough cause for anyone to go out on. And those who flash away in the conflict doing their duty in good company are not the most unhappy. You must be very brave my dear. My heart bleeds for you. We must at all costs win. Victory is a better boon than life and without it life will be unendurable. The British army has in a few weeks of war revived before the whole world the glories of Agincourt and Blenheim and Waterloo, and in this Norman[2] has played his part.

It rests with us to make sure that these sacrifices are not made in vain.

With deepest sympathy
Yours affectionately
Winston S C

Sir John French to Winston S. Churchill
(Churchill papers: 26/1)

25 October 1914   General Headquarters

My dear Churchill

Your letters are always a great help & strength to me. Thank you indeed for this last one.[3]

I wish you would try to take a less gloomy view of what these damned people chatter about! What does it matter.

I will gladly revise & forward Paris despatches if you think well & will rejoice to have an opportunity of expressing in no uncertain terms *my* opinion of your conduct & what it has meant to all of us now.

I tried hard to retain a hold on the Belgians and *with them* to operate alone on the Northern flank: but the French smelt a rat and sent *Foch* & a *mission* to take charge of the Belgians. I feel sure it was a political move. They were

---

[1] Leonie Blanche Jerome, 1859–1943. Churchill's aunt. Sister of Lady Randolph Churchill. She married Colonel John Leslie in 1884.

[2] Norman Jerome Beauchamp Leslie, 1886–1914. 2nd Lieutenant, Rifle-Brigade, 1905. Served in Egypt, 1908–10 and Bengal, 1912–14. Captain, May 1914. Killed in action, at Armentières, on the western front, 18 October 1914.

[3] Not found.

afraid of our developing a separate kind of campaign & they are determined to keep everything under their own control.

As the Belgians were practically the guests of France, using their territory and *Calais as a base*, I had no alternative but to gracefully 'submit'.

I have said nothing about it but I am sure this is what they meant.

I am however on the very best terms with Foch who is doing splendid work and will be at Ostend and probably Bruges within a week.[1]

The fighting is still severe. I've been at 2 points in the line to-day—but it is certainly slackening. The Germans will never get further West.

This is only a hurried line written in the watches of the night.

Yrs alys
JF

I hope you will see your way to come to us soon.

Winston S. Churchill to Sir John French

(*Copy, Churchill papers: 29/1*)

26 October 1914   Admiralty

. . . I do trust you realize how damnable it will be if the enemy settles down for the winter along lines which comprise Calais, Dunkirk or Ostend. There will be continual alarms and greatly added difficulties. We must have him off the Belgian Coast, even if we cannot recover Antwerp.

I am getting old ships with the heaviest guns ready, protected by barges with nets against submarines, so as to dispute the whole seaboard with him. On the 31st instant Revenge, four $13\frac{1}{2}$-inch guns, will come into action if required, and I have a regular fleet of monitors and 'bomb-ketches' now organized which they all say has hit the Germans hard, and is getting stronger every day. . . .

Winston S. Churchill to Rear-Admiral Hood: telegram

(*Hood papers*)

27 October 1914   Admiralty
11.30 pm

Certainly go on, husband ammunition till good targets show, but risks must be run and Allies' left must be supported without fail by the Navy. You have all done very well, and on land the line has been maintained. Keep it up.

[1] The Germans held both Ostend and Bruges until October 1918.

Sir John Jellicoe to Admiralty: telegram

(Copy, Churchill papers: 13/40)

27 October 1914   HMS Assistance
11.15 am

AUDACIOUS struck by mine or torpedo North latitude 55 degrees
40 minutes West longitude 8 degrees 20 minutes.

Fear she is sinking.

Small craft have been sent to her assistance.[1]

H. H. Asquith to Venetia Stanley

(Montagu papers)

27 October 1914   10 Downing Street

. . . Winston came here before lunch in a rather sombre mood. Strictly
between you & me, he has suffered to-day a terrible calamity on the sea,
which I *dare* not describe, lest by chance my letter should go wrong: it is
known only to him & me, and for a long time will & must be kept secret.
He has quite made up his mind that the time has come for a drastic change
in his Board; our poor blue-eyed German will have to go, and (as W. says)
he will be reinforced by 2 'well-plucked chickens' of 74 & 72. We both enlarged on the want of initiative & constructive thought of the present naval
advisors: if they had had any real insight, they wd. have begun 2 months
ago devising 'hen coops' & 'shoes', & other protective devices (e.g. torpedo-
proof harbours and refuges) against the submarine. It will be curious to see
how the public receives the changes of personnel when they are announced.
I can't help being very fond of him—he is so resourceful & undismayed:
two of the qualities I like best. . . .

Lord Stamfordham: memorandum

(Royal Archives)

27 October 1914   Windsor Castle

Today the King saw Mr Winston Churchill with regard to the position
of Prince Louis of Battenberg as First Naval Lord of the Admiralty.

Ever since the commencement of the War there has been, in certain
quarters, an inimical movement against him on account of his name and
parentage and this feeling has, to a slight extent, found expression in the

[1] For further references to the *Audacious*, see pp. 221–3, 228, 237, 263, 288–9, 297, 457 and
495–6.

Press. Meanwhile he has been assailed by anonymous letters and these attacks combined with the exacting duties and heavy responsibilities of his Office have no doubt affected his general health and nerves so that for the good of the service a change had become necessary. The First Lord then suggested to His Majesty that Lord Fisher should be brought back to the Admiralty as successor to Prince Louis and Sir Arthur Wilson as Chief of the Staff. This proposal was a great surprise to the King who pointed out to Mr Churchill his objections to the appointment. Lord Fisher has not the confidence of the Navy: he is over 73 years of age. When 1st Sea Lord he no doubt did much for the Navy but he created a state of unrest and bad feeling among the officers of the service—Mr Churchill represented that there was no one in the Admiral's rank fitted for the post in the present exceptional circumstance. Sir Hedworth Meux was spoken of, but Mr C declared that he could never work with him. His Majesty mentioned Sir Henry Jackson[1] but the First Lord, while admitting his scientific and intellectual capacity did not think he would do—The King also spoke of Sir Frederick Sturdee now Chief of the Staff as suitable for the Board but Mr Churchill did not agree—His Majesty concluded by saying he could not give his approval to the appointment until he had seen the Prime Minister.

Sir John Jellicoe to Admiralty: telegram
(*Copy, Churchill papers: 13/40*)

27 October 1914   HMS Iron Duke
4.35 pm

Submit every endeavour should be made to keep AUDACIOUS incident from being published.

Sir John Jellicoe to Admiralty: telegram
(*Copy, Churchill papers: 13/40*)

27 October 1914
10.10 pm

Regret report that AUDACIOUS has sunk. Believe that only one life lost. Hope loss can be kept secret.

[1] Henry Bradwardine Jackson, 1855-1929. Entered Navy, 1868. A pioneer of wireless telegraphy. Knighted, 1906. Chief of the Admiralty War Staff, 1912-14. Admiral, 1914. In August 1914 he was put in charge of planning the seizure of German colonies. First Sea Lord, May 1915-December 1916. President of the Royal Naval College, Greenwich, 1916-19. Admiral of the Fleet, 1919.

Winston S. Churchill to Sir John Jellicoe: telegram
(Copy, Churchill papers: 13/40)

27 October 1914   Admiralty

Private & Personal

It will be very difficult to keep AUDACIOUS secret though publication may for a time be prevented best chance is for you to send a wireless cypher signal saying damage to AUDACIOUS due to collision with derelict repairs will take at least three weeks or something of this sort.

We shall then use this as the official answer to all rumours and inquiries and possibly publish it later. Prefix letters F.K. to your reply.

Winston S. Churchill to Sir John Jellicoe: telegram
(Copy, Churchill papers: 13/40)

28 October 1914   Admiralty

I am sure you will not be at all discouraged by Audacious episode. We have been very fortunate to come through three months of war without the loss of a capital ship. I expected three or four by this time, and it is due to your unfailing vigilance and skill that all has gone so well. The Army too has held its own along the whole line, though with at least 14,000 killed and wounded. Quite soon the harbours will be made comfortable for you. Mind you ask for all you want.

H. H. Asquith to Venetia Stanley
(Montagu papers)

28 October 1914   10 Downing Street

. . . The disaster of wh. I wrote to you in veiled language yesterday was the sinking of the 'Audacious'—one of the best & newest of the super Dreadnoughts, with a crew of about 1000 and 10 13·5 inch guns, off the North coast of Ireland. They thought at first that it was due to the torpedo of a submarine, but it is now clear that she hit up against a new mine-field, laid by the Germans most unsuspectedly in those waters, which in the course of the day blew up 2 merchant ships. The mines must have been laid by vessels flying neutral flags, and as they were placed directly in the route which the great liners take, going from Liverpool to New York, they were probably not intended for the fleet. All the greater must be their satisfaction at such a valuable & unexpected bag. The 'Olympic' came up & took the Audacious in tow: she remained afloat for about 8 hours and the whole of her crew except one man were safely landed. But the ship itself sank before reaching the coast. It is far the worst calamity the Navy has so far sustained, as she cost at least 2½ millions. It is cruel luck for Winston.

Poor boy he has just been here pouring out his woes. (I ought to have said that after a rather heated discussion in the Cabinet this morning, we resolved *not* to make public the loss at this moment. I was *very* reluctant, because I think it bad policy on the whole not to take the public into your confidence in reverses as well as in successes. And I only assented to immediate reticence on the grounds (1) that no lives were lost and (2) that the military & political situation (especially as regards Turkey) is such that to advertise at this moment a great calamity might have very bad results. I am I confess rather uneasy about it, & I hope you think, on balance, that I was right. This is a huge parenthesis! Of course you will say nothing about the 'Audacious', till it is public property. Winston's real trouble however is about Prince Louis & the succession to his post. He *must* go, & Winston has had a most delicate & painful interview with him—the more so as his nephew Prince Maurice[1] was killed in action yesterday. Louis behaved with great dignity & public spirit, & will resign at once. Then comes in another trouble. W. proposes to appoint Fisher to succeed him & to get Wilson to come in also as Chief of Staff—which I think wd be very popular. But Stamfordham (who came to see me just before W) declares the King's unconquerable aversion to Fisher (he—the King—was always a Beresfordite in the old quarrels) and suggests nonsense people like Hedworth Meux & Sir Henry Jackson, whom W. will not have at any price. I said that nothing wd. induce me to part with W, whom I eulogised to the skies, and that in consequence the person chosen must be congenial to him. So there is for the moment a complete *impasse*, & it requires all my ingrained & much-tried optimism (wh. sometimes amuses you) to forecast a way of escape. Happily I have some experience in building bridges over gaping chasms: whether I can engineer this situation remains to be seen. . . .

Privately, we had a royal row at the Cabinet to-day between K & Ll. George, about Welsh recruiting & the Welsh Army Corps. They came to very high words, and it looked as if either or both of them wd. resign. The whole thing cd. be settled in 10 minutes by the exercise of a modicum of common-sense & imagination. K. is much the most to blame: he was clumsy & noisy: he

[1] Prince Maurice Victor Donald of Battenberg, 1891–1914. Lieutenant, King's Royal Rifle Corps, 1914. Grandson of Queen Victoria; son of Prince Henry of Battenberg. He died of wounds received in action in France.

has spent so much of his life in an Oriental atmosphere that he cannot acclimatise himself to English conditions. I have told Winston to go & see him, and try to infuse some sense of proportion. . . .

David Lloyd George to Winston S. Churchill

(*Churchill papers: 2/64*)

28 October 1914   11 Downing Street

My dear Winston,

I feel deeply grateful to you for the way you stood up for fair play to my little nationality this morning.[1]

I am in despair over the stupidity of the War Office. You might imagine we were alien enemies who ought to be interned at Frimley[2] until we had mastered the intricacies of the English language sufficiently to be able to converse on equal terms with an East End recruit.

I enclose copy of the order issued by the W.O. about the Welsh Army Corps. Under these conditions further recruiting is impossible.

Does K. want men? If he does not let him say so then we will all be spared much worry & trouble.

Why cannot he give us 18 battalions out of the 30 new battalions already formed in Wales. We could then send another division.

Ever sincerely
D. Lloyd George

Lord Stamfordham: memorandum

(*Royal Archives*)

28 October 1914   Windsor Castle

Lord Stamfordham saw the Prime Minister & told him that the King had been somewhat taken aback when, during an interview with the First Lord yesterday, the latter proposed to recall to the Admiralty Lord Fisher as successor to Prince Louis of Battenberg. The King appealed to the Prime Minister to prevent this step. His Majesty knows the Navy and considers that the Service mistrusts Lord Fisher and that the announcement of the proposed

---

[1] Kitchener had opposed the suggestion that a Welsh-speaking Army Corps should be established. In answer to Lloyd George's protest, he had apparently declared that, apart from the linguistic difficulties involved, the Welsh were not to be trusted *en masse*. There was a long and heated argument. J. A. Pease recorded in his diary: 'K said he would resign. PM said that was not practical.' (*Gainford papers*)

[2] Frimley, Surrey; site of an internment camp for aliens.

appointment would give a shock to the Navy which no one could wish to cause in the middle of this great War. It was also stated that Lord Fisher had become aged: he talked & wrote much but his opinions changed from day to day. Mr Asquith said he had never heard this before. The Prime Minister replied that he gathered from the First Lord that there was no one else suitable for the post—The Board was weak and incapable of initiative: the Navy had not fulfilled the hopes & expectations of the Country: anything that *had* been done was due to Mr Churchill—Mr Asquith believed that Lord Fisher's appointment would be generally welcomed by public opinion. He asked Lord S. whom he would suggest. Sir H. Meux would not do: tho' a personal friend of his. Mr Asquith said 'surely he would not inspire the confidence of the Navy'. Sir H. Jackson was able, but no personality. Sir F. Sturdee more suited to command a Fleet than to be in an office: he would be given a Fleet. Lord S. suggested that Sir F. Sturdee was not liked by the First Lord because he 'stuck up to him' but Mr Asquith did not agree. Lord S. said the appointment of Lord Fisher would place the King in a very painful position as the Navy would think His Majesty should not have sanctioned it. The PM replied that he himself would be in an equally awkward position as the refusal of Lord F. would mean the resignation of Mr Churchill. Lord S. pointed out that from what Mr Churchill had said to the King on the previous day he would not be sorry to leave the Admiralty as its work was uncongenial to him: he wanted to go to the War & fight and be a soldier. The Prime Minister scouted the idea and said Mr Churchill has a most intimate knowledge of the Navy & his services in his present position could not be dispensed with or replaced. The question was fully discussed and in answer to Lord S. Mr Asquith undertook to do nothing in a hurry but added that Prince Louis' retirement could not be delayed. Lord S. said he thought the King would prefer Sir A. Wilson to Lord Fisher as 1st Sea Lord.

Winston S. Churchill to Prince Louis

(*Copy, Churchill papers: 13/5*)

28 October 1914 Admiralty
Most Private

My dear Prince Louis,

The Prime Minister thought & I agree with him that a letter from you to me indicating that you felt that in some respects yr usefulness was impaired & that patriotic considerations wh at this juncture must be supreme in yr mind wd be the best form of giving effect to yr decision. To this letter I wd on behalf of the govt write an answer. This corrdce cd then be made public & wd explain itself.

I cannot tell you how much I regret the termination of our work together, & how I deplore the harsh & melancholy march of events wh lead to yr temporary withdrawal from active employment. I am sure however that you consult yr own happiness by the sacrifice wh you make.

Will you consider vy carefully whether there is any way in wh I can be of service, & will you tell me of any point wh I shd make in the letter wh I shall write.

No incident in my public life has caused me so much sorrow.

Yrs v sincerely
WSC

Prince Louis to Winston S. Churchill

(Churchill papers: 13/27)

28 October 1914   Admiralty

Dear Mr Churchill,

I have lately been driven to the painful conclusion that at this juncture my birth and parentage have the effect of impairing in some respects my usefulness on the Board of Admiralty. In these circumstances I feel it to be my duty, as a loyal subject of His Majesty, to resign the office of First Sea Lord, hoping thereby to facilitate the task of administration of the great Service, to which I have devoted my life, and to ease the burden laid on HM Ministers.[1]

I am, Yours very truly
Louis Battenberg
Admiral

Prince Louis to Winston S. Churchill

(Churchill papers: 13/27)

28 October 1914   Admiralty
Private

Dear Mr Churchill,

I would like to add a few words to my public letter, in response to your kind invitation. If on quitting office I could receive some sign indicating

[1] Commenting on this letter and Churchill's reply of 29 October 1914, quoted on page 229, *The Times* declared: 'Honest men will prefer the brevity of the retiring Admiral to the rhetorical document which accepts his decision.' Edward Marsh was so upset by this remark that he wrote to the Editor, Geoffrey Robinson, on 31 October that *The Times* was 'undermining the public confidence by an innuendo against the honour of a national leader at a time of crisis'. *(Copy, Marsh papers)*

that I still commanded the confidence & trust of HM the King & his Govt
it would have a great effect on my position in the country. I am ashamed to
have already so many initials after my name & there is hardly anything left
in Honours. What I should value above all else would be to admitted to the
Privy Council.[1] I may say that one or two of my predecessors were so honoured
in their time.

As regards my successor: Lord Fisher as l.S.L. with Sir A. Wilson as
C.O.S. would be ideal. If impossible then Sir A. Wilson sh be l.S.L. rather
than Ld F. The entire Navy would subscribe to this, I am sure. With you
would rest the task of over-ruling his well-known obstinacy.

Yrs as ever
LB

Winston S. Churchill to Prince Louis
(Milford Haven papers)

28 October 1914   Admiralty
Private

My dear Prince Louis,
The PM will charge himself with the duty of having you sworn a member
of the Privy Council subject to the King's approval.

I propose to ask Hedworth to remain at Portsmouth to the end of the
war; & thereafter, so long as it is in my power, that command will be
held at yr disposal.[2]

I shall write tomorrow a letter to you in acknowledgment of yr formal
letter to me.

I desire you to continue responsible until satisfactory arrangements are
made for a relief.

Yrs v sincerely
WSC

[1] At the outbreak of war Prince Louis had the following initials after his name: GCB,
GCVO, KCMG. He became a Privy Councillor on 5 November 1914.
[2] Prince Louis did not receive any further naval command.

Sir John Jellicoe to Winston S. Churchill: telegram

(*Copy, Churchill papers: 13/40*)

28 October 1914
1.00 am

Private & Personal

As ship has now gone will derelict stories be of any use? Hope that in any case press may be requested not to publish anything on the subject at all.

Prince Louis and Sir Frederick Sturdee to Sir John Jellicoe:
telegram

(*Copy, Churchill papers: 13/40*)

28 October 1914   Admiralty
12.05 pm

To ensure secrecy, will you endeavour to caution passengers & crew of OLYMPIC of the importance, in public interest, of keeping the loss secret as long as possible.[1]

OLYMPIC is being ordered to remain at Lough Swilly & discharge passengers until a safe passage has been found through mine field.

Winston S. Churchill to Sir John Jellicoe: telegram

(*Copy, Churchill papers: 13/40*)

28 October 1914   Admiralty
2.50 pm

Cabinet has decided that no publication of yesterday's affair should be allowed for the present in view of Military and Turkish situation. Use every endeavour to have matter kept secret locally.

[1] The sinking of the *Audacious* was witnessed by those on board the passenger liner *Olympic* (White Star Line), *en route* from New York to Liverpool. The *Olympic*, which rescued the crew of the *Audacious*, was then detained for several days in Lough Swilly, during which time no one was allowed to land. But a photograph of the sinking battleship, taken by one of the *Olympic's* passengers, was published in the *Philadelphia Public Ledger* on 14 November.

Sir Edward Grey to Sir Louis Mallet: telegram

(Draft, Foreign Office papers: 371/2144)[1]

28 October 1914   10 Downing Street

It is reported that four Turkish gunboats are intending to proceed from Alexandretta.

You should warn Turkish Government that, as long as German officers remain on 'Goeben' and 'Breslau' and Turkish fleet is practically under German control, we must regard movement of Turkish ships as having a hostile intention, and should Turkish gunboats proceed to sea we must in self defence stop them.

As soon as Turkish Government carry out their promise respecting German crews and officers and observe the laws of neutrality with regard to 'Goeben' and 'Breslau' and free the Turkish fleet from German control, we shall regard Turkish ships as neutral, but till then we must protect ourselves against any movements that threaten us.

Winston S. Churchill to Rear-Admiral Hood: telegram

(Hood papers)

29 October 1914   Admiralty
1.00 am

Save ammunition where possible, but don't lose any chance of hitting the enemy. Give your ships the following message: 'The inshore flotilla and squadron have played an appreciable part in the great battle now proceeding. You have shown the Germans that there is one flank they cannot turn.'

You have full discretion to go ahead.

Winston S. Churchill to Prince Louis

(Copy, Churchill papers: 13/27)

29 October 1914   Admiralty

My dear Prince Louis,

This is no ordinary war, but a struggle between nations for life or death. It raises passions between races of the most terrible kind. It effaces the old landmarks and frontiers of our civilization. I cannot further oppose the wish, you have during the last few weeks expressed to me, to be released from the

---

[1] This draft was handwritten by Grey, and initialled by Churchill.

burden of responsibility which you have borne thus far with so much honour and success.

The anxieties and toils which rest upon the naval administration of our country are in themselves enough to try a man's spirit; and when to them are added the ineradicable difficulties of which you speak, I could not at this juncture in fairness ask you to support them.

The Navy of to-day, and still more the Navy of to-morrow, bears the imprint of your work. The enormous impending influx of capital ships, the score of thirty-knot cruisers, the destroyers and submarines unequalled in modern construction which are coming now to hand, are the results of labours which we have had in common, and in which the Board of Admiralty owes so much to your aid.

The first step which secured the timely concentration of the Fleet was taken by you.

I must express publicly my deep indebtedness to you, and the pain I feel at the severance of our three years' official association. In all the circumstances you are right in your decision. The spirit in which you have acted is the same in which Prince Maurice of Battenberg has given his life to our cause and in which your gallant son is now serving in the Fleet.

I beg you to accept my profound respect and that of our colleagues on the Board.

I remain, Yours very sincerely
Winston S Churchill

Prince Louis to Winston S. Churchill
(Churchill papers: 13/27)

29 October 1914   Admiralty

My dear friend,

I am deeply touched by your letter, which shall be treasured by my sons.[1]

I beg of you to release me. I am on the verge of breaking down & I cannot use my brain for anything.

---

[1] Prince George Louis Victor Henry Sergius of Battenberg, 1892–1938. Prince Louis' elder son. Entered Navy, 1905. Lieutenant, 1914. Present at the battles of Heligoland, 1914; Dogger Bank, 1915 and Jutland, 1916. Knighted, 1916. Styled Earl of Medina, 1917. Succeeded his father as 2nd Marquess of Milford Haven, 1921.

Prince Louis Francis Albert Victor Nicholas of Battenberg, 1900–   . Prince Louis' second son. A Naval Cadet, 1913–15. Midshipman at Jutland, 1916. Assumed the surname of Mountbatten in 1917. Supreme Allied Commander, South-East Asia, 1943–6. Created Viscount Mountbatten of Burma, 1946. Viceroy of India, 1947. Created Earl, 1947. Governor-General of India, 1947–8. First Sea Lord, 1955–9. Admiral of the Fleet, 1956. Chief of the Defence Staff, 1959–65.

The C.O.S. can help you to carry out the War adm. 2.S.L. can sign any routine paper.

Do me the favour to assemble the Board for five minutes this afternoon. If you would merely read my letter to you & say that you have accepted it, not another [word], need, or indeed should be spoken & I can leave the room after a silent farewell handshake with my colleagues.

Yrs as Ever
Louis Battenberg

Prince Louis to Winston S. Churchill

(*Churchill papers: 13/27*)

29 October 1914   Admiralty

First Lord,

May I take it that the announcement of my resignation & the 2 letters will appear in tomorrow's morning paper? I want to warn my relations tonight in that case.

You will not misinterpret my silence when we meet here at 5. I cannot trust myself to speak for fear of breaking down. I am leaving London as soon as I have found some small house in the country where I can live.

My thoughts waking & sleeping will be with the fleet & those directing matters from here.

LB

H. H. Asquith to Venetia Stanley

(*Montagu papers*)

29 October 1914   10 Downing Street

. . . After lunch I went to see the King, on Winston's business. As you will see in your morning papers, the resignation of Prince Louis is a fait accompli, and the King agreed to make him a Privy Councillor, to show that there was no lack of confidence in his integrity & loyalty. Poor man, I am afraid he is broken-hearted, but he admits that he had become quite unfit for his work. It was a much more difficult job to persuade the Sovereign to consent to his being succeeded by Jacky Fisher. He gave me an exhaustive & really eloquent catalogue of the old man's crimes & defects, and thought that his appointment would be very badly received by the bulk of the Navy, & that he would be almost certain to get on badly with Winston. On the last point, I have some misgivings of my own, but Winston won't have anybody else, and there is no one among the available Admirals in whom I have sufficient confidence to force him upon him. So I stuck to my guns, and the King (who behaved very nicely) gave a reluctant consent. I hope his apprehensions won't turn out to be well founded.

Since I began this, I have had Grey & Winston with me, and W. read us a private letter he has just got from French,[1] who is extraordinarily confident, & talks of being in Bruges & Ostend in a week's time. . . .

Lord Stamfordham: memorandum
(Royal Archives)

29 October 1914   Windsor Castle

The King saw the Prime Minister who repeated much what he had said to Lord S. on the day previous in favour of Lord Fisher. The King declared that he eliminated all personal feelings: his one wish was that what *was* done should be in the best interests of the Navy. The Service did not trust Lord Fisher and HM feared his return to the Admiralty would be detrimental to the Navy. He could not however oppose his Ministers in this selection but felt it his duty to record his protest. The Prime Minister rejoined 'Perhaps a less severe term "misgivings" might be used by Your Majesty'. Later in the day the King signed the appointment and wrote as follows to Mr Asquith:

George V to H. H. Asquith
(Royal Archives)

29 October 1914   Buckingham Palace

Dear Prime Minister,

Following our conversation of this afternoon, I should like to note that while approving the proposed appointment of Lord Fisher as First Sea Lord, I do so with some reluctance and misgivings.

I readily acknowledge his great ability and administrative power but at the same time I cannot help feeling that his presence at the Admiralty will not inspire the Navy with that confidence which ought to exist, especially when we are engaged in so momentous a War.

I hope that my fears may prove to be groundless.

George R I

[1] Quoted on pages 218–19.

Sir Arthur Wilson to Winston S. Churchill

(*Churchill papers: 13/27*)

29 October 1914   Royal Naval Club
                                                   Portsmouth

Dear Mr Churchill,

With reference to our conversation last night I think you had better leave me to go on working much as I am doing now, except that I should like to have a room set apart for me near the War room, and a confidential clerk well acquainted with the different departments who could get me any information I want. I would then work simply as Fisher's slave to tackle any problems he likes to set me.

I do not want either pay or position, and I attach great importance to its not being known publicly that I have anything to do with the Admiralty until after Heligoland has been taken, as although I have not talked much, too many people know my ideas about Heligoland and they would be sure to begin discussing whether I was going to carry out my policy or not and then some clumsy newspaperman would mention it and give the show away. I am certain that I shall be more useful if I am kept as much as possible out of sight and not burdened with the care of any department.

                                                   Arthur Wilson

Sir Edward Grey to Sir Louis Mallet: telegram

(*Grey papers*)

29 October 1914   Foreign Office

I am waiting to hear what Russian attitude will be in face of attack by Turkish torpedo boats without provocation & without warning upon Russian ports & shipping.[1]

Unless Grand Vizier is strong enough to arrest & punish those responsible for this outrage & to make immediate reparation to Russia I do not see how war can be avoided, but we shall not take the first step.

[1] On 27 October 1914 the *Goeben*, the *Breslau*, the Turkish cruiser *Hamidieh*, and a division of Turkish destroyers all flying the Turkish flag and commanded by the German Admiral Souchon, sailed into the Black Sea. On 29 October they bombarded the Russian ports of Odessa and Theodosia; on 30 October they bombarded Sebastopol and Novorossiisk.

Sir Louis Mallet to Foreign Office: telegram

(*Copy, Foreign Office papers: 371/2145*)

29 October 1914   Constantinople
9.10 pm
Urgent
Confidential

. . . I have discussed the question with my French colleague and my Russian colleague.

In view of probability that attack on Odessa was carried out by Germans without full authority of Ottoman Government, we agreed to suggest to our Governments that they should instruct us to inform Ottoman Government that they must choose between rupture with Triple Entente or dismissal of German naval and military missions.

Sir George Buchanan to Sir Edward Grey: telegram

(*Copy, Foreign Office papers: 371/2145*)

29 October 1914   Petrograd

. . . Minister for Foreign Affairs, who is somewhat perturbed by Turkey's participation in the war, said that Russia would remain on the defensive, and that no troops would be diverted from German frontier. He believes that Russia has some 150,000 troops in Caucasus. Turkish action, he said, would unroll the whole Eastern question and entail final settlement of question of Straits. For this reason war is likely to be welcomed by large section of Russian public, who were afraid that Russia would gain no solid advantages from the war with Austria and Germany.

J. A. Pease: diary

(*Gainford papers*)

30 October 1914

. . . Position with Turkey very strained; and steps authorised to hold or fire on Turkish gunboats outside Alexandria and prevent their passing into Red Sea.

Sir Louis Mallet to Sir Edward Grey: telegram
(*Foreign Office papers: 371/2145*)

30 October 1914   Constantinople

In consequence of attack by Ottoman fleet on open part of Theodosia and on gunboat in the port of Odessa, Russian Ambassador has received instructions to leave Constantinople with all staff of embassy and consulates in Turkey, and to hand over Russian interests to Italian Ambassador.[1]

Following your instructions, I propose to ask for my passports also.

Sir Louis Mallet to Sir Edward Grey: telegram
(*Copy, Foreign Office papers: 371/2145*)

30 October 1914   Constantinople

Russian Ambassador asked for his passports this afternoon, and I and my French colleague have followed suit.

I hope to leave with Embassy Staff to-morrow night via Dedeagatch and Salonica. . . .

Sir Edward Grey to Sir Louis Mallet: telegram
(*Copy, Foreign Office papers: 371/2145*)

30 October 1914   Foreign Office

Russian Ambassador at Constantinople has been instructed by his Government, in view of hostile acts which have been committed, to leave Constantinople with all his staff and to take the necessary measures for the departure of Russian consuls, leaving protection of Russian subjects and interests to care of Italian Ambassador.

I am awaiting views of Russian Minister for Foreign Affairs as to the proposal put forward by you and your two colleagues in your telegram No. 1089; but should your Russian colleague leave you should yourself send in a note to the Sublime Porte to say that His Majesty's Government have learnt with the utmost surprise of the wanton attacks made upon open and undefended towns of a friendly country without any warning and without

[1] Camillo Eugenio Garroni, 1852–1935. Marquis. Prefect of Genoa, 1896–1912. Senator, 1905–35. Ambassador to Constantinople, 1912–15 and 1920–2. Headed the Italian delegation at the Conference of Lausanne, 1923–4; he was the Italian signatory of the Treaty of Lausanne with Turkey. A frequent speaker in the Senate, his main concerns were public administration and foreign policy.

the slightest provocation, constituting an unprecedented violation of the most ordinary rules of international law, comity, and usage. Russia, in conjunction with her allies France and Great Britain, has shown the utmost patience and forbearance in face of repeated violations of the rules of neutrality by Turkey, and in face of most provocative acts, amounting in reality to acts of hostility as in the invasion of the Sinai Peninsula by Bedouin tribes from Turkish territory. Such a situation cannot be prolonged, and it is evident that there is no chance of a return to a proper observance of neutrality so long as the German naval and military missions remain at Constantinople.

Unless, therefore, the Turkish Government will divest themselves of all responsibility for these unprovoked acts of hostility by dismissing the German military and naval missions and fulfilling their often repeated promises about the German crews of the 'Goeben' and 'Breslau', and will give you a satisfactory reply to this effect within twelve hours from the date of the delivery of the note, you should ask for your passports and leave Constantinople with the staff of the Embassy and such other British officials as you may consider it desirable should accompany you.

Winston S. Churchill to Lord Fisher

(*Admiralty papers: 137/96*)

30 October 1914   Admiralty

I.S.L.

Admiral Slade[1] shd be asked to state his opinion on the possibility & advisability of a bombardment of the sea face forts of the Dardanelles. It is a good thing to give a prompt blow.

WSC

Sir Edmond Slade to Winston S. Churchill

(*Admiralty Papers 137/96*)

30 October 1914   Admiralty

A bombardment of the sea face of the Dardanelles Forts offers very little prospect of obtaining any effect commensurate with the risk to the ships.

---

[1] Edmond John Warre Slade, 1859–1928. Entered Navy, 1872. Director of Naval Intelligence, 1907–8. Commander-in-Chief, East Indies, 1909–12. Knighted, 1911. Vice-Admiral, 1914. On Special Service in connection with Oil Fuel Supplies, 1912–14. Admiralty-nominated Director, Anglo-Persian Oil Company, 1914. Chairman, Diversion of Shipping Committee, 1916. Admiral, 1917.

The Forts are difficult to locate from the sea at anything like the range at which they will have to be engaged.

The guns in the Forts at the entrance are old Krupp and would probably be outranged by those in the Fleet, but it is not known where the new guns 16·5" Krupp said to have been mounted by the Germans are situated.

It may be possible to make a demonstration to draw the fire of these guns & make them disclose themselves trusting to lack of training of the gunners —but it would not be advisable to risk serious damage to any of the battle cruisers as long as the 'Goeben' is effective—*A little target practice from 15 to 12 thousand yards might be useful.*[1]

Other points at which they can be struck are:

1. A ship to be sent to Akaba to shell the wells and the stores said to be collected there.[2]
2. The force at Bahrein to be moved up to the bar of the Shatt al Arab at once to be ready to land directly the ultimatum expires.[3]
3. To send a ship to El Arish to command the coast road to Egypt—

E. J. W. Slade

Sir John Jellicoe to Admiralty: telegram

(*Copy, Churchill papers: 13/40*)

30 October 1914
12.35 am

Muster of ship's company of AUDACIOUS shows all hands were saved. Submit that when loss becomes public this fact may be announced to save anxiety on the part of relatives.

[1] Churchill underlined this sentence in red ink.

[2] Churchill wrote against this suggestion the one word 'Minerva'. The British light cruiser *Minerva*, commanded by Captain Warleigh, was at once ordered to go to Akaba, where, on 1 November 1914, she bombarded the town.

[3] On 7 November 1914 the Government of India landed a military force at Fao, at the head of the Persian Gulf. Basra was captured on 22 November, and a British officer, Major Brownlow, was appointed Military Governor. On 7 December, British control of the area was completed when the Turkish garrison at Kurna—at the confluence of the Tigris and Euphrates—surrendered. In one month of war, five British officers and six Indian soldiers were killed: there were over 300 Turkish dead.

Admiralty to all Admirals concerned: telegram

(*Copy, Admiralty papers: 137/96*)

31 October 1914   Admiralty
12.35 am

Orders sent Ambassador Constantinople 8.15 p.m. October 30 to present ultimatum to Turkey expiring at end of 12 hours. Do not yourself commence hostilities without further orders.

Admiralty to all ships: telegram

(*Copy, Admiralty papers: 137/96*)

31 October 1914   Admiralty
5.05 pm

Commence hostilities at once against Turkey. Acknowledge.

H. H. Asquith to Venetia Stanley

(*Montagu papers*)

31 October 1914   10 Downing Street

. . . The Turk has now under German pressure taken a hand, and interesting developments ought to follow. Greece is quite likely to come in, & it will become increasingly hard for Italy & Rumania to keep aloof. Few things wd. give me greater pleasure than to see the Turkish Empire finally disappear from Europe, & Constantinople either become Russian (which I think is its proper destiny) or if that is impossible neutralised and made a free port. . . .

Press Bureau statement

(*Foreign Office papers: 371/2144*)

31 October 1914
11.15 pm

The Foreign Office make the following announcement:—

At the beginning of the war, the British Government gave definite assurances that, if TURKEY remained neutral, her independence and integrity would be respected during the war and in the terms of peace. In this, France and Russia concurred.

The British Government have since then endeavoured with the greatest patience and forbearance to preserve friendly relations in spite of increasing breaches of neutrality on the part of the Turkish Government at Constantinople in the case of the German vessels in the Straits.

On Thursday, 29th October 1914, the British Government learnt with the utmost regret that Turkish ships of war had, without any declaration of war, without warning, and without provocation of any sort, made wanton attacks upon open undefended towns, in the Black Sea, of a friendly country, thus committing an unprecedented violation of the most ordinary rules of international law, comity and usage.

Ever since the German men-of-war, the 'GOEBEN' and 'BRESLAU', took refuge in Constantinople, the attitude of the Turkish Government towards Great Britain has caused surprise and some uneasiness. Promises made by the Turkish Government to send away the German Officers and crews of the 'Goeben' and 'Breslau' have never been fulfilled. It was well known that the Turkish Minister of War was decidedly pro-German in his sympathies, but it was confidently hoped that the saner counsels of his Colleagues, who had had experience of the friendship which Great Britain has always shown towards the Turkish Government, would have prevailed and prevented that Government from entering upon the very risky policy of taking a part in the conflict on the side of Germany.

Since the war, German Officers in large numbers have invaded Constantinople, have usurped the authority of the Government and have been able to coerce the Sultan's[1] Ministers into taking up a policy of aggression.

Great Britain, as well as France and Russia, has watched these proceedings patiently, protesting against the many acts which have been constantly committed contrary to neutrality, and warning the Government of the Sultan against the danger in which they were placing the future of the Ottoman Empire. Vigorously assisted by the Ambassadors of Germany and Austria,[2] the German military elements in Constantinople have been persistently doing their utmost to force Turkey into war, both by their activities in the service of the Turks and by the bribes of which they have been so lavish.

The Minister of War, with his German advisers, has lately prepared an armed force for an attack upon Egypt. The Mosul and Damascus Army Corps have, since their mobilization, been constantly sending troops South,

---

[1] Mehmed Reshad Effendi, 1844–1918. Succeeded his elder brother Abdul Hamid as Sultan, 1909. Known as Mehmed V. He had no influence on Turkish policy, which was firmly under the control of the Young Turks.

[2] Markgraf Johann Pallavicini, 1848–1941. Austrian Ambassador in Constantinople, 1906–18.

preparatory to an invasion of Egypt and the Suez Canal from Akaba and Gaza. A large body of Bedouin Arabs has been called out and armed to assist in this venture, and some of these have crossed the Sinai frontier. Transport has been collected and roads have been prepared up to the frontier of Egypt. Mines have been despatched to be laid in the Gulf of Akaba. The notorious Sheikh Aziz Shawish[1] has published and disseminated through Syria, and probably India, an inflammatory document urging Mahommedans to fight against Great Britain. Dr. Prueffer,[2] who was so long engaged in intrigues in CAIRO against the British occupation, and is now attached to the German Embassy in Constantinople, has been busily occupied in SYRIA trying to incite the people to take part in this conflict. Aggressive action was certain to be the result of the activity of the numerous German Officers employed in the Turkish Army and acting under the orders of the German Government, who thus have succeeded in forcing the hands of the advisers of the Sultan.

German intrigue cannot influence the loyalty to Great Britain of the 70 millions of Mahommedans in India and the feeling of the Mahommedan inhabitants of Egypt. They must look with detestation on misguided action under foreign influence at Constantinople, which will inevitably lead to the disintegration of the Turkish Empire, and which shows such forgetfulness of the many occasions on which Great Britain has shown friendship to Turkey. They must feel bitterly the degeneration of their co-religionists who can thus be dominated against their will by German influences, and many of them realize that, when Turkey is pushed into war by Germany, they must dissociate themselves from a course of action that is so prejudicial to the position of Turkey itself.

The Turkish Government, summarily and without notice, on Friday shut off telegraphic communication with the British Embassy at Constantinople. This is no doubt the prelude to further acts of aggression on their part, and the British Government must take whatever action is required to protect British interests, British territory, and also Egypt from attacks that have been made and are threatened.

[1] Sheikh Abdul Aziz Shawish, 1876–1929. Born in Alexandria, of Tunisian origin. Scholar, writer, journalist and politician, he taught for a while at Cambridge University. Government Inspector of Schools, Cairo. Editor of *al Liwa*. Imprisoned by the British Government; in exile in Constantinople, 1912. Employed by the Ottoman Government as a propaganda agent in Berlin, 1914–18. Returned to Cairo, 1919.

[2] Curt Prueffer, 1881–1959. Doctor of Philosophy, 1905. Served in the German Consulate-General, Cairo, 1907–14. German Foreign Office representative with the Turkish Fourth Army, 1914–17. Attached to the German Embassy, Constantinople 1917–20. Served in the Foreign Office, Berlin, 1920–4 and 1930–9. Consul-General Tiflis, Georgia, 1925–7. Minister, Addis Ababa, 1929–30. Ambassador, Rio de Janeiro, 1939–42.

Winston S. Churchill to Sir John Jellicoe: telegram

(*Copy, Churchill papers: 13/40*)

31 October 1914   Admiralty
2.30 am

Nothing has reached Germany yet, and here people who yesterday were fully informed believe report to be a hoax.

Hold OLYMPIC as long as you like, and make AUDACIOUS Officers wire reassuring telegrams to their relatives in response to enquiries.

Sir John Jellicoe to Winston S. Churchill: telegram

(*Copy, Churchill papers: 13/40*)

31 October 1914
3.00 am
Secret and Personal

I saw Mr. Schwab,[1] Head of Bethlehem Steel Works, today.

He has arrived in OLYMPIC to interview Secretary of State for War regarding certain contracts.

I have allowed him to land and have requested him to call on you in regard to certain propositions he has respecting sale of ships to British Admiralty and construction of new ships especially torpedo boat destroyers and submarines.

Sir Louis Mallet to Sir Edward Grey: telegram

(*Copy, Foreign Office papers: 371/2145*)

31 October 1914   Constantinople
Very Confidential

. . . United States Ambassador advises me in confidence to go as soon as possible. From information which is at his disposal there is no chance of favourable solution.

[1] Charles Michael Schwab, 1862–1939. President, Carnegie Steel Corporation, 1897–1903. President, United States Steel Corporation, 1901–3. Chairman, Bethlehem Steel Corporation, 1903–39. Coming to England on board the *Olympic*, October 1914, he witnessed the sinking of the *Audacious*; on reaching London he pledged the support of his factories to the allied cause. Built submarines for the Royal Navy in 5½ months, instead of the usual 14 months; they were assembled in Montreal to avoid breaching the neutrality of the United States. In charge of America's 'Shipbuilding Crusade', 1917–18. Hon Vice-President of the Iron and Steel Institute of Great Britain, 1926–39.

W.C.3—R

Winston S. Churchill to Lord Fisher
(Admiralty Papers 137/96)

31 October 1914   Admiralty

We ought to have a means of striking them ready prepared.

WSC

Lord Fisher to Vice-Admiral Oliver

31 October 1914   Admiralty

Have we anything prepared? Please consider the matter & discuss with me.

F

November 1914

Lord Fisher to Lord Esher

(*Esher papers*)

1 November 1914   Ritz Hotel
SECRET
Burn

My beloved Friend,

Thanks for your dear letter! Isn't it fun being back?

Some d——d fools thought I was dead & buried! I am busy getting even with some of them! I did 22 hours work yesterday but 2 hours sleep not enough so I shall slow down!

SECRET The King said to Winston (I suppose dissuading!) that the job would kill me. Winston was perfectly lovely in his instant reply:

'Sir, I cannot imagine a more glorious death'! Wasn't that delicious? but burn please!

Yours for ever more
Fisher

Winston S. Churchill to Vice-Admiral Carden: telegram

(*Draft, Admiralty Papers 137/96*)

1 November 1914   Admiralty

Without risking the Allied ships a demonstration is to be made by bombardment on the earliest suitable day by your armoured ships & the two French battleships against the forts at the entrance of the Dardanelles at a range of 24000–12000 yards.

The ships shd keep underway. Approaching as soon after daylight as possible.

A retirement shd be made before the fire from the forts becomes effective. The ships guns should outrange the older guns mounted in the Forts.

Latest information about guns herewith.

1 S.L. concurs.

WSC

Sir David Beatty to Ethel Beatty

(Beatty papers)

2 November 1914   H.M.S. Lion

They have resurrected old Fisher. Well, I think he is the best they could have done, but I wish he was ten years younger. He still has fine zeal, energy, and determination, coupled with low cunning, which is eminently desirable just now. He also has courage and will take any responsibility. He will recognise that his position is absolutely secure and will rule the Admiralty and Winston with a heavy hand. He has patriotism, and is a firm believer in the good qualities of the Navy, that it can do anything and will go anywhere, and please God we shall change our present method for a strong offensive policy.

H. H. Asquith to Venetia Stanley

(Montagu papers)

2 November 1914   10 Downing Street

. . . Winston is very angry about the torpedoing of the 'Hermes'[1] in the Straits of Dover. She was ordered to come back in the dark, when she would have been perfectly safe, but waited until daybreak & was caught. The Captain[2] will probably be court-martialled. On the other hand, he is pleased to think that he will at last catch the 'Königsberg': she is up a river in East Africa, & ought to fall an easy prey to the 'Chatham' (Clemmie has had a slight relapse, & cannot have us to dinner to-night).

I am just going to have a grand conference here about closing the North Sea: Jellicoe, Fisher, Winston, Grey, Kitchener & I. It will be interesting to hear the different points of view. . . .

Sir Edward Grey: note

(Foreign Office papers: 371/2145)

2 November 1914   Foreign Office

Tewfik should be told tomorrow that the only way to stop further hostilities is to inform his Govn't to send away the German missions.

EG

[1] The *Hermes* a seaplane carrier, was torpedoed eight miles west-north-west of Calais on October 30. Nearly all her crew were saved.

[2] Charles Laverock Lambe, 1875–1953. Entered Navy, 1889. Commander, 1908; Captain, 1916. Transferred to the Royal Naval Air Service, June 1916, with the rank of Wing-Captain. Colonel, Royal Air Force, 1918. Commanded RAF Halton, 1924–8. Air Officer Commanding Coastal Area, 1928–31. Knighted, 1931.

Winston S. Churchill to John Churchill
(*John Churchill papers*)

2 November 1914   Admiralty

My dear Jack,

I hear from Freddie [Guest] that they have had to put the regiment into the line; so I write this hoping you will tell them all that I shd be proud to be with them & that I am sure no part of the front will be more firmly maintained.[1]

God guard you.

Your loving brother
W

Winston S. Churchill: statement for the Press
(*Churchill papers: 13/29*)

2 November 1914   Admiralty

During the last week the Germans have scattered mines indiscriminately in the open sea on the main trade route from America to Liverpool via the North of Ireland. Two peaceful merchant ships have already been blown up with loss of life by this agency.[2] But for the warnings given by British Cruisers, other British and neutral merchant and passenger vessels would have been destroyed. These mines cannot have been laid by any German ship of war. They have been laid by some merchant vessel flying a neutral flag which has come along the trade route as if for the purposes of peaceful commerce and while profiting to the full by the immunity enjoyed by neutral merchant ships, have wantonly and recklessly endangered the lives of all who travel on the sea, regardless of whether they are friend or foe, civilian or military in character.

The operations of the British Fleet are hampered and spied upon by numerous trawlers and pseudo trading vessels under Dutch, Danish, Swedish or Norwegian flags, which report their movements and have frequently been

[1] On 30 October 1915 the Oxfordshire Hussars went into action for the first time, near Messines, south of Ypres. Jack Churchill took the first squadron forward to the front line. Five men were wounded that day; one later died of his wounds.

[2] On 26 October the French steamer *Amiral Ganteaume*, carrying 2,500 French refugees from Calais to Le Havre, struck a floating mine off Cap Gris Nez; over thirty lives were lost. The survivors were rescued by a British steamer. On 27 October the British steamer *Manchester Commerce*, carrying cargo from Manchester to Montreal, struck a mine near Tory Island. The captain and thirteen men were drowned; thirty of the crew were saved.

found operating in conjunction with German submarines. Minelaying under
a neutral flag and reconnaissance conducted by hospital ships and neutral
vessels are the ordinary features of German naval warfare.

In these circumstances, having regard to the great interests entrusted to
the British Navy, to the safety of peaceful commerce on the high seas, and
to the maintenance within the limits of International Law of trade between
neutral countries, the Admiralty feel it necessary to adopt exceptional
measures appropriate to the novel conditions under which this war is being
waged. They therefore give notice that the whole of the North Sea must be
considered a military area. Within this area merchant shipping of all kinds,
traders of all countries, fishing craft, and all other vessels will be exposed to
the gravest dangers from mines which it has been necessary to lay and from
warships searching vigilantly by night and day for suspicious craft. All merchant and fishing vessels of every description are hereby warned of the
dangers they encounter by entering this area except in strict accordance with
Admiralty directions. Every effort will be made to convey this warning to
neutral countries and to vessels on the sea, but from the 1st of November
onwards the Admiralty announce that all ships passing a line drawn between
the Shetlands and Ireland do so at their own peril.

Ships of all countries wishing to trade to and from Norway, the Baltic,
Denmark, and Holland are advised to come, if inward bound, by the English
Channel and the Straits of Dover. There they will be given sailing directions
which will pass them safely, so far as Great Britain is concerned, up the East
Coast of England to Farn Island [off the coast of Northumberland] whence a
safe route will if possible be given to Lindesnes [Norway]. From this point
they should turn North or South according to their destination, keeping as
near the coast as possible. The converse applies to vessels outward bound. By
strict adherence to these routes the commerce of all countries will be able to
reach its destination in safety, so far as Great Britain is concerned, but any
straying even for a few miles from the course thus indicated may be followed
by fatal consequences.

H. H. Asquith to Venetia Stanley
(*Montagu papers*)

2 November 1914   10 Downing Street
Midnight

. . . After I wrote to you this afternoon, we had our conference in the
Cabinet room at 5: a curious conclave. E. Grey & I, Winston, Kitchener,
Fisher, & Jellicoe (who appeared out of space, on terra firma for the 1st

time for 3 months). It went on for nearly an hour, & was quite interesting: I listened & didn't say much, but watched the different faces; K's, brick-red, short-nosed, blue-eyed; Fisher strangely un-English, twisted mouth, round-eyed, suggesting the legend (which is I believe quite untrue) that he had a Cingalese mother: Jellicoe, small, alert robin-eyed, of (it is said) gipsy parentage; Winston, whom most people wd. call ugly, but whose eyes, when he is really interested, have the glow of genius; and Grey with his well-cut, hawk-like visage, now rather pinched & drawn. . . . Our main topic was the closing of the North Sea to all vessels, except those wh. are willing to make their way along our carefully selected route. But there were lots of other things: and one felt at once the difference made by the substitution of Fisher for poor L.B—élan, dash, initiative, a new spirit. That is all to the good. . . .

Winston S. Churchill to Vice-Admiral Yashiro:[1] *telegram*

(*Copy, Churchill papers: 13/27*)

2 November 1914   Admiralty
Most Secret

Early in the New Year we hope to be strong enough to enter the Baltic and greatly to increase the severity of the naval pressure upon the Germans. By that time not only will Tsingtau have fallen but probably the German outlying cruisers will have been destroyed.[2] We shd. like our Japanese allies to look forward to this situation in order to consider how the powerful naval aid they are giving in the early stages of the war may be made to play a decisive part in its conclusion.

Winston S. Churchill to Vice-Admiral Yashiro: telegram

(*Copy, Churchill papers: 13/39*)

3 November 1914   Admiralty

Scharnhorst, Gneisenau, Nurnberg, Leipzig, Dresden have been located near Valparaiso coaling and provisioning. This Squadron is presumably concentrated for some serious operation. We are concentrating Glasgow,

[1] Rokurō Yashiro, 1861–1930. A 2nd Lieutenant in the Imperial Japanese Navy during the Sino-Japanese war, 1894–5. Captain, commanding the *Asama* during the Russo-Japanese war, 1904–5. Minister of the Navy with the rank of Admiral, 1914–16. He won fame by exposing a bribery scandal in the Imperial Navy early in 1914.

[2] Tsingtau, the German port on the China Coast, surrendered to a joint Anglo-Japanese force on 7 November 1914, after a two months' siege. The principal German cruiser at large, the *Emden*, was sunk off the Cocos Islands, on 9 November 1914.

Good Hope, Canopus, Monmouth & Defence on the S.W. Coast of S. America, hoping to bring them to battle. Konigsberg is effectively blockaded in Rufigi River near Dar-es-Salaam. There are therefore only Emden & Karlsruhe to be accounted for, and approximate position of both is known. We hope that the Japanese Admiralty may now find it possible to move some of their Squadrons Eastward in order to intercept the German Squadron and prevent its return to Asiatic or Australian waters. For instance, could Izumo & Newcastle form a junction off the W. Coast of N. America with two more Japanese ships and work down the Coast by the Galapagos Islands? Could the Sandwich Islands and the Society Islands be searched and guarded by other Japanese vessels to prevent all coaling facilities? We indicate our views in order to obtain yours and to concert common action.

Allan Maclean[1] *to Admiralty: telegram*
(*Churchill papers: 13/39*)

3 November 1914   Valparaiso
6.10 pm

Chilean Admiral[2] just informed me that German Admiral[3] states his ships met GOOD HOPE, MONMOUTH, GLASGOW and OTRANTO at sunset on Sunday north of Coronel in thick and wicked weather. Fight ensued.

After about one hour's action MONMOUTH turned over and sank. GOOD HOPE, GLASGOW and OTRANTO drew off into the darkness GOOD HOPE on fire. An explosion was heard. It is believed she sank. German ships engaged included SCHARNHORST, GNEISENAU, NURNBERG.

[1] Allan Maclean, 1858–1918. Entered Consular Service, 1893. Consul at Casablanca, 1893–1905; Bilbao, 1906; Danzig, 1910. Consul-General, Valparaiso, 1913–18.
[2] Luis Alberto Goñi, 1851–1928. Entered the Chilean Navy, 1866. In 1908 he headed the Chilean Naval Mission to London, which established important links between the British and Chilean Navies. Vice-Admiral, Commander-in-Chief of the Chilean Navy, 1913–16.
[3] Maximilian von Spee, 1861–1914. Entered German Navy, 1878. Chief of Staff, German North Sea Command, 1908–12. Commanded the German Far Eastern Squadron, 1912–14. Drowned, Battle of Falkland Islands, 8 December 1914.

Sir Frederick Sturdee, Lord Fisher and Winston S. Churchill to Captain
Leatham:[1] telegram

(*Copy, Churchill papers: 13/39*)

3 November 1914   Admiralty
6.20 pm

DEFENCE to proceed with all possible despatch to join Admiral Cradock
on West Coast of America.[2]

Lord Fisher and Winston S. Churchill to Sir Christopher Cradock: telegram

(*Churchill papers: 13/39*)

3 November 1914   Admiralty
6.55 pm

DEFENCE has been ordered to join your flag with all despatch. GLAS-
GOW should find or keep in touch with the enemy. You should keep touch
with GLASGOW concentrating the rest of your Squadron including
CANOPUS. It is important you should effect your junction with DEFENCE
at earliest possible moment subject to keeping touch with GLASGOW and
enemy. Enemy supposes you at Corcovados Bay. Acknowledge.

Sir Edward Grey to Sir George Buchanan, Sir Francis Bertie and
Sir Conyngham Greene

(*Foreign Office papers: 371/2145*)

4 November 1914   Foreign Office
Sir,
    Tewfik Pasha called upon me this afternoon, and informed me that he had
received instructions to ask for his passports, as His Majesty's Ambassador
had already left Constantinople.
    I expressed to Tewfik Pasha my personal regret at our official relations
being terminated, as he had always acted in a loyal, straightforward, and
friendly manner, and I had much appreciated the intercourse which we had

---

[1] Eustace La Trobe Leatham, 1870–1935. Captain, 1909. Commanded HMS *Defence*,
battle of the Falkland Islands, 1914. Present at the Battle of Jutland, 1916. Rear-Admiral,
1920. Vice-Admiral, 1925.

[2] This decision to reinforce Cradock was taken, unknown to the Admiralty, after Cradock
had been drowned and his squadron defeated off Coronel. This telegram was actually sent
from the Admiralty ten minutes *after* Consul Maclean, in Valparaiso, had telegraphed the
news of the defeat to London.

together during the past few years. I informed Tewfik Pasha that if his Government wished that hostilities between the two countries should cease, the only chance was to dismiss the German naval and military missions, and especially the officers and crews of the 'Goeben' and 'Breslau.' So long as German officers remained in complete naval and military control at Constantinople, it was clear that they would continue to make war against us.

I am, &c.

E. Grey

H.H. Asquith to George V
(*Royal Archives*)

4 November 1914   10 Downing Street

Mr Asquith, with his humble duty to Your Majesty, has the honour to report that the Cabinet met to-day.

Sir John French's telegram is the most satisfactory that we have received from him for some time. The French troops appear, at last, to be actively co-operating in the offensive; the enemy presents all the signs of weariness & demoralisation; and Sir John declares that both he & General Foch are of opinion that the movement towards Calais has been frustrated.

On the other hand, Mr Churchill had to report that the Navy had sustained a serious reverse near Valparaiso on the W. coast of S. America on Sunday last. Five German cruisers—the Gneisenau, Scharnhorst, Nuremberg, Dresden & Leipzig—encountered the Good Hope, Monmouth & Glasgow, and after a short engagement sunk the two former, & inflicted damage on the latter. The Good Hope was Admiral Cradock's flag-ship. This mishap is the more regrettable as it would seem that the Admiral was acting in disobedience to his instructions, which were express to the effect that he must concentrate his whole squadron, including the Canopus & Defence, and run no risk of being caught in a condition of inferiority. The whereabouts of the Canopus has not yet been ascertained. The Cabinet are of opinion that this incident, like the escape of the Goeben, the loss of the Cressy & her two sister-cruisers, and that of the Hermes last week, is not creditable to the officers of the Navy.

The motive for the appearance of German cruisers off Lowestoft yesterday is somewhat obscure: apparently they were engaged in laying mines. Their shooting was bad, & did little damage to the Halcyon, and on the appearance of the Undaunted & her two consorts, the German ships quickly retired into their own waters. Unfortunately, a British submarine was sunk through coming into contact with one of the newly laid mines.

The bombardment of one of the Dardanelles forts by the Anglo-French squadron resulted in the destruction of a magazine. In view of the probable appearance of the German squadron, lately at Valparaiso, on the Atlantic trade route, two battle-cruisers are being despatched from Admiral Jellicoe's fleet. . . .

The Cabinet came to the conclusion that a formal declaration of war against Turkey could no longer be postponed.

The scheme of Pensions for the widows & children of soldiers dying in the war was re-considered, and a minimum pension of 7/6 for a childless widow agreed to.

Sir Frederick Sturdee, Lord Fisher and Winston S. Churchill
to Sir John Jellicoe: telegram

(*Copy, Churchill papers: 13/39*)

4 November 1914   Admiralty
12.40 pm

Order INVINCIBLE and INFLEXIBLE to fill up with coal at once and proceed to Berehaven with all despatch. They are urgently needed for foreign service. . . .

Winston S. Churchill and Lord Fisher to Rear-Admiral Stoddart:[1] *telegram*

(*Copy, Churchill papers: 13/39*)

4 November 1914   Admiralty
1.35 pm

In view of reported sinking of GOOD HOPE and MONMOUTH by SCHARNHORST and GNEISENAU off Coronel November 1st., armoured ships on S.E. Coast America must concentrate at once.

CARNARVON CORNWALL should join DEFENCE off Montevideo CANOPUS GLASGOW OTRANTO have been ordered if possible to join you there. KENT from Sierra Leone also has been ordered to join your flag via Abrolhos.

Endeavour to get into communication with them. Enemy will most likely come on to the Rio trade route. Reinforcements will meet you shortly from England.

[1] Archibald Peile Stoddart, 1860–1939. Commanded HMS *Thrush* at the bombardment of the Palace at Zanzibar, 1896. Rear-Admiral, HMS *Carnarvon*, in the action off the Falkland Islands, December 1914. Rear-Admiral in the Home Fleet, Devonport, 1915.

Lord Fisher and Winston S. Churchill to Captain Luce[1] and Captain Edwards:[2]
telegram
(Copy, Churchill papers: 13/39)

4 November 1914   Admiralty
2.30 pm

You should make the best of your way to join DEFENCE near Montevideo. Keep wide of track to avoid being brought to action by superior force.

Winston S. Churchill and Sir Frederick Sturdee to HMS Canopus: telegram
(Copy, Churchill papers: 13/39)

4 November 1914   Admiralty
2.30 pm

In view of reported sinking of GOOD HOPE and MONMOUTH by SCHARNHORST and GNEISENAU on 1st November you should make the best of your way to join DEFENCE near Montevideo. Keep wide of track to avoid being brought to action by superior force.

If attacked however Admiralty is confident ship will in all circumstances be fought to the last as imperative to damage enemy whatever may be consequences.

H. H. Asquith to Venetia Stanley
(Montagu papers)

4 November 1914   10 Downing Street

. . . Poor Winston is in for a run of real bad luck, as tho' the sinking of the Hermes & the loss of the submarine yesterday were not enough for one week. I was saying at lunch to-day to Ll. George & Masterman (who both agreed) that one of the paradoxes of the War is that the Germans are as much better than *us* (what grammar!) on the sea, as we are than *them* on land. Fancy their being able last Sunday to get together 5 excellent cruisers outside Valparaiso on the W. coast of S. America, to engage our squadron in battle, & to sink 2 of our most useful cruisers—the Monmouth & the Good Hope (the latter the Admiral's—Cradock—flagship) & injure a third —the Glasgow. And all through sheer stupidity, for if the Admiral had

---

[1] John Luce, 1870–1932. Captain, commanding HMS *Glasgow*, 1912–16. Admiral Superintendent, Malta Dockyard, 1921–4. High Sheriff of Wiltshire, 1930–1.

[2] Herbert MacIver Edwards,   –1955. Lieutenant, Royal Navy, 1897. Commander, Signal School, Chatham, 1907. Captain, HMS *Otranto*, 1914. Chief Staff Officer, Naval Inter-Allied Mission of Control, 1918. Superintendent of Naval Establishments, Sydney, Australia, 1919–23. Rear-Admiral, 1924.

followed his instructions he would never have met them with an inferior force, but would have been by now on the other side of S. America with the Canopus & Defence, in overwhelming superiority. I am afraid the poor man has gone to the bottom: otherwise he richly deserves to be court-martialled. It is a poor consolation to know that the Königsberg is blocked in in her East African river, and that no less than 9 ships are hunting the elusive undefeated Emden. Moreover the operations outside Yarmouth yesterday, when the German shells nearly reached the shore, & their cruisers sailed away unharmed into the twilight, are far from glorious for the Navy. As I told Winston last night (and he is not the least to blame) it is time that he bagged something, & broke some crockery. The shelling of a fort at the Dardanelles seems to have succeeded in blowing up a magazine, but that is peu de chose. At any rate we are now frankly at war with Turkey.[1] . . .

Lord Kitchener to Winston S. Churchill

(Churchill papers: 13/43)

5 November 1914   War Office

My dear Churchill

I am very sorry to hear of the unfortunate Valparaiso action. What could the Admiral have been thinking of to take on such a vastly superior force in guns.

Yours very truly
Kitchener

Winston S. Churchill to Lord Kitchener

(Kitchener papers)

5 November 1914   Admiralty

My dear Kitchener,

Many thanks for the kindness of your letter.

Admiralty orders were clear. The Canopus battleship was sent him for his protection. He was told to keep concentrated & said himself he wd avoid division of force. Keeping together and scouting with the Glasgow he had a good chance of finding & holding them till reinforcements arrived.

As it was he had no chance at all.

It is vy disappointing. We had 8 separate forces awaiting them at different

---

[1] At a meeting of the Privy Council held at 11.00 am on 5 November 1914 the proclamations and orders in Council relating to the war with Germany and Austria–Hungary were extended to cover war with Turkey.

points, each of wh properly handled & concentrated cd have fought them
well.

A good many moves are necessary in consequence of this contretemps.

Yours vy sincerely
Winston S. Churchill

Winston S. Churchill to Sir John Jellicoe: telegram
(Churchill papers: 13/42)

5 November 1914   Admiralty
Secret & personal

From all reports received through German sources, we fear Cradock has
let himself be caught or has engaged recklessly with only MONMOUTH
and GOOD HOPE armoured ships against SCHARNHORT and GNEIS-
SENAU. Probably both British vessels sunk. Position of CANOPUS critical
and fate of GLASGOW and OTRANTO uncertain.

Proximity of concentrated German Squadron of 5 good ships will threaten
gravely main trade route Rio to London—essential recover control.

1st Sea Lord requires Invincible and Inflexible for this purpose.
Sturdee goes C-in-C South Atlantic and Pacific.
Oliver Chief of Staff.
Bartolome[1] Naval Secretary.

WSC

Captain Sinclair,[2] Vice-Admiral Oliver and Winston S. Churchill to
William Allardyce: telegram
(Copy, Churchill papers: 13/39)

5 November 1914   Admiralty

German cruiser raids may take place. All Admiralty colliers should be
concealed in unfrequented harbours. Be ready to destroy supplies useful to
enemy and hide codes effectively on enemy ships being sighted. Acknowledge.

---

[1] Charles Martin de Bartolomé, 1871–1941. Entered Navy, 1885. Commodore, 1914.
Churchill's Naval Secretary, November 1914–May 1915. Third Sea Lord, 1918–19.
Knighted, 1919. Rear-Admiral, 1919.

[2] Hugh Francis Paget Sinclair, 1873–1939. Entered Navy, 1886. Captain, 1909. Director
of the Mobilization Division, Admiralty War Staff, 1914–16. Rear-Admiral, 1920. Vice-
Admiral, 1926. Admiral, 1930. Knighted, 1935.

Winston S. Churchill and Lord Fisher to Vice-Admiral Yashiro: telegram
(*Copy, Churchill papers: 13/39*)

5 November 1914   Admiralty

In consequence of unsuccessful action off Chile and definite location of German squadron, we have ordered concentration off Montevideo of 'Defence', 'Kent', 'Carnarvon' and 'Cornwall'. These will be joined with all despatch by 'Invincible' and 'Inflexible' battle cruisers from England, and 'Dartmouth' light cruiser from East Africa, and remainder of defeated squadron from Chile. This assures the S. Atlantic situation. We now desire assistance of Japan in making equally thorough arrangements on Pacific side. We propose for your consideration and friendly advice the following: 'Newcastle' and 'Idzumo' to go South in company to San Clemente Island off San Diego California, there to meet 'Hizen' from Honolulu. Meanwhile 'Asama' will be able to effect internment or destruction of 'Geier'.[1] We also propose to move 'Australia' battle cruiser from Fiji to Fanning Island. By the time these moves are complete, probably by 17th November, we may know more of 'Scharnhorst' and 'Gneisenau' movements and a further concentration of 'Australia' and 'Asama' with 'Hizen', 'Idzumo' and 'Newcastle' will be possible either at San Clemente or further to the South, further movements depending on the enemy.

We should also like a Japanese squadron to advance to Fiji to take the place of the 'Australia' and so guard Australia and New Zealand in case the Germans return.

With regard to the Indian Ocean and Western Pacific, it is now known that 'Emden' is the only enemy ship at large. We therefore hope that the Japanese squadrons and vessels not involved in the Eastward movement will draw Westward into the vicinity of Sumatra and the Dutch East Indies in order to block every exit and deny every place of shelter up to the 90th meridian of East longitude.

British Admiralty are combining in Indian waters in search of 'Emden' the following light cruisers:—'Weymouth', 'Gloucester', 'Yarmouth', 'Melbourne', 'Sydney', and the armoured cruiser 'Hampshire' and Russian cruiser 'Askold'. These ships will be ready by the middle of November. Thus by concerted action between the allied fleets the 'Emden' should be speedily run down.

[1] The *Geier*, a German gunboat, had sailed from Singapore on 30 July 1914. In the middle of August three French destroyers searched for her in the Malacca Straits, but in vain. At the beginning of September the *Geier* captured a British merchant ship, the *Southport*, in the Eastern Caroline Islands. At the end of October, she was sighted by two Japanese warships, the *Asama* and the *Hizen*, off Honolulu but evaded them. On 8 November, chased by the *Asama*, the *Geier* sought refuge at San Clemente, California, and was interned by the United States Government.

H. H. Asquith to Venetia Stanley

(Montagu papers)

6 November 1914   10 Downing Street

. . . I found on descending to the Cabinet room Winston & Freddy Guest —the latter on a secret mission from Sir J. French. A *most* disagreeable affair. It has been reported to French (apparently by that poisonous mischief-maker Gen Wilson[1]) that when K. was at Dunkirk last Sunday, he asked the French Generals whether they were satisfied with Sir John, & even suggested as a possible successor Ian Hamilton[2] (whom K despises and would gladly kick round the Horse Guards Parade).[3] I don't believe there is a word of truth, or even a shadow of foundation for the story. But it appears to have given great distress to Sir J. F. (who is very sensitive) & led him to think that he had lost or was losing the confidence of the Government. Hence F. Guest's mission, wh. was to me & not to K. These noxious weeds only grow in prepared soil—in this case, apparently an estrangement, or at any rate a coldness, of long standing between French & K. I have written him (F.) what I think you would agree is a 'very nice' letter, & Winston is going to do the same: but we both feel a certain delicacy in doing this behind K's back, French being very anxious that he should not be told. . . .

Winston S. Churchill to John Churchill

(John Churchill papers)

7 November 1914   Admiralty

My dear,

I knew you wd distinguish yrselves. Tell my sqn how glad I am their first contact with the enemy was so creditable to them: & Nicholl[4] & the 2

---

[1] Henry Hughes Wilson, 1864–1922. Entered Army, 1884. Director of Military Operations, War Office, 1910–14. Lieutenant-General, 1914. Chief liaison officer with the French Army, January 1915. Knighted, April 1915. Commanded the 4th Corps, 1916. Chief of the Imperial General Staff, 1918–22. Shot dead by Sinn Feiners on the steps of his London house.

[2] Ian Standish Monteith Hamilton, 1853–1947. Entered Army, 1872. Major-General, 1900. Knighted, 1900. Chief of Staff to Lord Kitchener, 1901–2. General, 1914. Commander of the Central Force, responsible for the defence of England in the event of invasion, August 1914–March 1915. Commanded the Mediterranean Expeditionary Force, March–October 1915.

[3] Five months later Kitchener appointed Hamilton to command the allied forces at the Dardanelles.

[4] Charles Nicholl, 1880–1950. Solicitor. Entered the firm of Nicholl, Manisty & Co, in 1905, and remained a partner until his death. Major, Queen's Own Oxfordshire Hussars, 1914. Squadron-Leader, C Squadron (of which Captain V. Fleming was 2nd-in-Command and in which Lieutenant P. Fleming commanded 1st Troop), 1914–18. Lieutenant-Colonel commanding the Queen's Own Oxfordshire Hussars, 1919. Winston Churchill's solicitor, 1923–50. He was also solicitor to the 9th and 10th Dukes of Marlborough.

Flamingos,[1] I am so glad they are all right. I expect it is a stiff experience to stand up for a long time to that shell fire.

Goonie is vy brave, & we look after her here.

The Admiralty only sing one song. Pump troops into the Field Army.

I have my own troubles; but have no doubt we shall get the better of them. Keep a little in touch with French wh you get the chance.

With our best love, Yours always

W

H. H. Asquith to Venetia Stanley

(Montagu papers)

8 November 1914

The Wharf
Sutton Courtney
Berks

. . . There is no news this morning except the capture of Tsingtau by the Japs, which is all to the good. So far all the dramatic successes in the war have been won on land by the Russians & Japs, and on sea by the Germans. The sort of prolonged & bloody pull devil, pull baker, business, which has been & is going on in France & Belgium, does not appeal to people's imaginations. Winston of course would dearly love to break some crockery, as he nearly succeeded in doing at Antwerp. Between ourselves, Hankey is rather apprehensive that he may be drawn into some resounding adventure by the joint influence of those two unquenchable old sea-dogs, Fisher & Wilson. The latter, as I think I told you some time ago has long been advising the bombardment of Heligoland, and now that he has a room at the Admiralty and every facility for working out his plans, I believe he is quite willing himself to lead an expedition. He is a great tactician, but recent experience (particularly this blunder of Cradock's in the Pacific) makes me very distrustful of the competence of the subordinate Admirals. . . .

[1] Valentine Fleming, 1882–1917. Captain, Queen's Own Oxfordshire Hussars, 1909; Major, 1914. Conservative MP, 1910–17. Killed in action. Churchill wrote an obituary notice of Fleming in *The Times*, 25 May 1917.

Philip Fleming, 1889–1971. Brother of Valentine Fleming; known by Churchill as 'the lesser flamingo'. A merchant banker. Lieutenant, Queen's Own Oxfordshire Hussars, 1914; Major, 1917. High Sheriff of Oxfordshire, 1948–9.

Winston S. Churchill to John Churchill

(*John Churchill papers*)

9 November 1914   Admiralty

My dear,

I read yr letter with the deepest interest & pleasure. It is a great source of regret to me not to be with my squadron now. I feel so acutely the ignoble position of one who merely cheers from the bank the gallant efforts of the rowers. But I cannot stir. The combinations at this moment are of the highest interest and importance. Perhaps in a few weeks I may come & have a day with you all.

You must feel proud of the way in wh the regiment has taken its place in the line. It is always an honour to serve alongside the 9th [Lancers]. They are the best of all. I have known them long & though most I knew are killed, I am sure their peculiar virtue endures. I want the Oxfordshire to establish an enduring liaison with them, wh after the war will be much esteemed by both. All goes well. Have no fear for the result. We have got the dirty dogs tight. The end is a long way off: but it is certain tho' not in sight.

Goonie is vy good & brave. She is I think happy here and you cannot write to her (or me) too often. Every word is precious. Poor Gordon[1] is killed, also my friend Hugh Dawnay,[2] & the little de Gunzberg.[3] This is the latest casualty list. Hugo Baring[4] has arrived—wounded—almost the same as yr wound at Hussar Hill.[5] What a long way off that seems!

My dear I am always anxious about you. It wd take the edge off much if I cd be with you. I expect I shd be vy frightened but I wd dissemble.

With fondest love

Yours always

W

[1] Gordon Chesney Wilson, 1865–1914. Churchill's uncle by marriage; husband of Lady Sarah Spencer-Churchill. Entered the Army, 1887. Served as a Captain on Baden-Powell's staff at Mafeking, 1900. Major, 1903. Lieutenant-Colonel, Royal Horse Guards, 1914. Killed in action, 6 November 1914.

[2] Hugh Dawnay, 1875–1914. Second son of the 8th Viscount Downe. Lieutenant, Nile Expedition, 1898. ADC to Lord Roberts, South Africa, 1901. Major, 2nd Life Guards, August 1914. Killed in action, 6 November 1914.

[3] Baron Alexis de Gunzberg, 1887–1914. 2nd Lieutenant, Royal Hussars. Killed in action at Ypres, 6 November 1914.

[4] Hugo Baring, 1876–1949. 6th son of the 1st Baron Revelstoke. Lieutenant, 4th Hussars, 1896–8. Served in the South African War (severely wounded) and in the First War (wounded). Captain 1914; Major, 1918. A Director of Parr's Bank 1911–18, and of the Westminster Bank, 1923–45.

[5] Jack Churchill had been wounded in February 1900, in the South African war, during a skirmish at Hussar Hill in Natal. He had convalesced aboard the *Maine*, a hospital ship organized by his mother.

PS Speak to them all about my deep interest in the fortunes of the regiment. It is my fault you are in it all.

Sir John French to Winston S. Churchill

(*Churchill papers: 26/1*)

9 November 1914   Head-Quarters British Army

My dear Winston,

If I am too familiar in addressing you like this forgive me! I write as I feel—you have shown yourself to be one of the greatest friends I ever had in the world. I don't want to think again of what Freddy Guest told you— the truth is a complete mystery & must remain unsolved—for my part it is completely consigned to oblivion. It is for ever washed out of my mind by you & the Prime Minister & the delightful letters you have written me. I shall go forward with my work in the most complete confidence & hope.

'Allah requite them' my Friend 'I can't'! as the Afghan leader Shere Ali[1] said to his deliverer!

The Oxfordshires are doing splendid work with Allenby[2] who is taking good care of them.

I have your note about Samson & the Naval Aeroplanes—it shall be properly announced to-morrow.

Everything shall be as you wish.

Do try to come over here soon.

Yours alys

JF

[1] Shere Ali, 1825–79. Succeeded his father as Amir of Afghanistan, 1863. Recaptured Kabul from his rebellious half-brothers, 1866. After the rebellion of his son in 1870, turned towards Russia for support. Welcomed a Russian agent to Kabul, 1878, but refused to receive a British mission. The British advanced into Afghanistan, and defeated him at the Khyber Pass, November 1878. He fled to Turkestan, where he died.

[2] Edmund Henry Hynman Allenby, 1861–1936. Entered Army, 1882. Major-General, 1909. Commanded 1st Cavalry Division, British Expeditionary Force, 1914. Commanded the Cavalry Corps, 1914–15. Commanded 5th Army Corps, 1915. Knighted, 1915. Commanded 3rd Army, 1915–17. Lieutenant-General, 1916. General, 1917. Commander-in-Chief, Egyptian Expeditionary Force 1917–19. Received the surrender of Jerusalem, 9 December 1917. Drove the Turks from Palestine at the Battle of Megiddo, 19 September 1918. Created Viscount Allenby of Megiddo, 1919. Field-Marshal, 1919. High Commissioner for Egypt and the Sudan, 1919–25.

Vice-Admiral Oliver to Captain Grant[1] and Captain Luce: telegram

(*Copy, Churchill papers: 13/39*)

9 November 1914   Admiralty
3.10 am

Canopus to remain in Stanley Harbour. Moor the ship so that your guns command the entrance. Extemporise mines outside entrance. Be prepared for bombardment from outside the harbour. Send down your topmasts. Stimulate the Governor to organise all local forces and make determined defence. Arrange observation stations on shore to enable you to direct your fire on ships outside. Land guns or use boats torpedoes to sink a blocking ship before she reaches the Narrows. No objection to your grounding ship to obtain a good berth. Send Glasgow on to River Plate should she be able to get sufficient start of enemy to avoid capture if not moor her inside Canopus.

Repair your defects and wait orders.

Vice-Admiral Oliver, Lord Fisher and Winston S. Churchill to
Rear-Admiral Stoddart: telegram

(*Copy, Churchill papers: 13/39*)

9 November 1914   Admiralty
6.30 pm

'CANOPUS' and 'GLASGOW' expected to arrive Port Stanley on 8th. both ships must coal there.

'CANOPUS' cannot steam properly and has been ordered to remain in Port Stanley and defend herself and the town.

German ships may arrive Port Stanley on 10th and 'GLASGOW' has been ordered to remain unless she can get sufficient start of German Ships to ensure her escape.

Keep your ships concentrated off River Plate and remain long enough to enable 'GLASGOW' to rejoin you should she start.

Should you not get news of 'GLASGOW' after waiting a reasonable time retire keeping your forces still concentrated in advance of German Squadron and cover the coaling base at Abrolhos Rocks. Coal there if you have time before Germans arrive.

[1] Heathcoat Salusbury Grant, 1864–1938. Entered Navy, 1877. Captain, 1904. Nava Attaché, USA, 1912–14. Captain commanding HMS *Canopus*, 1914–16. In action at the Falkland Islands, 1914; Gallipoli, 1915; Gulf of Smyrna, 1916. Rear-Admiral, 1916. Second-in-Command, Dover, 1917. Senior Naval Officer, Gibraltar, 1917–19. Knighted, 1919. Vice-Admiral, 1920.

The colliers must be protected and you must engage the German Squadron if necessary to protect colliers.

Do not lose sight of the possibility of Germans not calling at Falklands and going North direct.

Keep Admiralty informed of your own and the Germans movements.

John Wilson[1] *to Edward Marsh*

(*Austen Chamberlain papers*)

9 November 1914   9 Egerton Place

Dear Mr Marsh,

Mr Chamberlain asks me to enquire—what day would be most convenient to Mr Churchill for the town's meeting which he has promised to attend at Birmingham.

The Lord Mayor writes to Mr Chamberlain that the meeting could be held in the Town Hall on practically any date in the near future.

Mr Chamberlain has engagements on Nov 21 & 28 which he would be reluctant to give up if other days are equally suitable to Mr Churchill, but he feels that he ought to meet Mr Churchill's convenience in the matter.

Please explain to Mr Churchill that Highbury is now dismantled, and that for this and *for other reasons Mr Chamberlain is unable to repeat his offer of hospitality, but if Mr Churchill thinks of spending the night in Birmingham Mr Chamberlain is sure that others would be glad to put him up.*

Yours faithfully
J. Wilson

Winston S. Churchill to Austen Chamberlain

(*Austen Chamberlain papers*)

10 November 1914   Admiralty

Dear Chamberlain,

I must really write to you about the letter wh Marsh received from your Secretary last night. I am afraid that in the pressure of business I did not fully appreciate its character.

I have looked at it again to-night, & I cannot altogether dismiss the impression that the passage underlined is a breach of customary manners. I have not sought yr hospitality on any occasion, & when you last invited me to Highbury I was vy sorry that my work prevented me from accepting yr invitation—as I wrote you at the time.

I am always on my guard against seeing offence where none is meant, &

[1] John Wilson, 1860–1938. Personal Secretary to Joseph Chamberlain, 1888–1914, and to Austen Chamberlain, 1914–34.

I hope that you will be able to reassure me, & let me add—acquit yourself of an intrusion upon me for wh you had no warrant.

Yours vy truly
Winston S. Churchill

Austen Chamberlain to Winston S. Churchill

(*Copy, Austen Chamberlain papers*)

11 November 1914   9 Egerton Place

Private

Dear Churchill,

When I last asked you to speak at Birmingham I also asked you to stay at Highbury. It was to me as I believe it was to you a great disappointment that these arrangements had to be abandoned for reasons which we discussed at the time. In now repeating to you, at the request of the Lord Mayor, the invitation to you to fix a date for a meeting, I thought it necessary, in order to guard against any possible misapprehension arising out of my previous letter to explain that I was unable to repeat my invitation to stay at Highbury but that I could easily make arrangements for your entertainment if you decided to stop the night in Birmingham.

There is in this no suggestion that you ever 'sought my hospitality', nor I hope any breach of good manners, though there is the recognition of a changed situation which, as you know, I did my utmost to prevent and am now anxious not to embitter. I therefore mark this letter 'private'.

Yours very truly
Austen Chamberlain

Winston S. Churchill to Sir Gilbert Parker[1]

(*Copy Churchill papers: 13/27*)

11 November 1914   Admiralty

Dear Parker,

You alarm yourself unnecessarily about American opinion, & the value attached to reports in American newspapers.[2] It is vy mischievious to discuss the strength in Capital units of Sir J. Jellicoe's fleet; & the Admy will take

---

[1] Gilbert Parker, 1862–1932. Born in Canada. Poet, novelist and traveller. His first poems, *A Lover's Diary*, were published in 1894. Conservative MP, 1900–18. Chairman of the Imperial South African Association. Knighted, 1902. In charge of American Publicity, 1914–17.

[2] On the previous day Parker had sent Churchill a letter from Ed L. Keen, General European Manager of the United Press Association of America, protesting against the 'stupidity' of the Admiralty's attempt to keep secret the sinking of the *Audacious*. 'The American public', Parker declared, 'will put the worst construction on our silence, and no after-explanation will enable us to regain their confidence in our willingness to take our gruel.' (*Churchill papers: 13/27*)

no responsibility for allowing or participating in such discussion now or at any future time. If the enemy choose to believe that the audacious has been sunk, let them do so, & make their plans accordingly. But let no Englishman or friend of England assist them to resolve their doubts. So far however this particular story does not seem to have reached their ears, altho' the rumours are as widespread & as circumstantial as those of the Russian troops from Archangel.

Yours vy truly
WSC

Winston S. Churchill to Vice-Admiral Carden: telegram
(Copy, Admiralty papers: 137/96)

13 November 1914   Admiralty

You must keep a concentrated force off Dardanelles to prevent egress of enemy. Subject to this make your proposals for injuring them.

Sir John French to Winston S. Churchill
(Churchill papers: 13/27)

14 November 1914   General Headquarters

My dear Churchill,

With reference to your note regarding naval aeroplanes and armoured motor cars.

In so far as the aeroplanes are concerned, it would be advisable to return them to England to refit, and that they should remain there until required for any definite enterprises against Zeppelins. Refitting in this country would increase the congestion behind the lines, and add to the difficulties of the Line of Communications.

Attacks on certain Zeppelin sheds will be undertaken by the Royal Flying Corps in the Field as soon as Zeppelins arrive in the sheds, and no doubt other objectives will come within reach as the Army advances. For these attacks the assistance of the Royal Naval Air Service would be very desirable, but in such case all arrangements for a 'jumping-off' place would be made by the Royal Flying Corps, and the Naval aeroplanes to be employed could fly over from Dover. Transport and land organization for these machines would not be required, as the detachment would be attached to the Royal Flying Corps for the period necessary for the execution of the particular enterprise.

The decision as to the time at which attacks on Zeppelin sheds should be delivered can best I think be made by me as steps can be taken here to verify the presence of the objective, and local weather conditions seriously affect the possibilities of success.

Now that the lines of battle in this theatre are continuous, there is no possibility of using the armoured cars in the manner originally intended. The value of these cars, when organized in a unit, has therefore diminished, and, I recommend that for the present they be returned to England where they can be repaired and if necessary re-armoured.

Yours sincerely
John French

Our roads are now terribly congested which is another reason for keeping this traffic off them as much as possible.

Winston S. Churchill to Sir John French: not sent

(*Churchill papers: 13/27*)

15 November 1914   Admiralty

My dear French,

I am sorry to trouble you with trifles but I must frankly say that the letter signed by you about the naval airmen is very disappointing to me. The Admiralty have done and will do the utmost in their power to support the expeditionary army, and we are taking an immense responsibility in acquiescing willingly in the denudation of this country of regulars at this critical time and really we have played your hand throughout as if it were our own.

I think the statement in your letter to the effect that a dozen naval aeroplanes and 15 motor cars refilling near Cassel [near St Omer] would congest your lines of communication cannot have emanated from you. It looks to me an instance of that inter-departmental friction which you and I have always laboured to discourage. The Naval Air department look upon the decision conveyed in this letter as a very poor recognition of the dangerous work they have done while at General Rawlinson's special request they continued with the 7th Division.

It seems impossible to maintain good comradeship between the Services. I telegraphed to you today the reasons which make it imperative for the Admiralty to keep themselves continually informed by aeroplane reconnaissance and attack of the German naval preparations in Ostende and Zee-brugge.

But in view of the wishes of the military wing the naval airmen have been ordered to keep entirely clear of the front and communications of the British army and to work only on the flank with the French and Belgians.

I trust this will remove the difficulties which are apprehended.

Winston S. Churchill to Sir John French
(*Copy, Churchill papers: 13/27*)

15 November 1914   Admiralty

Personal

Many thanks for your letter about the naval airmen. If the Military wing would assume sole responsibility for preventing Zeppelin bases being estab-lished in Belgium naval wing could be relieved of this duty. But I hope it is realised that there is no effective means of dealing with a Zeppelin raid in England after it has started & unless they are destroyed in their bases in Belgium or Germany serious injury may be done to London & our dock-yards. At present Admiralty is held responsible. Apart from this Admiralty feel it imperative to keep a squadron of aeroplanes on the French coast so long as Ostende & Zeebrugge are in German occupation for this is our only means of watching the development of their submarine bases there and other dangerous naval preparations, as well as spotting for British naval fire wh may be again required at any moment.

In these circumstances we propose to withdraw all naval aeroplanes and armoured cars to Dunkirk so as to keep quite clear of the British army and its communications: but to remain there for the present. I hope this meets the military view.

Sir John French to Winston S. Churchill
(*Churchill papers: 13/27*)

15 November 1914   Headquarters British Army

My dear Winston,

This is a very briefest line . . . to tell you that I am getting your brother Jack in here in a staff job for a few weeks. I see you are anxious about him and he's been with his reg doing very hard work for a month or so. . . .

Lord Fisher to Sir John Jellicoe

(*Jellicoe papers*)

17 November 1914   Admiralty

. . . Such a multitude of events incessantly interrupting and it dont do to lose the threads and I am also Winston's shadow on purpose. We yesterday 'speeded up' the Queen Elizabeth by a month—I hope you'll approve of her joining the Battle Cruisers. I listen with great interest day by day to A. K. Wilson, old Oliver & Bartholomé discussing your battle line. (We meet daily for an hour or two to discuss the world *'from China to Peru'*!—old A. K. W. wrote to Winston & the Prime Minister that he was now 'Fisher's Slave'! *Can you imagine A. K. W., being a slave*!!! but he works like a horse all day at all sorts of plans for the Belgian & German Coast attack. . . .) . . .

Winston S. Churchill to Sir John French

(*Copy, Churchill papers: 26/1*)

17 November 1914   Admiralty

My dear French,

When we met at the Aisne I promised you to organise an armoured motor car regiment for service with the army. This is now far advanced, & will comprise 8 sqns of 15 cars each—6 light with maxims, 2 heavy with 3 prs—together with all necessary vehicles & a total personnel of 1,200—already enlisted.

I was sorry to see in yr recent telm that you now attach vy little value to armoured cars. Certainly this does not tally with the infn we have recd from any qr. in wh ours have been engaged. Gen Rawlinson & the cavalry vie with the reports of the enemy (see enclosure[1]) in testifying to their effectiveness. No doubt during this period of deadlock & siege lines there is no scope, but the moment you move forward or back the use & convenience of these engines shd be apparent.

At any rate I am too far on to go back, & if when the force is completed you do not desire to have it with you, it can work with the Belgians. Perhaps you will let me know.

The latest types are well designed, & stand all bullets.

There are many signs here now of a possible naval movement combined with a raid large or small; & everything is being geared up for action.

This wd be their best moment from every point of view.

The continued prowess & valour of the army is wonderful. I hope the

---

[1] A German military report, procured by British intelligence.

territorials will win the respect of their professional comrades. Jack is having a lot of hard service & I feel vy anxious about him.

> With all good wishes, Believe me, Yrs vy sincerely
> WSC

Winston S. Churchill to Edward Marsh

(*Admiralty papers: 137/880*)

18 November 1914   Admiralty

Draft a letter to the War Office pointing out the dangers incurred by the convoy of transports in the Channel and the Atlantic, and urging that measures should be taken to reduce the amount of work to a minimum. Also point out that although in the case of a vital need like the reinforcement of the Army in the field there is justification in subjecting the troops to these risks, there is no such justification for doing so when it is merely a matter of administrative arrangements. It appears obvious that these troops could be organised and fitted out in the South of France in the same way as the Indians and complete their training there instead of making a double voyage across the danger areas in the Channel and the Atlantic.

> WSC

Winston S. Churchill to Lord Fisher and Admiral Oliver

(*Oliver papers*)

18 November 1914   Admiralty

First Sea Lord
Chief of Staff

. . . Considerably more than a week has passed since I minuted that Askold should be ordered to the Mediterranean. There or in Egyptian waters this Russian ship will have a chance of fighting against Turkey. To send her off to Hong-Kong is an altogether purposeless errand. Her stores should go on with the mines or in another vessel which keeps company with the mines from Vladivostock. No convoy is necessary; but if it were, the Clio or Cadmus, or some little vessel like them, could be used. The whole Japanese Navy is in the Pacific and Indian Oceans. They would quite willingly find a convoy for the mines and the Askold stores. The whole area of the sea, from the coast of Chili to the coast of Mozambique, has been cleared of the enemy. But for vague rumours of a possible armed merchant-man at large, there is not the slightest menace. We must profit from this situation to the full while it lasts, and this can only be done by moving every ship that is of any use promptly into waters where they are required. No one knows how many ships we shall want in Egypt when the Turkish invasion begins. There may also be massacres of Christians in the coast towns of Levant which will require vessels for immediate action there. All the ships out of the Indian Ocean that can play an effective part ought to be hurried home. The cruisers ought to steam at least 18 knots. Nearly all these ships have lost three or four precious days since the destruction of the Emden was known.

Winston S. Churchill to H. H. Asquith
(*Copy, Spencer-Churchill papers*)

18 November 1914   Admiralty

My dear Prime Minister,

As I hear that the Irish Viceroyalty is likely vy soon to be decided upon, I write to ask most earnestly that Ivor may not be overlooked. I do not attempt to go over again the ground I traversed with you when the last changes were made. But I feel that after his surrender of office 2 years ago to suit party convenience & the repeated hopes held out to him & to his friends, it wd be a vy hard thing to pass him finally over.

Now I have done my best & I will not take time to add words to this letter: for you know how strongly I feel abt the matter, & how sure I am that the choice wd be a right one.[1]

Yrs vy sincerely
WSC

Winston S. Churchill to Clementine Churchill
(*Spencer-Churchill papers*)

19 November 1914   Admiralty

Most Secret

My darling,

I have got some good news for Goonie. French has taken Jack on to the Staff. He has done this of his own accord & neither Jack nor I have ever asked for it. But I am vy thankful, because although there is always danger,

[1] Lord Wimborne's appointment as Lord Lieutenant of Ireland was announced by Asquith on 4 January 1915, and came into effect on 17 February 1915.

the risk is less & the work more interesting. Jack has done a lot of hard service & is quite entitled to use his good fortune.[1]

I was so delighted with your letter—— It gives me so much joy when I feel that with all my short comings, absorption, & sunlessness you can still find in me the pith & nourishment for wh your soul seeks in this vale.

The swine are concentrating at Wilhelmshaven, & the situation is thoroughly 'cat & mouse'. Which will be the mouse?

But I don't think they will dare the big coup. Still I must watch from minute to minute. All is well—— The loan & the taxes are going down like oil. No more news has arrived of any consequence. K. has moved his army about in gt excitement for the long looked for invasion. But no such luck.[2]

With tender love & many kisses
Ever your devoted & loving
W

Winston S. Churchill to Lord Fisher, Sir Arthur Wilson, and Vice-Admiral Oliver
(*Copy, Churchill papers: 13/29*)

19 November 1914   Admiralty

I begin to be extremely anxious about German submarines in the Channel. The Germans have now been for more than a month at Zeebrugge and Ostend, and we know that their submarines are passing in and out of the mined area. They must therefore be replenishing with oil and petrol from the shore, and from this handy base their action throughout the whole Channel is easy. The transport of troops is rendered much more dangerous, though of course moving at night reduces the risk; but very valuable ships fitting out to join the Fleet or refitting to go in and out of Portsmouth and Plymouth, and on any day someone may be caught. Plans should therefore be prepared to bombard Zeebrugge and Ostende as soon as possible in the most effective manner.

[1] Jack Churchill served on Sir John French's staff from November 1914 until March 1915, when he transferred to the staff of Sir Ian Hamilton, commanding the Mediterranean Expeditionary Force sent to Gallipoli.

[2] Clementine Churchill, who was at Lympne, replied that she felt 'anxious' about the outcome. 'The Germans are horribly powerful,' she explained, 'and cunning too; they have devoted for years past their best intellects to the preparations for this war, while we always think of soldiers & sailors as brave & bluff & simple, not to say *stupid*. . . .' (*Spencer-Churchill papers*)

Lord Fisher to Sir John Jellicoe
(*Jellicoe papers*)

20 November 1914   Admiralty

. . . we have a regular menagerie of 'charity admirals' employed & totally
unfitted for the work they are employed on—as the Admiralty is quite full
of young Naval officers who ought to be at sea—doing simply clerk's work
at the Admiralty. The corridors are crowded with them as I walk along! . . .

Winston S. Churchill to John Churchill
(*John Churchill papers*)

21 November 1914   Admiralty

My dear,

I had no direct hand in this, tho' I am heartily glad of it.

It is clearly your duty to go where you can be most use. I expect you will
do this work vy well and as more & more Territorials arrive its importance
will grow. Your brains & business training shd be useful & will find a wider
scope. You will know more of what is going on. Of course it is a pang with a
twinge of reproach in it, to part company with the regiment, and to them it is
a gt loss. But you are not in command & they will get on all right. If I cd pull
off a victory here over the dirty dogs I wd try to steal a holiday for a day or
two to visit them. But it is cat & mouse watching now—& I must take care
not to be the mouse!

Goonie was enchanted at the news. The war will be a long & cruel affair
& one wants, as Sunny says, about 4 lives to play the game out well.

You must be vy appreciative to French for the recognition he has accorded
you. In your position you will have lots of opportunities of helping the regiment & the Territorial interests in general. There will be plenty of chances of
being shot at before the end is reached.

With best love

Yours always
W

Colonel Seely to Winston S. Churchill

(*Churchill papers: 26/1*)

22 November 1914

My dear Winston,

A hundred days of war today so far as we are concerned, so naturally I think about you on whom so much depends for the days to come.

I have been with the French a good deal in these hard times, as well as with our own people. I did not know that men could be so brave or artillery so precise.

But this last is entirely an affair of observation at close quarters—the battery commander within 800 yards of the enemy trenches, conversing with his battery while he watches the shells burst is the man who dominates this phase of the war. For this he must have at least two telephones as the wires get cut by shells, and two spare instruments in case of accidents. This the best French divisions have, and the results are astonishing, as I have seen on two different occasions.

Our artillery is still short of telephones and wire, but I believe that all this will be repaired by the time you get this letter—at least so the C.R.A.[1] tells me who is keen about the business.

A French General said to me 'This war degenerates at all points into a war of seige, and the battery commander with his telephone in the front trench holds the grand secret.'

On the other hand there have been some very remarkable and old-fashioned infantry fights, as of course you know well, but mostly in wooded or broken country where artillery observation is more difficult.

At the south end of our line where I was last night, both sides are very busy with bombs of various descriptions and no doubt other destructive devices will come along as time goes on; but both sides change their methods simultaneously so equilibrium is maintained, at any rate in the Western theatre of war.

All the Territorials who have been in the trenches have done very well—by the way, I wish you would change the name—it never was a good one, and here on the continent it is misleading.

[1] Walter Fullarton Lodovic Lindsay, 1855–1930. Lieutenant, Royal Artillery, 1875. Major-General, Royal Artillery, attached to GHQ, August 1914–February 1915. Having been specially selected for this post by Sir John French, Lindsay was blamed for the lack of munitions in October 1914, at the first battle of Ypres, and was replaced. He was then given command of the 50th (Northumberland) Territorial Division. During the second battle of Ypres his infantry brigades were sent one by one into action, but never under his control. After the battle he broke down, and was sent home. He received no further military command. Knighted, 1915. Inspector, Royal Horse and Royal Field Artillery, War Office, 1915–16.

Your own regiment really did splendidly at a very critical time—everyone who was with or near them agrees in this. For myself I have been kept very busy obtaining information and writing reports as a consequence. This is my first off day for I don't know how long, so I have time to finish this letter. I long to see my children, but I won't ask for leave, or take it, if offered until we have bested these Germans.

Please give my kindest regards to your wife, and remember me to all our friends.

Yours ever

Jack

Valentine Fleming to Winston S. Churchill

(*Spencer-Churchill papers*)

November 1914

Any news from home is, as you may imagine, most welcome, for we live in an atmosphere of rumours of an astounding variety but of a uniform incredibility.

Well you will have heard of our first week's serious fighting. Let me give you some general impressions of this astounding conflict:—

1: First and most impressive the absolutely indescribable ravages of modern artillery fire, not only upon all men, animals and buildings within its zone, but upon the very face of nature itself. Imagine a broad belt, ten miles or so in width, stretching from the Channel to the German frontier near Basle, which is positively littered with the bodies of men and scarified with their rude graves; in which farms, villages, and cottages are shapeless heaps of blackened masonry; in which fields, roads and trees are pitted and torn and twisted by shells and disfigured by dead horses, cattle, sheep and goats, scattered in every attitude of repulsive distortion and dismemberment. Day and night in this area are made hideous by the incessant crash and whistle and roar of every sort of projectile, by sinister columns of smoke and flame, by the cries of wounded men, by the piteous calls of animals of all sorts, abandoned, starved, perhaps wounded. Along this terrain of death stretch more or less parallel to each other lines and lines of trenches, some 200, some 1,000 yards apart, hardly visible except to the aeroplanes which continually hover over them menacing and uncanny harbingers of fresh showers of destruction. In these trenches crouch lines of men, in brown or grey or blue, coated with mud, unshaven, hollow-eyed with the continual strain unable to reply to the everlasting run of shells hurled at them from 3, 4, 5 or more miles away and positively welcoming an infantry attack from one side or the other as a chance of meeting and matching themselves against *human* assailants and not against invisible, irresistible machines, the outcome of an ingenuity which even you and I would be in agreement in considering unproductive from every point of view. Behind these trenches, a long way behind, come the guns hidden in hedgerows and copses, dug into emplacements, concealed in every imaginable way from the aeroplanes which give their range; behind them again come the reserves and supports and masses of cavalry, or at least of their horses, for all the English cavalry are in the trenches; behind them again the forward supply and ammunition depots; next the Headquarters and last the big base, in our case on the coast.

2: Next to the destructiveness of the thing, what most amazes me is the number of non-combatants required to transport, to supply, to connect generally to provide and equip the comparatively small fighting line. Every road between the coast and the trenches hums with motor transport, every base is the centre of converging lines of supplies, every trench, every regimental, every brigade, every divisional, every army corps headquarters is connected and linked up with field telephones motor bicyclists and motor cars. In fact far more men in uniform are seen behind than in the actual fighting line, and what is satisfactory is that the whole machine appears to work admirably. It is a very different problem to tackle from the South African War. Here each battle is a prolonged bombardment of a series of carefully prepared positions; all the appliances of 20th century civilisation can be brought to work and the result is good.

It is wonderful to see the variety of uniforms and of faces, and to hear the babel of tongues at the big centres. In or on the way to the trenches people are either too tired or too frightened to talk, and all movements take place in the dark. One night last week, beautifully starlit, I was riding up the reverse slope of a wooded hill round which were encamped the most extraordinary medley of troops you could imagine, French Cuirassiers with their glistening breastplates and lances, a detachment of the London Scottish, an English howitzer battery, a battalion of Sikhs, a squadron of African Spahis with long robes and turbans, all sitting round their camp fires, chattering, singing, smoking, the very apotheosis of picturesque and theatrical warfare with their variety of uniforms, saddlery equipment and arms. Very striking it was to see the remnants of an English line battalion marching back from the trenches through these merry warriors, a limping column of bearded, muddy, torn figures, slouching with fatigue, with woolcaps instead of helmets, sombre looking in their khaki, but able to stand the cold, the strain, the awful losses, the inevitable inability to reply to the shell fire, which is what other nations *can't* do. It's going to be a *long long* war in spite of the fact that on both sides every single man in it wants it stopped *at once*.

Winston S. Churchill to Clementine Churchill
(Spencer-Churchill papers)

23 November 1914   Admiralty

My darling one,

This is an impressive letter from Val Fleming. What wd happen I wonder if the armies suddenly & simultaneously went on strike and said some other method must be found of settling the dispute!

Meanwhile however new avalanches of men are preparing to mingle in the conflict and it widens and deepens every hour.

The Friederichshafen raid by the naval airmen was successful, though it seems likely that one officer out of the 3 is lost, 120 miles into the heart of Germany![1]

My darling I cannot come to you today. The pressure is continual & there are operations pending wh require my constant presence. Come back home tomorrow to the basket. A very warm welcome awaits you from the kittens & from your devoted & loving

W

Sir Edward Grey to Winston S. Churchill
(Copy, Foreign Office papers: 372/570)

23 November 1914   Foreign Office

Mr Churchill

I suppose I can say that enquiry will be made of our aviators as to what has happened & if it is the case that Swiss territory has been flown over we will express regret and in any case give instructions to be careful not to do so again.

As to indemnity for the person killed we must know who he was & what he was doing [on] German soil.

EG

[1] On 14 November 1914 a Royal Naval Air Force expedition, led by Squadron-Commander Noel Pemberton Billing, left England for Belfort, a French fortress town near the border of Germany. On 21 November three aeroplanes flew from Belfort to Friedrichshafen, on the Lake of Constance, where they dropped nine bombs on the German Zeppelin sheds and a hydrogen factory. Two of the pilots returned safely; the third was shot down by German machine gun fire and shrapnel, and captured. For the area of the raid, see map 4 on page 1595.

Winston S. Churchill to Sir Edward Grey
(*Foreign Office papers: 372/570*)

23 November 1914   Admiralty

Sir Edward Grey.

The strictest instructions were given not to fly over Swiss territory: & we do not believe it was violated at any point.

At a great height the position of a machine flying near the frontier might easily be 'mistaken' by an ignorant or Pro-German observer.

No bomb was dropped on Swiss territory: & if a Swiss was killed in the Zeppelin factory, it serves him right.

WSC

H. H. Asquith to Venetia Stanley
(*Montagu papers*)

24 November 1914   10 Downing Street

. . . Winston is quite pleased with his raid on the Lake of Constance: a hydrogen factory wrecked, 1 Zepp. probably destroyed, and 2 out of the 3 aeroplanes safely back. As we have also bagged a good German submarine —U.18—charged & rammed by a small armed fishing trawler!, and Zeebrugge was heavily bombarded yesterday by 2 Duncans, the Navy is holding up its head. It is also quite possible that a real naval action off Heligoland may have begun to-day; but these things are so often announced & adjourned that one gets rather incredulous. . . .

H. H. Asquith to David Lloyd George
(*Lloyd George papers*)

24 November 1914   First Lord of the Treasury

Secret

My dear Ch of Ex,

I wish to have to-morrow (Wed) at *noon* a small conclave on the Naval and Mily. situation.

The only Ministers I propose to summon, beside yourself, are E. Grey,

K, & Winston. I hope that A. J. B.—who has given much care & expert knowledge to the matter—may also be there.

But of course we must preserve strict secrecy.

Yrs always
HHA

H. H. Asquith to George V

(*Royal Archives*)

25 November 1914   10 Downing Street

. . . Mr Churchill reported that the daring raid of airmen upon Fredrich-schafen had resulted in the wrecking of the hydrogen factory, and probably in damage to one of the Zeppelin ships.

The German submarine U18 was charged by one of the 80 armed trawlers in the region of Scapa Flow, and as she sank her crew were rescued by the destroyer Gary.

Two battleships of the Duncan class bombarded Zeebrugge and did considerable damage. . . .

War Council Meeting:[1] *Secretary's notes*

(*Cabinet papers: 22/1*)

Present: H. H. Asquith (*in the Chair*), *David Lloyd George, Winston S. Churchill, Lord Fisher, Sir Edward Grey, A. J. Balfour, Lord Kitchener, Sir James Wolfe Murray,*[2] *Lieutenant-Colonel Hankey* (*Secretary*)

25 November 1914   10 Downing Street

HOME DEFENCE

THE PRIME MINISTER said that, as the Admiralty and War Office had recently taken a good many steps in the direction of tuning up the arrangements for home defence, the moment appeared opportune for a general review of the dispositions made.

[1] This was the first formal meeting of a select group of Ministers and service chiefs, known as the 'War Council'. In May 1915 it was enlarged, and its name changed to the 'Dardanelles Committee'. In November 1915 it was reduced in size, and renamed the 'Cabinet War Committee'. In December 1916, when Lloyd George became Prime Minister, it evolved into the 'War Cabinet'.

[2] James Wolfe Murray, 1853–1919. Entered Royal Artillery, 1872. Knighted, 1902. Lieutenant-General, 1909. Chief of the Imperial General Staff, October 1914–September 1915. Special Mission to Russia, 1915–16.

MR. CHURCHILL sketched out the arrangements made by the Admiralty. He said that the defence of the coast was now entrusted to approximately 260 vessels, including battleships, cruisers, torpedo craft, and submarines, as well as some of the monitors and gunboats recently employed on the Belgian coast, which had now been allotted to coastal defence. These ships were disposed somewhat as follows:—

In the Straits of Dover.—5 battleships (4 Duncan class and His Majesty's ship 'Revenge,' employed in the bombardment of the Belgian coast); 12 French and 13 British submarines; 3 light cruisers and 24 destroyers; a seaplane station.

At the Nore.—10 battleships (Formidable and Lord Nelson classes); 6 submarines; 12 destroyers; and 20 torpedo-boats; a seaplane and airship station.

Based on Harwich.—4 cruisers of the Arethusa class; 22 of our best oversea submarines; 2 flotillas of destroyers (say 42 in all, of which 33 are fit for sea at any particular moment); also 3 (shortly to be increased to 6) of the new 'M' class destroyers of 37 or 38 knots, capable of remaining some time in the vicinity of the enemy's coast. These vessels are not allocated for local defence, but for reconnaissance duties in the North Sea (see below), and are only based on Harwich. There is also a seaplane station at Harwich.

Yarmouth.—7 destroyers; and a seaplane station. Some of the Harwich submarines are often here.

The Wash.—3 monitors.

In the Humber.—4 battleships of the Majestic class, anchored with nets out and steam up; 5 submarines; 2 scouts; 2 destroyers; 12 torpedo-boats; a seaplane station.

Whitby.—4 destroyers.

Hartlepool.—2 light cruisers and 1 submarine.

Sunderland.—2 submarines.

In the Tyne.—1 battleship, Majestic class; 4 submarines; and a seaplane station.

Blyth.—2 submarines.

In the Forth.—8 battleships, King Edward class; 3rd cruiser squadron (4 cruisers); 1 light cruiser; 6 submarines; 15 destroyers; 12 torpedo-boats; a seaplane station.

At Cromarty.—6 destroyers, and a seaplane station. } There are usually large
At Scapa Flow.—1 flotilla of destroyers. } numbers of vessels in these seas.

16 destroyers were being recalled from the Mediterranean to reinforce the coastal defence.

In addition to the above, there are aeroplane or seaplane stations at Hendon (12 machines), Clacton, and Kinnaird Head.

The Admiralty have established minefields at Sunderland, the Tyne, Blyth, and the Tay.

A regular system of reconnaissance is carried out by submarines, in addition to which destroyers and other vessels frequently carry out special reconnaissances, sometimes as far as the Heligoland Bight.

The whole of the above ships are entirely distinct from the main fleet under Admiral Jellicoe, which is maintained at an adequate superiority over the German High Sea Fleet.

Some of the Flag Officers afloat did not like these dispositions, considering that there was too much dispersion of force. The Admiralty, however, did not agree in this view. The force concentrated under the command of Admiral Jellicoe, which was our main force, was always maintained at a strength greatly superior to the German High Sea Fleet, and the dispersed ships were only our superfluous force. It was true that, if one of the dispersed battle squadrons was attacked by the German High Sea Fleet, it would be overwhelmed; but, in order to make such an attack the High Sea Fleet would have to approach within the radius of action of our submarines, and it would run a grave risk of incurring heavy losses. Having regard to the fact that it might subsequently have to encounter our main fleet, it was unlikely that this risk would be run, or that the High Sea Fleet would be used to convoy an invading army to our shores. But the squadrons of battleships now located in our east coast ports would be sufficient to deal with any of the old German armoured ships, which, owing to their smaller value, the Germans might employ to attack our coasts. . . .

THE DEFENCE OF EGYPT

MR. CHURCHILL suggested that the ideal method of defending Egypt was by an attack on the Gallipoli Peninsula. This, if successful, would give us control of the Dardanelles, and we could dictate terms at Constantinople. This, however, was a very difficult operation requiring a large force. If it was considered impracticable, it appeared worth while to assemble transports and horse boats at Malta or Alexandria, and to make a feint at Gallipoli, conveying the impression that we intended to land there. Our real point of attack might be Haifa, or some point on the Syrian coast. The Committee of Imperial Defence in 1909 had recommended that a serious invasion of Egypt could best be met by a landing at Haifa. (Minutes of 102nd Meeting approving the Report of Lord Morley's[1] Sub-Committee on Egypt, C.I.D. Paper 107–B.)

[1] John Morley, 1838–1923. Liberal MP, 1883–1908. Secretary of State for India, 1905–10. Created Viscount Morley of Blackburn, 1908. Lord President of the Council, 1910–14. Resigned from the Government in protest against the coming war, August 1914.

LORD KITCHENER agreed that later on we should probably have to make a diversion on the Turkish communications. The moment for it however had not yet arrived. Naval reconnaissance at El Arish had not discovered the presence of any considerable force. Aeroplane reconnaissance would however be made in a few days' time. For the moment time was required for the organisation of the considerable military forces now in Egypt.

MR. CHURCHILL suggested that at any rate tonnage should now be collected.

SIR EDWARD GREY pointed out that there was already a shortage of tonnage for mercantile purposes, due partly to military demands, and it was not expedient to aggravate this.

LORD FISHER asked whether Greece might not perhaps undertake an attack on Gallipoli on behalf of the Allies.

SIR EDWARD GREY explained that there was not much hope that Greece or Roumania could co-operate effectively with the Allies unless they were assured that Bulgaria would remain neutral. None of the Balkan States trusted the Bulgarian declaration of neutrality, nor would feel satisfied in taking action unless Bulgaria was actually committed to hostilities with Turkey. Bulgaria desired certain portions of Macedonia and Thrace, of which she considered that Greece and Serbia had unjustly deprived her after the war between the Balkan States and Turkey. The attitude of Serbia and Greece held out no hopes of an accommodation between the several Balkan States. In these circumstances he did not think we ought to count on the co-operation of Greece.

MR. CHURCHILL explained the naval situation in the Mediterranean. One of the British battle cruisers had been withdrawn to Malta for repairs. The other remained off the Dardanelles. The French navy had been asked to send 3 battleships to the Dardanelles, where, in addition to cruisers, there were 3 British and 3 French submarines.

For the defence of Egypt there were available the 'Swiftsure,' 'Proserpine,' and 'Doris.' The 'Ocean,' 'Minerva,' and 'Philomel' would also soon be available. The Malta torpedo-boat flotilla was on its way there, and a number of canal launches were being armed. The Austrian fleet was looked after by the French.

MR. BALFOUR asked whether the best method of defending Egypt was not by occupying the wells some 30 miles east of the canal. If these wells were held, an enemy with a long tract of sandy and almost waterless desert behind him would have great difficulty in advancing. Would it be possible to fill in the wells?

LORD KITCHENER said that the wells were too near the surface to be destroyed. He thought they were too far away from the canal to be held. At present he felt no anxiety about Egypt and the Suez Canal.

Sir Edward Grey to Grant Duff:[1] *telegram*
(*Draft, Foreign Office papers: 372/570*)

25 November 1914   Foreign Office

Swiss Minister[2] has made a protest here. I have replied that if British aviators have passed over Swiss territory I will on behalf of H.M. Govt. express unqualified regret & apologize, but that the strictest instructions have been given to our aviators not to fly over Swiss territory and when machines were flying at a great height their position might easily be mistaken by those observing from below.

Further enquiry would be made, but in any case if it occurred, it can be only have been by inadvertence.

EG

Winston S. Churchill to Sir Edward Grey
(*Churchill papers: 2/64*)

27 November 1914   Admiralty

Sir E. Grey

I hope not too much 'unqualified regret'.

The Swiss in these parts are vy pro-German.

Switzerland is lucky to have Englishmen fighting the battle of the small states. The least she can do is not be querulous. Everyone else is daring & struggling & suffering—& it is no time for hedging neutrals to give themselves airs.

Our position is that no British aviator crossed Swiss territory: & that even if so the international law on the subject is indeterminate.

WSC

Sir Edward Grey: note

I think to keep up forms the aviators might be told of the Swiss complaint & given an opportunity of denying it.

[1] Evelyn Mountstuart Grant Duff, 1863–1926. Entered Diplomatic Service, 1888. Consul-General, Budapest, 1911–13. Minister to the Swiss Confederation, 1913–16. Knighted, 1916. His brother Adrian was killed in action on 14 September 1914.

[2] Gaston Carlin, 1859–1922. Entered the Swiss Foreign Service, 1884. Minister to Rome 1895–1902. Minister to London, 1902–20. Minister to The Hague, 1920–2. Minister to Berlin, 1922.

C. P. Scott:[1] *notes of a conversation with Lloyd George*

(*Scott papers*)

27 November 1914

As to the War with Turkey, Lloyd George partly blamed Churchill also for that. The situation was not desperate even after the attacks by the Goeben on Russian Black Sea ports. They did not concern us and it was open to Russia to ignore them but the perfectly useless bombardment by the fleet of one of the Dardanelles Forts and the seizure of Akaba brought us at once into war.

Winston S. Churchill to Lord Fisher and Vice-Admiral Oliver

(*Churchill papers: 13/27*)

29 November 1914   Admiralty
Most Secret

The intercepted telegrams[2] shd not be copied: one copy only being made for circulation—the record preserved in the secret book.

Commander Hope[3] is to study the telegrams with the view of finding out *the general scheme* of the enemy, & tracing how far the reports of the telegrams have in the past been verified by recorded facts. But it is not necessary for him to write his views on each telegram as it arrives & not to transcribe large portions of these vy secret messages.

The telegrams when intercepted will go direct & exclusively to C.O.S. who will mark them 1.S.L. Sir A. K. Wilson, it being understood that deliveries are not to be delayed through the temporary absence of any of the addresees.

WSC

[1] Charles Prestwich Scott, 1846–1932. Editor of the *Manchester Guardian*, 1872–1929. Liberal MP, 1895–1906. A friend of Lloyd George, who often sought his advice.

[2] On 26 August 1914 the German light cruiser *Magdeburg* ran aground in the Gulf of Finland. On the body of a drowned German signalman the Russians found the secret cipher and signal books of the German Navy. In November they sent the books to the British Admiralty, and on 8 November 1914 a special intelligence branch was set up in Room 40 at the Admiralty to decode the messages. The existence of this 'priceless information' was known in the Admiralty only to those who worked in Room 40, and to Churchill, Fisher, Sir Arthur Wilson and Vice-Admiral Oliver.

[3] Herbert Willes Webley Hope, 1878–1968. Entered Navy, 1892. Commander, 1909. Admiralty War Staff, 1914. Captain, 1915. Rear-Admiral, 1926. President, Woolwich Ordnance Committee, 1928–31. Vice-Admiral, 1931. Admiral, 1936.

Sir John French to Winston S. Churchill
(*Churchill papers: 26/1*)

29 November 1914   Headquarters
                                                   British Army

My dear Winston,

... I am thinking as hard as I can as to future plans, but so much turns upon what is really happening in Poland that we can decide upon nothing definite till we know.[1] From my reliable information I gather that an advance by the coast on Ostend will be met by very extensive inundations which the Germans are preparing to effect when necessary from the numerous canals in that neighbourhood. This may have the effect of cutting off support by the Fleet.

There are other difficulties. But I'll write more later.

Yours ever
J F

Winston S. Churchill to Sir John French
(*Copy, Churchill papers: 26/1*)

29 November 1914   Admiralty
Most private & secret

My dear French,

The time to do a thing like that wd surely be if the enemy made a hard push at Arras & Verdun. All plans ought to be in readiness & the naval support worked out in detail. The Fire organisation is important.

If you like I will try to come over next Friday night (after the King's visit) and spend Saturday & Sunday at your H.Q. We cd then talk over all possibilities.

The idea of the lines congealing for the winter with those people in Ostende & Zeebrugge is very unpleasant to the Admiralty. Mining is no use agst submarines, and bombardment only gives temporary relief. I believe military & naval interests are at one in this matter.

You should touch on the matter to K, without reference to our correspondence, and then everything cd be put in train by the Admiralty to use or not to use as circumstances decide.

[1] The British hoped that Russian successes on the eastern front would force the Germans to transfer troops from the western front. But on 18 November 1914 the Germans had completed the encirclement of the Russian fortress of Lodz, in Russian Poland, and after more than two weeks of intense fighting, Lodz fell to the Germans on 6 December. As a result, all hope of a Russian advance into German Silesia was ended.

We have made very far-reaching plans to catch Scharnhorst & Gneisenau. There are good prospects on the whole. But the seas are broad.

I am so glad to congratulate you upon the Order of Merit which I understand the King is to bestow during his visit. The dauntless front you have maintained to all these perils and anxieties makes your countrymen forever your debtor.

Yours always
W

Vice-Admiral Oliver to Winston S. Churchill
(Churchill papers: 13/2)

30 November 1914   Admiralty

First Lord,

I propose to let the Transport Dept know that transports should be kept in Egypt in case they are required for an expedition.

Will it be sufficient to tell them to keep enough transports in Egypt for One Division of troops, as that is the smallest unit complete with all arms.

H. F. Oliver

Winston S. Churchill: note to Lord Kitchener

Had we not better keep enough transports congregated for 40,000 men: or shall we disperse them ready to assemble at short (? what) notice.

WSC

Lord Kitchener: note to Winston S. Churchill

I will give Admiralty full notice. I do not think transports need be obtained in Egypt yet.

K

Winston S. Churchill: note to Vice-Admiral Oliver

Keep for record.

WSC

Margot Asquith:[1] diary
(Margot Asquith papers)

30 November 1914

Winston Churchill was 40 today. I wrote and congratulated him on his youth. He has done a great deal for a man of 40. When I look round and see as I do a few young men of 35 with amazing brains and see how much less they have done knowing that superiority of character pure and simple

[1] Emma Alice Margaret Tennant, 1864–1945. Known as Margot, Asquith's second wife; they were married in 1894.

is not exactly what Winston has got 'I put myself this question' (as the dreary peer in the House of Lords started most of his speeches) . . .

What is it that gives Winston his preeminence? It certainly is not his mind. I said long ago and with truth Winston has a noisy mind.

Certainly not his judgment—he is constantly very wrong indeed (he was strikingly wrong when he opposed McKenna's naval programme in 1909 and roughly speaking he is always wrong in his judgment about people). It is of course his courage and colour—his amazing mixture of industry and enterprise. He can and does always—all ways put himself in the pool. He never shirks, hedges, or *protects* himself—though he thinks of himself perpetually. *He takes huge risks.* He is at his very best just now; when others are shrivelled with grief—apprehensive, silent, irascible and self-conscious morally; Winston is intrepid, valourous, passionately keen and sympathetic, longing to be in the trenches—dreaming of war, big, buoyant, happy, even. It is very extraordinary, he is a born soldier.

When he came back from Antwerp he sent in his resignation to Henry saying he wanted to join the Army and have a command of some sort—he did not care what. He confided this to Freddy Guest who spoke to me of it with grave anxiety. I reassured him by telling him Henry would not dream of accepting Winston's resignation.

The fall of Antwerp was a cause of real sadness to Winston.

He was subjected to violent abuse in long letters to the Morning Post from Walter Long and other Unionists[1]—the first departure from the political truce—but this did not affect him one hair, he is quite unsensitive which is also a help! . . .

Lord Fisher: memorandum

(Admiralty papers: 116/3454)

No date[2]

On the possibility of using our Command of the Sea to influence more drastically the Military Situation on the Continent

From the shape the war has now taken, it is to be assumed that Germany is trusting for success to a repetition of the methods of Frederick the Great[3]

---

[1] On 14 October 1914 the *Morning Post* published a letter from Walter Long, headed 'The Antwerp Blunder', in which Long criticized the despatch of the Marines to the city. This letter was followed by several more from Conservatives, all hostile.

[2] This memorandum, referred to by Fisher in his letter to Churchill of 2 January 1915 (quoted on p. 362), is undated. In August 1917 Fisher had it printed in the form quoted here, and added a note at the top of the memorandum which stated: 'This paper was first prepared in the early autumn of 1914'. It was probably written in late November 1914.

[3] Frederick the Great, 1712–1786. King of Prussia from 1740 until his death.

in the Seven Years' War. Not only are the conditions of the present war closely analogous—the main difference being that Great Britain and Austria have changed places—but during the last 15 years the German Great General Staff have been producing an elaborate study of these campaigns.

Broadly stated, Frederick's original plan in that war was to meet the hostile coalition with a sudden offensive against Saxony, precisely as the Germans began with France. When that offensive failed, Frederick fell back on a defensive plan under which he used his interior position to deliver violent attacks beyond each of his frontiers successively. By this means he was able for seven years to hold his own against odds practically identical with those which now confront Germany; and in the end, though he made none of the conquests he expected, he was able to secure peace on the basis of the *status quo ante* and materially to enhance his position in Europe.

In the present war, so far as it has gone, the same methods promise the same result. Owing to her excellent communications, Germany has been able to employ Frederick's methods with even greater success than he did; and at present there seems no certain prospect of the Allies being able to overcome them soon enough to ensure that exhaustion will not sap the vigour and cohesion of the coalition.

The only new condition in favour of the Allies is that the Command of the Sea is now against Germany, and it is possible that its mere passive pressure may avail to bring her to a state of hopeless exhaustion from which we were able to save Frederick in the earlier war. If it is believed that this passive pressure can achieve the desired result within a reasonable time, then there is no reason for changing our present scheme of naval operations. If, on the other hand, we have no sufficient promise of our passive attitude effecting what is required to turn the scale, then it may be well to consider the possibility of bringing our Command of the Sea to bear more actively.

We have only to go back again to the Seven Years' War to find a means of doing this, which, if feasible under modern conditions, would promise success as surely as it did in the eighteenth century.

Though Frederick's method succeeded, it was once brought within an ace of failure. From the first he knew that the weak point of his system was his northern frontier. *He knew that a blow in force from the Baltic could at any time paralyse his power of striking right and left, and it was in dread of this from Russia that he began by pressing us so hard to provide him with a covering fleet in that sea.*

Owing to our world-wide pre-occupations we were never able to provide such a fleet, and the result was that at the end of 1761 the Russians were able to seize the port of Colberg, occupy the greater part of Pomerania, and winter there in preparation for the decisive campaign in the following spring. Frederick's view of his danger is typified in the story that he now took to carrying a phial of poison in his pocket. Owing, however, to the sudden death of the Czarina in the winter the fatal campaign was never fought. Russia made peace and Prussia was saved.

So critical an episode in the early history of Prussia cannot be without an abiding influence in Berlin. Indeed, it is not too much to say that in a country where military thought tends to dominate naval plans, *the main value of the German Fleet must be its ability to keep the command of the Baltic so far in dispute that hostile invasion across it is impossible.*

If then it is considered necessary to adopt a more drastic war plan than that we are now pursuing, and to seek to revive the fatal stroke of 1761, it is for consideration whether we are able to break down the situation which the German fleet has set up. Are we, in short, in a position to occupy the Baltic in such strength as to enable an adequate Russian army to land in the spring on the coast of Pomerania within striking distance of Berlin or so as to threaten the German communications eastward?

The first and most obvious difficulty attending such an operation is that it would require the whole of our battle force, and we could not at the same time occupy the North Sea effectively. We should, therefore, lie open to the menace of counterstroke which might at any time force us to withdraw from the Baltic; and the only means of preventing this—since the western exit of the Kiel Canal cannot be blocked—*would be to sow the North Sea with mines on such a scale that naval operations in it would become impossible.*

The objections to such an expedient, both moral and practical, are, of course, very great. The chief moral objection is offence to neutrals. But it is to be observed that they are already suffering severely from the open-sea mining which the Germans inaugurated and it is possible that, could they be persuaded that carrying the system of open-sea mining to its logical conclusion would expedite the end of the present intolerable conditions, they might be induced to adopt an attitude of acquiescence. The actual attitude of the northern neutral Powers looks at any rate as if they would be glad to acquiesce in any measure which promised them freedom from their increasing apprehension of Germany's intentions. Sweden, at any rate, who would, after Holland, be the greatest sufferer, has recently been ominously reminded of the days when Napoleon forced her into war with us against her will.

In this connection it may also be observed that where one belligerent departs from the rules of civilised warfare, it is open to the other to take one of two courses. He may secure a moral advantage by refusing to follow a bad lead, or he may seek a physical advantage by forcing the enemy's crime to its utmost consequences. *By the half measures we have adopted hitherto in regard to open-sea mines, we are enjoying neither the one advantage nor the other.*

The main practical objections to the course proposed are two. One is the condition of the North Sea after war; but this in any case must be very bad; and here also it may be argued that any measure which will hasten the restoration of normal conditions for trade is worth considerable additional sacrifice of a temporary nature.

The other practical objection is the danger to the communications of our own fleet when it is in the Baltic. This appears serious in view of the difficulty of securing an advanced base so long as the Scandinavian Powers remain neutral; but possibly it may be overcome by restricting our mining to a certain latitude.

On the general idea of breaking up the German war plan by operations in the Baltic, it may be recalled that it is not new to us. It was attempted—but a little too late—during Napoleon's Friedland–Eylau campaign. It was again projected in 1854, when our operations in the Great War after Trafalgar, and particularly in the Peninsula, were still living memories. In that year we sent a fleet into the Baltic with the idea of covering the landing of a French force within striking distance of Petrograd, which was to act in combination with the Prussian army; but as Prussia held back, the idea was never carried out. Still, the mere presence of our fleet—giving colour to the menace—did avail to keep a very large proportion of the Russian strength away from the Crimea, and so materially hastened the successful conclusion of the war.

On this analogy, it is for consideration whether, even if the suggested operation is not feasible, a menace of carrying it out—concerted with Russia—might not avail seriously to disturb German equilibrium and force her to desperate expedients, even to hazarding a fleet action or to alienating entirely the Scandinavian Powers by drastic measures of precaution.

The risks, of course, must be serious; but unless we are fairly sure that the passive pressure of our fleet is really bringing Germany to a state of exhaustion, *risks must be taken to use our Command of the Sea with greater energy;* or, so far as the actual situation promises, we can expect no better issue for the present war than that which the continental coalition was forced to accept in the Seven Years' War.

December 1914

Lord Northcliffe to Lord Murray of Elibank[1]
(Copy, Northcliffe papers)

1 December 1914

Dear Lord Murray,

What the newspapers feel very strongly is that, against their will, they are made to be part and parcel of a foolish conspiracy to hide bad news.

I am quite well aware of Winston's great activity and immense enthusiasm, but I do not think he understands the English mind or can have thought out the Audacious matter very carefully. Thousands of American newspapers, containing the news, with photographs, have been sold during the last few days at the great hotels in London, Manchester, Liverpool, Amsterdam, Rotterdam, Paris and elsewhere. These newspapers, too, have a very large sale in Canada; and in Buenos Aires and other South American cities, as you know. The German newspapers are giving much more attention to the Audacious than they otherwise would, and are spreading the news in Italy, Spain and other countries.

The English people do not mind bad news. Inasmuch as the Germans know of the disaster there can be no possible reason for suppressing it. It is a boomerang policy that will hit this Government very hard in the course of the long war we are now commencing.

From the outset the Press Bureau treated the newspapers offensively, and went out of its way to be offensive. So far as the naval censors are concerned; a message I sent to a string of American newspapers in answer to a request from them, was altered so as to be meaningless, and the name of Lord Fisher, on which the whole message turned, was struck out.

Every newspaper man that I know regards Winston as responsible for many of the initial evils of the Press Bureau, and he himself is aware of his own letters to me about the Times by the special request in writing to Mr

---

[1] Alexander William Charles Oliphant Murray, 1870–1920. Liberal MP, 1900–5; 1906–10; 1910–12. Under-Secretary of State for India, 1909. Chief Liberal Whip, 1909–12. Created Baron Murray of Elibank, 1912. Director of Recruiting for Munition Works, 1915–16.

F. E. Smith, who not only made the request, but personally embellished and altered the article. My newspapers were held up in the House of Commons by Mr Asquith and others as having acted disloyally, and, in the House of Lords, by Lord Haldane, although they were all aware of the fact that Mr F. E. Smith asked the Times and my other newspapers to publish the article.

Some things are more than flesh and blood can stand. So far as I am concerned, I propose to keep aloof from members of this Government until the war is over. I have always liked Winston personally, and he knows that.

Very sincerely yours

Lord Murray of Elibank to Lord Northcliffe

(*Northcliffe papers*)

1 December 1914   47 Parliament Street
Confidential

Dear Lord Northcliffe,

I return the papers with thanks for letting me see them.

I quite share your view that it is absurd to suppress important news of this nature . . .

I think, however, you will now see a change of attitude which you will regard as satisfactory.

I hope sincerely that you will reconsider your present intention, as I feel that nothing but good can come out of a frank interchange of view between you and Winston at this moment. Mistakes he must make, but he knows that he is concentrating the whole of his powers and energy on a situation that, in spite of the fact that he has courage and never shirks responsibility, must be a great strain upon him and at times fills him with grave anxiety.

Personally, as an outsider, I regard it as of the highest importance to our country that in these critical days there should be a complete understanding between those who wield powerful influence and direct great organisations, and where mistakes have been made they should, if possible, be speedily corrected, otherwise they may become a positive national misfortune.

He is an old friend of mine and I know would be happy to come if I ask him—hence my note of yesterday to which I do not despair of receiving a favourable reply.

Sincerely your
Murray of Elibank

Meeting of the War Council: extract from Secretary's notes

(Cabinet papers: 22/1)

Present: H. H. Asquith (in the Chair), David Lloyd George, Lord Crewe, Winston S. Churchill, Lord Fisher, Sir Edward Grey, A. J. Balfour, Lord Kitchener, Sir James Wolfe Murray, Lieutenant-Colonel Hankey (Secretary)

1 December 1914   10 Downing Street

THE SEIZURE OF AN ISLAND OFF THE GERMAN COAST

MR. BALFOUR said that, if by allotting 20,000 men to the seizure of an island off the German coast, it was true that Home Defence would be effectively provided for, it would obviously be worth doing, as it would release some of the large numbers now retained for Home Defence. He questioned, however, whether it was really a substitute for Home Defence.

MR. CHURCHILL pointed out that the seizure and occupation of a suitable island might render possible the establishment of a flying base, by means of which the movements of the German fleet would be kept under constant observation. It would also enable us to keep large numbers of submarines and destroyers, including the older as well as the newer classes, constantly off the German ports. We could also drop bombs every few days. In these circumstances it would be very difficult for the Germans to prepare for invasion without our knowledge, or to escape from the North Sea ports. Invasion could then only come from the Baltic.

LORD FISHER pointed out the importance of adopting the offensive. The present defensive attitude of our fleet was bad for its *moral*, and did not really protect it from the attacks of submarines.

LORD KITCHENER dwelt on the military aspects of the proposal. To provide troops of the right quality for the enterprise it would be necessary to withdraw men from the continent. He doubted the expediency of this. Our rôle on the continent was to contain as large a German army as possible in order to prevent them from transferring sufficient troops to beat the Russians. If the Germans did transfer troops from West to East, replacing them with veterans and youths, it might be necessary for us to advance, and for this purpose we should require our best troops.

(Conclusion.)

After a more detailed discussion the question was adjourned. The Admiralty undertook to examine the question in detail and to report.

PROTECTION AGAINST AIRCRAFT

MR. BALFOUR asked whether adequate protection had been provided for oil tanks and other vulnerable points against aerial attack. He had felt some surprise that no attack had been made on Woolwich Arsenal or Thameshaven.

MR. CHURCHILL said the question had received careful consideration. As much as possible of the oil and petrol at Thameshaven had been moved to depôts in a more secure position. Possibly too much attention had been given to the defence of London, and it was open to question whether some of the guns allotted to London should not be moved to Woolwich. A large number of guns had been supplied for this purpose. At Portsmouth, for example, there were thirty anti-aircraft guns. It was, however, in his opinion, impossible to provide effectually by means of passive defences for every vulnerable point liable to aircraft attack. The best plan was to attack the sheds and bases of the enemy's aircraft, and this policy was being actively pursued.

Winston S. Churchill: memorandum

(Admiralty papers: 137/452)

2 December 1914   Admiralty

Sylt is 20 miles long, & in many places only $\frac{1}{2}$ a mile wide. On the seaward side there is at numerous points sufficient water close inshore for battleships to bombard from. On the land side it is protected by 8000 to 14000 yards of sand covered twice daily by the tide. These sands, the neighbouring island of Rom, & the mainland opposite Lister Deep for 6000 yards inland, can be dominated by the fire of warships lying in Lister or Romer Deep. This fire will also prevent reinforcements being brought to the enemy from one part of the island to another.

2. It is proposed to attack the Northern end of the island, overwhelming the enemy's guns by naval fire from positions to the North & the West, & thereafter under naval protection to land a Brigade of Infantry (4000) with engineers, & to occupy Listland, holding the narrow neck of the Island near Dovecot. It is proposed to establish an aeroplane, submarine, & destroyer base on the island & in Lister Deep, & thereafter to occupy the rest of the island of Sylt as convenient.

3. It is proposed to protect the island from *land* attack by naval fire whenever necessary, both from the seaward & inshore sides; to prevent enemy heavy guns being placed in positions on the mainland or on Rom to bombard Lister Deep; & to help in preventing all infantry attack across the

sands. It is believed that all these tasks can be easily discharged without any large or valuable naval force being required.

4. It is proposed to protect the island from seaward attack exclusively by the submarines & destroyers based on Lister Deep, & to make it self-contained & self supporting against any naval force which the enemy wd employ.

5. It is proposed to use the submarines destroyers and aeroplanes based on the island to maintain a regular observation & control upon the debouches of the Heligoland Bight, thus preventing any raid or invasion from putting to sea unperceived & without full warning.

Sequence of operations:

1) When the time for making the attack arrives, 6 oversea submarines will be working between Heligoland & Heever River & further East.

2) A submarine off Sylt report by W/T (or by pigeons) at night to a waiting destroyer that the weather is favourable & the wind Easterly.

3) The expedition will be composed as follows:—

A. *The bombarding force.*

4 Majestics or Royal Sovereigns lightened to 20 feet by caissons wh also protect against torpedoes.

3 Monitors

20 T.B.D.s.

B. *The landing force.*

4 small transports thoroughly equipped with landing facilities, carrying 4000 regular infantry with machine guns and sappers, in all 5000 men.

C. *The defending force.*

18 C Class submarines

1st & 3rd Destroyer Flotillas made up to 40 boats.

2 seaplane & aeroplane ships

6 sloops & gunboats.

3 Field batteries with diagroper instead of horses

4 6 in and 12 4.7 naval guns on land mountings or in flat-bottomed boats.

4) A and B parts of the expedition will sail to arrive off Sylt at daylight on the first day. 4 Battleships & 3 Monitors attack, from positions A & B as convenient, the Northern end of the island. No help can reach the enemy here, either from the mainland or along the island itself.

5) As soon as the enemy's artillery is silenced, probably in two hours from daylight, the troops land covered by the battleships on the western shore at convenient points & secure themselves in Listland.

6) At high water the Battleships pass inshore to Romer & Lister Deeps, & take stations to dominate the narrow part of Sylt at C, the approaches from the mainland both to Rom & Sylt, and the mainland opposite Lister Deep. The Monitors assist.

7) The occupation of the Northern end of the Island being completed during the day, C part of the expedition will have sailed so as to arrive at nightfall.

8) The occupation of the rest of the island can be effected as convenient, an additional brigade of Infantry (4000 men) being held ready to sail if necessary. The 9 battns of the Royal Naval Division (9000 men) are also available either to reinforce or to relieve the Infantry according to circumstances.

9) These operations will be covered by cruisers & battlecruisers, & by the Grand Fleet within supporting distance, & any attempt by the enemy's heavy ships to interfere with them will be met with superior force. There is no likelihood of S/M attacks during the 1st day, except from a chance patrolling boat. The troops shd all be on shore before S/Ms sent from Heligoland could arrive. If a S/M attack is seriously threatened, the transport can be run into shoal water.

Subsequent movements must depend on what the enemy does, but no difficulty wh cannot be met need be apprehended. An active patrol of destroyers near the bar will protect the anchorages in Romer & Lister Deeps from enemy S/Ms on the 2nd & 3rd days, & by the 4th day an anti-S/M net will have been placed across the entrance. The aeroplane station will be established in time to enable the battleships in Romer & Lister Deeps to prevent heavy guns being mounted within 6000 yards of the mainland shore. Infantry attacks across the sands at low water shd be easily repulsed by the rifle & artillery fire of the garrison supported by the Monitors, warships, gunboats & sloops. The artillery of the defence can be continually increased by field & heavy guns on shore or mounted in prepared horse-boats. Landings of enemy's infantry on the island of Rom can be prevented by gunboats monitors & destroyers firing from the North & by the close fire of the ships in Romer Deep. These cd certainly prevent heavy guns being brought across the sands. The railway line on the mainland can be broken up by the fire of the battleships in Romer Deep, & heavy guns on railway trucks, firing from that position, can be immobilized & dismounted. Attacks by enemy Destroyers & Light Cruisers can be met with great advantage by our similar vessels. Attacks by the enemy's heavy ships will always be notified in time by aeroplanes, & met by C Class S/Ms. The S/M &

Destroyer force can be augmented to any extent necessary to cope with the enemy. The more the enemy employs his naval force in the attack of Sylt, the greater the advantage to us, the provocation of such attacks being an essential object in itself. If very large military forces are diverted from other operations to attack Sylt across the sands, every advantage shd rest with us. Even if the enemy made a lodgement, he cd not possibly maintain himself under the cross fire of the warships, nor advance along the narrow neck to the N. end of the island. Finally, the force cd be withdrawn at any time without difficulty.

WSC

Winston S. Churchill to Sir Edward Grey
(*Admiralty papers: 116/1336*)

2 December 1914   Admiralty
Secret

Sir E. Grey.
1) The international Conference of 1910 reached no agreement on the subject of aeroplanes flying over neutral territory. There is therefore no international law on the subject, & no question can arise of breach of neutrality. It is vy important that this point shd be maintained, as we shall have to fly across the Maestricht appendix of Holland in order to attack Essen, in a few weeks time on a vy large scale.
2) Nevertheless the Br. aviators honestly tried to avoid Swiss territory, because the route across German territory was the best & shortest. They believe they succeeded.
3) We must not pay too much attention to pro-German Swiss.
4) Tell them to go & milk their cows.

WSC

Edward Marsh to Sir Edward Grey
(*Admiralty papers: 116/1336*)

2 December 1914   Admiralty

Dear Sir Edward,
    Winston asks me to send you this revised version of his minute of this afternoon. After studying the map, he feels obliged to withdraw the words 'and shortest'! but the rest of his argument holds good.

Yours sincerely
E. Marsh

Sir Edward Grey: note

I must see Winston tomorrow. The matter is getting very serious & we shall have a real row with Switzerland.

EG

Grant Duff to Sir Edward Grey: telegram

(*Copy, Admiralty papers: 116/1336*)

3 December 1914 Berne

British airmen crossed in direction of line from Schaffhausen to Lake Constance on return journey one of them was in Swiss territory nearly whole way.

Delay in answering Swiss protest creating bad impression here where any violation of Swiss neutrality much resented. As Government at present friendly it seems pity to delay apology. Press agitation increasing.

Grant Duff to Sir Arthur Nicolson: telegram

(*Copy, Admiralty papers: 116/1336*)

3 December 1914 Berne
Private

It is important to close aviation incident as the Swiss are just now very sensitive about their neutrality and Germans are exploiting matter.

There is no doubt whatever that our men flew over Swiss territory in several places.

Sir Edward Grey: note

I ought to have our aviators version, but my impression is that unless they are positive they did not fly over Swiss territory I had better express regret.

We dont want to claim the right to go over Swiss territory, nor to alienate Switzerland.

EG

Winston S. Churchill: note

I have sent an answer on other papers.

WSC

Winston S. Churchill to Lord Kitchener

(*Kitchener papers*)

3 December 1914   Admiralty

My dear Kitchener,

I hope to bring off my long delayed visit to France next Sunday—if all remains quiet here. The Prime Minister sees no objection & I hope you do not either.

I will take occasion to talk over with General Henderson[1] the W. Office proposal for our lending naval aeroplanes & pilots to the army. There is a good deal of jealousy between the head people in the two wings. But I have no doubt a friendly arrangement can be arrived at.

Till then I am delaying action on the official letter we have received from your office.

I have cut down Paris' despatch as you suggested.[2]

Yours vy sincerely
Winston S. Churchill

H. H. Asquith to Venetia Stanley

(*Montagu papers*)

4 December 1914   10 Downing Street

. . . V & I lunch to-morrow at the Admiralty with Winston & Clemmie. She (C) comes to the Wharf with me, & he (W) goes to France to see French. Kitchener, who spent the best part of an hour with me this morning, rather deprecates these frequent visits of W. to the front: the Army think that he mingles too much in military matters, & the Navy that he is too much away in what may be critical moments for them. I am so far disposed to agree that I think, after this, I shan't allow him to go again for a long time. . . .

[1] David Henderson, 1862–1921. Entered Army, 1883. Captain, 1890. Director of Military Intelligence, South Africa (under Lord Kitchener), 1900–2. Learned to fly, 1911. Advocated the formation of a Royal Flying Corps for the Army, 1912. Director-General of Military Aeronautics, 1913–18. Major-General, 1914. Appointed General Officer Commanding Royal Flying Corps, 5 August 1914; he took his force to France, 13 August 1914. Knighted, 1914. Lieutenant-General, 1918. Vice-President of the Air Council, January 1918; resigned, April 1918, after a disagreement with the Air Minister, Lord Rothermere. Director, League of Red Cross Societies, Geneva, 1920–1. His only son was killed in a flying accident in 1918.

[2] Major-General Paris' 'Confidential' report on the operations of the Royal Naval Division at Antwerp had been printed for the Cabinet on 13 October 1914. (*Admiralty papers: 116/3486*) It was issued to the public in December 1914, in an abbreviated form.

A. J. Balfour to Lieutenant-Colonel Hankey

(*Hankey papers*)

5 December 1914   Whittingehame

My dear Hankey,

. . . After leaving you last Tuesday evening I went to the Admiralty, and had a very long talk with Winston. I found him not only very much bent upon his scheme [a British landing at Sylt], in which I entirely sympathize with him, but in the mood which refuses to recognize even the most obvious difficulties. If he came to another meeting of the Defence Committee in this humour, I am certain that the whole time would be spent in quite futile discussion. . . . I am rather surprised that as Winston, by his own account, has been considering this scheme for a twelve month, all local details had not been thoroughly examined and tabulated. . . .

H. H. Asquith to Venetia Stanley

(*Montagu papers*)

5 December 1914   The Wharf

. . . I lunched with Violet at the Admiralty—only Goonie & M. Smith were there in addition to the Winstons. W. was just off to Dover, crossing to-night to see French. I strongly urged him to make a full announcement now about the 'Audacious' with a clear statement of the reasons for delay. His volatile mind is at present set on Turkey & Bulgaria, & he wants to organise a heroic adventure against Gallipoli and the Dardanelles: to wh. I am altogether opposed. . . .

Commodore Keyes[1] to Eva Keyes[2]

(*Keyes papers*)

7 December 1914

. . . I thought J F [Fisher] was going to start fresh with me—but no—he is determined to knock me out! Admiral Oliver . . . told me that JF had said

---

[1] Roger John Brownlow Keyes, 1872–1945. Entered Navy, 1885. Naval Attaché, Athens and Constantinople, 1905–7. Commodore in charge of submarines, North Sea and adjacent waters, August 1914–February 1915. Chief of Staff, Eastern Mediterranean Squadron, 1915. Director of Plans, Admiralty, 1917. Vice-Admiral in command of the Dover Patrol, 1918. Knighted, 1918. Created Baronet, 1919. Deputy Chief of the Naval Staff, 1921–5. Commander-in-Chief, Mediterranean, 1925–8; Portsmouth, 1929–31. Admiral of the Fleet, 1930. National Conservative MP, 1934–43. Director of Combined Operations, 1940–1. Created Baron, 1943.

[2] Eva Mary Salvin Bowlby, 1882–   . She married Roger Keyes in 1906. Their elder son was killed in action in Libya in 1941.

to him the night before 'Why is Keyes always at the Admiralty—why doesn't he go to sea like Tyrwhitt[1] and take command of his vessels at sea.' . . . I am sure he knows *that* isn't true—and that it is the way to hurt me most. . . . JF is an unforgiving unscrupulous devil and he will hunt me to the end, but I do feel that his re-appearance is for the good of the nation and that we shall make war now! That is the only thing that really matters or that I ought to care about.

Winston S. Churchill to Sir John French

(*Copy, Churchill papers: 26/1*)

8 December 1914   Admiralty
Most secret & personal

My dear French,
    Kitchener agrees entirely with yr view. We held an immediate conference with the P.M. & Sir E. Grey: & as the result the strongest possible telegram is being drafted. The Admy attach the greatest importance to the operation, & will aid in every way. We are already making the necessary preparation on an extensive scale. Later I will let you have vy full & clear details. The combination must be perfect.
    K. proposes to let you have the 27th Divn in time.
    The 4 Admy 6″ guns have been used to release 4 army 6″ guns employed on coast defences. This circumvents the ammunition difficulty.
    I hope you will continue to press the new plan hard both here at home & on the French Generals.
    Nothing cd exceed the urbanity of 'our mutual friend' on my return. I think the ungracious sentence was only habit, & indicated no deep design or feeling. I have purred like a cat, & shall continue to do so. We *must* all work together for the result.
    I cannot tell you how much I enjoyed our talks, & my visit to the front was pure delight.
    I shall try to come & see the working out of the plan, if all goes well.
    I am putting some experimental shields in hand, & will let you know about them later.

[1] Reginald Yorke Tyrwhitt, 1870–1951. Entered Navy, 1883. Commodore, commanding the Destroyer Flotilla of the First Fleet, 1913–16. Knighted, 1917. Created Baronet, 1919. Commanded the Third Light Squadron, Mediterranean, 1921–2. Commanding officer, coast of Scotland, 1923–5. Commander-in-Chief, China Station, 1927–9. Admiral, 1929. Commander-in-Chief, the Nore, 1930–3. Admiral of the Fleet, 1934.

I meant to tell you—but forgot—abt Reggie Barnes.[1] He is recovering here from his wounds. He will be back soon. He gives up the command of the 10th in April. I hope you will find some use for him. His many & high qualities are known to you.

Once more many thanks for yr hospitality & kindness to me.

Yours always
W

Lord Fisher to Winston S. Churchill
(*Churchill papers: 13/28*)

8 December 1914
3.30 am!!

Dear Winston,

Welcome back! I don't hold with these 'outings' of yours! I know how you enjoy them! Nor am I afraid of responsibility when you're away. But I think its too venturesome! Also it gives your enemies cause to blaspheme!

However, the leopard can't change his spots nor the Ethiopian his skins and you wont desist! Oliver is working out some scheme to give Jellicoe a destroyer Flotilla based on Rosyth & working with Bradford[2]—we kill thus 2 birds with one stone.

There are two very pressing matters—

I. The fortification of Scapa. Its too absurd that two fine Battleships should be doing what a hundred marines and half a dozen guns on shore could do better.

II. Our wireless abroad totally inadequate—we want high powered stations at (a) Falkland Islands. (b) Bathhurst (West Coast Africa). (c) Jamaica. (d) Fanning Island. (e) Bermuda.

Let us lose no time. If we don't get Scapa fortified in war & these 5 wireless we certainly shant get them hereafter. Besides this war is going to last now that the Russians have collapsed and Germany has a straight route to India.

Yrs F

I spent a maudlin hour yesterday with the King. His is quite mischievous.

[1] Reginald Walter Ralph Barnes, 1871–1946. Entered Army, 1890. Lieutenant, 4th Hussars, 1894. One of Churchill's close army friends, they went to Cuba together in 1895. Lieutenant-Colonel, commanding the 10th Hussars, 1911–15. Colonel, 1914. Brigadier-General, commanding the 116th and 14th Infantry Brigades, 1915–16. Major-General, 1916. Commanded the 32nd Division, 1916–17; 57th Division, 1917–19. Knighted, 1919.

[2] Edward Eden Bradford, 1858–1935. Entered Navy, 1872. Rear-Admiral, Home Fleet, 1909. Commanded the 3rd Battle Squadron, 1914–16. Knighted, 1916.

He told French that I had said 150,000 Germans would invade us! What I did say was that if 150,000 Germans did come they would never go back! I won't go any more. *I'll be sick!* . . .

Winston S. Churchill to Sir John French
(*Copy, Churchill papers: 26/1*)

9 December 1914   Admiralty
Personal & most Secret

My dear French,

Kitchener is sending you a copy of the telm we have fired off at the Fr Govt. I enclose the answer so far recd. Burn it please. I hope you will find means to press the policy on Joffre. Here everyone informed—5 only—is convinced & ready to press vy hard indeed. Please God we succeed. A good & brilliant operation is in sight, conducent immediately to the safety of this country & the general success of the war.

Meanwhile all the naval preparations are going forward; & I will to-morrow write to you in some detail abt them. The Admirals here are red hot for it.

If Joffre 'insists' that it is impossible to replace you in the line, wd it be conceivable to come round with part of yr force on to the sea-flank? I hazard this suggestion, because if the operation were successful, subsequent clearing up wd always be possible.

Yours always
W

George V to Winston S. Churchill
(*Churchill papers: 13/27*)

9 December 1914   Buckingham Palace

My dear Churchill,

I am delighted with the good news.[1] Sturdee has avenged poor Cradock & the loss of his ships. Please convey my hearty congratulations to Sturdee

[1] Admiral Sturdee's squadron was coaling at the Falkland Islands on 8 December when he sighted Admiral Spee's squadron. In the ensuing battle Sturdee lost no ships and very few men; four German warships were sunk and over 2,200 officers and men killed. The Admiralty were angry that Sturdee had allowed the fifth warship, the *Dresden*, to escape, and Sturdee received neither an Admiralty acknowledgement of the action nor any private letter of congratulation from either Churchill or Fisher. But the moral effect in England of the destruction of the same ships which scarcely a month before had defeated Cradock off Coronel was immense.

& his ships for this most opportune victory. I trust the remaining two German cruisers will be accounted for soon.[1] I wish also to congratulate you &
the Admiralty for the success of your well laid plans.

Believe me, very sincerely yours
George R. I.

Lord Haldane to Winston S. Churchill

(*Churchill papers: 13/27*)

9 December 1914   28 Queen Anne's Gate

My dear Winston,

Warmest congratulations on the great coup of which Masterton Smith has
told me.

It is a splendid result of fine strategy, for which the Navy and its First
Lord deserve the thanks and admiration of the nation. These they will
receive.

Ever yours
Haldane

Winston S. Churchill to Vice-Admiral Yashiro: telegram

(*Draft, Churchill papers: 13/29*)

9 December 1914   Admiralty

On behalf of the British Navy I heartily thank your Excellency for your
message conveying the congratulations of the Imperial Japanese Navy on the
action off the Falklands.

With the sinking of the Scharnhorst, Gneisenau, Leipsig, and Nurnberg,
the whole of the German Squadron based on Tsing-Tau at the outbreak of
the war has been destroyed, and that base itself reduced and captured. This
event marks the conclusion of the active operations in which the Allied
Fleets have been engaged in the Pacific for more than 4 months, and though
it has fallen to a British Squadron in the South Atlantic to strike the final
blow, it is largely owing to the powerful and untiring assistance rendered
by the Japanese Fleet that this result has been achieved. Had the enemy
turned westward again, the honours would have rested with the Japanese
and Australian Squadrons moving forward in the general combination.

[1] The *Dresden* was tracked down by the *Glasgow* in March 1915 and sunk at Juan Fer-
nandez Island. The *Karlsruhe* was destroyed in the Caribbean Sea by an internal explosion
on 4 November 1914; the British Admiralty only learnt of this late in March 1915.

The peace of the Pacific is now for the time restored, and the commerce of all nations can proceed with safety throughout the vast expanses from the coasts of Mozambique to those of South America. The expulsion of the Germans from the East is complete, and with good and vigilant arrangements all return should be rendered extremely difficult and hazardous.

I take the opportunity of your Excellency's cordial message to express on behalf of the British and Australian Navies our earnest recognition of the invaluable naval assistance of Japan.

Winston S. Churchill to Lord Fisher
(Fisher papers)

10 December 1914   Admiralty

My dear—This was your show & your luck.

I shd only have sent one Greyhound & Defence. This wd have done the trick.

But it was a sizzling coup. Your *flair* was quite true. Let us have some more victories together & confound all our foes abroad—& (don't forget)—at home.

I am not quite happy about Zeebrugge & have held back the letter till tomorrow. I am shy of landings under fire—unless there is no other way.

Yours ever
W

Winston S. Churchill to Sir John French
(Copy, Churchill papers: 13/27)

10 December 1914   Admiralty

My dear French,

The tides are favourable from the 14th onwards, but firing would begin later each day. A gale would interrupt the naval operations.

2 Battleships are all that can work off Ostende and Nieuport at one time. But arrangements would be made to replace any sunk or set on fire and to maintain the bombardment night and day as required. In addition 3 monitors, 2 gunboats, and 6 destroyers will be used. Total heavy guns 26 of which 9 very heavy. See attached note[1] by the Chief of the Staff.

This force should be sufficient to support the advance of the Army on Ostende.

Zeebrugge is the home of the enemy's submarines and it would add

[1] Not printed.

greatly to the safety of our ships if we could attack that place at the same time as you commence your advance with a sufficiently strong landing party to take and hold it until you came up.

The landing of this force would be covered by 2 other battleships, a number of destroyers, and 20 trawlers plated and fitted with maxims to keep down rifle fire—probably 10,000 men would be a suitable force for this purpose.

When Zeebrugge is in our hands the enemy's submarines will have no shelter to go to and we shall probably be able to drive them off or we may destroy some of them in the harbour, and when this is accomplished the ships will be able to keep abreast of your advance along the coast, and troops can be taken up to Bruges by the canal if necessary.

Please let me have your views and if necessary we can consult together on the details of a combined action.

Sir John French to Winston S. Churchill

(*Churchill papers: 26/1*)

10 December 1914   Headquarters
Secret

My dear Winston,

Yours of the 8th inst K. sent me the wire to the French and I have the reply which you enclosed. So far all seems to go well: but I fear Joffre & Foch will make difficulties. The preparations for a forward move, commenced as as I told you when you were here, had even then proceeded further than I thought and I'm afraid we must carry this thro' now from our present position.

I am in close consultation with Foch and shall hear at once what view Joffre takes. But if he agreed to an immediate change of our position the forward move now projected (and for which troops have been moved into position) would have to be postponed for several days. He will hardly agree to this and I'm not altogether sure that, from a general point of view, he would be right in incurring the delay. Supposing we attain our immediate objective in 3 or 4 days (say by Thursday 17th) I could then push Foch to make the change whilst if by chance (we can never be sure of anything in war) a further delay in getting forward comes about I could urge an immediate reversion to our new place.

I am just as anxious to get on the flank & work with our Navy as you are so you may be sure I shall let no opportunity slip or delay taking vigorous action longer than I can possibly help.

I enjoyed beyond measure having you here & shall look forward to your next visit.

I sent you a wire this morning expressing the pleasure we all feel at Sturdee's splendid victory.

Yrs always
JF

Sir Arthur Wilson to Winston S. Churchill
(*Churchill papers: 13/27*)

10 December 1914   Admiralty

I do not think we can do any good in the Baltic with any combined fleet of French and English such as we could make up even with the help of the Italians in the Mediterranean without reducing the North Sea Fleet below the safe limit until we have found some means of greatly reducing the danger from Submarines, or else of completely blocking the Canal.

A French Fleet in the Channel would however enable us to be more prodigal with our old battleships in bombarding operations, but we cannot even do that till they are properly **organized** and fitted for the purpose.

AKW

General Wilson: diary
(*Wilson papers*)

10 December 1914   St Omer

Sir J sent for me 10.00 am. It appears that he had advanced his theory, to Winston, of going on the left of the line so as to have ground for his cars! & the support of the Fleet. Winston fell in with this idiotic scheme, & went hot foot to London. He, K, Grey, Asquith put their heads together & sent off a kind of demand for this movement to the French Government. Meanwhile Sir J had got committed to the Messines attack. . . . The little fool has no sense at all. He told me he could take Ostend & Zeebrugge at once. And how? & if he did? He cannot read a map in scale. It really is hopeless.

Winston S. Churchill to Lord Fisher

(*Fisher papers*)

11 December 1914   Admiralty
Secret

I.S.L.

We ought without delay to order more 'Styx' class for heavy inshore work. There are, for instance, the four reserve 13·5″ guns of the Audacious which should certainly be mounted in new monitors. It should also be possible to draw from the reserve of 15″ guns, and to make in a short time 15″ or 18″ howitzers. We require now to make ships which can be built in 6 or 7 months at the outside, and which can certainly go close in shore and attack the German fleet in its harbours. These are special vessels built for a definite war operation, and we must look to them in default of a general action for giving us the power of forcing a naval decision at the latest in the autumn of 1915.

Our thought is proceeding independently on the same lines. I propose as a basis of discussion, that in addition to the 4 Schwab monitors, we prepare 8 more at a cost of not more than £700,000 apiece. These vessels should be armed either with 13·5″ or 15″ guns, two or four in each as convenient. Or, alternatively, they should be armed with four 18″ howitzers in separate Cupolas sunk low on their heavily armoured turtle backs. They should draw 8 feet at most and be propelled entirely by internal combustion at a speed not exceeding 10 knots; no funnels; three or four alternative telescopic masts for fire observation; strong crinolines 20 feet away all round to make them immune from mine or torpedo, etc. A third alternative variant would be two heavy guns in turrets in the centre and two mortars in 'cupolad' pits on each side of the deck.

Please consider these ideas. Let us discuss them together, and then bring them up at an early war conference. The root principle is to build vessels to be ready in June or July capable of going in to fetch them.

WSC

Winston S. Churchill to Sir John French

(*Copy, Churchill papers: 26/1*)

11 December 1914   Admiralty
Personal & Secret

My dear French,

I have sent you today a Memo through Kitchener showing in some detail the form naval assistance on the flank could take.

I was disappointed by your letter and do not quite know what is purposed now. But I wish you all good fortune in the coming battle from the depths of my heart. Your difficulties are great. All of us must look only to the great conclusion.

You must use the Navy or not as circumstances require. All our arrangements will be complete by the 15th. But weather introduces an element of uncertainty.

Yours always

W

Sir John French to Winston S. Churchill

(*Churchill papers: 13/27*)

11 December 1914   Headquarters
Secret

My dear Winston,

Foch has been with me today and urged the provision & use of some kind of Armoured Craft in the numerous Canals which traverse this country in all directions. I wonder if any of your Naval Experts could suggest the possible use & conversion of any such boat which you may happen to possess in store or otherwise.

I am sure they could be used with great effect.

This is only a short line to ask you to give a thought to this subject.

Foch thinks he can get something of the kind from the French Admiralty but I told him of your immense power of resource & that I would write to you about it. I have heard nothing yet from the French side about our new plans & in the meantime our fresh attack is imminent.

Of course your motor men—& all Naval people in our Employ—will receive full & sympathetic consideration.

Yrs always

J F

Winston S. Churchill to F. E. Smith

(*Birkenhead papers*)

December 1914   Admiralty

My dear—

I am coming over (DV etc) on Saturady night. I am vy anxious to see you and will wire from GHQ how and when. How are you doing under the military heel? We will have a good talk when we meet. I am getting on all right here in spite of some your party *swine*.

Your affectionate friend

W

Winston S. Churchill to Vice-Admiral Oliver

(*Churchill papers: 13/27*)

12 December 1914   Admiralty

Commodore S,[1] ought really to be able to do in one of those Zeebrugge submarines with his C Boats.

Surely one can lie off the entrance constantly—being relieved when necessary.

It is high time a result was achieved here.

WSC

Winston S. Churchill to Sir John French

(*Copy, Churchill papers: 26/1*)

13 December 1914   Admiralty

My dear French,

Of course we are disappointed here at the turn events have taken,[2] but we shall do our best to help the French in their feeble secondary 'dog-in-the-manger' attack on the left flank. The risks to the ships are much greater than they were last time. Many heavy guns are in position on the sea-front and there are at least 2 submarines at Zeebrugge.

Unless there is a genuine push made on this flank we cannot hang about day after day amid these perils.

Sir Arthur Wilson and I are coming over to Dunkerque Monday night—14th, and will watch the combined operations on the 15th.

---

[1] A reference to Commodore Keyes, the Commodore in charge of Submarines. For the subsequent controversy about Zeebrugge, and Churchill's defence of Keyes, see Churchill's undated letter to Fisher (quoted on p. 308), and his letters of 21 December (quoted on p. 324) and 23 December (quoted on p. 327).

[2] A more propitious turn of events had taken place that day at the Dardanelles, when the first Victoria Cross of the campaign was won by Lieutenant Norman Douglas Holbrook, whose submarine torpedoed the Turkish battleship *Messudiyeh*. To reach the battleship, Holbrook had taken his submarine, the B.11 under five lines of mines. On 22 December 1914 Churchill asked Carden to convey his 'warmest congratulations' to Holbrook, and added: 'The Captain is singled out for the VC because the whole conduct of the boat lay in his hands alone and success depended upon his judgment.' (*Churchill papers: 3/72*) Of the seventeen VCs conferred on the Royal Navy and Royal Marines between 1882 and 1916, ten were awarded for action during the Gallipoli campaign. Holbrook's only son was killed in action in 1945.

If you are making a move on your part, I should like you to send Seely for me in a motor-car so that I could come and join you for a few hours and watch what is going on.

I shall be in the harbour of Dunkerque till 7 a.m. Tuesday and after then Bridges at Furnes will know of my whereabouts. Will you send me an answer care of the British Consul, Dunkerque?[1]

Yours always
Winston S. Churchill

PS We are hard on the track of Dresden via the Magellan Straits and of Karlsruhe in the Bahamas.

Winston S. Churchill to Lord Fisher

(Fisher papers)

[?13] December 1914   Admiralty
Most Private

My dear, •

You have not given your mind to this.[2] Murder lurks in its heart.

Don't be crushed by Departmentalism. This naval war is different to all others. Victory feels a novelty and the unexpected. There is an idea to polish and perfect.

I can answer these rubbishy objections in half an hour. Am I to give the half hour, or are we to proceed on ruthless, r. and r. principles, and say to Keyes: 'Damned well do it or out you go'?

Yours
W

Winston S. Churchill to Sir John French: telegram
(Copy, Churchill papers: 13/27)

13 December 1914   Admiralty

Your request for armed craft for service on canals. 3 horseboats each fitted with one 4·7 gun and 2 maxims each towed by a steam cutter are

[1] Philip Charles Sarell, 1866–1942. Entered Consular Service, 1883. British Consul at Dunkirk, 1908–18. Consul-General, Tunis, 1920–3; Barcelona, 1923–6.

[2] I have not been able to find out what 'this' refers to; probably to correspondence between Fisher and Keyes concerning a submarine attack on Zeebrugge, such as Churchill referred to in his letter to Fisher of 12 December 1914. Unlike Churchill, Fisher had a poor regard for Keyes' abilities, and constantly entered into dispute with him (*see* Keyes' letter to his wife of 7 December 1914, quoted on pp. 297–8).

being prepared. If these answer a number of others can be got ready as required.

In addition 3 patrol launches mounting a three pounder and a maxim each are in hand.

These 6 boats should be ready at Furnes by the nineteenth.

If you or General Foch have any further suggestions for canal work please let us know.

The 3 Monitors can go up the canal from Zeebrugge to Bruges at the right time.

Winston S. Churchill to Sir John French: telegram

(*Draft, Churchill papers: 13/27*)

14 December 1914   Admiralty

In view of the low barometer and small scale of operations we have ordered only one battleship 2 gunboats & 6 Destroyers to fire tomorrow monitors being weather-bound.

Sir John French to Lord Kitchener: telegram

(*Copy, Churchill papers: 13/27*)

15 December 1914

The fleet action was most useful today. General Foch requests, and I recommend, that the same co-operation may be given tomorrow.

H. H. Asquith to Venetia Stanley

(*Montagu papers*)

16 December 1914   10 Downing Street

. . . I have just had a message from Winston—'Most Secret' so you had better keep it for the moment—that the 'game is afoot'. 3 German Dreadnoughts in action with our flotilla & 'shelling Scarborough'—3 cruisers firing towards Hartlepool—& the 'Roon' & 5 German destroyers sighted.

So the information was good, & there ought to be a 'considerable action' to-day. . . .

Meeting of the War Council: extract from Secretary's notes

(Cabinet papers: 22/1)

Present: H. H. Asquith (in the Chair), David Lloyd George, Lord Crewe, Winston S. Churchill, Sir Edward Grey, A. J. Balfour, Sir James Wolfe Murray, Lieutenant-Colonel Hankey (Secretary)

16 December 1914   10 Downing Street
Noon

THE BOMBARDMENT OF HARTLEPOOL, SCARBOROUGH, AND WHITBY.

MR. CHURCHILL communicated such information as had come to hand regarding the bombardment and its results. He explained that a division of the First Battle Fleet, a squadron of battle cruisers with armoured cruisers and light cruisers had been disposed with the object of intercepting the enemy's retreat and bringing him to action. In addition, part of the Second Battle Fleet had issued from the Forth to cut the enemy off from the North, and a destroyer force under Commodore Tyrwhitt had sailed from Harwich, and should before long establish contact with the division of battleships. In addition a submarine flotilla was off Terschelling on its way to intercept the enemy on his homeward route, though it was doubtful whether it would arrive in time. These dispositions justified the hope that, if the weather should prove favourable, the enemy would be intercepted on his return to port. It was believed that the enemy's object in making this raid was mainly as an act of retaliation for his recent defeat in the Falkland Islands; also to re-establish the prestige of the German navy in Germany and in neutral countries; and possibly to endeavour to influence the dispositions of our fleet and draw them into an area where they would be more accessible to the German submarines.

After some discussion,

THE PRIME MINISTER suggested an adjournment of the discussion on this question until further news was available.[1]

---

[1] At Hartlepool, during the German bombardment, 113 civilians were killed and 300 wounded. At Scarborough 17 civilians were killed and 60 wounded. At Whitby 3 civilians were killed and 4 wounded. At Hartlepool, for a few days, the local authorities had tried to minimize the number of dead. Among the buildings damaged were private houses, a barracks, a lighthouse, a school and a hotel.

Winston S. Churchill to Sir John French
(*Copy, Churchill papers: 13/27*)

16 December 1914   Admiralty

My dear French,

To-day a fine chance went astray.

I think I will come Thursday night to Dunkirk, & come on to you.

I cannot risk the ships unless there is a real push.

I will—if I may—communicate about my movements through Bridges.

Yours vy sincerely
Winston S. C.

Winston S. Churchill to H. H. Asquith
(*Asquith papers*)

17 December 1914   Admiralty

My dear Prime Minister,

The Germans are back in their harbours, & for the moment there is a lull. I propose if you see no objection to go over to Dunkirk tonight & spend tomorrow night at French's H'Quarters, returning Sunday. The attack wh has begun has now come to a complete standstill, & the whole question of the flank movement now comes up again. The clearance of the coast is a most serious matter for the Admiralty & I want to further it if possible. Yesterday was wearing: & a few hours of different surroundings will do me good.

Yours always
W

Winston S. Churchill to Lord Kitchener
(*Kitchener papers*)

17 December 1914   Admiralty

My dear Kitchener,

I propose to go tomorrow to Dunkirk to see what the position is.

Have you any objection to my staying with French as he wd like, or to my discussing with him the questions connected with naval co-operation on the sea-flank?

Things are quiet for the moment here. But I fear such a chance as yesterday is not to be counted on again. Directions have been given to place the 2 9·2's at your disposal. But the problem is where to put them.

I enclose you a copy of the telegram I have had to send in answer to yours from French.

Yours sincerely
Winston S. Churchill

Winston S. Churchill to Sir John French: telegram
(Kitchener papers)

17 December 1914   Admiralty

It is regretted that no ships can fire tomorrow. Monitors alone wd be knocked out by enemy's batteries. Revenge is damaged by shell fire under water & must refit. It is not justifiable to expose Majestic to submarine risks unless to support a real movement in which case every risk will be run & ample support provided.

H. H. Asquith to Winston S. Churchill
(Asquith Papers)

17 December 1914   10 Downing Street

My dear Winston,

I do not think that you ought to go again to French without first consulting Kitchener & finding that he approves.

Yrs always
HHA

Winston S. Churchill: note
My dear Prime Minister

I have always done this, and will do so now. I shall not go till tomorrow afternoon.

Yours always
W

Winston S. Churchill to Lord Kitchener
(Kitchener papers)

18 December 1914   Admiralty
Private

Dear Kitchener,

The question I asked was one wh you cd easily have answered yourself; & it was one upon wh yr wishes shd naturally prevail. It was not necessary

to trouble the Prime Minister; & some of the statements you appear to have
made to him are not well founded, & shd certainly in the first instance have
been made to me.

H. H. Asquith to Winston S. Churchill
(Churchill papers: 26/1)

18 December 1914   10 Downing Street

My dear Winston
   There can, of course, be no objection to your going to Dunkirk to look
into naval matters, but after talking with Kitchener, who came to see me
this morning, I am clearly of opinion that you should not go to French's
headquarters or attempt to see French.
   These meetings have in K's opinion already produced profound friction
between French & himself, & between French's staff & his staff, which it is
most desirable to avoid.
   Questions of concerted naval & military action can be best discussed and
arranged here.

                                                            Yrs always
                                                               HHA

H.H. Asquith to Venetia Stanley
(Montagu papers)

18 December 1914   10 Downing Street

   . . . I wrote to Winston as we agreed adding what you suggested about
the possibility of concerting naval & military action here at home. He has
just been to see me, very sore & angry with K, upon whom he poured a
kettle-full of opprobrious epithets. Of course he acquiesced in the decision,
and will not now go to Dunkirk till to-morrow, if even he goes then. . . .

Lord Kitchener to Winston S. Churchill: not sent
(Draft, Kitchener papers)

18 December 1914   War Office

My dear Churchill,
   I cannot of course object to your going over to discuss naval co-operation
with Sir J. French; but at the same [time] I think—I ought to tell you
frankly that your private arrangements with French as regards land forces

is rapidly rendering my position and responsibility as S of S impossible. I consider that if my relations with French are strained it will do away with any advantage there may be to the country in my holding my present position and I foresee that if the present system continues it must result in creating grave difficulties between French & myself. [I do not interfere with Jellicoe nor do I have a private correspondence with him.][1]

I am suggesting to the PM that you should take the WO and let Fisher be 1 Lord then all would work smoothly I hope.

Lord Kitchener to Winston S. Churchill
(*Churchill papers: 26/1*)

19 December 1914   War Office
Private

Dear Churchill,

I wrote an answer to your letter yesterday asking me about your visiting French, but before sending it to you I thought it advisable to show it to the P.M. He asked me not to send it and said he would speak to you on the subject which is one that has caused me considerable anxiety.

Yours very truly
Kitchener

Winston S. Churchill to Lord Kitchener
(*Copy, Churchill papers: 26/1*)

19 December 1914   Admiralty
Private

Dear Kitchener,

I have never visited French without yr assent, wh I supposed was freely given.

The statement that you seem to have made to the PM to the effect that I had been a cause of friction between you & French is not well founded. The exact contrary is true. The causes of any friction wh may exist are not difficult to see. They are all inherent in the situation. But I have on every possible occasion & by every possible means promoted that good will & confidence between you wh I regard as of the highest importance to the country. I know that what I say will be corroborated by French himself, & it can be proved without any difficulty.

---

[1] Sentence in square brackets deleted by Kitchener, before Asquith advised him not to send any of the letter.

The question rested obviously with you to decide. In the face of an objection by you I cd not have pressed my wishes in a matter of such a minor & personal character, whatever I might have thought. There was no need to make charges or statements of the character to wh I have referred. They are vy unfair to a colleague who has worked with you with the utmost loyalty.

Yours vy truly

WSC

H. H. Asquith to Venetia Stanley

(Montagu papers)

19 December 1914   10 Downing Street

. . . I have heard & seen nothing so far this morning [of] either of my stormy petrels—K & Winston, and I hope I shall make good my escape before either is well on the wing. Sir R. Brade[1] has just come in from K. with a message from French, who will be here by to-morrow night: so I shall see him Monday morning. Both K & French himself are anxious that his journey shd be kept a *profound secret*:—the Press Bureau is going to suppress any mention of it. . . .

P.S. I had closed this up but as the inevitable visit from K has now taken place I thought you wd. like to hear about it. W. seems to have sent him a pretty abusive letter last night, complaining of his speaking to me &c—a rather childish performance. K declares that he returned a 'soft answer'. Meanwhile for his own amusement, & the enlightenment of posterity, he (K) has been drawing up an imaginary account of how he secretly induced or bullied Jellicoe into, taking 300 War Office steamers & stowing them away off the S.W. coast of Ireland. In order to keep French's visit a secret we have arranged that K. shd meet him at Dover or Folkestone to-morrow morning, motor him to Broome,[2] and after they have confabulated there bring him over to me at Walmer, where if necessary I can put him up for the night, & he can be shipped off back to France next morning. . . .

I now hear that Winston is on his way over here: so I won't finally seal this up. Thank God he is not coming—after all. . . .

---

[1] Reginald Herbert Brade, 1864–1933. Entered War Office as a Clerk, 1884. Secretary of the War Office and Army Council, 1914–20. Knighted, 1914.

[2] In 1911 Kitchener had bought Broome Park, near Canterbury, and with it 500 acres of land. Between 1911 and 1916 he devoted his leisure time to reconstructing the interior of the house and beautifying the grounds. When he was created an Earl in July 1914 he had wanted to take the title 'Earl of Broome', but was persuaded by his friends that 'Earl Kitchener' would be a greater national asset.

Frederick Guest to Winston S. Churchill
(*Churchill papers: 26/1*)

19 December 1914   Headquarters

Dear Winston,

By the time you get this the chief will be in England and he has asked me to let you know what his plans are likely to be. After his talk with K & the P.M. he proposes to motor to his house at *94 Lancaster Gate* and remain there quietly for 48 hours. He hopes that he will see you and have some opportunity to talk things over with you. He is anxious to keep his visit and his whereabouts absolutely secret so do not send any letter addressed to him except by really trustworthy messenger. I am very anxious that he should be put au fait with all the European situation and should hear first hand either from the Foreign Office or the P.M. all there is to know about Russia etc. At present he only receives K's impressions which seem ill digested & pannicky.

It is most important for the nerves of any man with his responsibilities to know *really* what is going on elsewhere and what are the relative burdens that each member of the alliance has to bear etc, etc.

Now on to another point—You must not quarrel with or tread on K's toes. Nor must he encourage the Chief. I know that you never have done so in the past (in fact just the opposite) but I see signs of strained relationship between you and tremble for an explosion.

It is because you are so much the cleverer man of the three that the responsibility rests with you to keep the triumvirate together. Also you are the only politician of the group and can see further ahead. Our only consideration is how to 'beat the Bosche'—Forgive me writing plainly but an onlooker often sees most of the game & I have been watching & trying to help you all since the show began. Good bye little man & God bless you.

Yrs
Freddie

Lord Fisher to Lady Randolph Churchill[1]

(*Churchill papers: 28/84*)

19 December 1914   Admiralty

Dear Lady Randolph,

I cant dine out—I go to bed at 9.30—I get up at 3.30—I dont go any-where.

Winston is quite enough dissipation for me I want no more!

Yours in haste
Fisher

Lord Fisher to Lord Esher

(*Esher papers*)

19 December 1914   Admiralty

SECRET

My beloved E

. . . Everyone including the Prime Minister (with whom I was lunching yesterday & danced with his wife to a Moody & Sankey Hymn! SUCH A LOVELY VALSE!!!) consider I am Winston's facile dupe!

I am in the position of entering into a game of chess (against a good player) which has been begun by bloody fools! . . .

Winston S. Churchill to Sir John French: telegram

(*Draft, Churchill papers: 13/27*)

19 December 1914   Admiralty

We are receiving almost daily requests from the French for naval support on the Belgian coast. We regret we are unable to comply. The small vessels by themselves cannot free the new shore batteries and it is not justifiable to expose battleships to submarine perils unless to support a land attack of primary importance. If such an attack is delivered all the support in my memorandum forwarded to you through the S. of S. for War will of course be afforded. I should be glad if you would explain this to General Foch as it is painful to the officers concerned to have to make repeated refusals.

[1] Jennie Jerome, 1854–1921. Daughter of Leonard Jerome of New York. Married Lord Randolph Churchill, 1874. Mother of Winston and Jack Churchill. Editor of the *Anglo-Saxon Review*, 1899–1901. Married George Cornwallis-West, 1900; marriage dissolved, 1913. Married Montagu Porch, 1918.

Edward Smyth-Osbourne[1] to Winston S. Churchill

(*Churchill papers: 13/27*)

19 December 1914   HMS Invincible

Dear First Lord,

Thank you very much for your message which we were all very pleased to get. It was the greatest peice of luck the enemy delivering themselves into our hands as they did. I was expecting several weeks search for them & you can imagine our joy & surprise when they were reported just outside the harbour the morning after we arrived.

Capt Allen[2] did well & was lucky in sinking the 'Nurnberg' by himself & not having another of our ships with him to claim a share in his victory. Of course where two of our ships fired at the same enemy they both thought they had sunk her. I was positive we had sunk both the 'Scharnhorst' & 'Gneisenau' & was surprised later to find that the 'Inflexible' thought that they had had a great deal to do with it—possibly they had, & it does not matter much so long as it was done. I was amused & rather saddened by something I overheard the day after the Action— A boat from the 'Inflexible' came alongside & one of the boats crew starting bucking to some of our men who were looking over the side about what the 'Inflexible' had done & how lucky for the 'Invincible' that she was there, when one of our men asked 'Have you seen the "Goeben" lately' which silenced him & made all the poor fellows in the boat hang their heads.

The men we picked up out of the sea were very anxious to know whether we were going to shoot or hang them & quite believed the Germans were laying waste England. One of their Engineer Officers who was a bit too free with his revolver during the action, they say they popped into the furnace. They all cordially hated their officers but the discipline seemed to suit them as all their ships were fought marvelously to the end.

I must thank you for finding myself in the only ship which was present both in the Action off Heligoland & the F.I.S. & I trust that we will be home in time for 'The Day' in the North sea. . . .[3]

[1] Edward Smyth-Osbourne, 1884–1916. Entered Navy, 1900. Lieutenant, 1905. Served on the Admiralty Yacht *Enchantress*, 1912–13. Lieutenant-Commander, HMS *Invincible*, 1914–16.

[2] John Derwent Allen, 1875–1958. Entered Navy, 1888. Captain, commanding the Admiralty Yacht *Enchantress*, November 1913–August 1914. Commanded HMS *Kent* at the Battle of the Falkland Islands, December 1914. Commanded the *Vernon* Torpedo School-ship, 1922. Rear-Admiral, 1924. Vice-Admiral, 1929.

[3] After the battle of the Falkland Islands HMS *Invincible* returned to Rosyth for a refit. On 'the day', at Jutland, she formed part of the 3rd Battle Cruiser Squadron, when she was sunk. There were 1,026 British dead, including Smyth-Osbourne, and only six survivors. When the *Invincible* blew up, some of the sailors in the other British ships thought she was a German ship, and cheered wildly.

H. H. Asquith to Venetia Stanley

(*Montagu papers*)

20 December 1914   Walmer Castle

. . . I spoke very frankly to Sir J. F. about Winston's visits, & his intervention in military matters. I found that he was substantially of the same opinion, & with all his affection & admiration for W, estimates his judgment as 'highly erratic'. . . .

Lord Kitchener to Winston S. Churchill

(*Churchill papers: 26/1*)

20 December 1914   War Office
Private

My dear Churchill,
    I never said that you were trying to make trouble between French & myself. If you like we will talk it over.
    French is now here[1] so I hope we can get the matters that were troubling me settled up without friction.

                                                    Yours very truly
                                                    Kitchener

Lord Fisher to Sir John Jellicoe

(*Jellicoe papers*)

20 December 1914   Admiralty

. . . Winston has so monopolized all initiative in the Admiralty—and fires off such a multitude of purely departmental memos: (His power of work is absolutely amazing!) that my Colleagues are no longer 'superintending Lords' but only 'the First Lord's Registry'! I told Winston this yesterday and he did not like it at all but it is true! and the consequence is that the Sea Lords are atrophied and their departments run really by the Private Office

---

[1] On the morning of 20 December 1914 Sir John French crossed from France to Folkestone, where he was met by Kitchener. The two Field-Marshals went at once to Walmer Castle, to discuss with Asquith the question of munitions supply and the possibility of a German invasion of England. French then went to London, where he attended a War Council and was received by George V. He returned to France on 23 December.

and I find it a Herculean task to get back to the right procedure and quite possibly I may have to clear out & I've warned Winston of this. But please do not mention this to a soul—I only want to explain to you that I have so little time to write to you.

... Battenberg was a cypher and Winston's facile dupe! ...

Winston S. Churchill to C. C. Graham[1]
(Copy, Churchill papers: 13/27)

20 December 1914   Admiralty

My dear Mr. Mayor,

I send you a message of sympathy, not only on my own account, but on behalf of the Navy, in the losses Scarborough has sustained. We mourn with you the peaceful inhabitants who have been killed or maimed, and particularly the women and children. We admire the dignity and fortitude with which Scarborough, Whitby, and the Hartlepools have confronted outrage. We share your disappointment that the miscreants escaped unpunished. We await with patience the opportunity that will surely come.

But viewed in its larger aspect, the incident is one of the most instructive and encouraging that have happened in the war. Nothing proves more plainly the effectiveness of British naval pressure than the frenzy of hatred aroused against us in the breasts of the enemy. This hatred has already passed the frontiers of reason. It clouds their vision, it darkens their counsels, it convulses their movements. We see a nation of military calculators throwing calculation to the winds; of strategists who have lost their sense of proportion; of schemers, who have ceased to balance loss and gain.

Practically the whole fast cruiser force of the German Navy, including some great ships vital to their fleet and utterly irreplaceable, has been risked for the passing pleasure of killing as many English people as possible, irrespective of sex age, or condition, in the limited time available. To this act of military and political folly they were impelled by the violence of feelings which cd find no other vent. This is very satisfactory, & should confirm us in our courses. Their hate is the measure of their fear. Its senseless expression is the proof of their impotence & the seal of their dishonour. Whatever feats of

[1] Christopher Colborne Graham, 1857–1943. Mayor of Scarborough, 1913–19. Elected Alderman, 1918. He took an active interest in the Scarborough Sea Training School, and was President of the District Nursing Association.

arms the German Navy may hereafter perform, the stigma of the baby-killers of Scarborough will brand its officers and men while sailors sail the seas.

Believe me, dear Mr. Mayor, Yours faithfully
Winston S. Churchill

Lord Fisher to Winston S. Churchill
(*Churchill papers: 13/28*)

20 December 1914   Admiralty

Dear Winston

—I wrote a 'Hell and Damnation' letter to Sir John Bradbury[1] last night as I discovered that we had lost a mass of materials which had been available for instant purchase through Treasury opposition to our new wireless stations *and other purchasers have stepped in* (—*notably in the vital article of Dynamos—now sold to other purchasers*) *This will involve terrible delay!* Now as *without doubt* these wireless stations which I see my way to early completion (had these Dynamos been bought at once.) are vital to the successful conduct of the War (and I've informed Bradbury he will have the joy of forthcoming disasters registered to his Department). I think it would be a lovely opportunity for me to resign when you can have Sturdee as First Sea Lord!

Wilson seems to think we ought to have Beatty's [Battle Cruiser Squadron] down to Rosyth. I am thinking it over. *Jellicoe will* squeal! And the Rosyth defences are not as angelic as I was given to understand. (*Mr Bircham*[2] *is a fraud!*)

How this Scarborough massacre emphasises the Battle Cruiser!

I think the 32 Knot 'Rhadames' will want to be put in hand without delay—I see no escape—*The 'Queen Elizabeths' are too slow!* thanks to 6 inch guns and too much armour and too many Fads. I think the 'Rhadamanthus' could be built in 10 months if we put our minds to it. *No one will believe it possible—no one ever does when a big thing comes off!* The Dreadnought fired her

---

[1] John Swanwick Bradbury, 1872–1950. Entered Colonial Office, 1896; transferred to Treasury, 1898. Private Secretary to Asquith, 1905–8. Insurance Commissioner, 1911. Joint Permanent Secretary, Treasury, 1913–19. Knighted, 1913. Principal British Delegate to Reparation Commission, Paris, 1919–25. Created Baron, 1925. Chairman of National Food Council, 1925–29. Chairman, Bankers' Clearing House Committee, and President, British Bankers' Association, 1929–30, 1935–36.

[2] Francis Richard Sam Bircham. Lieutenant RNVR, 1914. Suggested the method for providing an anti-submarine obstruction for the Rosyth base, October 1914. Designed the Bircham Indicator Net, to detect the presence of submarines. Boom Defence Officer, Firth of Forth, 1915–16. Lieutenant-Commander, 1916. His commission terminated on 21 October 1915.

W.C. 3 — Y

guns in 15 months from the keel plate being laid and could have fought a battle!

Yours Fisher

Think it over about Sturdee!

H. H. Asquith to Venetia Stanley
(*Montagu papers*)

21 December 1914   10 Downing Street

. . . I thought Winston's letter about the 'Scarborough baby-killers' wh. I read in the train rather banal; a lot of cheapish rhetoric & an undertone of angry snarl! He appeared here in person soon after I arrived, and told me he had had an effusive reconciliation with K. It was all a 'quite trumpery misunderstanding' &c. He is going this afternoon to see French, who has dug himself in for the moment in his old lair at Lancaster Gate. . . .

By the way, Winston revealed to me as a *profound secret*, wh. he is not going even to breathe to Grey, that to-morrow (*Tues*) the Germans are contemplating a new naval adventure against us. So keep your eyes open, as I shall. I shall say nothing to any other human being. . . .

I am writing in the Cabinet room, at the beginning of twilight, and thro' the opposite window across the Parade I see the Admiralty flag flying, & the lights 'beginning to twinkle' from the rooms where Winston & his 2 familiars (Eddie & Masterton) are beating out their plans. The Bud[1] is back, but has a temperature (no wonder). . . .

Lord Fisher to Winston S. Churchill
(*Churchill papers: 29/1*)

21 December 1914

Dear Winston,

. . . We have got to get rid of our multitude of 'Canopi' et hoc genus omne! Scrap them all! *The scrapheap cries aloud!* A multitude of splendid seamen butchered in ships than can neither fight or run away! . . .

Look at the murdered Pegasus! All over the world we distributed Tortoises to catch Hares. *Bring them home and put them in the Zoological Gardens as specimens!*

Those minelayers of ours will be butchered if they go out. Send the mines in the 'L' class of destroyers—*they are all fitted to lay mines! The whole 'L' class to be* always out singly, independently *distributing bouquets of mines at the*

---

[1] Nellie Hozier, 1888–1957. Clementine Churchill's sister. Served as a nurse in Belgium, 1914. Captured by the Germans but released almost immediately. She married Colonel Bertram Romilly in 1915.

Amrum Light and far out to sea! Lock the Germans up! Do something!!!!! *We are waiting to be kicked!!!* Next kick this week!

Yours
F

Winston S. Churchill to Lord Fisher
(Fisher papers)

21 December 1914   Admiralty

My dear Friend,

This is *my* early worm—caught over-night.

Don't write too many letters to Admiralty folk in the dim dawn. It weakens your prestige. Write to me—who am your friend & who *am in the same boat.*

Or if you write them—burn them unsent. I often do this: & when I don't, Masterton-Smith & Eddie Marsh come & make me. •

We have got a monkey's puzzle to cuddle—& are doing it vy well.

A.K.W. [Wilson] & you are a splendid combination. We shall get our turn of luck.

Look at this[1] from Lady Jellicoe.[2] It makes me squirm!!!

Yours always
W

Winston S. Churchill to Lord Fisher
(Fisher papers)

21 December 1914   Admiralty

My dear Fisher,

I see no objection to laying down one or two secret minefields out from Heligoland tonight: or to laying some shield or barrier lines off weak points in our own coast. I expect we shall suffer inconvenience from it afterwards, but there is always a chance of a bag. It is like saving a few lottery tickets. But it is no substitute for going to work.

A policy of scattering a few bouquets of mines from destroyers & building fast ships that will not be ready until all is over, is only a partial solution of our problem. I am entirely opposed to the laying down of new Dreadnought ships at this stage. It will hamper more urgent work—in every direction. Long before they can be finished we shall have smashed up the German

---

[1] A Press appeal from Lady Jellicoe, in which she asked the public to send woollen socks and underclothes to the sailors of the Grand Fleet.

[2] Florence Gwendoline Cayzer. She married Jellicoe in 1902. Their son George Jellicoe (born 1918) was First Lord of the Admiralty, 1963–4. Lady Jellicoe's sister Constance was married to Admiral of the Fleet Sir Charles Madden.

Navy in harbour with our monitors, or they will have fought their battle on blue water, or peace will have been signed. I could never undertake to attempt to persuade the Cabinet to such a measure, after the immense programme of monitors & submarines th I have asked them for on the opposite policy—viz everything that can be finished in 1915, & nothing that can't.

You will have to beat & destroy them with what you've got in 1915: & God knows there is enough—if handled.

The key to the naval situation is an oversea base, taken by force & held by force: from wh our C class submarines, & heavily gunned destroyers can blockade the Bight night & day: & around wh and for wh a series of desperate fights wd take place by sea & land, to the utter ruin of the enemy.

But I cannot find anyone to make such a plan alive & dominant: & tell them our situation is as I have told you & as you justly say, that of waiting to be kicked, & wondering when & where. As long however as the priceless information lasts this is a pretty good game.

Keyes is a brilliant officer, with more knowledge of & feeling for *war* than almost any naval officer I have met. I think the work and efficiency of our submarines are wonderful.

I agree with you about scrapping some of the worthless old ships.

We must have a conference at 11. The signal looks right to reach Jellicoe tomorrow unless we definitely decide to refuse them to him.

It looks as if they were coming to the Christmas party. I trust so.

Yours always
W

Sir John French to Winston S. Churchill
(*Churchill papers: 26/1*)

20 December 1914   94 Lancaster Gate

My dear Winston,

I've just arrived & got your note. Motored up from Walmer Castle with K.

I must have some teeth looked at to-morrow morning & I am going to lunch with K at Carlton Gardens at 1.

Could you possibly manage to motor up here at 3.15? I want *much* to have a talk.

I'm dining quietly with some old friends to-night.

Yrs Always
JF

If I hear nothing to the contrary I'll expect you.

Winston S. Churchill to Lord Kitchener

(*Copy, Churchill papers: 26/1*)

21 December 1914   Admiralty
Most secret

My dear Kitchener,

I have had a good talk with French today. He says the question is: are the Russians so smashed that the whole weight is coming on our necks? If so then better not lengthen the line by the flank move, but simply hold on until we are all ready again. If not—if they are still a great effective force, then the flank move is a good one & could be well carried out. He does not yet believe abt the Russians, & thinks that it may turn out to be less bad than we now think.

What I want to say is this. We ought to settle tomorrow or Wed either to do the flank thing or simply stick it out on our existing line. If we decide yes on merits, the Govt ought to grapple with the French (les Francais) & get our army on the flank for the job. Now is the time, & It will take a good deal of doing. You must say. But if we miss this chance, then all we can do is to hold on—& I expect we can do this—till the Spring.

I hope you will get a decision taken one way or the other in the next 48 hours. These sporadic attacks at 40 officers a time, & 300 yards (lost again the next day) may keep the enemy on the qui vive, but they are a gloomy way of waging war.

I am so glad we had a good talk this morning.

French was enormously cheered & pleased by his drive with you.

Yrs vy truly
WSC

Don't bother to answer.

Winston S. Churchill to Lord Fisher

(*Fisher papers*)

22 December 1914   Admiralty
Burn

My dear Fisher,

I am wholly with you about the Baltic. But you must close up this side first. You must take an island & block them in à la Wilson; or you must break the canal or the locks, or you must cripple their Fleet in a general action.

No scattering of mines will be any substitute for these alternatives.

The Baltic is the only theatre in wh naval action can appreciably shorten the war. Denmark must come in, & the Russians be let loose on Berlin.

There are 4 good Russian Dreadnoughts.

Yours ever
W

Winston S. Churchill: Admiralty instruction
(Draft, Admiralty papers: 116/1351)

23 December 1914   Admiralty

There is no obligation to recognize a white flag, & this signal only acquires validity if recognized. Sir John French has found it necessary to order instant fire to be made on any German white flag, experience having shown that the Germans habitually & systematically abuse that emblem. Consequently any white flag hoisted by a German ship is to be fired on as a matter of principle. This does not mean that no surrender may be accepted from an obviously helpless ship. But officers will be held strictly responsible if mishap or disadvantage to HM ships results therefrom.

In all cases of doubt the enemy's ship shd be sunk.

In an action, white flags shd be fired upon with promptitude.

WSC

Winston S. Churchill to Lord Fisher
(Churchill papers: 13/28)

23 December 1914   Admiralty

Secret

My dear Fisher,

I am vy much interested by Jellicoe's letter. Many thanks for sending it to me.

I don't think that officers shd be got rid of for a single failure, unless there are other reasons for thinking they are incompetent. Men often learn by mistakes; & the anxieties of war are such that leaders must know they will be supported & not be worrying about their own positions & feeling themselves in personal jeopardy.

I cd not remove Warrender[1] now. He has been trained in Grand Fleet

---

[1] George John Scott Warrender, 1860–1917. Entered Navy, 1873. 7th Baronet, 1901. Rear-Admiral, 1908. Knighted, 1911. Commanded the 2nd Battle Squadron, 1912–15. Vice-Admiral, 1913. Removed from his command on Jellicoe's advice as a result of increasing deafness and absent-mindedness, December 1915.

work for 3 years & is well thought of in the Fleet. As for Carden—he has
never even commanded a cruiser Sqn. & I am not aware of anything that
he has done wh is in any way remarkable. You were vy angry with him
some time ago about circling Malta with his 3 submarines. Jerram[1] wd be a
far stronger candidate for a Battle squadron.

As for Keyes I think he has done vy well, & never failed us in any way.
All these three years I have watched his work with increasing confidence.
Merit, zeal & courage must not be easily overthrown by bad luck. The
Germans have missed many more shots than we have. And we have vy few
chances, & targets.

My note about the Queen Elizabeth was only 'for consideration' like your
early worms.

But observe.

Lion	New Zealand
Queen Mary	Inflexible
Princess Royal	Invincible
Tiger	Indomitable

Queen Elizabeth alone

Yours vy sincerely
Winston S. Churchill

Winston S. Churchill to Lord Kitchener

(Kitchener papers)

23 December 1914   Admiralty

My dear Kitchener,

I cannot for the life of me understand why the various naval units now
serving with the Army in France cannot be treated in the same way as naval
detachments have always been treated by the Army in Egypt, South Africa,
and many other campaigns. On returning to the Admiralty to-day I have
been shown numbers of precedents where small and large detachments of
sailors under the Naval Discipline Act, serving in their own units and under
their own officers in charge of guns, in charge of armoured trains, or as
infantry, have served all over the world side by side with their military

---

[1] Thomas Henry Martyn Jerram, 1858–1933. Joined Navy, 1871. Rear-Admiral, Second-
in-Command, Mediterranean Fleet, 1910–12. Vice-Admiral, Commander-in-Chief, China
Station, 1913–15. Knighted, 1914. Commanded Second Battle Squadron, 1915–16, leading
it at the battle of Jutland, 1916. Admiral, 1917.

comrades, receiving their orders from the military commander. I cannot understand why the precedents of the past should be thrown over entirely now and the choice put to every sailor of either becoming a soldier or being sent home. If the War Office have the absolute military command and the complete administrative control, why should the fact that these men are under the Naval Discipline Act and not under the Army Act be a source of trouble now, any more than it was on so many previous occasions. I am sure you would not wish your tenure at the War Office to be marked by an alteration of the customs which have so long been observed between the two services.

There are altogether five separate units, either out there or being prepared, which have to be considered.

(1) 3 armoured trains under Commander Littlejohns. These trains were formed for the defence of Antwerp, where they saw a great deal of fighting and then they were lent to Rawlinson at his request during the retreat and served with him all through the operations till he joined French's Main Army. Since then they have continued to work under the orders of the Commander-in-Chief and have, I regret to say, fired off a good deal of our ammunition. Both Rawlinson and French have at different times asked most emphatically that these trains should not be withdrawn. The Admiralty position is that they are at the service of the Army as long as they are required, but that we hope the expenditure of ammunition will be restricted as much as possible, and that when they are no longer required the naval ratings, guns, and ammunition may be returned.

(2) The 50 or 60 motor omnibuses, under Geoffrey Howard. This unit was originally formed when the Naval Brigade went over to Dunkirk. It has reached a very high state of efficiency. It was particularly asked for by the War Office when the flank movement from the Aisne took place. It has, I believe, rendered very useful service at different times. The omnibuses carry exactly a battalion and have carried in fact 14 or 15 battalions to critical points during the recent fighting with great punctuality and to general satisfaction. 70 motor lorries which were also in Admiralty possession were handed over as a free gift to the Army, but the motor omnibuses have been kept together as a small unit. Why this should excite so much ill-feeling passes my comprehension. The Naval Discipline Act is, for all disciplinary purposes, just as efficient as the Army Act. The officers and men obey every order they receive from the military authorities; they are only there for the purpose of obeying their orders. There is no question of laxity or misconduct of any kind. The only complaint I see in regard to it which has any foundation is the fact that the men get 10s. a day as compared with Army Service Corps drivers and those of the naval armoured motor-cars in England who

receive 6s. a day. I should propose to remove this anomaly by the process of offering to all the men a lump sum down to revert to the regular Army rates, and, if agreeable to you, I will arrange this with Howard.

The Admiralty position in regard to the motor omnibus unit is as follows:— We do not think that the officers and men ought to be broken up and dispersed or ought to be separated from their omnibuses. This was the first idea of using motor omnibuses in this way, and the unit having done good work and being a living organisation on which much trouble has been expended, ought to be treated with consideration. I shall require a Cabinet decision before I could agree to it being dispersed. Of course if it is no longer required by the Army, then I would propose that it should be sent to work with the Belgians, to whom it would be very useful, or, if they did not want it, it should come home and act as transport for the Royal Naval Division here.

(3) I understood that the question of aeroplanes had been satisfactorily settled. We have ceded to the Army 16 machines on which we had been counting for the Naval Wing and the aerial defence of this country. We have also offered a squadron of 12, subsequently to be raised to 16, machines of Army patterns for service in the field. All the details of this were worked out between Commander Longmore,[1] R.N., and Colonel Sykes,[2] and a written agreement was reached which I understood was satisfactory to both parties. The details of this agreement are in your possession. Under it military control for all essential purposes and full administrative uniformity in matters of supply are secured. The unit will be ready to the extent of 12 machines on the 10th January. The pilots comprise some of the best in the world. I stipulate expressly, however, that they shall be kept together as a unit and shall not be broken up and dispersed so as to destroy their identity as a single

[1] Arthur Murray Longmore, 1885–1970. Entered Navy, 1904. Squadron-Commander, Royal Flying Corps (Naval Wing), 1912; transferred to the Royal Naval Air Service, 1914. Commanded the No. 1 Royal Naval Air Service Squadron, Dunkirk, December 1914, and promoted Lieutenant-Commander, Royal Navy. Received no further air command until December 1917. Served at Jutland, 1916. Commanded No. 6 Wing, Otranto, December 1917; the Adriatic Group, May 1918. Lieutenant-Colonel (Wing-Commander), Royal Air Force, August 1918. Director of Equipment, Air Ministry, 1925–9. Commandant, RAF College, Cranwell, 1929–33. Air Officer Commanding Coastal Command, 1934–6. Knighted, 1935. Air Officer Commanding-in-Chief, Middle East, 1939–41. Inspector-General, RAF 1941. Vice-Chairman, Imperial War Graves Commission, 1954–7.

[2] Frederick Hugh Sykes, 1877–1954. Entered Army, 1901. Commander, Royal Flying Corps, Military Wing, 1912–14. Major, 1913. Commanded Royal Flying Corps, France, 1914–15. Colonel Commanding Royal Naval Air Service, Eastern Mediterranean, 1915–16. Brigadier-General, 1917. Deputy-Director, War Office, 1917. Served on the General Staff, Supreme War Council, Versailles, 1917–18. Major-General, 1918. Chief of the Air Staff, 1918–19. Knighted, 1919. First Controller-General of Civil Aviation, 1919–22. Conservative MP, 1922–8 and 1940–5. Governor of Bombay, 1928–33.

naval squadron among the various Army squadrons; and that they shall not be treated in any manner inferior to that in which Army squadrons are treated. If this arrangement, which has been come to satisfactorily, is now thought to be open to objection then it is much better to let the question drop altogether and allow the squadron to remain here, where it is needed for the aerial defence of this country.

(4) The armoured motor-cars. This is a very good force. It arose out of the practical experiences in connection with the need of establishing flying bases in Northern France while the Army was still near Paris, and it is believed to embody all the latest ideas. Altogether there are 15 squadrons, the majority of the cars being light and mounting maxims and the others being heavy and mounting 3 pounders. The squadrons are being equipped in every detail and the quality of the officers and men is high. 2 squadrons are already practically complete and the others will be completed in all respects at the rate of about one a week. Meanwhile they have all been trained with ordinary cars so that the only thing that delays their completion is the delivery of the armoured cars. It is obvious that quite apart from any use they may be put to in certain phases of the war on the Continent, they have also a value for home defence. Any squadrons or cars that may be ready will be placed instantly under the orders of the War Office in the event of a raid or invasion. If Sir John French at any time wants these cars abroad, and the War Office apply to the Admiralty for them, they will be placed at the disposal of the Army and will come under the orders of the Army in all respects, and will be supplied by the Army, who will draw upon our general stores of spare parts, etc., here and forward them through the regular channel.

(5) The 15″ howitzer will be fired for proof on Wednesday next. Assuming that the trials are satisfactory, 4 of these will be ready to take the field complete in all respects by the end of January, and the supply of ammunition has also been arranged for. The officers and men already appointed are either skilled artillerists or mechanicians, and a large proportion of the men come from the works where the guns have been made and therefore understand the methods by which the guns are parted and assembled. It is proposed to enlist all these men, except the naval officers, in the status of Royal Marines, who automatically come under the Army Act when on shore. No difficulty has ever been found before in naval officers serving with the Army.

This I think covers the whole ground and I can assure you that nothing is further from my thoughts or intentions than ever in any circumstances being lured into attempting to add to the number of naval units serving with the Army. I have, however, obligations to the officers and men of those which have been already formed, and have incurred responsibilities in regard to public money which I must make good. I think you will see that we ought to reach a definite agreement in regard to all of them so that there is a common principle and rule applied to all, and so that you and I are set free from the utterly disproportionate amount of work and worry in regard to them and from the jealousies with which people with nothing better to do are so fond of occupying themselves. If you will nominate someone from the War Office to meet the Secretary of the Admiralty, who will act for me, I suggest that a definite agreement should be drawn up which is not out of harmony with precedents of the past, which preserves the identity of these naval units, and which at the same time gives the fullest disciplinary and administrative control to the military authorities while they are serving in the field. All parties, whether at the Admiralty, the War Office, or in the field, can then be told that the matter is settled and that they need not argue about it any more.

Yrs vy truly
Winston S. Churchill

Lord Kitchener to Winston S. Churchill
(*Churchill papers: 13/27*)

23 December 1914 War Office

My Dear Churchill,

I am sorry to see by your letter that you have gone back upon what was agreed between us with regard to the future of the various formations that you have raised at different times for service with the Army.

The Navy and the Army have each their definite rôle to perform, and I think it is a good rule that the Admiralty and the War Office should confine themselves to the supply of the services required by their respective Departments. Armoured trains, 'bus transport, armoured motor cars are, or can be, provided by the War Office when required; they are subsidiary services pertaining to the Army on land, and not Naval services.

I look upon a Naval Brigade or Division of Bluejackets as on an entirely different footing from these irregular formations which have been attached to the Army in France as Naval units, and you may be sure that when a Naval Division is ready to take its place alongside the Army in the field, it will be cordially welcomed by the War Office, and all the traditional arrangements for its service with the Army will be strictly adhered to in the future as in the past.

I think I have proved my desire to see a Naval unit of this sort associated with the Army in the field by lending you many Army officers to assist you to prepare efficiently a Naval Division, at a time when these officers could be ill spared and were urgently needed by the Army in France.

If, however, as appears from the number of Naval officers employed with the formations we are discussing, you have more officers in the Navy than you require, I think it would be better, and only right, that they should be employed in preparing the real Naval unit which we hope to see with us some day, and so release the Army officers that you now have, who are so much required for service with the Army.

If these irregular formations are only a means to enable certain officers, and gentlemen without military experience and training, to get to the front and take part in the war,[1] then I think it is even more important, if they are to be kept on, that they should form part of the Army, and not claim to be separate entities under the control of the Admiralty; by control, I mean what you yourself state, viz:— that they cannot be broken up or used in any other way than as complete Naval units, even though the exigencies of the service may require this to be done.

I know how anxious you are to do all in your power to promote the success of our arms in France, and when I tell you that the morale of the Army in the field is affected by these irregular Naval additions and therefore its fighting power impaired, as well as that they cause discontent and give trouble to the staff entirely out of proportion to their utility, I think you will agree with me that it is essential that something should be done to regularise the situation.

Yours sincerely
Kitchener

Winston S. Churchill to Lord Kitchener
(*Copy, Churchill papers: 13/27*)

23 December 1914   Admiralty

My dear Kitchener,

It would be wrong to continue this discussion.

There are now abt 15 officers & 350 men paid by the Admy. serving with the army under yr orders.

Will you vy kindly say what you wish them to do. They can be recalled at once if you so desire; & in any case their *matériel* is at yr disposal.

Yrs sincerely
WSC

---

[1] Among Churchill's aristocratic friends serving as officers in Admiralty units by the end of 1914 were the Duke of Westminster, the Baron de Forest, and the Hon Eustace Twistleton-Wykeham-Fiennes.

H. H. Asquith to Venetia Stanley

(*Montagu papers*)

24 December 1914   10 Downing Street

. . . Winston came to see me, after I wrote yesterday, to report progress or rather (as usual) the lack of it. The information on wh. they were acting turned out to be either false or misrepresented, and nothing happened! W. has now got down in the South & within hailing distance an Admiral after his own heart—Lewis Bayly, who has taken the place of Burney sent North to join Jellicoe. Both are quite good officers, but, as W. expresses it, Burney belongs to the 'No' & Bayly to the 'Yes' school. So W. is now meditating fearsome plans of a highly aggressive kind to replace the present policy of masterly inactivity. The two old sea-dogs at the Admiralty are both of the forward school, and I expect the whole Navy is a little dispirited & chaffing under the sense of ill-luck and impatience at purely negative results. . . .

Lord Fisher to Winston S. Churchill

(*Churchill papers: 13/43*)

25 December 1914   Admiralty

Dear Winston,

I suggest to you to hold your hand about Cradock & the Falklands. No doubt the Dresden told all but yet there are always lingering doubts till you hear the other side. We ourselves unintentionally gave away the Invincible and Inflexible in our first communique and doubtless Tirpitz[1] saw it! But that is not the point—the point is there is inexplicable folly in the escape of the Dresden and the murder of Cradock best left alone—and you will also have to go back and explain *similar* past criminal follies also which time has eaten up. Hawke, Cressy, Aboukir, Hogue, Pegasus, the Scarborough butchery, the Goeben all will be resuscitated. So let your facile pen have a Christmas rest!

Yrs

F

[1] Alfred von Tirpitz, 1849–1930. As Chief of Staff of Supreme Naval Command 1892 he laid down plans for a powerful German Navy; as Secretary of State for Naval Affairs 1897 he supervised the construction of that Navy. He saw the Navy as an important instrument of diplomacy; not as a weapon of war. Favoured a fixed ratio for the Anglo-German Navies; wished to give up supplementary estimates in return for an Anglo-German Naval Agreement, 1912; in 1914 he advocated an early naval engagement to decide the war as quickly as possible. He resigned all offices on 15 March 1916. Entered politics as a Nationalist Member of the Reichstag 1924–8; urged German co-operation with Britain and the United States 1925–30.

Sir John French to Lord Kitchener: telegram

(Copy, Churchill papers: 13/27)

26 December 1914

We are not advancing along the Belgian coast from Nieuport as fast as we hoped to do. If a surprise bombardment by monitor and big gun ships could be undertaken, it would have a most beneficial moral and material effect. Will you please let me know if and when anything can be done in this way.[1]

H. H. Asquith to Venetia Stanley

(Montagu papers)

27 December 1914   Easton Grey
                                                             Malmesbury

. . . I must be rather in Winston's good books just now: he sent me quite an effusive Xmas telegram.[2] Frances[3] says that Eddie Marsh was in quite low spirits at the failure of another air coup. I hope this means the affair at Southend wh. was described in the papers; and not the enterprise, so often contemplated & never yet brought off, of a descent on the air sheds & factories at Cuxhaven. To-day we have brilliant sun & a clear air: good weather for flying! . . .

According to the latest conjectures from the various capitals, the probable dates of the 'coming-in' of the halting & wavering Powers are: Roumania, end of Jan; Italy, March; Bulgaria, not before March, if ever; Greece, as soon as she sees a prospect of making a good thing out of it. Of course Roumania & Italy are all important; their intervention would put an end to Austria, and in that case the Bulgarians would almost certainly come in & round on the Turks. All these little Powers hate one another cordially, but when the carcase is ready to be cut up each wants as big & juicy a slice as it can get. . . .

[1] The tides between 26 and 30 December were not favourable for naval action by heavy ships. During January 1915 the coastal advance was held up for political reasons. By the end of January plans to drive the Germans from the Belgian coast were shelved, as the Dardanelles expedition received priority for all naval reinforcements.

[2] Not found.

[3] Frances Graham, 1858–1940. She married Sir John Horner in 1883. Their home at Mells in Somerset was a centre of social entertainment. Their eldest son Edward was killed in action in 1917.

Winston S. Churchill to Sir John French

(*Draft, Churchill papers: 26/1*)

28 December 1914   Admiralty
Personal & Most Secret

My dear French,

I hope you will now get to the sea flank. I am vy sorry abt the losses. It was hard that you shd have been made to fight it out on that line. I expect the enemy got it as bad.

If you have to change yr Chief of Staff,[1] you ought to take the best man in the army among yr subordinates.[2] You must look forward to the time (now not vy distant) when 4 or 5 armies will be working under you. Haig[3] is without equal; & this is not a time when his personal feelings shd count a scrap. You must be freed from the minor worries. There is no comfort like really high ability working for one. This suggestion is personal & private.

[Freddie has been here today. I don't expect I shall come to you again for a long time—unless of course there are joint operations. It weakens my influence upon events to have to ask so small a thing from a colleague who is much better dealt with on even terms. You will comprehend!][4]

Abt the motor buses & other of my small interests now in yr charge, I have said to Kitchener 'Do what you like with them. It is a matter of honour & fair play.' We shall now see what that works out at.

I hope you will take good care of yr health & not let yrself be vexed by trifles—like I am fool enough to be. But still I try. All will go well: & the day will come when we shall have 'finally beaten down Satan under our feet.' Till then in all directions, & on all occasions, count on yr sincere friend

W

[1] Archibald James Murray, 1860–1945. Entered Army, 1879. Captain, 1887. Dangerously wounded while serving in South Africa, 1899–1902. Major-General, 1910. Knighted, 1911. Inspector of Infantry, 1912–14. Chief of Staff, British Expeditionary Force, August 1914–January 1915. Deputy Chief of the Imperial General Staff, February–September 1915. Chief of the Imperial General Staff, September–December 1915. General Officer Commanding in Egypt, 1916–17; and Aldershot, 1917–22.

[2] In January 1915 Sir Archibald Murray returned to England on account of ill-health. He was succeeded as Chief of Staff by Sir William Robertson, the Quartermaster General of the Expeditionary Force.

[3] Douglas Haig, 1861–1928. Entered the Army, 1885. Knighted, 1909. Chief of Staff, India, 1909–11. Lieutenant-General, 1910. Commander of the 1st Army Corps, 1914–15. His successful defence of Ypres, 19 October–22 November 1914, made him a national figure. Commanded the 1st Army at Loos, November 1915. Succeeded Sir John French as Commander-in-Chief, British Expeditionary Force, 19 December 1915. Field-Marshal, 1917. Created Earl, 1919.

[4] Churchill deleted this paragraph in the letter as finally sent.

H. H. Asquith to Venetia Stanley

(*Montagu papers*)

28 December 1914   10 Downing Street

. . . Eddie Marsh came to lunch & I cross-examined him about the sea-plane raid on Cuxhaven.[1] I am afraid that it was in essentials a coup manqué —out of 7 sea-planes 4 are lost, and 1 very good officer—the son[2] of Hewlett the novelist[3]. . . . It is very doubtful whether they did any effective damage at Cuxhaven—a thick fog (as usual) came on & they cd. not see what to aim at. But they believe they destroyed the gas-works, & seriously injured the aircraft sheds. The only satisfactory thing that I can see about the adventure is that it demonstrates the limitations of the Zeppelins, wh. fled like sea-gulls when they were fired at by our cruisers. Our Admiralty have not yet struck a streak of luck. . . .

Winston S. Churchill: memorandum

(*Churchill papers: 28/153*)

[28] December 1914   Admiralty

1. The War Office should be told that the Admiralty consider that the conditions under which large numbers of officers and men are now being sent each day across the Channel, are fraught with the gravest danger. They should be asked whether they consider the traffic is so necessary that it ought to be maintained. If so, the Admiralty will propose to take over the steamer themselves and run it as a transport. They will aim at running one boat each way in the 24 hours, but they cannot guarantee either the certainty or the punctuality of the service. On clear moonlight nights the service would probably have to be suspended; and in any case its suspension must be entirely at Admiralty discretion. It would also be necessary for the War Office to put

---

[1] For details of the Cuxhaven raid, see page 372, note 1.

[2] Francis Esmé Theodore Hewlett, 1891– . Entered Navy, 1908. Qualified as a pilot, 1911. Sub-Lieutenant, Royal Naval Air Service, 1912. Flight-Commander, 1914. On his return from the Cuxhaven raid his plane crashed into the sea, but he was picked up by a Dutch fishing vessel, and returned safely to British territorial waters. Squadron-Commander, 1915. Served in the Directorate of Aircraft Production, 1917–18. Lieutenant-Colonel, Royal Air Force, 1919. Commanded RAF Calshot, 1925. Group-Captain, 1929. Senior Equipment Staff Officer, Central Area, 1933.

[3] Maurice Henry Hewlett, 1861–1923. Keeper of Land Revenue Records and Enrolments, 1896–1900. Published his first novel, 1895. By the time of his death he had published forty volumes of novels and verse.

on board the boats a detachment of military police under an officer to maintain thorough discipline and absolute silence while the voyage is being made.

2. With regard to civilian traffic, we should point out to the Company the dangers, but say that if they wish to continue civilian traffic as hitherto, we shall raise no objection.

3. The War Office should be told that every effort should be made to reduce the number of military persons crossing by this route. Individual officers and men proceeding on leave or on special missions can be carried, but anything like the despatch of drafts, detachments, or details, should be prohibited, and should go by the regular transport service from Southampton. There would be no objection to individual officers not exceeding ten, including the King's Messengers, going by the civilian boat, if the War Office desire, but the number must be absolutely limited, and special permits should be issued by the War Office in each case. These officers should not show themselves on deck in khaki during the passage; they should either wear civilian clothes or remain below.

4. The Dunkirk service is reduced to a bi-weekly one unless any specia voyage is required for Admiralty purposes, and again will take place in the dark hours when there is no moon.

Lieutenant-Colonel Hankey: memorandum

(*Copy, Churchill papers: 2/89*)

28 December 1914

The remarkable deadlock which has occurred in the western theatre of war invites consideration of the question whether some other outlet can be found for the effective employment of the great forces of which we shall be able to dispose in a few months' time.

2. The experience of the offensive movements of the allies in this theatre within the last few weeks seems to indicate that any advance must be both costly and slow. Days are required to capture a single line of trenches, the losses are very heavy, and as often as not the enemy recaptures his lost ground on the following day, or is able to render the captured ground untenable. When viewed on a map the total gains (except possibly in Alsace–Lorraine) are almost negligible, and apparently incommensurate with the effort and loss of life. Moreover, the advance is so slow that the enemy has time to prepare fresh lines of defence in rear of his many existing lines to compensate for the trenches lost. The defensive power of modern weapons is so great that these attacks do not draw into the front trenches any large proportion of the enemy's armies, so that they do not seriously affect the *moral* of the mass of his forces, which are at any given moment outside the fighting line.

3. There is no reason to suppose that the enemy's successive positions can be captured merely by weight of numbers. The Germans themselves have proved to us the impracticability of this by the gallant, immensely costly, and wholly unsuccessful attempts to force the thinly held, hastily constructed, and incomplete positions occupied by the widely extended British army after our advance to Armentières and Ypres. In view of the German failure to penetrate our weakly held and partly fortified positions at this time, is there any reason to suppose (even assuming the superiority of British troops) that our armies, however much reinforced, will be able to drive the Germans from their fully prepared lines of entrenchments by mere weight of numbers?

4. Even at the present moment there are understood to be at least two British army corps always in reserve and out of the firing line, while only a small proportion of those army corps that are responsible for occupying the front are actually in the firing line. If, therefore, the new armies are thrown into France, all that can be done is to extend our lines and set free more French troops for an attack in some more promising quarter. But is it certain that a more promising quarter exists, or that the French want more troops?

5. If the deadlock on our side is complete, it is no less complete as regards the enemy. He has had bitter and costly experience of the difficulty of attacking entrenched positions, and, whatever force he brings to bear, there is no reason to suppose that he can penetrate our lines. We should ask nothing better than that he should hurl fresh masses to destruction on our impregnable positions.

---

6. Such deadlocks are not a feature peculiar to the present war. They have been the commonplace of wars in all ages. In the ancient wars it was usually before some great city, whose capture was indispensable to success, that the deadlock occurred. In the Peninsular War the lines of Torres Vedras provide one good example of such a deadlock. Chataldja is an instance from the recent Balkan Wars.

7. Two methods have usually been employed for circumventing an *impasse* of this kind. Either a special material has been provided for overcoming it, or an attack has been delivered elsewhere, which has compelled the enemy so to weaken his forces that an advance becomes possible.

---

8. In the ancient wars all kinds of devices were adopted to attack the enemy's ramparts when an *impasse* occurred. Special trains of battering rams, catapults, movable towers on wheels, with drawbridges, escalading ladders, Greek fire, the testudo or "tortoise," pent houses, special shields and armour

were among the means employed. Later on siege trains, sapping and mining, and hand grenades superseded the old devices, and these are still employed, though they are less effective against modern methods of defence.

9. Is it possible by the provision of special material to overcome the present *impasse*? Can modern science do nothing more? Some of the following devices might possibly be useful:—

(a.) Numbers of large heavy rollers, themselves bullet proof, propelled from behind by motor engines, geared very low; the driving wheels fitted with 'caterpillar' driving gear to grip the ground, the driver's seat armoured, and with a Maxim gun fitted. The object of this device would be to roll down the barbed wire by sheer weight, to give some cover to men creeping up behind, and to support the advance with machine-gun fire.

(b.) Bullet-proof shields or armour. Sir Edward Henry[1] has a most interesting bullet-proof shield designed after the Sidney Street affair. The War Office, however, consider it too cumbersome for use in the field. Possibly some similar, but less cumbersome, contrivance might be designed for use where the trenches, as at present, are only a few yards apart; only a proportion of the men need be armed with them, and these would shield others behind, who would be instructed to change places with the shield bearers when the first line of trenches was captured. Lord Esher has informed me that an officer has recently invented a light form of armour that covers the vital organs, and the French are reported in the newspapers to be employing a shield in the Argonne.

(c.) Smoke balls, to be massed in the trenches before an advance, and to be used if the wind is in a favourable quarter. They would be thrown by the troops towards the enemy's trenches to screen the advancing troops.

(d.) Rockets throwing a rope with a grapnel attached, which are being used by the French to grip the barbed wire, which is then hauled in by the troops in the trench from which the rocket is thrown.

(e.) Spring catapults, or special pumping apparatus to throw oil or petrol into the enemy's trenches. Sir John French (in his remarks on the recent experiments with burning oil) has asked if some such apparatus could be designed. It will be remembered that in one of their most recent official communiqués the French reported that their troops had been burnt out of their trenches.

---

[1] Edward Richard Henry, 1850–1931. Inspector-General of Police, Bengal, 1891. Commissioner, Metropolitan Police, 1903–18. Knighted, 1910. Created Baronet, 1918.

10. If these and other methods could be prepared secretly, and no hint of them allowed to leak out until the day or night of the attack, and if rumours were spread and dummy preparations made for an attack elsewhere, *e.g.*, on the Belgian coast, or the Frisian Islands, or in Schleswig-Holstein, these methods might have a fair chance of success. It must, however, be recognised that the preparations would take some months to complete, and they ought to be organised in concert with the French.

11. Is it not possible that a small expert Committee might be able to design devices suitable to the present situation? If formed it is indispensable that it should include officers of Royal Engineers personally acquainted with the conditions now prevailing at the front. The Committee would have to be given a free hand with a certain amount of money for experiment, and should have full authority to call to counsel any expert required.

---

12. The above proposals may perhaps be deemed fantastic and absurd. This brings us, therefore, to the consideration of the second method of sur-mounting an *impasse*, viz., the possibility of a diversion elsewhere.

13. Up to the present time the great Russian diversion has not proved sufficiently powerful to cause the enemy to denude his forces on the western frontier to a dangerous extent. Whether the German armies in the west actually outnumber the allies or not: whether they consist largely of half-trained forces or not—they appear none the less sufficient to hold the strong positions they occupy. Recent events give no ground to suppose that the eastern diversion will be sufficiently powerful in the near future to enable the allies to crush the German armies opposed to them in the western theatre of war. The Servian diversion, though extraordinarily valuable in weakening the Austrians, is probably too small to prove in any way decisive unless supported from elsewhere.

14. The only other areas from which a considerable diversion could be directed against Germany itself would be Schleswig-Holstein, which could only be reached through Denmark or through Holland. There appears to be no reasonable probability that either of these nations will voluntarily enter the war, and it would be inconsistent with our attitude toward the German violation of Belgium for us to force them to do so.

---

15. In our previous continental wars, when we have found ourselves un-able to inflict a direct defeat on our enemy in his own country, we have frequently resorted to diversions against his territory oversea, thus getting

into our possession assets to barter against his successes on the Continent of Europe when the arrangements for peace come to be discussed.

16. At the treaty of Aix-la-Chapelle in 1748, for example, the French, who had defeated the Duke of Cumberland and occupied Flanders, evacuated that country on condition that the British gave up Cape Breton Island. Many instances could be given of how we have re-established the balance of power in Europe by conquests beyond the seas, and this, combined with economic pressure, is the natural weapon of the Power that possesses command of the sea.

17. If our main military effort against German territory is unattainable for the present, the principal weapon remaining is economic pressure, and this, in the writer's opinion, is the greatest asset we have in the war. Economic pressure, however, appears to be breaking down to a certain extent owing to the enormous trade with Holland and Denmark, and at the best is a weapon slow in operation. In the meantime there is every reason for using our sea power and our growing military strength to attack Germany and her allies in other quarters. There is a wide field for such action, and some of the possible theatres of operations will now be examined.

---

18. Germany can perhaps be struck most effectively and with the most lasting results on the peace of the world through her allies, and particularly through Turkey.

19. Has not the time come to show Germany and the world that any country that chooses a German alliance against the great sea power is doomed to disaster? Is it impossible now to weave a web round Turkey which shall end her career as a European Power?

20. Greece and Roumania have hitherto hesitated to enter the war because Bulgaria, brooding on her wrongs, is supposed to be watching her opportunity to make good the gains she considers herself cheated of after the recent Balkan wars. Left to themselves these Balkan States, all of whom stand to gain from the ejection of Turkey from Europe and from the dismemberment of Austria, will be unable to realize their overwhelming opportunity, so great is their mutual distrust.

21. But supposing Great Britain, France, and Russia, instead of merely inciting these races to attack Turkey and Austria were themselves to participate actively in the campaign, and to guarantee to each nation concerned that fair play should be rendered. If the whole of the Balkan States were to combine there should be no difficulty in securing a port on the Adriatic, with Bosnia and Herzegovina, and part of Albania, for Servia; Epirus, Southern Albania, and the islands, for Greece; and Thrace for Bulgaria.

The difficult Dardanelles question might perhaps be solved by allowing more than one nation to occupy the north side and by leaving Turkey on the south, the Straits being neutralised.

22. If Bulgaria, guaranteed by the active participation of the three Great Powers, could be induced to co-operate, there ought to be no insuperable obstacle to the occupation of Constantinople, the Dardanelles, and Bosphorus. This would be of great advantage to the allies, restoring communication with the Black Sea, bringing down at once the price of wheat, and setting free the much-needed shipping locked up there.

23. It is presumed that in a few months time we could, without endangering the position in France, devote three army corps, including one original first line army corps, to a campaign in Turkey, though sea transport might prove a difficulty. This force, in conjunction with Greece and Bulgaria, ought to be sufficient to capture Constantinople.

24. If Russia, contenting herself with holding the German forces on an entrenched line, could simultaneously combine with Servia and Roumania in an advance into Hungary, the complete downfall of Austria–Hungary could simultaneously be secured.

25. Failing the above ambitious project, an attack in Syria would prove a severe blow to Turkey, particularly if combined with an advance from Basra to Bagdad by a reinforced army.

---

26. There remains the possibility of some co-operation with the Servian army against Austria, but this presupposes the entry of Greece into the war, or else action through Montenegro, and neither campaign would be easy to carry out.

---

27. A more decisive warfare against the remaining German colonies, to be carried out while the diplomatic and military preparations for the campaigns suggested above are in progress, might also be useful.

28. The loss of Tsing-tao has perhaps been the most grievous loss that Germany has suffered since the war began, the more grievous because it is never likely to be regained, and is therefore hardly an asset for us to barter with.

29. Germany's two largest colonies, however, still remain uncaptured, viz., German South-West Africa and German East Africa, while the capture of the Kamaruns is still incomplete.

30. General Botha's[1] forces will soon commence their serious campaign

[1] Louis Botha, 1862–1919. Commandant-General of the Boer forces in the South African war, 1900. First Prime Minister of the Union of South Africa, 1910–19.

against German South-West Africa. Would it not be worth while to strengthen his forces by the addition of (say) a division, so as to ensure that this great colony is in our possession when terms of peace are discussed?

31. Does not the same consideration apply to German East Africa? Presumably one division in each case (a small force as armies are counted in this war) would suffice to complete the business and to place a valuable asset in our hands.[1]

---

32. It is not suggested that the above campaigns should all be undertaken simultaneously. It is, however, suggested that, if our advance into Flanders and Germany cannot be effected either by superiority of numbers or by a preparation of special material, it would be wise without releasing our grip on the position in France to set to work at once, and in concert with our allies to choose a field, among those indicated above, for the employment of the surplus armies which will soon be available, and to make all preparations. Failing the invasion of Germany itself, which, in accordance with correct strategical principle, has hitherto been our aim, it is suggested that we should endeavour by the means proposed to get assets into our hands wherewith to supplement the tremendous asset of sea power and its resultant economic pressure, wherewith to ensure favourable terms of peace when the enemy has had enough of the war.

MPAH

Winston S. Churchill to H. H. Asquith

(*Copy, Churchill papers: 26/1*)

29 December 1914   Admiralty

My dear Prime Minister,

When Kitchener declared there was nothing in front of us but 'boys and old men', he was wrong; and when you and I agreed there was a fine and terrible army in our front, we were right. It has taken 5,000 men and more, in killed and wounded, to prove the simple fact.

I understand that Joffre told French he could take over the whole line

---

[1] The German Far Eastern territories had all surrendered before the end of 1914; Samoa on 20 August, German New Guinea and the Solomon Islands on 15 September, the Caroline Islands on 6 October and Tsingtau on 7 November. In Africa, only Togo had been captured by the Entente Powers, on 26 August. The German forces in South West Africa did not surrender until 9 July 1915, and some German troops held out in the Cameroons until 18 February 1916. In German East Africa a force of 200,000 Africans, under German command, continued to fight until 23 November 1918, twelve days after the armistice in Europe.

from La Bassee to the sea as soon as he had the troops. At least two more corps are required and these cannot, I presume, be supplied before March. In my judgment the flank move is a very different job to what it was when we first talked of it six weeks ago. The whole front and angle right up to the Dutch frontier is fortified line behind line; and although you can get on along the coast, the advantages to be gained are reduced as much as the difficulties are augmented—like the Sibylline Books (note the classic touch.)

I think it quite possible that neither side will have the strength to penetrate the other's lines in the Western theatre. Belgium particularly, which it is vital to Germany to hold as a peace-counter, has no doubt been made into a mere succession of fortified lines. I think it probable that the Germans hold back several large mobile reserves of their best troops. Without attempting to take a final view, my impression is that the position of both armies is not likely to undergo any decisive change—although no doubt several hundred thousand men will be spent to satisfy the military mind on the point.

For somewhat different reasons, a similar statement seems likely to be reached in the Eastern theatre. When the Russians come in contact with the German railway system, they are heavily thrown back. On the other hand, withdrawn into their own country they can hold their own.

On the assumption that these views are correct, the question arises, how ought we to apply our growing military power? Are there not other alternatives than sending our armies to chew barbed wire in Flanders? Further, cannot the power of the Navy be brought more directly to bear upon the enemy? If it is impossible or unduly costly to pierce the German lines on existing fronts, ought we not, as new forces come to hand, to engage him on new frontiers, and enable the Russians to do so too? The invasion of Schleswig-Holstein from the seas would at once threaten the Kiel Canal and enable Denmark to join us. The accession of Denmark would throw open the Baltic. British naval command of the Baltic would enable the Russian armies to be landed within 90 miles of Berlin; and the enemy, while being closely held on all existing lines, would be forced to face new attacks directed at vital points and exhaust himself along a still larger perimeter.

The essential preliminary is the blocking of the Heligoland debouch. The capture of a German island for an oversea base is the first indispensable step to all these possibilities. It alone can guarantee Great Britain from raid or invasion. It enables the power of our flotillas to be applied. Its retention by us would be intolerable to the enemy, and would in all probability bring about the sea battle. There is only one island (apart from Heligoland) which fulfils Mr Balfour's four conditions—Borkum. If Borkum were seized, it could be held without compromising the action of the Grand Fleet. If Borkum were held, it seems to me probable that a series of events would follow leading in a few weeks to German ships being driven altogether from the North Sea and into their harbours and mined and blocked therein.

There are three phases of the naval war, first the clearance of the seas and the recall of the foreign squadrons, that is nearly completed; second, the closing of the Elbe—that we have now to do; and third, the domination of the Baltic—that would be decisive.

Co-operation between the Admiralty and the War Office is difficult, owing to causes of which you are fully aware. The action of the allies proceeds almost independently. Plans could be made now for April and May which would offer good prospects of bringing the war to its decisive stage by land and sea. We ought not to drift. We ought now to consider while time remains the scope and character we wish to impart to the war in the early summer. We ought to concert our action with our allies, and particularly with Russia. We ought to form a scheme for a continuous and progressive offensive, and be ready with this new alternative when and if the direct frontal attacks in France on the German lines and Belgium have failed, as fail I fear they will. Without your direct guidance and initiative, none of these things will be done; and a succession of bloody checks in the West and in the East will leave the allies dashed in spirit and bankrupt in policy.

Yours &c
WSC

H. H. Asquith to Venetia Stanley
(*Montagu papers*)

30 December 1914   In train to London
Very secret

I have 2 very interesting memoranda to-day on the War—one from Winston, the other from Hankey—written quite independently, but coming by different roads to very similar conclusions. Both think that the existing deadlock in West & East is likely to continue, and W. points out that the flanking movement we urged on the French a month ago is much more difficult now that the Germans have fortified line by line almost the whole of Belgium. The losses involved in the trench-jumping operations now going on on both sides are enormous & out of all proportion to the ground gained. When our new armies are ready, as they will soon begin to be, it seems folly to send them to Flanders where they are not wanted, & where (in W's phrase) they will 'chew barbed wire', or be wasted in futile frontal attacks.

Hankey suggests the development of a lot of new mechanical devices, such as armed rollers to crush down barbed wire, bullet-proof shields & armour, smoke-balls, rockets with grapnel, petrol-throwing catapults &c. It will be strange if we are driven back to these Mediaeval practices.

But apart from this, both he & W. are for finding a new objective & a new theatre[1] for our new armies. H. wd. like them to go to Turkey & in conjunction with the Balkan States clear the Turk out of Europe. Germany, & what is left of Austria wd. be almost bound to take a hand.

W., on the other hand, wants (primarily of course by means of his Navy) to 'close the Elbe & dominate the Baltic'. He wd. first seize a German island —Borkum for choice—then invade Schleswig Holstein, obtain naval command of the Baltic, & thus enable Russia to land her troops within 90 miles of Berlin.

This plan (apart from other difficulties) implies either the accession of Denmark to the Allies, or the violation of her neutrality.

There is here a good deal of food for thought. I am profoundly dissatisfied with the immediate prospect—an enormous waste of life & money day after day with no appreciable progress. And it is quite true that the whole country between Ypres & the German frontier is being transformed into a succession of lines of fortified entrenchments. The nearest parallel is what Wellington did at Torres Vedras. I don't see the way to a decisive change before March, but I am sure that we ought to begin at once to devise, in concert with the French & the Russians, a diversion on a great & effective scale. . . .

Winston S. Churchill to H. H. Asquith

(*Asquith papers*)

31 December 1914   Admiralty

My dear Prime Minister,

Please see enclosure.[2] I have talked to Hankey. We are substantially in agreement and our conclusions are not incompatible.

I wanted Gallipoli attacked on the Turkish declaration of war. But Kitchener does not work far afield or far ahead, *vide* Antwerp. Meanwhile the difficulties have increased.

I look forward to yr Memo. But I think the War Council ought to meet daily for a few days next week. No topic can be pursued to any fruitful result at weekly intervals.

Best wishes for the New Year to you all,

Yours always
Winston S C

[1] For a map of the alternative war zones discussed at the beginning of 1915, see map 6 on page 1597.

[2] Hankey's memorandum of 28 December 1914 (quoted on pp. 337–43).

H. H. Asquith to Venetia Stanley

(*Montagu papers*)

31 December 1914   Walmer Castle

. . . I got a lot of figures this morning of which two I think will interest you. One is Winston's estimate of the men, (including wounded, prisoners, & refugees) horses, & stores wh. he has transported across the seas since the war began with (as he complacently notes) 'no fatal accident nor any loss due to the enemy'. The total is *men* 809,000: horses 203,000: stores 250,000 tons.[1] This is of course a record—especially when you come to think that large numbers have been brought from the ends of the earth across various oceans in wh. the German cruisers were still at large. . . .

Winston S. Churchill: memorandum

(*Churchill papers: 13/27*)

31 December 1914   Admiralty
Secret

The war will be ended by the exhaustion of nations rather than the victories of armies.

On both land fronts, especially the western, the fortified lines are being completed, & frontal advance by either side is practically impossible. Large reinforcements with abundant munitions will join the allies in the spring, & instead of spending them in costly frontal attacks, it will be better to engage Germany on new frontiers, & force her to exhaust her war energy at all points simultaneously along the longest lines the allies can develop.

With this object, the naval command of the Baltic must be secured, & the allied armies shd then attack both the Kiel Canal from Schleswig-Holstein, and Berlin from the Baltic shore. Both these new attacks are aimed at vital points, & Germany will be compelled to meet them with her utmost remaining strength.

In May 1915, if proper steps are taken meanwhile, the allies will be able to dispose of the resources & be in the position to develop the war on the two new fronts above specified.

But first the naval command of the Baltic must be secured.

---

[1] 'In circulating this paper to my colleagues,' Churchill wrote in his covering note of 29 December 1914, 'I observe that no fatal accident nor any loss due to the enemy has attended the movements of these large numbers across seas in which in most cases enemy vessels were present.' Churchill also stated that between 4 August and 30 November the Navy had transported 20,000 vehicles, 65,000 wounded, 5,000 refugees and 4,884 German prisoners. (*Cabinet papers: 37/122*)

The measures required, & their sequence, are as follows:—

1) The British must capture a German island for an oversea base as soon as possible; must mine on the most extensive scale the channels and rivers of the German coast; & from their advanced base must prevent the mines from being removed.

The only island that fulfils the necessary conditions (see Mr Balfour's paper)[1] is Borkum.

2) The German fleet having been effectually excluded from the North Sea by the blocking of the Heligoland Bight as above described, Schleswig-Holstein cd be invaded in force, & an advance made upon the Kiel Canal.

(If at any time the Kiel Canal can be cut, either by aerial attack or any other means, the German Navy is paralyzed. The cutting of the Canal is not however indispensable.)

3) As soon as a British army has established itself in Schleswig-Holstein, Denmark shd be invited to join the Allies, being promised naval & military protection, & her lost provinces after the war. On the accession of Denmark to the alliances, Funes Island can be occupied by British troops & the passage of the Great Belt secured.

4) A British fleet, strong enough to fight a decisive battle, shd then enter the Baltic & establish command of that sea, thus cutting Germany off from all Northern supplies.

5) It will then be possible to land a Russian Army at various points on the Baltic shore less than 100 miles from Berlin, as well as to threaten the whole Northern coast, immobilizing large numbers of German troops.

This plan of war combines all conceivable forms of pressure upon the enemy. It forces him to expend his strength simultaneously along the largest front. It attacks his vulnerable & vital points by the shortest routes. It cuts off his oversea supplies almost entirely. It destroys his political influence in the Baltic. It brings all the allied forces to bear, including the full power of the British Navy. If these movements were accompanied by the entry into the war of Italy & Roumania, the end wd not be long deferred.

It must be remembered first that we shall in May be dealing with an enemy already fully engaged on enormous fronts who cannot spare large numbers of good troops to meet new dangers; secondly that if he moves against a particular attack, it can immediately be converted into a fortified defensive against wh he wd uselessly expend his strength; & thirdly that the military mobility resulting from seapower applicable over a large area will counterbalance to a great extent the enemy's advantage of interior lines.

---

[1] Not printed; Balfour wanted an island off the German coast to be seized by the British as a base for further operations against Germany. Sir Arthur Wilson had favoured Heligoland; Churchill had earlier proposed Sylt.

The first & indispensable measure is the capture of Borkum. Apart from the general plan above described, it is necessary to the security of Gt Britain & the adequate discharge by the Navy of its duties. The British submarine force capable of action in German waters wd be quadrupled, all the B & C class boats becoming available. The superior gunfire of the British destroyer flotillas (nearly 3 times that of the German) cd be brought to bear on the German flotillas. Aerial reconnaissance & attack of the German harbours will be continual. Surprise, raid, or invasion wd be prevented. The military forces in England wd be liberated for oversea service in any direction required. A decisive naval action wd probably be forced in waters dominated by our flotillas of submarines & destroyers.

To capture Borkum, 3 infantry brigades of the highest quality are required. Two of these wd probably be released after the capture, their places being taken by less highly-trained troops.

Detailed plans for the operation will be submitted if the principle is approved. Upon these plans being found satisfactory the adoption or rejection of the enterprise shd depend.

WSC

Sir John French to Winston S. Churchill
(*Churchill papers: 26/1*)

31 December 1914   General Headquarters
Secret   British Army in the Field

My dear Winston,

This is in reality only a hurried line to wish you all good luck for 1915; but as I am writing I want to tell you quite privately how far my plans have progressed towards the object we both have so much at heart, namely a powerful advance Eastward along the coast, supported by the Navy.

I went to see Joffre on Sunday and had a long talk with him. He agreed in principle to the British Troops acting in conjunction with the Belgians on the left flank of the Allied line next to the sea; and it was arranged that I was to relieve all the French Troops to the north of me as quickly as the reinforcements coming to me would allow.

As, however, I now feel myself at liberty to enter into negotiations for combined action with the King of the Belgians, I have begun to do so through Bridges; and I have a scheme which, if the King will only accept, should enable me to take over the line within the next two or three weeks and find a sufficient reserve to enter energetically upon a land advance.

I feel I am writing rather in enigmas, but I do not like to tell you anything in detail until I am sure that the King of the Belgians will give his consent.

But if my suggestions are accepted and the plan comes off, I can assure you there will be a land force of sufficient size to justify a vigorous Naval support and to give good promise of success.

No one at home knows a word of this but you, so please destroy this letter when read. I will write privately again in a few days if my plans develop, and I have every hope they will.

Please convey my best wishes for the New Year to Mrs Churchill.

Yrs always
JF

Remember *no-one* knows of these ideas but you.

David Lloyd George: memorandum

(Harcourt papers)

31 December 1914   11 Downing Street
SUGGESTIONS AS TO THE MILITARY POSITION

Now that the new armies are in course of training and will, with the Territorials, be ready by the end of March to the extent of at least half a million men, I suggest that it is time the Government should take counsel with the military experts as to the use which shall be made of this magnificent force. It is a force of a totally different character from any which has hitherto left these shores. It has been drawn almost exclusively from the better class of artisan, the upper and the lower middle classes. In intelligence, education and character it is vastly superior to any army ever raised in this country, and as it has been drawn not from the ranks of those who have generally cut themselves off from home ties and about whose fate there is therefore not the same anxiety at home, the people of this country will take an intimate personal interest in its fate of a kind which they have never displayed before in our military expeditions. So that if this superb army is thrown away upon futile enterprises such as those we have witnessed during the last few weeks, the country will be uncontrollably indignant at the lack of prevision and intelligence shown in our plans. I may add that operations such as those we have witnessed during the past few months will inevitably destroy the *morale* of the best troops. Good soldiers will face any dangers and endure any hardships which promise ultimate progress, but this intermittent flinging themselves against impregnable positions breaks the stoutest hearts in the end.

There are therefore three or four considerations I wish to urge on the military situation.

I. STALEMATE ON THE WESTERN FRONT

I cannot pretend to have any military knowledge, but the little I saw and gathered in France as to the military position, coupled with such reading on the subjects as I have been able to indulge in, convinced me that any attempt to force the carefully prepared German lines in the west would end in failure and in appalling loss of life, and I then expressed this view to my colleagues. General Foch told me that there would be no more retreats on the French side, and I could well appreciate his confidence after I had driven past trench behind trench from Paris all the way to the Aisne. The French generals are confident that even if the whole of the German Army now occupied in Poland were thrown on the Western Front, the French and British troops would still be able to hold their own. The same observation, of course, must apply to the German military position. We were told the other day that the Germans had, during the last few months, prepared a series of trenches of the same kind on their side right up to the Rhine. After three or four months of the most tenacious fighting, involving very heavy losses, the French have not at any one point on the line gained a couple of miles. Would the throwing of an additional half-million men on this front make any real difference? To force the line you would require at least three to one; our reinforcements would not guarantee two to one, or anything approaching such a predominance. Is it not therefore better that we should recognise the impossibility of this particular task, and try and think out some way by which the distinct numerical advantage which the Allies will have attained a few months hence can be rendered effective?

2. EXTENSION, AND CONSEQUENT ATTENUATION, OF ENEMY'S FRONT

Another consideration which ought to weigh with us is the importance of attenuating the enemy's line by forcing him largely to extend it. The Germans now defend a front of 600 miles. No wastage in sight will so reduce their forces to such numbers as would make any part of this line untenable. The French returns of wounded prove that 79 per cent. of the wounded return to the line: 54 per cent. of the French wounded have already returned; 25 per cent. are convalescent and will soon be back. It is a fundamental mistake always committed by the press to exaggerate the enemy's losses; the slight and curable character of most wounds is always overlooked. But if the length of the German line is doubled, even at the present rate of attrition, it might become at an early date so thin as to be easily penetrable.

3. FORCING THE ENEMY TO FIGHT ON UNFAVOURABLE GROUND

The enemy is now fighting in country which is admirably adapted to his present entrenching tactics. He would be at a disadvantage if he were forced to fight in the open.

4. NECESSITY OF WINNING A DEFINITE VICTORY SOMEWHERE

There is another consideration which is political as well as military, but which nevertheless cannot be overlooked in an exhausting war like this, where we have to secure continuous exertion and sacrifice on the part of our people, and where we have also to think of hesitating neutrals with large armies who are still in doubt as to their action. There is a real danger that the people of Great Britain and of France will sooner or later get tired of long casualty lists explained by monotonous and rather banal telegrams from headquarters about "heavy cannonades," "making a little progress" at certain points, "recovering trenches," the loss of which has never been reported, etc., with the net result that we have not advanced a yard after weeks of heavy fighting. Britishers have ceased to be taken in by reports which exaggerate slight successes and suppress reverses; neutral states have never been deceived by these reports. The public will soon realise that the Germans are now in effective occupation of a larger proportion of Allied territory than they were in possession of at the date of the Battle of the Aisne. This is true of Belgium, of France, and of Poland. These occupied territories contain some of the richest coalfields and industrial centres in Europe, and the most sanguinary attacks have not succeeded in moving the Germans (on an average) a single yard out of these territories. A clear definite victory which has visibly materialised in guns and prisoners captured, in unmistakable retreats of the enemy's armies, and in large sections of enemy territory occupied, will alone satisfy the public that tangible results are being achieved by the great sacrifices they are making, and decide neutrals that it is at last safe for them to throw in their lot with us.

5. AN ALTERNATIVE SUGGESTION

Inasmuch as these objects cannot be accomplished by attacks on the Western Front, some alternative ought to be sought. I venture to make one or two suggestions. I have heard of a proposal that there should be an attack in the direction of Denmark upon the north coast of Germany. This proposal is associated with the name of Lord Fisher. For the moment I cannot venture to express any opinion upon it, as I should like to know more about the military and naval possibilities of such an enterprise. It strikes me as being very hazardous, and by no means certain to fulfil the purpose which its originators have in view. Schleswig-Holstein, with its narrow neck, could be easily defended by a comparatively small German force, strongly entrenched against a hostile army seeking to advance into Prussian territory, and there is no room for flanking operations. But at the present moment I would rather not criticise this plan. My purpose is rather to put forward another alternative, and I think more promising scheme for consideration by the Prime Minister and his advisers. It would involve *two independent operations* which would have the common purpose of bringing Germany down by the process of knocking the props under her, and the further purpose of so compelling her to attenuate her line of defence as to make it more easily penetrable. I will explain these two propositions in a little more detail.

6. THE FIRST OPERATION

I suggest that our new forces should be employed in an attack upon Austria, in conjunction with the Serbians, the Roumanians and the Greeks. The assistance of the two latter countries would be assured if they knew that a great English force would be there to support them. Roumania could put 300,000 men in the field, whilst retaining a sufficient force to keep the Bulgarians in check. As this move might decide the Bulgarians to remain honestly neutral, the Roumanians could spare another 200,000. The Greeks and Montenegrins have an army of 200,000 available. How many men could we spare? By the beginning of April we shall have in this country 700,000 men who will have undergone a six months' training. Of these 400,0000 would be Territorials, 200,000 of whom will have been in camp continuously for eight months. We shall have in France a force of 300,000 men, provided we do not waste it on barbed wire. The French can easily defend their lines against the troops which Germany can spare from defending Silesia after the Austrian armies have been withdrawn to defend their southern frontier. We should require 200,000 experienced troops to stiffen the new armies. We should thus have a force of 1,000,000 available. Four hundred thousand men might be left here as reserve to throw into France in case of need if the French were hard pressed before the southern diversion against Austria had developed. Some of them might be sent to Boulogne so as to be at hand in case of emergency. Subsequently this force could be used to reinforce the new Expeditionary Force from time to time. This would leave 600,000 available for the Austrian expedition. Gradually this force could be increased as the new armies were equipped.

This would mean an army of between 1,400,000 and 1,600,000 men to attack Austria on her most vulnerable frontier. Here the population is almost entirely friendly, consisting as it does of Slavonic races who hate both the Germans and the Magyars. We could send our troops up either through Salonika or, I believe, by landing them on the Dalmatian coast. We could seize islands there which might make an admirable base for supplies not far removed from the railway through Bosnia into Austria. This operation would force the Austrians to detach a considerable army from the defence of Cracow, and thus leave Silesia undefended. The Austrians could not withdraw the whole of their army to face this new attack, because in that case the Russians could pour through the Carpathians and capture either Vienna or Budapest. The front which would be developed would be much too lengthy for the Austrian forces to entrench and hold. The Germans would be compelled either to send large forces to support their Austrian allies or to abandon them. In the first case Germans would have to hold an enormous length of extended front, in the aggregate 1,200 miles, and the Allies would, for the first time, enjoy the full advantage of the superior numbers which by that time they can put into the field.[1] On the other hand, if the Germans decline to quit their own frontiers, and leave the Austrians to their fate, that empire would be rapidly disposed of as a military entity, and about 2,500,000 men (including Russians), engaged in the task of attacking it would be free to assail the Germans.

7. TWO INCIDENTAL ADVANTAGES OF THIS COURSE

1. Something which could be called a victory would be thus within our reach, and the public would be satisfied to support with all their resources the conduct of the War for a much longer period without grumbling or stint.

2. Italy would not only be encouraged by this formidable demonstration, she would be forced to come in in her own interest, because the operations would be conducted largely along the coast which she is looking forward to annexing to her kingdom, as the population is predominantly Italian. She must view with very great jealousy any occupation of this territory by Serbian troops, and Italian public opinion would not countenance any proposal on the part of the Italian Ministry to come to the aid of Austria if we made it clear that the whole of this littoral would become Italian territory if Italy helped to conquer it.

8. THE SECOND OPERATION

This involves an attack upon Turkey. There are four conditions which an attack on Turkey ought, in my judgment, to fulfil:—

1. That it should not involve the absorption of such a large force as to weaken our offensive in the main field of operations;

2. That we should operate at a distance which would not be far from the sea, so as not to waste too many of our troops in maintaining long lines of communication and so as also to have the support of the Fleet in any eventualities;

3. That it should have the effect of forcing Turkey to fight at a long distance from her base of supplies and in country which would be disadvantageous to her;

4. That it should give us the chance of winning a dramatic victory, which would encourage our people at home, whilst it would be a corresponding discouragement to our enemies.

[1] Lloyd George added in a footnote: 'The Germans would also render themselves liable to a dangerous attack in the rear from the immense forces which by that date Russia will have placed in the field'.

Perhaps I ought to add a fifth: it would be a great advantage from this point of view if it were in territory which appeals to the imagination of the people as a whole.

What operations would meet these conditions? It is supposed that the Turks are gathering together a great army for the invasion of Egypt. The sections show that they have collected something like 80,000 troops in Syria, and that they are slowly moving them along towards the Egyptian frontier. I would let them entangle themselves in this venture, and whilst they were engaged in attacking our forces on the Suez Canal, I would suggest that a force of 100,000 should be landed in Syria to cut them off. They could not maintain themselves in that country very long once their railway communications were cut. They would therefore be forced either to fight or to surrender. The distance from Constantinople to Syria would not permit them to bring up reinforcements in time to produce any impression upon the situation. A force of 80,000 Turks would be wiped out and the whole of Syria would fall into our hands. The pressure upon Russia in the Caucasus would be relieved; the Turkish Army in Europe could not effectively attack our lines of communication as they would be bound to take steps to redeem the situation in Syria, and, if possible, recover the country.

Unless we are prepared for some project of this character I frankly despair of our achieving any success in this War. I can see nothing but an eternal stalemate on any other lines. The process of economic exhaustion alone will not bring us a triumphant peace as long as Germany is in possession of these rich allied territories. No country has ever given in under such pressure, apart from defeat in the field. Burke was always indulging in prophecies of victory as a result of France's exhaustion. The war with France went on for twenty years after he indulged in his futile predictions. Germany and Austria between them have 3,000,000 young men quite as well trained as the men of the Kitchener Armies, ready to take the place of the men now in the trenches when these fall. At that rate the process of exhaustion will take at least ten years. In soil, in minerals, in scientific equipment, Germany is a country of enormous resources. In the number of men who have a scientific training it is infinitely the richest country in the world. That must not be left out of account when we talk about the process of exhaustion. No doubt they will suffer a good deal from lack of copper. We must not depend too much on this. German industries dependent on copper will suffer, but one way or another copper will be found for ammunition. Copper in small quantities will get in through neutral countries; neutrals cannot resist the prices offered by Germany for their copper supplies. Moreover, they have some copper mines in Germany. Some of them were working at a profit at the date of the War. There must be many more lower grade copper mines which would not have paid under ordinary conditions, just like the copper mines of North Wales, but which would become immediately profitable when the price of copper is doubled or trebled. Moreover, they have inexhaustible supplies of coal and iron, and as long as they have the Hungarian plains they can frugally feed themselves. There is an enthusiasm and a spirit, according to every testimony, which cannot be worn down by a two or three years' siege of German armies entrenched in enemy territory. The German spirit will not be broken by the bombardment of Dixmude or Roulers.

We cannot allow things to drift. We ought to look well ahead and discuss every possible project for bringing the War to a successful conclusion. Supply and ammunition difficulties, severe economic pressure, financial embarrassments, even privation and distress—nations will face them cheerfully as long as their armies in the field are in unbeaten possession of their enemies' land. But once defeat which is unmistakable comes their way, moderate economic troubles make a deep impression on their judgment. Such defeats are not to be compassed along our present lines of attack, and we ought to seek others.

If a decision were come to in favour of some such plan of campaign as I have outlined, it will take weeks to make the necessary preparations for it. I cannot recollect that in our discussions at the C.I.D. such an operation was ever contemplated. The ground therefore has not been surveyed. It would take some time to collect the necessary intelligence as to the country, so as to decide where to land the Army and what shall be the line of attack. Transport would have to be carefully and secretly gathered. Large forces might have to be accumulated in the Mediterranean, ostensibly for Egypt. It might be desirable to send an advance force through Salonika to assist Serbia. Military arrangements would have to be made with Roumania, Serbia, Greece and, perhaps, Italy. All this must take time. Expeditions decided upon and organised with insufficient care and preparation generally end disastrously. And as similar considerations will probably apply to any alternative campaign, I urge the importance of our taking counsel and pressing to a decision without delay.

D Ll G.

January 1915

H. H. Asquith to Winston S. Churchill

(Churchill papers: 13/46)

1 January 1915   Walmer Castle
Secret

My dear Winston,

I have read your mem[n] of yesterday.[1] Please have your detailed plans put in hand at once. We will have a War Council next week.

Yrs always
HHA

H. H. Asquith to Venetia Stanley

(Montagu papers)

1 January 1915   Walmer Castle
Midnight

. . . I have also received to-day two long mem[a]—one from Winston, the other from Lloyd George (quite good, the latter) as to the future conduct of the war. They are both keen on a new objective & theatre, as soon as our new troops are ready: W, of course, for Borkum & the Baltic: Ll. G. for Salonica to join in with the Serbians, & for Syria! I will bring them to you on Monday, & we can talk it all over. I am summoning our little 'War Council' for Thursday, & Friday to review the whole situation, & as there is a Cabinet on Wed. . . . .

[1] Churchill's memorandum of 31 December 1914 (quoted on pages 347-9).

Winston S. Churchill to Sir John French

(*Copy, Churchill papers: 26/2*)

1 January 1915   Admiralty
Private

My dear French,

It was a great delight to me to get your letter of good wishes for the new Year, wh I reciprocate from the bottom of my heart. Our friendship though begun late has grown strong and deep, & I feel sure it will stand with advantage all the tests of this remarkable time.

The coast game is I think more difficult now; & if done we must concert the naval measures with you to a nicety. Zeebrugge I feel sure shd at the critical moment—and as the thong of your attack—be assailed from the sea; and then kick back towards Ostende.

I had to ask Kitchener to send you a telegram today about the serious danger developing there by the submarine base. Today it has cost us a fine ship and 600 lives.[1] I think the telegram will strengthen your hands. I shall look forward to your full scheme. We shall be ready to run great risks in your support. I wonder when I shall be able to come to see you again. I must not put myself in a weak position vis-a-vis 'our mutual friend'. Here—within my own ramparts—I have a vy strong line whether for defence or offence. Yet it wd be a great relief to me to talk over with you the ideas wh are now coming to the fore, & wh will determine the scope and character of the war in the summer. Well perhaps a chance will come.

I have not got over those cruisers being lossed.[2] It is a recurring pang. Really with all yr stress, your game is not such a tricky one as ours. At least you can get results in proportion to your strength, whereas the caprice of fortune disposes absolutely with us of our strongest units.

I hope you feel as the result of your visit here how profoundly the Government appreciate the valiant & splendid part you have played, & enabled the British Army to play.

With all good wishes
Believe me, Yours always
W

---

[1] In the early morning of New Year's Day 1915 the pre-Dreadnought battleship *Formidable* was torpedoed south of the Devon coast. Only 200 of the 800 on board were saved. Her Captain, Arthur Loxley, signalled to another ship that she was not to stand by, lest she herself were torpedoed. Loxley was drowned when the ship went down.

[2] The three British cruisers, *Cressy*, *Hogue* and *Aboukir*, were sunk by a German submarine on 22 September 1914. 1,400 men were killed, 800 were saved.

Winston S. Churchill: memorandum

(*Churchill papers: 13/58*)

1 January 1915   Admiralty
Secret

Information from a trustworthy source has been received that the Germans intend to make an attack on London by airships on a great scale at an early opportunity.[1] The Director of the Air Department reports that there are approximately twenty German airships which can reach London now from the Rhine, carrying each a ton of high explosives. They could traverse the English part of the journey, coming and going, in the dark hours. The weather hazards are considerable, but there is no known means of preventing the airships coming, and not much chance of punishing them on their return. The unavenged destruction of non-combatant life may therefore be very considerable. Having given most careful consideration to this subject, and taken every measure in their power, the Air Department of the Admiralty must make it plain that they are quite powerless to prevent such an attack if it is launched with good fortune and in favourable weather conditions. . . .

Sir George Buchanan to Sir Edward Grey: telegram

(*Copy, Churchill papers: 26/4*)

1 January 1915   Petrograd
3.30 pm
Private and secret

Early this week position of Russians in the Caucasus gave cause for great anxiety, Turks having commenced enveloping movement seriously threatening Russian forces. Commander-in-Chief of army in the Caucasus[2] pressed most urgently for reinforcements, many Caucasian troops being now employed against Germans, but Grand Duke has told him he must manage to get on as he is. Grand Duke sent for General Williams[3] on Wednesday and officially informed him of above, and told him he was determined to proceed with his present plans against Germany and keep them unaltered.

[1] The first Zeppelin raid took place in the night of 19–20 January 1915, over the Norfolk towns of King's Lynn, Great Yarmouth and Sheringham. Four civilians were killed and seventeen injured.

[2] Ilarion Ivanovich Vorontzov-Dashkov, 1837–1916. Head of the Ochrana, the Russian Secret Police, 1881–97. Member of the Russian State Council, 1897. President of the Russian Red Cross, 1904–5. Viceroy of the Caucasus, 1905–15.

[3] John Hanbury-Williams, 1859–1946. Entered Army, 1878. Military Secretary to Sir Alfred Milner, 1897–1900. Knighted, 1908. Major-General, General Staff, War Office, 1914. Chief of British Military Mission, Russian Army in the Field, 1914–17. In charge of British Prisoners-of-War Department, The Hague, 1917–18; Berne, 1918.

Fourth Siberian Army Corps is now on the way to Warsaw and will be joined by Guard Army Corps when it is hoped to continue active operations against Germans and thus help to ease position of Allies, though in ordinary course it would be natural to send Caucasians to Turkish front.

Grand Duke however asked if it would be possible for Lord Kitchener to arrange for a demonstration of some kind against the Turk elsewhere, either naval or military, and to spread reports which would cause Turks, who he says are very liable to go off at a tangent, to withdraw some of the forces now acting against Russia in the Caucasus, and thus ease the position of Russia.

Lord Kitchener to Winston S. Churchill

(*Churchill papers: 13/46*)

2 January 1915   War Office

My dear Churchill,

You have no doubt seen Buchanan's telegram about the Russians & Turks. If not FitzGerald[1] is taking it over.

Do you think any naval action would be possible to prevent Turks sending more men into the Caucasus & thus denuding Constantinople.

Yours very truly
Kitchener

Lord Kitchener to Winston S. Churchill

(*Churchill papers: 26/4*)

2 January 1915   War Office

My dear Churchill,

I do not see that we can do anything that will very seriously help the Russians in the Caucasus.

The Turks are evidently withdrawing most of their troops from Adrianople and using them to reinforce their army against Russia probably sending them by the Black sea.

In the Caucasus and Northern Persia the Russians are in a bad way.

We have no troops to land anywhere.

A demonstration at Smyrna would do no good and probably cause the

---

[1] Oswald Arthur Gerald FitzGerald, 1875–1916. Lieutenant, Indian Army, 1897. A member of Lord Kitchener's staff, 1904–16. Lieutenant-Colonel, August 1914. Personal Military Secretary to Lord Kitchener, 1914–16. Drowned with Kitchener in HMS *Hampshire*.

slaughter of Christians. Alexandretta has already been tried and would have no great effect a second time.[1]

The coast of Syria would have no effect.

The only place that a demonstration might have some effect in stopping reinforcements going East would be the Dardanelles—particularly if as the Grand Duke says reports could be spread at the same time that Constantinople was threatened.

We shall not be ready for anything big for some months.

Yours very truly
Kitchener

Sir Rennell Rodd[2] to Sir Edward Grey: telegram
(Copy, Fisher papers)

2 January 1915   Rome
9.20 pm
Confidential

King of Italy[3] told me to-day that he understood that Germans had 39 submarines which did not appear on German Navy List.

There is a rumour here in official circles emanating I think from Minister of Marine[4] that Germans contemplate simultaneous submarine and aeroplane attack on our fleet in about a fortnight's time.

Lord Fisher to Winston S. Churchill
(Churchill papers: 13/56)

2 January 1915   Admiralty

Dear Winston,

For the past month I have been carefully following up the undoubted German submarine superiority in design—speed—efficiency & seaworthiness

---

[1] A reference to the exploits of Captain Larken, Commander of the light cruiser *Doris*, who on 18 December 1914 sent a landing party ashore at Alexandretta, and after two days of negotiation with the local Turkish authorities, obtained their agreement for the destruction of two railway engines and several military stores.

[2] James Rennell Rodd, 1858–1941. Entered Diplomatic Service, 1883. Knighted, 1899. Minister to Sweden, 1904–8. Ambassador to Italy, 1908–9. Conservative MP, 1928–32. Created Baron, 1933.

[3] Victor Emmanuel, 1869–1947. Became King of Italy following the assassination of King Umberto, 1900. Transferred Royal power to his son, Prince Umberto, 1944.

[4] Count Leone Viale, 1851–1918. Vice-Admiral, commanding the Italian force in the war against Turkey, 1911. President of the Supreme Naval Council, 1914. Minister of Marine, 1914–15.

and sea endurance—and today I will let you have the proposed action for consideration.

The apathy (*and indeed obstruction*) of Briggs[1] is the chief cause of our losing our immense lead over the Germans in 1910. They were literally NOWHERE! Also a very terrible error was committed in putting a purely ignorant officer[2] in charge of a purely technical business involving specialist and habituated knowledge of submarine service, but it's no use crying over spilt milk! I do hope under this proposed new procedure we shall 'knock out' the Germans (IF TIME PERMITS!).

Secondly today—the coastwise coal traffic must be dealt with or there will be a London panic for want of gas for the multitude of uses it now has in every house. . . .

Thirdly—if the Germans are really putting Torpedo tubes into Trawlers— the question of North Sea Fishing must be again considered as a vital danger to our Fleet.

For myself I think the whole North Sea ought to be cleared of everything and a mine blockade of the German ports established beginning with A. K. Wilson's excellent mining plan for the Amrum Light Channel which is just first rate. That will humbug the new American Transport Company three *of whose* ships have already passed through the merchant ship channel from Sylt to Hamburg with cotton & probably Copper underneath!

Alas, we only have 4,500 mines at present so we are forced to go slow!

Yours,

F

Postscript

I have again in this early morning again been reading over the paper I gave you with the heading:—

'On the Possibility of using our command of the Sea to influence more drastically the military situation on the Continent'[3]

and I prefer it without the alteration you suggested as regards mining and if you see no objection I would like to have it recorded as my opinion in regard to the future conduct of the war MORE ESPECIALLY AS REGARDS THE MINING POLICY—where I am quite aware I'm in a minority of one! (*but I've often been in that same minority so dont so much mind!*)

Mine laying is desirable from 3 points of view which are *impossible to evade!*

[1] Charles John Briggs, 1858–1951. Entered Navy, 1872. Captain, 1897. Rear-Admiral 1907. Controller of the Navy, 1910–12. Vice-Admiral commanding 4th Squadron, Home Fleet, 1912–14. Admiral, 1916.

[2] A reference to Commodore Keyes (see pages 307, 308, 324 and 327).

[3] Fisher's memorandum of late November 1914 (quoted on pp. 284–7).

I. To give the same trouble to all the German Fleet as the German Mines give to the British Fleet—and most especially to interfere with the unrestricted German egress of Submarines.

II. To protect the East Coast by hampering the approach there of the German Fleet and to prevent the German Minelayers freely operating there as they do now with both Warships & Trawlers

III. To blockade the German Ports & stop this American traffic now so abundantly in progress.

F

A. J. Balfour to Lieutenant-Colonel Hankey

(*Hankey papers*)

2 January 1915   Whittingehame
Private

My dear Hankey,

. . . Your Memorandum upon general Military Policy

I agree, and I fear that everybody must agree, that the notion of driving the Germans back from the west of Belgium to the Rhine by successively assaulting and capturing one line of trenches after another seems a very hopeless affair; and unless some means can be found for breaking their line at some critical point, and threatening their communications, I am unable to see how the deadlock in the west is to be brought to any rapid or satisfactory conclusion. If the Russians are as strong as 'hey profess to be, (of which so far I have seen no signs), they ought not to have the same difficulty in an 'offensive' on the Eastern frontier as we are experiencing on the Western;—for, when they have satisfactorily disposed of the Austrians, they might be able to do what the Allies cannot do in Flanders and in France, namely, turn the right flank of the enemy's lines and invade this country. Put the matter, however, as we like, no dramatic dénouement of the present situation seems to be in sight.

So far I am in entire agreement with your Memorandum: and I also agree with all your observations upon new contrivances for facilitating offensive warfare. But I am not sure that I see in your proposals for attacking the enemy elsewhere than in the North of Europe any solution of our difficulties. It is not that I deny the advantages of inducing the Balkan States, with the assistance of the Allies, to make a combined attack upon Turkey. On the contrary, I think such a policy would have very valuable results. But the questions involved are, I fear, so difficult that months of preliminary negotiation would be required to allay passions due to events in the past, and to arrange such a division of the spoils as would satisfy these jealous little States. And, in addition to these difficulties, there looms before us the menacing question of Constantinople. Who is to own it? And what is to be the international position of the Bosphorus? The solution you propose for the Dardanelles hardly applies to the other end of the Sea of Marmora.

Moreover, it must be remembered that Germany is perfectly indifferent to the fate of her Allies except in so far as her own fate is bound up with it. Were Turkey completely paralysed, the Russians could no doubt bring troops from the Caucasus to Galicia, and we could take troops from Egypt to German East Africa, or to some European theatre of operations. These would be very great advantages, but they would not finish the war.

I agree, however, that from the political and diplomatic point of view, it would be desirable to deprive Germany of everything she has to bargain with, and to hit Turkey as hard as we can, and wherever we can. But I fear operations like these, however successful, must be regarded as merely subsidiary.

Would it be quite impossible to land troops in Montenegro, and thus add strength to the Southern menace to Austria? I have no means here of forming any conclusion as to the practicability of such an idea; but, if it were within the range of possibility, it seems to me that it would not only hasten the Austrian débâcle, but might have the indirect effect of compelling Italy without further delay to take a hand in the game. Such an operation, could it be carried out, would surely have more effect upon the main theatre of operations than anything we can do in Syria or Africa.

These are very casual observations, and you must not take them too seriously. . . .

Yours sincerely
Arthur James Balfour

Sir Frederick Hamilton to Winston S. Churchill: memorandum

(Churchill papers: 26/3)

2 January 1915   Admiralty

STEEL SCREENS FOR INFANTRY

NO. I MODEL

Designed as the simplest to construct and to manipulate in the field.

It is 12 feet long by 6 feet high—will take 6 men abreast & will give protection to *at least* 25 men. I am not in favour of anything *less*.

Constructed for easy transport—ie remove *four* linch-pins and the whole thing lies flat & can be carried anywhere.

Ordinarily artillery wheels can be used, but much *flank protection* will be given if wheels are of steel plating.

Screens can be advanced over almost any ground as it weighs only 1000 lbs (or less) & can be lifted over anything. Wheels should be large.

Beardmour chrome steel weighs about 12 lbs per foot (resists German latest rifle or point blank).

Strongly deprecate having a *few* made & tried; recommend numbers more like 1000 with which 25000 infantry at least could advance.

I do not think they should be used from trench to trench, but fresh troops advance with them right over our trenches with all arrangements made for a rapid & prolonged advance. (Leaving our trenches manned.)

The first time they are used & proved successful will be the signal to Germany to turn out quantities, so they may prove a danger instead of an advantage to use unless we are prepared to follow up immediately.

I am strongly against any *partial* adoption.

As I have been an advocate of this principle & have been trying to find any flaw in it for the last 20 years I make no apologies for indicating how I think they should be used.

F C H

Winston S. Churchill to Lord Fisher, Sir Arthur Wilson
and Vice-Admiral Oliver

(*Copy, Admiralty papers: 137/452*)

3 January 1915   Admiralty
Secret

All preparations should be made for the capture of Sylt.

The best plan possible should be framed, even if not in all respects perfect. Then effort can be concentrated on overcoming the remaining difficulties.

All necessary appliances, and any likely to be useful, should be ordered *now*.

Among those which should be considered are the following:—

1. Monitors for shallow water bombardment and defence subsequently.
2. Shell gratings against howitzer fire built over vulnerable parts of the decks of the bombarding Squadron.
3. Transports for 12,000 infantry rendered unsinkable by crinolines and subdivision. Facilities for getting into boats quickly.
4. Flat bottomed craft for landing infantry. These should be plated against rifle fire, and should carry Maxims.

5. Shields for attacking enemy's defences.
6. Arrangements for making smoke and cutting it off when not required.
7. Indicator nets for submarines.
   Mining against submarines.
8. Towing charges and modified sweeps for destroyers acting against submarines in conjunction with indicator nets.

It may not be possible to wait for all the above appliances.

The plans should be aimed at two dates, viz:— March 1st and April 15th: and then it can be seen whether the advantage of waiting till all the appliances are made outweigh the dangers of continuing in our present situation.

In principle the following points are relied upon:—

1. That the gunfire of the bombarding Squadron and monitors, including old cruisers and the inshore bombarding flotilla, will, firing from several directions with cross and aerial spotting, subdue the fire of the batteries to allow

2. the transports to approach covered by darkness, and smoke, and sheltered by older cruisers, and land during the night after the bombardment 8,000 to 12,000 good infantry.

3. To resume the bombardment on the second day with the infantry attack upon all accessible points. The positions of the enemy's guns will then certainly be disclosed and reported by the troops; and the ships should be able to silence them quickly.

4. To press and nourish the attack with the utmost energy, reinforcing as may be necessary until the garrison is stormed or surrenders.

5. Meanwhile to keep the High Sea Fleet cooped up behind Heligoland by the activities for five days of 40 submarines—B, C and later classes, and by night 60 destroyers of the First Fleet flotillas to be used: the whole supported at a safe distance by the Grand Fleet and its cruisers about 56th parallel.

6. To protect the bombarding ships and waiting transports from submarines:
   (a) by minefields laid the night before the bombardment:
   (b) by the indicator nets:
   (c) by destroyers towing charges.

7. The island having been captured can be defended by submarines and inshore craft from any attack.

A resolve to have the island at all costs, coupled with exact and careful preparations, should certainly, with our great resources, be successful within three days of fire being opened.

WSC

Winston S. Churchill to Vice-Admiral Carden: telegram
(*Copy, Churchill papers: 13/65*)

3 January 1915   Admiralty
1.28 pm
Secret

Do you consider the forcing of the Dardanelles by ships alone a practicable operation.

It is assumed older Battleships fitted with minebumpers would be used preceded by Colliers or other merchant craft as bumpers and sweepers.

Importance of results would justify severe loss.

Let me know your views.

WSC

Lord Fisher to Winston S. Churchill
(*Churchill papers: 13/56*)

3 January 1915   Admiralty
Private and Personal

Dear Winston,

I've been informed by Hankey that War Council assembles next Thursday and I suppose it will be like a game of nine pins! Every one will have a plan and one ninepin in falling will knock over its neighbour!
I CONSIDER THE ATTACK ON TURKEY HOLDS THE FIELD!—but ONLY if it's IMMEDIATE! However, it won't be!—Our Aulic Council[1] will adjourn till the following Thursday fortnight!
(*N.B. When did we meet last? & (what came of it???)*)
We shall decide on a futile bombardment of the Dardanelles which wears out the irreplaceable guns of the 'Indefatigable' which probably will require replacement—what good resulted from the last bombardment?[2] Did it move a single Turk from the Caucasus? And so the war goes on! You want ONE man!

This is the Turkey plan:[3]—

I. Appoint Sir R. Robertson[4] the present Quartermaster General to command the Expeditionary Force.

[1] The Aulic Council, or Reichshofrat, was a judicial body of the Holy Roman Empire from 1497 to 1806. It had twenty members, six of whom had to be Protestants.

[2] A reference to the naval bombardment of the outer forts of the Dardanelles on 3 Nov. 1914.

[3] For a diagrammatic representation of Fisher's plan, see map 5 on page 1596.

[4] William Robert Robertson, 1860–1933. Entered Army as a Private, 1877. 2nd Lieutenant, 1888. Intelligence Department, War Office, 1900–7. Brigadier-General, 1907. Major-General, 1910. Commandant of the Staff College, 1910–13. Director of Military Training, War Office, 1913–14. Knighted, 1913. Quarter-Master-General, British Expeditionary Force, 1914–15. Chief of Staff, British Expeditionary Force, 1915. Chief of the Imperial General Staff, 1915–18. Commander-in-Chief, Home Forces, 1918–19. Commander-in-Chief, British Army of Occupation on the Rhine, 1919–20. Created Baronet, 1919. Field-Marshal, 1920.

II. Immediately replace all Indians and 75,000 seasoned troops from Sir John French's command with Territorials &c. from England (as you yourself suggested) and embark this Turkish Expeditionary Force ostensibly for protection of Egypt! WITH ALL POSSIBLE DESPATCH at Marseilles! and land them at Besika Bay direct with previous feints before they arrive with troops now in Egypt against Haifa & Alexandretta the latter to be a REAL occupation because of its inestimable value as regards the oil fields of the Garden of Eden, with which by rail it is in direct communication & we shove out the Germans now established at Alexandretta with an immense Turkish concession—the last act of that arch enemy of England Marschall von Bieberstein![1]

III. The Greeks to go for Gallipoli at the same time as we go for Besika, & the Bulgarians for Constantinople, and the Russians, the Servians, & Roumanians for Austria (*all this you said yourself!*)

IV. *Sturdee forces the Dardanelles at the same time with Majestic class & Canopus class!*[2] *God Bless him!*

But as the Great Napoleon said 'Celerity'!—without it—'FAILURE'!

In the history of the world—a Junta has never won! You want *one* man!

Yours

F

Winston S. Churchill to Sir John Jellicoe
(*Draft, Churchill papers: 13/46*)

4 January 1915   Admiralty
Private & Secret

My dear Jellicoe

I was vy glad to get yr letter of the 28th. Tho I do not bother you with correspondence it is a pleasure to hear from you, & an assistance.

[While the priceless infn lasts][3] we ought to rest our fleets & flotillas to the

---

[1] Marschall von Bieberstein, 1842–1912. German Ambassador to Constantinople, 1897–1912. His influence over Turkish policy was considerable. In 1908 Lord Kitchener entertained hopes of being sent to Constantinople as British Ambassador to counter von Bieberstein's influence.

[2] Both the Majestic and Canopus classes of battleship were of pre-Dreadnought design. The *Majestic* was launched in 1895 (with four 12-inch guns); the *Canopus* in 1897 (with four 12-inch guns). The *Dreadnought* was launched in 1906 (with ten 12-inch guns); by the outbreak of war a further thirty battleships had been launched or were being built (including ten with eight 15-inch guns).

[3] A reference to the intercepted and decoded German naval signals (see note on p. 281); Churchill deleted the three passages in square brackets before sending this letter.

utmost, & accumulate & conserve strength. But everything convinces me that we must take Borkum as soon as full & careful preparation can be made. The possession of an oversea base quadruples our submarines, making all our B & C boats available for service in German waters. It is the key not only to satisfactory naval policy but to future military action whether by the invasion of Schleswig–Holstein or (better perhaps) Oldenburg. Troops for Borkum will be available; & altho' the capture is a difficult operation I am sure we ought to make the attempt, & am also confident that means will be attained.

In balancing the risks of an offensive, one must not overlook the perils & losses of our present policy. [Even with the priceless infn,] the dangers of surrendering all initiative to the enemy are great & obvious. He strikes having prepared his trap for our counterstroke. We had bad luck on the 16th,[1] & I sympathize with you & yr Admirals in their disappt., but we also had good luck in avoiding mines, submarines, & an unexpected collision with the High Sea Fleet on one of our battle sqns. Even with an amazing advantage we missed our prey & incurred grave perils. [At any moment the infn may cease; & then we shd have to have a patrolling battle & battle cruiser sqn at sea frequently—with all the added dangers that implies.] New SMs are being built for Germany & must be finishing in a few months. Those they have increase in daring & skill each week.

I admire the patience you have shewn & the wonderful success wh has attended & rewarded yr efforts to guard the Grand Fleet from loss hitherto. Whatever happens we must keep that intact for the main decision. But I am sure that the time has come to seize an oversea base, to transfer our flotillas from our coasts to the enemy's, to block him in by mines close inshore wh are not only laid but guarded, & then to proceed to attack with a strong army his naval bases & the canal on wh his naval strength depends.

Later on I will send you a paper dealing more precisely with these points. Meanwhile speak to no one of this.

Yours vy sincerely
WSC

---

[1] A reference to the Scarborough raid of 16 December 1914, in which the British naval forces involved failed to intercept the German battle cruisers which had bombarded Scarborough, Hartlepool and Whitby. 'Yesterday morning,' George V wrote in his diary on 17 December, 'four large German cruisers, it being foggy, appeared off the east coast of Yorkshire about 8.0 o'clock, & shelled Hartlepool & Scarborough for 40 minutes, doing considerable damage, killing about 40 women, children & civilians and maiming & wounding about 400. This is German kultur.' (*Royal Archives*)

Lord Fisher to A. J. Balfour
(*Balfour papers*)

4 January 1915   Admiralty

We have a War Council and we are going to meet next Thursday, and our proceedings remind me of a game of ninepins! One ninepin in falling knocks over its neighbour, and so on! Plans *ad infinitum*! (and I'll back my Winston against the field!). . . .

The purpose of my letter, which really was solely begun to urge on you the peculiar merit of Hankey's Turkey Plan. *I do hope you will give it all your support.* . . .

Lieutenant-Colonel Hankey to A. J. Balfour
(*Balfour papers*)

4 January 1915

. . . I find that there is a very general feeling that we must find some new plan of hitting Germany. You have already received my own ideas on the subject. The First Lord has also written a paper or a letter to the P.M. pressing his own favourite plan with some important extensions. Mr Lloyd George has also written to the P.M. urging developments,—rather on my lines I gather. Meanwhile my information is that Italy and Greece are rather cooling down. . . .

Winston S. Churchill to Lord Fisher
(*Copy, Churchill papers: 13/46*)

4 January 1915   Admiralty
Secret

My dear Fisher,
    We must be agreed on certain points:—
1. No landing at Zeebrugge except as an incident in a general British advance & at the desire of Sir J. French.
2. Failing any British advance along the coast only do Sir A. Wilson's bombardment & blocking the canal business. But do this on the 14th.
3. If the Army cannot or will not advance along the coast there is no use in sending more reinforcements to France.
4. Borkum is the key to all Northern possibilities whether defensive agst raid

or invasion, or offensive to block the enemy in or to invade either Oldenburg or Schleswig-Holstein.

5. Ask that a Regular division of Infantry be assigned to the capture of Borkum, & that plans be made on that basis for action at the earliest moment.

6. While we have the priceless information, take all the rest we can for our heavy ships & flotillas, keep them in harbour & get ready for the offensive.

7. I think we had better hear what others have to say about the Turkish plans before taking a decided line. I wd not grudge 100,000 men because of the great political effects in the Balkan peninsula: but Germany is the foe, & it is bad war to seek cheaper victories & easier antagonists.

This is however a vy general question.

8. With regard to mining you shd put forward definite & practical proposals.[1]

Yours ever
Winston S. Churchill

Lord Fisher to Winston S. Churchill

(*Churchill papers: 13/56*)

4 January 1915   Admiralty

First Lord,

In reply to your memorandum herewith of this date it seems necessary to lay down in the first place what the British Naval Policy is.—

(a) In the first place that policy is to conserve our Naval Superiority over the Germans and in no wise jeopardise it by minor operations whose cumulative effect is to wear out our vessels and incur losses in ships and men— We cant afford any more losses or any further deterioration except for absolutely imperative operations.

(b) No landing expedition on the North Sea Coast can be entertained during the winter months which however should be utilised in preparing for such expeditions in the Spring.

(c) If there is not going to be any military advance along the Coast I see no advantage in what would be a futile bombardment of Zeebrugge which may well be accompanied by the loss of some of our bombarding vessels because it is now an expected event instead of being a pure surprise as was the case on the previous occasion.

(d) I agree that Borkum offers great possibilities but it's a purely military question whether it can be held.

---

[1] In a covering note, Churchill wrote to Fisher: 'Please return this to me with your remarks. We never seem to settle anything.' (*Churchill papers: 13/46*)

(e) Your remarks I absolutely concur in '*to take all the rest we can for our heavy ships and* FLOTILLAS, keep them in harbour and get ready for the offensive'.

(f) Herewith is the mining statement. These opinions I have held since the war began.

(g) I also attach the Baltic paper.

(h) The Naval advantages of the possession of Constantinople and the getting of wheat from the Black Sea are so overwhelming that I consider Colonel Hankey's plan for Turkish operations vital and imperative and very pressing.

(i) I think such feats as the recent air attack on Cuxhaven[1] most necessary & consider an attack should be made on Jan 10th which I understand is feasible.

I think this deals with all your remarks.

F

Lord Fisher to Winston S. Churchill

(*Churchill papers: 13/56*)

4 January 1915   Admiralty

First Lord,

These are my views about Minelaying—

F

MINELAYING

The German policy of laying mines has resulted in denying our access to their harbours—has hampered our submarines in their attempts to penetrate into German waters—and we have lost the latest type of Dreadnought & many other war vessels and over 70 merchant vessels of various sizes.

As we have only laid a patch of mines off Ostend (whose position we have notified) the Germans have free access to our coasts to lay fresh mines and to carry out raids and bombardments. We have had to our own immense disadvantage in holding up our coastwise traffic to extinguish the navigation lights on our East Coast so as to impede German ships laying mines.

At times we have had completely to stop our traffic on the East Coast

---

[1] On Christmas Day, 25 December 1914, nine seaplanes, supported by Commodore Tyrwhitt's Harwich force, attacked the German Zeppelin sheds at Cuxhaven. A dense frost fog made it impossible to locate the sheds. When, however, one of the seaplanes flew over the Schillig Roads, it so alarmed the German battle cruiser *Von der Tann* that she fouled another cruiser and both were severely damaged. Only two of the British planes returned safely to their carriers; the rest had to land in the sea. One pilot was rescued by Commodore Keyes in the torpedo boat destroyer *Lurcher*; three by Lieutenant-Commander Nasmith in the submarine E. 11; the fourth by a Dutch trawler.

because of German Mines—and the risk is so great that freights in some cases have advanced 75 per cent—quite apart from shortness of tonnage. The Germans have laid mines off the North of Ireland and may further hamper movements of shipping in the Atlantic.

The German Minelaying policy has so hindered the movements of the British Fleet by necessitating wide detours that to deal with a raid such as the recent Hartlepool affair involves enormous risks while at the same time the German Fleet can navigate to our Coast with the utmost speed and the utmost confidence. They know that we have laid no mines and the position of course of their own mines is accurately charted by them—indeed we know this is a fact. Our Fleet on the contrary has to confine its movements to deep water or slowly to grope its way behind minesweeping vessels.

There is now no option but to adopt an offensive mine laying policy. It is unfortunate however that we only have 4900 mines at present available—on Feb. 1st (together with 1000 mines from Russia) we shall have 9110 and on March 1st we shall have 11,100 mines. This number however is quite inadequate but every effort is being made to get more. Also *Fast* Mine layers are being procured as the present ones are very slow and their coal supply very small—so at present we can only go very slow in mine laying but carefully selected positions can be proceeded with. We must certainly look forward to a big extension of German Mine laying in the Bristol Channel & English Channel & elsewhere in view of Admiral Tirpitz's recent statements in regard to attacking our commerce.

Neutral vessels now pick up Pilots at the German Island of Sylt and take goods unimpeded to German Ports ostensibly by carrying cotton but more probably copper &c. and thus circumventing our economic pressure. This would be at once stopped effectually by a Mine laying Policy. Nor could any German Vessels get out to sea at speed as at present—they would have to go slow preceded by mine sweeping vessels and so would be exposed to attack by our submarines

F

Lord Fisher to Winston S. Churchill
(*Churchill papers: 13/56*)

4 January 1915   Admiralty

First Lord,

On Dec 26 the Admiralty had reliable information of a Zeppelin Attack on London on the largest scale with both naval and military German Zeppelins.

This is Jan 4 and the Public are not aware of what is impending nor any step taken as regards reprisals in notifying the German Government.

There are at least 20 Zeppelins available for this attack on London and each Zeppelin can carry a ton of explosive.

It is asserted by the experts that one ton of explosive would completely wreck the whole of the Admiralty buildings—this is quoted merely to indicate the terrible massacre resulting from the dropping of these 20 tons of explosive anywhere in the London Area. There is no defence against an air raid on London except reprisals to be officially announced beforehand to the German Government.

As this step has not been taken I must with great reluctance ask to be relieved in my present official position as First Sea Lord—because the Admiralty under present arrangements will be responsible for the massacre coming suddenly upon and unprepared for by the Public.

I have allowed a week to elapse much against my judgment before taking this step to avoid embarrassing the Government. I cannot delay any longer.

F

Winston S. Churchill to Lord Fisher

(*Copy, Churchill papers: 13/56*)

4 January 1915 Admiralty

My dear Fisher,

The question of aerial defence is not one upon wh you have any professional experience. The question of killing prisoners in reprisal for an aerial attack is not one for the Admiralty and certainly not for you to decide. The Cabinet alone can settle such a matter.

I will bring your views to their notice at our meeting tomorrow.

After much reflection I cannot support it. I am circulating a paper giving the facts about a Zeppelin raid as far as we can estimate them.

I hope I am not to take the last part of your letter seriously. I have always made up my mind never to dissuade anyone serving in the department over wh I preside from resigning if they wish to do so. Business becomes impossible on any other terms.

But I sympathise with your feelings of exasperation at our powerlessness to resist certain forms of attack: and I presume I may take your letter simply as an expression of those feelings.

Yours vy sincerely
Winston S. Churchill

Sir John French to Winston S. Churchill

(*Churchill papers: 26/2*)

4 January 1915   General Headquarters

My dear Winston,

I received your very welcome letter of the 1st, and I thank you with all my heart.

The telegram which you sent me through Kitchener about the 'Formidable' came at a most opportune moment. It enabled me to put forward views which I have strongly held for some time.

I am enclosing *for your own private information* copies of two memoranda[1] which I am sending to Kitchener tomorrow (5th) by Murray, my Chief of the Staff. They express my views on the general situation, my ideas as to the methods of employment of the 'New' Army, and the plans of action I am preparing in conjunction with the French.

You will see that what you describe as the 'Coast Game' is the most prominent feature in my proposed operations.

Please on no account let it be known to anyone that I am corresponding with you on the subject. There will be a tremendous fight over the demands I make as to the methods of employment of the 'New' Army; and on the result of that the necessary supply of men to enable me to take the offensive within the next three or four weeks will greatly depend.

When that tremendous point at issue is satisfactorily settled I will tell the Secretary of State for War that I must be put into the closest touch with you and the Admiralty for the carrying out of plans in which the Navy will take so important a part.

I am sending a copy of the enclosed memoranda to the Prime Minister to-day, and I am telling Kitchener that I have done so; and it would be well if you could get the PM to show you these papers as soon as possible, so that you may have knowledge of them otherwise than you have learnt from me.

The man who has been conducting the smaller operation at Nieuport, in which the Navy have assisted, is, as I think you know, General De Mitry.[2] He is a good man and has good troops with him, although they are numerically weak. Joffre will consent to leave him there to act in conjunction with me. I have told him privately, through Bridges, of my proposed plans, and have requested him to pave the way as much as he possibly can by keeping, and as far as possible extending, his present line. I want to support him with

---

[1] Not printed; Kitchener wished his volunteers to be sent to France as a complete Army Corps. Sir John French wanted the new men to be incorporated into his existing Armies.

[2] Marie Antoine Henri de Mitry, 1857–1924. Commanded the 6th Cavalry Division, 1914. Commanded the 2nd Cavalry Corps, 1914–16. Commanded the 6th Army Corps, December 1916. Commanded the 7th Army, October 1918.

as many heavy guns as I can get together, which may enable us to knock out some of the enemy's heavy artillery which might otherwise do considerable damage to the Fleet.

The discussion of all further details must be postponed until the questions raised in the enclosed memoranda are settled and I know what troops I can depend upon getting for trench work at once, so as to relieve my two best Army Corps for the offensive operation.

As regards our meeting. Can you not manage to come over to Dunkirk on Naval business? I will meet you there This can be managed as often as you like quite easily.

Please remember that *no-one* must ever know that this present communication has passed between us and will burn the letters & papers when done with.

Yrs always
JF

Sir Henry Jackson: memorandum[1]
(*Copy, Churchill papers: 2/82*)

5 January 1915 Admiralty

. . . 6. From the above rough estimate, the risk to a battle squadron rushing the Straits under favourable circumstances can be approximated. I have put it at six ships out of the eight, *hors de combat*, and the other two severely damaged. On the other hand, much damage should have been inflicted on the forts; and a second squadron following closely to the heels of the first, and in the same channel, might get through with much less damage.

Light cruisers and other unarmoured craft, must be expected to suffer more heavily, and would follow the two squadrons at their highest speed.

9. It may be deduced that it would be unwise to attempt the operation with less than two complete battle squadrons and two cruiser squadrons, to give any chance of meeting the enemy squadron at an advantage, and dominating the city of Constantinople; and it is open to consideration whether the attempt should not preferably be preceded by long range bombardment of the forts in the Narrows as at the entrance, so as to reduce the volume of fire in the 'approach'.

---

[1] The first five points are missing in the printed copy of this document in the Churchill papers, and point 9 follows immediately after point 6. I have been unable to find a fuller version of this memorandum in the Admiralty archives, or among Jackson's own papers at the Naval Record Centre.

10. A methodical bombardment would entail the expenditure of a large amount of ammunition and wear of heavy guns, and also some losses, but it would enable the attacking squadron to replenish before making the passage and to start fair from the Narrows, and expend much less ammunition during the last rush, and then be in a better position to engage the enemy naval forces. It may be reasonably expected their forces would endeavour to meet our squadron as it emerged from the Straits into the Sea of Marmora, before we had time to reform in that sea and recover from the effects of the fire of the batteries.

To arrive off Constantinople with depleted magazines and ships almost out of action from gun fire, and with shore batteries still intact both in front and rear, would be a fatal error, and tend to annul the effect of the appearance of the squadron, as soon as its real state was known.

H. B. Jackson

Winston S. Churchill to H. H. Asquith

(*Copy, Churchill papers: 13/44*)

5 January 1915   Admiralty

My dear Prime Minister,

I entirely agree with Colonel Hankey's[1] remarks on the subject of special mechanical devices for taking trenches. It is extraordinary that the Army in the field and the War Office should have allowed nearly three months of trench warfare to progress without addressing their minds to its special problems.

The present war has revolutionised all military theories about the field of fire. The power of the rifle is so great that 100 yards is held sufficient to stop any rush, and, in order to avoid the severity of the artillery fire, trenches are often dug on the reverse slope of positions, or a short distance in the rear of villages, woods, or other obstacles. The consequence is that the war has become a short range instead of a long range war as was expected, and opposing trenches get ever closer together for mutual safety from each other's artillery fire. The question to be solved is not therefore the long attack over a carefully prepared glacis of former times, but the actual getting across of 100 or 200 yards of open space and wire entanglements. All this was apparent more than two months ago, but no steps have been taken and no preparations made. It would be quite easy in a short time to fit up a number of steam tractors with small armoured shelters, in which men and machine guns could

---

[1] In Hankey's memorandum of 28 December 1914, paragraphs 8 to 11 (quoted on pp. 338–340).

be placed, which would be bullet-proof. Used at night they would not be affected by artillery fire to any extent. The caterpillar system would enable trenches to be crossed quite easily, and the weight of the machine would destroy all wire entanglements. 40 or 50 of these engines prepared secretly and brought into positions at nightfall could advance quite certainly into the enemy's trenches, smashing away all the obstructions and sweeping the trenches with their machine-gun fire and with grenades thrown out of the top. They would then make so many points d'appui for the British supporting infantry to rush forward and rally on them. They can then move forward to attack the second line of trenches. The cost would be small. If the experiment did not answer, what harm would be done? An obvious measure of prudence would have been to have started something like this two months ago. It should certainly be done now.

The shield is another obvious experiment which should have been made on a considerable scale. What does it matter which is the best pattern? A large number should have been made of various patterns: some to carry, some to wear, some to wheel. If the mud now prevents the working of shields or traction engines, the first frost would render them fully effective. With a view to this I ordered a month ago 20 shields on wheels to be made on the best design the Naval Air Service could devise. These will be ready shortly, and can, if need be, be used for experimental purposes.

A third device which should be used systematically and on a large scale is smoke artificially produced. It is possible to make small smoke barrels which on being lighted generate a great volume of dense black smoke which could be turned off or on at will. There are other matters closely connected with this to which I have already drawn your attention, but which are of so secret a character that I do not put them down on paper.

One of the most serious dangers that we are exposed to is the possibility that the Germans are acting and preparing all these surprises, and that we may at any time find ourselves exposed to some entirely new form of attack. A committee of engineering officers and other experts ought to be sitting continually at the War Office to formulate schemes and examine suggestions, and I would repeat that it is not possible in most cases to have lengthy experiments beforehand. If the devices are to be ready by the time they are required it is indispensable that manufacture should proceed simultaneously with experiments. The worst that can happen is that a comparatively small sum of money is wasted.

Winston S. Churchill

Winston S. Churchill to Sir John French: not sent

(*Churchill papers: 26/2*)

5 January 1915   Admiralty
Personal & Secret

My dear French,

I will tell the Prime Minister that I have heard from you & that you wd like him if he thinks fit to show me the memorandum you have forwarded.

It certainly raises all the issues. There is much to be said for the interpolating of the 1st new army in the units & under the staff organisation of those already familiar with the conditions of this war. But you are right to be under no illusions as to the differences of opinion wh will be aroused by it.

Discussion here has turned rather to looking for other theatres of war: for the employment of the new armies. Some point to Emden & Wilhemshaven & the direct invasion of Germany there, others to Schleswig Holstein with the consequent opening of the Baltic & the exposure of the Baltic shore to Russian oversea attack. Competing schemes turn to the capture of Constantinople & an advance via Belgrade from Cple & Salonika; or to an invasion of Austria from the Adriatic shore.

There is a general feeling that a condition of stalemate has been reached in France & Flanders—certainly in Flanders: & that we ought not to play the German game by incurring vy heavy losses in driving them (if we can) from one entrenched position to another. Nothing is decided: but this view is vy strongly held. The war council is to meet on Thursday. Before anything is settled I shall press that you shd come over to some later meeting. Of course if there were good prospects of a fruitful offensive in Flanders or on the French front, that wd hold the field.

But I fear that the losses wd not be repaid by gains, except perhaps along the coast; & that is not the job it was.

The need of clearing the coast is however a vy real one, and if you are in a position to effect this with naval aid, the operation wd have paramount claims.

My dear friend this letter is only to keep you *au fait*. Please let it be entirely between us two—& do not let the speculative ideas I have put down dissuade you from the development of your immediate plans.

Yours always
W

PS I send this by Archie Sinclair[1] who rejoins tomorrow—I will write again as soon as I see good occasion.

WSC

Lord Fisher to Winston S. Churchill

(Fisher papers)

5 January 1915   Admiralty

For information of the First Lord in the hope that futile bombardments will be discouraged especially as Admiral Hood writes that Colonel Bridges tells him that these bombardments result in nothing as the Army does not take advantage of them. Our stock of Heavy Gun ammunition and the life of our big guns is limited & should be reserved for the 3 great prospective operations in the spring and our margin of Battleships has also to be considered.

F

Winston S. Churchill to Lord Fisher

(Fisher papers)

5 January 1915   Admiralty

Many thanks. I have always kept myself fully informed on these points.

I do not agree that the bombardments wh have taken place have been *futile*. On the contrary the results have fully justified the expenditure of ammunition.

The armament of the monitors has been settled & the ships selected.

WSC

Vice-Admiral Carden to Winston S. Churchill: *telegram*

(Copy, Churchill papers: 13/65)

5 January 1915   HMS Indefatigable
2.20 pm
Secret

With reference to your telegram of 3rd inst, I do not consider Dardanelles can be rushed.

They might be forced by extended operations with large number of ships.

---

[1] Archibald Henry Macdonald Sinclair, 1890–1970. Entered Army, 1910. 4th Baronet, 1912. ADC to Colonel Seely, 1915–16. Captain, 1915. 2nd in Command of the 6th Royal Scots Fusiliers, while Churchill was in command, January–May 1916. Squadron-Commander, 2nd Life Guards, 1916–17. Major, Guards Machine Gun Regiment, 1918. Served under Churchill, Ministry of Munitions, 1918–19. Churchill's personal Military Secretary, War Office, 1919–21. Churchill's Private Secretary, Colonial Office, 1921–2. Liberal MP, 1922–45. Secretary of State for Scotland, 1931–2. Leader of the Parliamentary Liberal Party, 1935–45. Secretary of State for Air, 1940–5. Created Viscount Thurso, 1952.

Winston S. Churchill to Vice-Admiral Carden: telegram
(*Copy, Churchill papers: 13/65*)

6 January 1915   Admiralty
1.45 pm
Secret and Personal

Your view is agreed with by high authorities here. Please telegraph in detail what you think could be done by extended operations, what force would be needed and how you consider it should be used.

H. H. Asquith to Venetia Stanley
(*Montagu papers*)

6 January 1915   10 Downing Street

... Winston came in this morning & told me 2 new & not very agreeable Naval stories. The first was that on the luckless day of the Scarborough bombardment, part of the German fleet was picked up by Goodenough[1] & his light cruisers. He saw some of them in the mist & at once opened fire on them with two of his ships: if he had gone on, the rest of the two fleets wd. have been attracted by the noise & come up, and there might have been a general engagement in wh. we were bound to score. Unfortunately Beatty with his battle cruisers—not hearing or knowing of the firing—signalled to G's two unengaged cruisers to sheer off: the message was by some fool's mistake miscarried to G; who thereupon (as he supposed in obedience to orders) ceased firing & drew away. I don't think in the circumstances he was to blame; but Fisher & I fancy Winston think otherwise. Anyhow it was a piece of real bad luck. W's other story was about the 'Formidable' & shows that the Admiral—Bayly—was seriously at fault. It was a horrible night & he ought to have taken his squadron of 8 battleships into Portland, where they wd have been quite secure. Instead of that he moved them in a close column towards Torbay, and when they were in the full glare of the Start lighthouse (one of the most powerful) & steaming at only 10 knots, the German submarine found the last ship in the line—the Formidable—an excellent target, and drove 2 torpedoes home. Wasn't it tragic? ...

[1] William Edmund Goodenough, 1867–1945. Entered Navy, 1882. Captain, 1905. Commodore commanding 2nd Light Cruiser Squadron at Heligoland Bight action, 1914; at Dogger Bank action, 1915; and at battle of Jutland, 1916. Superintendent, Chatham Dockyard, 1918–20. Knighted, 1919. Vice-Admiral, 1920. Commander-in-Chief, Africa Station, 1920–2. Commanded Reserve Fleet, 1923–4. Commander-in-Chief, the Nore, 1924–7. Admiral, 1925.

Winston S. Churchill to H. H. Asquith

(*Copy, Churchill papers: 13/44*)

6 January 1915   Admiralty

Prime Minister,

I have read the memorandum from Sir John French which you showed me this morning. I do not feel convinced that the organization which the Commander-in-Chief outlines, is the best which could be devised for utilising the troops of the new army. But I think there is a great deal to be said for the principle which Sir John French advocates, of intermingling units from the new armies with those of the regular forces now serving in the field. It is undesirable that British armies serving side by side in one theatre of the war, should show great differences in character, experience, and training; and that the British line should be maintained at one part over a very large front by army corps which have seen all the hardest fighting, while another equally large section of the front is to be held by an army or armies who come entirely new to active service, whose training though excellent has been very short, and who necessarily lack in their brigade, divisional, and army corps staffs, officers of the highest professional experience. Such a system might produce very great unevenness in the line; would certainly not give the new troops the best chance of distinguishing themselves; and may easily, through a retirement of so large a section of the line, lead to a general defeat. The problem is no doubt a difficult one; but I think that the preponderance of military opinion in this and other countries would advocate the formation of an army in the field whose army corps at any rate, and probably whose divisions, were equal in quality. I can quite understand the misgivings of a Commander-in-Chief who contemplates one portion of his forces consisting entirely of new troops and inexperienced staffs, while the other consists exclusively of tried and seasoned units under the staffs who have been in continual contact with the actual conditions of the present war. I believe also that it would be taken as a great compliment by the troops of the new army if they were to be brigaded with, and enabled to serve alongside of the regular battalions who have covered themselves with so much distinction. I cannot consider that it would be a reasonable thing to segregate the two forces. It might easily lead to a very unpleasant rivalry and friction between 'French's Army' and 'Kitchener's Army' instead of all serving harmoniously together as the British Army. The danger seems to me to be serious and real, and I think we should take timely steps to avoid it. The sound and accepted principle of military organization is undoubtedly that young troops should be brigaded with seasoned troops, and that young troops specially need experienced and trained staff organization. Marked differences between large portions of an army are detrimental to military efficiency, and add an immense complication to its tactical employment.

Acting on the above principle, I think it was a pity that the three divisions of British troops from India, the 27th, 28th, and 29th, which consist exclusively of regulars serving with the colours without any admixture of reservists, should have been sent abroad without any admixture into their cadres of the well-trained recruits of the new armies. If every company in these three divisions had been divided into two and then raised to full strength by the addition of an equal number of soldiers from three divisions of the new army, we should have had six divisions almost immediately ready which would have been almost as good as the original divisions mobilised in England on the declaration of war, and certainly far more ready to take the field immediately than any homogeneous force raised since August. As it is, the 36 battalions of these three divisions do not contain a single reservist, and differ in that respect from every other unit employed by any country in the field. It seems to me a waste of our very small number of regular soldiers serving with the colours to use them concentrated in this way instead of using them as cadres on which to build the excellent material now coming to hand. This, however, is a digression, though it illustrates the same principle.

On the other hand, I agree entirely with Lord Kitchener that the new armies and the territorials should not be absorbed piecemeal into the existing army and I should deprecate in principle any departure from the accepted and well-known organization of brigades, divisions, and army corps. Marked and serious divergence of opinion between the Commander-in-Chief and the armies in the field, on the one hand, and the Secretary of State and the forces raised in England, on the other, ought to be prevented. I would therefore propose for your consideration, and subsequently for that of the Cabinet, a middle course. As soon as the first new army is ready to go out, let two battalions from every brigade of the first new army change places with two battalions of the corresponding brigades of the first army now in the field. This would secure an absolutely even level over the whole of the 36 brigades; and if there was a proper interchange of officers between the regular and new staffs, two armies would have been created exactly equal in quality, both of a very high standard, and both directed by experienced staffs, instead of one veteran and professional army, and the other recruit and emergency army. When the second new army was ready to go out, the same process should take place with the second regular army. I am sure that this is the right way, and the only way to attain a large homogeneous army capable of acting together against the enemy in April and May; and I do not think any considerations of sentiment, still less any supposed rivalry between the army now training at home and the army now in the field, ought to prevent us from taking the best steps open to us to increase our military power.

WSC

Lord Fisher to Winston S. Churchill and Vice-Admiral Oliver
(*Churchill papers: 13/56*)

6 January 1915   Admiralty

First Lord

I think before the proposed bombardment of Zeebrugge is again discussed it should be carefully considered what certain losses we have to face in capture of Borkum, in attack on Dardanelles and forcing the passage—in Baltic operations—and (I HOPE) in landing & covering a British army landed in the Spring in Schleswig Holstein to advance on the Kiel Canal. No one can question that whatever damage is inflicted at Zeebrugge can be quickly repaired by the Germans—unless the army join with the Fleet to hold it— are we going to bombard it every 3 weeks?

F

P.S. I strongly supported the previous bombardment of Zeebrugge and I would strongly support it now but have we the margin of ships in view of impending great operations? *and the men and officers!*

Meeting of the War Council: extract from Secretary's notes
(*Copy, Cabinet papers: 22/1*)

Present: H. H. Asquith (in the Chair), Lord Haldane, Lord Crewe, Winston S. Churchill, A. J. Balfour, Lord Fisher, Sir Arthur Wilson, David Lloyd George, Sir Edward Grey, Lord Kitchener, Sir James Wolfe Murray, Lieutenant-Colonel Hankey (Secretary)

7 January 1915   10 Downing Street
Noon

THE DEFENCE OF LONDON AGAINST AIRSHIPS

THE PRIME MINISTER drew attention to a note by the First Lord of the Admiralty on this question. From this he gathered that, notwithstanding the elaborate preparations described therein, there was no assurance that London would not be subjected to aerial attack.

LORD KITCHENER confirmed the views expressed in the Admiralty Memorandum, which, he said, were concurred in by the War Office Aeronautical Department. The question was largely one of intelligence. The airships, starting from the Rhine, would probably call somewhere in Belgium for fuel. If news could be obtained of this, the army aircraft in Flanders would attack them. It was possible that the enemy's airships might sail here with the wind, relying on their means of propulsion to get them home again.

LORD FISHER said the Admiralty had reliable information that an attack would be made, first by the German naval Zeppelins on some east coast town, and subsequently a combined attack by naval and military airships on London. He thought that they would probably wait for still, frosty weather, and come at night.

MR. CHURCHILL explained the arrangements made for the defence of London against aerial attack. A special detachment of aircraft (ten aeroplanes) was stationed at Dunkirk, whose primary functions were to prevent the completion of airship bases in Belgium, and to attack any airships which might call in that country for supplies. A special intelligence system had been organized in connection with this service. It was not impossible, however, that German airships might attack London without alighting in Belgium. To meet this contingency there were some sixty aeroplanes always ready in the triangle enclosed between London, Sheerness, and Dover. The moment a hostile airship was sighted the alarm would be given and the aeroplanes would ascend. Those on the coast would probably not be able to rise sufficiently high to attack the airships on their approach, but would be ready for them on their return; those at Hendon, however, should be ready to attack the airships as they neared London. These aeroplanes were armed with rifles firing incendiary bullets, which, in the course of experiments, had proved their capacity to destroy a balloon. In addition, he believed that some flyers were prepared to charge a Zeppelin. Within the same triangle there are 9—3-inch, 39—6-prs., and 28 pompom guns—a total of 76 anti-aircraft guns. In London itself there are 2—3-inch, 4—6-pr., and 6 pompoms, with 13 searchlights. The 3-inch is a powerful and accurate long-range gun. The pompoms were now being provided with incendiary shell. Notwithstanding these preparations, if the enemy thought it worth while to attack London merely for the purpose of injuring and terrorising the civil population and damaging property, there was no means of preventing it. In order to reduce the loss of life to a minimum, instructions had been published by the police warning the populace to remain indoors. The Fire Brigade had worked out careful plans for meeting a simultaneous outbreak of a number of fires.

MR. BALFOUR asked whether, having regard to the experience of the seaplane raid on Cuxhaven, ships had much to fear from airships.

MR. CHURCHILL said they had not much to fear. All the more modern ships had already been armed with anti-aircraft guns.

SIR ARTHUR WILSON said that in the course of the raid the cruisers had little difficulty in driving off the airships.

LORD HALDANE pointed out that the bombs dropped from an airship would burst without penetrating into the ship, and would therefore do less damage than a shell.

SIR EDWARD GREY criticized the system of permitting rows of lights along the roads through the parks.

MR. CHURCHILL said that the system of lights had been most carefully and systematically worked out. The object aimed at was to spread the lighting evenly. Otherwise the dark gaps caused by the parks would enable an enemy to locate his position.

LORD CREWE questioned whether airships could navigate by night with sufficient accuracy.

LORD FISHER said that in order to reach London they would only have to follow the course of the Thames.

THE PRIME MINISTER said that two conclusions presented themselves to his mind:—
1. It was necessary to have a complete system of intelligence and communication.
2. The responsibility for action must be clearly defined.

MR. CHURCHILL said that on the question of responsibility the War Office, before the outbreak of war, was the Department responsible for Home Defence. When war commenced, however, the War Office were so engrossed with the arrangements for the transportation of the Expeditionary Force to France that the Admiralty had offered to undertake the aerial defence of London.

LORD KITCHENER said that the Army would be able to reinforce the Navy to some extent. The system of communications had proved very satisfactory.

LORD CREWE asked if any arrangements had been made for warning the civil population of an impending attack by ringing bells, &c., so that they might take cover.

MR. CHURCHILL said that the expediency of this was not quite certain. The question was being examined.

LORD HALDANE suggested that arrangements ought to be considered for transferring public offices elsewhere in the event of their destruction.

THE PRIME MINISTER thought this might be left until the event occurred.

MR. CHURCHILL mentioned that on the occasion of the recent air raid up the Thames Valley thousands of shots had been fired, but no one had been damaged by accident. There had been not a single complaint.

(*Conclusion.*)

No further action can be taken at present.

THE GENERAL POLICY OF THE WAR

... LORD KITCHENER ... For Home Defence it was considered that we ought to work up to a figure of approximately 500,000 men, and in addition about 370,000 men were required for Special Reserve services for the original Army and the new Armies combined. There would therefore eventually be 870,000 men at home.

THE PRIME MINISTER asked how the figure of 500,000 for Home Defence was arrived at.

MR. CHURCHILL said that this figure appeared to exceed any estimates made in the course of enquiries made by the Committee of Imperial Defence. The Navy was prepared to protect the country against organized invasion, and 500,000 therefore seemed rather a large figure.

LORD KITCHENER said that 500,000 was only a conventional figures towards which his arrangements aimed. It could not in any case be realized before the autumn and it appeared unnecessary at present to discuss the matter further.

MR. BALFOUR suggested that some part of the Special Reserve might be counted on for Home Defence. If the country was in danger, any forces of the kind would unquestionably be called on to defend it.

LORD KITCHENER agreed. He pointed, however, to the difficulty of counting a force whose numbers varied from day to day and whose organization was not well adapted to work as an army.

THE PRIME MINISTER concluded from Lord Kitchener's remarks that the military reinforcements regarded by Sir John French as indispensable for the capture of Zeebruge could not be supplied without dislocating the organization not only of the existing Territorial Force, but also of the future Armies.

MR. CHURCHILL said that he did not wish to challenge this opinion, but, before finally rejecting Sir John French's proposal, it was necessary to consider what was involved. The main object of the proposal was to clear the coast of the enemy's forces, and the Admiralty attached great, though not supreme, importance to this. If Sir John French could only reoccupy Zeebrugge on condition that he was supplied with fifty additional battalions, and, if Lord Kitchener was unable to provide these, the Admiralty would have to do their best to deal with Zeebrugge themselves. This, however, could only be effected by running great risks and probable losses, if naval means only were employed. Moreover, the damage that could be occasioned by the fleet would only be temporary, so long as the Germans remained in occupation of the Belgian coast. It must be recognized that in abandoning the offensive project against Zeebrugge the communications of the army and British commerce up channel were jeopardized.

LORD KITCHENER said that the provision of reinforcements of troops was not the only difficulty. Sir John French required in addition a supply of gun ammunition equal to fifty rounds per day per gun for a period which might reach ten or twenty days. It was impossible to calculate how long offensive operations, once commenced, might last before the object was attained; it was, however, evident that the breaking off of such operations before accomplishment, owing to lack of artillery ammunition, and not on account of a successful termination or a convenient pause in the operations having been reached, might lead to a serious reverse being sustained by our forces. Every effort was being made in all parts of the world to obtain an unlimited supply of ammunition, but the result was still far from sufficient to maintain the large number of guns now at the front adequately supplied with ammunition for offensive purposes. The present rate of output was about thirteen rounds per gun per day.

MR. LLOYD GEORGE suggested that, before a final decision was arrived at, it was desirable to consider the large question of the future employment of the new Armies. If our army on the Continent was to be thrown away and shattered in an operation which appeared to him impossible, the war might continue indefinitely, or at any rate for two or three years more. Was it impossible, he asked, to get at the enemy from some other direction, and to strike a blow that would end the war once and for all? If some new plan should be decided on, every man would be required for it in April or May, and the loss of some fifty battalions of Territorial troops would be very severely felt. . . .

MR. CHURCHILL said that the great point was this: Is General Joffre going to take the offensive, or will the Germans be left to take it? The latter was most desirable, if the Germans would only oblige us by doing so. But if the Allies are to take the offensive, he hoped we should not shatter our armies on wire entanglements, but would advance in co-operation with the fleet.

LORD KITCHENER thought it probable that the Germans would shortly take the offensive. He did not feel very much certainty about General Joffre's offensive; he had several times announced his intention of taking the offensive but hitherto, very little result had ensued, and the recent offensive in Alsace appeared already to have been checked.

(*Conclusion.*)

The proposal contained in Sir John French's Memorandum of the 3rd January (C.I.D. Paper G–1) to take the offensive against Zeebrugge is not approved, as the advantages would not be commensurate with the heavy losses involved.

THE PROPOSED CAPTURE OF AN ISLAND

THE PRIME MINISTER asked the First Lord whether the Navy could do anything to circumscribe the activities of the Germans at Zeebrugge?

SIR EDWARD GREY suggested that the Admiralty should not be pressed to explain their plans in detail.

MR. CHURCHILL said that he attached greater importance to the seizure of an island on the German coast. Effective action by the Navy in limiting the operations of the German fleet depended to a great extent upon our being able to seize and hold an island possessing the requisite qualifications. There was only one suitable such island.[1] The problem of effecting its capture was difficult, but the difficulties were not insuperable. Unquestionably certain risks of loss would be run, but this would not involve serious risk to our main fighting fleets. If an island were occupied, the whole of the B and C class submarines, which at present were unable to be employed on the German coast, could be based on it; and the dangers of any German ship which put to sea would be correspondingly increased. The island would also be a useful base for aircraft, which could reconnoitre the German ports. Invasion would then become impossible, and the risk of raids enormously reduced, as we should soon discover if preparations of this kind were in progress. It was anticipated that about a division of troops would be the largest force that could be employed in the enterprise, and, if it succeed, the Army would be fully recouped by the greater security of and the fewer troops required for Home Defence. A large amount of detailed work would be required before the plans were ready and, if this expedition were approved in principle, the Navy would desist from risking heavy ships at Zeebrugge.

[1] The island was Borkum. For security reasons, Churchill did not name it at the War Council. He informed Sir John French of its name on 11 January 1915.

LORD FISHER said that two or three months would be required before the Navy was ready to carry out the proposed operation.

(*Conclusion.*)

The proposed attack on an island is approved in principle, subject to the feasibility of the plan when worked out in detail. The Admiralty to proceed with the making out of plans.

Winston S. Churchill to H. H. Asquith

(*Copy, Churchill papers: 26/2*)

7 January 1915   Admiralty
Secret

My dear Prime Minister,

The following points seem to arise out of our talk today:—

1: We are to remain on the defensive in France & await another German attack.

2: If Joffre advances meanwhile, we shd only demonstrate & fire our cannons. No more local frontal attacks. Anything aggressive must be on the coast. That or nothing.

3: If we are to remain on the defensive, *query* ought we not to get into a more comfortable, dry, habitable line—even if we have to retire a few miles. (Our troops are rotting.)

4: The Indians must winter elsewhere. Query Smyrna?

5: Zeebrugge to be left to the Navy: you all expressing yr wishes that we shd try if possible to bring it up.

6: You must all recognize the disadvantage and danger of its remaining in enemy hands, and not blame us for the consequent menace to communications.

7: 'Sylt'[1] to be taken as soon as arrangements can be made. Admiralty may count on the necessary military aid, up to one division.

8: The intermingling of the Kitchener & Regular armies at any rate by brigades must be further considered.

Yours always

---

[1] The code name for the German island of Borkum.

Meeting of the War Council: extract from Secretary's notes

(Copy, Cabinet papers: 22/1)

*Present: H. H. Asquith (in the Chair), Lord Haldane, Lord Crewe, Winston S.
Churchill, A. J. Balfour, Lord Fisher, Sir Arthur Wilson, David Lloyd George, Sir
Edward Grey, Lord Kitchener, Sir James Wolfe Murray, Lieutenant-Colonel Hankey
(Secretary)*

8 January 1915
Noon   10 Downing Street

THE GENERAL POLICY OF THE WAR

... MR. LLOYD GEORGE laid stress on the great losses that would be
entailed in any attempt to break through the German lines in France. He
reminded the Council that as far back as 1879 the Russians, under one of the
best generals they ever had,[1] had been held up by the Turks at Plevna.
Since then the power of the defensive had enormously increased. The
Germans had lines and lines of entrenchments. To attempt a decisive
attack and to fail would produce the worst possible physical and moral effect
on the Allied armies. Was there, he asked, no alternative theatre in which
we might employ our surplus armies to produce a decisive effect? He suggested that an attack on Austria might produce the desired effect. This
would extend the front of the enemy and enable the superior forces at the
disposal of the Allies to be brought to bear. Austria was the weakest part
of the hostile combination and had already suffered heavily. There were
great racial antagonisms in the Austrian Empire. The population of the south
was largely Slavonic in origin and hated the Teutons. If a British Expeditionary Force landed in Southern Austria it might expect to receive a
sympathetic greeting. Further, it would have to encounter a nation inferior
to Germany in military efficiency and from the point of view of staff and
training. An attack on Austria would probably compel Roumania and Italy
to join in the war in order to obtain their share of the spoils. In fact, we
ought to make it clear that no nation that declined to take part in the war
should derive any benefit from it. This plan, therefore, would enormously
increase the military strength of the Allies by bringing in other nations.
The result of these combinations would be that Austria would have to withdraw her armies from the north to meet the menace in the south. This would

---

[1] Mikhail Dimitrievich Skobelev, 1843–82. Lieutenant-General at the siege of Plevna,
September–December 1877. Defeated the Turks near the Shipka Pass, January 1878. A
leading panslavist, in 1882 he forecast a desperate strife between Teuton and Slav.

materially assist the Russian plan, enabling them to invade Silesia, as at present it was the Austrians who stood between Russia and Silesia.

The moment Austria was knocked out, Germany would be entirely isolated. Not only would she lose the military strength of Austria, but she would be cut off from her supplies of Hungarian wheat and Roumanian oil.

He realized that the difficulty of an attack of the kind suggested was mainly one of lines of communication. He understood that the Salonica railway, though a good railway of German construction, had only a single line of track, and it would be difficult to supply a large army along it, particularly if the Greeks also had to be supplied by it.

An alternative line of approach would be from Ragusa, and this might be used to supplement the Salonica line, giving two lines of communication.

THE PRIME MINISTER said he had been at Ragusa the previous year,[1] and had penetrated some distance inland. The railway was of narrow gauge, and there was only one road, which, though a good one, ran through difficult and mountainous country.

LORD KITCHENER read a letter dated the 2nd January, 1915 in which Sir John French, in reply to a letter from him, examined the whole military situation. The gist of this letter was somewhat as follows:—

The impossibility of breaking through the German lines by direct attack is not admitted. Recently rain and fog have been the principal difficulty. It is largely a question of larger supplies of ammunition, and specially of high explosives. Until the impossibility of breaking through on this side was proved, there could be no question of making an attempt elsewhere. Ultimate victory must be sought for in the eastern theatre of war.[2] In the western theatre a German victory would be decisive, but a victory of the Allies, who might drive the Germans back to the Rhine, would not be decisive. A crushing defeat, however, of the French would be very dangerous and embarrassing to our own safety, and must be made impossible. For these reasons not a man could be diverted from France to any other theatre of operations without the consent of the French, and this would never be obtained.

Moreover, only first line troops could be used for an offensive in any other theatre of war, and this would mean withdrawing them from France. Even

---

[1] In May 1913 Asquith was Churchill's guest on board the Admiralty yacht *Enchantress*. Together with Margot and Violet Asquith, Edward Marsh and James Masterton-Smith, they spent three weeks cruising in the Adriatic and Mediterranean. They visited the Dalmatian ports of Austria–Hungary (including Ragusa—now Dubrovnik), as well as Greece, Sicily and Malta.

[2] In contemporary discussions, the phrase 'eastern front' refers to the Russian front. The area of attack on Austria and Turkey was known as the 'southern front'. It was only after the war that those who advocated an attack on Turkey came to be called 'easterners'.

then we should almost certainly arrive at a condition of stalemate, similar to that already reached in France.

If, however, these arguments were brushed aside, it would be necessary to consider what other theatres of war were open to us.

Russia, Denmark, Holland, and the North Coast of Germany must be ruled out for obvious reasons. Italy would be a good point from which to attack; but, if Italy entered the war she would not require troops to support her. Istria and Dalmatia must be ruled out, owing to the danger from mines and submarines. An attack with Greece and Serbia via Salonica was, perhaps, the least objectionable proposal, but the lines of communication would be long and difficult. To attack Turkey would produce no decisive result, and would be to play Germany's game.

Summing up, Sir John French expressed a strong preference for the employment of our armies in France.

Lord Kitchener then read a second (anonymous) Memorandum, arriving at much the same conclusion:

THE PRIME MINISTER said that Sir John French's Memorandum was a very able statement of the case against action outside France.

MR. CHURCHILL suggested that the proposals for an attack from the south should form the subject of careful Staff examination.

LORD KITCHENER gave the results of a preliminary examination of these questions in the War Office. Attack from Italy, Trieste, and Fiume might be ruled out, as the co-operation of Italy would be necessary, and Italy's forces were sufficient without assistance.

Ragusa was an impossible sea base, owing to the difficulty of the country inland; the inferior railway; the ease with which it could be destroyed by the enemy; and the lack of sufficient roads. It had also been provided with artillery defences since the war began.

Salonica could only be used if Greece were an ally; the single line of railway leading to Serbia could only support, at the outside, an army of 200,000 men; the bridges would be liable to attack by komitajis.

The Dardanelles appeared to be the most suitable objective, as an attack here could be made in co-operation with the Fleet. If successful, it would re-establish communication with Russia; settle the Near Eastern question; draw in Greece and, perhaps, Bulgaria and Roumania; and release wheat and shipping now locked up in the Black Sea.

LIEUTENANT-COLONEL HANKEY pointed out that it would give us the Danube as a line of communication for an army penetrating into the heart of Austria and bring our sea power to bear in the middle of Europe.

LORD KITCHENER thought that 150,000 men would be sufficient for the capture of the Dardanelles, but he reserved his final opinion until a closer study had been made.

MR. LLOYD GEORGE expressed surprise at the lowness of the figure.

ALEXANDRETTA

LORD KITCHENER suggested an attack on Alexandretta as a minor but useful operation requiring from 30,000 to 50,000 men. It would strike an effective blow at the Turkish communications with Syria.

THE PRIME MINISTER read a telegram from the acting High Commissioner in Egypt (Sir M. Cheetham),[1] which had arrived that morning, advocating an attack on Alexandretta.

MR. CHURCHILL suggested that the Indians, who were suffering from the effects of the hard climate in France, might be removed and devoted to an attack at Alexandretta, returning to France in the spring.

LORD KITCHENER said that the climate of the hills around Alexandretta was more rigorous than that of France. He agreed that it was desirable temporarily to withdraw some of the Indian battalions who were affected by the climate. For this purpose he proposed to withdraw three battalions, and to send them to Egypt as a sanatorium. When the General Officer Commanding in Egypt[2] reported that they were sufficiently fit to form part of the defence force in Egypt, three good Indian battalions would be withdrawn to replace them in France. In any case, if other battalions, over and above the three referred to above, were sent to Egypt, it would be on the understanding that they were to be replaced from Egypt. He thought that it would have a bad political effect to withdraw the Indian troops from France.

LORD CREWE concurred that the effect in India would be very bad. The position of the Sultan as head of the Mahommedan religion had not been affected by the war, and, if Indians were used as the sole force to attack Turkey, the effect on the Mahommedan races of India might be serious.

---

[1] Milne Cheetham, 1869–1938. Entered Diplomatic Service, 1894. Counsellor of Embassy, Cairo, 1911–19. Chargé d'Affaires, Cairo, in Kitchener's absence, 1914. Knighted, 1915. Minister to Peru and Ecuador, 1919–20; to France, 1921–2; to Switzerland, 1922–4; to Greece, 1924–6; to Denmark, 1926–8.

[2] John Grenfell Maxwell, 1859–1929. Entered Army, 1879. Governor of Pretoria, 1900–2. Knighted, 1900. Major-General, 1906. Lieutenant-General commanding the forces in Egypt, 1908–12, and 1914–15. Commander-in-Chief, Ireland, 1916; Northern Command, 1916–19. General, 1919. A member of Lord Milner's mission to Egypt, 1919–20.

SIR EDWARD GREY said it was important not to lose sight of the political considerations involved in an expedition of this kind. If it was announced that there was no intention of a permanent occupation, the population would become restless and anxious as to what would happen after our departure. On the other hand, a permanent occupation would probably secure the support of the civil population, but there then would arise the possibility of friction with France.

LORD CREWE suggested the expediency of conferring with France and Russia in order to obtain their consent.

LORD KITCHENER said that in any case it would not be expedient to take any action until after the Germans had delivered another big attack on the west. If this failed, we could proceed with some of the plans suggested. In the meantime the possibility of an attack at Alexandretta would be studied.

(*Conclusion.*)

The possibility of an attack on Alexandretta to be studied by the Admiralty and War Office.

HOLLAND

MR. CHURCHILL said he fully agreed in the proposal to study the suggested operations in the Mediterranean. He urged, however, that we should not lose sight of the possibility of action in Northern Europe. As an instance of the attractiveness of such operations, he mentioned that the distance from Emden to Berlin was exactly half the distance from Sir John French's headquarters to Berlin. Was there no possibility that Holland might enter the war on the side of the Allies? He understood that earlier in the war Holland had considered the matter, but had declined. Possibly, however, if given a military guarantee that we could bring a certain force into the field, Holland would change her mind. There were indications that Germany was very anxious about Holland, and Dutch public opinion was only held from declaring for the Allies by fear of the consequences. If Holland could be induced to enter the war the advantages would far outweigh those of the Mediterranean; we could then have an island as a naval base without fighting for it, and our armies, in conjunction with the Dutch, could attack towards Essen.

LORD KITCHENER agreed. The effect would, he thought, be decisive.

SIR EDWARD GREY said that, as soon as we were in a position to guarantee military assistance to Holland on a sufficient scale, he would be prepared to sound the Dutch Government. It would be necessary to satisfy Holland that there was no prospect that she would share the fate of Belgium.

ZEEBRUGGE

MR. CHURCHILL asked the views of the Council as to whether the risk of a naval attack on Zeebrugge ought to be run in order to avoid ultimate risk from submarines.

SIR EDWARD GREY suggested that the opinion of the Admiral who would have to carry out the operation should be obtained.

MR. BALFOUR asked whether, if Zeebrugge was bombarded, the risk to transports and other ships in the channel would be materially reduced.

LORD FISHER thought not. In his opinion the results of a successful operation would not justify the danger involved.

(*Conclusion.*)

The question is mainly a naval one. The Admiralty should destroy the resources of Zeebrugge, if they think it can be done without excessive risk.

Winston S. Churchill to Sir John French

(*Copy, Churchill papers: 26/2*)

8 January 1915   Admiralty
Secret

My dear French,

Your memorandum was circulated to the Cabinet & the War Council. Kitchener also read to the War Council this morning the correspondence you have just sent me. No one cd say that he did not place us fairly in possession of yr views. Your letter in answer to his made a profound impression. On the other hand he demurred vy strongly to sending the 52 territorial battns, saying that their despatch now wd dislocate all his arrangements for the future, whether in regard to the expansion of the army for foreign service, or the provision for home defence. He also read a letter from you, written a few days before yr memm, abt artillery ammunn, & proved, I thought successfully, that it was physically impossible to satisfy these requirements. Both these conditions, i.e. the 52 battns & the ammunn, were, he said, according to you indispensable to the coast offensive. Secondly, he adduced a great mass of evidence showing the probability of a renewed German assault upon the Anglo-French lines in the near future, against wh every preparation must be made. To this end he was going to send you the 28th & 29th Divns & the Canadians in the course of the next 6 weeks. In view of this vy strong case, the opinion was that we had no choice but to await this new attack before attempting an offensive move ourselves. Great doubt was thrown, & naturally exists here, on the ability & even the intention of Joffre to make a really strong offensive himself; & even if his offensive were launched, it was said that the coast attack by the British wd not be an integral part of his plans.

The PM, while not dissenting from the general opinion, stated that he had written to you, hoping that you cd come over early next week, provided the military situation permitted. I strongly urge you to do this if you can. Another meeting of the War Council will be held, at wh you and, I gather, any officer you might bring with you, wd be present. The question of how the new army was to be interwoven with the existing army was not discussed at length. I send you a note wh I have prepared on the subject, a copy of wh I have given to the PM & to Kitchener. Kitchener tells me that he certainly contemplates the mingling of the armies by divns, but does not want to go beyond this, & that anyhow he does not want any public announcement at the present time wh wd impair the enthusiasm & esprit de corps of the new forces. Please do not let it be known to anyone that I have sent you a copy of my note; for it might only lead to unnecessary trouble.

I am bound to say that I do not think that anyone cd complain of the way in wh Kitchener stated yr position, tho' the differences of view were apparent. If you find it possible to come over, I expect we can get to a general agreement. If not, I will come over to Dunkirk & we can meet at Furnes. My only desire is to keep us all together, & to see that you are properly sustained in your great task. If it is true that the Germans are going to attack, then it wd be much better to give them another good bleeding before clearing the coast, urgent tho' that be. But is it true? I send you one or two other papers of interest, wh please treat as entirely personal & secret. Above all, my dear friend, do not be vexed or discouraged. We are on the stage of history. Let us keep our anger for the common foe. I have kept Freddie back to bring this to you, & am sending him over in a destroyer tonight.

Don't fail to come if you possibly can. I can fetch you at Calais or Boulogne any time after dark, & bring you here with the utmost speed & little risk.

Yours always

Sir John Jellicoe to Winston S. Churchill
(Churchill papers: 13/46)

8 January 1915   Home Fleet

My dear Mr Churchill,

Your letter of the 4th was very welcome. I know you are far too busy to write much, and as I so constantly write to the 1st Sea Lord I do not trouble you with letters.

The difficulty I see about Borkum is its retention when taken. I do not doubt that we can capture it, though probably we should lose heavily in the process. But the losses might well be worth the gain if we could keep it. That is my doubt. If we can capture a very strongly fortified base 240 miles from home, I cannot see that the Germans will have much difficulty in retaking it, when it is only 60 miles from them, and the fortifications weakened or even destroyed in the process of capture. If the fleet is to hold it we shall certainly lose very heavily as the submarines would flock there in dozens.

I make these remarks of course in ignorance of the plan, which will no doubt be very carefully thought out & I shall be much interested to see it. I do not for a moment wish to appear to be in opposition to the idea. I only point out the difficulties of retention after capture as they appear to me, without a full knowledge of the scheme. I have tried to work out a plan myself, but I can't get anything that is satisfactory. Sylt seems to me more feasible & strikes at a flank, from the naval point of view, but from the military stand point is I suppose not so good. . . .

Yours very sincerely
J. R. Jellicoe

Sir John French to Winston S. Churchill

(*Churchill papers: 26/2*)

9 January 1915   Headquarters British Army

My dear Winston,

Thank you very much for sending me the papers[1] which I have kept absolutely secret and now return by Freddie Guest.

He will explain my views generally to you & tell you of my proposed plan to come before the War Council. There is one point I want particularly to mention. Kitchener apparently told the Council that I had said that a certain supply of Arty & Ammunition was necessary for the prosecution of the 'Coast' Campaign—and that such a supply was 'physically impossible'. I mentioned particularly in my memorandum that I had arranged with the *Belgians* to supply the guns & with *the French* to supply the ammunition.

I also told Murray (my C of S) to tell K verbally how this was going to be done.

---

[1] Papers brought by Frederick Guest from Churchill to Sir John French on 6 January. French wrote in his diary that day: 'These documents were very *secret* and included a memo. by himself to the P.M., and memos. on the general situation by L.G. and Hankey. I agree partly with Winston's memo. but entirely disagree with the other two.' (quoted in Gerald French *The Life of Field-Marshal Sir John French*, London 1931, p. 272)

As to the '52 *Battalions*'—I could do with less and I feel sure they could be supplied.

I have gone carefully into this '*German Threat*' with my Intelligence people and I will show the Council when I meet them that the War Office information as to this is entirely wrong & unfounded. I got the details of what he has produced to the Cabinet under this head to-day from him and I have refuted the conclusions point by point.

I shall be greatly disappointed if we don't bring off our joint enterprise as I have been preparing for it energetically—altho' with the utmost secrecy.

Freddie will tell you anything else.

Yours always
JF

Lord Fisher to Winston S. Churchill
(*Churchill papers: 13/56*)

9 January 1915   Admiralty

My dear Winston,

In view of Kitchener joyfully accepting Alexandretta as an excellent and easy subsidiary operation capable of instant effect, *I suggest that not a single day be lost in pushing it* by at once asking Kitchener for a high military officer to work in conjunction with Sir H. Jackson in scheming out all necessary preparations & suggest that Kitchener should be pressed to make it a purely local expeditionary force working from the magnificent harbour & base of Alexandria, where with speed & secrecy all could be prepared as regards construction of troop boats and horse boats and armed flat bottomed boats for covering the landing and the transports all quietly collected there by one's & two's. If done quickly & suddenly a very small force will no doubt suffice, *but we ought to push on*, & I do hope Sir Edward Grey wont be meally mouthed about the French. We've not got a single advantage from the French Fleet that I can see! & apparently the French Fleet in the Adriatic has been a laughing stock to the Italians according to the Rome newspapers.

Anyhow I hope you'll push Kitchener all you can to make it a local expeditionary force acting from Alexandria, & press him for instant action & *put on Jackson!*

I don't think that you at all realize that your Dutch project will sweep the board on May 1st (when all chance of Holland being frozen is past!). All other schemes will be swallowed up by it & it will mean THE END OF THE WAR! provided we put our shoulders to the wheel & prepare our transport arrangements & their convoy for 750,000 men being landed at Antwerp,

Rotterdam, Amsterdam, and all the other spots (however small) along the Dutch Coast—LAND EVERYWHERE! AT ONCE! *sudden—secret—subtle*—our 3 watchwords!

    Push Alexandretta!

                                                                    Yours

                                                                    F

Margot Asquith: diary
(Countess Oxford and Asquith papers)

10 January 1915

... WINSTON said to me: I've given up all desire for that[1] now (he used to say he would like this above all things)—do you think this is a sign of more modesty or more ambition?

MARGOT: More ambition certainly—no one sinks into greater insignificance than a retired viceroy (aged in arteries, pickled by the climate, poor and bewildered by another kind 'of political public life—he retires to small and drab quarters in Eaton Place).

WINSTON: My God! This, this is living History. Everything we are doing and saying is thrilling—it will be read by a thousand generations, think of *that*!! Why I would not be out of this glorious delicious war for anything the world could give me (eyes glowing but with a slight anxiety lest the word 'delicious' should jar on me). I say don't repeat that I said the word 'delicious'—you know what I mean. . . . .

F. E. Smith to Winston S. Churchill
(Churchill papers: 26/2)

10 January 1915   France

My dear W.

Our General[2] says that with his A.C.[3] & 25,000 Territorials he cd take Smyrna & hold a wide range of trenches round it against 100,000 Turks.

[1] The Viceroyalty of India. In 1910 Churchill had expressed an interest in succeeding Lord Minto as Viceroy; Minto's successor, Lord Hardinge, was expected to retire in 1915. He was in fact succeeded by Lord Chelmsford in April 1916.

[2] James Willcocks, 1857–1926. Entered Army, 1878. Knighted, 1900. Lieutenant-General, 1908. Commanded Northern Army, India, 1910–14. Commanded the Indian Corps on the western front, 1914–15. He asked to be relieved of his command following the promotion of Sir Douglas Haig, who was junior to him, as commander of the 1st Army; his request was granted. General, 1916. Governor of Bermuda, 1917–22.

[3] The Indian Army Corps. Originally of 24,000 men, it reached the western front in October 1914. It saw action in the first battle of Ypres, October–November 1914, at Festubert, November 1914, at Givenchy, December 1914, and at Neuve Chapelle, March 1915, when over one-tenth of the Corps were killed. After further heavy losses at Loos, September 1915, the Indians were withdrawn from France and disbanded. Subsequently, Indian troops

He says the morale of his troops would be superb in that climate & against that enemy.[1]

Yrs
FE

Of course W [Willocks] has mentioned it to no one.

Winston S. Churchill to Sir John French

(*Copy, Churchill papers: 26/2*)

11 January 1915   Admiralty
Secret & Personal

My dear French,

I have received both yr letters & have had a talk to Freddie; & in addition a long talk à trois with Gen Murray & PM. The impression the PM & I formed was I think this:—It is attempting too much to (1) take over the Ypres salient from the French and also (2) to make the coast attack. Either may be possible, but our resources do not cover both. Of these alternatives we were not at all attracted by the first. It is a bleak & dreary rôle for the Br Army simply to take over more & more of this trench warfare, so harassing to the troops & so unrelieved by any definite success. The Coast on the other hand offers not only the prospect of a definite success, but relief from a grave danger wh threatens our sea-communications etc. Therefore it seemed to us that in order to make the coast movement you ought either to make Joffre relieve you from taking over the Ypres salient, or, if you take it over, make him relieve you (say) on the point La Bassée Armentières. However, I rejoice to think we shall be able to talk on all this together.

I am in entire agreement with the notes you so kindly sent for my perusal. I argued in the War Council strongly against deserting the decisive theatre & the most formidable antagonist to win cheaper laurels in easier fields. The only circs in wh such a policy cd be justified wd be after every other fruitful alternative had been found impossible. I do not at all relish the idea of our new armies being consumed in doing what the Germans have failed in, viz frontal attacks on successive lines of entrenchments.

---

fought at Gallipoli, Salonika, Mesopotamia and Palestine. While serving on the western front they suffered 10,000 deaths. F. E. Smith served on the Corps Staff from October 1914 until May 1915, having been asked by Kitchener to be in charge of maintaining and preserving the Corps records—a task similar to that which Sir Max Aitken carried out for the Canadian troops in Flanders.

1 Churchill, who had himself raised this suggestion at the War Council on 8 January (see p. 394), showed this letter to Asquith on 13 January.

Let the G's do it if they will, as often as they like. I favour remaining in the N. theatre, but endeavouring, as our numbers & resources increase, the lengthen the G. line & compel him to expose new surfaces to the waste of war. It is clear that there are 4 possible lines of activity in this direction: (1) if we cd get command of the Baltic, the Russian armies cd threaten the whole Baltic shore, & Berlin at close quarters. (2) A landing in Schleswig wd directly threaten the Kiel Canal, & bring Denmark out on our side. (3) A landing at Emden wd strike at Wilhemshaven & at the German heart. Yr headqrs are twice as far from Berlin as Emden is.

All these 3 operations depend on a naval situation not yet realized. But the Capture of Borkum (always to be referred to as 'Sylt') was approved in principle by the War Council; & if this cd be achieved in March or April, it may be found possible to establish a control on the German rivermouths vy different from that wh now exists. Therefore I do not exclude these possibilities; tho it is premature to build on them now.

But after all the greatest hope in the N is (4) bringing Holland in. If in the summer we are in a position to offer Holland the protection of an army of 700,000 or 800,000 men, it is by no means impossible that she might join the Allies. Her fate is bound up in our victory. One of the reasons why I favour the Coast opern is that it is a step in the direction of Holland, & that every yard of Belgian soil cleared shows the Dutch that England never deserts her friends. It is not until all the Northern possibilities are exhausted that I wd look to the S of Europe as a field for the profitable employment of our expanding milty forces. But plans shd be worked out for every contingency.

Yours always
W

Winston S. Churchill to Sir John Jellicoe
(Copy, Churchill papers: 13/46)

11 January 1915   Admiralty
Secret & Strictly Personal

My dear Jellicoe,

I was thinking of the island operations as the first step in an aggressive warfare which would, as it proceeds, cow the enemy; beat him into his ports, and mine and wire him in there. Except for that purpose, the capture would be a mere burden. Tyrwhitt's Xmas Day experiences show that the presence of 8 or 10 hostile S/Ms deters the Germans from using their heavy ships.[1] Without generalizing from one example, I believe this is a new and true fact. No one on either side will willingly take heavy ships into waters where he knows there are 8 or 10 hostile S/Ms.

Having taken the island in question, we must make it the most dreaded lair of S/Ms in the world, and also the centre of an active mining policy. 30 B. & C. class S/Ms working up towards Heligoland in reliefs, combined with the mining of certain channels and bombarding areas, the whole supported by 2 flotillas of the best destroyers and backed by a squadron of old battleships, would constitute a defence which it would not be worth while for German heavy ships to challenge, and which small ships could not face.

I do not think the scheme can hold unless the island when taken can be made self-supporting. The freedom of the Grand Fleet must not be compromised. It must be kept to meet the High Sea Fleet.

I have heard a great deal about not fighting in waters dominated by the enemy's torpedo craft. But suppose we established ourselves at this island (we call it 'Sylt') strongly enough to make the surrounding waters *our* torpedo-infested area, would not the unfavourable situation be offered to the Germans? It seems to me only necessary to dominate the area with flotillas to make the German face at his very doors the dangers he now invites us to come across the seas to seek. Once established there, we should confront him with all the ugliest propositions. If he sends minesweepers out, destroyers will sink them. If he sends transports covered by bombarding battleships, what more could our S/Ms ask? Once we have got there, it is he who has to run the risks; and surely he would be compelled to do so. In remembering 'Sylt', he would lose sight of England. Our position there would be intolerable to him. He would have to come to attack us, not at any point he chose on our sparsely guarded coast, but where he would have to face a concentrated swarm of S/Ms; and every movement outward, no matter what the object, would have to pass and return through this peril.

Why should we be afraid of proximity? Suppose Harwich were pulled out right up to the island and we had to hold it and fight it out at close quarters, should we not rejoice? We have only to make our position good and really get started there with a complete outfit of S/Ms, destroyers, mines, monitors and aircraft, to quell them. Instead of their making it not good enough for us to send our heavy ships into the North Sea by scattered S/M activity, we would make it too dangerous for them to send heavy ships out of their rivermouths.

Remember that by proximity we quadruple our S/M force, and we apply that force not dispersed over wide areas but swarming in a small bight which

[1] On 25 December 1914 Commodore Tyrwhitt had provided the supporting force for the air raid on the German Zeppelin sheds at Cuxhaven (*see* p. 372, *n1*).

is itself their very throat. And all the time we keep the vital units remote and intact in case through desperation they dash out. But we ought certainly not to rest content with the capture of the island or its retention. After they have lost 3 or 4 big ships in trying to come near it, we shall have established an ascendency. It would be easy to advance, to fight their destroyers unceasingly, to occupy other islands of little consequence to us but vital to them, to sweep our own channels through their minefields, to lay our mines in the mouths of their rivers, and to prevent our mines from being removed.

This is the only aggressive policy which gives the Navy its chance to apply its energy and daring, and in 6 weeks of fierce flotilla warfare we could beat the enemy out of the North Sea altogether.

No, I have no doubts about the subsequent stages. 'C'est le premier pas qui coute'. The bombardment, the holding off the enemy's S/Ms., the landing of troops, the storming of the gorges of the batteries, the getting well established there; all these seem to me most anxious steps—but once there, in full force and fettle, the path is clear.

I am grieved about Bayly. I am doing my best for him,[1] not for his own sake but because to terrorize admirals for losing ships is to make sure of losing wars; but he outraged every principle of prudence and good seamanship without the slightest military object.

Always write me what you think. The machine is working far better than it ever worked before. Arthur Wilson rules our councils in tactics, and is incomparably superior to anyone I have seen. Fisher you know. You simply cannot compare Oliver and Sturdee in the transaction of business. The conduct of the Fleet is in your hands. I really do not think I should do much good by dressing the window with Warrender and Gamble[2] just because they have hoisted their flags afloat.

While the intercepts last we can husband our strength, and move only when there is a real cause. I daresay we shall get another chance, and this time I hope you will have it all in your own hands.

With every good wish

Yrs vy sincerely

WSC

[1] Churchill appointed Bayly President of the Royal Naval College at Greenwich on 18 January 1915, sixteen days after he had been ordered to haul down his flag. On 20 July 1915 he was appointed Vice-Admiral Commanding the Coast of Ireland, holding this command until 1919. He was promoted Admiral in 1917.

[2] Douglas Austin Gamble, 1856–1934. Entered Navy, 1870. Captain, 1899. Member of the Naval Intelligence Department, 1893–96. Knighted, 1909. Naval Adviser to Turkish Government, 1909–10. Rear-Admiral, 1910. Commanded 6th Cruiser Squadron, 1910–14; 4th Battle Squadron, 1914–15. Accompanied Churchill to Paris for the Anglo-Italian naval negotiations of May 1915. Admiral, 1917.

Vice-Admiral Carden to Winston S. Churchill: telegram

(*Copy, Churchill papers: 13/65*)

11 January 1915   HMS Indefatigable
Secret and personal

In reply to your telegram of 6th January. Reference to N.I.D.[1] report
No. 838 Turkey Coast Defence 1908. Possibility of operations:
A. Total reduction of defences at the entrance.
B. Clear defences inside of Straits up to and including Kephez Point battery
No. 8.
C. Reduction of defences at the Narrows Chanak.
D. Clear passage through mine field advancing through Narrows reducing
forts above Narrows and final advance to Marmara.

Term defences includes permanent semi-permanent and field works also
guns or howitzers whose positions are not yet known.

Whilst A and B are being carried out a battleship force would be employed
(in) demonstration and bombardment of Bulair line and coast and reduction
of battery near Gaba Tepe. Force required: 12 battleships of which four
fitted with mine-bumpers. Three battle cruisers; two should be available on
entering Marmara. Three light cruisers. One flotilla leader sixteen destroyers
one depot repairing ship six submarines four seaplanes and the 'Foudre'.
Twelve mine sweepers including perhaps four fleet sweepers one hospital
ship six colliers at Tenedos Island two supply and ammunition ships. The
above force allows for casualties.

Details (of) action. Frequent reconnaissance by seaplanes indispensable.

A. Indirect bombardment of forts, reduction completed by direct bombardment at decisive range; torpedo tubes at the entrance and a gun commanding
minefield destroyed: minefield cleared.
B. Battleships preceded by mine-sweepers enter straits working way up
till position reached from which battery No. 8 can be silenced.
C. Severe bombardment of forts by Battle Cruisers from Gaba Tepe
spotted from battleships, reduction completed by direct fire at decisive range.
D. Battleships preceded by sweepers making way up towards Narrows.
Forts 22 23 24 first bombarded from Gaba Tepe spotting for 22 by seaplanes
then direct fire. Sweep minefields in Narrows, the fort at Nagara reduced
by direct fire battle force proceeds to Marmara preceded by mine-sweepers.

Expenditure on ammunition for 'C' would be large but if supplies sufficient

---

[1] The Naval Intelligence Department of the Admiralty; from 1914 to 1919 the Director of
Naval Intelligence was Captain William Reginald Hall (whose father had been DNI from
1882 to 1887). The director in 1908 had been Captain Slade (*See* p. 236 *n*1)

result should be successful. Difficulty as to 'B' greatly increased if GOEBEN assisting defence from Nagara. It would unless submarine attacks successful, necessitate employment of battle cruisers from Gaba Tepe or direct.

Time required for operations depends greatly on morale of enemy under bombardment, garrison largely stiffened by the Germans, also on the weather conditions. Gales now frequent. Might do it all in a month about.

Expenditure of ammunition would be large. Approximate estimate of quantity required being prepared. Disposition of squadron on completion of operations. Marmara   2 battle cruisers 4 battleships 3 light cruisers 1 flotilla leader 12 T.B. destroyers 3 submarines 1 supply and ammunition ship four mine sweepers collier.

Remainder of force keeping straits open and covering mine sweepers completing clearing minefield.

Winston S. Churchill to Sir Frederick Hamilton: not sent

(*Churchill papers: 13/46*)

12 January 1915   Admiralty

My dear Second Sea Lord,
    You told me this morning that Sir John Jellicoe only had 22 Dreadnoughts to the German 20, & pointed out what a narrow margin that was. Happily the case is vy different. The Germans have only 16 Dreadnought battleships to Sir John Jellicoe's 22. If you count Battle cruisers on one side, you must count them on the other, which wd make the numbers Germany 20, Gt Britain 28. This is as you say a bad moment for us. Still, in view of these figures, together with the enormous superiority in weight of metal, and the presence of the 8 King Edwards, I do not think there ought to be any need for anxiety.

Yours vy truly
Winston S. Churchill

Lord Fisher to Vice-Admiral Oliver

(*Oliver papers*)

12 January 1915   Admiralty
RUSH

Dear Oliver,
    I've told Crease to find out from Percy Scott and the Gunnery Experts if anything to prevent Queen Elizabeth giving all her ammunition at the

Dardanelles Forts instead of uselessly into the ocean at Gibraltar and to let you know. If this is practicable she could go straight there, hoist Carden's flag & go on with her gunnery exercises and free the Indefatigable to go to Malta to refit and allow Inflexible to come straight home from Gibraltar to join the Second Battle Cruiser squadron.

Perhaps you'll think over this. . . .[1]

Meeting of the War Council: extract from Secretary's notes

(*Copy, Cabinet papers: 22/1*)

Present: H. H. Asquith (in the Chair), Lord Haldane, Lord Crewe, Winston S. Churchill, A. J. Balfour, Lord Fisher, Sir Arthur Wilson, David Lloyd George, Sir Edward Grey, Lord Kitchener, Sir James Wolfe Murray, Lieutenant-Colonel Hankey (Secretary) In attendance: Sir John French,[2] Brigadier-General MacDonogh[3]

13 January 1915   10 Downing Street

THE ZEEBRUGGE PLAN

MR. CHURCHILL said that from the Admiralty point of view it was unfortunate that the question of clearing the enemy out of the Belgian coast was inextricably bound up with the future of the New Armies. This latter question was not urgent in the same sense as the former. He suggested that the two questions might be separated. The number of battalions (fifty) asked for by Sir John French could be reduced, if Sir John French was not bound to assist General Joffre by taking over a portion of the part now occupied by the French armies. If Sir John French, owing to his promise of co-operation with General Joffre, did not feel himself able to make the suggestion, it was at any rate open to the British Government to

[1] The *Queen Elizabeth*, which had not yet fired her 15-inch guns, was scheduled to do so at dummy targets off Gibraltar. Fisher's proposal that she should go instead to test her guns at the Dardanelles was accepted. That same day Fisher wrote to Sir William Tyrrell: '. . . if the Greeks land 100,000 men on the Gallipoli Peninsula in concert with a British naval attack on the Dardanelles I think we could count on an easy and quick arrival at Constantinople.' (*Foreign Office papers: 800/107*)

[2] Sir John French had arrived in London on the previous day, 12 January, when he wrote in his diary: 'Winston Churchill came to see me at 6.30. *He* was bent upon the attempt to capture Ostend and Zeebrugge. He thought the time was not yet ripe to consider a diversion of our troops to other more distant theatres.' (quoted in Gerald French *The Life of Field-Marshal Sir John French*, London 1931, p. 273)

[3] George Mark Watson MacDonogh, 1865–1942. Lieutenant, Royal Engineers, 1884. Brigadier-General, General Staff, War Office, 1914–15. Major-General, 1916. Director of Military Intelligence, 1916–18. Knighted, 1917. Lieutenant-General, 1919. President, Federation of British Industries, 1933–4. Member, Central Committee for the Regulation of Prices, 1939–41. Member of the Finnish Aid Bureau, 1940.

say that they attached greater importance to the clearance of the coast than to an extension of the line. In this case fewer battalions would suffice.

LORD KITCHENER said that the question of the reinforcements depended to some extent upon the time within which the operation was to be carried out. It was his intention to send out two divisions of Territorials ultimately as part of his programme. These could not be despatched at once, but it was just possible that, by an acceleration of the programme, two divisions might be despatched by the middle of February. . . .

MR. CHURCHILL said that the clearance of the coast would be a first-class victory, constituting a material and inestimably valuable protection to the lines of communication.

SIR EDWARD GREY thought that the operation was worth attempting, if a loss of only 8,000 men was involved.

MR. LLOYD GEORGE said that it would only be a minor operation and without any material effect on the final result of the war. How, he asked, did Sir John French think that the German resistance was to be finally broken?

SIR JOHN FRENCH said that, if the weather would improve, General Joffre had a fair chance of breaking through both at Arras and near Rheims. At present advance was almost impossible owing to the mud. If he could only force his way along the coast to the Dutch frontier, he would hold an important salient from which to operate against the German lines of communication.

MR. CHURCHILL said that the naval co-operation in the advance along the coast was dependent on weather.

LORD KITCHENER asked whether, in the event of his reaching the Dutch coast, Sir John French felt confident of his ability to hold the line if the Germans considered it essential to re-establish themselves there and made a determined attack.

SIR JOHN FRENCH was sure that he would be able to hold the line. . . .

MR. BALFOUR asked for an expression of the Admiralty's views on the Zeebrugge plan.

MR. CHURCHILL said that the Admiralty would welcome it, if it could be carried out successfully. If Zeebrugge continued to be developed as a German naval base, it entailed great disadvantages on the Navy. There would probably be a series of depressing incidents. The Admiralty, however, could not regard the matter as one of absolutely vital importance from a naval point of view. The possession of Zeebrugge by the Germans would not kill our naval supremacy.

LORD KITCHENER said that, from the War Office point of view, he was prepared to carry out what Sir John French proposed. He proposed that all arrangements should be made for this, but that the final decision should be postponed until next month (February).

SIR EDWARD GREY agreed with Lord Kitchener. For the moment, this was the only offensive movement within our capacity and it should be prepared for. There was, however, no necessity to take a final decision at present. In the meantime he would be glad if the Admiralty could consider the feasibility of effecting something at Cattaro, or elsewhere in the Adriatic, with the object of drawing Italy into the war. We ought also to consider what we should do in the event of a complete stalemate. For this purpose we should study the possibilities of (a) co-operation with Serbia and (b) an attack on the Gallipoli Peninsula.

THE DARDANELLES

MR. CHURCHILL said he had interchanged telegrams with Vice-Admiral Carden, the Commander-in-Chief in the Mediterranean, in regard to the possibilities of a naval attack on the Dardanelles. The sense of Admiral Carden's reply was that it was impossible to rush the Dardanelles, but that, in his opinion, it might be possible to demolish the forts one by one. To this end Admiral Carden had submitted a plan. His proposal was first to concentrate his fire on the entrance forts. When they were demolished he would proceed to deal with the inner forts, attacking them from the Straits and from the seaward side of the Gallipoli Peninsula. This plan was based on the fact that the Dardanelles forts are armed mainly with old guns of only thirty-five calibre. These would be outranged by the guns of the ships, which would effect their object without coming within range. Three modern ships, carrying the heaviest guns, would be required for reducing some of the more modern works, and about twelve old battleships would deal with the remainder. These could now be spared for the task without reducing our strength in the main theatre of war. Among others, he mentioned the 'Triumph', 'Swiftsure', 'Goliath', 'Glory', and 'Canopus', all of which had been employed hitherto for trade protection. Four of the Majestic class, which were to have been 'scrapped', their 12-inch 'guns being utilized for monitors, could also be made available, though this would entail a delay in the completion of the monitors. Two battle-cruisers were, he said, already in the Mediterranean. The new battle-cruiser, 'Queen Elizabeth', was already to be sent to Gibraltar for gun trials, and it would be feasible to allow her to conduct her trials against the Dardanelles forts, instead of against a target.

The Admiralty were studying the question, and believed that a plan could be made for systematically reducing all the forts within a few weeks. Once the forts were reduced the minefields would be cleared, and the Fleet would proceed up to Constantinople and destroy the 'Goeben'. They would have nothing to fear from field guns or rifles, which would be merely an inconvenience.

MR LLOYD GEORGE liked the plan.

LORD KITCHENER thought it was worth trying. We could leave off the bombardment if it did not prove effective.

SIR EDWARD GREY said that the key for bringing in Italy was Cattaro.

MR. CHURCHILL said that the French were already at Cattaro in great strength. It would be awkward for the British Fleet to take any action there so long as the French remained there.

MR. BALFOUR asked why the French had failed at Cattaro.

MR. CHURCHILL said it was due to the Austrian submarines, which had seriously injured one of the best French battleships.

SIR EDWARD GREY said he was very anxious to do something to force Italy's hand. Her present plan appeared to be to keep out of the war and to secure her own settlement. It was necessary to take some action to compel her to participate in order to obtain a suitable settlement.

LORD KITCHENER said that the Italian Military Attaché[1] appeared to think that Italy was on the verge of war.

SIR JOHN FRENCH, in reply to Mr. Lloyd George, said that complete success against the Germans in the Western theatre of war, though possible, was not probable. If we found it impossible to break through, he agreed that it would be desirable to seek new spheres of activity—in Austria, for example.

MR. CHURCHILL said that we ought not to go South until we are satisfied that we can do nothing in the North. Was there, for example, no possibility of action in Holland?

SIR EDWARD GREY postulated two conditions which must apply before he could approach Holland—
  1. That we should have some successes during the next few weeks.
  2. That we should be in a position to send assistance to the extent of 3–400,000 men.

[1] Edoardo Greppi, 1867–1952. Count of Busseto and Corneliano. 2nd Lieutenant, Artillery, 1885. Major, 1913. Italian Military Attaché, London, 1914–17. Lieutenant-Colonel, 1915. Served with the Italian forces in France, 1917–18. General of Brigade, 1929.

MR. LLOYD GEORGE said that he wanted us to take some steps, though not irrevocable ones, to prepare for a campaign against Austria. Not only should the question be studied, but actual preparations should be made. For example, rolling-stock would have to be manufactured for the Salonica railway, and perhaps barges built for the Danube. Any waste there might be would not be very serious.

MR. CHURCHILL agreed that preparations should be made. At the worst they would be a good feint.

SIR JOHN FRENCH said that the French Government would not like it if we were to divert troops to some theatre of war other than France.

ALEXANDRETTA

LORD KITCHENER repeated the reasons given at a previous meeting in favour of an attack on Alexandretta. He said that a very good scheme had been worked out.

MR. CHURCHILL said there were no difficulties from a naval point of view.

LORD KITCHENER said it would be kept in mind. The troops in Egypt were not yet sufficiently trained to carry it out.

(*Conclusions.*)

1. *That all preparations should be made, by concert between the Naval and Military authorities, including making ready for the despatch of 2 Territorial divisions, without guns, to reinforce Sir J. French by the middle of February, for an advance along the line Dixmude to the Dutch frontier. The actual decision whether the circumstances call for such an operation can be postponed till the beginning of February.*

2. *That the Admiralty should consider promptly the possibility of effective action in the Adriatic—at Cattaro, or elsewhere—with the view* (inter alia) *of bringing pressure on Italy.*

3. *That the Admiralty should also prepare for a naval expedition in February to bombard and take the Gallipoli peninsula, with Constantinople as its objective.*

4. *That if the position in the Western theatre becomes in the spring one of stalemate, British troops should be despatched to another theatre and objective, and that adequate investigation and preparation should be undertaken with that purpose, and that a Sub-Committee of the Committee of Imperial Defence be appointed to deal with this aspect of the situation.*

H. H. Asquith to Venetia Stanley
(*Montagu papers*)

13 January 1915   10 Downing Street

... We are now (4 p.m) in the midst of our War Council, wh. began at 12, adjourned at 2, & is now sitting again. Sir J. French is here & sits next me. A most interesting discussion, but so confidential and secret that I won't put anything down on paper, but I will talk fully to you to-morrow (if we meet then) or if not in the course of our drive on Friday.

Later. The Council is now over, having arrived harmoniously at *4* conclusions suggested by me, wh. will keep both Navy & Army busy till March. I am keen to tell you all about it, & see if it meets with your approval.

... I maintained an almost unbroken silence until the end, when I intervened with my conclusions but, except for one or two furtive glances at your letter, (wh. only arrived at 3) I kept a careful watch on the rest. French sat next to me on one side & A.J.B. on the other; next to French *K*, then old Jacky Fisher, Winston & Sir A. Wilson (the Naval Trinity); and beyond them Crewe, Grey, & Ll. George. You won't often see a stranger collection of men at one table. Of the lay disputants the best were A.J.B & Ll. George. French & K were polite & almost mealy-mouthed to one another. Happily the great question upon wh. they are nearly at daggers-drawn (how the new 'K' armies are to be organised—as separate entities, or intermingled with the old units) tho' broached, was tacitly postponed to a later & more convenient date. Winston (if such a phrase is possible) showed a good deal of rugged fluency. ...

Winston S. Churchill to Lord Fisher and Vice-Admiral Oliver
(*Copy, Churchill papers: 2/74*)

13 January 1915   Admiralty

In future, the Mediterranean plan discussed to-day will always be referred to as 'Pola'.[1]

2. Sir Percy Scott has been cautioned as to secrecy. He is going out to assist in regulating the Director in 'Queen Elizabeth' but wishes to return from Gibraltar.

3. As Sir H. Jackson is sick, the detailed proposals should be worked out by C.O.S. and orders drafted both as regards the concentration of the ships and the regulation of the gunnery.

[1] There is no evidence to suggest that the naval attack on the Dardanelles was referred to by the code name 'Pola' again, except in paragraph six of this same letter. Pola was an Austro-Hungarian port on the Adriatic coast.

4. The orders for concentrating the Fleet required cannot be delayed. It is not necessary to delay the preliminary bombardment of the entrance until all the ships have arrived; but the ships should start for the various Mediterranean ports at once.

5. The question of a base on a Turkish island should be considered. We also want a landing place for aeroplanes on Tenedos.

6. D.A.D. should be instructed to hold 'Ark Royal' with 8 seaplanes and aeroplanes in readiness for service in Egypt. We cannot rely on French seaplanes for our spotting. The Army have developed a system of wireless telephone from aeroplanes spotting for artillery, which is most effective. Full details of this should be at once obtained, and some of the machines fitted accordingly. Meanwhile the French should be asked not to fly over the Pola area, as it will only lead to the mounting of A.A. guns and complicate spotting later. Admiral Carden should be informed of this.

7. The auxiliary vessels asked for by Carden should be specified and put under orders. He has already 'Sapphire' and 'Dublin'. 'Doris' will make the third Light Cruiser. As the river-boats come home from China, they must stop with the 7 'Beagles' already available. One 'E' boat from home, or if suitable, the 'S' boat, and 2 'C's' should be sent to meet 'A.E.I.'. Let a regular scheme of movement and concentration be prepared.

8. Proposals for mine-sweepers should be made, and Malta Dockyard should prepare to fit mine-bumpers.

9. Admiral Carden's proposals should be carefully analysed by an officer of the War Staff in order to show exactly what guns the ships will have to face at each point and stage of the operations, the character of the guns, and their range; but this officer is to assume that the principle is settled, and all that is necessary is to estimate the force required.

10. This enterprise is regarded by the Government as of the highest urgency and importance. A telegram should be drafted to Admiral Carden approving his proposals and informing him of the forces which will be placed at his disposal. No order should go out to him or anyone else until his answer about ammunition expenditure is received, and until the whole scheme can be considered finally in draft.

Commodore de Bartolome will keep in touch with the details on my behalf. I hope that definite orders may be issued in 2 or 3 days.

WSC

In view of the danger of enemy submarines being sent from the Adriatic, speed and secrecy are essential. The mine-sweepers should take a supply of Bircham indicator nets.

Winston S. Churchill to the Russian people: telegram
(*Copy, Churchill papers: 26/2*)

13 January 1915   Admiralty

The wonderful exertions of Russia in the cause of the Allies have enabled her to sustain the war against three hostile Empires with general success often made glorious by victory during five most critical months in 1914. The time gained has enabled Great Britain to train and equip large armies which will soon enter the conflict, and has enabled both France and Great Britain to develop and create the means of producing war material on a scale hitherto only practised by Germany.

The dawn of the New Year[1] lighting the immense field of battle shows unmistakeably that our side is the stronger. Our resources are within reach and inexhaustible; our minds are made up. We have only to bend forward together laying aside every hindrance, keeping nothing back, and the downfall of German ambition is sure.

God bless Russia and the Russian people so nobly doing their duty in the common cause.

Winston S. Churchill

Vice-Admiral Carden to Winston S. Churchill: telegram
(*Copy, Churchill papers: 13/65*)

13 January 1915   HMS Indefatigable
Secret and Personal

. . . High speed considered necessary in the two capital ships required for meeting GOEBEN in Marmara. QUEEN ELIZABETH very desirable should certainly shorten operations. French battleships are included in total. Submit that operations should not be commenced until the whole force is ready. Estimated there are now eight lines of mines altogether in various parts of Dardanelles, total about 330 mines.

Winston S. Churchill to H. H. Asquith, Sir Edward Grey and Lord Kitchener
(*Churchill papers: 2/82*)

14 January 1915   Admiralty

We consider that no useful means can be found of effective naval intervention in the Adriatic at the present time. The French have a large superiority

[1] The Russian New Year fell, in 1915, on 13 January. The Russian calendar did not adjust to the world method of dating until after the Revolution of November (October) 1917.

of naval force there now, including Dreadnoughts and large numbers of destroyers. Their operations make no progress through the absence of a friendly army and the presence of hostile submarines. The bombardment of the forts at Cattaro would be a sterile operation attended by great risk from submarines and some damage from gunfire. The entry of the harbour would lead to nothing by itself. Unless therefore adequate military force is forthcoming to storm and hold the forts after bombardment, there are no means of producing good results. The same is true of Pola[1] but in a greater degree. The attempt at a demonstration would probably lead to waste of ammunition and loss of ships; & would produce an effect the exact opposite of what is desired.

While the French have ample force for any preventable step in this quarter, we cannot provide any squadron comparable to theirs.

The attack on the Dardanelles will require practically our whole available margin. If that attack opens prosperously it will very soon attract to itself the whole attention of the Eastern theatre, and if it succeeds it will produce results which will undoubtedly influence every Mediterranean power.

In these circumstances we strongly advise that the Adriatic should be left solely to the French and that we should devote ourselves to action in accordance with the third conclusion of the War Council, viz:—the methodical forcing of the Dardanelles.

Pressure shd be put upon the French to be more active.[2]

WSC

Winston S. Churchill to Vice-Admiral Carden: telegram

(*Copy, Churchill papers: 13/65*)

14 January 1915   Admiralty
Secret and Personal

Your scheme was laid by the First Sea Lord and myself before the Cabinet War Council yesterday and was approved in principle.

We see no difficulty in providing the force you require including the QUEEN ELIZABETH by the 15th February.

We entirely agree with your plan of methodical piecemeal reduction of forts as the Germans did at Antwerp.

We propose to entrust this operation to you.

Admiral de Robeck will probably be your second in command.

[1] The 'real' Pola, against which Grey in particular was anxious to see British naval action, in order to encourage Italy to join the Allies.

[2] This last sentence was added at Fisher's suggestion.

The sooner we can begin the better.

You will shortly receive the official instructions of the Board.

Continue to perfect your plan.

Lord Fisher to Winston S. Churchill

(Churchill papers: 13/56)

14 January 1915   Admiralty

My dear Winston,

. . . . It is sad that Jellicoe has sciatica. His enclosed letter this moment arrived. If only he could get his 'Zareba' finished he could sleep quiet in his bed! but the delay is incredible and deplorable and I cannot understand Jellicoe's praise of Colville[1] who has shown such utter want of energy and resource in dealing with the Submarine Defence of Scapa Flow—Every week the report shows utter stagnation!

I presume you've sent Bayly's letter round to all the Sea Lords for their opinions—and Oliver ought to report on Bayly's statement that submarines were negligible, which of course condemns him, as he stated in my presence his knowledge of them and he omits 'Mid-Channel' though that was wrong for a continued perambulation backwards & forwards over the same ground —I think it's undignified to argue—he has lost our confidence and that is sufficient reason for his removal—*and no other reason should be given him*! When you give your housemaid warning—however excellent she may be—you haven't to explain. You don't like her so she goes!

Yours

F

For a wonder I'm writing near midnight![2]

---

[1] Stanley Cecil James Colville, 1861–1939. Entered Navy, 1874. Naval ADC to King Edward VII, 1905–6. Knighted, 1912. Vice-Admiral Commanding the 1st Battle Squadron, 1912–14. Admiral, on Special Service with the Grand Fleet, 1914–16. Commander-in-Chief, Portsmouth, 1916–18. First and Principal Naval ADC to King George V, 1919–22.

[2] Fisher's usual habit while First Sea Lord was to go to bed in the early evening, but to be at work between three and four each morning.

Sir John Jellicoe to Winston S. Churchill

(*Churchill papers: 13/46*)

15 January 1915   Home Fleet

My dear Mr Churchill,

Yours of the 11th for which I thank you, has arrived. I hope I have not given the impression that I do not realise the immense advantages that such a base would confer on us. I am very fully aware of them. I believe also that the operation is probably feasible, so long as we are prepared to accept heavy losses, principally naval losses, and provided an adequate military force is used. I feel fairly certain that we should require the best troops for the work. Marines would be good, but I don't imagine we have nearly a sufficient number available. My recollection is that Sir L Bayly's committee mentioned something like 12000 as required.[1] My real doubt is as to whether we could hold what we secured. The preparation of new defences would take time, and during that time the island must be defended by the Navy. We should not be able to maintain a force of small craft I fear there until we had secured it as a base, with all necessary supplies to keep the small craft going. Consequently *our* small craft would be working during this period from a great distance & would be trying to fight an enemy in very great numerical superiority who would be close to their own base & their supplies. I feel very doubtful whether under these conditions we should not find that after all our expenditure of personnel & material, a retirement might not become necessary, or even worse, the place be recaptured. It is very difficult to express an opinion of much value on this point without knowing the details of the proposed arrangements, but this is how it strikes me.

To put it plainly, my fear is that *our* line of communications during the first week or so after the operation would be very long, very open to attack by submarines and destroyers, whilst the enemy's would be very short. He would have an immense numerical superiority in both submarines & TBD's since in these early days we could use only oversea submarines & our large TBD's. *He* could use all his submarines and even torpedo *boats*. Our large ships could not work on the lines of communication because of this submarine & TBD menace. His would not need to do so.

I give you my views for what you think they are worth. At the same time as I said earlier, if we *could* get established firmly the advantages are immense.

I do hope we are doing everything possible to restore some sort of

---

[1] In January 1913 Churchill had instructed Sir Lewis Bayly to study the possibility of British offensive action against a number of points on the German, Dutch, Danish, Norwegian and Swedish coasts. Bayly's reports were submitted to Churchill later that year. Churchill sent them to Asquith on 31 July 1914, with a covering note (printed on pp. 6–7).

superiority, or at any rate equality in the particular areas in which the Germans have such a great advantage over us viz submarines (suited for oversea work) and mines. We realised early last year or before that how sadly we had dropped behind in submarines, but I fancy we never quite realised that our deficiency in this area was so great as it is. Not only are we all behind in *numbers* but also in quality. Our SM's cannot look at the weather that the Germans seem to revel in. Our speed is far lower & our torpedoes not nearly as efficient. Thank goodness the personnel is all right.

In mines we are apparently in a very bad way. I can only imagine that lack of mines prevents us from mining effectively the East End of the English Channel. We *must* do it, or our transports will sooner or later be torpedoed. I can't imagine that there is any difficulty about tides. Properly moored mines should stand easily the Channel tides & weather. The Russians would think nothing of the difficulties. I trust we are manufacturing mines as fast as we possibly can.

I still hope to see mines in the vicinity of Heligoland. *Why dont we block Zeebrugge.* This has got to be a war of small craft & mines for some time yet & the more we get the better. If I only had 2 more TBD flotillas here I could make the life of the German submarines most unpleasant. As it is I have to husband my destroyers for the fleet action. The weather up here kills them off so fast that I hardly like to use them even for screening ships out of harbour. The Germans on the other hand never let a ship move without an escort of TBD's. Our ships run immense risks from submarines which *they* never take, simply because we have not got the craft.

If you look at the daily returns of movement of German ships for Jany 10th for instance you will see that there are apparently 77 sea going TBD'S at this moment available for ships in the Elbe or Jade, viz the High Sea Fleet. At Scapa I have 16, at Cromarty 16, and at Rosyth none, only 7 30 knotters that are not fit to go outside May Island. This is where we are so handicapped. Of course none of us realised I fear what great seagoing qualities the German submarine possessed, so we can't complain. But we ought to try to make up deficiencies at full speed. I hope I shall not have wearied you with all this. We are very fit up here. My only trouble is that of refits. I shall be happier when Monarch returns[1] & I can go ahead again. With all good wishes.

Yours very sincerely
J. R. Jellicoe

[1] The battleship *Monarch*, of the Grand Fleet, was temporarily out of action, having been in collision with the battleship *Conqueror* on 27 December 1914. She rejoined the Grand Fleet on 20 January 1915. Both ships were present at the battle of Jutland, 31 May to 1 June 1916.

H. H. Asquith to Venetia Stanley

(*Montagu papers*)

15 January 1915   In train [going from
                                                London to Walmer Castle]

... I don't believe I had time to tell you of my talk this morning with
Lloyd George and the 2 Buxtons, who were both shot (one in the lungs) by
a young Turk at Bucharest some weeks ago, and have employed their time
of convalescence in going round the Balkan States, & interviewing the leading so-called 'statesmen' of that devil's kitchen. They are strong pro-Bulgars,
and are quite sure that if we offered (1) Bulgaria, the slice of Macedonia,
Irredenta which (Monastir &c) the Serbs stole from her 2 years ago
(2) Servia, Bosnia & a good bit of the coast of Dalmatia (3) Roumania,
Transylvania & one or two oddments & (4) Greece, Southern Albania,
Rhodes & the other islands, & perhaps Smyrna & a strip of the shore of
Asia Minor in that region—we could bring the whole lot in to fight on our
side. They all hate one another & are as jealous as cats—particularly the
Serbians & Bulgarians; but in the case of the 2 latter we cd. save them from
the repulsive necessity of fighting side by side, by putting them back to back
—the Serbs going for Austria & the Bulgars for Turkey. This (with our
Gallipoli enterprise, of wh. of course I did not tell them) might conceivably
make a huge & even decisive diversion. It wd certainly compel Italy to
come in.

On the whole (tho' the difficulties are prodigious) I am attracted by the
plan. ...

Sir Henry Jackson to Vice-Admiral Oliver

(*Copy, Churchill papers: 2/82*)

REMARKS ON VICE-ADMIRAL CARDEN'S PROPOSALS
AS TO OPERATIONS IN DARDANELLES

15 January 1915   Admiralty

Concur generally in his plans. Our previous appreciations of the situation
differed only in small details.

(*a*) and (*b*) Reduction of defences at the entrance and inside the Straits
up to Kephez battery and the destruction of minefields.

The French and British armoured vessels at the Dardanelles, and the
'Foudre' with seaplanes, should be able to deal with (*a*), *i.e.*, defences at the
entrance, on similar lines to the previous bombardment which under unfavourable conditions of light seems to have been effective.

Reconnaissance is, however, necessary after every series of attacks, as it may result in the saving of large quantities of ammunition.

In the previous bombardment,[1] four rounds per turret gun were allowed in the British ships, *i.e.*, sixty-four total. If these succeeded in putting Fort Seddul Bahr, with its six heavy guns out of action, the result is satisfactory, and gives us some data to go on; say, ten rounds per gun at extreme range, as an average.

It is noticeable that the guns of the fort succeeded in dropping projectiles alongside our battle cruisers, up to a range of 12,300 yards.

This may be taken as near their extreme limit of range, and is good for the old pattern of guns mounted.

It would not, therefore, be prudent to close to less than 13,000 yards in future bombardments of forts with similar guns, in the early stages.

It will be essential to close them in the latter stages to ensure every gun being destroyed.

A reconnaissance by seaplane should be made before getting to close range.

For (*b*) the necessary sweepers, munitions, &c., should be despatched without delay; and the minefields should be cleared, mostly at night, under the cover of the guns of the squadron, before risking a new battleship in these mined waters, *i.e.*, if it be decided to send one out to assist in the reduction of the batteries. She might, with advantage, commence her operations from outside, off Gaba Tepe, destroying the signal station, and bombarding any fort which is situated on the top of the ridge, and visible from the sea. The experience thus gained would show the practicability of continuing this indirect attack on other forts in the Narrows, as proposed in (*c*); or whether it would be necessary to resort solely to direct attack at 15,000 yards, and above, from ships anchored in Aren-Kioi Bay, until the forts at the Narrows and the batteries on the surrounding heights are silenced.

There will probably be at least 200 guns of 6-inch and above to be silenced, and many of these will be concealed and probably protected from direct gun fire.

If it requires ten rounds per gun on board to put each gun on shore out of action, 2,000 rounds will, at least, be required, and this must be from heavy guns with long range. In addition to this the final destruction of the forts and field artillery in entrenchments at short range will require a considerable quantity of ammunition for the smaller as well as the larger guns.

I do not think the operation should be attempted unless we are prepared to expend 3,000 rounds of ammunition for the primary armament, and a

[1] The naval bombardment of 3 November 1914.

similar number of rounds for the secondary armament, besides the loss of some vessels.

Seaplanes with incendiary and other bombs should be in readiness to assist by every means in their power in the work of destruction and reconnaissance.

I would suggest (*a*) might be approved at once, as the experience gained would be useful. It should be carried out under favourable conditions of light, and with spotting ships, and continued till all guns at the entrance are permanently silenced.

Winston S. Churchill to Sir Edward Grey

(*Grey papers*)

16 January 1915   Admiralty

My dear Grey,

I see every advantage in Greece coming in and no disadvantage.

It will be necessary quite soon to apprise France & Russia of our Dardanelles intentions. I am preparing you a paper on this subject.

Yours vy sincerely

Winston S. Churchill

Winston S. Churchill to the Comte de Saint-Seine

(*Copy, Churchill papers: 2/82*)

16 January 1915   Admiralty

Secret

1. The British Government find it necessary to take offensive action against Turkey in the near future. The Admiralty have in consequence decided to attack the Dardanelles forts, and force, if possible, a passage into the Sea of Marmora. It is proposed to achieve this by a gradual and methodical reduction of the forts by naval bombardment, taking three or four weeks if necessary, and using a number of the older battleships, supported by 2 battle cruisers and the very long-range fire of the 15-inch guns of the 'Queen Elizabeth'. In all, 15 battleships or battle-cruisers, 3 light cruisers, 16 destroyers, 6 submarine, 1 seaplane ship, and a large number of mine-sweepers and auxiliaries are required, having regard to the expected casualties and the need of fighting the Turco-German fleet immediately on entering the Sea of Marmora. This fleet will be assembled between the 7th and 15th February, and it is hoped that the attack will follow immediately. The scheme of these

operations has been prepared by Vice-Admiral Carden, now commanding the Allied fleets at the Dardanelles.

The Admiralty do not wish, in view of this very important operation, that any change in the local command in that portion of the Mediterranean should be made at the present time. They hope, however, that the squadron of French battleships, together with the French submarines and destroyers and the seaplane ship 'Foudre', will co-operate under a French rear-admiral.

As the degree of the opposition to be met with cannot be anticipated, it is most undesirable to announce the full scope of the operations beforehand, and secrecy is, of course, vital.

2. The War Office also consider it necessary during the month of February to occupy Alexandretta and the surrounding district in order to cut the Turkish railway communicating at this most important strategic point. If this operation should take place it would be convenient that the disembarkation at Alexandretta and the maintenance of the British force on shore should be covered by British ships, and some of the older vessels now in Egyptian waters would probably be used for this purpose.

3. The Admiralty hope that the French fleet will be able to supply a squadron to watch and act as may be necessary along the whole of the Syrian coast from Latakia to the Egyptian frontier. It would be equally agreeable to them whether this squadron were a separate command under a French vice-admiral acting in co-operation with Vice-Admiral Peirse[1] or whether it was commanded by a French rear-admiral under Admiral Peirse's orders.

4. The conventions agreed to on the 6th August, 1914, between the British and French Admiralties had reference only to the naval conduct of a war against Austria and Germany, and from that point of view they still hold good. The entry of Turkey into the war confronts the Allies with new dangers and an entirely different situation in the eastern basin of the Mediterranean. The spheres of activity of the two navies require some further definition with a view to the energetic prosecution of the war, but the Admiralty still consider that agreeably with those spheres of activity the general direction of the operations should belong to France.[2]

---

[1] Richard Henry Peirse, 1860–1940. Entered Navy, 1873. Vice-Admiral Commanding-in-Chief, East Indies Station, 1913–16. Knighted, 1914. Commanded Allied Naval Forces on the Suez Canal, 1914–16. Naval member, Board of Invention and Research, 1916–18. Admiral, 1918.

[2] Kitchener noted at the end of Churchill's copy of this letter: 'I agree.' Churchill noted on 18 January 1915: 'P.M. has also seen and concurs.' Masterton-Smith noted that same day: 'First Sea Lord has seen, and concurs.'

Winston S. Churchill to Sir Edward Grey
(*Copy, Churchill papers: 2/82*)

16 January 1915   Admiralty

My dear Grey,

I propose to give this note, on behalf of the Admiralty, to the French naval Attaché. He says it is all they want. Kitchener agrees.

Yours always
WSC

Sir Edward Grey: note

I agree.
But we must also say something to Russia, not necessarily in detail, or she will think we are stealing a march to forestall her at Constantinople. The peg to hang our communication on would be the Grand Duke's appeal to us some days ago to make a diversion to prevent Turkish pressure in the Caucasus.

EG

Cornelia, Lady Wimborne[1] to King Alphonso XIII of Spain
(*Copy, Churchill papers: 2/65*)

17 January 1915   Admiralty

Señor!

I fear you may think that I have been a long time answering yr letter. It arrived just at Xmas time when everybody had dispersed for the holidays, & it was some time before I cd see Winston who then asked for a little time to consider yr letter.

He has asked me to tell you that he is immensely reassured & comforted by what you say, & that he knows well that strict neutrality is the least that you personally desire on our behalf! He has, as I am sure you know Señor, a vy deep admiration for you, & has the happiest recollection of his time at Madrid last year—he so often talks of you & yr kindness to him—of yr drive together & of the delightful talks he had with you.[2]

---

[1] Lady Cornelia Henrietta Maria Spencer-Churchill, 1847–1927. Churchill's aunt; eldest daughter of the 7th Duke of Marlborough. She married, in 1868, Ivor Bertie Guest (1835–1914), who was created 1st Baron Wimborne in 1880.

[2] Churchill had spent the Easter of 1914 in Madrid. He played polo, and also had a long conversation with Sir Ernest Cassel about a possible meeting with Grand Admiral von Tirpitz to discuss the reduction of Anglo-German naval rivalry. On returning to London in May 1914, Churchill found Sir Edward Grey sceptical about the value of such a meeting.

He tells me to say that with regard to the wireless messages the situation in foreign waters has become greatly eased by our recent naval victories, nearly all the German ships having been sunk; but as far as Madrid is concerned he thinks there is no doubt that from the point of view of neutrality vy unfair use is being made by the German Ambr[1] of the wireless installation there. If this is so, the injury we sustain thereby is considerable, for whereas owing to our control of wireless stations all over the world the use of the Madrid installation wd be of comparatively small importance to us, to Germany—owing to her lack of such facilities elsewhere—yr wireless, if accessible to them becomes of paramount importance or confers a vy substantial benefit upon her, depriving us of the legitimate advantage wh our supremacy at sea shd give us.

I shd say here that W repeatedly impressed upon me that it is not only the present inconvenience wh worries him, but also the fear of what unfavourable impression may result in the public mind here if after the war yr strict neutrality can be questioned. Opinion here has warmly welcomed the good relations between the two countries wh it is believed you have done all in yr power to promote; & wd sadly deplore any incident wh cd tend to cloud the fair prospect.

When I told W of what you said as to Germany's promises & the unfortunate effect they have had on the country, he replied that promises are generally a sign of weakness & being extremely easy to make are a vy cheap form of benevolence! It is all vy well for Germany to make these promises, but how is she going to keep them? Her doom, he says, is sealed, she is beat—England cd go on fighting her alone at sea if it were necessary—she has got no chance at all.

As regards what you say Señor about the Kameroon[2] he says if Spain were to come in on our side—we don't ask this, we only plead for strict neutrality—of course she wd share in the advantages of victory.

This I think is the substance of what W said. I hope that I have been able to put it clearly Señor—it has been such a joy to me to think that I might be of the slightest service to you in this matter.

[1] Maximilian Prince of Ratibor and Corvey, 1856–1924. Entered German Foreign Ministry, 1880. Served in St Petersburg, Vienna, Constantinople, London (1887–8), Rome and Budapest. Minister, Athens 1902–6; Belgrade, 1906–8, Lisbon, 1908–10. Ambassador, Madrid, 1910–20.

[2] In 1919 the Cameroons were divided between Britain and France, as Mandates under the League of Nations. The British Mandate ran along the eastern border of Nigeria; the French Mandate, which covered the majority of the former German colony, included Duala, its capital and principal port. Spain, having remained neutral throughout the war; received no German territory.

Lieutenant-Colonel Hankey to A. J. Balfour

(Balfour papers)

17 January 1915[1]   2 Whitehall Gardens

... (1) The XXIXth Division, now forming part of Sir John French's army to be despatched to Lemnos at the earliest possible date. It is hoped that it may be able to sail within 9 or 10 days.

(2) Arrangements to be made for a force to be despatched from Egypt, if required.

(3) The above forces, in conjunction with 4 battalions of Royal Marines already despatched, to be available in case of necessity to support the naval attack on the Dardanelles.

(4) Horse boats to be taken out with the XXIXth Division, and the Admiralty to make arrangements to collect small craft and lighters in the Levant. ...

H. H. Asquith to Venetia Stanley

(Montagu papers)

17 January 1915   Walmer Castle

... Winston arrived at last—just before 8 p.m.—having dropped Clemmie at Gravesend with a headache—& having had a lot of minor adventures with a bad chauffeur in the dark. He was in good form & contributed to our amusement. After dinner we played Bridge—Winston & Violet against the Assyrian[2] & me. ...

I sent all the other men away after dinner to have a talk with W. He is quite determined—and I think rightly—whatever the Army may do—to bombard & if possible destroy Zeebrugge, wh. becomes more menacing & dangerous day by day.

---

[1] The notes taken by Hankey at the meetings of the War Council were not printed until 1916, when the Dardanelles Commission of Inquiry began to collect evidence. After each meeting, Hankey would circulate those who had been present with a brief note such as this one, to remind them of what had been decided. See also Hankey's letter to Churchill of 1 February 1915, quoted on page 477.

[2] Edwin Samuel Montagu, 1879–1924. Liberal MP, 1906–22. Financial Secretary to the Treasury, February 1914–February 1915; May 1915–July 1916. Chancellor of the Duchy of Lancaster, February–May 1915; January–June 1916. Minister of Munitions, July–December 1916. Secretary of State for India, June 1917–March 1922. He married Venetia Stanley in July 1915.

Winston S. Churchill to Sir John Jellicoe
(*Copy, Churchill papers: 13/46*)

18 January 1915   Admiralty
Most Secret

My dear Jellicoe,

1) Surely the difficulty of communications during the first week wd. not be great. The flotillas only require their depôt ships to be self-supporting for a considerable period. The 'B' and 'C' class can remain at sea a week and would then return to their new home. If we had 30 submarines on the spot, there wd. be no serious German superiority. Besides S/M do not fight each other.

As for destroyers our two best flotillas can fight the whole German destroyer fleet with great advantage so long as it is a question of gunfire. You will find it much cheaper to let them do this than to face German torpedo activities in a fleet action.

I expect we shall have to wait till 4 or 5 heavy Monitors are ready at the end of April. Proximity to the enemy's guns from shore water, probably only partially commanded, coupled with immunity from mines and S/M are decisive advantages.

Therefore Bayly will have the Monitors there. I have not been so upset over anything so much as that since I have been here.

2) 56 destroyers and 75 additional S/M are under construction to finish this year. But let me repeat that what our S/M lack is not numbers but targets. As to mines—you know my views. We have never laid one we have not afterwards regretted. It is a delusion to suppose that mines will stop S/M unless strung together on a regular net. The Bircham Indicator Net is a far better game. Nevertheless 4 months ago I ordered 15,000 more mines which are now coming in in increasing numbers. Mine in haste and sweep at leisure! It wd be folly to mine while the good information lasts.

3) I cannot understand where all your destroyers have gone to. I make out you have 70 and yet you tell me you have only 32. The 1st flotilla will reach you shortly & you will then have almost all there are.

4) I am so glad you will rest for a few days at the end of the month. Your health and poise are vital to us. While the 'good information' lasts is the time to rest—only moving on certainties. Many thanks about the rifles and with all good wishes.

Believe me Yours very sincerely
Winston S. Churchill

H. H. Asquith to Venetia Stanley

(*Montagu papers*)

18 January 1915   Walmer Castle

... Winston did not arrive till dinner time, having 'inspected' some of his side shows on the way & had some motor mishaps. (I find I've told you this already). H.J.[1] watched him with much curiosity & not a little bewilderment. We (the two V's [Violet Asquith and Viola Parsons[2]] & I) asked him this morning after Winston had gone what he thought of him. He answered in his pauseful oracular way: 'I never had the lively interest of seeing so much of this remarkable young man before'. Then after some compliments to W, and comparing him favourably with his father, he added: 'I confess I am often struck at the limitations with which men of power pay the price for their domination over mankind'. W's 'limitations' would be quite a good subject for a character sketch. ...

There is really no political news, this morning, except a message from young Geo. Trevelyan[3] who is on a Balkan pilgrimage & at present in Servia. He is very much afraid that the Serbs will be overwhelmed by the new attack wh Austria is preparing unless some one comes at once to their assistance; Roumania for preference, next Greece. Another indication of the importance of getting the caldron to brew the right mixture without any further delay.

Winston tells me that they have recalled Lewis Bayly from the command of the Channel Fleet as a consequence of his loss of the 'Formidable', & have put Admiral Bethell in his place. It is rather disquieting, for Bayly was supposed to be almost the pick of our younger Admirals, & Bethell, whom I used to see on the C.I.D. is to my thinking no flier. We really seem to have better reserves in the way of Commanders in the Army than in the Navy. ...

---

[1] Henry James, 1843–1916. Author and novelist. Born in the United States. He became a British subject in July 1915, when Asquith was one of his sponsors.

[2] Viola Tree, 1884–1938. Daughter of the actor Sir Herbert Beerbohm Tree; herself an actress. Married Alan Parsons, 1912.

[3] George Macaulay Trevelyan, 1876–1962. Historian. Accompanied R. W. Seton-Watson on a mission to the Balkans, 1914–15. In charge of the 1st British Ambulance Unit for Italy, 1916–17. Professor of Modern History, Cambridge, 1927–40. Master of Trinity College, Cambridge, 1940–51.

Lord Fisher to Winston S. Churchill
(*Churchill papers: 13/56*)

18 January 1915   Admiralty

First Lord

I have no wish whatever to cold-douche any projects for our being troublesome to the enemy in the following remarks. . . .

But I desire to emphasize the necessity of sticking to the enemy's vitals! I am not minimizing the coming Dardanelles operation, but I wish to aggrandize the great big fact that 750,000 men landed in Holland, combined with intense activity of the British Fleet against, say, Cuxhaven, would finish the War by forcing out the German High Sea Fleet and getting in rear of the German Armies! The First Lord has twice put before the War Council and Dutch Project and no one 'gainsaid' it! Is it going to be done? Great preparations are involved. The frost so deadly to Holland is over in May. Cannot a definite decision be reached?

F

Winston S. Churchill: memorandum
(*Admiralty papers: 116/1278*)

18 January 1915   Admiralty

The general condition of our airship service and the fact that so little progress has been made by Vickers in the construction of the rigid airship now due, makes it necessary to suspend the purely experimental work in connection with airships during the war and to concentrate our attention on the more practical aeroplane in which we have been so successful.

1. The Director of Contracts[1] should, in conjunction with D.A.D. make proposals for suspending altogether the construction of the Vickers rigid airship. The material which has been accumulated should be stored and the shed in which it is being constructed should thus be set free.

2. The repairing staff of the airships which is now at Farnborough should be moved with the utmost despatch to Barrow and should be accommodated in the neighbourhood of the new rigid airship shed and make the shed their repairing shop. Arrangements should be made to this effect with Vickers, so that we take over this shed completely from them during the war.

---

[1] Frederick William Black, 1863–1930. Entered the Colonial Office, 1880; transferred to the Admiralty, 1883. Director of Naval Stores, 1903–6. Director of Naval Contracts, 1905–15 and 1918–19. Knighted, 1913. Mission to the USA, 1917–18. Resigned from the Admiralty 1919. Managing Director, Anglo-Persian Oil Company, 1919–23.

3. The Farnborough sheds are to be handed back to the Army as soon as possible, thus meeting their urgent demands.

4. Messrs Vickers are to be urged to expedite as much as possible the two non-rigid airships they are building at the old Admiralty shed at Barrow. These when completed will give us five airships (3 Parsevals and 2 Astra Torres), besides the small military ones. These five airships will be accommodated 3 in the wooden shed at Kingsnorth and 2 at the old Admiralty shed at Barrow. The iron shed at Kingsnorth will thus become available for the large aeroplanes which are now being delivered.

5. Temporary housing accommodation for the aeroplane staff is to be at once provided near Kingsnorth, which is to become an aeroplane as well as an airship base.

6. There is scarcely any advance since I visited these sheds in early July. The roads are to be made without further delay, and I await proposals for completing all the existing contracts by the end of February.

7. The personnel of the Royal Naval Airship Service is to be reduced to the minimum required to man and handle the 5 airships. The balance, including especially the younger naval officers, are to be transferred to the aeroplane section. The military officers are to remain with the airships. I am not at all convinced of the utility of keeping this detachment at Dunkirk, and unless they are able to show some good reason for their existence they should be withdrawn.

WSC

Lord Fisher to Sir John Jellicoe

(*Jellicoe papers*)

19 January 1915   Admiralty
PLEASE BURN

My dear Jellicoe,

... It's amusing how Winston makes out that in all types you are ever so much stronger than when you assumed command of the Fleet. I simply keep on reiterating, '*He has only 29 battleships available at present.*' He can't get round that fact! So goes off on another attack on your arrangements: 'Why do you send so many away at once for repairs and refit?' Because you can't help it! Then the complaint is that you run the ships to death! that they never get rest! etc., etc. And now the Cabinet have decided on taking the Dardanelles solely with the Navy, using 15 battleships and 32 other vessels, and keeping out there three battle cruisers and a flotilla of destroyers—*all urgently required at the decisive theatre at home!* There is only one way out, and that is to resign! But you say '*no*', which simply means I am a consenting party to what I absolutely disapprove. *I don't agree with one single step taken*, so it is fearfully against the grain that I remain on in deference to your wishes. *The way the War is conducted both ashore and afloat is chaotic! We have a new plan every week!* . . .

Yours

F

Captain Richmond: diary

(*Richmond papers*)

19 January 1915

He [Fisher] is simply paving the way for defeat. And this is the master-mind which his worshippers would have us believe to be so steeped in strategy! In reality he does nothing: he goes home and sleeps in the after-noon. He is old & worn out & nervous. It is ill to have the destinies of an empire in the hands of a failing old man, anxious for popularity, afraid of any local mishap which may be put down to his dispositions. It is sad.

Winston S. Churchill to the Grand Duke Nicholas

(*Draft, Churchill papers: 2/82*)

19 January 1915   Admiralty

The Admiralty have considered with deep attention the request conveyed through Ld Kitchener from YIH for naval action against Turkey to relieve pressure in the Caucasus.[1] They have decided that the general interests of the Allied cause require a serious effort to be made to break down Turkish opposition, in addition to the minor demonstration of wh Ld Kitchener tele-graphed to YIH. It has therefore been determined to attempt to force the passage of the Dardanelles by naval force. [The method chosen is the sys-tematic & deliberate reduction of the forts by the long range fire of the 15″ guns of the 'Queen Elizabeth', followed up by direct attacks by old battle-ships][2] It is expected that the operation will take 3 or 4 weeks, & it is hoped that it may be similar in character to the methods by wh the Germans destroyed seriatim the forts of the outer line at Antwerp. The Admy are accordingly in process of assembling in the Meditn a fleet of 12 battleships, of wh 2 will be Dreadnoughts, [including the 'Q. Elizabeth'][2] 3 light cruisers,

[1] This refers to the Grand Duke's request telegraphed to London by Sir George Buchanan from Petrograd on 1 January 1915 (quoted pp. 359-60).

[2] For reasons of security, the two passages in square brackets were both deleted by Churchill before the telegram was sent.

16 destroyers, 4 submarines, 1 seaplaneship, & a large number of mine-sweepers & other auxiliaries. This concentration will be complete in the middle of February, & it is expected that the attack will begin soon after then.

A French Sqn of battleships & a French flotilla have also been invited to co-operate. As it is impossible to measure beforehand the degree of resistance wh the Turkish forts will offer, it is most undesirable that the full scope of the operation shd become known beforehand, & secrecy is vital.

The force available allows for casualties, & for the destruction of the Turco-German fleet if & when the Sea of Marmora is reached.

The Admy hope that the Russian Govt will cooperate powerfully in this operation at the proper moment by naval action at the mouth of the Bos-phorus, & by having troops ready to seize any advantage that may be gained for the allied cause. It wd probably be better to defer Russian action until the outer forts of the Dardanelles have been destroyed, so that if failure shd occur at the outset, it will not have the appearance of a serious reverse. But it is our intention to press the matter to a conclusion, & at the right moment the intervention of the Russian Fleet will be most desirable.

H. H. Asquith to Venetia Stanley
(*Montagu papers*)

20 January 1915   10 Downing Street

. . . We had a long talk about the Balkans & Greece & how to bring them in. Grey is anxious to be able to dangle before the Greeks Cyprus as a lure. It is not worth much to us, indeed nothing—tho' Kitchener is very loth to part with it, because it is on the high road, via Alexandretta, to Meso-potamia, where we now straddle across the Tigris & Euphrates. Grey thinks it wd have a good moral effect to show that we were really prepared to part with something we have, instead of merely carving out & distributing other people's possessions. . . .

Hankey came to me to-day to say—*very privately*—that Fisher, who is an old friend of his, had come to him in a very unhappy frame of mind. He likes Winston personally, but complains that on purely technical naval matters he is frequently over-ruled ('he out-argues me'!) and he is not by any means at ease about either the present disposition of the fleets, or their future movements. Of course he didn't want Winston, or indeed anybody to know this, but Hankey told him he shd pass it on to me. Tho' I think the old man is rather unbalanced, I fear there is some truth in what he says; and I

am revolving in my mind whether I can do anything, & if anything what?
What do you say? . . .

Winston S. Churchill to Lord Fisher and Vice-Admiral Oliver

(*Copy, Churchill papers: 2/74*)

20 January 1915   Admiralty
Most secret

The attack on the Dardanelles should be begun as soon as the 'Queen
Elizabeth' can get there. Every effort will be made to accelerate her departure, so that fire can be opened on Feb. 15th. It is not desirable to concentrate the whole fleet of Battleships required for the operation at the Dardanelles at the outset. This would only accentuate failure, if the forts prove
too strong for us. 'Indefatigable', 'Queen Elizabeth', and 3 or 4 other British
Battleships, with the mine-sweepers and the 'Ark Royal', will be sufficient
at the outset, having regard to the French ships available. The rest of the
fleet should be distributed between Malta, Alexandria and Alexandretta,
from which points they can be readily concentrated as soon as progress
begins to be made.

As soon as the attack on the Dardanelles has begun, the seizure of Alexandretta should take place. Thus if we cannot make headway in the Dardanelles, we can pretend that it is only a demonstration, the object of which
was to cover the seizure of Alexandretta. This aspect is important from an
Oriental point of view.

All preparations for the attack on the Dardanelles are to proceed in
general accordance with my minutes of the 12th and 16th January.[1] The
C.O.S. has already given the necessary orders, and the ships are moving.
Sir H. Jackson will study, and advise the Board upon, this operation, raising
all points of detail which require attention. He will also watch and study the
naval part in the seizure of Alexandretta, and will confer with the War
Office as may be necessary.

As soon as 'Indefatigable' is relieved by 'Inflexible', Vice-Admiral Carden
may proceed as he proposes to Malta, refit 'Indefatigable' and make all
necessary preparations of special appliances for protection against mines,
mine-sweeping, etc., returning to the Dardanelles about the 12th, when
'Inflexible' will immediately rejoin the Grand Fleet.

---

[1] These appear to be Churchill's minute to Fisher and Oliver of 13 January 1915 (quoted
on pp. 412–13) and his note to the French Naval Attaché of 16 January, which was approved
by Asquith, Kitchener and Grey (quoted on pp. 421–2).

Rear-Admiral de Robeck will hoist his flag in one of the Battleships detailed for the Dardanelles as soon as possible, and will proceed to Malta to concert the operation with Vice-Admiral Carden.[1]

WSC

Winston S. Churchill to Lord Kitchener
(Copy, Churchill papers: 13/46)

20 January 1915   Admiralty
Secret

My dear Kitchener,
Until the bombardment of the Dardanelles forts has actually begun, we cannot tell how things will go. We must guard against the appearance of a serious rebuff: and we shall therefore at the outset only use the battleships needed for the initial stage, keeping the rest of the fleet spread between Malta, Alexandria, and Alexandretta, whence they can concentrate very quickly. It is also very desirable that the Alexandretta operation should be so timed as to be practically simultaneous with the attack on the Dardanelles, so that if we are checked at the Dardanelles, we can represent that operation as a mere demonstration to cover the seizure of Alexandretta. I believe this aspect is important from an oriental point of view.

Could you therefore arrange this and let me have your Alexandretta dates? We are aiming at the 15th February for opening fire on the Dardanelles.

Yours sincerely
WSC

P.S. I am sending a copy of this letter to the Prime Minister to keep him informed.

Winston S. Churchill to Lord Fisher
(Churchill papers: 13/56)

Secret and Personal
20 January 1915   Admiralty

You seem to have altered your views since taking office about the relative strengths of the British and German Grand and High Sea Fleets. In November you advised the removal of 'Princess Royal', 'Inflexible', and 'Invincible',

---

[1] Fisher noted at the end of this minute, in his own handwriting: 'The First Sea Lord concurs.'

W.C. 3—FF

together with 8 'King Edwards' and 5 'Duncans', a total of 18 capital ships from the Grand Fleet, some for temporary duties of importance, but the battleships for permanent service in the south. These dispositions were carried out. Since then the Commander-in-Chief has received back the 8 'King Edwards' and the 'Princess Royal'; he has gained the 'Indomitable'; he has received the 'Warrior', 'Duke of Edinburgh', 'Black Prince', 'Gloucester', 'Yarmouth', 'Caroline', 'Galatea', 'Donegal', and 'Leviathan' together with 16 destroyers additional and, I think, about 50 extra trawlers and yachts.

These are immense additions to his strength, and I know of no new circumstances which have arisen or of reinforcements which have reached the enemy which ought to make us anxious now, if we were not anxious before.

However, in view of your minute and of the importance of re-assuring the Commander-in-Chief so far as possible, it seems to me that the following arrangements might be made:—

1. The 1st Destroyer Flotilla to join the Grand Fleet as soon as 'Penelope' and 'Inconstant' arrive at Harwich. (We cannot allow our forces there to be reduced to a point at which we are powerless even to reconnoitre the enemy).

2. 'Galatea', 'Caroline', 'Cordelia', and 'Phaeton' to form a new Light Cruiser Squadron for the Grand Fleet as soon as possible.

3. The 1st Cruiser Squadron to be retained by the Commander-in-Chief until the new Light Cruiser Squadron has been formed.

4. I cannot understand his complaint about 'Hannibal' and 'Magnificent'. These vessels have been asked for to prevent barrier-breaking ships approaching the booms and as defences against destroyer attack. The 6″ guns of the 'Crescent' and 'Royal Arthur' now on their way North are ample for this purpose, and there can be no need whatever for 12″ gun ships in those positions. The Commander-in-Chief's views about the complements should, however, be met, the complements strengthened accordingly, and the two present captains of 'Magnificent' and 'Hannibal' transferred to the new vessels.

5. As soon as convenient the 2 'Lord Nelsons' and the 6 remaining 'Formidables' forming the 5th Battle Squadron should be transferred from Portland to Rosyth, where they could set the 3rd Battle Squadron free to rejoin the Commander-in-Chief at Scapa or Cromarty.

6. The battle cruisers ought to be kept together, as then we shall always have a force strong enough to beat the whole of the German fast vessels. They will be quite out of reach for any action to protect the coast of England if they go to Cromarty, which is the same distance from Heligoland as Scapa. I therefore think they should not be divided or moved from the Forth unless Admiral Beatty reports that he finds the navigational conditions dangerous. The outer line defences of the Forth are now nearly completed. There is a

considerable force of trawlers, torpedo boats, destroyers, and submarines there under the direction of Admiral Lowry,[1] who has shown himself to be a most energetic and capable officer. I see no reason why they should be mined in there more than at Cromarty, and in any case they ought never to proceed to sea without the channels being properly swept beforehand. There is good seaplane protection at the Forth which can be reinforced if necessary.

7. The refit of 'Invincible' should be accelerated to the utmost. The necessary additional fitters asked for should be sent from home to Gibraltar. The 'Inflexible' can sail for home on the 12th February. 'Australia' can stand by to reinforce the Grand Fleet in case of a casualty until either 'Invincible' or 'Inflexible' have got home.

I hope you will consider that these measures meet the case put forward in your minute.[2]

WSC

Lord Fisher to Winston S. Churchill
(*Churchill papers: 13/56*)

20 January 1915   Admiralty

First Lord,

You have marked enclosed 'Personal' so I expect you wish it returned to you & not sent to C.O.S. for execution as I think the measures you mention meet the case put forward in my minute—As you rightly say it is of the highest importance to re-assure the Cmdr in Chief. I would like on his behalf (so frequently re-iterated to me) to press for return of Blenheim & the Destroyer Flotilla from Dardanelles replacing them by French Destroyers. The whole Turkish Naval Force is quite a negligible quantity even with German officers (with the 'Goeben' 'knocked out' as we know her to be!) & therefore French Destroyers & French Submarines if more are wanted should be called upon. The Australian Submarine ought to come home to the much required submarine duties in the North Sea. I understand she is the best we have and therefore inexcusable to waste her on the Turks.

F

[1] Robert Swinburne Lowry, 1854–1920. Entered Navy, 1867. Captain, 1896. Assistant Director of Naval Intelligence, 1897–1900. Rear-Admiral in the Channel Fleet, 1907. Commanded 2nd Cruiser Squadron, 1908–10. Admiral, 1913. Knighted, 1913. Admiral Commanding in Scotland, 1913–16. Commander-in-Chief, Rosyth, 1916.

[2] Earlier that day Fisher had written to Churchill about Jellicoe's 'temporary depression' and had warned that 'such a state of mind is infectious and may easily spread through the Grand Fleet'. He had gone on to agree with Jellicoe's complaint that as far as destroyers were concerned, Jellicoe was 'undoubtedly weak', and adding several other points of unease about his shortage of light cruisers, and the insecurity of their base in the Firth of Forth, which had led to several 'sudden panics'. (*Churchill papers 13/65*)

Lord Fisher to Sir John Jellicoe

(Jellicoe papers)

21 January 1915   Admiralty

My dear Jellicoe,

. . . This Dardanelles operation, decided upon by the Cabinet, in its taking away 'Queen Elizabeth', 'Indefatigable' and 'Inflexible' and 'Blenheim', with a flotilla of destroyers arranged to have been brought home, is a serious interference with our imperative needs in Home waters, and I've fought against it 'tooth and nail'. But, of course, if the Government of the Country decide on a project as a subject of high policy, one can't put oneself up to govern the diplomatic attitude of the nation in its relation with foreign powers, and apparently the Grand Duke Nicholas has demanded this step, or—(I suppose he would make peace with Germany which is really on the tapis in Russia through the herculean efforts of M. de Witte,[1] the Finance Minister, who is a German through and through!) The making of peace with Germany behind our backs by France and Russia is really quite a possible event, I hear, as Germany has got *the one thing* she wanted, in Antwerp and the Belgian coast, and on peace being made she would compel Holland to join Germany with an independence like Bavaria.

I fully enter into all your feelings as regards the German High Sea Fleet with its '*selected*' moment and you with your '*average*' moment. On the other hand, you have enormously increased the power of your individual ships since the beginning of the war by the additions of 'Erin', 'Benbow', 'Tiger', and other new vessels. After all, the immense superiority of the $13\frac{1}{2}$-inch guns *must* tell, and the German Fleet, since I came to the Admiralty, *have never once*, either in the Baltic or North Sea, been out to exercise—three months with never one single day's tactics! while you seem hardly ever to be in harbour for more than a week at a time! I'm now trying to get the 'Warspite' pushed on to join you sooner.

I just abominate the Dardanelles operation, unless a great change is made and it is settled to be made a military operation, with 200,000 men in conjunction with the Fleet. I believe that Kitchener is coming now to this sane view of the matter . . .

Yours always

Fisher

[1] Sergei Yulievich Witte, 1849–1915. A leading figure in the development of Russian railways. Minister of Finance, 1903–5. Prime Minister, 1905–6. He spent the rest of his life in the political wilderness, bitter that the Tsar had failed to appreciate his qualities, and ventilating his bitterness in his memoirs (which were published in English in 1921). He died of meningitis on 12 March 1915.

Lieutenant-Colonel Hankey to A. J. Balfour

(*Balfour papers*)

21 January 1915

. . . I have recently seen a good deal of Lord Fisher. I discussed with him the strategical situation which arose on the day of the Hartlepool raid, and put to him the danger which was explained to you by Beatty without mentioning any names. Lord Fisher said that in his opinion a great mistake had been made; he said that he had been overruled, but that the First Lord had afterwards confessed to him that a mistake had been made in not utilising the whole of Jellicoe's Fleet. Fisher, I find, frequently disagrees with statements made by the First Lord at our War Council. I wish he would speak up. . . .

H. H. Asquith to Venetia Stanley

(*Montagu papers*)

21 January 1915   10 Downing Street

. . . the main point is to do something really effective for Servia, which is threatened by an overwhelming inrush from the Austrians reinforced by some 80,000 Germans. If she is allowed to go down, things will look very black for us, and the prestige of the Allies with the wavering & hesitating States will be seriously, if not mortally, impaired. I have urged Grey to put the strongest possible pressure upon Roumania & Greece to come in without delay, & to promise that if they will form a real Balkan *bloc*, we will send troops of our own to join them & save the situation. I am sure that this is right, and that all our 'side-shows'—Zeebrugge, Alexandretta, even Gallipoli—ought to be postponed for this.

You may ask—Where are we to get the troops? They must come either from those wh. we already have in France, or from those wh. we were going to send there. . . .

There are two fatal things in war—one is to push blindly against a stone wall, the other is to scatter & divide your forces in a number of separate & disconnected operations. We are in great danger of committing both blunders: to neither of which it seems to me is Winston properly alive. Happily K. has a good judgment in these matters—never impulsive, sometimes inclined to be over cautious, but with a wide general outlook wh. is of the highest value. . . .

Lord Fisher to Winston S. Churchill

(*Churchill papers: 13/56*)

22 January 1915   Admiralty

My dear Winston,

I have got a cold in the head—nothing more—I caught it in the First Lord's room! (Page[1] has it like an oven often and you dont know it!) Please dont attempt to catch it by seeing me as there is nothing on except those d—d mines which you are all quite determined shant be put down!

There never was such a wily stratagem as laying down empty mines for a fortnight to see what happens! Well, they are coming over to celebrate the Emperor's Birthday (Zeppelin, Derfflinger & Co.) and there wont be any mines to stop them—that's all!

I've had a 'spiffing' letter from Queen Alexandra[2] about the Zeppelins— she's buying rockets to fire at them & wants me to join in—I've told her she'd better be in the basement than on the roof! and that she had best go to the Green Bank Hotel at Falmouth.

I'm so glad you've given Jellicoe soothing syrup.

Yours
F

H. H. Asquith to Venetia Stanley

(*Montagu papers*)

22 January 1915   10 Downing Street
4.00 pm

. . . I had Grey & Ll. George & Hankey here, to talk over the Servian business, which pre-occupies me a good deal. If we are to send a Corps (50,000 or 60,000 men) to help at the critical time & place, Hankey calculates that it will take at least 6 weeks from to-day to get it there. Plans have to be worked out at the W.O, the actual transport by sea takes at the least a fortnight, stores have to be accumulated, & a large margin allowed for unforeseen delays & accidents. War is a tiresomely slow business under

---

[1] A servant at Admiralty House, the First Lord's residence adjoining the Admiralty. When Clementine Churchill visited Admiralty House later in 1915, while her husband was in the trenches, she wrote to him—on 9 December 1915—of how 'everything there was very quiet & solemn except old Page who frisked about like a faithful old dog & plied me with tea & arm chairs near the fire'. (*Spencer-Churchill papers*)

[2] Alexandra Caroline Mary Charlotte Louise Julia, 1844–1925. Daughter of Prince Christian of Schleswig–Holstein–Sonderburg–Glücksburg (later King of Denmark). Married Edward, Prince of Wales (later Edward VII), 1863. Queen consort, 1901–10. Founded the Queen Alexandra Imperial Military Nursing Service, 1902. A friend of Lord Kitchener, she placed herself at the head of the memorial appeal after his death in June 1916.

modern conditions, tho' I dare say actually a good deal faster than it ever was before; but then we are accustomed to quickness & hurry.

In view of the urgency of this, it looks as if Sir J. French's proposed operation would at any rate have to be postponed. Winston meanwhile is quite prepared to do a lot of bombarding—there and elsewhere.

After that, I presided for nearly 2 hours over a Committee on Food Prices: quite a business-like body, Crewe, Runciman, Bron [Lord Lucas], the Assyrian [E. S. Montagu], with Hopwood & Bluey [Harold Baker].[1] As there was no rhetorician present,[2] we went over practically the whole ground, and came to a few modest & sensible conclusions. There is no doubt that we are at last beginning to feel the pinch of war, mainly because all the German ships wh. used to carry food are captured or interned, and the Admiralty has commandeered for transport &c over 1000 of our own. Further, the Australian crop has failed, & the Russian (wh. is a very good one) is shut up, until we can get hold of Constantinople, & open the Black Sea.

Winston arrived about 1.30 and groused a little about my demand that Jellicoe shd come up next week to the War Council. He is all for having French at these gatherings, but doesn't like his own man to be summoned & cross-examined.[3]

He stayed to luncheon, where we had Sir D. Henderson who goes back to the front to-morrow morning. He is in my judgment a long way the best instructed & most level headed of our Generals: in fact (if Robertson is unavailable) he clearly ought to succeed Murray as Chief of the Staff. W & I discussed with him the whole position at the front: he does not favour the forward move at present. He thinks the new men who come out excellent material: the difficulty (of course) is to get really good officers. . . .

Winston S. Churchill to H. H. Asquith

(*Copy, Churchill papers: 13/46*)

22 January 1915   Admiralty

My dear Prime Minister,

I should personally like very much to have Sir John Jellicoe up to London for a few days, as there are a number of minor matters which would gain

---

[1] Harold Trevor Baker, 1877–1960. Liberal MP, 1910–18. Financial Secretary, War Office, 1912–15. Member of Army Council, 1914–15. Inspector of Quartermaster General Services, 1916.

[2] Neither Churchill nor Lloyd George was a member of the Cabinet Committee on Food Prices.

[3] On the previous day Asquith had written privately to Churchill, asking that Jellicoe attend the War Council to be held on 28 January.

sensibly from being talked over: but I feel difficulty either in directing him to come or in leaving it to his judgment.

There is no similarity between the position and functions of a naval Commander-in-Chief and of a modern General in the field. Military operations take a long time to develop and to carry through. The situation changes by gradations. The directions from the commanding General are given by telegraph or telephone. The larger the army, the less direct is his contact with it, and the longer are the phases of every operation. All the instant emergencies are dealt with by brigade, divisional, and army corps commanders. With the Fleet, on the other hand, it is nothing or everything. The Grand Fleet has always been kept at four hours notice to proceed to sea. Sir John Jellicoe in the letter which I read to you expresses the opinion that he ought not to be more than two hours away from his flagship, even during the short period of rest we have pressed him to take. At any moment, night or day, news may arrive which will require the whole fleet to proceed to sea immediately. This has happened several times already in the course of this war; while the number of alarms which led to nothing is of course more than numerous. The information which would require this immediate action might possibly come to the Commander-in-Chief through the presence of hostile vessels in his area, or a submarine alarm, but much more probably in present circumstances it would come to him through us. We should receive a message which would require the whole fleet to be sent to sea at once; and the great battle for the naval supremacy of the world might begin in twelve hours and be over in two. I must impress upon you that this may happen at any moment without any previous apparent change in the situation, which would pass at one step from absolute inertia to supreme crisis.

The leadership of a fleet is personal in a sense and degree quite different to that of a large modern army. On an emergency arising, or on a signal being received from the Admiralty, he himself takes his fleet out of harbour, in itself a critical operation complicated by danger from mines, submarines, and weather. He leads that fleet himself personally. They follow his flag in action. He manœuvres them as quickly and easily as a cavalry regiment would be handled by its Colonel. They all move in one body in a strict drill formation; and he gives with his own lips the actual executive words which regulate their direct attack upon the enemy.

When Lord Fisher became First Sea Lord, the matters to be discussed were so serious that we took the extraordinary step of inviting Sir John Jellicoe to come South to consult with us. This was before the Germans had attempted any raid upon our coast, and after a long period of complete passivity on their part. Before he could return to his flagship, the enemy made their abortive attack on Yarmouth. The whole fleet was sent to sea without the flagship; and if the enemy had intended a decisive operation, either the opportunity of bringing him to action would have been missed, or the decisive battle of the war would have been fought without the Commander-in-Chief, and under an admiral by whom it has very rarely been exercised. In consequence of this experience, we arranged that if any further consultation was necessary, we should go up to him and not bring him down to us. More than a month has passed since the raid on the Hartlepools, and although on two occasions since then we have had to order the fleet to stand by, and on two other occasions it has had to proceed in a great hurry to sea on account of submarine alarms, nothing of note has actually occurred. But the 27th of this month is the Emperor's birthday, and it is quite possible that something may be attempted then which would require the immediate movement of the whole fleet.

In these circumstances, it is no use my telegraphing to Sir John Jellicoe saying 'if you think you can get away, do so'. He knows perfectly well that he ought not to leave, and we know well that we ought not to direct him to leave, unless there is a graver military need for his presence here, than there is for his presence with his fleet. I think it is very likely that he could come down South for a few days and nothing would happen; but there is no assurance at all of this; and if the enemy puts to sea in his absence, events of the utmost consequence might take place almost immediately, under conditions which would rob the fleet of a very great advantage, and which would commit them to the supreme test under strange hands. Believe me it is not out of any desire to raise difficulties that I put these considerations before you. Still less do I wish to prevent the fullest interrogation of the Commander-in-Chief by yourself or any other member of the War Council. Nothing would give me greater pleasure than for yourself, or Mr Balfour, or Lord Kitchener, to visit Sir John Jellicoe or meet him on shore in close proximity to his ships, and discuss with him fully any and every aspect of the naval war. Although Sir John Jellicoe has expressed in minor matters some wishes which we have not yet been able to meet, particularly in regard to the number of destroyers permanently attached to the Grand Fleet, and has evinced some discontent with the slow progress made in spite of all our efforts in rendering Scapa Flow submarine proof, we believe that entire unity of thought on the main strategy of the war exists between himself and the Admiralty. The most intimate relations of personal friendship prevail between him and the First Sea Lord; they write to each other every day, and sometimes several times a day. I also maintain a close and cordial correspondence, both by letter and telegraph, with him. I know of no reason, either personal or of policy, which requires external intervention; but if such intervention were necessary, it would be much more in accordance with the public interest and safety that members of the War Council should visit Sir John Jellicoe than that he should be brought down here.

The First Sea Lord desires me to say that this letter has his full agreement.

If, having considered these views fully, you still wish Sir John Jellicoe to attend the meeting next Thursday, I am willing to take the responsibility of directing him to do so provided no change in the situation occurs in the interval.

H. H. Asquith to Venetia Stanley

(*Montagu papers*)

22 January 1915   10 Downing Street
Midnight

. . . I went to dinner to K's: he has a house (No. 2) in Carlton Gardens.[1]
. . . The other colleagues there were Haldane, Grey, Ll. George & Winston. Millerand, the French War Minister, was of course the principal guest, and he was accompanied by Cambon & one or two French officers. I sat next him at dinner & had quite an interesting conversation. He can't speak a word of English, but was apparently able to follow my French. He was all against the proposed démarche of Sir J. F., and says that Joffre is anxious that we should pour all our troops during the next month into his theatre, in order that he may be able to organise & carry out a really effective coup. Of course I put to him strongly the Balkan situation, and the irreparable disaster wh. wd. be involved, in the crushing of Servia. He purported to be quite alive to this, but not 'dans ce moment' &c. Ll George (with the aid of an interpreter) & E. Grey after dinner pressed our point. . . .

Lord Fisher to Winston S. Churchill

(*Churchill papers: 13/56*)

23 January 1915   Admiralty

Dear Winston

When Bartolomé appeared last night with the mine chart my heart was glad and my glory rejoiced! I make no criticism—half a loaf is better than

[1] On 6 August 1914 Kitchener took up residence at 2 Carlton Gardens, which was lent to him by Lady Wantage until he could find a London house of his own. He made no effort to find one; but in March 1915 moved to York House, St James's Palace, which had been put at his disposal by the King. Both houses were only a few minutes' walk from the War Office.

no bread and we shall get on! No one believes me that things done in a hurry are always done the best. *It's a Nelsonic Maxim!* Imagine if (*as desired*) the Invincible & Inflexible had stayed at Plymouth till FRIDAY Nov. 13 instead of sailing as they did in a devil of a hurry on the Wednesday previous!!! We have struck oil in Admiral Ommanney.[1] Oliver tells me he knows more abt handling a Fleet than anyone in the Navy! *Why is he not in a Battle Squadron then?* Put him in place of Warrender—Warrender to Greenwich—Bayly to Monitors—Jerram to Mines like Ommanney—let those ideas germinate!

I hope you will make a big fight before surrendering over the military retreat from the Zeebrugge bombardment. Remember wht the Dutch officer told us of the last bombardment—that if only 10,000 English or French Troops could have been landed *then* there would certainly have been a German Rout! It's simple folly not to use the British Army to win back the Sea Frontier to the Dutch border instead of (*to use your own words*) playing the ignoble petty part of occupying a small sector of the French line in its most damnable part! Is there no Marlborough to be had anywhere? I think really we should fight to the death over this matter because so vitally affecting the Navy to get to the Dutch Frontier. Is the British Navy to be absolutely ignored as to its vital necessities considering that but for it the German Army would be on the Cotentin Peninsula and Joffre at Elba!

France & Russia owe all to the British Navy and they flout us.

I think we should tell Jellicoe to absolutely object to leave his command for any purpose whatever especially as his second in command[2] has only lately joined. The case is not similar to French coming over—his army occupies $\frac{1}{10}$th of the fighting line—Jellicoe occupies $\frac{10}{10}$ths! Thats the difference!

I am really alright this morning but prudence & the experts say to me, 'Stay at home till Monday'! but I will be getting on with things— Warspite & the new Light Cruiser. *Wait till you see the model!!!* 33 knots 23 feet draught of water Four 15 inch guns, and built by Cammel Laird in 11 months! OH! MY!!! What a surprise for Tirpitz!!!

Yours

F

---

[1] Nelson Ommanney, 1854–1938. Entered Navy, 1867. Rear-Admiral, 1908. Admiral Superintendent, Chatham Dockyard, 1909–12. Vice-Admiral, 1913. Retired, 1915. Served at Admiralty, 1915–18. Admiral, 1917. Knighted, 1919.

[2] Vice-Admiral Sir Cecil Burney (see p. 25 *n.1*.)

Winston S. Churchill to Lord Fisher and Vice-Admiral Oliver
(Churchill papers: 13/65)

23 January 1915 Admiralty

When 'Inflexible' arrives at Dardanelles, Adl Carden must shift his flag to her & send 'Indefatigable' to refit. If Adl Carden needs to be at Malta to make his preparations, he must wait at Dlles until relieved by Adl de Robeck. In the absence of Adl Carden, Adl de Robeck will have temporary rank of V.A. It is imperative that we shd continually retain a battle-cruiser & a VA off the Dlles. I cannot run the risk of the French obtaining command.

WSC

Sir John French to Winston S. Churchill
(Churchill papers: 26/2)

23 January 1915 General Headquarters
Secret

My dear Winston,

I returned last night from French Headquarters where I had a long conference with Joffre. Just after I got here you spoke on the telephone. In reply to your query I told you that I should still be prepared to take part in joint operations, to commence about the middle of March, but that owing to French demands elsewhere I could only do so with about two thirds of the force which I had hoped to employ.

After I returned here from London Joffre came to see me, and was anxious to know how far the reinforcements which I have been promised will enable me to assist him. We had a long discussion and, although we were in complete accord as we always have been as to the main issues, our views on certain points were a little divergent. When he left he sent me a memorandum embodying the substance of his conversation to which I replied in like manner. I hope to show you both these documents sometime.

The chief point about them is that the French do not attach anything like so much importance to the coast operation as we do, and what they really want above all things is to be completely relieved in the North and their troops set free to strengthen their line elsewhere and support a possible offensive movement.

The situation was, of course, stated with the usual French conversational 'embroidery', in the employment of which they are masters when they want to gain their point.

The upshot of it all was that I agreed to meet Joffre at Chantilly, which I did on Thursday; and there it was finally arranged that I should only employ one British Corps (instead of two) for any offensive operation I might want to undertake, and use the other to relieve more French troops.

In view of the situation as I know it to be really, I think this was quite a just and right compromise.

I may tell you therefore, finally, that I am prepared to commence a joint operation between the 10th and 15th March; the forces employed will probably be one British Cavalry Corps, one British Army Corps, De Mitry's detachment of about 10,000, whatever Naval land contingent you can give me, and the bulk of the Belgian Army.

This force will be supported by (I hope) four or five 9·2″ Howitzers and as many of the 15″ guns as you will have let me have by that time.

Whether we can do all that we intended to do (i.e. secure a line of entrenchments stretching across from Dixmude to the Dutch Frontier) depends upon the result of my investigations (now being carried out) of our ability to inundate a large part of the country.

Belgian troops can be thoroughly trusted behind inundations, and 56,000 of their infantry will go a long way towards filling up the line.

I have made a kind of 'Treaty' with Joffre on paper, which we have both signed, and it includes a clause which gives me a free hand to work as I think best with the King of the Belgians.

Do you remember, in one of your early letters, telling me you heard that I was a 'grabber' of troops?

You then expressed a favourable opinion as to the use which might be made of the Belgian Army.

You recommended me to come up here and 'grab' them.

You will see that I have endeavoured to act strictly up to your advice.

Just as I am sending this letter I hear that the arrival of the 9·2″ Howitzers is to be delayed for three or four weeks. I really think this is too bad. We *must* have power to keep down the enemy's long range artillery fire, and at present we have only got this one 9·2″ Howitzer and the eight 6″ guns.

May I appeal to you and Bacon[1] to come to the rescue and send us one or two of the 15″ guns which you are preparing? You see in all my troubles I fall back upon you.

[1] Reginald Hugh Spencer Bacon, 1863–1947. Entered Navy, 1877. Started the Submarine Service, 1903. Naval Assistant to Sir John Fisher, 1905. First Captain of the *Dreadnought*, 1906. Director of Naval Ordnance and Torpedoes, 1907–8. Rear Admiral, 1909. Retired from the Navy to become Managing Director of the Coventry Ordnance Works, 1910–15. Colonel commanding Royal Marine Heavy Howitzer Brigade, 1915. Vice-Admiral commanding the Dover Patrols, 1915–18. Knighted, 1916. Admiral, 1918. Controller, Munitions Inventions, 1918–19. Naval historian; biographer of Lord Fisher.

Good bye my dear Friend—Let me know if you go to Dunkirk & I'll come
& see you

Yrs always

JF

Winston S. Churchill to George V

(Royal Archives)

24 January 1915   Admiralty
10.11 am
Secret

Sir,

An action is in progress in the North Sea between the British & German
battle cruisers with light cruisers & destroyers on both sides.[1] We have a
good superiority plenty of daylight and plenty of sea-room. I will send Your
Majesty a further report presently.

I remain Your Majesty's devoted servant

Winston S. Churchill

Winston S. Churchill to Sir Edward Grey

(Grey papers)

24 January 1915   Admiralty

Dear Grey,

This is a very unpleasant & unfair reply to my communication.[2] The
French Naval Attaché here refused to deliver it at first, & was supported
by Cambon; but Augagneur has now insisted. He has been urged by Cambon
to come over here, & will arrive Tuesday morning. I have simply said that
I am delighted he is coming, & reserve all matters for discussion till we meet,
& hope he will dine with me on Tuesday night. Please come too (8.30).

I attach what is called the Convention of the 6th of August. This is a
working arrangement dealing with conditions wh existed at the beginning
of the war. It is obviously capable of being modified or cancelled on both

[1] This was the action of the Dogger Bank, which resulted in the sinking of the German
armoured cruiser *Blücher*. A thousand Germans were killed or taken prisoner; fifty British
sailors were killed or wounded. As a result of the action, the Commander of the German
High Sea Fleet, Admiral Ingenohl, was relieved of his command on 2 February. Sir David
Beatty's flagship, the battle cruiser *Lion*, was so badly damaged that she was out of action
for four months.

[2] On 21 January the French Minister of Marine, Victor Augagneur, had written to the
French Naval Attaché in London, the Comte de Saint-Seine, insisting that all naval operations in the Mediterranean 'must be prepared and planned' by France. (*Copy, Churchill
papers: 13/36*)

sides at any time. It cd not have any bearing upon the new conditions created by the entry of Turkey into the war. It is absurd for the French to claim that henceforward we are to make no movement in the Mediterranean except by their directions & under their command. That wd be to inflict on Gt Britain, as the forfeit for her services to France, conditions wh cd not be extorted from her by any power by war. The French ships placed under our direction have done little or nothing in the Channel & foreign waters, & we are ready to release them at any time. The French Fleet moreover has itself done nothing in the Mediterranean. We are quite capable of conducting the Dardanelles operation without any assistance, & I only suggested the French co-operation out of loyalty & politeness.

It is curious that on Nov 21st we asked the French to release our battle cruisers & to relieve our Admiral off the Dardanelles, in order that we might use all our force to catch Admiral von Spee's Squadron. They declined however, & begged us to leave our ships & retain the command. This we did, tho' under some strain. Now the outer seas are clear, & we have ample forces available. All plans for the attack on the Dardanelles are moving forward, & I have every expectation of opening fire on the 15th. I hope I may count on you to see me through with these people.

You will no doubt have heard of the battle cruiser action this morning in the North Sea, in wh the German cruiser 'Blücher' (almost a battle cruiser) was sunk, & two other German battle cruisers seriously damaged. On our side the 'Lion' is damaged, but is coming home at 12 knots. Beatty shifted his flag to the 'Princess Royal', & is I trust unhurt. No details of the flotilla & light cruiser fighting have yet come to hand. The significance of this fierce & well-fought fight between the best & newest ships in the world is that our preponderance was only 5 to 4, & the Germans thought of nothing but flight; whereas in the general battle our preponderance ought certainly not to be less than 6 to 4.

Come round & see me if you feel inclined. I shd like to have a talk.

Yours ever

W

Winston S. Churchill to Sir John French
(*Copy: Churchill papers: 26/2*)

24 January 1915   Admiralty
Secret

My dear French,

Of course yr decision is a heavy blow to us. But I am not going to waste time & strength about choses jugées.

Two 15″ howitzers complete with 150 rounds of ammunition for the two will be at yr disposal in France thoroughly equipped on Feb 15th, if you claim them through W.O. Thereafter we work up from 10 to 15 rounds a day.

Millerand has been over here. The French are all vy self centred & vy much inclined to regard the British & Belgians as pawns in their game. As for the Navy, it is only the table on wh the chess board stands!

The result of the decision (wh I shall not dispute) is that we must vy soon attempt a dangerous operation, wh can, at the best, bring only a partial & transient remedy.

Today a chance offered: but only one forfeit cd be exacted. I had hoped for more. We hit them vy hard. But their strong armour protected their motive power: & they fled so fast, we cd not obtain a decision. Still 'Blücher' was a fine ship; quite the equal of our 'Invincible'. If I can get a day or two next week, I will try to come out & have a talk. K. assures me that he has no objection. It is only a qn of the cat & mouse game here.

I send you some pictures of the big cannons.

Always yr sincere friend
W

H. H. Asquith to Venetia Stanley
(*Montagu papers*)

25 January 1915   Walmer Castle

... While we were at dinner last night a messenger arrived from the Admiralty with a letter to me from Winston, giving a narrative of the naval battle in the North Sea. The 'Lion'—Beatty's flagship—was a good deal damaged tho' not disabled: her speed was reduced to 12 knots from (I suppose) 26: and Beatty transferred his flag to the 'Princess Royal'. None of this appears in the official account published to-day—from wh. one wd. gather that none of our ships had been touched. Don't you think this kind of secrecy is quite puerile? It is not the least likely to deceive the Germans, who no doubt know perfectly well that they hit and injured the 'Lion', and when the truth comes out people here will say with justice that they have been treated with lack of candour. I am all for telling the worst at once, aren't you? All the same, it was the best thing—at least the most successful—the Navy has done so far. The German squadron was no doubt out for another 'Scarborough' raid. ...

Lord Fisher to Winston S Churchill
(*Churchill papers: 13/56*)

25 January 1915   Admiralty
Private & Personal

My dear Winston,

We must not say that our wireless turned back the Germans—the fact is (*though I had intended to bury the fact*) and it is solely my fault we put the rendezvous for Beatty *in front* instead of *behind* the enemy, *but I beg you not to say a word on this to anyone* and least of all to Oliver or Wilson—as they came over with the chart to my house at 2.20 P.M. and I deferred to their joint certainty—I mention this as it may recoil upon us that ours was the initial error—though it may truly be said it avoided mine laying and a massacre to turn them back but it would have been worth a massacre to have got between them and their home! . . .

I cant at all understand Admiral Stoddart's movements[1] and his inexcusably keeping ships together & his not communicating with our Minister in Chile[2] who also seems a bloody fool like most of our foreign representatives who have all lived so long in foreign parts that they've ceased to be Englishmen! If our Minister in Chile had been worth his salt he would have bought up all the telegraph people and when the Germans had enjoyed every liberty to their hearts content and the Dresden 31 hours cypher telegraphing and a Chilean Cruiser discovering her & not telling us before she went to Punta Arenas our effete Minister permits without a protest the utmost rigour of the law against us & our consul[3] at Punta Arenas prohibited telling us news of Dresden in cypher with the £5000!

Yours
F

Winston S. Churchill to Vice-Admiral Carden
(*Copy, Admiralty papers: 137/96*)

25 January 1915   Admiralty
Personal and secret

I am expecting you to formulate all your requests for mine-sweepers mine-bumpers, and all special appliances in the greatest possible detail.

[1] From December 1914 to March 1915 Rear-Admiral Stoddart, commanding the South Atlantic and Pacific Stations, was searching for the German light cruiser *Dresden* (the only German ship to have escaped after the Falkland Islands battle on 8 December 1914). The *Dresden* was found, and sunk herself, on 14 March 1915 (*see* p. 635).

[2] Francis William Stronge, 1856–1924. Entered Foreign Office, 1878. Minister to Colombia, 1906–11; to Mexico, 1911–13; to Chile, 1913–19. Knighted, 1919.

[3] Charles Amherst Milward. British Vice-Consul at Punta Arenas, Straits of Magellan, Chile, 1903–10; Consul, 1910–15.

W.C.3—GG

Malta must execute them if possible but we will supplement her resources from England. This is a great opportunity and you must concentrate absolutely upon it. We shall give you ships enough to be independent of the French. Sir Henry Jackson who examined for the Board all Naval questions connected with the East, is in general agreement with your plans. You should telegraph fully for everything you want that cannot be supplied locally. Every effort is being made to accelerate departure of QUEEN ELIZABETH.

Official orders will reach you in due course.

Winston S. Churchill to H. H. Asquith, Lord Kitchener and Sir Edward Grey
(Churchill papers: 13/54)

25 January 1915   Admiralty
Secret

Details of concentration for attack upon Dardanelles herewith as prepared by Chief of Staff.

Kindly return.

Arrangements sh'd enable fire to be opened on Feb 15.

WSC

Vice-Admiral Oliver: memorandum[1]
(Churchill papers: 13/54)

25 January 1915   Admiralty

Albion	left St Helena 20th Jany for Malta, she has £4,000,000 for England which will be landed at Gibraltar or transferred to another ship.
Canopus	on passage to St Vincent for Malta.
Ocean	In Egypt, ready.
Vengeance	on passage to Gibraltar for Malta. Rear-Admiral de Robeck has been ordered to transfer his flag to her & has arrived at Gibraltar.
Inflexible	Arrived at Tenedos 26th Vice-Admiral Carden ordered to ship flag to her.
Indefatigable	Goes to Malta to refit & return to Tenedos, orders given.

[1] In the summer of 1916, when Churchill was preparing his evidence for the Dardanelles Commission, he wrote at the end of this memorandum: 'Note: To the above fleet the First Sea Lord added "Lord Nelson" & "Agamemnon".'

Swiftsure	In Egypt ready.
Triumph	Coaling at Colombo, on passage to Medn.
Dartmouth	At St Vincent on passage to Malta.
Irresistible	At Sheerness fitted with Mine Bumper, goes to Medn after Zeebrugge.
Cornwallis	At Quiberon Bay firing goes from there to Malta.
Prince George	being fitted with mine bumper at Devonport. Takes Howitzers to Malta, & 2 sets of mine bumping gear for other ships.
Majestic	at Portland takes Howitzers to Malta.
Amethyst	Working up drills after commissioning, now at Gibraltar.
Sapphire	Leaves Devonport tomorrow for Med.
Queen Elizabeth	To be ready 27th.
Dublin	At Tenedos.
Blenheim	At Tenedos.
12 Destroyers	do
3 ,,	refitting at Malta.
1 ,,	at Gibraltar.
Swanley	fitting at Malta as Depot.
Ark Royal (9 Seaplanes)	having guns fitted before going out.
Berrinia Submarine *A.E. 2.* }	At Aden on passage.
3 B. Class	At Gibraltar.
Doris	Syrian coast.
1 Yacht } 21 Trawlers	Collecting at Devonport docking as required & storing, go out in batches of seven.
24 French Trawlers in Medn Ports. }	Being fitted with sweeping gear.

H. F. Oliver

Lord Fisher to Winston S. Churchill

(*Churchill papers: 13/56*)

25 January 1915   Admiralty

First Lord,

I have no desire to continue a useless resistance in the War Council to plans I cannot concur in, and I would ask that the enclosed may be printed and circulated to its members before the next meeting.

F

Lord Fisher: memorandum

(*Copy, Cabinet papers: 42/1*)

25 January 1915   Admiralty
Secret

MEMORANDUM BY THE FIRST SEA LORD ON THE POSITION OF THE BRITISH FLEET AND ITS POLICY OF STEADY PRESSURE

At recent meetings of the War Council projects have been discussed for joint naval and military operations against places on the coast as well as for similar operations by the Navy alone. Up to the present, however, no clear statement has been made at the War Council as to what our naval policy in this war is to be. Some statement of principle appears a fundamental necessity to any decision in regard to naval action against coast fortifications.

Our naval policy must be regulated by that of the enemy. It is the policy of Germany to avoid a decision at sea and to keep the command in dispute as long as possible while they concentrate their offensive powers on the army ashore. This defensive attitude has been adopted deliberately, notwithstanding that it has involved the sacrifice of the whole of the German mercantile shipping and oversea trade, and has subjected Germany for six months to the whole pressure of our sea power. This tremendous sacrifice has been imposed on Germany by two causes; first, by her numerical inferiority to our fleet; and, second, because an unsuccessful action and the destruction of the High Sea Fleet might place Germany in a position of naval inferiority to Russia, and expose the Baltic coast to invasion; and since the time of Frederick the Great Germany has always been nervous of this flank, but on this subject I have presented another paper.

The deliberate adoption of the defensive, being contrary to the tradition of German military policy, and involving such sacrifices and losses, must be most galling to the German people. They only await a favourable moment to pass from the defensive to the offensive. They have already endeavoured without success to scatter our naval strength by attacks on our trade, and not much more successfully to reduce our main strength by submarines and mines.

Of all strategical attitudes that of a naval defensive as adopted by Germany is the most difficult to meet and the most deeply fraught with danger for the opposing belligerent, if he is weak ashore as we are, and the enemy strong ashore as Germany is. Nevertheless, all through our history we have had to encounter similar situations. The policy of the French in nearly all our naval wars was the policy which Germany has now adopted. Our reply to-day must be the same as our reply was then, namely, to be content to remain in possession of our command of the sea, husbanding our strength until the gradual pressure of sea power compels the enemy's fleet to make an effort to attack us at a disadvantage.

In the seven years war the French preserved their fleet from a decision for five years. Nelson was off Toulon for two years. By comparison, the six months during which Sir John Jellicoe has had to wait are short, and they have been relieved by incidents which have considerably diminished the enemy's forces.

The pressure of sea power to-day is probably not less but greater and more rapid in action than in the past; but it is still a slow process and requires great patience. In time it will almost certainly compel the enemy to seek a decision at sea, particularly when he begins to realise that his offensive on land is broken. This is one reason for husbanding our resources. Another reason is that the prolongation of war at sea tends to raise up fresh enemies for the dominant naval power in a much higher degree than it does on land owing to the exasperations of neutrals. The tendency will only be checked by the conviction of an overwhelming naval supremacy behind the nation exercising sea power.

We play into Germany's hands if we risk fighting ships in any subsidiary operations such as coastal bombardments or the attack of fortified places without military co-operation, for we thereby increase the possibility that the Germans may be able to engage our fleet with some approach to equality of strength. The sole justification of coastal bombardments and attacks by the fleet on fortified places, such as the contemplated prolonged bombardment of the Dardanelles forts by our fleet, is to force a decision at sea, and so far and no further can they be justified.

So long as the German High Sea Fleet preserves its present great strength and splendid gunnery efficiency, so long is it imperative, and indeed vital, that no operation whatever should be undertaken by the British Fleet calculated to impair its present superiority, which is none too great in view of the heavy losses already experienced in valuable ships and invaluable officers and men, whose places cannot be filled in the period of the war (in which respect the Navy differs so materially from the Army). Even the older ships should not be risked, for they cannot be lost without losing men, and they form our only reserve behind the Grand Fleet.

Ours is the supreme necessity and difficulty of remaining passive, except in so far as we can force the enemy to abandon his defensive and to expose his fleet to a general action. In the French wars we aimed at this by cutting off the enemy's trade and by joint naval and military operations against his territory.

We are already, to a great extent carrying out the first method. To cut off the enemy's trade we ought to aim at a complete closing of the North Sea, and the declaration of a blockade. The machinery of a blockade is already established and maintained between Scilly and Ushant, and between the Hebrides and Norway. It is remarkable and beyond all praise and admiration how our patrols have, in the furious gales that have continuously raged all this winter, so completely blocked the passages into the North Sea as to identify every steamer that has sailed from foreign ports for the North Sea. Difficulties with neutrals and adherence to an absolute international law based on the conditions of a century ago, and quite inapplicable to technical developments of modern naval warfare, have alone prevented us from declaring an actual blockade.

The second method of forcing the fleet out, that is to say, by attacks on the enemy's territory, is difficult. Attacks on German colonies are not sufficient to tempt it out, and joint operations against continental Germany are impracticable in view of the enemy's strength in submarines.

It has been said that the first function of the British Army is to assist the fleet in obtaining command of the sea. This might be accomplished by military co-operation with the Navy in such operations as the attack of Zeebrugge, or the forcing of the Dardanelles, which might bring out the German and Turkish fleets respectively. Apparently, however, this is not to be. The English Army is apparently to continue to provide a small sector of the allied front in France, where it no more helps the Navy than if it were at Timbuctoo.

Being already in possession of all that a powerful fleet can give a country, we should continue quietly to enjoy the advantage without dissipating our strength in operations that cannot improve the position.

Fisher

Margot Asquith: diary
(*Countess Oxford and Asquith papers*)

25 January 1915

LLOYD GEORGE: McKenna's judgement is 1,000 times better than Winston's! . . . Really if it wasn't for Winston's affectionate quality and good temper I sometimes think I can hardly do with him! . . .

Winston, like all really self-centred people ends by boring people. He's as you say, such a child! Would you believe it, he, Neil Primrose[1] and I dined

---

[1] Neil James Archibald Primrose, 1882–1917. Younger son of the 5th Earl of Rosebery. Liberal MP, 1910–17. Captain, Buckinghamshire Hussars, 1914. Married, 1915, Lady Victoria Stanley, only daughter of the 17th Earl of Derby. Parliamentary Under-Secretary, Foreign Office, February–May 1915. Parliamentary Military Secretary, Ministry of Munitions, September–December 1916. Parliamentary Secretary, Treasury, December 1916–May 1917. Killed in action, November 1917.

at the Cafe Royal and had a very nice evening. I suddenly saw Winston get sulky—what for I had no notion! Neil said to him 'Shall I motor you home?' —Winston answered crossly 'No' and got into my taxi. I said to him 'Now what *is* the matter with you?' He said in a sulky angry voice, 'didn't you hear the young pup say to me *I don't agree with you*?*.

Of course I roared with laughter, it's so childishly absurd. Luckily Winston has got no rancour and has a really good heart, these make him lovable. . . .

*　　　*　　　*

MARGOT: I don't think he [Fisher] is much use now, though he is awfully clever and vital.
LLOYD GEORGE: He is not at all gaga.
MARGOT: No, not at all, only he sees things much more coloured than they are, and is so inventive and extravagant and coarse, has bad judgment.
LLOYD GEORGE: I am not a good judge of his brains, I'm so fond of him, but I am glad Sir Arthur Wilson is there. . . .

Sir George Buchanan to Sir Edward Grey: telegram
(*Copy, Churchill papers: 26/2*)

25 January 1915　　　　　　　　　　　　　　Petrograd
Personal & Most Secret

General Williams has sent me memorandum by Grand Duke to the following effect on proposed operations against Dardanelles:—

Memorandum begins by stating appeal to Allies for help was made because H.I. Highness was determined not to weaken forces operating against Germans and Austrians. Appeal was not accompanied by any suggestion as to the method of execution as Russia had not the means of directly assisting in carrying out a plan of action against Turkey.

Russian Dreadnoughts were not finished: they had no submarines of modern type and only an insufficient number of swift Destroyers. Their Fleet was therefore not more than equal of Turkish Fleet and that only when all the ships were together. Russian ships only carry four days coal and coaling at sea in the Black Sea was rendered impossible in the winter by bad weather. The nearest Russian base was moreover 24 hours from the entrance of the Bosphorus. Guns of the Bosphorus Batteries as compared both in number and power with those placed in Russian ships were such as to give little hope of a successful attack by the latter.

Reinforcement of Black Sea Squadron by Dreadnought 'Imperatritza Maria'; by submarines of modern type, and by Destroyers would of course change all this; but these reinforcements would not be completed until the month of May.

The most effective assistance which could be given to Allied Fleet after forcing of Straits would be for Russia to land troops. This was however impossible as it would necessitate at least two Army Corps being withdrawn from the principal theatre of war. This was, Memorandum continues, clear and truthful statement of Russia's position and of the reasons which prevented her from helping the Allies, great as was her desire to do so.

Memorandum concludes by stating in opinion of the Grand Duke any military action against Turkey of the kind contemplated would be bound to have important results for the Allied cause. It could not be hoped to crush Turkey in the Caucasus—even capture of Erzeroum would not effect object. But a successful attack against Turkey would react on the principal enemy (German) line; it would paralyze Turkey; and would infallibly be a deciding factor in determining the attitude of neutral States in the Balkans.

In forwarding me above Memorandum General Williams stated in conversation with himself the Grand Duke had spoken in very much the same sense as above but that H.I. Highness had strongly emphasized telling effect which successful carrying out of operations contemplated would have on Turkey and Balkans.

Sir Edward Grey to Winston S. Churchill
(*Churchill papers: 26/2*)

26 January 1915 Foreign Office

Submitted *for your consideration.*

This is the Russian reply about Dardanelles. It shows that, though Russia cannot help, the operation has her entire good will & the Grand Duke attaches the greatest importance to its success.[1]

This fact may be used with Augagneur to show that we must go ahead with it & that failure to do so will disappoint Russia & react most unfavourably upon the military situation, about which France & we are specially concerned just now.

I should not communicate the text of the Russian Memo: to Augagneur —the Grand Duke doesn't like his military information being given to foreign or even Russian Ministers.

EG

[1] Grey wrote at the end of this letter: 'I have kept one copy [of the Russian reply] with my private papers—no other copy exists: it is therefore for you to communicate one to Kitchener & the P.M. if you wish. I regard the document as belonging to you.'

H. H. Asquith to Venetia Stanley

(Montagu papers)

26 January 1915   10 Downing Street

. . . I find myself immersed in all kinds of affairs. First, I am going to send to Winston to say that he must now publish without any concealment or reserves a full account of Sunday's battle. I gather that the 'Lion' tho' not very seriously injured had to be towed home, & did not get there (Rosyth) until early this morning: also that a few men were killed on the 'Tiger'. . . .

Sir Edward Grey to Winston S. Churchill

(Churchill papers: 13/46)

26 January 1915   Foreign Office

I hear with joy that all the ships are back. I do hope you will now kill the German lie about having sunk one of our cruisers by telling the whole story of the fight. I hear the Germans now say that they *saw* our cruiser sink & unless we convince people that we are telling the whole story the German lie will get believed even here.

By the whole story I mean when the fight began, how the Germans ran so that the fight was sheer pursuit, why we would not pursue after them, the exact damage done to our ships & men by gunfire & how comparatively slight it was; the nature & cause of injury to the Lion, but for which bit of bad luck we should have inflicted grievous loss on the Germans with hardly any injury to ourselves.

Dont forget that though our silence about the Audacious has left the Germans uncertain as to her real fate, it has impaired all over the world the credit attached to our official statements & we have got to re-establish it by telling the whole story in a case like this. Forgive if I urge this unnecessarily; it seems to me very important.

EG

Winston S. Churchill to Lord Fisher

(*Fisher papers*)

26 January 1915   Admiralty
Personal

First Sea Lord,

There is no difference in principle between us. But when all your special claims are met, you must let the surplus be used for the general cause.

I suggest I show your Memo & my comment to the Prime Minister: instead of printing & circulating the documents. You & I are so much stronger together.

WSC

Winston S. Churchill to Sir Edward Grey and Lord Kitchener

(*Churchill papers: 13/54*)

26 January 1915   Admiralty

I had a long discussion this morning with the French Minister of Marine. There wd be no difficulty in arriving at agreement on the following lines:—

1) The British to have the command at the Dlles & to undertake the operation at their discretion. The French sqn. there will cooperate, but the extent of its cooperation will be defined after the French naval authorities have examined the general plan.

2) The British Vice Admiral will continue to command in Egypt, but a French VA will command in the Levant, not only as I had proposed from Latakia to Jaffa, but including Alexandretta. Any military operation on the Levantine coast shd be a subject of discussion first between the two govts. & the French wish to participate in any occupation of Alexandretta.

Lord Kitchener informs me that he cannot now fix any date for the Alexandretta expedition, so it appears unnecessary to make precise conditions about it.

I think it would be a good thing if you both had a talk with M. Augagneur.

WSC

Sir Edward Grey: note

I think it important to let the French have what they want in this Memo even about Alexandretta. It will be fatal to cordial cooperation in the Mediterranean & perhaps everywhere if we arouse their suspicions as to anything in the region of Syria. I hope you will close with this proposal. If it is not agreed to I foresee very untoward consequences. I am to meet M. Augagneur at dinner (am I not?) tomorrow, Wednesday.

EG

Winston S. Churchill to Lord Kitchener
(*Copy, Churchill papers: 13/46*)

27 January 1915   Admiralty

My dear Kitchener,

Some time ago before the recent arrangements in regard to the supply of explosives, I arranged with the French authorities with a view to meeting their urgent need for lyddite, that if they supplied the Admiralty with 150 tons of guncotton we would in exchange cede to them 150 tons of lyddite on which we were counting to fill our mines. Guncotton will do for filling mines, but lyddite is required for the French shells. My people in the Admiralty now report that the War Office have interposed a veto on the transaction, and that the filling of the mines, which is a very urgent matter, is being delayed in consequence.

It is very inconvenient that ordinary matters of inter-departmental business should require personal discussion between us. The Admiralty have been willing to acquiesce in the War Office obtaining the general control of the production of explosives: but it has always been understood, and is indeed obviously right, that our special requirements should receive the fullest consideration. I am sure that this is your wish and intention.

I do not wish to trouble you to go into the details of the question yourself: I have no doubt it will be sufficient if you put your people in friendly relations with mine.

Commodore de Bartolomé to Lord Fisher
(*Copy, Admiralty papers: 116/3454*)

27 January 1915
11.30 pm

Dear Lord Fisher,

The First Lord desires me to say that he has just seen the Prime Minister, and the latter wishes to see you and the First Lord at 11.10 a.m. tomorrow, before the Meeting of the Council. He considers it imperative that you and the First Lord should both be present at the Meeting.

Yours sincerely
C. M. de Bartolomé

Lord Fisher to Winston S. Churchill

(*Churchill papers: 13/56*)

28 January 1915   Admiralty
Strictly Private & Personal

My dear Winston,

I entreat you to believe that if as I think really desirable for a complete '*unity of purpose*' in the War that I should gracefully disappear and revert to roses at Richmond[1] ('*The heart untravelled fondly turns to home*') that there will not be in my heart the least lingering thought of anything but regard and affection and *indeed much admiration* towards yourself.

Late last night quite spontaneously I got these words (*absolutely unsolicited*) from Jellicoe to whom I had said not one word about the 'Inflexible' being detailed to Dardanelles or about the 'Indefatigable' or Destroyers or submarines AE 2 or indeed anything beyond the 'Elizabeth' going to the Mediterranean for gun practice & why shouldn't she use her practice shots on the Dardanelles etc and the possibilities flowing from it.

'The Battle cruiser action shewed very conclusively the absolute necessity for a *big* preponderance of this type of ship and I hope will at any rate result in no diversion of *ANY* "Queen Elizabeths" or *ANY* Battle Cruisers *FROM THE DECISIVE THEATRE*. It might easily have been a disaster. Had we lost the Lion victory would have been turned into a defeat.'

Yours F

My position is quite clear:—

I make no objection to either Zeebrugge or Dardanelles if accompanied by military cooperation on such a scale as will permanently hold the Belgian coast to the Dutch Frontier and our permanent military occupation of the Dardanelles Forts pari passu with the Naval bombardment. Simultaneous Military & Naval actions but no drain thereby on Grand Fleet Margin so therefore *no modern vessels at Dardanelles*.

I shall not as arranged with you attend the War Council and am going down to Richmond.

---

[1] In 1912, when Fisher was appointed Chairman of the Royal Commission on Fuel and Engines, he went to live at Langham House, Ham Common, near Richmond in Surrey. He lived there until October 1914 when, as First Sea Lord, he moved to Archway House, adjoining the Admiralty. While First Sea Lord he occasionally went to Langham House at weekends.

Lord Fisher to H. H. Asquith
(*Copy, Fisher Papers*)

28 January 1915   Admiralty
Private and Personal

My dear Prime Minister,

I am giving this note to Colonel Hankey to hand to you to explain my absence from the War Council. I am not in accord with the First Lord and do not think it would be seemly to say so before the Council. His reply to my memorandum does not meet my case. I say that the Zeebrugge and Dardanelles bombardments can only be justified on naval grounds by military co-operation, which would compensate for the loss in ships and irreplaceable officers and men. As purely naval operations they are unjustifiable, as they both drain our naval margin — not too large in view of collisions, such as 'Conqueror' and 'Monarch', mines and submarines, such as 'Audacious' and 'Formidable', and other previous great losses, and fools as admirals, such as Bayly and others, who can no more account for beforehand than for Sir Redvers Buller,[1] who, with a Victoria Cross, was seized with mental paralysis on the field of battle at Colenso and Spionkopf!

We are at this moment vitally in want of destroyers, wrongly kept at the Dardanelles in opposition to my representations. We are sending our best submarine to the Dardanelles and our largest and most valuable battleship, the 'Queen Elizabeth', with the only 15-inch guns ready at present, besides sending other battle cruisers now there against my protest. What will our officers and men say to me if I agreed to those 15-inch guns being in Asia Minor, when at any moment the great crisis may occur in the North Sea and the German High Sea Fleet be driven to fight by the German Military Headquarters as part of some military operation? I am very reluctant to leave the First Lord. I have a great personal affection and admiration for him, but I see no possibility of a union of ideas, and unity is essential in war, so I refrain from any desire of remaining as a stumbling block.

The British Empire ceases if our Grand Fleet ceases. No risks can be taken.

Yours truly
Fisher

Postscript. Since my conversation with the First Lord last night and the sending to you of my memorandum, I have got these quite spontaneous and un-

---

[1] Redvers Henry Buller, 1839–1908. Entered Army, 1858. Received the Victoria Cross in 1879, during the Zulu War. General, commanding the forces in South Africa, 1899–1900. His attempts to relieve Ladysmith were checked by the Boers on 15 December 1899 at Colenso, and on 24 January 1900 at Spion Kop.

solicited words from Sir John Jellicoe in a letter just come: 'The battle cruiser action [Dogger Bank] showed most conclusively the absolute necessity of a BIG preponderance of these ships and I hope will at any rate result in no diversion of any "Queen Elizabeths" or any battle cruisers from the decisive theatre (the North'Sea). Had we lost the "Lion", the victory would have turned into a defeat.'

Winston S. Churchill to Lord Fisher

(*Fisher papers*)

28 January 1915   Admiralty
Private

My dear Fisher,
 The Prime Minister considers your presence at the War Council indispensable, & so do I. He will receive us both at 11.10 so that we can have a talk beforehand.
 You have assented to both the operations in question & so far as I am concerned there can be no withdrawal without good reason from measures wh are necessary, & for wh preparations are far advanced.
 I wd infinitely sooner work with you than with Sturdee who will undoubtedly be forced upon me in the eventuality of wh you write so lightheartedly.

Yours ever
W

H. H. Asquith to Venetia Stanley

(*Montagu papers*)

28 January 1915   10 Downing Street
 ... Another personal matter which rather worries me is the growing friction between Winston & Fisher. They came to see me this morning before the War Council, and gave tongue to their mutual grievances. I tried to compose their differences by a compromise, under which Winston was to give up for the present his bombardment of Zeebrugge, Fisher withdrawing his opposition to the operation against the Dardanelles. When at the Council we came to discuss the latter—wh. is warmly supported by Kitchener & Grey, & enthusiastically by A.J.B—old 'Jacky' maintained an obstinate and ominous silence. He is always threatening to resign & writes an almost daily

letter to Winston, expressing his desire to return to the cultivation of his 'roses at Richmond'. K. has now taken up the role of conciliator[1]—for wh. you might think that he was not naturally cut out! . . .

Meeting of the War Council: extract from Secretary's notes
(Copy, Churchill papers: 2/86)

Present: H.H. Asquith (*in the chair*), Lord Haldane, Lord Crewe, Winston S. Churchill, A. J. Balfour, Lord Fisher, Sir Arthur Wilson, David Lloyd George, Sir Edward Grey, Lord Kitchener, Lieutenant-Colonel Hankey (*Secretary*)

28 January 1915   10 Downing Street
11.30 a.m.

THE DARDANELLES

MR. CHURCHILL said that he had communicated to the Grand Duke Nicholas and to the French Admiralty the project for a naval attack on the Dardanelles. The Grand Duke had replied with enthusiasm, and believed that this might assist him. The French Admiralty had also sent a favourable reply, and had promised co-operation. Preparations were in hand for commencing about the middle of February. He asked if the War Council attached importance to this operation, which undoubtedly involved some risks?

LORD FISHER said that he had understood that this question would not be raised to-day. The Prime Minister was well aware of his own views in regard to it.

THE PRIME MINISTER said that, in view of the steps which had already been taken, the question could not well be left in abeyance.

LORD KITCHENER considered the naval attack to be vitally important. If successful, its effect would be equivalent to that of a successful campaign fought with the new armies. One merit of the scheme was that, if satisfactory progress was not made, the attack could be broken off.

MR. BALFOUR pointed out that a successful attack on the Dardanelles would achieve the following results:—

It would cut the Turkish army in two;
It would put Constantinople under our control;

---

[1] Fisher had tried to leave the War Council in the first few minutes, as he objected to any discussion of the Dardanelles, about which he had protested to Asquith and Churchill in the Prime Minister's study just before the War Council opened. He left the table, but was followed by Kitchener who went up to him, and persuaded him to stay. But he took no part in the subsequent discussion.

It would give us the advantage of having the Russian wheat, and enable Russia to resume exports;

This would restore the Russian exchanges, which were falling owing to her inability to export, and causing great embarrassment;

It would also open a passage to the Danube.

It was difficult to imagine a more helpful operation.

SIR EDWARD GREY said it would also finally settle the attitude of Bulgaria and the whole of the Balkans.

MR. CHURCHILL said that the naval Commander-in-Chief in the Mediterranean had expressed his belief that it could be done. He required from three weeks to a month to accomplish it. The necessary ships were already on their way to the Dardanelles. In reply to Mr. Balfour, he said that, in response to his inquiries, the French had expressed their confidence that Austrian submarines would not get as far as the Dardanelles.

LORD HALDANE asked if the Turks had any submarines.

MR. CHURCHILL said that so far as could be ascertained they had not. He did not anticipate that we should sustain much loss in the actual bombardment, but, in sweeping for mines, some losses must be expected. The real difficulties would begin after the outer forts had been silenced, and it became necessary to attack the Narrows. He explained the plan of attack on a map.

SIR EDWARD GREY thought that the Turks would be paralyzed with fear when they heard that the forts were being destroyed one by one.

THE NAVAL CAMPAIGN

MR. CHURCHILL sketched out his views of the naval campaign. The ultimate object of the Navy was to obtain access to the Baltic. First, however, as had been explained at a previous meeting, it was necessary to seal up the enemy so far as the North Sea was concerned, and for this purpose an island was required. The attack on a German island, however, would have to be postponed until some of the new monitors were ready. These vessels would be practically unsinkable by mines, and would be able to operate in shallow water where submarines could not operate. Six would be ready by May and fourteen by July. Once we had secured possession of an island, we could proceed to lock the enemy in with mines, submarines, and wire nets. When that was complete we could proceed to the Baltic. To sum up, the naval campaign, he said, consisted of three stages—

1st Phase: The clearing of the outer seas, which was practically complete.

2nd Phase: The clearing of the North Sea.

3rd Phase: The clearing of the Baltic.

This latter operation was of great importance, as Germany was, and always had been, very nervous of an attack from the Baltic. For this purpose special vessels were required, and the First Sea Lord had designed two light cruisers armed with four 15-in. guns apiece, 33 knots speed, and light draft, costing about 1,000,000*l.* apiece.

LORD FISHER said they could be built in eleven months if the usual formalities of tenders, &c., could be dispensed with. Two firms had offered to complete them within this period.

MR. LLOYD GEORGE said that, if the First Lord would send him a Memorandum, he would sanction this expenditure.

Meeting of a Sub-Committee of the War Council: Secretary's notes

(Copy, Churchill papers: 2/86)

Present: Lord Kitchener (in the Chair), David Lloyd George, A. J. Balfour, Winston S. Churchill, Sir James Wolfe Murray, Lieutenant-Colonel Hankey (Secretary). In attendance: Major-General Callwell

28 January 1915   War Office
4.00 p.m.

LORD KITCHENER said that this meeting had been arranged as the result of the fourth conclusion reached at a meeting of a War Council on the 13th January which was as follows:—

'*That if the position in the Western theatre became in the spring one of stalemate, British troops should be despatched to another theatre and objective, and that adequate investigation and preparation should be undertaken with that purpose, and that a Sub-Committee of the Committee of Imperial Defence be appointed to deal with this aspect of the situation.*'

The General Staff had carefully examined the question from the following three points of view:—

Attack on Austria from the Adriatic, assuming Italy to be an ally.
Attack on Austria in co-operation with the Serbian army, using Salonica as a base.
Attack on Turkey.

He then read a Memorandum prepared by the General Staff.

THE ADRIATIC

MR. CHURCHILL pointed out that any landing in the northern half of the Adriatic would be very dangerous owing to Austrian submarines, unless

W.C.3—HH

Pola had first been reduced. The reduction of Pola, however, would be an operation of the first magnitude. He did not think that Italy would undertake it.

SERBIA

GENERAL CALLWELL said that the Greek army would put about 200,000 men in the field. They had fought well in the Balkan wars.

LORD KITCHENER said that the Serbian army was short of mounted troops, and this was a deficiency which it would not be very difficult for us to make up.

MR. LLOYD GEORGE suggested a landing at Dedeagatch and co-operation with Bulgaria in an attack on Adrianople. This would have the double effect of drawing Bulgaria into the war and of opening up a second line of railway to Nish.

LIEUTENANT-COLONEL HANKEY asked if the General Staff had considered the kind of transport that would be required in Serbia. Would our ordinary military transport be serviceable on the Serbian roads?

LORD KITCHENER said that the Serbian roads were all right.

MR. BALFOUR asked whether the Danube presented a formidable military obstacle.

LORD KITCHENER pointed out that the Austrians had apparently found no difficulty in effecting a passage.

GENERAL CALLWELL was sure that no special difficulty ought to be encountered.

MR. CHURCHILL suggested that special river monitors or gunboats ought to be provided for use on the Danube.

MR. LLOYD GEORGE asked if they could be built in sections and sent to the Danube by rail from Salonica if necessary.

MR. CHURCHILL thought this was quite practicable.

LORD KITCHENER said that the gunboats used in the Omdurman campaign[1] had been built in sections and transported by rail above the

---

[1] It was Beatty who, when a Lieutenant, had commanded several gunboats used during the Nile campaigns of 1896 to 1898. He was promoted Commander in November 1898, at the age of 27, over the heads of 395 senior officers on the Lieutenant's list. In *The River War* (published in 1900), Churchill described Beatty in action on the gunboat *Abu Klea* in 1896, and in the gunboat *Tamai* in 1897 (vol, 1 pp. 267, 336). In the latter action, the other gunboat involved, the *El Teb*, was commanded by Lieutenant Hood, who in 1914, when a Rear-Admiral, became Churchill's Naval Secretary (he was killed at Jutland).

cataracts and then fitted together. These vessels, however, had only been bullet-proof and not shell-proof.

MR. CHURCHILL suggested that a dozen should be built.

MR. LLOYD GEORGE agreed.

MR. BALFOUR said that the conclusion he drew from this and previous discussions was that the Adriatic should be ignored; that the naval bombardment of the Dardanelles should be attempted; and that in any case a force should be landed at Salonica.

MR. LLOYD GEORGE said that he was very anxious to send an army to the Balkans in order to bring all the Balkan States into the war on our side and settle Austria. M. Venizelos had recently offered to come into the war without conditions, provided that Roumania did likewise.

MR. CHURCHILL said that if we sent troops they ought to be our best.

LORD KITCHENER agreed that it was very desirable to send troops to the Balkans in order to determine the attitude of the Balkan States. He was, however, not quite sure that the right moment had arrived. It was very difficult to get British troops out of France, and he was sending his last man to France. He expressed the view that ultimately we might send an army of 500,000 men to Serbia, and if the Dardanelles were open we could maintain it there. He asked what was Admiral Troubridge's mission in Serbia.

MR. CHURCHILL said that already there was a small naval detachment in Serbia with some torpedoes for the purpose of attacking the Austrian gunboats. He was now sending some further naval detachments with 8—4·7-inch guns. Admiral Troubridge was to command the whole force.

MR. LLOYD GEORGE asked how soon an army corps could be sent to Salonica.

LORD KITCHENER said that there was no pressing necessity, as an Austro-German invasion was impossible owing to the snow.

MR. CHURCHILL suggested the despatch of a brigade as an earnest of our intention to send more. They need not go further than Salonica, and would be sent solely on political grounds.

MR. LLOYD GEORGE agreed.

LORD KITCHENER said that if troops were sent at all they ought to be followed up shortly by other troops.

MR. LLOYD GEORGE said we ought to offer an army corps to Serbia at once, naming the probable date of arrival.

MR. CHURCHILL said this would have a very bad effect on the French. 'Nous sommes crucifiés,' was their complaint, and they wanted every available man.

LORD KITCHENER thought that in a month's time the French difficulty would have been cleared up, and the German attack would be over.

GENERAL CALLWELL expressed doubts as to whether the Germans intended to attack.

MR. CHURCHILL said that, in his opinion, the Germans intended to press towards the Balkans. He asked why the two Territorial divisions should now be sent to France. They were to be sent with the sole object of rendering possible the Zeebrugge offensive movement, and not merely to strengthen the line. Now that this project had been abandoned, there was no excuse for deranging Lord Kitchener's military organization by sending these troops out.

LORD KITCHENER agreed. In his opinion, it ought now to be sufficient to send the Canadians, and the 29th Division might be kept back.

(*Conclusion.*)

After some discussion it was agreed to ask the Prime Minister to assemble an immediate meeting of the War Council for the purpose of discussing whether instructions should not be sent to Sir John French informing him that the Zeebrugge offensive operation was not to be undertaken, and that the reinforcements intended to enable him to undertake this operation would not be sent.

Meeting of the War Council: extracts from Secretary's notes
(*Copy, Churchill papers: 2/86*)

Present: H. H. Asquith (in the Chair), Lord Haldane, Lord Crewe, Winston S. Churchill, A. J. Balfour, Lord Fisher, Rear-Admiral Oliver,[1] *David Lloyd George, Sir Edward Grey, Lord Kitchener, Lieutenant-Colonel Hankey (Secretary)*

28 January 1915   10 Downing Street
6.30 pm

GUNBOATS FOR THE DANUBE

MR. CHURCHILL said that the Sub-Committee which had met earlier in the afternoon had been in favour of the construction of some river gunboats, which could be sent out in sections and conveyed by rail to the Danube.

[1] Oliver had in fact been promoted to the rank of Vice-Admiral in October 1914, on becoming Chief of the Naval Staff.

LORD FISHER said that a conference would be held at the Admiralty on the following day to consider the design.

MR. LLOYD GEORGE supported the proposal.

(*Conclusion.*)

The Admiralty to order a dozen river gunboats.

NAVAL ATTACK ON ZEEBRUGGE

MR. CHURCHILL said that the Admiralty had decided to abandon for the present the suggested naval attack on Zeebrugge, and, pending the completion of monitors, to limit our activities to aerial attacks. It might, however, be necessary to reconsider this.

THE DARDANELLES

MR. CHURCHILL said that the Admiralty had decided to push on with the project approved at the meeting held on the 13th January, to make a naval attack on the Dardanelles.

ADMIRAL OLIVER said the first shot would be fired in about a fortnight. Ships were on their way, and the intensity of the attack would increase. He said that the Naval Commander-in-Chief wanted to use Port Mudros, in Lemnos Island, which now belonged to the Greeks. He would have then 16 destroyers, 24 French and 21 British minesweepers, and other small craft. A base was required for these vessels. Hitherto ships had anchored under Tenedos for coaling, or wherever they could find smooth water.

THE PRIME MINISTER asked whether the use of Lemnos would not involve a breach of neutrality.

SIR EDWARD GREY said that the Germans, on behalf of the Turks, had already protested against the use of Mytilene by the Allied fleets. They had been informed of this by the French crew of the French submarine which had been wrecked in the Dardanelles. No doubt they would also protest against the use of Lemnos. He was willing to sound the Greek Government on the subject.

MR. LLOYD GEORGE suggested that a better plan would be to sound them through the British Admiral lent to the Greek Navy (Rear-Admiral Mark Kerr).

MR. CHURCHILL agreed to do this.

Conclusions

1. *Mr. Churchill to visit Sir John French as soon as possible, with the purpose of explaining to him that, in consequence of the postponement of the proposed offensive*

movement from Dixmude to the Dutch frontier, it was desired not to send him, for the present, any reinforcements except the Canadians. The troops would either (a) be kept in this country in readiness to proceed to France, if necessity should arise, or (b) be sent to Sir John French on the distinct understanding that they might be withdrawn in a month. Further, he was to explain to Sir John French the importance of a diversion in the Balkans designed to draw the various Balkan States into the war, and to consult with him as to the best way of inducing the French Government to adopt a similar view.

2. Sir Edward Grey to sound M. Venizelos as to whether he shared the Greek Minister in London's[1] view that 5,000 British troops at Salonica would be of value.

3. The Admiralty to order twelve monitors, to be built in sections, capable of being transported to Salonica and sent thence by rail to Serbia, where they would be fitted together for service on the Danube.

4. The Admiralty to sound the Greek Government through Admiral Mark Kerr as to their willingness to allow Port Mudros in Lemnos Island to be used as a base by the Allied fleets.

Lord Fisher to Sir John Jellicoe

(*Jellicoe Papers*)

29 January 1915   Admiralty

. . . I had fierce rows yesterday with Winston & the Prime Minister. . . . I was 6 hours yesterday with them at War Council and sat till 8 pm! They are a 'flabby' lot! . . .

Lord Esher: diary

(*Esher papers*)

29 January 1915   2 Tilney Street

I saw Fisher this morning; he was in low spirits, and said that for the first time in his life he was a pessimist. At the bottom of this lies the indecision on very material points affecting the Navy. He finds Winston very brilliant, but too changeable; he has a different scheme every day.

Yesterday, the Aulic Council sat till eight o'clock; Fisher got so irritated that he rose at one moment and walked to the window. Lord K. got up and asked him what was wrong, and he said that he would have to resign. Earlier on, the Prime Minister had an interview with Fisher and Winston, and acted as arbitrator upon their differences.

[1] John Gennadius, 1844–1932. Member of the Greek Delegation to the Congress of Berlin, 1878. Minister to London 1910–18. In 1918 he was made Honorary Greek Minister for life. He had married, in 1902, an English wife, and lived in Surrey from 1918 until his death.

Winston has gone abroad to see Sir John, and possibly on to see Joffre.

In the afternoon, Lord K. sent for me, and plunged at once into high strategy. He dislikes more than ever the attack upon Zeebrugge; the more he considers it, the more he feels that even in the event of an attack being successful, which is more than doubtful, it could lead to no result adequate to the loss of life. At the same time, he also dislikes very much now having to send out the number of troops he is supposed to have promised. . . .

Lord Fisher to Winston S. Churchill

(*Churchill papers: 13/56*)

29 January 1915   Admiralty

Dear Winston,

Bigge [Lord Stamfordham] in the Peers Gallery last night asked me when the Falkland Islands Despatches were going to be made public as the King wanted to know. I told him I could not say—and asked him in return if the Germans ever published their despatches and whether we were really at War? He looked glum and spoke no more. It will take the gilt off the gingerbread when the despatches are published—both Dec 8 & Jan 24:—

Dec 8 at 8 A.M. Extreme visibility—smooth water, blue sky & bright sun and united till after dinner! at 4 P.M. thick pea soup & the 'Dresden' lost to sight.

However the 'Kent' will pull us up!

Jan 24. Well! Why did they leave off?

There's a 'halo' round Dec 8 & Jan 24 now!

Answer as you said in your speech—the people dont understand we are at war!

The utmost bounds of the imagination wont allow one to fancy reading German despatches!

What to the lay mind may mean nothing gives away a great deal to the expert! Anyhow I suppose the despatches will be sent to Jellicoe for excision both Dec 8 & Jan 24.

I hope you were successful with Kitchener in getting a Division sent to Lemnos *tomorrow*!

Not a grain of wheat will come from the Black Sea unless there is military occupation of the Dardanelles!

And it will be the wonder of the ages that no troops were sent to cooperate with the Fleet with half a million of soldiers in England!

Yours

F

The War of Lost Opportunities!!!
Why did Antwerp fall?
We propose to order 200 Troop boats on Wednesday besides the oil engine
Barges from the Rhine but I will bring you the model for approval.
(The Horse boats[1] might go at once to Lemnos—as somebody will land at
Gallipoli some time or other!)

David Lloyd George to Winston S. Churchill

(*Churchill papers: 26/2*)

29 January 1915   Treasury Chambers

My dear Winston,

The Sophia telegram (No 14)[2] in last night's gives ominous significance to
the warnings you uttered at yesterday's Committee as to the danger of our
coming too late to the rescue of Servia.

Are we really bound to hand over the ordering of our troops to France as
if we were her vassal. We have already sent her thrice our promise. Strategy
in France must necessarily be hers to declare. Outside we are free after taking
counsel with her to take our own course. French dilatoriness timidity and
selfishness helped to lose Antwerp. It would be criminal folly if we allowed
it to compel us to look on impotently while a catastrophe was being prepared
for the Allies in the Balkans.

Ever yours
D. Lloyd George

Lord Fisher to Winston S. Churchill

(*Fisher papers*)

29 January 1915   Admiralty
SECRET

First Lord—

I have arranged this morning a scheme of gunnery trials for Queen Elizabeth which will expedite her arrival at the Dardanelles and only involving
48 hours stay at Gibraltar. It is hoped she leaves day after tomorrow for

---

[1] These horse boats had already been sent to Alexandria on Fisher's suggestion, to be
ready for any possible military landings against Turkey.

[2] On 29 January Sir Henry Bax-Ironside telegraphed from Sofia to Sir Edward Grey:
'Bulgarian Government have sent Director of Public Debt and a German named Von
Mach, who was for some years in Bulgarian army and has since been correspondent of
"Cologne Gazette", to Berlin to negotiate respecting temporary financial advance. Amount
asked for is 100,000,000 fr.' (*Foreign Office papers: 371/2250*)

Gibraltar—She will probably require a couple of days of Malta so she should arrive Dardanelles about Feb. 14 dependent on gun trials at Portland.[1]

F

H. H. Asquith to Venetia Stanley
(Montagu papers)

30 January 1915   Walmer Castle

. . . I don't think I told you—for it happencd after I wrote on Thursday—that we had a second meeting of the War Council before dinner, and despatched Winston to go & see Sir J. French—in order that both he & Joffre may realise the importance we all attach to being able to send at any rate 2 Divisions to help the Servians, instead of continuing to pour every available man into the North of France. I don't know whether Winston has yet returned, or how he fared with his mission. I suppose I shall hear to-morrow. Curiously enough it was K. who suggested that he should go & pressed it hard.

Winston & Fisher have for the time at any rate patched up their differences, tho' F is still a little uneasy about the Dardanelles. . . .

Lord Fisher to Winston S. Churchill
(Churchill papers: 13/56)

30 January 1915   Admiralty

Dear Winston,

This to reach you on arrival (at whatever hour that may happen) to say I've ordered Sir Arthur May[2] the M.O.G. to get the very best specialist in London to the Caledonian Hotel at Inverness to see Jellicoe who evidently has been maltreated for Piles (*only I dont want to say this publicly*) and has an abscess (so Lady Jellicoe writes me who is with him). They have called in another local man who hopes all will yield to treatment without an immediate operation. Jellicoe's staff ought to have put him to bed instead of his walking about in the wet and damp trying to tinker up the Conqueror (as he is worth 20 Conquerors) till at last he dropped with pain & fatigue, but

---

[1] On January 31 Churchill noted on this letter, 'Good', and returned it to Fisher.

[2] Arthur William May, 1854–1925. Entered Royal Naval Medical Service, 1878. Director-General, Medical Department, Royal Navy, 1913–17. Knighted, 1914. Surgeon-Vice-Admiral, 1914.

he is an indomitable little man as Nelson suffered likewise before him off Toulon! . . .[1]

'Queen Elizabeth' will reach Dardanelles on Feb.14. thanks to Percy Scott.

Tirpitz is fulfilling his threats and his submarines are off Liverpool necessitating further dispersion of Destroyers away from the decisive theatre where they are so vitally essential. But we are the lost 10 Tribes of Israel so we shall finish all right I suppose.

Yours
F

Winston S. Churchill to Lord Kitchener
(*Copy, Churchill papers: 26/2*)

31 January 1915   Admiralty

My dear Kitchener,

Two points require your attention.

1) Transports crossing the Channel often behave in a very careless way. The men sing songs—there is lots of talking in loud tones—lights are often shown on the upper deck—[& the transports frequently go only 6 miles an hour. We find it necessary to arrange to put a naval Captain or acting Captain on board each, in order to ensure the observance of all precautions;][2] & we hope that you will have very strict orders given to ensure silence & secrecy, and in fact all the precautions of a night march in an enemy's country.

2) There is a strong difference of opinion between the C in C Home Fleet and the C in C Devonport[3] & other naval authorities on the one hand, & the military authorities on the other, about the use of search lights at defended ports. As these ports are defended in order to make the warships safe, we think that the naval view ought to prevail. I do not go into the merits here; but the position is that the War Office say that they will not take responsi-

---

[1] In July 1797 Nelson's right arm was shot through by the Spaniards at Tenerife. The amputation was done quickly, badly, and in the dark. He was invalided home, and was in extreme pain for many months. In April 1798, still in pain, he returned to sea, hoisting his flag in the *Vanguard* off Toulon, determined to bring the French fleet to action. In May his ship was dismasted and had to go to Sardinia to be refitted. He searched for the French in the Mediterranean throughout June and July, finding them off Alexandria and defeating them on 1 August 1798 at the battle of the Nile.

[2] In the version of this letter as sent, Churchill deleted the passage in square brackets.

[3] George Le Clerc Egerton, 1852–1940. Entered Navy, 1866. 2nd in Command, Atlantic Fleet, 1906–07. Vice-Admiral, Commander-in-Chief, Cape of Good Hope, 1908–10. Knighted 1910. 2nd Sea Lord, 1911–12. Admiral Commanding Plymouth and Commander-in-Chief, Devonport, 1913–16.

bility for the defence of harbours if Jellicoe's wishes about search lights are met. It does not much matter who takes responsibility so long as the ships are safe; & if our views are deferred to in a matter like this by the War Office, it is clear that the blame for anything going wrong in consequence must rest with us.

I should be very much obliged if you would give these two matters your consideration.

Yours very truly

Winston S. Churchill to Lord Kitchener
(*Churchill papers: 13/46*)

31 January 1915   Admiralty
Secret

My dear Kitchener,

I had several conversations, as desired by the War Council and yourself, with Sir John French during the two days I was at his headquarters. He hopes very much that the arrangements he has made with Joffre will be allowed to go forward. These arrangements comprise Joffre relieving him on the frontage of one corps on the extreme right of the British line, and French relieving Joffre on the frontage of two corps from Wytchaete round the Ypres salient to Dixmude. This achieves the important object of giving the British General control of all troops, including the Belgian army and some French detachments, from a point south of Armentières to the sea. If this arrangement were altered Joffre would be greatly disappointed. It would be useless for Sir John French to address him on the subject; and if it were decided not to send the four divisions as arranged, the matter would have to be settled between the Governments.

When this operation of relieving the two French corps has been completed, Sir John French will have five British corps, strengthened by twenty-four territorial battalions, in the line, and two corps and the cavalry in reserve. With this he would feel secure. He cannot recommend any weakening of this force; nor on strategic grounds does he favour a diversion in South-Eastern Europe. But if the Government wish him to hold two of these four divisions of reserve at their disposal from the middle of March onward, he would do so, and the divisions could be withdrawn if required, provided, of course, that no great emergency, either defensive or offensive, was occurring on his front. I pointed out at this stage that by the 15th March we should be within measurable distance of the reinforcements provided by the new army, and

that therefore the withdrawal of the two divisions would only make it necessary to bridge over a gap of from three to five weeks during which the reserve
would be weakened before they would be replaced. He agreed that this could
be accepted, subject to emergencies. I consider, therefore, as the upshot of
my conversations, that we should be justified in counting on two divisions
being available from the Expeditionary Army from the 15th March on, in
the absence of emergencies, though it would be most necessary to replace
them as soon as possible.

I was very much impressed with the Field-Marshal's great desire to meet
the wishes of the Government, even when he could not share our views.

Yours sincerely
Winston S. Churchill

February 1915

Lieutenant-Colonel Hankey to Winston S. Churchill
(Admiralty papers: 116/3491)

1 February 1915
SECRET

First Lord

On writing up some minutes for the three Meetings of the War Council and its Sub-Committee last Thursday, I find that, apart from your own visit to Sir John French, the following conclusions involving action by the Admiralty or by yourself were agreed to:—

1) *The Press Bureau.* The First Lord to ask for the explanations of the Director of the Press Bureau in regard to the Daily Mail's indiscretion of 28 Jany 1915.[1]

2) *Monitors.* The Admiralty to order twelve river monitors or gunboats to be built in sections, so as to be capable of transport by ship and rail.

3) The Admiralty to ask Admiral Mark Kerr to sound the Greek Government as to their willingness to allow Port Mudros in Lemnos Island to be used as a base by the allied fleets.

I thought it advisable to send you a reminder in case any of these items should have been overlooked.

M. P. A. Hankey

Winston S. Churchill to Sir John French
(Copy, Churchill papers: 26/2)

2 February 1915   Admiralty

My dear French,

I have had the enclosed pile of Balkan telegrams prepared for you to look through. They will show you why a sabre stroke is needed to cut the tangle.

---

[1] At the War Council on 28 January Churchill had drawn attention to an item in the *Daily Mail* which, he said 'ought not to have passed the Press Bureau'. It was a report that the British battle squadron had left its base, having been 'apprised of the movements of the enemy's fleet'. It listed the names of the five battleships of the squadron, and the order in which they had put to sea. Churchill noted on this document: '*Done*'. But it is not clear what was done.

Pray let me have them back after you have looked through them, for I have no other copy.

I am arranging to have Bacon sent over to you almost immediately. The guns can shoot 11,000 yards instead of 9,000 as promised. The iron girder platforms are a complete success. Everything will be ready on the 15th for their despatch. I shall be most interested to know where you put them and I hope I may find an opportunity of watching them practice.

'Dardanelles' goes forward steadily and all the ships are sailing.

I hope you are all right now. I have not mentioned your being laid up to anyone.

Poor Jellicoe has had to have a slight operation and is out of it for 3 weeks. This also is a secret.

Yours always
W

Vice-Admiral Oliver: memorandum[1]
(Copy, Churchill papers: 2/82)

2 February 1915   Admiralty
Most Secret

The forts at the entrance to the Dardanelles are armed with 28 cm. guns, the extreme range of which is believed to be about 12,500 yards. The Allied Fleet on the 2nd November, 1914, did not come under serious fire until within 12,300 yards.

It is not proposed to carry out heavy bombardments from a fleet under way entailing very large expenditure of ammunition.

The method proposed is to anchor a ship, such as 'Queen Elizabeth', at a range which cannot be reached by the guns in the forts, and to place other ships in suitable positions for accurately marking the fall of the shot, and also to use seaplanes for marking.

The firing will only take place when the weather and light are favourable, and will be carried out with the greatest care and deliberation, shot by shot. The object will be to try and obtain a very high proportion of hits to rounds fired.

When each fort in turn at the entrance has been subjected to this slow, deliberate bombardment, and the forts are considered to be out of action, a squadron of older battleships will be sent closer in to draw the fire of the forts.

---

[1] Churchill sent copies of this memorandum to Asquith, Grey, Kitchener and Balfour, with a covering note, dated 2 February, that 'All preparations are moving forward and it is expected that operations can begin on the 15th instant'. (Churchill papers: 26/3)

If the fire is serious the ships will withdraw out of range and the long-range bombardment from ships at anchor will be resumed.

When the ships can approach to within range of the forts without drawing heavy fire the forts will be subjected to fire from the secondary armament at a suitable range for accurate shooting, and all range-finding positions, search-lights, and other accessories will be destroyed.

Mine-sweeping will be undertaken and a swept channel will be buoyed, and one or two old battleships will follow the mine-sweeping vessels to keep down the fire of field guns, machine guns, or infantry in trenches.

A large number of Maxim guns will also be used from small vessels and steam-boats, and the mine-sweeping vessels will be protected from rifle and machine-gun fire by steel plates.

When the entrance has been gained the mine-sweeping will be continued, the seaplanes will be used to find any guns concealed in the hills, and they will be deliberately shelled by the ships, and those which are behind hills will be dealt with by the howitzers which have been provided.

The ships will gradually make their way up the Dardanelles—perhaps a mile a day, perhaps more, perhaps less.

When the ships come to a range at which they can reach Kephez Point they will silence the guns there by the same deliberate plan as was adopted for the entrance forts.

The forts at Chanak and Kilid Bahr and those further up the Dardanelles will be reduced in the same manner, and indirect fire will also be used from ships anchored off Gaba Tepe.

It is expected that the slow, irresistible destruction of the forts by vessels which cannot be reached effectively by their fire will have a great effect on the morale of the garrisons of those forts which have yet to be attacked, and will go far to shake the confidence of the Turks in their German advisers, and it may possibly result in an overthrow of the German rule in Constantinople.

The ships it is proposed to employ are:—

'Queen Elizabeth'	..	..	..	15-inch guns.
'Swiftsure'	..	..	..	10-inch and 7·5-inch guns.
'Triumph'	..	..	..	
'Cornwallis'	..	..	..	
'Irresistible'	..	..	..	
'Ocean'	..	..	..	
'Albion'	..	..	..	12-inch guns.
'Canopus'	..	..	..	
'Vengeance'	..	..	..	
'Majestic'	..	..	..	
'Prince George'	..	..	..	

'Amethyst' .. ..)
'Sapphire' .. .. |
'Dublin' .. .. } Light cruisers.
'Doris' .. ..)
'Blenheim' .. .. Destroyer depôt.
'Swanley' .. .. Destroyer and trawler depôt.
'Soudan' .. .. Hospital ship.
'Ark Royal' .. .. Seaplane ship (6 seaplanes).
16 destroyers.
1 yacht .. ..)
21 trawlers .. .. } for mine-sweeping.

1 'E'-class submarine.
5 'B'-class submarines.

Two battalions of Royal Marines will also be provided for any small landing operations which can be carried out under the fire of the ships' guns, such
as destroying mining stations and fire-observation stations.

The support which would be most useful from the French Marine would
be—

2 battleships, with guns which could be used at a range of about 16,000
yards.
Small cruisers.
Destroyers.
Submarines.
Seaplanes.
Mine-sweeping vessels.

The British force is well provided with older battleships, but is weak as
regards small cruisers, destroyers, and mine-sweeping vessels, and assistance
in this direction will be most valuable.

Sir Edward Grey to Winston S. Churchill
(*Churchill papers: 26/3*)

2 February 1915   Foreign Office

To my lay mind the operation seems to be well planned. I hope however
that these detailed plans will be communicated to as few persons as possible
here outside the Admiralty.

The sooner they can be put in execution the better as some striking offensive is necessary to counteract the effect, that the presence of German troops
on the Balkan frontiers is having in the Balkans.

The Austro-German objective now is to overawe Roumania & Greece, to attract Bulgaria & to steady the Turks by an offensive against Serbia. If we can succeed in forcing the Straits or even creating a scare at Constantinople before this offensive can make headway we shall have done much to discourage if not to paralyze it.[1]

EG

Winston S. Churchill to David Lloyd George
(*Copy, Churchill papers: 13/47*)

3 February 1915   Admiralty
Secret

My dear Chancellor of the Exchequer,

I ask for your covering authority, as desired by you, to the following alterations and additions to the programme of new construction.

1. The two battleships 'Renown' & 'Repulse' already approved by Parliament but not begun are to be converted into battle-cruisers with 6—15″ guns instead of 8 & the greatest possible speed. This involves no financial effect.

2. 2 additional Monitors with the spare 15″ guns & turrets for the 'Repulse' & 'Renown' are being made at a cost (including guns) of £450,000 each (ready in April).

3. 2 'Light' cruisers of the greatest speed carrying 4—15″ guns apiece are to be built as explained by me to the War Council. The cost of these ships will be about £1,200,000 apiece as far as can now be ascertained.

Secrecy is important & I suggest that Treasury authority shd be given by your personal acknowledgement of this note, all financial & business details being settled according to rule in the Admiralty.

Yours vy sincerely

Winston S. Churchill: memorandum
(*Churchill papers: 13/54*)

3 February 1915   Admiralty

Every opportunity should be taken of impressing on the officers and men that the success of naval operations and their own safety from avoidable risks depends on secrecy, silence, and suddenness. The less said to outsiders about

[1] On 3 February Kitchener noted after Grey's remarks: 'I agree with above.'

naval matters, by speech or letter, even after a fight, the better. Many of
the most harmful disclosures are made innocently and unwittingly. Officers
and men should also be cautioned that they are not in any circumstances to
write letters which have the slightest reference to naval operations, without
submitting them to the Censor beforehand. The surreptitious conveyance of
uncensored letters for postage on shore by persons having access to H.M.
ships is forbidden.

It is better if necessary to leave some officers and men on shore than to
advertise the departure of H.M. ships. When instructions or information
about putting to sea are received from their Lordships by flag officers or
others in separate commands, it is usually not necessary for them to take any
immediate action other than that of raising steam swiftly and unostenta-
tiously. It should not be suggested to the men that any special operation is
expected. The ordinary routine should be varied as little as possible compatible with military needs. When it is necessary to explain matters to Captains while in harbour, this should always if possible be done verbally or by
letter, and not by signal. On the other hand, from time to time when no
operation is in contemplation, a false impression may be created at thickly
populated places like the Forth, by firing a gun, hoisting the Blue Peter,
raising steam, etc. Such measures tend to mystify and mislead the enemy,
baffle his spy organization, and tend to destroy his confidence in it.

Captain Richmond to Rear-Admiral Leveson
(*Copy, Richmond papers*)

3 February 1915   Admiralty

... We should concentrate our attention on crushing the Turkish naval
force in order to give Russia complete command in the Black Sea: so that she
can carry her troops in safety from Odessa, Sevastopol, Novorosiisk by sea to
Batoum or Trebizond.

Subsidiary, but connected with this, we require to liberate the trade in the
Black Sea so that Russian grain can reach England & France.

Both of these require the forcing of the Dardanelles in order to destroy the
Turkish fleet & obtain a safe passage: besides cutting off European Turkey
from Asiatic Turkey & preventing further supplies reaching the Turkish
army in Asia Minor &c.

Therefore urge the Greeks to assist us at once in the Dardanelles operations
with any army, which they should land on the northern side of Gallipoli
peninsula while our fleet is occupying the forts on the Dardanelles side.

H. H. Asquith to Venetia Stanley
(*Montagu papers*)

3 February 1915   10 Downing Street

... The Turks have been trying to throw a bridge across the Suez Canal & in that ingenuous fashion to find a way into Egypt. The poor things & their would-be bridge were blown into smithereens, and they have retired into the desert.

Winston S. Churchill to Rear-Admiral Kerr: telegram
(*Copy, Admiralty papers: 137/96*)

3 February 1915   Admiralty

Will you discreetly and informally sound Greek Government as to their willingness to allow Port Mudros in Lemnos to be used as a base by allied fleets. As an alternative you might mention Skyros Island which is understood to be sparsely inhabited by peasants.

H. H. Asquith to George V
(*Royal Archives*)

3 February 1915   10 Downing Street

Mr Asquith with his humble duty to Your Majesty has the honour to report that the Cabinet met yesterday.

Lord Kitchener & Mr Churchill communicated information as to the German air-raid of the previous night. The balance of evidence inclines to the conclusion that the invaders were air-ships & not aeroplanes; the damage to life & property was very slight.

The question of the contracts with the Marconi Company for the erection of Imperial wireless stations was again discussed. It was agreed that for the moment strategic must be regarded as overriding commercial considerations. The new contract with the Admiralty provides for the most important strategic requirements, but as the Company insist that they are entitled to whatever advantages they have under the old contract with the Post Office, & will claim damages if it is repudiated, it was resolved not to proceed with the proposed determination of the latter.

Considerable discussion took place on the possible expediency of offering Cyprus to Greece, as an inducement to her to join the allies. Lord Kitchener thinks that under present & probable conditions Cyprus has some strategic value.

H. H. Asquith to Venetia Stanley
(Montagu papers)

4 February 1915   H of C

. . . I did not know until your letter to-day[1] that you liked Winston *quite* so much as all that . . . But I quite agree with what you say as to the difficulty of having a 'nice' talk with him. He never gets fairly alongside the person he is talking to, because he is always so much more interested in himself and his own preoccupations & his own topics than in anything his neighbour has to contribute, that his conversation (unless he is made to succumb either to superior authority or to well-directed chaff) is apt to degenerate into a mono-logue. It is the same to a certain extent in the Cabinet. And to do him justice I don't think it makes any difference to him whether his interlocutor is the dreariest dry as dust (like our friend Telemachus Shuttleworth[2]) or the most charming of women. . . .

Rear-Admiral Kerr to Admiralty: telegram
(Admiralty papers: 137/96)

4 February 1915   Athens

In view of reports published lately that allied submarines have been using Mitylene as a base I do not think the present time propitious for asking Greek Government for further concessions in Lemnos and it may have effect of taking away secret understanding now in force allowing British destroyers use of Mudros in Lemnos.

Sir Francis Elliot to Sir Edward Grey: telegram
(Admiralty papers: 137/96)

4 February 1915   Athens

I concur German and Turkish Ministers[3] make frequent representations respecting our use of Mitylene to which Greek Government return evasive replies. Moreover it seems inexpedient to call attention too openly to incon-sistency of our conduct with protest against the use of French ports by Russian fleet during the Russo-Japanese war.

[1] Like the majority of Venetia Stanley's letters to Asquith, this one does not appear to have survived.

[2] Ughtred James Kay-Shuttleworth, 1844–1939. Liberal MP, 1869–80; 1885–1902. Chancellor of the Duchy of Lancaster, 1886. Created Baron Shuttleworth, 1902. Lord-Lieutenant of Lancashire, 1908–28.

[3] The German Minister to Athens (1912–15) was Count von Quadt von Wykradt und Isny. The Turkish Minister (1914–15) was Ghalib Kemaly Bey.

Winston S. Churchill to Eleutherios Venizelos: telegram

(*Copy, Churchill papers: 28/153*)

5 February 1915   Admiralty
Personal & Secret

We contemplate an important operation against the Dardanelles to be undertaken soon. A British fleet of a dozen battleships and numerous minor vessels is now assembling in the Mediterranean & will be aided by a French squadron. Secrecy is essential. We require the temporary use of a harbour near the 'Dlles' where our small craft and auxiliaries can shelter. Best of all wd be Lemnos, failing that Mitylene. We ask you to assist us by allowing us to use this temporary base. If a formal consent is inconvenient in existing circes. any procedure wh commends itself to you will be carefully followed by us. I shd not have troubled Y.E. on such a matter but for its imminent & vital consequence.

Admiralty to Vice-Admiral Carden

(*Copy, Churchill papers: 2/82*)

5 February 1915   Admiralty

DARDANELLES OPERATION ORDERS

The British Force will consist of the following ships:—

QUEEN ELIZABETH	..	.. .. 15-inch guns.
INFLEXIBLE	..	.. .. 12-inch guns.
SWIFTSURE	..	.. .. 10-inch and 7·5-inch guns.
TRIUMPH	..	.. „ „
CORNWALLIS		} 12-inch—40 calibre guns.
IRRESISTIBLE		
OCEAN		} 12-inch—35 calibre guns.
ALBION		
CANOPUS		} 12-inch—35 calibre guns.
VENGEANCE		
MAJESTIC		⎱ 12-inch—35 calibre guns.
PRINCE GEORGE		⎰ 6 inch howitzers.
DORIS.		
AMETHYST.		
SAPPHIRE.		
DUBLIN.		
BLENHEIM		} Destroyer depôts.
SWANLEY		

ARK ROYAL .. .. .. Seaplane ship.

8 Destroyers (BEAGLE Class).
8 ,, (RIVER Class). Including Wear.
1 Yacht (in charge of trawlers).
21 Mine-sweeping trawlers.
6 submarines, viz.: AE. 2 and 2 B. Class from Gibraltar, B. 9,
    B. 10, B. 11.

'Queen Elizabeth' has been detailed on account of her long range 15-inch guns.

It is particularly important that her guns should not be unduly worn nor a large quantity of her valuable ammunition expended.

She should not be risked in positions which have not been thoroughly swept free from mines.

With seamanlike precautions it is quite possible to anchor vessels in any depths which obtain in or about the Dardanelles. Given fine weather and good conditions of visibility, and the ship anchored in view of but out of range from the fort, she is to attack; the destruction of the fort will be entailed if from five to ten of 'Queen Elizabeth's' heavy shell can be dropped in it.

Very careful arrangements will be required to mark the fall of shot by means of anchored marking ships and seaplanes.

To reduce the expenditure of ammunition and wear of the 15-inch guns and obtain the greatest percentage of hits to rounds fired, salvoes should not be fired, and full charges should not be used whenever the range of the fort's guns permits the ships to be anchored within a distance which permits of the use of reduced charges.

The problem of destroying a fort from a ship at a fixed range, at which she cannot be hit, is a different one from that of ships under way engaging each other, because time does not enter into the calculation, and the range is a fixed quantity.

If, say, five gun salvoes are fired from 'Queen Elizabeth' it is hardly possible that more than one hit per salvo will be made (after straddle is obtained) owing to the guns not shooting together at long range, due to the spread in elevation. Four rounds will be wasted for every hit made in addition to the rounds used before the straddle is obtained. The shell-smoke and dust from the misses will render marking difficult, and more time will be required for the smoke to clear and the target to become visible.

If a single gun is used, hitting should be established in four or five rounds, and a very high percentage of the subsequent rounds should be hits. Personal and other errors will also be reduced proportionately.

The 38-centim. howitzers which destroyed the Antwerp forts by indirect fire, used about five rounds to establish hitting and five further rounds to destroy the fort. It is to be expected that 'Queen Elizabeth', using direct fire at older forts, will equal this performance at a fixed range if accurate marking is ensured and the greatest care and deliberation is used.

When the same conditions apply similar methods should be followed in using the fire of the 12-inch guns in other vessels. Their ammunition is limited, though not to the same extent, and wasteful expenditure of ammunition may result in the operations having to be abandoned before a successful conclusion is arrived at.

In the case of indirect fire having to be used from ships, it is recognised that the expenditure will be considerable. For indirect fire the older ships should be preferred, if possible, to the 'Queen Elizabeth'.

A base should be seized and garrisoned. Any convenient Turkish island should be selected.

The entrance forts at Cape Helles and Kum Kale should be deliberately bombarded at long range from an anchored vessel or vessels. After this, some of the older battleships should approach nearer to draw the fire of the forts and silence any remaining guns. If the fire is found to be still considerable, they should withdraw and the fort should be subjected to further deliberate long-range fire from anchored ships.

Sweeping to approach the entrance will then be necessary, and it is to be expected that the sweeping vessels will be fired at by guns placed in other positions than the forts. These will require to be dealt with by vessels covering the sweeping vessels, and as probably no very large guns will be in other positions than the forts, 6-inch and 7·5-inch guns should be sufficient to deal with them.

As the sweeping vessels close the entrance, it is to be expected that they will come under machine-gun and infantry fire, and air reconnaissance will be advisable to locate the trenches.

The trenches and the positions of the torpedo-tubes will require to be well searched with fire.

Should it not be possible to locate the torpedo-tubes and destroy them by gun-fire, it may be necessary to land men, if the enemy's infantry can be kept at a sufficient distance by shell and machine-gun-fire.

If there is any doubt as to the torpedo-tubes being destroyed, it may be possible to take ships past them by securing colliers or other merchant-vessels alongside.

Vessels covering the mine sweepers will be exposed to attack by drifting mines, especially when at anchor. Torpedo-nets will be some protection against pairs of mines, connected by lines, coming alongside when the connecting rope takes across the stem.

It may be advisable to prepare buoys to be laid ahead of vessels anchoring in the Dardanelles to catch drifting mines, and also to make use of fishing-nets between buoys to intercept mines. Concrete blocks could be used as moorings for the buoys.

Drift nets have been found efficacious in the North Sea as a means of clearing away moored mines. They are allowed to drift with the tide, and foul the mines and break them adrift.

Nets might be laid at night by shallow draught vessels or picket-boats above the minefields to drift down with the current.

There may be considerable difficulty in dealing with observation mines, owing to the depth at which they may be moored.

The cables will probably have to be crept for with explosive grapnels, but it may be possible also to sweep with mine-sweeping vessels to a sufficient depth.

When the defences at the entrance are put out of action the operations will probably develop into a slow methodical progress of perhaps a mile a day, silencing fire of concealed guns and keeping down fire from trenches or machine-gun pits which will inconvenience the mine sweepers.

It is not expected or desired that the operations should be hurried to the extent of taking large risks and courting heavy losses. The slow relentless creeping forward of the attacking force mile after mile will tend to shake the moral of the garrisons of the forts at Kephez Point, Chanak, and Kilid Bahr, and will have an effect on Constantinople.

The forts at Chanak and Kilid Bahr appear to be open to bombardment by long range direct fire from ships anchored on the European and Asiatic shores respectively, but the difficulty of ensuring accurate marking will be considerable.

Indirect fire from an anchorage off Gaba Tepe should be effective against the works on the Asiatic side, but it would appear difficult to ensure its effect against the works at Kilid Bahr. This will be apparent if the trajectory curve is plotted in relation to a vertical section of the intervening hills. But there is no reason it should not be tried, and anchorage positions may be found where the trajectory curves will have the best clearance over the intervening ridges.

The possibility of increasing the effective range of the older ships by listing them should be borne in mind. This was practised at Tsing-tau recently.[1]

[1] Three months earlier, on 7 November 1914, the German port of Kiaochow (Tsing-tau) on the China coast had been occupied by British and Japanese troops after a two-month siege. It had a population of 84,000 Chinese, 1,700 German civilians, and about 2,000 German soldiers.

H.M.S. 'Triumph' took part in the reduction of Tsing-tau, and the experience gained by her captain[1] and officers should be made use of.

Two battalions of Royal Marines are being sent out to Malta under Brigadier-General Trotman.[2] Their transports should be retained so that they can at any time be moved to the Dardanelles. They will be of service as garrison for the base or for any small landing operation of a temporary nature in circumstances where they can be efficiently protected by the guns of the fleet against superior Turkish forces.

They should not be landed against superior forces or entrenched positions in circumstances where they cannot be efficiently supported by the ships' guns without first obtaining Admiralty sanction.

Twenty additional maxim guns are being sent with the Royal Marine Force, either for use when landed or for use in small craft, to keep down rifle fire.

So far as can be ascertained no submarines have as yet been put together at Constantinople, but when operations against the Dardanelles commence it is to be expected that Germany will endeavour to either send submarines to the Mediterranean or to influence the Austrians to send them out of the Adriatic.

As a measure of precaution submarine indicator nets are being sent out. They can be either moored or used as drift nets, and will betray the presence of a submarine to the boats watching the nets, and possibly permit of explosive charges being used to destroy her.

An arrangement is being made to establish agents in the Greek islands to watch for and report submarines or vessels supplying them, and prevent them establishing secret bases.

A number of merchant vessels have been altered to represent 'Dreadnought' battleships and cruisers, and are undistinguishable from them at 3 or 4 miles' distance.

A squadron of these vessels will be sent out to Tenedos Islands. They should be used with due precaution, to prevent their character being discovered, and should be shown as part of the Fleet off the entrance to the Dardanelles, as if

---

[1] Maurice Swynfen Fitz-Maurice, 1870–1927. Assistant Director, Intelligence Division, Admiralty War Staff, 1912–14. Captain, HMS *Triumph*, 1914–15. Principal Naval Transport Officer, Dardanelles and Salonika, 1915–16. Chief of Staff, Eastern Mediterranean, 1916–17. Senior Naval Officer, Coast of Palestine, 1918. Director of Naval Intelligence, 1921–4. Commander-in-Chief, African Station, 1924–7. Knighted, 1925. Vice-Admiral, 1926.

[2] Charles Newsham Trotman, 1864–1929. Lieutenant, Royal Marine Light Infantry, 1882. Brigadier-General, 1914. Commanded Royal Marine Brigade, Royal Naval Division, 1915, at Gallipoli and Salonika. Commanded 190th Infantry Brigade in France, 1916. Commanded Portsmouth Division, Royal Marine Light Infantry, 1917–19. Knighted, 1921. General, 1923.

held in reserve. They may mislead the Germans as to the margin of British strength in Home Waters.

The mine-sweeping trawlers will require a depôt ship for provisions, pay, and medical attendance, and as 'Blenheim' will suffice for the destroyers, the 'Swanley', or one of the supply ships, should be used for them, unless it is preferred to attach them to the battleships as tenders.

The bombardment of the forts at the entrance need not be delayed until the arrival of all the ships and can be commenced as ships become available.

The French Minister of Marine has been requested to provide two battle-ships, with as long-range guns as possible, and as many small cruisers, des-troyers, sea-planes, and submarines as possible, as the proportion of small ships to large ships in the British Fleet is not as large as is thought desirable.

Admiralty announcement[1]

(Churchill papers: 13/47)

6 February 1915   Admiralty

Germany has declared that the English Channel, the North and West coasts of France, and the waters round the British Isles, are a 'war area', and has announced her intention of torpedoing at sight without regard to the safety of the crew any merchant vessel under any flag found there. As it is not in the power of the German Admiralty to maintain any surface craft in these waters, this attack can only be delivered by submarine agency. The law and custom of nations in regard to attacks on commerce have always presumed that the first duty of the captor of a merchant vessel is to bring it before a Prize Court, where it may be tried and condemned or released, and the sinking of prizes is in itself a questionable act, to be resorted to only in extra-ordinary circumstances and after provision has been made for the safety of all the crew or passengers (if there are passengers on board). The responsibil-ity for discriminating between neutral and enemy vessels, and between neutral and enemy cargo, obviously rests with the attacking ship, whose duty it is to verify the status and character of the vessel and to preserve its papers before sinking or even capturing it. So also is the humane duty of providing for the safety of the crews of merchant vessels, whether neutral or enemy, an obligation upon every belligerent. It is upon this basis that all previous discussions of the law for regulating warfare at sea have proceeded.

A submarine is, however, by her nature incapable of fulfilling any of these obligations. She enjoys no local command of the waters in which she operates.

[1] This announcement was drafted by Churchill after consultations with three Cabinet colleagues: McKenna, Runciman and Simon. It was then approved by Grey.

She has no prize courts to which she can take her captures. She has no prize crew which she can put on board a prize. She has no effective means of discriminating between a neutral and an enemy vessel. She is unable to receive on board for safety the crew of the vessel she sinks. Her methods of warfare are therefore entirely outside the scope of any of the international instruments regulating operations against commerce in time of war.

For these reasons the British Government cannot recognize attacks by submarines on merchant ships as a legitimate means of warfare.

It is evident that since Germany has openly freed herself from the restrictions not only of law and custom at sea, but of common humanity, special measures willl be required on the part of her opponents, and these may in some respects involve a departure from previous practice.

Directions have therefore been given to the British fleets and squadrons to detain and take into port all ships carrying goods of presumed enemy destination, ownership, or origin. It is not intended to confiscate such vessels or cargoes unless the Prize Court condemns them on grounds independent of this announcement, but Great Britain will reserve the right to requisition these vessels and cargoes.

H. H. Asquith to Venetia Stanley

(*Montagu papers*)

6 February 1915   Walmer Castle

. . . We talked (you & I) no politics yesterday, except personal things, such as Winston for India. He (W) has sent me to-day his proposed counter-blast to the truly absurd German 'blockade' of our seas & coasts. In effect it comes to this—that we shall seize and detain all ships containing cargo of a useful kind (particularly food) going to Germany, or presumed—wherever ostensibly going—to have a German destination. I am rather disposed to confine it in the first instance to food. We shall get into the devil's own row with America if we seize all the cotton shipped from the Southern States directly or indirectly to Germany. . . .

Winston S. Churchill to Sir Edward Grey

(*Grey papers*)

6 February 1915   Admiralty

My dear Grey,

We cannot really undertake to allow American journalists to photograph 'Tiger' and 'New Zealand' in order to correct German lies. It would be quite ineffective as the Germans would say that these photographs had been taken before the action and the correspondent had been bribed. And every time they asserted a ship had been sunk we should be invited to repeat the process and charged with concealment if we refused. What does it matter what they think or say? We have got them 'down' at sea and everyone knows it all over the world.

The more I see of war the more I realize that when you are winning, explanations are unnecessary, and when you are losing they are futile.

Admiral Beatty's despatches will be published in due course and ought to be our last & only word upon this subject.

Our information about damage to 'Derfflinger' and 'Seidlitz' and their casualties is certainly correct.

Yours ever
W

Sir Henry Bax-Ironside[1] to Sir Edward Grey: telegram

(*Copy, Churchill papers: 26/4*)

6 February 1915   Sofia

German and Austrian policy now is to crush Serbia as soon as possible and to bring their troops to Serbian Bulgarian frontier which is only some twenty miles from Widin. Bulgaria would then be faced with three alternatives. First to allow passively passage of our enemies' troops into Turkish territory, secondly to oppose them and thirdly to join with them. Temptation to adopt latter course will be very strong and it could be done indirectly by occupying Macedonia.

It would seem more than ever desirable to render Serbia effectual support.

Winston S. Churchill to Vice-Admiral Carden: telegram

(*Copy, Churchill papers: 2/88*)

6 February 1915   Admiralty

Personal and Secret. I propose to send out as your Chief of Staff Commodore Keyes. Let me know by telegram whether this suits you.[2]

[1] Henry George Outram Bax-Ironside, 1859–1929. Entered Diplomatic Service, 1883. Minister at Sofia, 1910–15. Knighted, 1911.

[2] Carden accepted Keyes, who served as Chief of Staff at the Dardanelles from February 1915 to January 1916. In October 1915 Keyes returned to London to put to the Admiralty his plan for a renewed attack by ships alone, but it was not approved by A. J. Balfour, then First Lord.

2. You should keep me closely informed daily of progress of operations. Do not hesitate to send full telegraphic reports, and inform me of all your difficulties.

3. Is everything progressing satisfactorily, and are all your wants being supplied? I attach great importance to fire being opened punctually on the 15th, by which time 'Queen Elizabeth' should have arrived.

Sir Francis Elliot to Sir Edward Grey: telegram
(Grey papers)

6 February 1915   Athens
Private & Secret

Owing to attitude of Bulgaria and Roumania, Monsieur Venizelos does not wish to be drawn into war.

He thinks that if Greece went to war without Roumania, there would be less chance of the latter coming in.

He would be prepared to withdraw Greek ships and troops from Lemnos on some pretext and, when it was occupied by His Majesty's ships, to send a formal protest for the sake of appearances.

His Majesty's Government might declare that they occupied Lemnos since the Turks regarded it as theirs: if they protested it would be a recognition of annexation.

But he feels that it would be disloyal and improper for him to consent to any such arrangement without consulting the King,[1] whose approval he is confident of obtaining.

Sir Edward Grey to Sir Francis Elliot
(Copy, Grey papers)

7 February 1915   Foreign Office

Procedure proposed by Mr Venizelos wd be acceptable, except that it wd not do for Greece to make even a formal protest against use by Br ships of harbour at Lemnos.

If Gk Govt addressed an enquiry to HMG they wd be ready to evacuate harbour on being assured that Turkish Govt had formally recognized the

---

[1] Constantine, 1868–1923. Became King of Greece in 1913, when he was created a Field-Marshal in the German Army. Vetoed Greek co-operation in the Dardanelles campaign, 1915. Refused to help the Allied Army at Salonika, 1916–17. Forced to leave Greece by the Allies, 1917. In exile, 1917–20. Returned as King, 1920. Abdicated after a military revolt, 1922.

island as belonging to Greece, but wd consider themselves entitled to make use of harbour as long as Turkey claimed it, & while they were at war with Turkey. HMG wd agree not to claim any rights in Lemnos after the war, as they have already been a party to decision of Powers not yet accepted by Turkey that the Island shd be ceded by Turkey to Greece. British use of the island will be brief, & only for the purpose of specific operation; but use is desired as soon as possible, as action is imminent. M. Venizelos can consult the King as he desires, but infn as to impending attack upon Dlles must be kept vy secret.

Vice-Admiral Carden to Winston S. Churchill: telegram
(Copy, Admiralty papers: 137/96)

7 February 1915   H.M.S. Inflexible
Secret and Personal

Everything progressing well to make beginning on February 15th.

H. H. Asquith to Venetia Stanley
(Montagu papers)

7 February 1915   Walmer Castle

. . . I have talked a lot of shop with Haldane about Serbia, Bulgaria &c. His idea of the most effective stroke that cd. be put in for Serbia is that an Entente force—say 1 Russian Corps 1 French Divn & 1 English Divn should promptly appear on the scene. The Bulgarians will never fight against the Russians, and the Roumanians, who are for the moment in a funk & very much 'off colour' could hardly fail to be drawn in. There is a good deal to be said for this. No real fighting can begin in Serbia until well on in March when the spring has set in. . . .

Sir George Buchanan to Sir Edward Grey: telegram
(Copy, Churchill papers: 26/4)

7 February 1915   Petrograd

. . . His Excellency [Sazanov] said he had just received a telegram from Headquarters stating that Grand Duke could not divert any troops beyond a regiment of Cossacks for service in Balkans. To send a small detachment would be to expose it to almost certain risk of reverse and he required all the men he could get for service in the main theatre of war. His Imperial Highness believed that Austrians and Germans were concentrating all their efforts against Russians in Galicia and that they could not at present undertake anything very serious against Serbia.

Minister for Foreign Affairs then raised question whether we ought not after all to make a definite offer of territorial compensation to Bulgaria. Outlook at Sofia was at present so bad that it could hardly be made worse and he personally was in favour of making final effort to save the situation. Long discussion followed in which the French Ambassador[1] expressed himself unfavourably to our taking any further action at Sofia. I said that I personally agreed with Minister for Foreign Affairs and thought any offer which we might make to Bulgaria ought to be accompanied by serious warning as to consequences of throwing in her lot with our enemies.

Finally Minister for Foreign Affairs said that he would think the matter over and let us know his decision to-morrow.

Winston S. Churchill to H. H. Asquith

(*Copy, Churchill papers: 13/47*)

7 February 1915   Admiralty

My dear Prime Minister,

More than three weeks ago you told me of the vital importance of Servia. Since then nothing has been done, & nothing of the slightest reality is being done. Time is passing. You may not yet feel the impact of the projectile. But it has already left the gun & is travelling along its road towards you. Three weeks hence you, Kitchener, Grey will all be facing a disastrous situation in the Balkans: & as at Antwerp it will be beyond yr power to retrieve it.

Surely in your position you cannot be content to sit as a judge pronouncing on events after they have taken place.[2]

Unless we are prepared to run a risk & play a stake the Balkan situation is finished fatally for us.

With regard to your letter about the 'Audacious': I arranged some time ago

---

[1] Maurice Georges Paleologue, 1859–1944. Entered French Diplomatic Service, 1883. Minister in Sofia, 1909–12. Director of Political and Commercial Affairs, French Foreign Office, 1912–14. Ambassador at St Petersburg, 1914–17. Secretary-General, Ministry of Foreign Affairs, for a few months in 1920.

[2] Churchill deleted this sentence before sending the letter to Asquith.

not to publish any more Navy Lists during the war.[1] I don't know who studies them except the German Admiralty and the Archbishop of Canterbury.[2]

Yours always
W

Lord Fisher to Winston S. Churchill

(*Churchill papers: 13/56*)

7 February 1915   Admiralty
Early

Dear Winston,

I am reading the 'proof' of Sturdee's fight. I never in my life read anything so astounding as follows with his enemy in sight and lovely weather so evanescent and rare off Cape Horn!

'I determined not to press the action at once and accordingly at 11.32 A.M.' (having sighted the enemy at 8.20 A.M.!!!!) 'made the signal "Ship's Company have time for the next meal" ' I hope he wont do this in the Latitude of Heligoland! The King told me he said to Sturdee 'Dont you realise why the Admiralty kept on telegraphing to you to ask your reasons for not sending a ship immediately at close of action to Puntas Arenas? The "Dresden" was able to tell the German Admiralty you only had about 20 rounds of ammunition left and if the German Battle Cruisers had been sent they could have finished you off' and besides without the Dresden no one knew that the 'Invincible' & 'Inflexible' were there?

Sturdee replied, 'that after such an action & getting 4 out of 5—it all escaped him.'

When Hardy told Nelson that 15 ships had struck their colours at Trafalgar he said 'That wont do—we want the 20'! *and he got them before he died!*

BUT WHO TOLD THE KING OF OUR REPEATED TELEGRAMS TO STURDEE?[3]

I've always told you we have a big spy somewhere in Admiralty!

Yours
F

---

[1] On 6 February Asquith had written to Churchill to ask him to remove the entry for the *Audacious*—sunk in October 1914—from the Navy List. 'I thought it had been allowed to drop out,' he wrote from Walmer Castle, 'but the Archbishop . . . reports that it is causing the greatest disquietude to many of our best friends in America, who do not know what to . say when they meet the enemy in the gate.' (*Churchill papers: 13/47*)

[2] Randall Thomas Davidson, 1848–1930. Dean of Windsor, and Domestic Chaplain to Queen Victoria, 1883–91. Bishop of Rochester, 1891–95. Bishop of Winchester, 1895–1903. Archbishop of Canterbury, 1903–28.

[3] The King's information came from Sir Francis Hopwood (see also pp. 175–6).

Page 7 of Sturdee.

'The weather changed after 4 P.M. and the visibility much reduced: further the sky was overcast & cloudy thus assisting the Dresden to get away unobserved!'

If Sturdee had begun at 8.20 A.M. when 'the visibility was at its maximum & the sea was calm, with a bright sun, a clear blue sky and a light cold breeze from the North West' *See page 4.* instead of waiting till afternoon, we should have had the Dresden! '*We suffer fools gladly*'! *What will the Germans make of our Admirals when they read Sturdee's Report and Beatty's Report!* . . .

Sir John Maxwell to Lord Kitchener: telegram
(Copy, Crewe papers)

7 February 1915   Egypt

Numbers of Anatolian Turks of good quality well clothed, fed and equipped are deserting. All say large numbers wish to desert from fourth Army Corps and few wish to fight English or invade Egypt. They state officers are bad and do not look after men, and also that the intention is to retire to Bir Saba, reorganise and come on again, but they do not think the men will follow.[1]

H. H. Asquith to Venetia Stanley
(Montagu papers)

8 February 1915   House of Commons

. . . I had rather an interesting luncheon at Edward Grey's: Delcassé,[2] Cambon, Kitchener & Winston. Winston was very eloquent in the worst French you or anyone has ever heard: s'ils savent que nous sommes gens qu'ils peuvent conter sur' ('count on') was one of his flowers of speech. We were all agreed that (1) the Serbian case is urgent (2) we must promise to send them 2 divisions—1 English 1 French—as soon as may be to Salonica, & *force in* the Greeks & Roumanians (3) we must try our damnedest to get the Russians to join if possible with a corps, not of their good troops, but drawn from the vast reservoir they can't at present get to the front or use against Germany & Austria. Ll. George thinks he has got Sir J. French's assent to this; but I have told K to send for him & he is coming over to-night on one of Winston's Destroyers. . . .

[1] This telegram, with its implications about the poor morale of the Turksih troops on the Sinai front, was circulated by Kitchener to members of the War Council before their meeting of 9 February.

[2] Théophile Delcassé, 1852–1923. French Minister of Foreign Affairs, 1898–1908 and 1914–19. Principal French architect of the Anglo-French *Entente* of 1904.

W.C.3—KK

George V to Winston S. Churchill
(*Churchill papers: 13/47*)

8 February 1915   Buckingham Palace

My dear Churchill

Your mind can be entirely at rest. I have not mentioned our conversation of this evening to a soul & I quite realise the extreme importance of secrecy in regard to the operation in Mediterranean. Any information you give me of a confidential nature is quite safe with me. The only persons I should ever speak to on these subjects are the 1st Sea Lord & sometimes Stamfordham who is absolutely trustworthy.

I was much interested by all you told me this evening & I only hope that our various schemes for overcoming the enemy may prove successful.

Believe me very sincerely yrs
George R

H. H. Asquith to Venetia Stanley
(*Montagu papers*)

9 February 1915   10 Downing Street
3.00 pm

. . . At 5 we have a War Council at No 10, wh. Sir J. French has come over to attend. The main question of course will be how soon & in what form we are able to come to the aid of Serbia, & whether & how far the French & Russians will join in. French will no doubt kick even at a single Division being abstracted from his forces, but he must be made to acquiesce in this. The two danger points at this moment are Serbia, & Mesopotamia, where we have a rather weak Indian force at the confluence of the Tiger & Euphrates, threatened by what is reported to be a heavy Turkish advance. Our men must be reinforced promptly from India & possibly from Egypt, whence the Turks have for the moment retreated baffled & broken.

I can't help feeling that the whole situation in the Near East may be vitally transformed, if the bombardment of the Dardanelles by our ships next week (*Secret*) goes well. It is a great experiment. . . .

I have thought a good deal of what you said about Winston & India. He has never hinted at anything of the kind, & of course it couldn't come off unless Hardinge's[1] term was extended to well over the finish of the War. I

---

[1] Charles Hardinge, 1858–1944. Entered Foreign Office, 1880. Knighted, 1904. Ambassador at Petrograd, 1904–6. Permanent Under-Secretary of State for Foreign Affairs, 1906–10. Created Baron Hardinge of Penshurst, 1910. Viceroy of India, 1910–16. Reappointed Permanent Under-Secretary of State for Foreign Affairs, 1916–20. Ambassador to Paris, 1920–3.

gather that you are rather in favour of it. It would, of course, for the time close down his political chances here, and no one ever comes back from India into English politics without a considerable handicap. On the other hand, it is not easy to see what W's career is going to be here: he is to some extent blanketed by E. Grey & Ll. George, & has no personal following; he is always hankering after coalitions and odd re-groupings, mainly designed (as one thinks) to bring in F. E. Smith & perhaps the Duke of Marlborough. I think his future one of the most puzzling personal enigmas in politics—don't you?

. . . The only exciting thing in prospect (after seeing you on Friday) is what will happen in the Dardanelles next week. This as I said is supposed to be a secret, and indeed I believe it isn't known to some members of the Cabinet, tho' Violet heard Louis Mallet talking about it most indiscreetly at dinner one night. If it is successful, it will smash up the Turks, and, incidentally, let through all the Russian wheat wh. is now locked up & so lower the price of bread. But it is full of uncertainties. . . .

H. H. Asquith to Venetia Stanley
(*Montagu papers*)

9 February 1915   10 Downing Street
Midnight

. . . We had a longish War Council, which lasted from 5 to 7. French was there, as always optimist, quite convinced that the Germans couldn't even break through in France or Flanders, certain that the Russians were doing well in the Eastern theatre, and altogether sceptical as to a German-Austrian attack on Serbia. He told us, among other things, that Joffre was equipping himself with a full apparatus for bridging the Rhine!

With some difficulty we brought him to the point of agreeing to send *one* division to Salonica, if he got a good Territorial Division in exchange.

The result is—that we try the Dardanelles bombardment next week, & with the French, & we hope & believe the Russians, make the Serbian démarche by or about the beginning of March. . . .

Vice-Admiral Carden to Winston S. Churchill: telegram
(*Churchill papers: 2/88*)

9 February 1915

Personal and Secret. As mine-sweepers cannot be ready before the 19th, we shall not be prepared to start before that date.

It is essential for moral effect, to make real progress, and reduce ammunition expenditure, that the operation should be continuous. Presence of minesweepers required for this purpose.

By same date—but not before—the seaplanes will be available.

H. H. Asquith to Venetia Stanley
(Montagu papers)

10 February 1915   10 Downing Street

... A destination & use has at last been found for Winston's squadron of armoured motors, which has been lying practically derelict at Wormwood Scrubs for the last 2 or 3 months. They are to be sent out to take part in the War in German *South West Africa*, with Josiah Wedgwood[1] as first & Francis McLaren[2] as second in command! I doubt whether there [are] any roads in the country, but I suppose they may be able to trek across the veld & the scrub. ...

A secret telegram came this morning, wh. has only been seen by Winston Grey, K & me, from the Admiral (Carden) that the business out there, wh. was to have been begun next Monday, has had to be postponed for a few days, as the requisite mine-sweepers could not be got together sooner. I hope it won't be delayed any longer, as it is all important as a preliminary to our démarche in the Balkans. So far it has been on the whole a well kept secret. ...

Lieutenant-Colonel Hankey to A. J. Balfour
(Balfour papers)

10 February 1915   2 Whitehall Gardens

... I am convinced that an attack on the Dardanelles is the only extraneous operation worth trying. From Lord Fisher downwards every naval officer in the Admiralty who is in the secret believes that the Navy cannot take the Dardanelles position without troops. The First Lord still professes to believe that they can do it with ships, but I have warned the Prime Minister that we cannot trust to this. ...

[1] Josiah Clement Wedgwood, 1872–1943. Liberal MP, 1906–19. Commanded armoured cars in France, Antwerp, Gallipoli and East Africa, 1914–17. Assistant Director, Trench Warfare Department, Ministry of Munitions, 1917. War Office Mission to Siberia, 1918. Labour MP, 1919–42. Vice-Chairman of the Labour Party, 1921–4. Chancellor of the Duchy of Lancaster, 1924. Created Baron, 1942.

[2] Francis Walter Stafford McLaren, 1886–1917. Liberal MP, 1910–17. Lieutenant, RNVR, 1914. Served with the Armoured Car Squadron, Gallipoli Peninsula, 1915. Flight-Lieutenant, Royal Flying Corps, 1916. Killed in action, 1917.

Vice-Admiral Carden to Winston S. Churchill: telegram

(*Copy, Admiralty papers: 137/96*)

10 February 1915   HMS Indefatigable
Noon
Secret and Personal

I have arranged that QUEEN ELIZABETH, now carrying out gunnery practice at Gibraltar, shall pick me up at a rendezvous South of Malta on 15th February.

I shall arrive Tenedos A.M. 17th and commence operations 19th.

Winston S. Churchill to Walter Runciman

(*Runciman Papers*)

12 February 1915   Admiralty
Secret

My dear Walter,

It is most important to attract neutral shipping to our shores, in the hope especially of embroiling the U.S. with Germany. The German formal announcement of indiscriminate submarining has been made to the United States to produce a deterrent effect on traffic. For our part, we want the traffic—the more the better; & if some of it gets into trouble, better still. Therefore do please furbish up at once your insurance offer to neutrals trading with us after February 18th. The more that come, the greater our safety & the German embarrassment. Please act promptly so that the announcement may synchronize with our impending policy.

I was vexed about yr taking Hopwood away for 10 days without mentioning it, so that I only found out his absence by a breakdown in Admiralty work.[1] But the times are too serious, & the days are too full, to fight about that.

Yours very sincerely
Winston S. Churchill

---

[1] With Asquith's approval, Runciman had asked the Civil Lord of Admiralty, Sir Francis Hopwood, to join Board of Trade negotiations with the Trades Unions. 'I fear that I took for granted all was in order,' he replied on 15 February, '. . . Please forgive me.' (*Churchill papers: 13/47*)

Winston S. Churchill to Andrew Bonar Law: telegram.
(Bonar Law Papers)

12 February 1915   Admiralty

Please enable me identify ship to which you referred last night[1] so that I can have actual facts investigated. Churchill

Winston S. Churchill to Andrew Bonar Law
(Bonar Law Papers)

12 February 1915   Admiralty

Dear Bonar Law,

I hope you will be able to give me the facts. It is always vy unfair to state a case in detail & then refuse to let the details be checked.

Vy likely you are right, & a better procedure shd have been adopted. But a 'hard case' apart from the actual facts is absolutely intangible.

The Admiralty Transport Department were inclined to think they had done rather well—if only the facts were known—; & 'incapacity' is a severe expression. I am bound to look after their claims to consideration, otherwise believe me I wd not trouble you.

Yours sincerely
Winston S. Churchill

Andrew Bonar Law to Winston S. Churchill
(Churchill papers: 13/44)

13 February 1915

Pembroke Lodge
Edwardes Square
Kensington

Dear Churchill,

I am obliged by your letter, the temperateness of which, and the reasonableness of your request I fully recognise. I have read over the report of what I said the other day, and I really think that if I were to raise the subject at all I could hardly have done it more temperately. The real point I tried to make was not that the officials of the Admiralty who are responsible for this work are to blame, but that it is work which no amount of ability would enable them to perform without the necessary experience.

---

[1] Bonar Law had complained in the House of Commons on 11 February that the Admiralty Transport Department were making inefficient use of merchant ships commandeered for war services. He had quoted a letter from a shipowner who had referred to the Department's 'incapacity'.

Let me give you an illustration from my own experience. The business firm with which I was connected till I became an Under-Secretary[1] at one time bought a steamer and we thought we could manage her. We made a complete mess of it, losing money every year, and at last we handed her over to be managed by a firm of shipowners, and from that moment she began to pay and pay handsomely.

I am sure that my friend[2] would have no objection to giving the name of the steamer, if I had not quoted the extract from his letter. But he is a prominent man, and as it happens, a supporter of your Party, and I am afraid that he will not allow me to give the name of the steamer which will identify him.

I have asked him to telegraph, but so far have not received a reply. If he declines I shall ask him to allow me to give you the name privately, and you could then easily have enquiry made into the case by including the name of this steamer with other vessels. Indeed, I would suggest to you that as the best method of testing this whole matter, you should take from the list of chartered steamers ten or a dozen vessels at haphazard and ask that a return should be given to you of the way in which they have been employed every day since they came on Government charter.

The Prime Minister said that a Committee had been formed to help the Admiralty. I do not much believe in Committees; but I feel quite certain that if you could get the right man—a really competent shipowner—and place him at the head of the Department dealing with chartered ships with complete power you would effect an immense saving. It is not a question of getting a business man, but of getting the right business man. The friend whose letter I quoted would be an ideal man; but of course I have no reason to believe that he would be willing to sacrifice his own business and devote himself to such work. If, however, he could not do it I am sure that there are others who would be competent to undertake it.

If you would like to discuss the matter with me, or better still with my friend, I shall be glad to arrange a meeting.

Yours sincerely
A. Bonar Law

[1] In 1875, at the age of sixteen, Bonar Law had entered the Glasgow firm of William Kidston & Company, Iron and Steel brokers. In July 1902, when he was appointed Parliamentary Secretary at the Board of Trade, he retired from active business; but he retained his directorships until 1911, when he was elected Leader of the Conservative Party in the House of Commons.

[2] Joseph Paton Maclay, 1857–1951. Shipowner. Created Baronet, 1914. Minister of Shipping, 1916–21. Created Baron, 1922. Of his three sons, one, Ebenezer (born 1891), was killed in action in France, 1918; another, William Strang (born 1895), died of wounds received at Gallipoli, 25 June 1915.

PS I have now received a telegram from my friend permitting me to give the name of the steamer, but adding that it would be better for me to wait till I receive his letter. I shall therefore give you the information on Monday.

ABL

Winston S. Churchill to H. H. Asquith

(*Cabinet papers: 37/124*)

13 February 1915   Admiralty

Prime Minister,

I have had a talk with Sir Francis Hopwood about the Labour Organization Inquiry, of which he is a member.

It seems to me most important that energy should not be diverted into the labyrinth of difficulties concerning the frontiers between different classes of Trade Union labour. The questions thus raised are of the greatest intricacy, and touch at every point the deepest prejudices and interests of the classes of workers affected. The gain to national industries for war purposes is on the other hand comparatively small.

A far more fruitful field lies in concentrating the whole labour forces upon Government work, as opposed to 'merchant work'. It is suggested that the principle we have followed with so much advantage with regard to the railways, requires to be extended during the continuance of the war to shipping and shipbuilding. At present we have the power to requisition any ships we choose for Government service, and have requisitioned one-fifth of the entire tonnage for military and naval purposes. Owing to the great rise in freights, the profits made by shipowners whose vessels have not been requisitioned, promise to be greatly in excess of those obtained from the Government under requisition charters, although Government prices afford a fair and even a handsome profit. This is unjust in principle; it creates a feeling of injustice in practice; and it is detrimental to national interests.

The time has now come when we ought to do what it would have been well to have done at the very beginning, namely, to take over the whole British mercantile marine for the period of the war for national purposes. According to the regular scales in force, this assures a complete equality of treatment to all, and prevents altogether the upward movement freights. On the other hand, the fullest incentive is left to active trading. The shipowners would continue to run their ships, which would be re-chartered to them by the Government merely for working purposes, in exactly the same manner as the railway companies run their trains under a similar arrangement.

If the existing law does not allow of this, or if it would be a hard construction of the existing law to use it for such a purpose, power should be taken under an amendment to the Defence of the Realm Act similar to that which gives us control of the railways.

I pass over the intermediate link in the shape of transport workers at the docks, as this has already been to some extent the subject of treatment at your hands, and because it is not directly connected with Admiralty affairs.

What is done to shipping should also be done to shipbuilding. We cannot allow labour to be consumed at the present juncture on any class of vessels not necessary for our immediate national or military needs. We should, therefore, obtain legislative power to requisition for use or suspension, all shipbuilding work now in progress in the country. All hulls within, say, three months of completion should probably be finished for national transport purposes. All the rest should be left where they are at any moment when it is convenient to divert the labour from them; and the representatives of a Government committee should have the power to suspend all further work upon them without notice, holding the shipbuilder free from actions for damages for breach of contract. In other words, a moratorium for the execution of such contracts would be instituted by law.

The physical transference of labour from merchant work to Government work consequent upon the above operations, could be harmoniously effected by the payment of a subsistence allowance of 1l. a week for men moving from one district to another, who thus have to keep up two homes. This principle has already been adopted by us for some months past in the dockyards, and has enabled us to secure without difficulty the labour we require. Short-term contracts of three to six months should be made with the men, and they should be guaranteed continuous employment during that period.

I have only attempted to deal with the great group of industries and questions with which the Admiralty is primarily connected; and I suggest to you that they form a category which stands out plainly by itself.

Sir Francis Hopwood informs me that if the Trade Union leaders are right in what they say, a transference of this character from merchant work to national work would supply completely the deficiency of labour so far as all forms of shipbuilding are concerned; and as shipbuilding is the key to a great number of subsidiary and ancillary industries of all kinds, a similar transference from those to the corresponding employments where the War Office need labour would also be effected.

These matters are of the highest importance now. At the beginning of the war, people were prepared to accommodate themselves to any change, however far-reaching, and expected great changes would follow; but now things would appear to be settling down into an everyday atmosphere, although the crisis and emergency of the war are in no respect abated.

WSC

Winston S. Churchill to Walter Runciman

(*Runciman Papers*)

13 February 1915   Admiralty

My dear Walter,

I cannot tell what the effect of the German SM attack on trade may be. It is quite possible that we shall lose 15 or 20 ships in the first week, when all their submarines may be out. But this effort cannot be maintained; & the exertions which can be required of these small craft are limited. I hope therefore you will now allow the insurance rates to be put up until we have had a proper experience of the new conditions. For this, time is necessary; & I wd ask you to let the Admy have an opportunity of expressing their views before you decide on any advancement of the rates.

Thank you very much for your letter received today.

Yours ever
Winston S. Churchill

Sir Francis Elliot to Sir Edward Grey

(*Copy, Churchill papers: 13/51*)

13 February 1915   Athens
Personal & Secret

M. Venizelos & the King agree to procedure proposed. Orders will be sent at once to withdraw ships & men from Mudros Bay, men going from town of Lemnos except a few left in charge of the stores. Batteries will be left all standing & M. Venizelos requests they may be looked after.

The King has not been told that attack on the Dardanelles is impending, but newspapers note Fleet has been strengthened.

Sir Henry Jackson: memorandum[1]

(*Copy, Churchill papers: 2/82*)

13 February 1915   Admiralty

ATTACK ON CONSTANTINOPLE

It seems desirable in the proposed attack on the Dardanelles forts to take every possible advantage of their obsolescent design, so as to reduce the amount of damage they can inflict on the bombarding vessels.

[1] On 15 February Carden was sent a copy of this memorandum, with a covering note from Oswyn Murray, Assistant Secretary at the Admiralty, informing him that: 'The suggestions contained in this paper are not to be regarded as orders from their Lordships, and may be adopted by you or not, at your discretion.' (*Copy, Churchill papers: 2/82*)

A careful study of the I.D. [Intelligence Department] reports shows in many cases the forts are not constructed to be able to reply at all to a flank or rear attack at long range, owing to the limited arc of training of their guns, which are so placed as to bear on vessels passing them at moderate or short ranges only.

It is possible some of these defects may have been reduced, and also that the defences have been supplemented by concealed batteries of howitzers. To discover these, thorough aerial reconnaissances should be carried out before commencing operations, and additional units told off to deal with these at the same time or previously to the final bombardments.

As regards the passage of the Bosphorus, a study of the forts shows they are in most cases open to attack from the rear, with little chance of making an effective reply, and the principle danger will be from concealed howitzer batteries on the surrounding heights. However, if these forts are to be reduced, they can be much more easily and safely attacked from the Constantinople than from the Black Sea end.

I am dealing with the Dardanelles in detail. Some notes I have prepared on the attack of the forts are herewith for consideration.

NOTES ON ATTACK OF DARDANELLES FORTS

1. Cape Helles—

Armament—

No. 1	..	..	.. 2—24 centim., training from S.W. to S.E.
„ 1B	..	..	.. Supposed to contain 6-inch howitzers.
„ 2	..	..	.. Field guns only.
„ 3	..	..	..$\begin{cases} 6—28 \text{ centim.} & 5 \text{ training W. to S.} \\ 2—15 \quad „ & 3 \text{ training S.W. to E.} \end{cases}$

The position from which bombardment should commence against No. 1, 1B, and 3 partly depends on armament of 1B. This should be previously investigated by sea-plane, and if only 6-inch howitzers exist, as supposed, these may be engaged at long range at same time as No. 1 by another vessel.

Under this supposition, the position to anchor should be about 6 miles west of Cape Helles lighthouse, in 40 fathoms at 11,800 yards from No. 1B; 13,500 yards from No. 1; and 15,500 yards from the nearest fort on the Asiatic side.

Spotting ship for No. 1B, N.N.W., out of range; for Nos. 1 and 3, probably S.S.W., out of range, *after* the Asiatic forts have been silenced, will be the best positions.

Full charges from 12-inch VIII, 10-inch, and 7·5-inch guns would suffice. As far as can be judged from the profile, there would be no need to shift berth till Nos. 1, 1B, 2, and 3 were silenced; but the Asiatic forts must be engaged at the same time, and also silenced before the land can be closed for the final bombardment and landing of a demolition party.

2. Asiatic Side: Kum Kale—

Armament—

No. 4 ..	..	2—24 centim., training from W. by S. to N.N.E.
„ 5 ..	..	Field guns.

8—28 centim.	2 training from S.W. to N.W.
	2 „ „ W. to N.
„ 6 .. .. 1—15 „	2 „ „ N. to E.
	3 „ „ N.W. to N.E.

And field guns.

Bombarding position should be S.W. by W., 6 miles from No. 4, amongst the Rabbit Islands, in 9 fathoms; 14,300 yards from No. 6.

A position further to the south would mask the fort by the land and town of Reni Shehr.

The same guns as for 1 to 3 will suffice.

When this fort is silenced, No. 6 should be closed on a bearing about S.W., outside the arc of training of any of its guns.

If such a position can be obtained, the fort can be closed to 6,000 yards and reduced charges used.

It contains 9 heavy guns and would require a considerable amount of ammunition, but apparently it can be attacked from the rear without any of its guns being able to fire on a bearing south of S.W. The spotting vessel might be near the position of the squadron attacking the northern forts.

GENERAL REMARKS

The position of the field guns may be changed from that shown on the charts, and the forts must probably be subjected to a severe bombardment at short range with secondary armament to destroy these movable light guns before the demolition party is landed.

Every gun must be damaged to such an extent as to prevent the possibility of its being used again.

Owing to the construction of the forts, some of the ready magazines will probably be struck and exploded during the bombardment.

Ships required: 1 Battle Squadron of 8; two to bombard the northern and two the southern forts; each pair assisted by 1 spotting vessel and one vessel to bombard any enemy concealed positions, which may be disclosed during the operations.

The destruction of the outer defences will permit the squadron to enter the Straits for a short distance, with due precautions as to fixed and floating mines, and attack by concealed batteries and field artillery.

The details of the next batteries to be attacked are not known, but they do not appear to be armed with guns over 6-inch calibre.

Sweeping for mines will be necessary, and should be carried out at night, and every advantage taken of thick weather, which is more prevalent in late winter than at other times.

Screening the sweepers from sniping and attack by field artillery with searchlights may be found practicable, concentrated beams from high searchlights being thrown up the channel between the shore and the sweepers. The enemy searchlights must also be attacked and destroyed by light cruisers or destroyers.

It may be found possible to seize a high look-out and spotting station on shore, if the peninsula is not strongly occupied by military forces.

The channel should be well swept up to the Dardanus No. 8 Fort, if possible, before further bombardment of the inner defences is carried out. The Fort Dardanus guns should be bombarded as soon as the channel is cleared from mines and is within range.

The two 6-inch guns mounted in it, though commanding the channel, offer good targets and should not give much trouble. Four other 6-inch guns are reported to be mounted in a new battery near them, and there is another 6-inch battery on the northern shore, nearly opposite.

Nos. 9, 13, and 19 are the next batteries to be dealt with, but must be considered with the other powerful forts at the narrows.

No. 9, Tekeh: Armament probably ten 15-centim. guns and four 15-centim. howitzers, commanding the channel, but offering good targets. These must be bombarded from long range from ships which are also outside the range of the guns from Nos. 13 and 19. The latter fort, Hamidieh I, contains two 35-centim. and seven 24-centim. long-range guns, the former training from S. 50° W. to N.W., the latter from S. 30° W. to W., approximately; the front of the fort faces W.S.W.

A position bearing S. 35° W. from the fort in Aren Kios Bay at about 16,000 yards range can be used as an anchorage. This will be in dead water as regards the 35-centim. guns, and will render it necessary for the 24-centim. guns to be fired in extreme angles of bearing, to the detriment of the men working the guns on the flank. The whole armament will also be attacked from the flank, and 15,000 yards is beyond the range of the 24-centim. and ·24 guns; but the guns in forts to its rear have probably considerably greater ranges.

The large area of this fort renders it also a suitable target for indirect fire at long range; and the fire of the ships in the Straits may well alternate with that from a vessel anchored in 25 fathoms outside the Straits at a distance of about 10 miles, on a W.N.W. bearing, the ships inside spotting, if no shore spotting station can be seized and used for the purpose.

The reduction of this powerful fort may take some time, but it is one of the most destructive to ships, which must pass its heavy guns at short range.

No. 13, Rumili Medjidieh, must be dealt with at the same time. It is on the opposite shore to No. 19; faces the Straits; and is not open to a flank attack, except on its two eastern guns. It will require long-range bombardment at 17,000 to 18,000 yards, and though it offers a good target, will probably require a large number of heavy shell to complete its destruction. Spotting for elevation will be difficult, unless a shore spotting station has been secured. This fort is supported by No. 16 Hamidieh II, a few hundred yards in its rear; and as this fort mounts a couple of 35-centim. guns, training from S.S.W. to east, it is necessary to select an anchorage in dead water from these two guns; that is, as close to the N.W. side of the channel as is practicable, but keeping Nos. 13 and 16 in view.

When No. 13 is silenced, No. 16 can subsequently be closed in dead water, and dealt with.

It may be found possible to attack some of these forts in rear by firing over the peninsula, as for No. 16. Local reconnaissance alone will show whether this is practicable or not.

No. 17, Fort Namazieh: Armament 13 guns of 21 to 28 centim., and three 21-centim. howitzers.

One half of the guns covers the southern approach, and the other half covers the narrowest part of the channel.

The former support Nos. 13 and 16, and must be dealt with by long-range bombardment; which, at the same time, will probably be efficacious in damaging the guns on the other face. It is, however, a powerful work, and will require a large expenditure of heavy gun ammunition. It cannot be ascertained from the chart if it is open to bombardment from seaward over the peninsula.

Compared with the above, the 6-inch armaments of Nos. 11 and 18, and the field-gun batteries of minor importance, but they may give some trouble unless they have been silenced before the ships get within range of their guns.

No. 20, Fort Hamidieh III: Armament two 35-centim., two 24-centim. guns, and four 15-centim. howitzers. It is 2,000 yards to the rear of No. 19, and can be left till this and the forts on the opposite shore have been silenced, so far as the guns commanding the channel are concerned. It should then be attacked from beyond the range of its 24-centim. guns, from a position in Kephez Bay, on which its 35-centim. guns cannot bear, and should alternately be attacked over the peninsula from seaward. It offers an excellent target with its old castle in the middle of the fort.

When the guns in the above-named forts have been silenced, extensive sweeping operations will again be necessary for the squadron to proceed toward Kephez Bay for action against Nos. 23 and 24.

The former of these, apparently, is armed with only howitzers, but the latter carries eleven guns of 21- to 28-centim., and three 15-centim. guns. Eight of these guns command the channel, but are, apparently, only of L 22 pattern, with a range not exceeding 14,000 yards. The remaining guns will receive the fire from their flank and rear.

Long range bombardment from a range of 15,000 yards, or over, will be necessary, and the fort destroyed before the ships can approach Sari Siglar Bay to deal with No. 22 on the opposite shore, and to the north of the Narrows.

These guns mostly do not command the channel, and can probably be silenced by a flank attack from Sari Siglar Bay, but the range will be short, as the fort will not be visible till within 6,000 yards on a bearing in which two 24-centim. guns can reply to the ship's fire.

When the forts at the Narrows are silenced, and the channel cleared of mines, ships can move into Sari Siglar Bay and attack the No. 30 fort, Nagara Kallosi, at a range of 18,000 yards on a S. by W. bearing, which position will be in dead water to all but two of its seven 24-centim. guns.

When these have been silenced, Dardan Bay can be entered and the remaining batteries attacked. These are Nos. 28, 31, 32, 34, and 35, which contain no guns over 6-inch calibre.

This would complete the operation as far as the known gun defences in the Straits are concerned. The Princes Island defences would, however, have to be silenced later before approaching Constantinople.

General Remarks.—Bearings, training of guns, and ranges above quoted are approximate, and are only to be considered as a guide for preparing detailed orders.

The general scheme is first to totally destroy the outer defences to enable the squadrons to enter the Straits, and then attack the forts in detail at distances beyond the range of the old heavy guns mounted in them, and to take every advantage of dead water whilst carrying out a slow and deliberate bombardment from ships at anchor.

The first attack on the forts at the Narrows should be commenced not inside the line between Tott's Battery, Achilleum, *i.e.*, at a range of about 20,000 yards from the outer forts guarding the Narrows.

Every ship carrying out long-range fire should have another ship specially told off to deal with sniping and fire from concealed batteries directed at the firing ship; she should not anchor.

The employment of the Marine Brigade must depend on the number and position of the enemy forces on the Peninsula and the Asiatic shore. If these can be held by the Brigade, the work of demolition of the forts and guns may be thoroughly completed as the operations proceed, and look-out spotting stations established.

Owing to the prevailing northerly winds and south-westerly current, it is probable that the fore-turret guns and starboard batteries will get an undue share of the firing. To prevent disablement of guns from this cause, reduced charges should always be used if the range permits it.

The provision of the necessary military forces to enable the fruits of this heavy naval undertaking to be gathered must never be lost sight of; the transports carrying them should be in readiness to enter the Straits as soon as it is seen the forts at the Narrows will be silenced.

To complete their destruction, strong military landing parties with strong covering forces will be necessary. It is considered, however, that the full advantage of the undertaking would only be obtained by the occupation of the Peninsula by a military force acting in conjunction with the naval operations, as the pressure of a strong field army of the enemy on the Peninsula would not only greatly harass the operations, but would render the passage of the Straits impracticable by any but powerfully-armed vessels, even though all the permanent defences had been silenced.

The naval bombardment is not recommended as a sound military operation, unless a strong military force is ready to assist in the operation, or, at least, follow it up immediately the forts are silenced.

H. B. Jackson

H. H. Asquith to Venetia Stanley

(*Montagu papers*)

13 February 1915   10 Downing Street

. . . I have just been having a talk with Hankey, whose views are always worth hearing. He thinks very strongly that the naval operations of which you know should be supported by landing a fairly strong military force. I have been for some time coming to the same opinion, and I think we ought to be able without denuding French to scrape together from Egypt, Malta & elsewhere a sufficiently large contingent. If only these heart-breaking Balkan States could be bribed or goaded into action, the trick wd. be done with the greatest of ease & with incalculable consequences. It is of much importance that in the course of the next month we should carry through a *decisive* operation somewhere, and this one would do admirably for the purpose. . . .

My main anxiety just now is about Serbia. Apart from the typhus & the small pox, they are very badly off both for food & clothing. We are sending them 50,000 great coats, & from Egypt 5000 tons of flour. I have just been reading a letter from George Trevelyan—the clever one—who is there for F. Acland.[1] He says that, tho' stout & stiff, the Serbs are a very mercurial & impressionable people, and is very strong on the moral effect which the appearance of even a small contingent of British troops wd. produce. As you know we have decided on this in principle, but the wheels of diplomacy move with damnable slowness, and even the Greeks (not to speak of Bulgarians & Roumanians) require to be 'menagés' in every kind of way. What a true saying was Lord Carnarvon's[2] as far back as 1878—'the crux of the Eastern problem is that the Turks are half-dead and the Christians are only half-alive'. In the 40 years, or so, that have since passed, the Turks have become at least three quarters dead, & the Christians, though much more than half alive in force & fighting power, are more distrustful of one another, & more quarrelsome among themselves, than they have ever been before. . . .

Captain Richmond: diary

(Richmond papers)

14 February 1915

. . . Thirty thousand men at the Dardanelles next week would make more impression on the continental campaign than five times that number on the banks of the Yser. . . . Think of 50000 troops, or confound it even 5000, landed at Alexandretta today! Why the garrisons would surrender like gentlemen. . . . It would be worth shoving 20000 of the Egyptian army on board any ships they can get hold of & rushing up to Alexandretta at once. . . .[3]

[1] Francis Dyke Acland, 1874–1939. Liberal MP, 1906–10; 1910–22; 1923–24 and 1932–39. Parliamentary Private Secretary to Haldane, 1906–8. Financial Secretary, War Office, 1908–10. Under-Secretary of State for Foreign Affairs, 1911–15. Financial Secretary Treasury, February–June 1915. Succeeded his father as 14th Baronet, 1926.

[2] Henry Howard Molyneux Herbert, 1831–1890. 4th Earl of Carnarvon, 1849. Secretary of State, 1866–67, 1874–78. Resigned, 1878, in opposition to Lord Beaconsfield's policy on the Eastern question.

[3] On 14 February, in a memorandum entitled 'Remarks on Present Strategy', Richmond insisted that 'the bombardment of the Dardanelles, even if all the forts are destroyed, can be nothing but a local success, which without an army to carry it on can have no further effect.' 'Your Memo. is absolutely A.1 and is most opportune,' Hankey wrote to Richmond on 15 February: 'I am sending it to Jacky. You are preaching to the converted but it may ginger him up. As a matter of fact things are going much better than you think. More I cannot say in a letter.' Fisher also wrote—briefly but enthusiastically—on 15 February: 'YOUR PAPER IS EXCELLENT.' (*Richmond papers*)

Winston S. Churchill to Andrew Bonar Law

(*Bonar Law papers*)

15 February 1915   Admiralty

My dear Bonar Law,

Many thanks for your speech today,[1] which will be of definite value in our policy against the enemy.

I am vy anxious you shd have every opportunity of satisfying yourself about the collier question: you must realize that it is vital to us to keep something like 400,000 tons of coal afloat, 'idle', in reserve at the various fleet bases. This of course is wholly wasteful & uneconomic. It is merely necessary. I don't wish to obtrude confidential information upon you, in case it might hamper yr freedom of criticism. But if you like I shall be glad to send you a full memorandum on the general collier question as well as on the particular points you have mentioned; & if there are any points in this wh require further explanation, I shall be very happy to put you in contact with persons who can give you the fullest information.[2]

Yours sincerely
Winston S Churchill

F. E. Smith to Winston S. Churchill

(*Churchill papers: 26/2*)

15 February 1915   St Verrant

My dear Winston,

I liked your speech on the Navy particularly the sentence about Jellicoe's fleet in the Northern mists which recalled Mahan's[3] famous rhetoric.[4]

[1] On 15 February Bonar Law spoke on the Navy Estimates debate in the House of Commons, immediately after Churchill. He criticized the Admiralty's Transport Department for its inefficient use of merchant shipping. 'To win the War,' he declared, 'is more important than to win it cheaply.'

[2] Bonar Law was not satisfied with this reply, writing to Churchill on 17 February: 'I am really convinced that immense sums of money could be saved by an organisation which would prevent three steamers being kept available where two would do the work....' (*Churchill papers: 13/44*) But Churchill had confidence in his arrangements, and made no changes in the organization of the Admiralty Transport Department.

[3] Alfred T. Mahan, 1840–1914. Entered the United States Navy, 1856. Retired with the rank of Rear-Admiral, 1896. Naval historian; author of twenty major works. His best known book, the *Influence of Sea Power Upon History*, was published in 1890.

[4] On 15 February Churchill introduced the Navy Estimates for 1915–16 to the House of Commons. In the course of his speech he referred to the Grand Fleet as 'lost to view amid the northern mists, preserved by patience and seamanship in all its strength and efficiency, silent, unsleeping, and, as yet, unchallenged'.

Everyone is groping here with no plan & no prospects. I shudder for fear our new million get swallowed up here if the Germans can match them with another million or even (as defensive lines) with 500,000.

Why dont you make a deal on any terms with Italy for joint action in the Spring & send the new army to Italy to break through in the North Munichwards? Probably this is impracticable but so apparently is everything. The result is certain but Russia is disappointing. We make no progress here & haven't in the least conquered the offensive.

Ever yours affectionately

FE

Vice-Admiral Oliver to Graeme Thomson
(Copy, Churchill papers: 2/82)

16 February 1915   Admiralty

D. of T.

The First Lord has seen Lord Kitchener and desires me to say that the preparation of the transports for the 29th Division is to be put in hand at once, including shipping the horse boats and getting the vessels to Avonmouth ready for the troops.

H. F. Oliver

Winston S. Churchill and Vice-Admiral Oliver to Vice-Admiral Carden: telegram
(Admiralty papers: 137/96)

16 February 1915
Secret

Greek Govt have agreed to use of Lemnos Island as a base for Allied Fleet and are arranging to withdraw their ships and men from Mudros Bay with the exception of a few men left in charge of stores.

The batteries will be left all standing and Mr Venezelos requests that they may be looked after by the British.

Communicate with Sir F. Elliott Athens and arrange the earliest possible date on which to take over Lemnos Island from the Greeks. The Marine Brigade should be landed there on that date and the place taken over.

You should be careful to meet the wishes of the Greek authorities in every way possible and treat them with due consideration.

R. A. Wemyss will be sent out as Governor and S.N.O. at the Base and Brigadier General Trotman will command the troops.

You should telegraph if any additional officers are required for administrative duties and should communicate with the High Commissioner Cyprus[1] and obtain the loan of an official from him to be attached to the staff of R. A. Wemyss in an advisory capacity.

Proper arrangement should be made for the administration and policing of the Island.

Meeting of the War Council: conclusions
(Copy, Cabinet Office papers: 22/1)

Present: H. H. Asquith (in the Chair), David Lloyd George, Winston S. Churchill, Lord Fisher, Sir Edward Grey, Lord Kitchener

16 February 1915   10 Downing Street

Conclusions[2]

1. The XXIXth Division, hitherto intended to form part of Sir John French's Army, to be despatched to Lemnos at the earliest possible date. It is hoped that it may be able to sail within nine or ten days.

2. Arrangements to be made for a force to be despatched from Egypt, if required.

3. The whole of the above forces, in conjunction with the battalions of Royal Marines already despatched, to be available in case of necessity to support the naval attack on the Dardanelles.

4. Horse-boats to be taken out with the XXIXth Division, and the Admiralty to make arrangements to collect small craft, tugs, and lighters in the Levant.

5. The Admiralty to build special transports and lighters suitable for the conveyance and landing of a force of 50,000 men at any point where they may be required.

Lord Esher: diary
(Esher papers)

16 February 1915

The Dardanelles are to be tried three days hence. A landing force will be composed of the 29th Division, but they cannot be there in time. Lord K's words to Winston were: 'You get through! I will find the men.'

[1] John Eugene Clauson, 1866–1918. Entered Army, 1885. Major, 1900. Assistant Secretary, Committee of Imperial Defence, 1904–6. Lieutenant-Governor, Malta, 1911–14. Knighted, 1913. High Commissioner and Commander-in-Chief, Cyprus, 1914–18.

[2] On 17 February Hankey wrote up these conclusions, with a covering note: 'This Meeting commenced as an informal conference between one or two Ministers, others subsequently being called in. The decisions arrived at were of such importance that it has been recorded as a full Meeting of the War Council. The decisions were communicated to the Secretary (who was not present) by the Prime Minister.' (*Cabinet papers: 22/1*)

H. H. Asquith to Venetia Stanley
(*Montagu papers*)

17 February 1915   10 Downing Street

. . . 3 of the Sea planes which took part in yesterday's raid[1] have not returned, & the Admiralty fear that they may be lost. The pilot of one of them
was Gilbert Murray's[2] (of Oxford) son,[3] who was reputed to be a very good
young officer. The war just at present, tho' not fertile in incidents of a dramatic kind, is very costly: K. told me yesterday . . . that in the last *10 days*
Sir J. French's force has lost 100 officers and about 2600 men. And very little
that is ostensible to show for it. Meanwhile the Russians seem to be doing
badly: happily they have wonderful powers of recuperation, and those
wretched little Balkan States . . . are bickering and cowering & holding their
hands after the Italian pattern. It is a sorry spectacle, & makes me sad.

The Dardanelles affair will begin—we hope—on Friday morning. It is an
absolutely novel experiment, & I am curious & rather anxious to see how
it develops. . . .

H. H. Asquith to Winston S. Churchill
(*Churchill papers: 13/47*)

17 February 1915   10 Downing Street
Secret

My dear Winston,

Kitchener has just been to see me in a state of some perturbation. He has
just received two official letters from French, in which he announces that
you have offered him a Brigade of the Naval Division, and 2 squadrons of

---

[1] On 16 February 1915 forty naval aeroplanes and seaplanes dropped bombs on the
German-held ports on the Belgian coast, including Ostend and Zeebrugge.

[2] George Gilbert Aimé Murray, 1866–1957. Classical scholar. Regius Professor of Greek
at Oxford, 1908–36. In 1915 he published a small volume in support of Grey's Foreign
Policy, which estranged him from his radical friends. Chairman, League of Nations' Union,
1928–40. President, United Nations Association, 1947–9. His wife, Lady Mary Howard,
eldest daughter of the 9th Earl of Carlisle, was a cousin of both Clementine Churchill and
Venetia Stanley.

[3] Denys George Murray, 1892–1930. Son of Professor Gilbert and Lady Mary Murray;
a cousin of Clementine Churchill. Educated at Winchester and New College, Oxford.
Flight-Lieutenant, Royal Naval Air Service, 1914. Reported missing, February 1915, during
an air raid on German positions in Belgium. He fell into the North Sea, drifted towards the
shore for two hours, and was picked up by a Dutch torpedo-boat. Interned in Holland for
two years, when he was repatriated. After hospital treatment, served with various Royal Air
Force units in England, 1917–18. Retired, 1919.

armoured cars. Kitchener is strongly of opinion that French has no need of either. But, apart from that, he feels (& I think rightly) that he ought to have been told of, & consulted about, the offer before it was made.

I hope you will go & see him & put things right.

Yrs always
HHA

Winston S. Churchill to H. H. Asquith
(*Copy, Churchill papers: 13/47*)

17 February 1915   Admiralty

My dear Prime Minister,

Kitchener's obvious course would have been to send me copies of French's official letters and ask me what I had to say about them. Until I see them I cannot discuss them. If Kitchener raises the subject with me I shall be delighted to go into it with him, and I suggest to you that you should recommend him to do this.

The whole thing is a mare's nest. I have no power to offer any troops to Sir John French. All I can do is to hand over to the War Office, when they ask me for them, any Admiralty units which may be thought to be of use to the Army in the field.

As a matter of fact I have been contemplating, as you know and as Kitchener knows, quite a different destination for the naval brigades. [I think you are rather precipitate in assuming I have transgressed the strictest limits of inter-departmental etiquette.][1]

I wish you had heard what I had to say before assuming that I was in the wrong.

This is not the first time that Kitchener has troubled you about matters which a few moments' talk with me would have adjusted. I do not remember that I have ever claimed your aid against any colleague otherwise than in Cabinet.

Winston S. Churchill to Lord Kitchener
(*Copy, Churchill papers: 13/47*)

18 February 1915   Admiralty

My dear Kitchener,

If our operations at the Dardanelles prosper, immense advantages may be offered wh cannot be gathered without military aid. The opportunity may

---

[1] Churchill deleted the sentence in square brackets before sending this letter to Asquith.

come in 3 weeks time; And I think at least 50,000 men shd be within reach at 3 days notice, either to seize the Gallipoli Peninsula when it has been evacuated, or to occupy C'nople if a revolution takes place. We shd never forgive ourselves if the naval operations succeeded & the fruits were lost through the Army being absent.

In these circumstances I hope earnestly that you will send the 29th Divn complete either to Alexandria or Lemnos as convenient. Before it arrives, we shall know how the naval operations are going to turn out. The attitude of the Greeks may also have become defined in a satisfactory manner.

The troops can always live in the transports for 10 days or a fortnight, all the material can be left on board, only the horses & men being exercised on shore to keep them fit. It seems to me from what you said this morning that the 50,000 men cd be provided as follows:

1) 29th Division, 18,000.

2) Australians or other troops from Egypt. 22,000.

3) 9 battns. of R N Divn & details, 10,000

                               ————

                              50,000

You wd then have a force within 2 days steam of Salonica or C'nople, wh having regard to the political circs of Turkey & the Balkans, might produce vy great results.

Winston S. Churchill to Lord Fisher and Vice-Admiral Oliver

(*Churchill papers: 13/54*)

18 February 1915   Admiralty
Confidential

1) Tomorrow afternoon AGRM [Adjutant-General Royal Marines] will assemble Gen Paris, Commodore Backhouse,[1] Col Ollivant and any staff Officers required for the purpose of concerting the following movement:—

2) Two Battns R.M. will land at Lemnos on the 22nd or as soon after as convenient (This has been already arranged). The remaining two Battns RM & the 5 naval Battns 'Hood', 'Howe', 'Anson', 'Drake' & 'Nelson' will embark for Lemnos on Sat February 27th together with a signal company 2 engineer cos 2 AS companies ambulance & ordnance party.

---

[1] Oliver Backhouse, 1876–1943. Brother of Roger Backhouse, Lieutenant RN 1898; Captain, 1914. Commanded the Second Naval Brigade, 1914. Served with the Royal Naval Division at the siege of Antwerp, October 1914 and at the Dardanelles, 1915. Commanded HMS *Orion*, battle of Jutland, 1916. Commanded HMS *Royal Sovereign*, allied occupation of Constantinople, 1919–20. Captain Superintendent, Sheerness Dockyard, 1923–5. Admiral Superintendent, Devonport Dockyard, 1927–31. Vice-Admiral, 1929. Admiral, 1934.

3) A memm has been prepared by Col Ollivant under the direction of the 1st Lord covering the various points of details wh require decision.

4) The Divn will be formed in 3 brigades, a RM Brigade of the 3 Bns under Gen Trotman, a naval Brigade of 3 Battns under Commodore Backhouse and a mixed Brigade of 2 Naval & one marine Bn under Gen Mercer.[1] The existing Brigade Staff & organisations will be maintained.

5) The Division will not require artillery, as it will operate solely under the guns of the fleet. It will be kitted & equipped in all respects necessary to enable it to operate within their range. The Board will inspect the Divn complete in all details and Wed & Thurs next, according to the weather at Blandford.

6) Subject to the course of events, it is intended that the Divn shall rendezvous at Blandford on or before May 1st, & shall then find the 3 remaining Battns viz 'Benbow' 'Collingwood' & 'Hawke', fit to take the field with them and all transport store & equipment for a Divn on army scale perfected. AGRM will submit the names of a Commandant & staff to carry on the training of the Blandford Camp.

7) Besides the three above mentioned Battns left behind there will be at Blandford immediately formed 2 reserve Btns from the Crystal Palace & subsequently two more, it being intended to reduce the Crystal Palace to a minimum. The Marines will provide from their own depots for the replenishment of the fighting force. They will also provide the 300 officers and men, as verbally arranged by 1L with AGRM to fortify the 3 Btns 'Benbow', 'Collingwood' & 'Hawke'.

8) Machine guns: 20 machine guns have gone with the 2 leading Btns, of the marine Brigade. 4 machine guns per battn will be immediately issued to the remaining Btns now under orders to embark. Total 48 for the Divn in addition to this a machine gun Brigade of 24 auxiliary will be provided by DAD & will embark with the Divn. All machine guns taken are to be capable of firing Mark 11 wh is the only ammun to be permitted in the force.

9) The arrangements in regards to the supply of tropical kit already explained are to be additional to the above for 2 Battns the kit being kept on board.

10) D. of T will provide the necessary transport for sailing in the dark hours of the 27th inst. Ammunition Mark VI from the reserve at Woolwich approximately 1,5000,000 rounds, the 2,5000,000 rounds now with the Divn

---

[1] David Mercer, 1864–1920. Lieutenant, Royal Marines Light Infantry, 1883. Brigadier-General, Commanding the 1st Royal Naval Brigade, Royal Naval Division, 1914–16. Commanded the 1st Brigade at Anzac, 1915. Major-General, 1916. Adjutant-General, Royal Marines, 1916–20. Knighted, 1918.

the 1,500,000 with the 2 landing Battns & 500,000 rounds from Malta will be sufficient having regard to the fact that the Fleet by DAD will be separately provided.

11) 1,000,000 rounds must be provided from surrender by the fleet in home water, from remnants in Depots and from reserves returned from Hongkong for the musketry training of the units at Blandford.

12) Report to be presented tomorrow night 1st December printed states both of the RND & the organisation left at home, to be ready by Sat midday.

H. H. Asquith to Venetia Stanley

(Montagu papers)

18 February 1915   10 Downing Street

. . . I am rather vexed with Winston who has been tactless enough to offer Sir John F. (behind K's back & without his knowledge) a brigade of his Naval Division, and 2 squadrons of his famous Armoured Cars which are being hawked about from pillar to post. K. came to me & complained very strongly both of the folly of the offer itself & of its being made without any previous consultation with him.

French was evidently very puzzled what to do with these unwelcome gifts—the Naval battalions being still raw & ragged, and the only use he would suggest for the cars being to remove from them their Maxim guns for the use of his troops. The whole thing is a bad bêtisse. . . .

Kitchener takes rather a gloomy view of the Russian situation. The Germans have undoubtedly given them a bad knock & taken a large number of prisoners: happily the weather there is still very wet, and the country being sodden as well as naturally swampy & wooded, the German pursuit will be hampered, & the Russians may be able to get back into cover. They tell us they have 900,000 men in reserve at this moment, ready to fight, and clothed & equipped—except that they have *no rifles*. You remember a similar tale of woe about 2 months ago. One never knows what to believe of what they say, or what to expect they are capable of doing.

We are at the moment confronted with all sorts of difficulties—not 'single spies but in battalions'—in all parts of the world—Persian Gulf, South Africa, not to mention Serbia and the Dardanelles. The French & the Russians are both rather *mauvais coucheurs*, (of the two I think, between you & me, that the Russians are the straighter) and you know what I think of the Balkan lot.

Then we have got to make effective reprisals against the German 'blockade', & this brings us into all sorts of possible troubles with the neutrals &

especially America. Winston, McKenna, Ll George &c are full of blood and thunder, but they haven't half thought out the thing & its consequences: and so I determined to have a second Cabinet this afternoon, and a War Council to-morrow morning. . . .

Winston S. Churchill to Lord Kitchener

(*Copy, Churchill papers: 13/47*)

18 February 1915   Admiralty

My dear Kitchener,

With regard to the armoured cars, I told French that if he wanted them, and you approved, I shd be delighted to hand two squadrons over to the War Office. They were made originally for the Army abroad, & some time ago you told me that when he wanted them he shd have them. The matter rests with you, and I see French says in his letter that it is 'subject to the concurrence of the Army Council'. My conversation with French was of course quite unofficial.

I also had a talk with F. abt the future of the RN Divn. Four battns are under orders for Lemnos; 3 have not yet recovered from their losses at Antwerp. The other 5 are good, & almost ready. We discussed whether they wd be of use to him, & how they cd be used. But this was only in the air; & so little did I consider myself to have made a firm offer, even unofficially, that I am as you know contemplating quite a different immediate destination for them. I did not expect him to make an official request to you for the 5 bns; tho I thought he wd write a private letter to you abt the armoured cars.

I cannot conceive that this shd be any cause of quarrel between us; or why Murray shd take offence at French's application. At the beginning of the War 100 men of the Somersetshire L I were actually put on board HMS *Triumph*, & sailed as part complement without the Admty even hearing of it till afterward. So far from being offended, we were vy grateful.

I think Murray is rather inappreciative in his reference to maxims. In his minute he agreed only to receiving ½ of our orders for maxims from Vickers, altho we had precedence. Altogether so far we have only received 34. Meanwhile we have handed over to the WO 50 maxims, wh are I believe already at the front. The maxims with which the armoured cars are armed have come from the fleet.

You must know what care I have taken in these last few months to avoid anything wh cd cause difficulties with the WO. Even little things, such as whether Adl Bacon shd go over to France to find out where French wanted the howitzers put, or whether Capt Guest shd go to the Dlles,[1] I have sent specially over to obtain yr permission.

Théophile Delcassé to Sir Edward Grey
(*Churchill papers: 13/54*)

18 February 1915   Paris

Après délibération le gouvernement a décidé de préparer une division qui sera concentrée à Lemnos.

Je vous serais obligé de demander au gouvernment britannique si l'opération navale contre les forts des Dardanelles est ajournée jusqu' à l'envoi ou 'arrivée des divisions.

Winston S. Churchill to Sir Edward Grey
(*Churchill papers: 13/54*)

19 February 1915   Admiralty

The naval operations having begun cannot be interrupted but must proceed continuously to their conclusion, as every day wd add to the dangers of the arrival of German or Austrian submarines, & any lull in the attack prejudicing the moral effect of the Turkish capital.

WSC

Lieutenant-Commander Wedgwood to Winston S. Churchill
(*Churchill papers: 13/47*)

19 February 1915   R.N. Armoured Cars
                                                          Holkham
                                                          Norfolk

Dear Churchill,

I am afraid that the S° African venture must be 'off', or they would have wired by now.[2]

---

[1] Guest had not gone to the Dardanelles, but remained on Sir John French's staff at St Omer.

[2] That same day, 19 February, General Smuts telegraphed to Churchill that it was uncertain whether the armoured cars could be used 'to the best advantage' in South Africa, and that he and General Botha 'thought it was a private patriotic enterprise which was not required for European theatre but did not understand that it was a naval unit under Admiralty control'. To this Churchill replied on 23 February in a 'private and personal' telegram to Botha: 'Squadron of armoured cars can be placed at yr disposal without disadvantage to other interests provided with your local knowledge that you think German S.W. Africa practicable for them.' (*Churchill papers: 13/47*) Botha did not think so; and the cars were sent instead, under Wedgwood's command, to the Dardanelles.

I do beg you therefore to let this Squadron be one of those sent with Rimington[1] to France.

It would be too awful if we lost that chance too, & were left here.

Westminster was always going to take our two squadrons, and it was only because that seemed hopeless that S° Africa was tried.

Please don't leave me in this country now. The Squadron will mutiny, which I ignore, but I myself should be seriously incommoded,—& I do want to get at them again.

Yours always
Josiah C. Wedgwood

Margot Asquith: diary
(Countess Oxford and Asquith papers)

19 February 1915

Henry said to me in the motor:

Winston just now is absolutely maddening, how I wish Oc had not joined his beastly Naval Brigade! He is having a great Review of them today. He inspects the Brigade in a uniform of his own which will cause universal derision among our soldiers!

Clemmy said some time ago that inventing uniforms was one of Winston's chief pleasures and temptations.

He has just emerged from a fearful row with K. by the skin of his teeth[2] and has now let himself into another.

M: do tell me.

H: K. has just been to see me about it. Sir John wrote from St. Omer and tells K. that Winston has offered him 9000 of his Naval Brigade ready to go into action at once in the trenches—and a squadron of armed motor cars and French asks if he may be allowed to remove the guns and use the motors which shows what he thinks of the use of these expensive follies—!

K. is of course furious—and says to me he wonders what Winston would

---

[1] Michael Frederic Rimington, 1858–1928. Entered Army, 1881. Major-General, 1910. Inspector-General of Cavalry, India, 1911–15. Lieutenant-General commanding the Indian Cavalry Division in France, 1915. Commanded the Reserve Cavalry Centre attached to Headquarter Units, France, 1916. Knighted, 1921.

[2] For over a week Churchill and Kitchener had been in dispute about the purchase of rifles from abroad. Churchill believed that Kitchener was making insufficient efforts to obtain Brazilian rifles, then on the market, for the British Army. 'I do beg you not to let this opportunity slip,' Churchill had written on 13 February, 'soon the chance may be gone for ever.' (Kitchener papers) But Kitchener had refused to be hustled into action, being sceptical of the Brazilian offer.

say if he—K.—was always writing to Jellicoe offering to do this and that. Of course Winston is intolerable. It is all *vanity*—he is devoured by vanity.

M: It was curious to me to see how depressed he was when I congratulated him on his remarkably good naval speech in the House on Monday night (8th February 1915).

H: It was merely because he thought the newspapers should have praised it *more*—he is quite childish. I have written him a very stiff letter. Its most trying as K. and he had got a 'modus vivendi'.

Winston S. Churchill to Lord Kitchener
(Copy, Churchill papers: 13/47)

19 February 1915   Admiralty

My dear Kitchener,

You have known for months past of the armoured cars & the naval battalions, & what was the intention with which they were called into being. It has always rested & now rests exclusively with you when & how they shall join the Army.

So far as the cars are concerned I shd be glad if you found it possible to send over 2 squadrons. I have heard indirectly that one of the Cavalry Generals—Rimington—is vy anxious to work them with his cavalry division so as to be able to make use of them if the armies begin to manœuvre.

However if you do not wish them to go—please tell me—as I will try to find some other employment for them.

With regard to the naval battalions I suggest that you might tell French that circumstances have now arisen wh have led the Admiralty to direct their troops to the S. of Europe temporarily so that the question of their employment in France is suspended.

It wd be a great pity to have an argument on the letter of a phrase. If his letters had begun 'I have heard that there are some armoured cars available which the Admiralty have prepared & etc.' instead of by talking about 'the offer of the First Lord of the Admiralty' this whole wearisome incident wd have been avoided. . . .

Yours sincerely
Winston S. Churchill

Winston S. Churchill to Vice-Admiral Carden: telegram

(*Draft, Admiralty papers: 137/109*)

19 February 1915   Admiralty
1.30 am

Report at nightfall 19th effects of bombardment & thereafter report fully
every day. Possibility of an attack by S/Ms from Adriatic cannot be wholly
excluded & you shd bear this in mind. Thirdly the instructions given you are
to be taken as a guide & not as a rule, & you are not prohibited from using
Director fire of Q. Elizth in special circumstances.

                                                                        WSC

Vice-Admiral Carden to Winston S. Churchill: telegram

(*Churchill papers*)

19 February 1915

Personal and Secret. Bombardment commenced 8 a.m. to-day.[1] Aircraft
reconnoitred yesterday.

Winston S. Churchill to Lord Fisher and Vice-Admiral Oliver

(*Admiralty papers: 137/1089*)

19 February 1915   Admiralty

Smoke may be useful in the Dardanelles to cover minesweeping and other
operations. Dr Fowler,[2] of the Hydrographic Department, ought to set to
work and draft a telegram to Malta providing for a sufficient quantity of
smoke-making material, so that when the wind is favourable, it can be used
from trawlers etc., to obscure the view of the field armies on the Gallipoli
Peninsula and Asiatic bank.

I suggest Dr. Fowler should prepare this telegram fully to-day, and submit
it to COS.

                                                                        WSC

[1] This was the same day on which, in 1807, Admiral Duckworth had successfully passed
the Straits. But he had been caught by a head wind when only eight miles from Constantinople, and after waiting a week in vain for a favourable wind, had retired, losing 150 men
in repassing the Dardanelles' batteries. Contemporary critics of Duckworth suggested that
had he taken 10,000 troops on board they could have landed on the shore of the Marmara
and marched on Constantinople.

[2] George Herbert Fowler, 1861–1940. Zoologist and oceanographer. Edition, *Science of the
Sea*. Served in the Hydrographic and Naval Intelligence Departments of the Admiralty,
1914–18.

Meeting of the War Council: Secretary's notes

(*Copy, Churchill papers: 2/86*)

Present: H. H. Asquith (*in the Chair*), A. J. Balfour, Lord Haldane, Lord Crewe, Winston S. Churchill, Lord Fisher, Sir Arthur Wilson, David Lloyd George, Sir Edward Grey, Lord Kitchener, Sir James Wolfe Murray, Lieutenant-Colonel Hankey (*Secretary*) *In attendance:* Major-General Callwell

19 February 1915   10 Downing Street

THE DARDANELLES

LORD KITCHENER said that the latest information from Egypt was that the Turks were retiring from the Canal. There appeared to be no intention of an advance by the Turks in greater force than before. For repelling such attacks, or even stronger attacks, the garrison of Egypt was sufficient without the assistance of the Australians and New Zealanders, who numbered 39,000 in all, and were regarded as an army corps. He was inclined to substitute these troops for the XXIXth Division in support of the naval attack on the Dardanelles. They would arrive at Lemnos sooner than the XXIXth Division, as the latter would in any case have to go first to Alexandria to land its horses and impedimenta, which could not conveniently be landed at Lemnos owing to the absence of facilities. The XXIXth Division would be held in readiness to proceed later to the East, if required. In view of the recent Russian set-back in East Prussia, he was averse to sending away the XXIXth Division at present.

GENERAL WOLFE MURRAY said that it was only proposed at present to send the infantry of the Australians and New Zealanders, numbering 30,000. The cavalry would then be left in Egypt. This would leave 44,000 men for the defence of Egypt, including Indians and Territorials.

MR. CHURCHILL said it would be a great disappointment to the Admiralty if the XXIXth Division was not sent out. The attack on the Dardanelles was a very heavy naval undertaking. It was difficult to over-rate the military advantages which success would bring. Its importance could only be appreciated by considering the question as a whole from the point of view of the Allies. In France there was a complete deadlock; the Russians were arrested. At what point, then, could a favourable blow be struck by the Allies? The reply was the Dardanelles. In his opinion, it would be a thrifty disposition on our part to have 50,000 men in this region. The Russian estimate of the force necessary to capture Constantinople and open the Dardanelles and Bosphorus was two army corps. He had hoped strongly, therefore, that we should have 50,000 men within reach of the Dardanelles, which could be concentrated there in three days. He was sending out the ten trained battalions of the Naval Division. Neither these, however, nor the Australians and New Zealanders, could be called first-rate troops at present, and they required a stiffening of regulars. He did not insist that the troops must be landed at Lemnos. He would be quite content if they were sent to Alexandria, where the men and horses could be landed for exercise while the heavy gear was left on board. We should never forgive ourselves if this promising operation failed owing to insufficient military support at the critical moment.

LORD KITCHENER said that in case of emergency more troops might be spared from Egypt.

LORD CREWE asked that the position in Mesopotamia should not be lost sight of. The general opinion was that the force operating there ought to be strengthened by the addition of two brigades from India, which would raise it to a total strength of two divisions. Lord Kitchener, he said, held the view that India ought to be content with a smaller garrison than in normal times, and even to run some risks in order to secure the position in Mesopotamia. Lord Kitchener, however, had given him to understand that as soon as Egypt was safe he would send some troops back to India.

LORD KITCHENER said this was still his intention.

MR. BALFOUR suggested that, if the Gallipoli Peninsula was occupied, and our passage through the Dardanelles secured, we should obtain all we required. He queried, therefore, the need for two army corps.

MR. CHURCHILL said it was necessary to have a sufficient reserve of men on the spot.

LORD KITCHENER said that the War Committee ought to consider very seriously before advising the removal of the XXIXth Division to the East. The situation in Russia had greatly deteriorated during the last week or two. The Russians had lost very heavily in men, and, what was more serious, they had lost heavily in rifles, of which they were short. If the Germans could inflict a sufficiently decisive defeat on the Russians they would be in a position to bring back great masses of troops very rapidly to France, and there would be a great demand for reinforcements in the Western theatre of war.

MR. LLOYD GEORGE agreed that the position was very serious. Russia might receive a knock-out blow, and her offensive would be delayed for three months or longer. Czernowitz had already fallen. If the Russians were driven out of Galicia, and to the line of the Bug in Poland, the position of the Allies would be very grave. Had we to admit that we were impotent in view of such a contingency? In his opinion, the Germans would not send their forces West, but would endeavour to smash Serbia and settle the Balkan question. The view appeared now to prevail that Germany would aim at the conquest of the north-east corner of Serbia with a view to establishing through communication and direct access to Bulgaria, and thence to Constantinople. If we had some troops in the East, as proposed by Mr. Churchill, they would be available either for Constantinople or, if that operation failed, to support the Serbians. We certainly ought to make some effort to retrieve the situation in the East.

THE PRIME MINISTER agreed, but considered that the most effective way would be to strike a big blow at the Dardanelles.

LORD KITCHENER agreed with the Prime Minister. If the fact of not sending the XXIXth Division would in any way jeopardize the success of the attack on the Dardanelles he would despatch it. He doubted whether the Germans would attack Serbia, as suggested by Mr. Lloyd George.

SIR EDWARD GREY pointed out that, according to the Greek estimate, fifty days would be required to transport the Greek army to Serbia up the Salonica Railway.

THE PRIME MINISTER read a telegram received from Greece the general effect of which was that Greece required fifty days to transport her army to Serbia; that it would depend on a single line of railway; that in fifteen days Bulgaria could reach Veles on three lines of advance; but that, if Bulgaria attacked Serbia, the Greeks would be able to attack them from the south.

MR. CHURCHILL suggested that General Joffre had sent out General Pau[1] with instructions to 'spike our guns' by forcing his views on the Greek General Staff.

LORD KITCHENER said he had every intention of supporting the Dardanelles operation, but he considered two divisions on the spot to be sufficient at first. There was no object in sending out troops from here which we might require.

MR. BALFOUR said that, if the Navy was successful at Gallipoli, the effect would be almost as great as the occupation of Constantinople.

MR. LLOYD GEORGE suggested that we ought to send more than three divisions. It was worth while to take some risks in order to achieve a decisive

---

[1] Paul Marie César Gerald Pau, 1848–1932. Lieutenant, 1869. Lost his right hand during the Franco-Prussian War, 1870. Member of the Conseil Supérieur de la Guerre, 1909. Passed into the Reserve, 1913. Recalled, 1914. Commanded the Army of Alsace, August–October 1914, reoccupying part of the Province. On several missions outside France, 1915–16, before finally leaving the Army, 1916.

operation, which might win the war. From the discussion he gathered that the maximum force available for operations in the East was as follows:—

The Australians and New Zealanders (including mounted troops)				39,000
The XXIXth Division..	..	..	..	19,000
Naval Division ..	..	..	..	10,000
Marines ..	..	..	..	4,000
French Division..	..	..	..	15,000
Russians..	..	..	..	10,000
Total ..	..	..	..	97,000

SIR EDWARD GREY asked if we were safe in the West.

MR. LLOYD GEORGE said he had spoken on this subject with a great many officers who had been at the front. There was a general agreement that our army could not carry out a successful attack without a very heavy loss of life, and the same was true of the French Army. No doubt it was also true of the Germans. For the Germans to attack, therefore, would be the best thing that could happen. It was just as costly for them to try and break us as for us to try and break them.

LORD KITCHENER did not think that either side as yet had made a really determined effort to break through. The Germans would make quite a different kind of attack from any hitherto attempted in the West, if they meant business.

MR. CHURCHILL suggested that, where such large forces were in question, the retention of the XXIXth Division was unlikely to make the difference between success and failure.

MR. BALFOUR asked when the New Armies would be ready.

LORD KITCHENER said that the 10th April was the present date for the first army, but there might be minor hitches postponing it a little. He thought it probable that the Germans had a pretty good idea of this date, and that all their plans hinged on it. His view was that the Germans had precipitated their attack on the Russians, notwithstanding that the season was unfavourable, hoping to defeat the Russians and to hurry troops back to the West before our New Armies were ready to take the field.

SIR EDWARD GREY expressed the opinion that in the contingency contemplated the Austrians would attack the Serbians in force while the Germans came to the West.

MR. CHURCHILL said that a comparatively small force would be sufficient to finish off Serbia. He felt that the whole situation in the East had changed very much to our disadvantage in the last month. The Russians had sustained reverses; the Greeks and Roumanians were now rather lukewarm; and Bulgaria had rather veered over towards our enemies.

LORD KITCHENER said it was precisely these reasons which led him to wish to retain the XXIXth Division at home, in order to assist in meeting any resulting emergency which might arise in the West.

SIR EDWARD GREY said that a great deal in the Balkans was staked on our attack on Constantinople. If there was a fair prospect of success it would be worth taking some risk.

LORD KITCHENER said that his point was that we had enough troops to ensure success, provided that the navy was successful, without sending the XXIXth Division.

MR. BALFOUR suggested that, if the XXIXth Division was sent to Malta, it would be available either to reinforce the troops sent against the Dardanelles or to go to France, arriving at either destination within a few days.

LORD KITCHENER replied that the French railway communications were so slow that it would be quicker to send troops to the North of France by sea than to rail them through France. He had a difference of opinion with his advisers on this point, and a test had been made which had proved the truth of this. In fact, therefore, the XXIXth Division would be too far away at Malta to be of value as a reinforcement to our army in France.

THE PRIME MINISTER said that the general situation would be vitally affected by the issue of the Dardanelles operation. Success would probably change the attitude of the Balkans, which, from our point of view, was very unsatisfactory.

MR. CHURCHILL suggested that all preparations for the despatch of the XXIXth Division should go forward. The fitting of the transports, which had already commenced, should be continued. In four or five days we should have made some impression on the forts, and should have a good idea as to whether we were likely to achieve success by naval means. He wished, however, to lay stress on the fact that the navy could only open the Straits for armoured ships, and could not guarantee an unmolested passage for merchant ships unless the shores of the Dardanelles were cleared of the enemy's riflemen and field guns.

THE PRIME MINISTER then read some extracts from C.I.D. Paper 92–B, dated the 20th September, 1906, on the subject of 'The Possibility of a

Joint Naval and Military Attack upon the Dardanelles', tending to show that military co-operation was essential to success.[1]

LIEUTENANT-COLONEL HANKEY explained that C.I.D. Paper 92–B had been withdrawn from circulation owing to its extreme secrecy at the time when it was written. Though not exactly applicable to the present problem, he had thought it worth while to bring it to the notice of the War Council. He also drew attention to the conclusions reached at the 92nd meeting of the C.I.D., held on the 28th February, 1907.[2]

(There was some more or less desultory discussion at this point on C.I.D. Paper 92–B and the question of how far it was applicable to present conditions.)[3]

LORD HALDANE said that we had not yet settled how many troops we should require, or the precise purpose for which they were to be used.

LORD KITCHENER considered three divisions to be ample.

MR. CHURCHILL recalled the various phases of the question. The first proposal was to send no troops at all, leaving the Dardanelles to be dealt with by the Navy. The next phase was that the XXIXth Division only was to be sent to Salonica in the view of thereby involving Greece in the war. Then the situation had again changed by the Russian defeat in the East, and it became desirable to ensure success in the Dardanelles. If this operation was successful, it was possible that the Greeks might change their minds, and that a complete change might be brought about in the Balkans.

LORD KITCHENER said that the Russian reverse in the East might be followed by further defeats, and this might react in the West in such manner as to make us very short of men. Nevertheless, if events should show it to be necessary, he was prepared to send the XXIXth Division to the East.

LORD HALDANE wanted to know what was the precise function of the three divisions estimated by Lord Kitchener.

[1] The paper to which Asquith referred was in fact circulated to the CID on 20 December 1906. It had been written the previous day, signed by General Sir Neville Lyttelton (1845–1931), Chief of the General Staff, 1904–8. Its author was Charles Callwell.

[2] The Committee of Imperial Defence meeting of 28 February 1907, at which Fisher, Grey and Hankey were among those present, had concluded 'that the operation of landing an Expeditionary Force on or near the Gallipoli Peninsula would involve great risk, and should not be undertaken if other means of bringing pressure to bear on Turkey were available.' (*Churchill papers: 2/74*)

[3] In a memorandum of 1 September 1916 Hankey informed the Dardanelles Commissioners that several points of contrast had been discussed between conditions in 1907 and 1915. These included, he wrote, the adverse effect on Turkey of the severe defeats in the Balkan Wars, the fact that Turkey was at war on three other fronts (the Caucasus, Egypt and Mesopotamia), the hope that as a result of aircraft reconnaissance the value of naval bombardment was greatly increased, and the belief that the development of the submarine would greatly harass Turkish communications with Gallipoli. (*Copy, Churchill papers: 2/85*)

LORD KITCHENER said that a force up to this size might be required to secure the passage of the Dardanelles after the fall of the forts.

MR. CHURCHILL said that no one could foretell the results of success in a country like Turkey. He did not ask for troops actually to be sent to the Dardanelles, but only that they should be within hail. It might give us a tremendous opportunity. Some risks must be run in any military operation. In his opinion, the main risk in this case was that the horses and men of the XXIXth Division would get out of training through being cooped up on board ship.

LORD KITCHENER repeated that he was ready to send the XXIXth Division in case of necessity, but he did not want to send it just yet. He wished to wait until the Russian situation cleared up. Much depended on whether the Russians could hold the line of the Niemen. The Germans, in his opinion, knew quite well that the Russians had 900,000 men in reserve without rifles. Unfortunately, many rifles must have been lost in recent reverses. The question was one of grave anxiety. It was possible, of course, that the Russians might be able to hold out. On the last occasion that the Germans had penetrated towards the Niemen, the Russians had recovered and driven them back into East Prussia. Then, however, they had had large reserves; but now the situation was different, and their reserves had been thrown in on the Warta. We ought, therefore, not to speculate on the Russians holding out. The Russian military attaché[1] had come to him with a new scheme for obtaining rifles, and he had promised to co-operate, but he was not at all sanguine of obtaining them. In the meantime the Russian output of rifles was limited to 45,000 a month.

LORD FISHER asked how many troops were to be sent from Egypt. The transports to carry a force from Egypt would in the main have to be sent from this country, and it was important for the Admiralty to know the exact 'state' of the force. It would be three weeks before the transports reached Alexandria.

SIR EDWARD GREY asked that they should take out some coal to Egypt.

LORD FISHER agreed.

MR. BALFOUR suggested that the War Council ought to be informed what would be the precise political effect of an occupation of the Gallipoli Peninsula combined with naval command of the Sea of Marmora. He wished that the Foreign Office would prepare a Memorandum on the subject.

---

[1] Nicholas S. Yermoloff, 1854–1924. Russian Military Attaché in London for over twenty-five years, until the revolution of 1917. Lieutenant-General; honorary Knight Commander of the Victorian Order. He died in exile in London.

MR. CHURCHILL said it ought to give us control of Turkey.

LORD KITCHENER expected that in this event the Turkish army would evacuate Europe altogether.

MR. BALFOUR asked if we should be bound to afford military protection to the Christian population of Constantinople.

SIR EDWARD GREY said that they would have to take their chance.

MR. LLOYD GEORGE said we ought to have more detailed information of Russia's ability to carry on the war. We wanted to know how many men Russia had left. A few weeks ago we understood they had 1,200,000 men. Since then they were reported to have lost 400,000 men. If this were true, they would now only have 800,000 men left. How could we make plans when one of our Allies kept us entirely in the dark?

SIR EDWARD GREY asked how we could get the information. We telegraphed every day on the subject. He asked whether General Wolfe Murray, who knew Russia and the Russian language, could suggest any way of doing it.

GENERAL WOLFE MURRAY replied that he had no suggestion to make.[1]

MR. LLOYD GEORGE said that the Russian Minister of Finance,[2] who was himself kept entirely in the dark, had told him that the Russian War Office counted for nothing, and that the Grand Duke Nicholas was the only person who knew the truth. He pointed to the extraordinary discrepancy in the estimates of the Russian strength. The Russians themselves had told the French a few weeks ago that they would have 3,000,000 men in the field by March.

MR. CHURCHILL said that the Russians were holding a very long line of some 500 miles. It was clear, therefore, that they must have a good deal more than 800,000 men in the field.

(*Conclusion.*)

Transports to be prepared:—

1. *To be sent out to Alexandria to convey the Australian and New Zealand troops to Lemnos.*

2. *To take the XXIXth Division to the Mediterranean, if required.*

No final decision to be taken at present with regard to the XXIXth Division.

---

[1] It was for remarks such as these that Churchill used to refer to Wolfe Murray as 'sheep' Murray.

[2] Peter Bark, 1858–1937. Russian Minister of Finance, 1914–17. In exile in England from 1917 until his death, he was knighted by George V in 1935.

Winston S. Churchill to Lord Kitchener

(*Copy, Churchill papers: 13/47*)

20 February 1915   Admiralty

My dear Kitchener,

I hope your letter means that the 'advance party' from Egypt will be ready as soon as transport for 10,000 men is assembled at Alexandria. It costs nothing to be ready.

If the Turks clear out of the Gallipoli peninsula we ought at least to have a force that can prevent it being re-occupied. As to cutting off their retreat— that is much more ambitious, and only a good General on the spot can judge that. It may be that a part will go and the next might be cut off.

I should be very glad if you could see your way to place a good General at the side of the Admiral as quickly as possible. You spoke the other day of General Hunter-Weston.[1] Would it not be possible to send him or someone like him out at once to take command of whatever troops, including the Naval Division, may arrive?

40,000—this is what we are providing transport for. It is for you to send as many as you can or choose. It is much better to have too much transport than too little. . . .

The operations yesterday were delayed by weather.

Yours sincerely
Winston S. Churchill

Winston S. Churchill to Lord Kitchener

(*Copy, Churchill papers: 13/47*)

20 February 1915   Admiralty

My dear Kitchener,

I send you a copy of my minute about transport for the Mediterranean. It is possible that the operations at the Dardanelles may go much more rapidly than has been expected. In this case it would be vital to have enough men to hold the lines of Bulair. There will be 2,000 Marines at Lemnos, but that is not enough, and I ask you to organize in Egypt 8,000 or 10,000 men

[1] Aylmer Hunter-Weston, 1864–1940. Entered Royal Engineers, 1884. Served on Kitchener's staff in the Sudan, 1898. Chief Staff Officer to Sir John French's Cavalry Division in South Africa, 1900. Brigadier-General commanding 11th Infantry Brigade, August 1914; promoted Major-General for distinguished service in the field. Commanded the 29th Division at the landing on Cape Helles, April 1915; promoted Lieutenant-General for the successful landing. Commanded the VIIIth Corps at the Dardanelles and in France, 1915–18. Knighted, 1915. Conservative MP, 1916–35.

who could in an emergency be despatched much earlier than the others. If the operations take a normal course, this would not be necessary, but it appears to me to be an indispensable precaution. Transports are being provided accordingly.

I shall be glad to have an answer to my letter of yesterday.

Yours very truly
Winston S. Churchill

Winston S. Churchill: minute[1]
(Churchill papers: 13/54)

20 February 1915   Admiralty
Secret
Please return

1. Transports should be provided for seven battalions and details of the RND, approximately 8,000 men, leaving Avonmouth on Saturday the 27th for Lemnos.
2. All preparations are to be made to embark the 29th Division independently of the above with the least possible delay. The despatch of this Division is not, however, finally decided.
3. There should be accumulated at Alexandria by Saturday the 27th inst, sufficient transport to carry 8,000 or 10,000 infantry. This may be wanted in a hurry if the Dardanelles operations take a favourable turn. This transport must be found locally. The transports which carry the two Marine battalions and some of the ships in the Egyptian Prize Courts might be available.
4. The emergency action provided for in par 3 may not be required, as the operations in the Dardanelles may take a leisurely course. In that event the ships collected for the emergency would form part of a larger fleet of transports which is to be collected without delay for the transport of approximately 40,000 men, details of which will be given by the War Office.

WSC

---

[1] Churchill sent one copy of this minute to Kitchener, and another to Graeme Thomson, the Director of Transports at the Admiralty, who noted on it later that day: 'Action is proceeding with all possible dispatch.' *(Churchill papers: 13/54)*

Lord Kitchener to Winston S. Churchill
(*Churchill papers: 13/54*)

20 February 1915   War Office

My dear Churchill,

I have telegraphed to Maxwell about the force in Egypt. The French are in a great way about so many troops being employed as you told them of.

I have just seen Grey about it & hope we shall not be saddled with a French contingent for the Dardanelles.

I do not quite understand what you mean by holding the lines of Bulair. Is it to prevent the 75,000 Turks from escaping? I hardly think we should have enough for this at night if they determined to get through.

In your enclosure you mention 40,000 men. This is new to me.

I have already finished the two cases. I have told French he cannot have the battalions & we are willing to ask for the cars. I cannot make out why I have only just got your letter of yesterday. Sorry to hear you are ill.

Yours very truly
Kitchener

Lord Fisher to Winston S. Churchill
(*Churchill papers: 13/56*)

20 February 1915   Admiralty

Dear Winston,

I suggest to you you should deal directly with Kitchener to stop the transport of troops during this bright moon or we shall have a calamity bigger than the Formidable and even more inexcusable! the only exception I would make would be allowing the sailing of the Transport conveying the Base Staff for the Dardanelles under special precautions—all the Cross Channel steamers should be commandeered for the transport of troops including all the Irish and Isle of Man boats and their impedimenta sent over in the transports in the few dark hours that may be. . . .

Lord Kitchener to Sir John Maxwell: telegram
(*Copy, Churchill papers: 2/88*)

20 February 1915   War Office

The Naval Squadron is proceeding with the bombardment of the Dardanelles, and during the first day they have silenced one fort and severely damaged another. In order to assist the Navy in their undertaking a force is being concentrated in Lemnos Island to give any co-operation that may be required and to occupy any captured forts.

At present 2,000 Marines are concentrated on the Island, to be followed about 13th March by 8,000 more.

You should warn a force of approximately 30,000 of the Australian and New Zealand contingents under Birdwood[1] to prepare for this service. We shall send transports from here to convey these troops to Lemnos, which should arrive at Alexandria about 9th March. You should, however, communicate through the Navy with Admiral Carden, commanding at the Dardanelles, as he may require a considerable force before that date and in order that you may send him what he most requires.

You should not, therefore, wait till the transports arrive from here but should take up any transports you can obtain and despatch units to Lemnos immediately. Admiral Carden and myself should be kept fully informed of the numbers and time of despatch of any troops you send.

It will be necessary for specially competent officers to be selected for this first detachment as, until the main force under Birdwood joins them, they will have to act independently. Admiral Robinson[2] will be able to give you details of the ships available for transport at Egyptian ports.

You should bear in mind that, at the outset, it will be Infantry that will, no doubt, be most required. But the force had better be accompanied by some of the Indian mountain guns if they can be spared. Any sappers competent in demolition should also be sent with the first detachment, and special officers for Intelligence work. . . .

We are telegraphing to you separately as to Base Staff, details and supplies, which we are sending from here.

[1] William Riddell Birdwood, 1865–1951. Lieutenant, Royal Scots Fusiliers, 1883. General Officer commanding the Australian and New Zealand Army Corps (ANZAC), 1914–18. Lieutenant-General commanding the ANZAC landing, 25 April 1915. Commander-in-Chief of the Allied forces at the Dardanelles, October 1915–January 1916. Knighted, 1913. Field-Marshal, 1925. Commander-in-Chief, India, 1922–30. Master of Peterhouse, Cambridge, 1931–8. Created Baron, 1938.

[2] Henry Russell Robinson, 1856–1942. Entered Navy, 1870; retired with the rank of Rear-Admiral, 1908. Director-General of Ports and Lighthouses, Egypt, 1909–20. A Pasha of Egypt. Knighted, 1917.

J. C. C. Davidson[1] to Edward Marsh

(*Admiralty papers: 116/1336*)

20 February 1915   Colonial Office

My dear Marsh,

We have just received a minute from Sir Edward Grey with reference to the telegram from Cyprus of which I sent you a copy this morning. The minute runs as follows: 'Sir Edward Grey is unaware that any British Governor or Official is to be appointed to Lemnos & strongly deprecates any such announcement.'

In view of this does the 1st Lord wish us to instruct Clauson to hold his hand as regards Wemyss' advisory official Lukach[1] and to send no one at present.

Yours

J. C. C. Davidson

I understand that you received a similar expression of Sir E. Grey's opinion.

Sir Edward Grey to Winston S. Churchill

(*Admiralty papers: 116/1336*)

20 February 1915   Foreign Office

Dear Churchill,

I am aghast at this telegram. Do please remember that all Greece agrees to is the use of the harbour at Lemnos by our ships.

We do not take charge of the Island & no Governor must be appointed or official steps commenced to take over the Island.

A real catastrophe may be provoked if you go beyond the agreement with Greece & I may have to say that my position is impossible & I must resign.

Our ships can use the harbour that is all we have at present from Greece & I warned you verbally the other day that no Governor must be appointed

---

[1] John Colin Campbell Davidson, 1889–1970. Private Secretary to successive Colonial Secretaries: Lord Crewe, 1910; Lewis Harcourt, 1910–15; and Bonar Law, 1915–16. Private Secretary to Bonar Law, 1916–20. Conservative MP, 1920–3 and 1924–27. Chancellor of the Duchy of Lancaster, 1923–4 and 1931–7. Created Viscount, 1937. Chairman of the Unionist Party, 1927–30. Controller of Production, Ministry of Information, 1941.

[2] Harry Charles Lukach, 1884–1969. A traveller in eastern Europe, the Balkans, Turkey and Alaska. Joined the colonial service, 1908. Assistant Secretary to the Governor of Cyprus, 1912–15. Served as political officer on HMS *Doris*, January–February 1915. Political Officer on the staff of Admiral Wemyss, 1915–16, and of Admiral Robeck, 1916–19. Changed his surname to Luke, 1920. British Chief Commissioner in the Caucasus, 1920. Assistant Governor of Jerusalem, 1920–4. Colonial Secretary, Sierra Leone, 1924–8. Chief Secretary, Palestine, 1928–30. Lieutenant Governor of Malta, 1930–8. Knighted 1933. High Commissioner, Western Pacific, and Governor of Fiji, 1938–42.

by us. To appoint a Governor wont help us to take the Dardanelles: we want the use of the harbour without titles & other useless things.

Y sincerely
E. Grey

Winston S. Churchill to Sir Edward Grey
(*Admiralty papers: 116/1336*)

20 February 1915   Admiralty

My dear Grey,

The original telegram from the Greeks said that they wd go out on the 22nd leaving their batteries all standing, & that they wished us to look after the guns. Lemnos is also to be used for a British & probably a French Division to concentrate at. It is therefore quite clear that something must be meant beyond the use of the waters of Mudros Bay, & that the shore landing places, camping grounds, & defensive positions round that bay are also comprised. In these circumstances it was thought that the Admiral appointed to look after the base & harbour, which will be used by a fleet of nearly 70 British ships apart from French, shd have at his hand some skilful official versed in the problems of a Turco-Greek island. The Chief of the Staff therefore telegraphed to the Vice Admiral advising him to apply to the Governor of Cyprus, for some competent official.

Shortly after this another telegram arrived from Greece, speaking of the transference being limited to Mudros Bay; & I also had my talk with you about a Governor. In consequence, Adl Wemyss was told that he wd not be appointed Governor of Lemnos, but merely Senior Naval Officer at Mudros; & all that you wished in this respect is being done.

Admiral Carden will be informed accordingly.

At the same time it seems clear that there must be some Governing authority in this island, especially if it is to be used as a cantonment for troops, as all sorts of questions as between Turks & Greeks, British & French, will have to be settled by the S.N.O.; & it is certainly desirable that he shd have the advice of people who understand this part of the world.

The only workable theory is that Lemnos is a Turkish island in British naval occupation. Any theory that it is a Greek island, or a Turkish island in Anglo-Greek occupation, is plainly inadmissible.

Yours very sincerely
Winston S. Churchill

P.S. I presume the enclosed telegram to Carden will meet your views. Would you please send it back with this letter of which I shd like to keep a copy.

Admiralty to Vice-Admiral Carden: telegram
(*Copy, Admiralty papers: 137/109*)

20 February 1915   Admiralty

Occupation of Lemnos must be kept to the minimum compatible with Naval and Military necessities. Our presence there is somewhat irregular, and every effort must be made not to compromise Greece. Everything must be as informal as possible. Admiral Wemyss will be appointed S.N.O. Mudros Bay and not Governor of Lemnos. It is necessary however that he should have a competent adviser with local knowledge and Colonial Office is being asked to place Mr Lukach's services at his disposal. You should be careful that nothing is done or said to give impression that occupation is other than purely temporary.

Sir Edward Grey to Winston S. Churchill
(*Admiralty papers: 116/1336*)

20 February 1915   33 Eccleston Square[1]

Dear Churchill,

The telegram to Carden will meet the case. Let everything in the way of administration be as informal as possible & nothing said about it outside.

For years the Admiralty (notably Fisher) have spoken of having Lemnos & if we announce urbi et orbi (Marsh will translate) that we have appointed a Governor not only the Greeks but the French & Russians will think we have bagged Lemnos & mean to keep it & that we are out for grab & not for the common cause & the very success of our operations at the Dardanelles will be watched with suspicion by our own friends. So do make your Admirals careful to keep all their action at Lemnos within the limits necessary to use the island for strategic purposes & to say as little as possible. I have suggested an addition to the telegram to Carden for this purpose.

I enclose a minute for the C.O. to correct one that I sent there in haste this morning.

So sorry to hear of your influenza; but if you have really smashed up three forts in the first day it should be a good tonic.

Y sincerely
E. Grey

---

[1] The house in which Churchill had lived from 1909. He moved to Admiralty House in 1913. Grey rented it from Churchill until 1917. In the inter-war years, after Churchill had moved to Chartwell, 33 Eccleston Square became the Headquarters of the Labour Party.

Lord Fisher to Winston S. Churchill

(*Draft, Admiralty papers: 137/109*)

20 February 1915   Admiralty

First Lord,

Propose to send [following] telegram:

In view of the 'Queen Elizabeth' only being able to use one set of engines she must not be risked in narrow waters.

Fisher

Winston S. Churchill to Vice-Admiral Oliver

(*Admiralty papers: 137/109*)

20 February 1915   Admiralty

Before sending this, I shd like to know whether 'Q. Elizth' will not be required to fire from just inside the entrance towards the forts at the narrows, or whether she can do all her work from outside & by firing across the peninsula—I think fort 19 or 20 (the one with the castle in it) requires to be brought under fire at 18000 yards. Can anything but 'Q.E.' do this? I quite agree she shd not go through the narrows, & I shall be glad if without spoiling the show she can be kept outside altogether.

WSC

Lord Fisher to Winston S. Churchill

(*Churchill papers: 13/56*)

20 February 1915   Admiralty

Dear Winston,

As I have always (*before the Balkan War and when Admiral in the Mediter-ranean*[1]) been an '*out and out*' Bulgarian this paper[2] has my deepest sympathy and fullest concurrence with the Bulgarian Minister of War.[3]

We have done nothing else this whole war but lose opportunities! As I told you last night the one most awful thing in war is '*the careful man*'! He's

[1] Lord Fisher, then Vice-Admiral Sir John Fisher, was Commander-in-Chief in the Mediterranean from 1899 to 1902. He was promoted Admiral in 1901.

[2] It is not clear to which particular memorandum Fisher is referring. In return for being willing to attack Turkey, the Bulgarians had sought a British promise of Turkish territory, including Adrianople, and an Anglo-French guarantee that Serbia would not attack them. Fisher, Churchill and Lloyd George all believed that Britain should do its utmost to bring Bulgaria into the war. But Grey was sceptical of any such agreement having its desired result.

[3] Ivan Ivanovich Fitscheff, 1860–1931. Studied in Italy at the Staff College, Turin, in the 1880's. Chief of the Bulgarian General Staff, 1908–14. An opponent of rash ventures in foreign affairs. Minister of War, 1914–15. Bulgarian Minister in Bucharest, 1921–3.

the man with the one talent! Shove him into outer darkness where there is grinding and gnashing of teeth!

Yours,

F

Winston S. Churchill to Lord Kitchener

(*Kitchener papers*)

22 February 1915   Admiralty

My dear Kitchener,

I have had a talk with Lord Moulton[1] this afternoon upon the Cordite question. I am getting vy anxious about this. The new factory requires a great effort to create, & will certainly not be ready in time. Your urgent needs have practically cut us off from the source of war supplies to wh we had any right to look. I think the cordite problem requires to be treated as a whole. The Army can use cordite, or other propellents, wh the Navy could not without undue risk to the ships. A new factory may be able to make some kinds for the Army, & Waltham Abbey may be the only factory capable of making other kinds for the Navy. Anyhow I suggest to you that Moulton should take over propellents of all kinds as well as high explosives, & let us have a large & coordinated scheme of action. Moulton says he can easily do it, & he wd like to do it. If you see no objection to this, I shall be very glad.[2] After June our shell will be ahead of the propellent, & the demands upon us may at any time become very large.

Yours very truly
Winston S. Churchill

Winston S. Churchill to Lord Kitchener

(*Churchill papers: 13/45*)

22 February 1915   Admiralty
Not sent

My dear Kitchener,

The Royal Naval Division 12,000 strong will be fed on & from their transports till they are joined by or join up with a military force. Thereafter

[1] John Fletcher Moulton, 1844–1921. Mathematician and barrister. Liberal MP, 1885–86, 1894–95, 1898–1906. Knighted, 1906. Created Baron, 1912. Lord Appeal in Ordinary, 1912. Chairman of the Committee on Chemical Products, 1914. Chairman of the Committee on High Explosives, 1914. Director-General, Explosives Supplies, Ministry of Munitions, 1915.

[2] On 23 February Kitchener replied to Churchill, agreeing that Lord Moulton should 'help you to push forward your new cordite factory and also . . . to assist us to start another factory for us'. (*Churchill papers: 13/47*)

it would be better if you fed everyone landed. I understand your people will find it quite easy to provide for 12,000 extra to whatever you have now ordered.

There ought to be a good general at Carden's side as soon as possible. You spoke the other day of Hunter-Weston. Could not he or someone equally competent be sent to take command of whatever troops arrive including the Royal Naval Division. He will then be able to judge what ought to be done & what force is required.

The delay in the bombarding is due to weather & must be faced.

The actual result of the first day's firing seems satisfactory.

I provided transports for 40,000 men from Egypt because 39,000 was the figure mentioned by Murray less some casualties; & it costs little to have a margin in hand.

Yours sincerely
Winston S. Churchill

Lord Fisher to Sir John Jellicoe

(*Jellicoe Papers*)

22 February 1915   Admiralty

12,000 soldiers from Egypt join Carden on March 2nd. . . .

Myself I think it utter folly to publish a word about the bombardment & more especially the names of ships[1] but it is all Foreign Office business & pressure from Russia and France. We are their facile dupes! . . .

David Lloyd George: memorandum

(*Copy, Churchill papers: 21/38*)

22 February 1915

SOME FURTHER CONSIDERATIONS ON THE CONDUCT
OF THE WAR

. . . We have hitherto proceeded as if the war could not possibly last beyond next autumn. We should now take exactly the other line—assume that it will last not merely through the year, but conceivably through next year as well. Capital therefore ought to be spent on laying down machinery

---

[1] On 20 February the Admiralty had given to the Press details of the bombardment of 19 February, including the names of the ships, the range of the guns, and the general effects of the bombardment, in which the magazine of one of the forts, at Sedd-el-Bahr, had been blown up. This Press statement was much criticized, both as boastful, and as premature; many critics believed that Churchill was principally responsible for it, although this letter suggests otherwise.

which will enormously expedite the output of rifles, cannon, and all other machinery and munitions of war towards the latter end of the year and the beginning of the next. If it turns out that my estimate errs on the side of pessimism the worst that happens will be that we shall have spent a considerable amount of money, we shall have caused a considerable amount of inconvenience to the population. But all that is nothing compared with the disaster of having to face another year of war with inadequate preparation. This the public will never forgive after the warning we have received, nor ought they to be expected to forgive.

But what is to be done in the meantime? It looks as if during the best part of the present year the Allies must content themselves to be in a position of military inferiority to Germany. During this period the best we can hope for is that we shall be able to hold our own. Can we even accomplish this without summoning some fresh forces to our aid? Having regard to the overwhelming forces at the disposal of Germany there is at least an element of doubt. There are only two directions in which we can turn for any prospect of assistance—the Balkan States and Italy. The Balkans we might conceivably have brought in some months ago, but the Allies have been unfortunate in this quarter. We have only succeeded in bringing in the Turks against us without engaging any other Balkan Power on our behalf. Is it too late to do anything now? Lord Kitchener pointed out the other day at the Council that the Germans had taken risks by attacking the Russians with their full forces before they were quite ready, in order to be prepared to meet the attack of our reinforcements in April. With the one exception of our initial action against Turkey where our promptitude was unmistakable, our risks have all been in the contrary direction; we have generally taken them too late. The momentous step we have taken in attempting to force the Dardanelles must have a decisive effect one way or the other on the Balkans. Are we prepared for either or for any event?

If this great movement succeeds—then, if we are prepared to take immediate advantage of it—its influence may be decisive as far as the Balkan States are concerned. This means that if we have a large force ready, not merely to occupy Gallipoli, but to take any other military action which may be necessary in order to establish our supremacy in that quarter, Roumania, Greece, and, I think, very probably, Bulgaria, will declare for us. If, on the other hand, we have no force on the spot adequate to cope with the Turkish army, it may be that most of the effect of such a brilliant *coup* might be lost. To bring Bulgaria, Roumania, and Greece in with Serbia means throwing an aggregate army of 1,500,000 on to the Austrian flank. This will not only relieve the pressure on Russia, but indirectly on France. It will tend to equalise things, and thus give us time to re-equip the Russian Army.

Now let us take the other contingency—the failure of the Dardanelles effort. Unless it is at once countered, such a failure will be disastrous in the Balkans, and might very well be disastrous throughout the East. The Bulgarian general pointed out that not merely Bulgaria, but Roumania and Italy have a good deal to gain in the way of territory by throwing in their lot with Germany. There is only one guarantee against a catastrophe being precipitated in that quarter as the result of a repulse in the Dardanelles. There must be a strong British force there available to support our friends. Is it quite out of the question that we should anticipate our April preparations by three or four weeks and thus follow the German example of taking risks so as to arrive in time?

The sending of a large expeditionary force undoubtedly involves large preparations—ships, transports to carry troops and their equipment to Salonica or Lemnos, also preparations for transporting them up country; and the Committee of Imperial Defence decided some weeks ago that these preparations should be immediately undertaken, so that if an expedition were at any time determined upon, no delay need ensue owing to lack of sea or land transport. I understand that the Admiralty have done all that was entrusted to them in this respect; I know nothing of the steps taken by the War Office respecting the railways and the roads.

My final suggestion is that a special diplomatic mission, based on our readiness to despatch and maintain a large expeditionary force in the Balkans should immediately be sent to Greece and Roumania to negotiate a military convention. Germany has not depended upon her ordinary diplomatic representatives where the situation presented any great possibilities, friendly or hostile to her welfare. She sent Von der Goltz[1] to Constantinople, Sophia, and Bucharest; Von Bülow[2] to Italy; Dernburg[3] to America. She has not

[1] Colmar von der Goltz, 1843–1916. 2nd Lieutenant, Prussian infantry, 1861. Wounded in the Austro-Prussian war, 1866. Fought in the Franco-Prussian war, 1871. Professor, Potsdam Military School, 1871. Author of several works of military history and strategy, 1873–83. Attached to the Turkish Army, to reorganize the military establishment of Turkey, 1883–96. Lieutenant-General, 1896. Field-Marshal, 1913. Governor General of German-Occupied Belgium, August–November 1914. ADC to the Sultan, November 1914. Commanded the 1st Turkish Army, Mesopotamia, April 1915–April 1916; forced the surrender of the British forces at Kut-el-Amara, December 1915.

[2] Bernhard Heinrich Karl Martin, Prince von Bülow, 1849–1929. Imperial Chancellor, 1900–9. Lived in retirement at his villa in Rome, 1909–14. Temporarily in charge of the German Embassy, Rome, August 1914–May 1915; active in the negotiations between Austria and Italy, but unable to prevent Italy from entering the war on the side of the Entente. Lived in Berlin, 1915–18. Returned to Rome, 1919–29.

[3] Bernhard Dernburg, 1865–1937. Of Jewish extraction, he emigrated from Germany to the United States as a young man, and was engaged in banking. Returned to Germany in the 1890s. Financier. Director of the German Colonial Office, 1906–10. Sent to the USA, 1914, to win American support for Germany. A Democratic Representative in the Reichstag, 1919–33. Minister of Finance, 1919.

depended upon her Bax-Ironsides in critical situations. No doubt they are very good men in their way, but the mere fact that they have remained so long in inferior diplomatic berths proves that, in the opinion of the Foreign Office, their qualities are not of the first order.[1]

DLlG

Lord Fisher to Sir John Jellicoe

(*Jellicoe papers*)

23 February 1915 Admiralty

... Winston has been 3 days in bed with Influenza but it dont lessen the activities of his pen!! ...

Winston S. Churchill: memorandum

(*Churchill papers: 21/38*)

23 February 1915 Admiralty
Secret

1. For us in the present period the decisive point, and the only point where the initiative can be seized and maintained, is in the Balkan Peninsula. With proper military and naval co-operation, and with forces which are available, we can make certain of taking Constantinople by the end of March, and capturing or destroying all Turkish forces in Europe (except any that may shut themselves up in Adrianople). This blow can be struck before the fate of Serbia is decided. Its effect on the whole of the Balkans will be decisive. It will eliminate Turkey as a military factor.

2. The following military forces (at least) are available immediately:—

		Men
In England { 29th Division / Another Territorial Divn. }		33,000
Under orders for Lemnos RN Division		11,000
From Egypt—		
2 Australian Divisions and Cavalry		39,000
French Division ,, ,,		18,000
Russian Brigade ,, ,, ,, (say)		8,000
	Total	109,000

---

[1] On 23 February 1915, after reading this memorandum, Fisher wrote to Lloyd George: 'I am in complete accord with your phenomenal paper! Yesterday I had to write these words to a most influential personage:—' "*Rashness in War is Prudence, and Prudence in War is Criminal. The Dardanelles futile without soldiers!*" ' (*Lloyd George papers*)

3. All these troops are capable of being concentrated within striking distance of the Bulair Isthmus by the end of March if orders are given now. As soon as the Dardanelles are open, they can occupy Constantinople, taking the lines of Chataldja in reverse. Operating from the Constantinople peninsula and protected on three sides by the Allied fleets, they would be in a position to compel the surrender of any Turkish forces in Europe. This army is also well placed for future contingencies which cannot now be foreseen.

If Bulgaria comes in on our invitation issued from Constantinople to occupy up to the Enos–Midia line, our army can proceed through Bulgaria to the aid of Serbia; or (b) if Bulgaria is merely confirmed in a friendly neutrality but Greece comes in, they can proceed through Salonica to the aid of Serbia; or (c) if Roumania comes in, they can proceed to the front via Constanza and Bucharest—if this thought a better line. They can make any of these three moves either simultaneously with, or in advance of, the despatch of a larger force.

WSC

Victor Augagneur to the Comte de Saint Seine: telegram
(*Copy, in translation, Churchill papers: 13/65*)

23 February 1915 Ministry of Marine
Paris

The strength of French troops sent to the Dardanelles comprises one division complete in all respects viz:—18,000 men and 5,000 horses.

Lieutenant-General Birdwood to Vice-Admiral Carden: telegram
(*Copy, Churchill papers: 13/54*)

23 February 1915 Egypt

In anticipation of embarking a large force from here I am ordered to communicate with you as to your immediate requirements. I can have ready at short notice a mixed brigade of infantry, sappers and artillery. In what order would you like these sent? It would greatly help if you could give me an indication of the place of disembarkation.

Vice-Admiral Carden to Lieutenant-General Birdwood: telegram
(*Copy, Churchill papers: 13/54*)

23 February 1915 Dardanelles

I have been directed to make preparations for landing a force of 10,000 men if such a step is found necessary; at present my instructions go no further. If such a force is sent I would propose landing it at Seddelbahr with the object of occupying the Gallipoli peninsula as far east as the line Suandere River–Chana Ovasi. The garrison of the peninsula is about 40,000 men. If the troops are sent they must be prepared to undertake all land transport and staffing of base at Seddelbahr. They should bring all available horse boats with them. Prior to landing on the peninsula the troops would have to live in their transports.

Winston S. Churchill to Vice-Admiral Carden: telegram, not sent
(*Draft, Churchill papers: 13/54*)

24 February 1915 Admiralty

Lord Kitchener has asked me to ascertain your views on the following points affecting military cooperation:

What are strength & composition of Turkish troops on the Gallipoli peninsula according to yr latest information?

What are yr views about the aid which might be given you by a military force?

For instance cd troops help yr operations at a critical moment by attacking the forts in rear? At what point in the operation if at all do you contemplate the occupation of the Bulair lines? Do you expect that any land operations on the Asiatic side will be necessary?

I recognize that you can only give general answers to these questions.

WSC

Winston S. Churchill to Lord Kitchener
(*Kitchener papers*)

24 February 1915 Admiralty

My dear Kitchener,

I send you a copy of a secret and personal telegram I am sending to Carden. In view of his telegram to Birdwood which answers some of the questions you wished me to ask him, I think it better that he and the General should have an opportunity of discussing the situation before inviting any further statement of his views on military co-operation. I am not therefore sending the telegram I showed you in Cabinet this morning. I send you also a copy of an official telegram which I have had sent on the definite operations proposed by Carden in his telegram to Birdwood.

I am sorry to trouble you about recruiting but your people have begun to take persons engaged in Admiralty work to which we could not possibly agree.

Yours very truly
Winston S. Churchill

Winston S. Churchill to Vice-Admiral Carden: telegram
(*Copy, Churchill papers: 13/54*)

24 February 1915   Admiralty
10.30 pm
Secret and Personal

The operation on which you are engaged consists in forcing the Dardanelles without military assistance, as generally described in your telegram No 19 of the 11th January and in your instructions from the Admiralty. It is not proposed at this stage to use military force other than parties of Marines landed to destroy particular guns or torpedo tubes. On the other hand, if your operation is successful, we consider it necessary that ample military force should be available to reap the fruits. The following military forces are therefore being moved or held ready to move to within striking distance:—

Royal Naval Division	8,500
2 Australian Divisions	30,000
A French Division	18,000

It is also possible that the 29th regular Division of 18,000 will be sent from England. You will receive full details of these movements, but they do not affect your immediate operations. It has been arranged that 10,000 troops should be held ready, part in Egypt, part in Lemnos, for unexpected contingencies, should your operations proceed more rapidly than had been estimated. But it is not intended that they should be employed in present circumstances to assist the Naval operations which are independent and self-contained.

General Birdwood, who will command the army, is leaving to-night in the 'Swiftsure' to join you. You should discuss the whole position with him, and if you are of opinion that the army can help your operations, you may make recommendations. An official telegram is also being sent you on this subject.

WSC

Sir Henry Jackson to Vice-Admiral Carden: telegram
(*Draft, Churchill papers: 13/54*)

24 February 1915   Admiralty

Referring to telegrams exchanged between you and General Birdwood as to employment of military forces in Dardanelles operations:—the War Office consider the occupation of the southern end of the peninsula to the line Suandere–Chana Ovasi is not an obligatory operation for ensuring success of first main object which is to destroy the permanent batteries.

Though troops should always be held in readiness to assist in minor operations on both sides of the straits in order to destroy masked batteries & engage enemy forces covering them, our main army can remain in camp at Lemnos till the passage of the straits is in our hands when holding Bulair lines may be necessary to stop all supplies reaching the peninsula.

You should discuss the operation with General Birdwood on his arrival before deciding any major operation beyond covering range of ships guns and report conclusion arrived at.[1]

H. B. Jackson

Lord Kitchener to Sir John Maxwell: telegram
(*Copy, Churchill papers: 2/88*)

24 February 1915   War Office

It is clearly essential that General Birdwood should get into personal consultation on the spot with Admiral Carden. In concerting operations he should be guided by the following considerations. The object of forcing the passage of the Dardanelles is to gain an entrance to the sea of Marmora with the view of ultimately gaining possession of the Bosphorus and over-awing Constantinople. The forcing of the Dardanelles is an operation to be effected mainly by naval means, and one which when successful will doubtless

[1] This draft by Sir Henry Jackson was telegraphed to Carden that evening, signed jointly by Vice-Admiral Oliver and Churchill. Its text was unchanged. (*Copy, Churchill papers: 13/65*)

be followed by the retirement of the Gallipoli garrison. So far as our information of the situation goes, it does not appear to be a sound military undertaking to attempt a landing in force on the Gallipoli peninsula, the garrison of which is reported to be 40,000 strong, until the naval operations for reduction of the forts have been successful and the passage has been forced. The entrance of the Fleet into the Sea of Marmora would probably have the effect of rendering the Turkish position in the Gallipoli peninsula untenable and of enabling a force to occupy the peninsula if considered necessary. But to land with 10,000 men in face of 40,000 Turks while naval operations are still incomplete seems extremely hazardous. If it can be carried out without seriously compromising the troops landed for the purpose, there would be no objection to the employment of a military force to secure hold of forts or positions already gained and dominated by naval fire so as to prevent their re-occupation or repair of damage by the enemy. Having regard to the foregoing, the first step which seems to be desirable is that the brigade, &c., about to be despatched from Alexandria should be sent to Lemnos, where it will be close at hand in case of need, and to hold remainder of Australian and New Zealand force in readiness to embark at Alexandria at short notice. •

General Birdwood should report as early as possible the result of his conference with Admiral Carden, and he should also give his views as to the number of troops required for the above purposes; further, if it should prove possible to send increased forces, he should report how he thinks they could best be utilized for the prosecution of further enterprise after the passage of the Dardanelles has been forced, stating what views are held on this subject by Admiral Carden or others of local experience as to subsequent events in Constantinople.

Birdwood should also inform me privately whether from the results of the bombardment up to date he considers that the forcing of the passage will require the landing of a considerable force to take the forts in reverse, or whether he thinks that the naval operations will succeed without having resource to such a step.

Eustace Tennyson-d'Eyncourt to Winston S. Churchill

(*Admiralty papers:116/1339*)

24 February 1915

First Lord,

Enclosed is a brief Report of the recommendations of the Committee which went into the question of the design of a Land Ship in accordance with your instructions.

If the course suggested is adopted very little time will be lost. The 25 ton model we propose will not only be a model for further development, but will also be a tractor of real military value, carrying 50 men with machine guns &c, capable of negotiating enemy trenches.

If you can give your approval to our proposal, the necessary work can be put in hand at Lincoln at once.

E. H. T. d'Eyncourt

Eustace Tennyson-d'Eyncourt: minutes

(*Copy, Admiralty papers: 116/1339*)

24 February 1915   Admiralty

LAND SHIPS

A Meeting was held in the Office of the D.N.C. on Monday the 22nd instant.

Present:—

> Director of Naval Construction.
> Colonel Crompton[1] C.B.
> Colonel Dumble.
> Major Hetherington.[2]

Much discussion on the subject of a large Land Ship took place, confined mainly to the chief difficulty i.e. the best form of making contact with the ground, whether by wheels or some pedrail device greater in length and strength than any hitherto made.

At first it was decided to make small models, one with wheels and one with a caterpillar but later it was considered better to make them of an appreciable size so as to be fairly considered as practical working models. Trials with these machines would determine the respective merits of the large wheel and the caterpillar. The weight of such working models was

---

[1] Rookes Evelyn Bell Crompton, 1845–1940. As a naval cadet he served in the Crimean War, 1856. Lieutenant, Rifle Brigade, 1864; while in India he constructed a steam road-train capable of 30 miles an hour. Retired with the rank of Captain, 1876. Engineer-in-Chief, Stanton Ironworks Company, 1877. Played a leading part in introducing electric lighting to England in the 1880s; he installed electric lighting at the Law Courts (1883), Victoria Station and Buckingham Palace. President, Institution of Electrical Engineers, 1895 and 1908 Colonel Commanding motor transport, South Africa, 1900–2. Consulting Engineer to the Road Board, 1910. He played a leading part in the development of the 'tank', 1914–17.

[2] Thomas Gerard Hetherington, 1886–1951. Joined Royal Flying Corps on its formation, May 1912. Attached to the Royal Naval Air Service for experimental work, 1914–15. Air Attaché, Washington, 1926–30; Rome, 1931–5.

considered to be about 25 tons. This weight coincides approximately with the calculated weight of a machine suitably armoured against Infantry fire and available for attacking and crossing a trench.

The two working models arrived at independently are almost identical in principle, wheels being used in one case and a caterpillar in the other. The machine with wheels actually exists at Lincoln at this moment as a number are being built for Admiral Bacon.

With a view to such eliminating trials at the earliest possible moment we recommend

(1) That one of the Tractors at Messrs Foster and Company's Works, Lincoln, be selected for this work at once and that the Firm be instructed to carry out the Committee's recommendations.

(2) That the Committee be empowered to order a similar working model fitted with some form of caterpillar supporting and propelling device from such firms as they may suggest.

H. H. Asquith to Venetia Stanley
(*Montagu papers*)

24 February 1915   H of C

... The gale has at last abated in the region of the Dardanelles, and the ships were going to resume this morning their pounding of the forts. Winston is sending off his Naval Division on Saturday to be at hand when the military part of the operations becomes ripe. ...

A much more serious thing is coming on at 6, when we have another War Council. We are all agreed (except K) that the naval adventure in the Dardanelles shd be backed up by a strong military force. I say 'except K', but he quite agrees in principle. Only he is very sticky about sending out there the 29th Division, which is the best one we have left at home. He is rather perturbed by the strategic situation both in the East & West, and wants to have something in hand, in case the Germans are so far successful against Russia for the moment, as to be able to despatch Westwards a huge army—perhaps of a million—to try & force through Joffre & French's lines.

One must take a lot of risks in war, & I am strongly of opinion that the chance of forcing the Dardanelles, & occupying Constantinople, & cutting Turkey in half, and ranging on our side the whole Balkan peninsula, presents such a unique opportunity that we ought to hazard a lot elsewhere rather than forgo it. If K can be convinced, well & good: but to discard his advice & overrule his judgment on a military question is to take a great responsibility. So I am rather anxious. . . .

Meeting of the War Council: extract from Secretary's notes
(*Copy, Cabinet Office papers: 22/1*)

Present: H. H. Asquith (in the Chair), A. J. Balfour, Lord Haldane, Winston S. Churchill, Lord Fisher, Sir Arthur Wilson, David Lloyd George, Sir Edward Grey, Lord Kitchener, Sir James Wolfe Murray, Lieutenant-Colonel Hankey (Secretary)

24 February 1915   10 Downing Street

THE DARDANELLES AND MESOPOTAMIA

MR. CHURCHILL said that the naval bombardment had been suspended, owing to a gale and low visibility. Admiral Carden had reported that the attack could only be continued under these conditions at the expense of a great waste of ammunition.

SIR EDWARD GREY said that the delay was unfortunate from a political point of view. He proposed to send a confidential telegram to Athens and Sofia, announcing the reason for the delay and stating that no ship of the Allies had been hit, if this was correct.

MR. CHURCHILL said that no ship had been hit, though they had closed to 10,000 yards and used their medium armament.

MR. BALFOUR asked whether the Navy had sufficient ammunition for the operations, and whether the guns would not be worn out?

MR. CHURCHILL said that 28,000 rounds of heavy gun ammunition had been provided. This was considered ample. The question of wear and tear of guns had been carefully considered.

THE PRIME MINISTER reminded the War Council of the following conclusions reached at the last meeting of the War Council:—

'*Transports to be prepared:—*
'1. *To be sent out to Alexandria to convey the Australian and New Zealand troops to Lemnos.*
'2. *To take the XXIXth Division to the Mediterranean, if required.*'

He asked what action had been taken.

MR. CHURCHILL said that, immediately after the meeting of the War Council, the First Sea Lord had issued instructions for the preparation of transports for:—

1. The XXIXth Division.
2. A force up to 40,000 men from Egypt.
3. The Naval Division.

Owing to the rapid progress made on the first day of the bombardment, it had appeared possible that events might develop more rapidly than had at first been anticipated. The Director of Transports had therefore been asked to ascertain whether some ships could be obtained in Egypt, and had succeeded in chartering several. This would enable the Admiralty to embark 10,000 men by Saturday, the 27th March, from Egypt. 2,000 Marines had already arrived at Lemnos.

LORD KITCHENER said that he had instructed General Maxwell in Egypt to take up transports, and to get the Australians and New Zealanders ready for embarkation. A brigade had either been embarked or was about to embark, and would be despatched to Lemnos forthwith.

LORD FISHER said that the 10,000 men referred to by the First Lord as about to leave on Saturday, the 27th February, would include the brigade referred to by Lord Kitchener.

MR. BALFOUR asked if the strength of the garrison of the Gallipoli Peninsula was known.

LORD KITCHENER said that our intelligence on this point was not very good. The garrison was believed to be 40,000. He was, however, making inquiries from the Greek General Staff, who had had their eye on Gallipoli for a long time, and from the British Admiral. He also would be glad to learn the views of the British Admiral as to the possibilities of landing a force to attack the forts in rear, and as to the possibility of holding the Bulair lines.

LORD HALDANE asked if the Turks could be driven out of the Gallipoli Peninsula by naval attack alone?

LORD KITCHENER said that, in his opinion, if the fleet succeeded in silencing the forts, the garrison of Gallipoli would probably be withdrawn. Otherwise they would run the risk of being cut off and starved out.

He then referred to the present condition of Egypt. According to the latest reports, the Turks were likely to make another attack on the Suez Canal position from the direction of El Arish and Nekl. It was undesirable, therefore, to withdraw too many men from Egypt, more especially as the population were not to be depended on too surely, and had not shown themselves so averse to the prospect of Turkish rule as might have been expected. It was essential that we should be safe in Egypt, and for this reason the brigade of Indian troops, which he had promised to send back to India, could not be spared yet.

As regards India, he had asked the India Office to tell the Viceroy that any disaster or failure in Mesopotamia would be more dangerous than internal trouble. His intention in advising this was that the Viceroy should send more troops to Mesopotamia. The Viceroy had replied that he quite agreed, and hoped that the War Office would send more troops to Mesopotamia. The War Office, however, had no troops to spare. He thought that further pressure ought to be put on the Viceroy.

MR. LLOYD GEORGE suggested that the Mesopotamian expedition was merely a side-issue. The Turks knew how far reaching the effect of a disaster there would be, and would spare no efforts to bring it about. The Mesopotamian force ought, in his opinion, to be withdrawn and concentrated on the Dardanelles.

LORD KITCHENER said that it ought either to be reinforced or withdrawn. At present it consisted of 1 division and 1 brigade, with some heavy guns, occupying strong positions but rather spread out.

LIEUTENANT-COLONEL HANKEY suggested that it would appear a very proper use to make of our sea-power, having drawn about 60,000 Turks into Mesopotamia, to withdraw and concentrate on the Dardanelles, which was at present the decisive point in the East.

MR. LLOYD GEORGE concurred.

MR. CHURCHILL thought we ought not to give up Basra and Kurna. This provided an additional reason for sending the XXIXth Division to the East. When they arrived in Egypt, an Indian brigade could be released for service in Mesopotamia or India. The main reason, however, was that with a comparatively small number of troops we might be in Constantinople by the end of March. No one could tell how far-reaching the results of such an operation might be. Moreover, we were now absolutely committed to seeing through the attack on the Dardanelles. He would like to send out at once all the available troops, concentrating there the XXIXth Division, a Territorial Division, the Naval Division, two divisions from Egypt, a French and a Russian Division, making altogether more than 100,000 men. It was not a question of sending them immediately to the Dardanelles, but merely of having them within reach. If an immediate decision was taken, all these troops would be in the Levant by the 21st March.

LORD KITCHENER asked if Mr. Churchill now contemplated a land attack.

MR. CHURCHILL said he did not; but it was quite conceivable that the naval attack might be temporarily held up by mines, and some local military operation required. He asked how 2 divisions could make the difference between success and failure in the Western theatre of war, especially as, by the middle of April, 4 divisions of new army would be available.

LORD KITCHENER asked what Mr. Churchill proposed these large forces should do, when they reached the Dardanelles?

MR. CHURCHILL said they would have several choices. If the fleet got through the Dardanelles, they could be put into Constantinople. Or they could be put into European Turkey towards the Bulgarian frontier; Bulgaria could then be invited to take possession up to the Enos–Media line as a condition of joining the Allies. The Allied forces could then be sent up through Bulgaria to Nish. Another plan would be to send them to Salonica in order to influence the Balkan States. Or they might be sent up the Danube, if Roumania joined the Allies.

LORD HALDANE asked whether the Turks had not 200,000 troops in Thrace?

LORD KITCHENER said the number was about 150,000.

LORD HALDANE asked if the risk to the British forces would not be very great?

MR. CHURCHILL admitted that there was some risk. On the whole, however, it was less than the risk run at the beginning of the war in sending 4 divisions to the Continent

MR. LLOYD GEORGE agreed that a force ought to be sent to the Levant, which could, if necessary, be used after the Navy had cleared the Dardanelles, to occupy the Gallipoli Peninsula or Constantinople. He wished to know, however, whether, in the event of the naval attack failing (and it was something of an experiment), it was proposed that the Army should be used to undertake an operation in which the Navy had failed.

MR. CHURCHILL said this was not the intention. He could, however, conceive a case where the Navy had almost succeeded, but where a military force would just make the difference between failure and success.

MR. LLOYD GEORGE hoped that the Army would not be required or expected to pull the chestnuts out of the fire for the Navy. If we failed at the Dardanelles we ought to be immediately ready to try something else. In his opinion, we were committed by this operation to some action in the Near East, but not necessarily to a siege of the Dardanelles.

MR. BALFOUR said that, if the fleet failed in the Dardanelles, the Government would have a very serious decision to take.

LORD KITCHENER said he would risk a good deal in order to open up the Dardanelles. He was, however, still unable to understand the purpose for which so many troops were to be used. In his opinion, once the British fleet had forced its way through the Dardanelles, in fact, as soon as the forts were clearly being silenced one by one, the Gallipoli garrison would evacuate the peninsula; the garrison of Constantinople, the Sultan, and not improbably the Turkish army in Thrace, would also decamp to the Asiatic shore. In any case, if we had patience and negotiated wisely, the Turkish forces at Chatalja would probably surrender. How then could the large forces contemplated by Mr. Churchill be employed until the time for decisive operations in the heart of Europe had arrived? What was to be done while the troops were waiting?

MR. CHURCHILL said the troops would be required to support our diplomacy.

THE PRIME MINISTER said that at the last meeting the main reason for doubts about the expediency of sending the XXIXth Division was that the Russian position in East Prussia and Poland had been precarious.

MR. LLOYD GEORGE pointed out that the reports were very conflicting, and we had no real knowledge.

LORD KITCHENER said that he was now less anxious about the position in Russia and its possible effect on our position in France. The Russians had received a bad knock, but not the disaster he had feared. But he wished to point this out as an illustration of the rapidity with which the situation changed and the desirability of keeping a reserve in hand.

SIR EDWARD GREY said that it was not impossible that we might have a *coup d'état* in Constantinople, if success was achieved at the Dardanelles.

LORD HALDANE suggested that the XXIXth Division should be sent to Egypt, which should become a great *place d'armes* for our troops in the East.

LORD KITCHENER said that he was prepared to send the XXIXth Division, if necessity was shown. He felt that, if the fleet would not get through the Straits unaided, the army ought to see the business through. The effect of a defeat in the Orient would be very serious. There could be no going back. The publicity of the announcement had committed us.

SIR EDWARD GREY said that failure would be morally equivalent to a great defeat on land.

MR. CHURCHILL said that our one aim in this operation should be to get the Balkans out. The capture of Constantinople was a means to this end. The presence of 100,000 men would have a great moral effect. Up to now our diplomacy had been paralysed because we had had nothing to offer. If we could make an offer we might bring out a million men in the Balkans. He would be willing to send a quarter of a million men to effect this result, if we had them.

LORD KITCHENER agreed, but pointed out that we had not the men available. We were, he said, acting prematurely. It was no use bargaining unless we had a really large force to offer.

MR. BALFOUR said that our *immediate* objective was Constantinople, in order to open the Black Sea, obtain the Russian wheat, and obtain a line of communication with Russia. Our ultimate object might be a much larger operation.

THE PRIME MINISTER asked whether the question of opening the Bosphorus had been considered.

LORD KITCHENER said that it was easy by comparison with the Dardanelles.

MR. CHURCHILL said he was advised that most of the Bosphorus forts faced the opposite way and could be attacked in rear. He again appealed for a large force to be sent, only to be utilized in case of necessity.

THE PRIME MINISTER said the force it was at present proposed to send consisted of the Australians, New Zealanders, Naval Division, and Marines. He asked if these were good enough. The Marines were the only seasoned troops.

LORD KITCHENER said they were quite good enough if a cruise in the Sea of Marmora was all that was contemplated.

THE PRIME MINISTER asked who was to command the military force.

LORD KITCHENER said that Lieutenant-General W. R. Birdwood, who now commanded the Australians and New Zealanders—a corps command—would be Commander-in-Chief. If the XXIXth Division was sent, he proposed that General Hunter-Weston should command it.

MR. CHURCHILL said he would like to have a General sent to join Admiral Carden at once. Lord Kitchener wished him to ask Admiral Carden a number of questions, many of which referred to military matters on which a naval officer's opinion was of no great professional value.

THE PRIME MINISTER suggested that General Birdwood should be sent up to join Admiral Carden.

LORD KITCHENER agreed, and undertook to issue the necessary instructions at once.

MR. CHURCHILL undertook to notify Admiral Carden.

(*Conclusion.*)
General Birdwood to be instructed to proceed to join Admiral Carden before the Dardanelles. The decision as regards the XXIXth Division to be postponed until the next meeting.

A. J. Balfour: memorandum

(*Copy, Churchill papers: 2/89*)

24 February 1915   2 Whitehall Gardens
Secret

THE WAR

I think it may help us to a sound decision next Friday if we bear clearly in mind that the forcing of the Dardanelles is the preliminary stage of *two* military operations, which are quite separable in fact, and ought to be separated in our thoughts. I will call them respectively the Bosphorus operation and the Balkan operation.

By the Bosphorus operation I mean the control of the Sea of Marmora, the Bosphorus, and Constantinople. Were this carried out successfully, although it stood alone, we should paralyse Turkey; we should secure free communications with Russia, with all that this carries with it; we should have defeated the German ambitions in the Near East; we should (I believe) have secured the neutrality of Bulgaria; and we should have shown to all the world what sea power means.

These advantages are not easy to over-estimate. Yet I fully admit that they would be far surpassed if we could bring to a successful issue the second, or Balkan policy. This policy aims at nothing less than bringing into the struggle at least Roumania and Greece, possibly Bulgaria, and uniting the whole of the South-East of Europe with Britain and France in a combined action against the Central Powers.

If this could be successfully effected, its influence on the fortunes of the war must be great, and might be decisive.

It is unfortunately extremely difficult—perhaps at this moment impossible —to work out all the elements in the complicated problem which it presents. The course of events depends upon the policy of three small States, who, from the very necessities of their position, are obliged to incline to that side in the European struggle which they think is likely to win, and whose views are largely swayed by the small local hopes and hatreds. It is impossible in such circumstances clearly to think out a course of a military campaign in these regions until we know *who* is going to fight on our side and *when*. And our difficulties are not diminished by the fact that, on the most sanguine estimate which we dare make, the number of Anglo-French troops which could take part in the Balkan operations would only be a relatively small fraction of the troops which the Balkan States themselves have at their disposal.

This is a very important point which I think we are apt to forget. Wellington's army in the Peninsula, though not large, was the only one that could stand up against the French. It was the controlling military factor in the situation. This can never be parallelled in South-East Europe. The Roumanian, Bulgarian, and Greek armies are not only separately and collectively larger than any that the Allies, for a long time to come, can put into this theatre of operations, but they form very efficient fighting units. Our superiority is a naval and financial one, supported, no doubt, by immense, but distant, reserves of power.

The conclusions I draw are as follows:—

We *must* send as many troops as may be required to make the Bosphorus operation, to which we are now committed, a success. But whether we should send more than this number depends upon the answer to two questions which I think we have not yet sufficiently discussed: (*a*) Do we want the Balkan States to join us at once? and (*b*) Would sending 110,000 men induce them to join us?

As regards (*a*), I should like very much to know whether it would be to our interest that Roumania, for example, should declare war within the next month. Would it not expose her to being crushed before Russia was strong enough to come to her assistance? And would any force which we could conceivably send through the Bosphorus be sufficient to turn the scale?

If these questions, and other parallel questions with regard to Greece, be answered in the negative, it would seem that the maintenance for the present of Balkan neutrality is to our advantage, and that nothing would be gained by sending to the East more troops than are required for what I have called the Bosphorus operation.

If, on the other hand, it is desirable to induce Greece and Roumania to take immediate action, and if sending 110,000 men, instead of 40,000, is going to make the difference, then it might be proper to take risks in the West, and to send every man we can spare to aid in the Balkan operations.

I am not sure that sending troops much in excess of what are required for the Bosphorus operation would really give the impression of military strength. The difference between the smallest force which it is proposed to send and the largest force which we can afford to send is, I gather, somewhere about 70,000 men. This, speaking from recollection, is about one-seventh of the Bulgarian army and about one-tenth of the Roumanian army. I find it difficult to believe that this would be regarded as a very important addition to the local armies; or that, if the Balkans remained obstinately neutral, it would add to our prestige to have them encamped in the neighbourhood of the Sea of Marmora, doing nothing, while important fighting was going on elsewhere. It is certainly arguable (I do not put it higher) that to carry out the Bosphorus operation effectively and rapidly, to provide all the troops that may be required for this purpose, and (this feat accomplished) to negotiate with Servia, Greece, and Roumania as to the next step to be taken, might give better results *even as regards the Balkan operation* than the alternative course. But this turns upon questions, diplomatic as well as military, on which I am not competent to offer an opinion.

Only one further observation would I make, which points in the direction of not being niggardly as regards the number of troops we send or their quality. We are all agreed that, whatever else is done, the Bosphorus operation must be carried through to a successful termination. This may involve a pitched battle with Turkish troops in the neighbourhood of Constantinople; and, so far as I could gather from our last discussion, we have no very precise information as to the number and quality of the Turkish troops with which, in such circumstances, we might have to deal. Evidently we must work with ample margins, for a check there might amount to a disaster.

AJB

Winston S. Churchill to H. H. Asquith, David Lloyd George and A. J. Balfour
(*Churchill papers: 2/81*)

25 February 1915   Admiralty
Secret

1. *Russia.*—We must not expect Russia to invade Germany successfully for many months to come. But though the Russian offensive is paralysed, we may count on her not only maintaining a successful defensive, but effectively containing and retaining very large German forces on her front. There is no reason to believe that Germany will be able to transfer to the West anything like 1,000,000 men at any time; nor anyhow that German forces large

enough to influence the situation can arrive in the West before the middle of April.

2. The Anglo-French lines in the West are very strong, and cannot be turned. Our position and forces in France are incomparably stronger than at the beginning of the war, when we had opposed to us nearly three-fourths of the first line of the German army. We ought to welcome a German assault on the largest possible scale. The chances of repulsing it would be strong in our favour; and even if its success necessitated retirement to another line, the superior losses of the Germans would afford good compensation. The issue in the West in the next three months ought not to cause anxiety. But, anyhow, it is not an issue which could be decisively affected by four or five British divisions.

3. For us the decisive point, and the only point where the initiative can be seized and maintained, is in the Balkan Peninsula. With proper military and naval co-operation, and with forces which are available, we can make certain of taking Constantinople by the end of March, and capturing or destroying all Turkish forces in Europe (except those in Adrianople). This blow can be struck before the fate of Serbia is decided. Its effect on the whole of the Balkans will be decisive. It will eliminate Turkey as a military factor.

4. The following military forces (at least) are available immediately:—

	Men
In England {29th Division / Another Territorial Division} . . .	36,000
Under orders for Lemnos: RN Division . . .	12,000
From Egypt: 2 Australian Divisions . . .	39,000
French Division . . . . . (say)	20,000
Russian Brigade . . . . . (say)	8,000
Total	115,000

5. All these troops are capable of being concentrated within striking distance of the Bulair Isthmus by 21st March if orders are given now. If the naval operations have not succeeded by then, they can be used to attack the Gallipoli Peninsula and make sure that the fleet gets through. As soon as the Dardanelles are open, they can either (a) operate from Constantinople to extirpate any Turkish forces in Europe; or (b) if Bulgaria comes in at our invitation to occupy up to the Enos–Midia line, they can proceed through Bulgaria to the aid of Serbia; or (c) if Bulgaria is merely confirmed in a friendly neutrality, but Greece comes in, they can proceed through Salonica to the aid of Serbia.

WSC

Vice-Admiral Carden to Winston S. Churchill: telegram

(*Copy, Churchill papers: 13/65*)

25 February 1915
12.20 a.m.

If only 10,000 men are sent I propose at first to base them on Mudros and make occasional feints in Xeros without actually landing troops. If it becomes necessary to prevent serious interference with fleet by concealed guns, force could be landed at Seddulbahr to occupy the Peninsula up to the line Suandere River–Chanaovasi being supported on both flanks by ships. A landing at Seddulbahr and maintenance after landing being as dependent on weather I do not intend to take this step unless essential. I have informed General Officer Commanding Egypt that force should be sent to Port Mudros as soon as possible in order to be instantly available, should be entirely independent of fleet for all supplies. . . .

Vice-Admiral Carden to Winston S. Churchill: telegram

(*Copy, Churchill papers: 13/65*)

25 February 1915
6.30 am

Extreme urgency. Weather same as yesterday I do not intend to commence in bad weather leaving result undecided as from experience on first day I am convinced that given favourable weather conditions reduction of forts at the entrance can be completed in one day. . . .[1]

Vice-Admiral Carden to Winston S. Churchill: telegram

(*Copy, Churchill papers: 13/65*)

25 February 1915
8.30 pm
Extremely urgent

Forts at the entrance of Dardanelles Nos: 1, 3, 4 & 6 are reduced.

Sweeping operations commenced covered by a division of battleships & destroyers.

Details follow.

[1] Churchill circulated this telegram to Asquith, Grey, Kitchener and Lloyd George.

Winston S. Churchill to Vice-Admiral Carden: telegram

(*Copy, Churchill papers: 2/88*)

25 February 1915   Admiralty
Personal and Secret

Good! We are following your operations with great interest, and full confidence reposed in your resolution and judgment.

C. P. Scott to Winston S. Churchill

(*Churchill papers: 13/47*)

26 February 1915   The Manchester Guardian
                                                    3 Cross Street
                                                    Manchester

My dear Churchill,

We received the enclosed communication from the Press Bureau late last night.[1] We are most anxious to carry out the wishes of the Admiralty and to do what is best in the public interest, but I don't think the circular as it stands is likely to secure these objects.

To begin with I find it is variously interpreted by different papers— that some take it as an instruction, some as a suggestion as to which they are at liberty to exercise their discretion. But if some papers fail to act upon it strictly others will follow suit and very soon it will be hardly acted upon at all.

Further I don't think the policy suggested, if intended to be strictly observed, is practicable. It is hardly possible that if a great liner or any other valuable ship were sunk with the loss of many lives the press should ignore the matter till the Press Bureau announced it at the end of perhaps a week. But if strict observance is not required then the whole matter becomes one of discretion, and different papers will exercise their discretion very differently.

I venture to suggest that nothing is gained by the delay of a week or by any delay at all and that all that is needed is that the losses as they occur should be day by day reported in the briefest and most unsensational way consistent with a full disclosure of the material facts and exactly in the form (including if desired the headlines) in which the Press Bureau sends them. Then you would get uniformity and at the same time the public mind would remain undisturbed because it would be known that nothing was being kept back.

[1] The Admiralty had asked newspapers not to report that ships had been sunk by submarines until details of the sinkings had been officially announced by the Admiralty through the Press Bureau.

On the other hand if nothing is to be published for days or for a week all sorts of wild rumours will circulate and be believed and the very object of appeasement which the Admiralty has in view will be wholly defeated.

May I add that if something of this kind is done a skilled pressman should be employed for drafting the announcements and that he should be instructed to give all the essential facts, however baldly.

Forgive me for troubling you personally, but the matter is of so much consequence that it seemed best to go to you direct.

Yours sincerely,
C. P. Scott

There is just one other point against keeping back the news of losses till the end of the week. If the submarines make at all a good daily bag the accumulated total will come as rather a shock on an unexpectant public.

Meeting of the War Council: Secretary's notes
(Copy, Churchill papers: 2/86)

Present: H. H. Asquith (in the Chair), Lord Haldane, Lord Crewe, Winston S. Churchill, A. J. Balfour, Lord Fisher, Sir Arthur Wilson, David Lloyd George, Sir Edward Grey, Lord Kitchener, Sir James Wolfe Murray, Lieutenant-Colonel Hankey (Secretary)

26 February 1915   10 Downing Street

THE DARDANELLES

LORD KITCHENER drew attention to the serious position in Russia. According to the latest information, German troops had crossed the Niemen at one point, and they were close to the Warsaw–Petrograd Railway in the vicinity of Grodno. If they succeeded in getting astride this railway, it would probably involve a Russian retirement from the Warsaw line, as the troops in this region were dependent on this railway for their supplies. The Russians were believed to be short of supplies, but it was extremely difficult to obtain accurate information. The representatives sent over by the Russian Government appeared to know neither what they possessed nor what they required. The Russian military attaché, however, represented that they were short of nearly everything, especially rifles and artillery ammunition. We had done everything we could to help them. He now proposed to ask the French to assist them.

MR. CHURCHILL read a series of telegrams from Admiral Carden regarding the second day's operations against the Dardanelles. All the outer forts were now reduced, mine-sweeping had commenced, and as soon as the intervening minefields had been cleared up the battleships would attack the forts at the Narrows.

THE PRIME MINISTER asked what Mr. Churchill meant by the word 'reduced' in regard to the forts.

MR. CHURCHILL said that they were completely demolished so far as further hostilities were concerned.

LORD HALDANE asked if there was any risk of a Turkish military field force being able to approach the entrance to the Dardanelles by land and cut off the retreat of the ships which had entered the Straits by using heavy field artillery.

MR. CHURCHILL said that even 6-inch guns were not easy to move about.

LORD KITCHENER said that, once the fleet was through the Straits, the Bulair lines would become untenable, and the Turks would probably evacuate the Gallipoli Peninsula.

LORD HALDANE suggested that Turkish guns might be brought up on the south side.

LIEUTENANT-COLONEL HANKEY said he understood the roads on this side were very bad.

MR. CHURCHILL said that the Navy were only attempting to force a passage for armoured ships, the passage of which could not be interfered with by field artillery.

LORD KITCHENER said that if the forts were reduced the requisite military effect would be gained.

MR. CHURCHILL said that Admiral Carden, having heard that General Birdwood was to visit him and that military forces were to be sent, had proposed to land troops on the Gallipoli Peninsula in order to capture and hold the end of the peninsula. The Admiralty, however, had replied in the sense that the scope of the present operations was limited to a naval bombardment, except if it was necessary to land marines to capture single works or observation stations for mines or torpedo stations; that the military forces were not intended to participate in the immediate operations, but to enable him to reap the fruits of those operations when successfully accomplished. They had also sent particulars of the troops allotted to this expedition, viz., the Australians and New Zealanders from Egypt (30,000), the Naval Division (10,000), the Marines (4,000), with possibly the XXIXth Division of regular troops.

He (Mr. Churchill) wished to make the strongest possible appeal that the

XXIXth Division would not be withheld. In three weeks' time Constantinople might be at our mercy. We should avoid the risk of finding ourselves with a force inadequate to our requirements and face to face with a disaster. At the previous meeting Lord Kitchener had asked him what was the use to be made of any large number of troops at Constantinople. His reply was that they were required to occupy Constantinople and to compel a surrender of all Turkish forces remaining in Europe after the fleet had obtained command of the Sea of Marmora. With an army at hand this could be accomplished either by fighting, or by negotiation, or by bribery. The Chatalja lines would be occupied from the reverse side, the flanks being commanded by men-of-war. Subsequently, if Bulgaria joined the Allies, we should be in a position to push the troops up through Bulgaria to Serbia. Or, if Roumania came in, they could be sent up the Danube or by rail through Roumania. The actual and definite object of the army would be to reap the fruits of the naval success.

LORD KITCHENER said that if every man who could be spared were sent to the Dardanelles, the maximum number would be 89,500, composed of the XXIXth Division, a Territorial Division, the Australasian Corps, the Naval Division, the Marines, and a French Division. If this force became engaged in serious military operations a large amount of ammunition would be required, and this could not be spared. He had two objections to the despatch of the XXIXth Division and the Territorials. First, he considered it a serious risk to send away the only troops we had available as a reserve to send over to France until the Russian situation had cleared up; and second, he felt convinced, from his knowledge of Constantinople and the East, that the whole situation in Constantinople would change the moment the fleet had secured a passage through the Dardanelles. We should be in a better position to judge the situation when the defences at the Narrows began to collapse. He suggested that the 33,000 men available from the XXIXth Division and the Territorials would not be likely to make the difference between success and failure. He had no intention at present of moving either the XXIXth Division or the Territorials to France without consulting the War Council, but he did not wish at present to send these troops to the East. He wanted to await two events, viz.: (1) the clearing up of the situation in Russia, and (2) some signs of a probable result in the Dardanelles.

MR. BALFOUR suggested that, if the purely naval operation were carried out, the following results would be attained: the command of the Sea of Marmora would be secured; the Turkish troops remaining in Europe would be cut off; the arsenal and dockyard at Constantinople could be destroyed; the conditions of the Turks would become worse every day they held out; the Bosphorus could be opened; a line of supply for war-like stores opened up with Russia; and wheat obtained from the Black Sea.

MR. CHURCHILL said that no wheat could be obtained. Merchant-ships could not make the passage, as they would be liable to be sunk by field guns and howitzers. The passage would only be open to armoured ships and transports, for which special arrangements and convoy would be required. It might even be necessary to land the troops opposite the Bulair lines, and march them across to other ships in the Sea of Marmora.

SIR EDWARD GREY said that what we really relied on to open the Straits was a *coup d'état* in Constantinople.

LIEUTENANT-COLONEL HANKEY suggested that the probable main use of troops at Constantinople was to open the Dardanelles and Bosphorus to all classes of ship. First it might be necessary to clear the Gallipoli Peninsula. Once this was acccomplished, the forces could be withdrawn from there, unless it was necessary to defend the Bulair lines. Next it might be necessary to clear out the position south of the Dardanelles. Probably no very large force could be brought here by the enemy, as the line of communication along the south of the Sea of Marmora was long and difficult, and the normal route for supplying the troops in this region, which was by sea, would not be available. With the advantage of free movement by sea it ought not to be difficult to cut off and isolate the Turkish troops south of the Dardanelles. Once this was done the passage of the Dardanelles would be safe for all traffic, though it might be necessary to leave behind a small force to secure it. Similar operations might be necessary in the Bosphorus.

LORD KITCHENER considered it unlikely that the Turks would move any considerable force to the southern side of the Dardanelles. Their aim would probably be to concentrate on a defensive line to defend Ismid and Brusa.

MR. CHURCHILL considered it probable that the Turks have an army of 40,000 men on the south side of the Dardanelles.

LIEUTENANT-COLONEL HANKEY said that we had information of entrenchments between Besika Bay and the forts to the south of the Dardanelles, which pointed to the probability of a strong garrison.

MR. CHURCHILL said that if we were successful and the Dardanelles defences collapsed suddenly, as was by no means impossible, it was probable that we might cut off the Turkish army before it could cross to the Asiatic shore.

MR. LLOYD GEORGE asked how many men would be available in the next fortnight.

LORD FISHER said only 10,000 from Egypt and 2,000 Marines, all of whom would be available very shortly. It was impossible to send the transports back to Egypt for more troops, as the original force would have to live on board, there being no accommodation in Lemnos. The other transports would not reach Egypt for two or three weeks.

LORD KITCHENER, in reply to Mr. Balfour, said that if field operations became necessary the force in the Dardanelles could be reinforced by 8,000 Australian and New Zealand mounted troops, who were very good soldiers and did not form part of the garrison of Egypt.

MR. CHURCHILL did not believe that the Turkish army would have time to escape from Europe. It was a formidable operation to move 150,000 men with all its equipment and stores. He believed that, the moment it became clear that our fleet was likely to get through the Dardanelles, things would go with a run, and the Turkish army would be cut off.

MR. BALFOUR asked whether, in this event, the Turks were likely to surrender, or to fight with their backs to the wall.

LORD KITCHENER thought it probable that the Sultan, the Government, and the principal generals would evacuate Constantinople and go over to Asia. The Turkish army would be deserted, and would probably surrender.

MR. LLOYD GEORGE thought it more probable that the Turks would make a stand, as they had done in the Russo-Turkish war and at Chatalja in the recent Balkan wars.

MR. CHURCHILL said that he saw no risk of a repetition of Admiral Duckworth's expedition to Constantinople, but if we had insufficient troops the Germans would soon discover it and would tell the Turks, and we should accomplish nothing.

LORD KITCHENER said that, without the XXIXth Division, we should have two-thirds of the force contemplated.

MR. LLOYD GEORGE asked how many men Mr. Churchill would like to send, supposing he had a perfectly free hand.

MR. CHURCHILL said he would like to send the XXIXth Division and a Territorial Division, which could both be transported to the Dardanelles by the 21st March. The transport for the XXIXth Division was actually ready now.

LORD KITCHENER said that the XXIXth Division was also ready to embark, but, if serious and prolonged operations were contemplated, sufficient ammunition was not available.

MR. CHURCHILL said that it appeared to be only a question of whether the XXIXth Division fired away its ammunition in the West or in the East. Ammunition would be required, wherever the division was sent.

LORD KITCHENER explained that ammunition was being accumulated in France. At present, this amounted to 600 rounds per field gun. If the XXIXth Division went to France, it would merely mean that the ammunition would have to be spread over more guns.

MR. LLOYD GEORGE pointed out that the XXIXth Division were the only regular troops available for the Dardanelles.

THE PRIME MINISTER asked what was the position as regards the despatch of French troops.

LORD KITCHENER said he had no knowledge.

MR. CHURCHILL said that the French naval attaché had received a telegram from his Minister to the effect that the French intended to embark a division.

SIR EDWARD GREY said he had no knowledge of the matter, but promised to make inquiries.[1]

MR. LLOYD GEORGE said that as many men as possible, including the XXIXth Division, ought to be sent to the East, in order to bring Greece into the war.

LORD HALDANE said that, without a success in Russia, the Balkan States would not come in.

SIR EDWARD GREY agreed. The Russian situation overhung everything.

MR. LLOYD GEORGE said that this made it more important than ever to bring the Balkan States in. He proposed that a special envoy should be sent to the Balkans.

SIR EDWARD GREY said it would be useless merely to send one diplomatist instead of another. It was possible that Mr. Lloyd George himself, if he could be spared, might accomplish something.

MR. LLOYD GEORGE said that the despatch of 100,000 men, following close on the fall of the Dardanelles, ought to produce a great effect in the Balkans.

MR. CHURCHILL said that the important point to remember was the

[1] Hankey added a footnote at this point, which read: 'A telegram containing full details was received in the course of the day from France, so these inquiries were not made'.

time taken to transport troops to the East. His suggestion was to get the men into transports. They could then be brought back to France very quickly in case of need. The only thing lost would be that they would not be quite so near to France, and the men and horses would deteriorate as regard physical condition. If the necessary forces were not available on the spot, we might fail to reap any advantage from a naval success.

THE PRIME MINISTER said that the whole question at issue was whether the difference between 69,000 men and 85,000 men would prejudicially affect the operation.

MR. LLOYD GEORGE said that he had discussed the question with Sir William Robertson, the Chief of Staff to Sir John French. General Robertson had said that, in order to make sure of bringing in the Balkan States, he would spare two divisions. It would be good business and good strategy. In his own opinion, 85,000 men would have a much better chance of achieving this than 69,000. He would prefer, however, to bring the force up to 100,000.

MR. CHURCHILL said that 85,000 men were enough and 63,000 were not.

THE PRIME MINISTER said that the quality of the XXIXth Division appealed to him far more than the actual numbers. There were no other regular troops available, and man for man they were probably far superior to any other troops who would be engaged. In fact, they were the only first-class seasoned men available.

LORD KITCHENER said that, in view of the opinions expressed at this War Council, he felt he was accepting a considerable responsibility in not sending the XXIXth Division at once to the East. He was, however, not willing to accept the much greater responsibility of giving up the power to reinforce in the West, if and when the line was broken, having special regard to the somewhat precarious position of the Russian Army. If once our line was broken in the West by masses of German troops brought from Russia, a period of manoeuvring would begin. He wanted to have in hand a mobile reserve to throw in at any threatened point. Once he felt quite secure about the French position, he would be prepared to send the troops to the East.

MR. BALFOUR said we were under an honourable obligation to keep our part of the line intact.

SIR EDWARD GREY said he was most concerned about the position in the West.

MR. CHURCHILL said that the XXIXth Division would not make the difference between failure and success in France, but might well make the difference in the East. He wished it to be placed on record that he dissented altogether from the retention of the XXIXth Division in this country. If a disaster occurred in Turkey owing to insufficiency of troops, he must disclaim all responsibility.

LORD KITCHENER said that he could not change his position, which had been thought out very carefully.

MR. CHURCHILL said he could not understand Lord Kitchener's point of view. At a meeting of the War Council held on the 9th February it had been agreed to send the XXIXth Division to Salonica, in order to entice Greece into the war. In fact, this Division had been hawked round the Balkans. Now, that a real and decisive opportunity for using it had arisen Lord Kitchener declined to send it.

LORD KITCHENER said that the new factor which influenced him was the deterioration of the Russian position. If the Russians gave way, the Germans would be in a position to bring back great masses of troops, and, if we had no reserves, the position might be one of tremendous danger.

MR. CHURCHILL asked what was the earliest possible moment that the German troops, after crushing the Russian army, and being transported from one end of Germany to the other, could appear in great masses in the Western theatre of war. In his opinion, they certainly could not be brought back before the end of March, and he understood that four divisions of the New Army would be available early in April.

LORD KITCHENER said that very careful calculations would be required before he could answer this question.

MR. BALFOUR suggested that Roumania should be sounded as to her position in the event of the Dardanelles being forced.

SIR EDWARD GREY said he would be prepared to make inquiries at Bucharest as soon as the Admiralty were in a position to say the attack on the Dardanelles was likely to succeed.

MR. CHURCHILL said he could not as yet offer any assurance of success. All that we could say at present was that the reduction of the outer defences gave a good augury of success. The real difficulty would arise when the narrows at Chanak were attacked. Once through these, there would only be a few forts to deal with, and Constantinople might be reached in a few hours. He would prefer to wait before any inquiries were made at Bucharest.

LORD KITCHENER thought that the reduction of the defences at the Dardanelles was likely to take some time. He thought it probable, therefore, that the XXIXth Division would arrive as soon as it was wanted, if the situation enabled it to be spared, and in this event he would send it at once. He hoped therefore that the Dardanelles attack would be carried out slowly and systematically, and would not go with a rush.

SIR EDWARD GREY said that if the Russians were still able to hold Warsaw and the success of the Dardanelles attack brought about a *coup d'état* in Constantinople, the moment would be favourable to make inquiries at Bucharest.

THE PRIME MINISTER said that we had a double object in attacking the Dardanelles. First, we wanted to bring about a *coup d'état* in Constantinople; and second, we wanted to bring in the Christian Balkan States. To make an appeal before we had brought off our *coup* would be to appear cap in hand, and he thought it should be postponed.

MR. LLOYD GEORGE said that, in his opinion, the collapse of Russia was so imminent that we ought to lose no time in sending a special mission to the Balkan States to try and induce them to come in before it was too late.

LORD KITCHENER objected to the term 'collapse'. The Russian position was difficult and dangerous, but 'collapse' was too strong a word. In his opinion, the Russians had done very well. The Germans had been astonished at their powers of resistance.

MR. CHURCHILL agreed with Lord Kitchener. It was a great mistake to take too pessimistic a view of the Russian situation. It was their national tradition always to come up to the scratch again after defeat. Even if Warsaw fell, there would still be a great Russian army requiring very large forces to contain it.

MR. LLOYD GEORGE adhered to his view that Russia was on the verge of a collapse. Not only was the strategical position critical, as pointed out by Lord Kitchener, owing to the propinquity of the Germans to the Warsaw–Petrograd Railway, but the Russians were reported to be short of rifles, ammunition, and military stores of all kinds.

LORD KITCHENER admitted that he had no real knowledge of the Russian position in regard to equipment. He did not believe that the Russians knew themselves. He suggested that a special mission should be despatched to the Balkans and Russia. It should consist, not of a diplomatist, but of some person having the full authority of the Government, and knowing exactly what was in the Government's mind. In the Balkans the object should be to arrange terms on which the Balkan States would be willing to join the Allies. In Russia the object would be simply to obtain information as to the situation of the Russian army. He felt sure that the Grand Duke Nicholas would give information to a properly accredited representative, who should be accompanied by an experienced military officer, to prevent his being 'spoofed'.

MR. BALFOUR saw advantages in the despatch of a mission to South-East Europe to obtain information, and to get a general view of the situation, so as to advise the Government what offers could be made with some prospects of success. Such a mission would have the double advantage of visiting all the States concerned (whereas a diplomatic representative was usually only well-informed about the country to which he was accredited), and of returning to discuss the matter at home.

SIR EDWARD GREY felt doubtful as to the value of such a mission. The Germans had sent out Field-Marshal von der Goltz, but he had done them no good. The French had just sent General Pau. Last October the Prime Minister had suggested to send Sir Maurice de Bunsen[1] to the Balkans; if he had gone it was quite possible that his instructions would have had the effect of alienating Serbia, and inducing her to make peace with the enemy, owing to the concessions she was to be asked to make to Bulgaria. The fact was that the only consideration likely to influence these States was a success, and they were all waiting on the result of the Russian campaign. If Warsaw fell, there was very little prospect of any assistance from the Balkan States. So far as information was concerned, he had sent Mr. G. H. Fitzmaurice,[2] the late chief dragoman of the British Embassy at Constantinople, to Sofia. He had great knowledge of the Near East, and would be able to furnish full information. He was to join the Commander-in-Chief of the Mediterranean Fleet in the event of the Dardanelles being forced. A larger mission would probably lead to intrigue and difficulties.

LORD KITCHENER said that it would be impossible for the proposed mission to obtain information in Russia. The Grand Duke Nicholas would merely pass them on to the Artillery Department in Petrograd, where they would be told nothing. He thought it would, however, be advisable to write to the French and ask them to make every possible effort to send supplies to Russia, which he believed they were in a position to do.

(*Conclusion.*)

A communication to be sent to the French requesting them to make every possible effort to send necessary supplies to the Russian army.

[1] Maurice William Ernest de Bunsen, 1852–1932. Entered the Diplomatic Service, 1877. Secretary of Embassy at Constantinople, 1897–1902. Knighted, 1905. Ambassador, Vienna, 1913–14. Created Baronet, 1919.
[2] Gerald Henry Fitzmaurice, 1865–1939. Entered Diplomatic Service, 1888. Held various Consular posts throughout the Ottoman Empire, 1890–1905. A British Consul, Constantinople, 1905–14 and 1919–21.

MR. BALFOUR said that, in the event of success attending the naval attack on the Dardanelles and a consequent *coup d'état* in Constantinople the ascendant party would no doubt ask what terms would be offered. There would then be a difficult question to answer, which ought to be considered beforehand.

SIR EDWARD GREY said that conversations on the subject with Russia had already taken place. Russia insisted that the *status quo* must on no account be guaranteed.

H. H. Asquith to Venetia Stanley

(Montagu papers)

26 February 1915   10 Downing Street

. . . Margot & Violet have both been away at Poole seeing the last of Oc, before he starts to-morrow for 'Aleppo',[1] or more literally Lemnos at the mouth of the Dardanelles. Their lot includes Patrick Shaw Stewart,[2] Rupert Brooke & Charles Lister:[3] how lucky they are to escape Flanders & the trenches and be sent to the 'gorgeous East'. . . .

The War Council lasted nearly 2½ hours. Winston was in some ways at his worst—having quite a presentable case. He was noisy, rhetorical, tactless, & temperless—or full. K, I think on the whole rightly, insisted on keeping his 29th Division at home, free to go either to the Dardanelles or to France, until we know (as we must in the course of the next week) where the necessity is greatest. The Russians are for the moment retiring & out-manœuvred: tho' one knows that they have a curious knack of making a good recovery. And the difference between sending to the Dardanelles at once 60,000 troops (which we can certainly do) & say 90,000 cannot, I think, for the moment at any rate be decisive. Ll. George is (between us) really anxious to go out

[1] 'Aleppo' was the code name used by the War Office and Admiralty for the destination of the Mediterranean Expeditionary Force.

[2] Patrick Houston Shaw-Stewart, 1888–1917. Fellow of All Souls, Oxford, 1909. Joined Barings, the merchant bankers, 1911. A Managing Director of Barings from 1913 until his death. A friend of the Asquiths, and of Edward Marsh. Sub-Lieutenant, Royal Naval Division, September 1914. Embarkation officer, Ostend, October 1914. Lieutenant-Commander, Gallipoli, 1915. Attached to the French forces at Salonica, 1916. Killed in action in Flanders, December 1917. 'No one ever looked forward to his life more,' Lady Cynthia Asquith wrote in her diary on 4 January 1917, 'or coveted a glorious death less.'

[3] Charles Alfred Lister, 1887–1915. 2nd son and heir of the 4th Baron Ribblesdale. Entered Foreign Office, 1910. Attaché, Rome, 1910–13. 3rd Secretary, Constantinople, 1913–14. Lieutenant, Royal Marines, 1914. Served with the RND at Gallipoli; twice wounded, May and June 1915. Killed at Gallipoli, 28 August 1915. His elder brother, Thomas, was killed in action in Somaliland, 1904. On the death of their father in 1925 the Barony became extinct.

as a kind of Extra-Ambassador & Emissary, to visit Russia & all the Balkan States, & try to bring them into line. Grey is dead opposed to anything of the kind. We accepted K's view as right for the immediate situation to Winston's immense & unconcealed dudgeon. . . .

Sir John Maxwell to Lord Kitchener: telegram
(*Copy, Churchill papers: 2/88*)

26 February 1915   Egypt

I have received a Note on the question of forcing the Dardanelles from Colonel Maucorps,[1] of the French Military Mission, late Military Attaché at Constantinople, which I will send home for your information.

The following is briefly his opinion:—A military expedition is essential for opening the Dardanelles passage for the Allied Fleet, and it would be extremely hazardous to land on the Gallipoli peninsula as the peninsula is very strongly organized for defence. The garrison of the peninsula is 30,000 strong, composed of the 9th Division of the 3rd Army Corps with reserve formations, under the command of Djevad Pasha, who is an excellent and very energetic officer; and Bulair Lines have been re-made and armed. A landing in the vicinity of Bessika Bay, although it might be opposed, presents far less difficulty, and an army landed there would advance supported on its left flank by the Fleet, and could act in co-operation with the Fleet.

After destroying the forts Sed-ul-Bahr and Erthogroul on the European side and the forts of Koumkale and Orhanie on the Asiatic side, the main objective of the Fleet would be the removal of the successive lines of mines in the Narrows south and north of Khilid Bahr and south and north of Tchanak Kali, and the progressive silencing of the forts on either side.

This operation would be materially assisted by the Expeditionary Force without its meeting the organized resistance of the peninsula, and, moreover, the guns of the Fleet could enfilade any lines of entrenchments. From the vicinity of Tchanak Kali the Expeditionary Force would attack the rear of the Turkish batteries, co-operating with naval attack, but at least one battery of heavy artillery is needed. Once the lines of mines are removed the Allied Fleet could pass through, even though the passage had to be made under the fire of the batteries on the heights on the European side above Khilid.

---

[1] Edmond Frederick Maucorps, 1867–1922. French Military Attaché, Constantinople, 1910–14. Major, African Section, French General Staff, November 1914. Colonel, Mission to Egypt and the Dardanelles, 1915. Commanded a sequence of artillery regiments, 1916–19.

On the Asiatic side the Turkish force is about 30,000 strong, made up of the 7th Division of the 3rd Army Corps with reserve formations, but it would be easy for the Turks to pass from one side to the other, and therefore it is necessary to make a diversion at the Gulf of Saros. Colonel Maucorps suggests that the Greeks might undertake this. It would also be necessary for the Russians to make a simultaneous demonstration on the Black Sea near Constantinople, as it would be quite easy for the Turks to send reinforcements by sea from Constantinople.

The passage having been forced a solid naval base could be established on the Asiatic side at Panderma, or the islands of Marmora; and with the assistance of the Fleet the military force could mask Bulair Lines and compel the Gallipoli garrison, their means of supply being cut off, to surrender, or else undertake any other operation that might be decided upon.

Lord Kitchener to Lieutenant-General Birdwood: telegram
(*Copy, Churchill papers: 2/88*)

26 February 1915   War Office

The forcing of the Dardanelles is being undertaken by the Navy, and as far as can be foreseen at present the task of your troops, until such time as the passage has actually been secured, will be limited to minor operations, such as final destruction of batteries after they have been silenced under the covering fire of the battleships. It is possible, however, that howitzer batteries may be concealed inland with which the ships cannot deal effectively, and if called upon by Admiral Carden, you might have to undertake special minor operations from within the straits for dealing with these. Remember, however, that there are large enemy military forces stationed on both sides of the straits, and you should not commit yourself to any enterprise of this class without aerial reconnaissance and assurance of ample covering fire by the Fleet. At any time during the bombardment of the Dardanelles you can, of course, apply for and obtain any additional forces from your corps in Egypt that you may require up to the total of its strength.

It is anticipated that when the forcing of the Narrows is practically assured the Turks will probably evacuate the Gallipoli peninsula, and a small force at Bulair will then be able to hold it. You should take note of positions at which you may be able to land artillery in order to dominate the east side so as to prevent enemy on that side from harassing shipping passing up and down the channel. I anticipate that the gradual overpowering of the batteries by naval fire will exert great moral effect upon the Turks, and the more gradual and certain the naval operations, the greater will be the effect produced. The Admiral is arranging for a ship to watch Bulair, and it might be well to induce the enemy to believe that landings are under consideration at this point threatening his retreat out of the peninsula.

Please keep me fully informed of your operations referring to War Office Map G.S. 2285. I should like you to send me, as soon as you can get into touch with local information, an appreciation of what will be likely to happen in Constantinople, and whether you consider that more than 64,000 troops will be required for operations at Constantinople after the channel has been forced. While your troops are at Port Mudros rapid embarkation and disembarkation should be practised on any beaches that may be available, the operation being carried out under service conditions and in face of pretended opposition. You might specially earmark one brigade and perfect it in this work.

Winston S. Churchill to John Churchill
(John Churchill Papers)

26 February 1915   Admiralty
Secret

My dear,

I am deeply interested by all you write about the big cannons.[1] I expect it will work out right in the end: & I shall be vy glad to hear they have opened their mouths. Keep a little in touch with French when opportunity serves.

The Dardanelles delay through weather from the 19th to the 24th inclusive was vy vexatious to me, & hard to bear. But now they have moved forward again, & so far everything shows the soundness of the plan. I have had many difficulties in trying to keep people up to the scratch. The capacity to run risks is at famine prices. All play for safety.

The war is certainly settling on to a grim basis, & it is evident that long vistas of pain & struggle lie ahead. The limited fund of life & energy wh I possess is not much use to influence these tremendous movements. I toil away. LG has more true insight & courage than anyone else. He really sticks at nothing—no measure is too far reaching, no expedient too novel. I am afraid yr losses have been vy heavy lately—& for so little result.

---

[1] The 15-inch howitzers, commanded by Colonel Bacon. Only one arrived in France in time to take part in the battle of Neuve Chapelle in March 1915, but according to the British Official History of the War, 'Its ammunition was faulty and there was not much of it'. (J. E. Edmonds and G. C. Wynne *Military Operations France and Belgium 1915*, vol. 1, p. 83, *n*3)

Never mind we will find ways & means to bring them low. I shd like to see you home for a little—if you cd come away on leave. Goonie is here & I expect shares this view! Mind you let me know beforehand, so that I can perhaps manage to help you across.

It is not so safe as it was. I think they must be strained for food etc in Germany. Their submarine blockade cannot at all affect the real position here.

I cannot measure the true American intent—I have a feeling that an incident might turn them rather powerfully our way.

Dear Jack do write to me. I am so glad to hear from you.

With best love, Ever & always yours
W

Bacon if an optimist, is a practical optimist.

Sir Mark Sykes to Winston S. Churchill
(Churchill papers: 26/2)

Central Station Hotel
Newcastle-on-Tyne

26 February 1915

My Dear Winston Churchill,

I see by the papers that there has been liveliness in the vicinity of the Dardanelles, though what it portends I know not, but as you bore with me the last time, I venture again to write of certain things passing through my mind.

A. Have you got with our forces in the Mediterranean sound political advisers, such as accompany our troops on extra-Indian expeditions? If not there are two men now in London whose knowledge would be invaluable to your people in the Ægean, the one is Mr Lamb[1] of the consular service, the other Mr Weakly.[2] I only accidently heard they were home, between the two of them there is nothing they do not know of the working of the Near Eastern mind, or the Balkan mind either—of course it is very impudent of me to mention this, but in these times of stress men get overlooked, particularly civilians.

B. Owing to the affair in East Prussia and the German financial manœuvre

---

[1] Harry Harling Lamb, 1857–1948. Entered Consular Service, 1879, as a Student Interpreter, Constantinople. Served in Consulates throughout the Ottoman Empire, 1884–1907. Consul-General, Salonika, 1907–13. Foreign Office, London, 1914–18. British Mission, Bulgaria, 1919. Knighted, 1919. Consul-General, Smyrna, 1921–3.

[2] Ernest Weakley, 1861–1923. Commercial Attaché for European and Asiatic Turkey and Bulgaria, resident at Constantinople, 1897–1914.

in Sofia, I feel Constantinople and the Dardanelles becomes increasingly more important, but also do I feel that the blow delivered there should be hard, decisive, and without preamble. Morally speaking every bombardment which is not followed by a passage of the Dardanelles is a victory in the eyes of the mass of Turkish troops around the Marmora. It is worth considering that the Turks are accustomed to thinking in terms of passive defence—Plevna, Erzerum, and Chatalja each make Turks think a long resistance or repulsed attack all that can be wished for.[1] Therefore do I think that 'reconnaisance' and 'harassing' are things to be used as sparingly as tactical requirements will allow. Turks always grow formidable if given time to think, they may be lulled into passivity, and rushed, owing to their natural idleness and proneness to panic, but they are dangerous if gradually put on their guard.

During the Balkan war, they were at one moment ready to abandon Constantinople but in 18 days they had recovered and were ready to fight to their last man.

I suggest there are two ways. (1) To take the Gallipoli peninsula and begin negotiating with Bulgaria, or, (2) to play the great stroke and take Constantinople by a combined attack by sea from North and South. This of course depends on Russia's power to produce men, 80,000 troops can take and hold the Gallipoli Peninsula, but to hold Constantinople requires a larger force—at least 200,000 since the Turks must have large forces both in Asia and Europe.

But whichever way is taken, I am sure that it should be done as near as possible in one bound, I am certain the Turks think they are secure because they believe England and Russia distrust each other too much to attack either the straits or the capital.

Abdul Hamid's[2] reign inured the Ottoman mind to demonstrations and manœuvres, also I am growing convinced that Bulgaria will not move until she sees some reason for doing so—at present she knows of no real allied success on land—why should she even negotiate with people who cannot touch their enemies territories. The Bulgarian only knows that Servia is pretty well done up, that France is invaded, that Belgium is overrun, and that the Russian frontier is not intact—and in spite of an attack on the Suez Canal and an invasion of the Caucasus the Dardanelles and Constantinople are not threatened.

[1] During the Russo-Turkish war (1877–8) the Turks tenaciously defended Plevna (July–November 1877), Erzerum (October–November 1877) and the Chatalja Lines (January 1878), but were defeated at each.

[2] Abdul Hamid, 1842–1918. Sultan of Turkey, 1876–1909. Prorogued Parliament, 1878; ruled autocratically for thirty years. Forced to restore the Constitution by the Young Turks, 1908. Deposed, 1909.

The whole panorama becomes quite different in the face of an occupied Gallipoli Peninsula and a Turkish capital at the mercy of an invader. Then there would be some inducement to move and daily I become more and more sure that the war will not end until the Balkan States are mobilised against Austria—save by the starving out of Germany which is an uncertain and wearing method for us meaning months perhaps years of siege and exhausting petty conflicts. As time goes on without any results, the people of this country will grow sick and irritable, and there will be more and more danger of a feeling of suspicion and friction growing up between the French and English. No doubt we can starve Germany out, and will do in the end if no other means avail, but one can never forget that the starving out of Germany will not be retarded by gaining successes and strategic advantages in the Mediterranean and Marmora—Wellington's campaign in the Peninsula was no mistake in our Napoleonic war, and here is another Peninsula far easier of access with far greater prizes in it, one of course must beware of parallels but the instance is to me too striking not to mention it.

The evening papers are just in, and perhaps my letter is ridiculous in view of what to-morrow's may contain, I write as one in the dark to one who is in the light, still you will forgive me.

If one has spent from the age of 9 to 37 watching & wondering & listening, one cannot help being interested in the sequel to Gibbon's Decline & Fall, particularly when one sees the page of the last chapter turning over.

Yours very sincerely
Mark Sykes

H. H. Asquith to Venetia Stanley
(Montagu papers)

26 February 1915   In train [from London
                                                   to Walmer Castle]

. . . The Naval Division starts on Sunday night from Avonmouth. Margot saw them reviewed yesterday first by Winston & then by the King: Oc's battalion, called the 'Hood' seems to be admittedly the best. At the eleventh hour it seems to have been discovered that they were without either doctor or drugs, & Clemmie showed a good deal of resource, with the result that they will pick up some necessary 'details' at Malta, but it doesn't look as if the organisation was well thought out. Rupert Brooke is quite convinced that he will not return alive. . . .

Winston was rather trying to-day & I felt constrained to talk to him afterwards a little for his soul's good: a task wh. as you know I do not relish, & in which I fear do not excel. . . .

Vice-Admiral Carden to Winston S. Churchill: telegram[1]

(*Copy: Churchill papers: 13/65*)

27 February 1915   H.M.S. Inflexible
11.05 am

Sweeping carried inside Straits up to 4 miles from entrance.
No mines found.

'ALBION' and 'MAJESTIC' supported by 'VENGEANCE' entered to limit of swept area shelled Fort No. 8 and new batteries on Asiatic shore, fire ineffective from Fort No. 8 which was hit several times by 'ALBION'.

Two batteries apparently 6 inch and some field guns on hill S.W. of Arenkioi caused considerable annoyance and small material damage but no casualties.

Aerial reconnaissance failed to locate these batteries in the morning.

These will be dealt with tomorrow.

Demolishing party were landed 2.30 pm. from 'VENGEANCE' and 'IRRESISTIBLE' at Kum Kali and Seddulbahr respectively as enemy had been seen retiring from these localities after being shelled from inside Straits.

Forts Nos. 1, 3 and 4 were demolished, 6 partially.

Two new 4-inch guns concealed near Tombachilles were destroyed.

These had been firing on our ships and minesweepers, and could not be located.

Four Nordenfelts covering entrance were destroyed.

Enemy encountered in Kum Kali village were driven out over Mendere Bridge which was partially destroyed.

Our casualties here 1 killed 3 wounded.

Winston S. Churchill to the Grand Duke Nicholas: telegram

(*Copy, Churchill papers: 13/47*)

27 February 1915   Admiralty
Personal & Secret

The progress of an attack on Dlles is encouraging & good, & we think the Russian Black Sea Fleet shd now get ready at Sebastopol to come to the entrance of the Bosphorus at the right moment, of wh we will send notice.

Any Russian troops that can be spared shd also be ready to embark.

Although the hardest part of the task is not yet begun; progress may be quicker than we expected.

[1] Churchill circulated this telegram to Asquith, Kitchener, Grey, Lloyd George, Balfour, Lansdowne and Bonar Law.

Winston S. Churchill to Vice-Admiral Oliver

(*Oliver papers*)

27 February 1915   Admiralty

Make it clear to W.O that Admiralty desire the whole French division at Lemnos without delay.

WSC

Graeme Thomson to Winston S. Churchill

(*Churchill papers: 2/82*)

27 February 1915   Admiralty

As regards paragraph 2 of your minute of 20th instant, my report above indicates broadly what has been done. In greater detail following action has been taken:—

1. The Australian fitted transports (16 in number), now in England, have been kept with their fittings standing, and coaling and general preparations have been pressed forward.
2. Four infantry ships have been set aside coaled and stored ready for service.
3. The limiting factor in quick despatch is fitting for horses, but if a really urgent move of 29th Division is contemplated, the Australian ships can be used, ignoring the grave objection that they have not finished discharging their cargo, part of which will have to remain in the ships.

It will be seen, therefore, that while definite orders were not given till today to prepare ships for this specific purpose, the situation has been kept well in hand ready for instant action.

Immediately after receipt of your minute of 20th, Colonel Fitzgerald came over from Lord Kitchener and informed me that the 29th Division were not to go. Shortly afterwards Lord Fisher came over and made the same statement (see my blue pencil note made at the time). I had every reason to suppose that these conversations represented the latest orders, though I take blame for not asking for your written confirmation.

Winston S. Churchill to Lord Kitchener
(*Churchill papers: 13/47*)

27 February 1915   Admiralty

My dear Kitchener,

The War Council on the 18th instructed me to prepare transport inter alia for the 29th Division, and I gave directions accordingly. I now learn that on the 20th you sent Col FitzGerald to the Director of Transport with a message that the 29th Division was not to go, and acting on this the transports were countermanded without my being informed. It is easy to see that grave inconvenience might have resulted from this if it had been decided at Friday's council to send this Division at once.

I have now renewed the order for the preparation of the transports; but I apprehend that they cannot be ready for a fortnight. It now seems very likely that the passage of the Dardanelles will be completed before the end of March, and perhaps a good deal earlier.

May I also ask to be informed of any instructions given to the French Division. I understand that the War Office do not wish them to come to Lemnos. The absence of any British regulars seems to make the presence of the French specially necessary; and I trust they may not be prevented from coming until at any rate the matter can be discussed in Cabinet.

Yours very truly
Winston S. Churchill

Lord Kitchener to Winston S. Churchill
(*Churchill papers: 13/47*)

27 February 1915   War Office

My dear Churchill,

I do not remember telling Fitzgerald to say anything about the 29th Division transport. I will ask him when he comes in. I could not well have done so as I did not know myself.

I saw Colonel Valentin[1] this afternoon. He had previously seen Genl Callwell. I understood the Admiralty wished the French division to go to Mytelene so as not to crowd up Lemnos. Col Valentin spoke of the first detachment going to Lemnos if Mytelene was not arranged for in time to

[1] Joseph Bernard Valentin, 1863–1938. Colonel, French Army, 1914. Commanded 32nd Infantry Brigade, 1914. ADC to General D'Amade, the Commander of the French Expeditionary Force to the Dardenelles, 1915; visited London 26 February 1915 to discuss questions of disembarking troops and the establishment of bases. General of Brigade, 1917.

receive them & this was agreed to—Col Valentin said the first part of the division was leaving on the 2nd March.

There is no idea of preventing or delaying their coming.

Yours very truly
Kitchener

Winston S. Churchill to Graeme Thomson
(*Churchill papers: 2/82*)

27 February 1915   Admiralty

You should not have disregarded the definite instructions of my minute; but should immediately have reported to me the message received from Colonel Fitzgerald.

Please proceed in accordance with my minute of the 20th February, 1915, *i.e.*, order and fit out the transports for the 29th Division, reporting to me when they can be ready.

The Australian ships should not be used if inconvenient.

Winston S. Churchill: note
(*Churchill papers: 21/38*)

27 February 1915   Admiralty
Secret

I circulate to my colleagues the enclosed note, which I wrote a few days ago.[1]

I must now put on record my opinion that the military force provided, viz two Australasian divisions supported by the nine naval battalions and the French division, is not large enough for the work it may have to do; and that the absence of any British regular troops will, if fighting occurs, expose the naval battalions and the Australians to undue risk.

Even if the Navy succeed unaided in forcing the passage, the weakness of the military force may compel us to forgo a large part of the advantages which would otherwise follow.

WSC

[1] The memorandum of 23 February (printed on pp. 547–8). Churchill wrote on his note: 'Tell Hankey to circulate to War Council only.' But later he added 'Put up' and 'Hold'. The memorandum was circulated, as there is a copy of it in the Public Record Office (*Cabinet papers: 37/124*), and Churchill later referred to it in his statement to the Dardanelles Commission of Enquiry (see p. 1571).

Lord Fisher to Sir John Jellicoe

(*Jellicoe papers*)

28 February 1915   Admiralty

. . . There is no one directing our public affairs who has '*the courage of a louse or the backbone of a slug*' (I've told you this before!) except Winston whose courage is that of the Evil one!

Winston S. Churchill: memorandum

(*Churchill papers: 21/38*)

Confidential   Admiralty
28 February 1915

OBSERVATIONS UPON THE UNITED STATES NOTE OF THE 22nd FEBRUARY, 1915[1]

The first and most important point which issues from the note of the United States Government is its strongly unneutral character. It is an unblushing attempt to assist our enemy by using German threats and illegal actions as a means to force the Allies to abate some of the pressure they are bringing to bear on Germany.

There is no complaint made against the Allies that they have acted in a manner inconsistent with the recognised principles of international law, and, in fact, it would be impossible to make out a good case if the matter is approached from the point of view of strict law. It is true we have departed from some of the provisions of the Declaration of London in certain details, but it must be remembered that the Declaration of London was a compromise and a pendant to the conventions signed at The Hague in 1907. It has not been ratified, and, even if it had been, Germany has flagrantly broken every convention that has been made for the more humane conduct of war, so that it is unreasonable to expect us to remain with our hands tied by what we had conceded in order to arrive at the compromise. We may therefore consider ourselves as standing only on what we have always considered as representing international law, which is in the main the same as the United States conceptions. So far, we have not acted in any way outside those conceptions, and the United States has tacitly acknowledged that this is in fact the case.

---

[1] The British blockade of the North Sea involved the treating of all cargoes going to neutral ports as if they were intended for Germany, and therefore subject to seizure and detention. The United States Government held this to be contrary to the Declaration of London (1909), and protested to the British on 22 February. But the British Government insisted on maintaining the blockade as an essential part of its war strategy.

On the other hand, Germany has deliberately broken the engagements agreed to in the conventions; she has, for instance:—

1. Laid mines broadcast in the open sea without due notice to neutrals.
2. Bombarded undefended towns with loss of life to civil population.
3. Dropped bombs on undefended towns and villages.
4. Fired a torpedo at a hospital ship.
5. Attacked and sunk undefended and unresisting merchant vessels, neutral as well as belligerent, without warning or attempting to save the crew.
6. Used a means of attack calculated to inflict unnecessary suffering, viz., spray of burning or corrosive liquid.—(Official French report.)

It has been always recognised in war, even in the middle ages, that deliberately to kill an unresisting enemy was murder. It has been reserved for the 20th century to find a so-called highly civilised European State claiming this as a legitimate act of war. The United States, in this last note, make themselves a party to these proceedings, because they suggest that if Great Britain and her Allies will abandon methods of warfare which are perfectly legitimate, but which cannot be effectively countered by the enemy except by illegitimate means, that then the enemy should cease to do these acts and agree to be bound by the recognised rules of war, to which they are already supposed to be parties, and which they invoke on every possible occasion when they think it is favourable to them.

A great deal is made of the freedom of supplies to the civilian population, but the question arises, what is the civil population in a war in which the whole nation is taking part? The plea was quite good enough in the days when the fighting forces only formed a small proportion of the whole population, and the civil life of the State was only partially diverted to the maintenance of the war. In the present war the whole of the manhood of Germany, without exception, is engaged in the war. Those that are not fighting are producing the means to fight, or are doing other services which are indispensable to the fighting machine. Even women and children are not exempt from this law, and it is therefore difficult to see how the old distinction between civil and military population can be maintained.

The position is not even the same as in Belgium. There the civil population that we are feeding are, we hope, taking no part in the war, and may therefore be fairly considered to be outside the scope of military operations. But everything that is done to assist the civil population of Belgium indirectly helps the German operations.

It is just as if we were to be asked to draw a distinction between the civil and the military population of a beleagured town. The Germans have not done so in Belgium, and notably so in Antwerp and Brussels, where they have requisitioned the whole of the foodstuffs belonging to the town, and left the civil population starving, only to be relieved by the Allies and neutrals.

It seems as if the claim of the Germans through the United States is that the German civilian population is to be free to support the war in every way and to be untouched by any of the disabilities of a state of war, while they are to be absolutely free to starve, oppress, or murder the civilian population of their enemies as they please.

In conclusion, it may be as well to see what are the causes at work in the United States that have brought about this note. It is probably inspired by the strong German element in the administration, and in trade working on the fear of the community as to what is going to happen to American ships and American trade.

It is partly fear of what the Germans may do in sinking vessels, it is also partly fear of what the Allies may do by way of reprisals. It must be obvious to them that one side in the struggle cannot tear up all rules of humanity and not expect the other to take retaliatory measures, and between the two, neutral trade which was beginning to boom is bound to suffer.

There is also the fear of what the German vote in their country may do. The German is nothing if not an organiser, and it is becoming evident that the German-American is not at all pleased with the course of events, and would like to force the administration to take steps much more definitely in their favour than is warranted by the attitude of neutrality adopted by the Government.

In short, the effect of the note would be very different from what the United States Government profess to expect, and, far from being in the interests of humanity, will only tend to prolong the war and increase the loss of life. Their own experience which led to the campaign in Georgia should convince them that under certain conditions this is the quickest and most humane way of terminating hostilities.

Sir Francis Elliot to Sir Edward Grey: telegram
(*Admiralty papers: 116/1336*)

28 February 1915   Athens

Operations against the Dardanelles are followed with intense interest here and there is a rapidly growing feeling that capture of Constantinople ought not to take place without Greek co-operation.

Winston S. Churchill to Sir Edward Grey

(*Grey papers*)

28 February 1915   Admiralty

This requires most careful constn. I regard it as essential that Bulgaria shd be invited to occupy up to the Enos–Midia line & told that if she does not take this, it will be otherwise disposed of. I hope the answer will not be sent till we have had a talk.

WSC

Winston S. Churchill to Vice-Admiral Carden: telegram

(*Copy, Admiralty papers: 137/109*)

28 February 1915   Admiralty
Personal and Secret

What is your latest estimate of number of days required excluding bad weather days to enter the Marmora.

WSC

Winston S. Churchill to Vice-Admiral Oliver, Sir Henry Jackson and Lord Fisher

(*Admiralty papers: 137/1089*)

28 February 1915   Admiralty
Secret & Urgent

Let me have a report as soon as possible upon the measures necessary to reduce the Bosphorus forts by an attack from Admiral Carden's fleet after entering the Marmara.

The Russian Fleet shd be made to cooperate by attacking the Black Sea entrance.

WSC

Winston S. Churchill to Sir Edward Grey

(*Copy, Churchill papers: 26/2*)

28 February 1915   Admiralty
Secret

My dear Grey,

Shd we get through Dardanelles, as is now likely, we cannot be content with anything less than the surrender of everything Turkish in Europe. I shall tell the Admiral after destroying the Turco-German fleet to push on at once to attack Bosphorus, & thus cut off the retreat of the army. Their capitulation is then only a question of time. The terms of an armistice might be considered as follows:—

1. Surrender as prisoners of war of all Turkish forces in Europe.

2. Surrender of all arms, arsenals, armaments, ships etc in Europe.

3. Surrender of fortress of Adrianople & military positions affecting the control of the Bosphorus.

4. Allies to occupy & administer militarily the Turkish territories in Europe.

5. Bulgaria to occupy the Chatalja line by leave of the Allies.

6. Surrender of all German officers & men in Turkey whether in Europe or Asia as prisoners of war.

7. Subject to the above, an armistice for Turkey in Asia. All troops on both sides to advance no further; to retire if convenient; & no hostilities to take place, pending the general settlement.

I look forward with much hope to the delivery of Adrianople by the British to the Bulgarian army. But celerity & vigour are indispensable.

Remember C'nople is only a means to an end—& the only end is the march of the Balkan States against the Central powers.

Yours always
WSC

March 1915

1 March 1915   Admiralty

My dear Kitchener,

A squadron of 12 naval aeroplanes complete in all details with one supporting squadron of armoured cars can sail about the 5th or 6th instant for service in Turkey. They will be commanded by Commander Samson and will be under the orders of the G.O.C. to scout for the army.

I propose also to place the Royal Naval Division under the orders of General Birdwood or whoever you appoint for these operations: but I must have liberty to withdraw them by the middle of April in order that they may complete at home for other duties.[1]

Will you say whether these arrangements are convenient to you in principle. The details can then be settled.

Yours vy truly
Winston S. Churchill

Lieutenant-Colonel Hankey: memorandum

(Copy, Churchill papers: 2/89)

1 March 1915   2 Whitehall Gardens
Secret

AFTER THE DARDANELLES. THE NEXT STEPS
NOTES BY THE SECRETARY TO THE COMMITTEE OF IMPERIAL DEFENCE

A certain amount of reluctance must be felt in setting out to discuss a future, contingent on military operations, the outcome of which cannot be forecasted with any certainty. The action to be taken after the conclusion of the present operations against the Dardanelles ought, no doubt, to be

[1] The Royal Naval Division remained at the Dardanelles until the evacuation of the Gallipoli Peninsula in January 1916, when it went to the western front.

considered under two heads according as they result in success or failure. The present notes deal only with the contingency of success. A further note will be prepared, if and when the War Council desire, to examine the situation in the event of failure, and what alternatives are open to retrieve it.

2. After writing the minutes of the last three meetings of the War Council two main impressions are left on the mind—first, that a successful passage of the Dardanelles would open the way to military results which cannot be overestimated, and second, that these results can only be achieved if the right steps are thought out at once and acted on the moment that success is certain. This is the justification for these notes, in which an attempt is made to indicate what these steps should be, the various suggestions made at the War Council, being as far as possible taken as a guide.

3. It will conduce at every stage to a correct decision if it is laid down clearly what is the ultimate goal which we seek to attain by the Dardanelles operation. If this is kept constantly in view time will not be lost nor energy wasted in the inevitable intermediate stages. The scheme of these notes, then, will be—first, to state the ultimate object which the War Council have in view, and then to examine the steps required to give effect to it in the second stage which follows the opening of the Dardanelles.

The Ultimate Object

4. At the fourteenth meeting of the War Council, held last Friday, the Prime Minister stated that the immediate object of the Dardanelles operation was to open the sea road to the Black Sea, but that the ultimate object was to bring in the Balkan States. Nearly every member of the War Council mentioned that as our ultimate aim. Some members went further, and suggested that we might find scope in the Near East for the employment of the new armies. As Mr. Lloyd George has repeatedly pointed out, the employment of British military forces in the Balkans is probably indispensable if we are to secure the adherence of the Balkan States to the cause of the Allies. Probably, therefore, the War Council will accept the view that the ultimate object of the operations now commenced is to open the way for military operations against Austria, in which a British army will, it is hoped, co-operate with the armies of Roumania, Servia, and perhaps Greece.

5. If this view is accepted, the question arises for consideration whether the moment success is assured an emissary (as proposed by Mr. Lloyd George) should not be despatched to the Balkan States to offer a great scheme of co-operation. It would be difficult to convey the ideas of the War Council by telegraph to our diplomatic representatives, who would not have the complete knowledge possessed by (say) a member of the War Council.

And, as pointed out by Mr. Balfour, a special emissary would be able to visit all the States concerned, and would return to discuss the matter with the War Council.

6. Such an emissary would be in a far stronger position if armed with something more than promises for a more or less distant future, and the prestige attaching to the forcing of the Dardanelles. For example, the despatch of a naval flotilla to the Danube immediately after the opening of the Dardanelles might be of great assistance to him, as it would not only be of great material help in the defence of Servia, but would be an earnest of our intention to intervene effectively. It is understood, however, that the shallow depth in the Iron Gates canal will prevent effective naval co-operation until the new gunboats are ready. It is not known whether the military situation would enable existing light craft to be lightened and brought through the Iron Gates, but it is a question which deserves immediate study.

7. Although the appearance even of a small flotilla capable of dealing with the Austrian monitors would greatly help our emissary, he would not be in a bad position if he was only in a position to announce the possibility of a substantial military force being sent within some stipulated time. The amount of such military force and the time within which it can make its appearance is a question which Lord Kitchener alone can decide. The emissary should explain the advantages of an offensive alliance. A British force, supported by a powerful flotilla, would form the centre of the Allied army. On the left the Serbians and Greeks would penetrate into Bosnia and Herzegovina. On the right the Roumanians would form a connecting link with the Russian armies in the Carpathians. The British forces would turn the flank of the enemy's forces opposing the Roumanians, which would enable the Roumanians to threaten the communications of the enemy's forces operating in the Carpathians. All the time the Franco-British armies would be exerting continual pressure in the west, and the Russians, even if driven back to the line of the Bug, should be able to contain considerable armies of observation.

8. It is suggested that the Admiralty might consider the possibility of finding some vessels which could be lightened sufficiently to pass through the Iron Gates canal without waiting for the new gunboats, and should consult with our Allies on the subject. It is also suggested that the War Council might consider the selection of a suitable emissary, to be despatched the moment success is achieved in the Dardanelles, if that fortunate moment should arrive.

9. Having indicated the ultimate aim of the operations in the Near East, and some of the steps which might be prepared for on the wider issue, the

situation likely to arise immediately after the forcing of the Dardanelles will be examined. The plan followed will be to discuss certain hypothetical situations. In the event they may never arise, but they form a convenient form in which to bring out certain factors in the problem, which in any case must be considered. First, however, it will be pertinent to state certain physical and military considerations bearing on the problem.

The Sea Defences of Constantinople

10. The following distances are important:—

> The length of the Dardanelles: about 35 sea miles.
> The length of the Sea of Marmora: about 115 miles.
> The length of the Bosphorus: about 17 miles.

The Dardanelles are 4,000 yards wide at the entrance. At the Narrows, which are now being attacked, the width is 1,400 yards; at the Nagara bend, opposite Nagara Point, and 4 miles above the Narrows, the width is 2,200 yards, and above this the Straits have an average width of $3\frac{1}{2}$ miles. The depths are very great.

11. The main defences of the Dardanelles, as is well known to the War Council, are at the Narrows, and extend from there to Nagara Point. An important point, to which allusion will be made later, is that the defences and military forces on both the European and Asiatic sides of the Straits are normally supplied by sea from Constantinople. There is only one metalled road leading from the Gallipoli Peninsula to the mainland, and that road approaches close to the sea, and can probably be rendered useless by ships' fire. From the Asiatic side there is no metalled road towards Constantinople.

12. These points are of considerable importance, because if the sea route from Constantinople to the Dardanelles is interruped by the passage of our fleet, and if a ship is sent into the Gulf of Xeros to command the high road to the mainland, the forces defending the Straits are practically isolated. The problem of reducing them thus resolves itself into the destruction of their supplies. The bulk of these might be found at one of the towns on the Straits. There should be little difficulty in discovering from the inhabitants, who are mainly Greeks, where their supplies are, and, in the event of resistance, they might be attacked by incendiary bombs dropped from seaplanes.

13. A further point worth noting is that, for telegraphic communication with Constantinople, the Dardanelles defences depend on a cable landed on the Asiatic side from Nagara Point and overhead land wires across the Bulair neck. Once the fleet is through, it will be easy either to cut the communications or to utilise them for sending false messages.

14. The garrison of the Dardanelles is stated by the Greek General Staff to consist of one division (10,000 men) on the Gallipoli Peninsula, and one division on the Asiatic side. These figures are obviously exclusive of the large artillery force required to man the forts. These figures are low, compared with the estimates hitherto given to the War Council, and 10,000 men is a small field force to defend a peninsula 52 miles long with numerous landing places. The Greeks, however, ought to be well informed, as the greater part of the civilian population on both sides of the Dardanelles is Greek. When the writer was Intelligence Officer to the Mediterranean Fleet[1] he found that Greek information on Turkish garrisons, &c., was usually reliable. The garrison might, of course, have been reinforced, but against this is the consideration already alluded to, that if the fleet forces a passage, the garrison of the Dardanelles is practically isolated.

15. Unless it is considered an unwarranted interference with the men on the spot, it might be worth while to warn the Admiral, as soon as he anticipates success, to send a ship to the head of the Gulf of Xeros, in order to prevent the escape of troops from Gallipoli, or their reinforcement from the mainland, by the Kavak road. He might also be warned to seize the end of the cable and telegraph as soon as practicable.

16. The Bosphorus, as already stated, is 17 miles long. At the narrowest point it is only 700 yards wide, but the average breadth is $1\frac{1}{2}$ miles. The depths are very great. It is important to note that the defences are all situated in the 7 miles nearest to the Black Sea, and most of the works face only towards the east. There have been rumours of the hasty mounting of guns at the Princes Islands, and at other places near Constantinople, but there are not likely to be any very formidable defences at the east end of the Bosphorus.

The Main Objective of the Fleet

17. The naval Commander-in-Chief, if he succeeds in forcing the Dardanelles, will have one primary and immediate object—to seek out and destroy the Turco-German Fleet, and more particularly the 'Goeben'.

18. It would be presumptuous to attempt to suggest how this would be accomplished. It will depend a good deal on the action of the enemy, who may escape into the Bosphorus, or endeavour to elude our fleet in the Sea of Marmora in a desperate attempt to escape to the Mediterranean. It may be supposed, however, that the Admiral will leave some units of his con-

---

[1] Hankey, who had been promoted Captain in 1899, served from 1900 to 1901 as Intelligence Officer to the Commander of the Mediterranean Fleet, Lord Charles Beresford, and to Beresford's Flag Captain, R. S. Lowry, a former Director of Naval Intelligence.

siderable fleet, including perhaps some submarines, to prevent this latter eventuality, and to ensure that his communications are kept open.

19. It is suggested that the Russians (if this has not been done) might be asked to send their Black Sea Fleet to the neighbourhood of the Bosphorus to prevent egress on that side.

Subsidiary Objectives

20. Before discussing the possible terms to be offered to Turkey, if the Dardanelles defences are successfully reduced, it will be useful to indicate a number of military operations which, though secondary in importance to the destruction of the Turco-German Fleet, are nevertheless of vital importance to the ultimate goal discussed in the early paragraphs of these notes. Some of these operations will probably require military co-operation.

21. *The clearance of the Gallipoli Peninsula and of the Defences on the Asiatic side of the Dardanelles* comes first of these. It is desirable, as soon as possible, to effect this, in order, whatever may be the result of the negotiations at Constantinople, to have a safe and uninterrupted line of water communication to Constantinople.

22. If, as anticipated, the Admiral leaves his older ships to guard the Straits, while he goes in pursuit of the 'Goeben', the Senior Naval Officer at the Dardanelles might be instructed to demand the surrender of the garrisons. Failing compliance, he should be instructed to institute a blockade and to endeavour to ascertain the whereabouts of the supplies and to destroy them, if possible, by bombardment or by incendiary bombs dropped from aircraft. It is a matter for consideration whether it would be worth while to attack with military forces at this stage, though this might become necessary.

23. *Turkey's Arsenals* are all situated on the shores of the Sea of Marmora and, as soon as forces can be spared, they should either be destroyed, or (a much better course if practicable) they should be occupied and held by a military force. These manufacturing establishments consist of:—

The Naval Dockyard, situated in the Golden Horn, which turns out all kinds of warlike stores;

The Tophane Arsenal, situated at the south-western end of the Bosphorus on the water's edge. It turns out various munitions of war;

The Zeitun Burnu cartridge factory and steelworks and the Zeitunlik powder factory, both the latter being situated on the Sea of Marmora, close to deep water, and not far from San Stephano.

All the above are entirely at the mercy of a fleet having command of the Sea of Marmora, and steps should be taken at the earliest possible opportunity to deprive Turkey of their use, and, if possible, to place their resources at the disposal of the Allies. It should be particularly noted that, apart from the above, Turkey has no establishments for the manufacture of arms or ammunition. Their output is understood to be rather small, as Turkey has drawn her main supplies of ammunition for some years from Krupp's, but under efficient management perhaps the production could be increased.

24. *The isolation of Constantinople* is another object that should be effected at the earliest possible moment.

25. On the European side communication with the rest of Turkey is supplied by one railway, which runs for several miles along the coast. At Kuchuk Chekmeje, some 5 miles along the coast to the west of Constantinople, this railway is crossed within a few hundred yards of the beach, on flat land, by the only good metalled road leading from Constantinople. At this point both railway and road communication can be interrupted from the sea, and Constantinople partially isolated. The telegraph lines to the interior also run along the coast. These could be cut, and the Russians might be asked to cut the German cable to Roumania, thus cutting off Turkey from Europe.

26. It might be worth while to warn the Admiral to effect this interruption as soon as he felt able to do so, in order to secure as much rolling-stock as possible, and to prevent the escape of Germans, Turkish notables, &c., before the reckoning.

27. Communication with Haidar Pasha, the terminus of the railway on the Asiatic side, will, of course, be interrupted the moment a fleet appears off the Golden Horn.

28. It might, however, be worth while to warn the Admiral to interrupt the railway, which runs for many miles along the shores of the Sea of Marmora, by destroying a length of permanent way, in order to prevent the removal of rolling-stock and the escape of persons of the type alluded to above in paragraph 26.

Negotiations

29. Having forced the Dardanelles, destroyed the Turco-German Fleet, isolated the garrisons at the Dardanelles or secured their surrender, seized or destroyed the Turkish arsenals and isolated Constantinople, the Admiral would be in a fine position to commence negotiations.

30. It is suggested for consideration that a first-rate diplomatist, versed in Turkish methods, should be sent out to assist him, unless Mr. Fitzmaurice is considered to have sufficient weight. If this suggestion is adopted, he might be sent to Salonica or Athens at once to await events.

31. It is also for consideration whether the Admiral should not be instructed to refuse to enter into any negotiations with the Germans in Constantinople, though there are arguments both ways.

32. It may well happen that the course of events might by this time have led to a *coup d'État* in Constantinople. Whether this is so or not, whether the negotiations are conducted with a Government under German domination or with a more friendly administration, terms may have to be offered, and there seems to be no particular reason why in the one case they should differ from the other in material points.

33. The writer is not specially qualified to express views on what these terms should be. The question, however, has already been discussed briefly at the War Council; it concerns naval and military as well as political interests, and may therefore be considered within the purview of the Committee of Imperial Defence. In any case it is imperative that the Turks should not be allowed to procrastinate, and that we should not lose time in making up our mind. The following tentative suggestions are therefore put forward as a basis for discussion.

34. The principles on which we should base our conditions might, perhaps, be summed up as follows:—

(1.) No attempt must be made at this stage for the *final* solution of the difficult Turkish problem. An interim arrangement of a non-committal character must be made. This was made clear at the last meeting of the War Council.

(2.) An absolutely safe line of communications must be obtained between the Mediterranean and Black Sea for the remainder of the war.

(3.) Turkey must at once be freed from German influence.

35. Conformably to the above principles it is suggested that Turkey should be offered a *truce* on some such terms as the following:—

(a.) The final settlement to be left in abeyance for the present.

(b.) The Turkish fleet and all naval material to be surrendered to the Allies.[1]

(c.) The defences and material of the Dardanelles and Bosphorus to be surrendered to the Allies.[1] All Turkish troops to be withdrawn from the Dardanelles and Bosphorus.

(d.) The Turkish expeditions in the Caucasus and against Egypt and Mesopotamia to be at once recalled.

[1] In the memorandum as printed, Hankey included the following footnote at this point: 'If this is rejected, purchase might be offered, or it might be merely requisitioned or borrowed for the tenure of the war to "save the face" of the Turkish negotiators.'

(*e.*) The demobilisation of the Turkish army.

(*f.*) The hire for the period of the war, or sale to the Allies, of Turkish rifles and other weapons.

(*g.*) The Turkish naval dockyard, arsenal, powder factory, shell factory, and clothing factory to be placed under officers appointed by the Allies and worked in their interest.

(*h.*) The persons of all German and Austrian born officers in the army and navy, and of all German and Austrian born officials in any branch of the Turkish administration (whether such persons are Turkish subjects or not) to be handed over to the Allies as prisoners of war. Lists of all other persons of German and Austrian origin in Turkey to be compiled and handed over to the Allies, such persons to be dealt with as decided by the Allies.

(*i.*) All German and Austrian concessions in Turkey to remain in abeyance for the duration of the war. Such concessions to be worked under the supervision of the Allies in the interest of Turkey.

(*j.*) German officials to be replaced by nominees of the Allies (*e.g.*, by Belgians).

(*k.*) Free passage up the Dardanelles by the ships of the Allies.

(*l.*) The Allies to have the right to place a garrison in Constantinople during the war.

There would probably be necessary provisions for financial control and for making good damage to British, French, and Russian railways and other commercial concerns in Turkey. The writer, however, is not qualified to go into these questions.

36. It is suggested that the British Government should decide what terms it desires, and should communicate them, as soon as there is a reasonable prospect of success, to our Allies prior to informing the Admiral.

In the Event of Refusal

37. If the Allies' terms are refused, which probably depends on the extent of the German domination, the following operations would be desirable and should be proceeded with:—

(*a.*) The final elimination of the garrison of the Dardanelles and the occupation of the Bulair lines.

(*b.*) The opening of the Bosphorus.[1]

[1] In the memorandum as printed, Hankey included the following footnote at this point: 'It is possible that it may be considered desirable to reduce the Bosphorus defences before negotiations are commenced, in order to hustle the Turks and to prevent them bringing fresh guns and howitzers into position. This depends on a detailed examination of the project.'

(*c.*) The occupation or destruction (if not already carried out) of the various armament works, and the entire isolation of Constantinople.

(*d.*) A naval blockade.

(*e.*) The occupation of the country on either side of the Bosphorus, in order to secure a free passage for wheat and transports. This might involve extended military operations, though the Turkish communications would be weak and vulnerable. This would probably involve the despatch of military reinforcements.

38. Summary of proposals put forward for consideration:—

(*a.*) The despatch of an emissary to be sent to the Balkans, not immediately, but if and when success in the Dardanelles is assured. (Paragraphs 5, 6, and 8.)

(*b.*) The despatch, if physically possible, of a flotilla to the Danube as soon as the route to the Black Sea is open. (Paragraphs 6, 7, and 8.)

(*c.*) To suggest to the Admiral that he should send a ship to the head of the Gulf of Xeros to command the high road past Kavak, and to prevent the escape or reinforcement of the Dardanelles garrison; also to seize the cable end at Nagara, and cut the land lines from the Dardanelles to Constantinople. (Paragraph 15.)

(*d.*) To ask the Russians to send the Black Sea Fleet to seal up the Black Sea entrance to the Bosphorus, and to cut the cable connecting Constantinople with Roumania. (Paragraph 19.)

(*e.*) To draw the Admiral's attention to the secondary objectives discussed in paragraphs 20 to 28.

(*f.*) To send a diplomatist versed in Turkish methods to Athens or Salonica to assist the Admiral as soon as negotiations commence. (Paragraph 31.)

(*g.*) To consider the terms to be offered to the Turks when negotiations commence. (Paragraphs 33 to 36.)

N.B.—Some general instructions might be sent to the Admiral for his guidance in the event of a successful forcing of the Dardanelles.

MPAH

Sir Edward Grey to Sir Francis Elliot: telegram[1]

(*Copy, Churchill papers: 26/4*)

1 March 1915   Foreign Office
11.30 pm
Private and Secret

Proposed cooperation of a Greek Army Corps in Gallipoli peninsula would be readily accepted.

Admiralty strongly urge that Greece should give naval as well as military aid in operation now proceeding at the Dardanelles.

The Greek battleships and cruisers and the excellent and efficient Greek flotillas of destroyers, the Greek submarines and small craft can play a useful part.

The Turkish resistance, however, is less than was expected, and if Greece is to share in the prestige of victory no time should be lost in taking part in the operations. You should inform Monsieur Venizelos verbally.

I have not mentioned Monsieur Venizelos's proposal to French or Russian Governments, but they must be taken into confidence as soon as possible.

Sir Francis Elliot to Sir Edward Grey: telegram

(*Copy, Churchill papers: 26/4*)

1 March 1915   Athens
12.20 pm
Private and Secret

Monsieur Venizelos has just made following proposal: After premising that he entirely shared view of General Staff as to impossibility for Greece of sending an army to Serbia, he stated that he was ready to submit to the King and to support if necessary by a threat of resignation offer of free passage through Salonika for allied forces. Further he would propose to offer co-operation of a Greek army corps of three divisions on Gallipoli peninsula. This he does not regard as a contradiction of his refusal to co-operate with Serbia because this army corps would be available for operations against Bulgarian rear in case of necessity.

---

[1] The second, third and fourth paragraphs of this telegram were drafted by Churchill, and sent by him to Asquith, who forwarded them to Grey. (*Churchill papers: 13/54*)

H. H. Asquith to Venetia Stanley

(Montagu papers)

1 March 1915   10 Downing Street

. . . Winston is breast-high about the Dardanelles—particularly as to-night we have a telegram from Venizelos announcing that the Greeks are prepared to send 3 divisions of troops to Gallipoli. It is really *far* the most interesting moment up to now in the War. . . .

Julian Corbett[1] to Lord Fisher

(Copy, Churchill papers: 13/54)

1 March 1915
Secret
Nanshan and Bulair

Referring to our conversation this morning[2]—the point is the nervousness of troops in a peninsula when the surrounding waters are occupied by the enemy and there is a possibility of a force being landed so as to cut their line of retreat.

By taking advantage of this the effective strength of a landing force can be greatly increased.

The last example is that of the Japanese operations against Nanshan—the neck of the Kwang-tung Peninsula.[3]

By a naval demonstration in rear of the Russian defending army they frightened the Russians into withholding the supports intended to reinforce the position and were thus able to carry it by assault.

---

[1] Julian Stafford Corbett, 1854–1922. Naval Historian. Barrister, 1877–82. Special Correspondent, *Pall Mall Gazette*, Dongola Expedition, 1896. Lecturer in History, Royal Naval War College, 1903. Admiralty representative, Historical Committee of the Committee of Imperial Defence; on 27 August 1915 he agreed to undertake an official naval history, and began work on 17 March 1916. Knighted, 1917. Author of the first three volumes of *Naval Operations*, part of the Official History of the Great War, published in 1920, 1922 and 1923 (posthumously); the 4th and 5th volumes were written by Sir Henry Newbolt, and published in 1928 and 1931.

[2] Fisher and Corbett had discussed the possibility of landing troops on the Bulair Isthmus, to cut off the Turkish forces on the Gallipoli Peninsula.

[3] In a successful attempt to isolate the Russian forces at Port Arthur, the Japanese 2nd Army under General Oku landed on 5 May 1904 on the Kwang-tung Peninsula and advanced to Nanshan, at the narrowest point of the isthmus. On 26 May, after a bloody battle, the Russians defending Nanshan retreated, leaving the Japanese in control of the Isthmus. The Japanese, who lost 4,500 out of the 30,000 troops engaged, were too exhausted to pursue the Russians towards Port Arthur. The Russians lost 1,500 men, out of 3,000 engaged.

The device, however, was not used adequately. For we now know from Russian sources that had the Japanese actually begun to land troops, or if they had even had transports with their demonstrating ships, the Russians would at once have evacuated the position and retired their whole force into Port Arthur.

As Nan-shan is to Kwang-tung Peninsula, so is the Bulair Neck to the Gallipoli Peninsula. The analogy suggests that if a landing is desired anywhere at the extremity of the Gallipoli Peninsula, the real operation should be disguised by an effective threat against or in rear of the Bulair Neck. The result which the Japanese example promises is the evacuation of the peninsula and an unopposed landing.

An account of the Kwang-tung affair will be found in *Maritime Operations in the Russo-Japanese War*, I. D. 944, vol. 1, chap. XV, and especially pp. 261–3, where the whole affair is criticised. Also appendix H, and Map D, (in separate case). It seems especially worth study at the present time.

Winston S. Churchill to Sir Edward Grey
(*Copy, Churchill papers: 26/2*)

2 March 1915   Admiralty
Secret

My dear Grey,

Dardanelles & C'ple

We must not disinterest ourselves in the final settlement of this region. In principle of course Russia's claims are recognised. But if they are to be satisfied the Br Naval position in those waters must also be safeguarded. It is not the time to talk of Lemnos. I consider we shd keep to the rule that all territorial accessions can only be settled at the general peace.[1]

It was a pity that we let the Russians talk of 'giving' us Egypt. We have had it for years *in fact*, & wanted no victorious war to give it to us *in form*.

[1] Unlike Churchill, Fisher was a strong advocate of annexing Lemnos, as were Sir Henry Jackson and Rear-Admiral Limpus. On 19 February 1915 Limpus had written to Churchill from Malta: 'I venture to suggest that we ought to acquire Lemnos Island. It is more valuable to us as a Sea Power than is Cyprus. The time of turmoil & general War seems to present a better opportunity of acquiring it than peace time would.' (*Churchill papers: 13/47*)

Certainly we must not let ourselves be pushed out of all interests here by
the statement that Egypt is our prize. That wd be paying for Egypt twice
over.[1]

I am having an Admy paper prepared abt the effect of a Russian control
of the Straits & Cple. I hope you will not settle anything further until you can
read it. English history will not end with this war.

I am glad to say that the attack on the *Dlles* has been resumed.

Yours ever

W

Sir Edward Grey to Winston S. Churchill

(*Churchill papers: 26/2*)

2 March 1915   Foreign Office
Private

Dear Churchill

I have seen the son[2] of the American Ambassador at Constantinople to
thank him for the way his father has helped & protected British subjects in
Turkey.

He says that it would probably prevent a massacre at Constantinople if
the American Ambassador could have an assurance that in the event of no
resistance being offered to the passage of the Fleet & no attack made upon it,
we should not bombard Constantinople or destroy the Mosques.

Of course any assurance needs to be carefully worded, but as I assume we
dont intend to bombard Constantinople, if it doesn't resist & keeps quiet
when we get there, we might perhaps settle some formula at the War Council
tomorrow.

Yours sincerely

E. Grey

---

[1] Since the British occupation of 1882, Egypt had been ruled by the British Agent (or
Consul-General), who acted as adviser to the Khedive. Under the Anglo-French Convention
of 1904 France had recognized the 'permanency' of Britain's occupation, in return for
British recognition of France's predominant position in Morocco. In December 1914 Britain
declared a Protectorate over Egypt (which France at once recognized) and replaced the
Khedive Abbas Hilmi by Hussein Kamel Pasha.

[2] Henry Morgenthau Jr, 1891–1967. Born in New York City. A student at Cornell Uni-
versity, 1909–10 and 1912–13. Lieutenant, United States Navy, 1917–18. Publisher of the
American Agriculturist, 1922–33. Chairman of the Federal Farm Board, 1933. Secretary of the
United States Treasury, 1934–45. General Chairman, United Jewish Appeal, 1947–50.
Chairman, American Financial and Development Corporation for Israel, 1951–4.

Winston S. Churchill to Graeme Thomson
(*Churchill papers: 2/82*)

2 March 1915   Admiralty

Transport for the 29th Division is to be ready on the 15th.

In addition to this, transport is to be provided *as soon as possible* (using and replacing if necessary the transports of the 29th Division) for carrying the Yeomanry Cavalry Division to Turkey.

Please report how this can be done.

Report also dates of transports arrived at Alexandria for the Australian Army.

WSC

Sir Ian Hamilton to Winston S. Churchill
(*Churchill papers: 26/2*)

2 March 1915   1 Hyde Park Gardens

My dear Winston,

You asked me yesterday what sort of a fellow was Birdwood. I replied a very charming fellow, which was true.

But I feel I ought to have given you *more insight* to guide you in your dealings with a man I have known well for many years.

Birdwood has had a brilliant staff career vide Pages 31–2 of big official Army List. He is tactful and quick but not strong. He was Military Secretary to Lord K. both in South Africa and in India.[1]

His weak point for a big war command is that with all his brilliant service he has never *commanded* anything in war; that he has never even *commanded* anything in peace except, for less than two years, a brigade.

His strong point for your business is that he will not quarrel with anyone, not at any price.

Yours ever
Ian Hamilton

[1] Birdwood, then a Major, served as Kitchener's Military Secretary in South Africa in 1902. Promoted to Lieutenant-Colonel, he went with Kitchener to India, where he served as both his Assistant Military Secretary and Interpreter, 1902–3. Promoted Colonel, he was again Military Secretary to Kitchener in India, 1905–7.

Lord Fisher to Winston S. Churchill
(Admiralty papers: 116/1681)

2 March 1915   Admiralty

Dear Winston,

I earnestly press you to hire Sir Trevor Dawson[1] AT ONCE to go to America as our *'Buyer'*. I quite understand about Pierpoint Morgan[2] being our Financial man over there with full powers—*but you want a* 'PUSHER' like Dawson WHO WILL GO EVERYWHERE AND BUY EVERYTHING!—just see how we have been held up for nets while the Newton works in New Jersey could supply millions of yards! & no doubt there are endless other items like nitro glycerine—pistols—rifles—AND INDEED EVERYTHING—and even steel plates that we are waiting for in our new vessels we are hustling and as my American friends tell me the whole American nation are intensely wanting to help us! (*no doubt they appreciate the dollars!!*) and you yourself acutely remarked yesterday *the more vast our orders the more vast will be the American bias towards England*—! THIS IS A BIG WAR! so send Sir Trevor Dawson by the ADRIATIC sailing TOMORROW *Wednesday* from Liverpool for New York with carte blanche *to buy everything appertaining to war.*

Yrs
F

Send him and then arrange afterwards to get the necessary authority for his proceedings— '*Munitions are the breath of war!*' what use millions of Russians without rifles or our monitors without cordite.

Sir Thomas Cuninghame[1] to Sir Edward Grey: telegram
(Copy, Churchill papers: 26/4)

2 March 1915   Athens

In conversation with officers of Greek General Staff I learnt view that

[1] Arthur Trevor Dawson, 1866–1931. Lieutenant, Royal Navy, 1887. Experimental Officer, Royal Ordnance Factories, 1892–6. Joined Vickers Ltd, as Superintendent of Ordnance, 1896. Director of Vickers, and of Armstrong Ltd, 1910–31. Knighted, 1909. Created Baronet, 1920.

[2] John Pierpont Morgan, 1867–1943. Son of the American financier John Pierpont Morgan (who died in 1913). Chairman of the Board of the U.S. Steel Corporation, and of Morgan, Grenfell and Co. of London. In 1919 he was awarded an honorary doctorate at Cambridge University (England), and in 1930 a Doctorate of Civil Law at Oxford. His London home was at 12 Grosvenor Square, and he had a country house in Hertfordshire.

[3] Thomas Andrew Alexander Montgomery Cuninghame, 1877–1945. Entered Army, 1897. Succeeded his father as 10th Baronet, 1897. Military Attaché, Vienna, with the rank of Major, 1912–14. General Staff Officer, French General Headquarters, September 1914–February 1915. Military Attaché, Athens, February 1915–March 1916. Lieutenant-Colonel, General Staff of the 34th Division, 1917. British Representative, American Staff College in France, 1918. British Military Representative in Austria, 1919–20. Military Attaché, Vienna and Prague, 1920–3.

present Naval operations should be assisted by land operations is universal. Plan they suggest is to disembark four of five divisions at Southern extremity of peninsula and advance against the heights east of Maidos.

Three successive defended positions would have to be carried, but Turks could not develop large forces owing to lack of space for deployment.

If simultaneously an attack by a separate and sufficient force was made against lines of Bulair, either by disembarking troops North of lines or at head of Gulf of Xeros, Turks would have to abandon Maidos region or run risk of being cut off and total result of diversion would be augmented.

Greeks do not think threat of bombardment of Constantinople by Fleet would have much effect upon Turkish resistance owing to number of German officers with the troops, but a definite military success might have great effect. . . .

Vice-Admiral Carden to Winston S. Churchill: telegram
(Copy, Churchill papers: 13/65)

3 March 1915
12.45 am

Operations 1st March 11 a.m. TRIUMPH, OCEAN and ALBION entered Straits and engaged battery No. 8 and guns at White Cliff. They were fired at by field guns and howitzers. Seaplane in the evening reported many fresh gun positions prepared but no guns in them and line of seventeen mines located across Straits on a line N.W. of Battery No. 8, mines appeared near surface. Mine-sweepers covered by destroyers swept to within 3,000 yds. of Cape Kephez during the night 1st–2nd March, they were fired at. ALBION had 1 officer, 4 men wounded; TRIUMPH and OCEAN also were hit, the latter one slightly wounded.

Mine sweepers doing excellent work. Four French battleships are off Bulair to demonstrate, reconnoitred landing place and bombarded guns seen. Material destroyed near entrance guns 6 in. to 11 in. 19, below 6″ 11, Nordenfelt 4, searchlights 2. Magazine(s) of forts Nos. 6 and 3 destroyed.

Vice-Admiral Carden to Winston S. Churchill: telegram
(Copy, Churchill papers: 13/65)

3 March 1915
1.50 am

CANOPUS, SWIFTSURE, CORNWALLIS entered Strait today and engaged fort 8 which now mounts seven guns. Fort 9 opened heavy fire using six guns some of which ranged to 11,000 yards. Field batteries and howitzers also opened fire. Ships withdrew 5.30 p.m. after inflicting damage on fort 9 which ceased firing 4.50 p.m. All three ships were hit several occasions one man slightly wounded. Sweepers working to-night. Seaplanes were unable to fly on account of weather.

Meeting of the War Council: extract from Secretary's notes

(*Copy: Cabinet Office papers: 22/1*)

Present: H. H. Asquith (*in the Chair*), Lord Haldane, Lord Crewe, Winston S. Churchill, A. J. Balfour, Lord Fisher, Sir Arthur Wilson, David Lloyd George, Sir Edward Grey, Lord Kitchener, Sir James Wolfe Murray, Lieutenant-Colonel Hankey (*Secretary*)

3 March 1915   10 Downing Street

THE DARDANELLES

MR. CHURCHILL read two messages regarding the progress of the bombardment of the Dardanelles forts, the net result of which was that forts 8 and 9 were in process of being destroyed, and that the forts at the entrance had been practically demolished.[1]

SMYRNA

MR. CHURCHILL then informed the War Council that orders had been sent on the previous evening for two battleships and an armoured cruiser to bombard Smyrna. The primary object of this operation was to smash the forts and prevent Smyrna from being used as a base for submarines. It was feared that Austrian submarines might come from Pola, and a submarine, the nationality of which was uncertain, had been seen off Tangier. The delays caused by bad weather in the bombardment of the Dardanelles increased the anxiety regarding the possible appearance of submarines. The orders for the forces attacking Smyrna were to destroy the forts deliberately by long-range bombardment, but to land no troops.

MR. BALFOUR suggested that the Greeks should be asked to attack Smyrna. This might have a double effect: first it would get rid of the Russian objections to the co-operation of Greece, as suggested by M. Venizelos, on the Gallipoli Peninsula; and second, it would probably force Italy to take part in the war.

MR. CHURCHILL said that the Greek fleet had not yet been put at our disposal, and the bombardment of Smyrna was required immediately.

[1] A Press communiqué to this effect was issued by the Admiralty on 4 March.

THE FUTURE OF CONSTANTINOPLE

SIR EDWARD GREY said that Greece would want to co-operate in the Gallipoli Peninsula. We are approaching a point at which we should have to say to Russia what we were willing to concede in regard to the Straits. What Russia required was access to the sea, and this implied a route of access which she can control. It was absurd that a huge empire such as Russia should have only ports that were icebound part of the year, such as Archangel and Vladivostock, or ports such as those in the Baltic and Black Sea, which were liable to be closed in time of war.

MR. BALFOUR said that he himself had no objection to Russia having an outlet which no one else could control, but he was not very anxious that Russia should herself be able to control the outlet from the Black Sea.

LORD HALDANE suggested that the Suez Canal provided a useful analogy. We might concede to Russia a privileged position such as we ourselves occupied in Egypt, the Dardanelles and Bosphorus being neutralized.

SIR EDWARD GREY said that some months ago, when the question was first discussed, M. Sazonoff had been willing to agree to the neutralization of Constantinople. Now, however, he said that there was a growing feeling in Russia that they ought to control the Straits.

MR. CHURCHILL said that we should stick to our general principle that the settlement of all territorial questions should be left until the end of the war, but suggested that we might in the meanwhile signify that we were in sympathy with Russian aspirations. He considered it absurd to compare Egypt with Constantinople.

MR. LLOYD GEORGE said it was clear that Russia wants territory.

SIR EDWARD GREY was not certain that we could leave the question to be settled at the eventual peace negotiations. It was very important to avoid anything in the nature of a breach with Russia, or any action which would incline Russia to make a separate peace. He had asked for the French view. There was great satisfaction in Paris that we were taking the lead in this matter, but this made it important for us to avoid being manœuvred by the French into a position of opposing Russia. It would never do for us to drift into a position of again checking Russian aspirations in the Dardanelles as we had in the past.

LORD HALDANE said this was the more important, because Germany would seize any opportunity to conclude a separate peace with Russia.

LORD CREWE suggested that perhaps some arrangement might be made with Roumania, as a condition of her entering the war. Roumania had a great interest in keeping the Straits open at all times, and some treaty might be made to which she was a party.

SIR EDWARD GREY pointed out that treaties were apt to be disregarded in war.

MR. LLOYD GEORGE said that, if this were the case, the only question which arose was as to who should control this passage.

LORD HALDANE said that, even if Russia controlled the Straits, the British and French fleets, if they had command of the sea, could always close the exit.

MR. CHURCHILL agreed. It would, he said, be impossible to prevent Russia from closing access to the Black Sea, but we could prevent them from coming out.

MR. BALFOUR suggested that the Gallipoli Peninsula might be internationalized.

LORD KITCHENER suggested that the Gallipoli Peninsula should be handed over to Greece.

LORD FISHER said that all our requirements would be met if we obtained possession of Lemnos, which would enable us to control the exit from the Black Sea.

SIR EDWARD GREY reminded the War Council that we had promised Greece that our occupation of Lemnos would be only temporary, and that we would lay no permanent claim to it.

LORD FISHER suggested that this might be got over by bartering Cyprus for Lemnos, or by obtaining a lease.

SIR EDWARD GREY said he would try to stave off the question of any permanent territorial settlement with regard to Turkey until after the war. He would approach M. Sazonoff in some such terms as these: 'You say that Russian sentiment will insist on the occupation of Constantinople by Russia. My personal opinion is that the British Government will not interpose a veto. But public opinion in this country will insist on all sorts of economic questions being settled. France will say that Syria must be earmarked for her. We ourselves have up to now asked for nothing, and have only declared a protectorate over Egypt. We should have to consider our claims in Asia Minor. British opinion, however, had entirely changed in regard to a Russian occupation of Constantinople, and he personally did not anticipate any veto to it.'

AFTER THE DARDANELLES. THE NEXT STEP

MR. LLOYD GEORGE asked if it was intended that an Allied force should occupy Constantinople?

MR. CHURCHILL said that a change had occurred. In consequence of the success of the bombardment of the outer forts Russia was preparing to embark an army corps at Batoum.

SIR EDWARD GREY read a telegram confirming this.

MR. CHURCHILL said that Russia had always been favourable to the proposed attack on the Dardanelles. With a Russian army corps, three divisions from Greece, a French division, and our own troops from Egypt, we should dispose of from 120,000 to 140,000 men. The Greeks were quite close; 4,000 men from Egypt and 2,000 Marines were at Lemnos. 4,000 Marines and the Naval Division had sailed from this country.

LORD KITCHENER said that 6,000 more men were waiting at Alexandria, to proceed as soon as asked for.

MR. CHURCHILL said that the transports would be ready to embark either the XXIXth Division or a mounted Territorial brigade by the 15th March, but if both these forces were to go a further delay of a fortnight would be occupied in collecting the necessary transport.

LORD KITCHENER proposed to leave the question open until the 10th March, when he hoped to have heard from General Birdwood.

He suggested that it would be a good plan to announce that we were coming as the ancient friend of the Turks, &c. It would be quite easy to get this information through by means of aeroplanes. There are also other channels by which it could be passed through.

MR. CHURCHILL reminded Sir Edward Grey that some time ago he had suggested that the Foreign Office should prepare a leaflet.[1]

SIR EDWARD GREY said that, after listening to this discussion, he thought a leaflet would be either very misleading or so offensive as to fail in its object.

MR. BALFOUR suggested that we might promise not to damage mosques or private buildings at Constantinople if no rising or opposition was made.

[1] A proclamation to be dropped into Adrianople by aeroplane had been drafted at the Admiralty in February 1915 by the Assistant Director of Operations, Captain Richmond. Part of it read: 'When Germany is beaten, as she is going to be, who will have a word of pity for her miserable allies . . .? The forts of the Dardanelles lie in ruins: the great guns are silent never to speak again. . . .' (*Richmond papers*)

LORD KITCHENER did not agree in this. He suggested that the American Ambassador in Constantinople should be asked to prepare transports, to which the European population could be sent in the event of disturbance.

SIR EDWARD GREY said that he had seen the son of the American Ambassador in Constantinople, who was in London. He had said that his father believed he might be able to avert a massacre if he could issue an assurance that no damage would be done to Constantinople if the Allies were not attacked there.

MR. BALFOUR suggested that the Admiral should receive orders to cut the bridges on his arrival at Constantinople. He understood that by this means great difficulties were placed in the way of a massacre of Europeans, as the native quarter would be separated from the European quarter.

MR. CHURCHILL said that he thought it would be a mistake to give any assurance whatsoever to Turkey. He then outlined the action to be taken by our fleet, if and when the Dardanelles were forced. The first thing to be attempted would be the capture or destruction of the Turco-German fleet. A battle might take place either in the Dardanelles or the Sea of Marmora, or the enemy might seek to escape into the Black Sea. He hoped in this latter event that its egress would be barred either by mines or by the Russian fleet. The second step would be the destruction of the defences of the Bosphorus. This was not so easy as appeared at first sight, owing to the difficulty in attacking some of the forts from a distance. As soon as the fleet was through the Dardanelles, the Turkish lines of communication would be cut at Bulair, and the garrison of the Gallipoli Peninsula would be isolated. In addition, it might be possible to cut some of the bridges on the line between Adrianople and Constantinople by means of aircraft. The prize we ought to seek from this action was nothing less than the occupation by the Allies of Turkey in Europe. All must pass into our hands, and we ought to accept nothing less.

MR. BALFOUR said that he hoped that the railways running along the shore of the Sea of Marmora on both the European side and the Asiatic side would be cut.

LORD KITCHENER said this would be done at once if the Turks resisted.

He then discussed the question of the command of the military forces of the Allies in this expedition. The French had agreed that the supreme command should be vested in a British officer, notwithstanding that the

French general (d'Amade)[1] was senior to General Birdwood. For the present, therefore, he proposed to leave General Birdwood in command. Later on, however, particularly if the forces increased, it might be necessary to send a more senior general, for which purpose he proposed Sir Ian Hamilton.

MR. LLOYD GEORGE asked if General Birdwood was highly thought of.

LORD CREWE said he was considered the best general in India, though he lacked experience of a high command on active service.

MR. CHURCHILL pointed out that the Russians might send a very senior general. The Greeks also might send a senior man. It might be advisable to send a very senior general now, in order to avoid the risk of an attempt on the part of the Allies to outbid one another in the seniority of the generals.

LORD KITCHENER thought that all difficulties were covered by the French consent to allow us to have the supreme command.

MR. BALFOUR suggested that the road on the Asiatic shore of the Dardanelles should be broken up directly the ships effected a passage. This would prevent the possibility of field guns and howitzers being brought in to embarrass us after the Straits had been forced. The road round the head of the Gulf of Xeros ought also to be broken up so that nothing could pass in or out of the Gallipoli Peninsula. He asked whether the Admiralty anticipated opposition from howitzers.

MR. CHURCHILL said that the longer the delay the greater was the chance of such interruptions. He had obtained six howitzers, which had been mounted on board some of the ships, for the special purpose of dealing with the shore howitzers. As regards the road round the head of the Gulf of Xeros, four French battleships were already there. The road on the Asiatic shore would also be dealt with.

LORD KITCHENER anticipated that, when the forts began to fall, the garrison would either surrender or slip out over the Bulair lines in small parties by night.

MR. CHURCHILL said that we ought to be content with nothing less than the surrender of Turkey in Europe. Everything in Turkey in Europe comes from Asia, and we should cut them off from there. Now that the

[1] Albert Gérard Léo d'Amade, 1856–1941. 2nd Lieutenant, 1876. French Military Attaché with the British Forces in South Africa, 1899–1900. French Military Attaché, London, 1901–4. Commanded a detachment of French troops at Casablanca, 1906–9. Commanded the Territorial Divisions of the North, near Arras, 1914. Commanded the French Expeditionary Corps at the Dardanelles, 24 February–15 May 1915, when he was relieved of his command. He received no further active military command. On a military mission to Russia, 1915. In 1923 he published a booklet, *Constantinople et Les Dardanelles*.

Greeks had expressed their intention of joining we should have plenty of men available. Everything in Europe, arsenals, arms, and even the fortress of Adrianople, ought to fall into our hands. Constantinople was only a step towards the Balkans. If we granted Turkey an armistice it should be on the condition of the military surrender of Turkey in Europe. We might, however, permit Turkey temporarily to hold on to Turkey in Asia.

LORD KITCHENER said the first step to insist on was the surrender of the German officers in Turkey. After that the Turks would be no good.

MR. CHURCHILL said that it was quite possible that Turkey might sue for peace, whereas the Russian proposals only contemplated an armistice.

SIR EDWARD GREY suggested that the evacuation of the line of the Bosphorus and Dardanelles by Turkey, and the withdrawal of their army to a certain distance behind that line by their army, ought to meet our needs.

LORD KITCHENER said that, if we could get the Germans out, Turkey would probably sue for peace. There would then be no need of an armistice.

MR. CHURCHILL suggested that we ought to hire the Turkish army as mercenaries.

MR. LLOYD GEORGE said that the Turks had never been any use as mercenaries. In their own country they fought well, but not when employed as mercenaries.

SIR EDWARD GREY said we should have to pay rather a heavy price politically to secure Turkish co-operation.

LORD CREWE considered that it would be quite impossible to settle the question of Turkey in Asia during the war.

THE PRIME MINISTER expressed the view that the Turks and their German masters would not give in easily. He asked if they would not in all probability mine the arsenal?

SIR EDWARD GREY said they were reported already to have mined the British and French Embassies.

LORD KITCHENER said it would not be easy to mine the arsenal and blow it up at precisely the right moment.

SIR EDWARD GREY said that, from the Balkan point of view, he hoped we should get through the Dardanelles before the Russians met with another reverse.

LORD FISHER said it was even more important to get through before the arrival of Austrian submarines.

SIR EDWARD GREY said that the psychological moment was the fall of the defences at the Narrows. We could then invite Bulgaria to take the Enos–Midia line, on condition that they joined the Allies. We might also get in touch with Italy.

MR. LLOYD GEORGE said that we ought to give a pledge to Bulgaria that, as a condition of her joining, she should, in the final settlement, receive the portion of Macedonia lost after the last Balkan war, provided that Serbia obtained Bosnia and Herzegovina. There should be no bargaining with Serbia, who should be told that we had secured her safety and the cause of the Allies by this move, and that she would have to accept it.

SIR EDWARD GREY said the difficulty was that Bulgaria wanted something on account.

THE PRIME MINISTER said it was by no means improbable that Bulgaria was already on the move.

LORD KITCHENER said he would not be surprised if they were to seize Adrianople.

SIR EDWARD GREY explained our present position towards Bulgaria. He had told the Bulgarian Minister[1] quite plainly that he must know what conditions they desired before he could do anything. If he knew this, he could approach Serbia, but it was useless to do this unless he knew what they wanted. If we considered their proposals reasonable we could go to Serbia, and say they must accept them. He had arranged for this offer to be conveyed to the Opposition, as well as to the Government in Bulgaria.

MR. LLOYD GEORGE said that if Bulgaria came into the war *now* her co-operation would be worth more than later on. He asked if it was correct that there are 300,000 Turks in Thrace, as stated in a recent telegram.

LORD KITCHENER thought this unlikely. In any case, the Turkish troops were not good ones. He felt convinced that the Bulgarians would be at them. It would be a mistake to make further overtures to Bulgaria unless we were certain of getting through the Narrows.

THE DANUBE

MR. BALFOUR asked how we were getting on as regards the preparations for action on the Danube.

LORD FISHER said that the monitors had been ordered, but that their construction was being very seriously delayed by strikes.

MR. CHURCHILL said that we ought not to make the main line of advance up the Danube. We ought not to employ more troops in this theatre of war than are absolutely essential in order to induce the Balkan

[1] In 1915 the Bulgarian Minister in London was Pancho Haji-Mischeff.

States to march. He was still of opinion that our proper line of strategy was an advance in the north through Holland and the Baltic. This might become feasible later on when our new monitors were completed. The operation in the East should be regarded merely as an interlude.

Leverton Harris[1] to Winston S. Churchill

(Churchill papers: 13/48)

3 March 1915   Admiralty

My dear Winston,

I have this morning concluded the biggest copper deal in the world's history.

The British Govt.—without spending one penny—has now the absolute control of 95% of the American Export trade—& the remaining 5% are clamouring to come in.

I have got in all the Guggenheims &—Steins.

This represents control of (according to 1913 exports) 95% of 380,000 tons or over 26 million pounds worth of copper per year—so long as the war lasts. All shipments are to be licensed by our consul at N. York & are to be only to the Allies & to actual consumers in those neutral countries whose prohibitions of export are effective & you will give a guarantee not to re-export.

I will circulate a paper tonight in the meantime you might like to inform your colleagues on the front bench.

In addition all copper at Gibraltar is to come to England or France & the Govt is to have the OPTION of purchase, & further we are to be well paid for bringing it home & no claims for detention are to be made.

I am really delighted & I know you will be.

Yrs
Leverton Harris

[1] Frederick Leverton Harris, 1864–1926. Conservative MP, 1900–6; 1907–10; 1914–18. Honorary Commander, RNVR, 1915. Parliamentary Secretary, Ministry of Blockade, 1916–18.

Winston S. Churchill: memorandum

(*Churchill papers: 21/38*)

3 March 1915 Admiralty

ARMAMENT FIRMS

I see great difficulties in the Government acquiring temporary ownership and control of the armament producing firms. No analogy can be drawn between these firms and the railways. The railways are monopolies which have grown up on the basis of definite Acts of Parliament, and which are discharging on a somewhat reduced scale in time of war exactly the same functions as they have discharged in peace. The approach of the calamity of war led the railways to expect a diminution in their profits to an extent which no one could measure, and for them to be guaranteed at the outset practically what they would have made had peace continued, was a proposition to which they were naturally ready to agree. The shipowners also at the beginning of the war would have been very glad to be guaranteed the profits which they had made in the previous year, and at the outset were delighted to be chartered by the Government. Now that the seas are practically safe and freights have advanced far beyond the generous rates paid by the Government, the shipowners make grave complaints when their ships are requisitioned. Yet shipowners are only conducting in time of war the same work as in time of peace on a reduced scale, and their only contribution to the national industry has been to exact larger profits for the same or less service. I think, therefore, there is a good case for taking over the means of transportation both by sea and land. It would be equitable to the private interests concerned, and beneficial to the State.

But the armament firms have embarked upon an enormous and highly speculative business of expansion necessitating the most far-reaching and intricate financial and commercial arrangements. They are discharging an immense variety of operations which have grown up anyhow under the pressure of the emergency. It was in the nature of their business that war should be a time to them of exceptional profit. They have certainly made astonishing exertions. They have got a great mass of definite contracts from the State which cannot be repudiated, and on which, if they fulfil them, they are entitled to their reward. If these firms are deprived of the profits they may reasonably expect to make from the contracts into which the State has entered with them, they will be discontented; and, without going into questions of equity and public good faith, if they are discontented, it is certain that the production of armaments will be paralysed. If, on the other hand, a financial arrangement is made with them with which they are satisfied, we may be perfectly certain that the State will be the loser. It is quite impossible to estimate, except after a prodigious enquiry, what their profits actually are in relation to their expenses, their exertions, and their risks. Their finance is of the utmost complexity. They have an enormous volume of Government contracts; they have secondary contracts with hundreds of firms; they have all sorts of private arrangements with particular subsidiary firms; they have a large volume of foreign business; and for all of these they are answerable to their shareholders. It is customary to talk of this question in terms of Vickers and Armstrongs. A study of the business even of these two firms alone will reveal complications and ramifications of the most extraordinary character. But there are at least 500 firms now under contract with the Admiralty, apart from the War Office, for the production of armaments, all of which are in exactly the same moral position as Vickers and Armstrongs. If the plant, property, and good-will of these firms is to be acquired by the State, it can only be done by virtue of either an act of confiscation, which means a quarrel fatal to the organisation of armament production, or by compensation on terms which are bound to be most wasteful to the State. Look at our position with the Marconi Company. Look at every State purchase of land or private business.

The Admiralty do not admit that their contracts (the larger part of which were made in time of peace) have not been settled thriftily, and we shall court at the proper time close investigation of all our business transactions. We therefore do not consider, so far as we are concerned, that the workmen of armament firms have any grievance against their employers on the ground of excessive profits. Class envy and an anti-war spirit, seeking a permissible form of expression, may lead a small section of the workmen in these industries to make out that their complaint is that they are working for the profit of private employers, and not for the State. My own view is that workmen do not care very much whether they are working for the State or for a private employer. What they care for is good wages and good conditions of labour. Certainly there is great discontent very often in Government factories, and there are signs of agitation at the present time in the Royal dockyards, in spite of large concessions which have been made year after year. I believe it to be a delusion to suppose that by pandering to socialistic ideas in regard to State ownership of armament firms, we should produce any appreciable improvement in the spirit of the discontented minority of workmen. The process of taking the armament firms over would either impose a blighting check on production, or be a very bad bargain for the State, and the addition which would be made to the work of the Admiralty officials and to my own personal work of general supervision would be one quite impossible to face in time of war. Either the transformation would be a pretence—i.e., the firms would get in the form of compensation the profits they were going to make anyhow, and the management would remain wholly unaltered except in name—or you would have a complete collapse of the existing system by which the life and power of the Navy have been maintained. I am not personally anxious to have anything to do with either of these alternatives.

I do not believe in socialistic production, but in private enterprise and private thrift regulated and restrained by private interest. There is a great gulf fixed between transportation and production. If we attempt to cross it while we have the daily conduct of the war on our hands, in order to satisfy the sulky spite of a very small section of discontented workmen, a catastrophe will follow. We have got to use private enterprise and we have got to pay private enterprise; and, where a vast degree of new exertion and invention is required from private people, with great changes in their business arrangements and new risks, we must expect to pay handsomely. The armament firms have long been the object of animadversion from a certain small political section. I have never believed that the complaints against them were just or well founded. Where should we be without them now? Private enterprise has produced these magnificent establishments, has localised in this country the great warship building trade of the world, and has given us a reserve of ships of the most powerful character, available without the slightest effort on our part in the hour of need. I am not at all prepared to say that they are not entitled to reap some measure of exceptional profit from the present emergency.

And, after all, a much simpler and more effective remedy can be found in a proper combination of rewards and penalties. I am in favour of the Chancellor of the Exchequer's Bill, the essence of which is compulsory arbitration in the event of labour disputes during the war—and for the purposes of the war only—by the Board of Trade, with penalties on masters and men who do not obey the award. This will enable any excessive profits which the employers are found to be making in particular cases to be shared as a result of awards with the workmen, and it will bring home to the workmen and employers the resolve of the State that production shall go on uninterruptedly. I think we should not grudge the employer his legitimate profit, and we are bound to enlist his wholehearted energies in the management and development of his business. A special system of State bonuses to the workmen should also be instituted and paid to all men who keep good time. There are a variety of ways of doing this. In cases where the completion of a ship makes a definite break in the labour system a bonus should be distributed as a lump sum if the work is completed punctually. But the principle that the State will reach out over the employer and give the workmen special premiums during this exceptional period for sustained exertion will be found an easy solvent of the main difficulties, and will make the workman feel, in the most pleasant and satisfactory of ways, that he is a worker in the national cause. If a system of compulsory arbitration, gilded by State bonuses to the workmen and sustained by a restriction of public house hours, is inaugurated, it will secure almost all the results desired.

WSC

Sir Edward Grey to Sir George Buchanan and Sir Francis Bertie: telegram
(Copy, Churchill papers: 26/4)

2 March 1915   Foreign Office
Private and Secret

There are indications that Greece may wish to participate in operations at the Dardanelles. If so it is most important readily to accept her co-operation and thereby to secure her coming out on the side of the Allies.

His Majesty's Government have said nothing to any Power about the future of Constantinople and the Straits except what I have said to Russian Minister for Foreign Affairs,[1] and should Greece ask for conditions as to her co-operation I propose to say nothing except in consultation and agreement with Russia and France.

Lord Fisher to Winston S. Churchill
(Churchill papers: 13/56)

3 March 1915   Admiralty
First Lord,

I concur in your proposal to remit this question[2] for careful study by Sir A. K. Wilson, with whom I have on many occasions discussed it in general terms. (*The whole problem depends on the efficiency of our arrangements for protection against submarines—an effective means of protection is not yet in sight.*)

This operation would necessarily await the trend of events in the Dardanelles. We must know what forces remain before embarking on a new undertaking.

[1] Since 1908 Grey had based his eastern policy upon eventual Russian control of the Straits. On 12 November 1914 he had informed the Russian Government: 'We regard the conduct of the Turkish Government as having made a complete settlement of the Turkish question including that of the Straits and Constantinople in agreement with Russia inevitable.' 'We must carry out our promises of 1908 . . . in terms acceptable to Russia,' he telegraphed to Sir Francis Bertie on 18 December 1914; and on 14 January 1915 he assured the Russian Foreign Minister, Sazonov, that whatever territorial changes took place in Turkey, 'all I said . . . about the settlement of Constantinople and the Straits at the end of the war holds good as far as we are concerned'. (*Grey papers*)

[2] The proposed attack on Borkum (see pp. 389, 732-8).

We are now committed to the Dardanelles at all costs so must anyhow wait till middle of May, by which time events in Holland may quite change the position and indicate Terschelling as our base.

Sir Francis Elliot to Sir Edward Grey: telegram
(*Copy Churchill papers: 13/45*)

3 March 1915   Athens
11.30 pm
Private and Secret

Russian Minister[1] tells me that his Government have informed British and French Governments that in no circumstances will they allow Greek soldiers to enter Constantinople.

This attitude creates a very serious situation for I am convinced that prospect of entering Constantinople as conquerors weighs more with the King and his people than that of any material advantage to be obtained by the war. The war fever is mainly of sentimental origin.

If they are told of veto of Russia (which must be represented as veto of the Three Powers) before they actually join us I believe effect will be to stop them from doing so. If they are not told they will have been allowed to join under false pretences and disillusion will be still greater. In both cases there will be a strong revulsion of feeling against the Entente Powers and probably the resignation of Venizelos.

If therefore decision of the Greek Government be in favour of war I earnestly trust Russian Government will be brought to withdraw their veto against entry of the Greeks into Constantinople. No objection will be made to stipulating that occupation would not be permanent (such as was made in January with regard to Gallipoli) since no practical Greek dreams of re-establishing Byzantine Empire.

My French colleague[2] entirely agrees with me. My Russian colleague cannot be made to understand effect of tradition and sentiment on Greek feeling.

[1] Alim Pavlovich Demidov, Prince of San Donato, 1868. Traveller and taxidermist. Author of several books on hunting in the Caucasus (1898), Mongolia (1900) and Kamchatka (1905). Counsellor, Russian Embassy, Paris, 1910–12. Minister in Athens, 1912–17.
[2] Gabriel Pierre Deville, 1854–1940. French Minister to Athens, 1909–15.

Sir Thomas Cuninghame to Sir Edward Grey: telegram
(*Copy, Churchill papers: 13/45*)

3 March 1915   Athens
11.30 pm
Private and Secret

Difficulty at present is threefold. Objection of General Staff concerns dispersion of forces, the wish of the King for war and the expectation of people is for advance on Constantinople. Object of Russia is to (group omitted ? prevent) entry of Greeks into that city.

It is suggested that all these difficulties would be met by acceptance, for purposes of co-operation, of one Greek Division only in addition to the fleet.

Minimum force with which disembarkation on Gallipoli Peninsula should be attempted is four Divisions and if three of these were British or Anglo-French and only one Greek, objection of Russia might be overcome. . . .

Reports here agree that Turks are not a formidable enemy.

Lieutenant-General Birdwood to Lord Kitchener: telegram
(*Copy, Churchill papers: 2/88*)

3 March 1915   Mudros
6.15 pm

I anticipate, that if required to land by the Navy, we shall not be able in taking concealed guns or howitzers to restrict movements to minor operations, as any guns are sure to be in strong positions and very numerous, and would be covered by strongly entrenched infantry, who in some places would doubtless be able to command coast fort guns which might have been reduced by the Navy. With the exception perhaps of two Mounted Brigades I shall probably be taking with me in the first instance my whole corps; there will not at first be much scope for Mounted Brigades, and one of these lately arrived from Australia is but little trained. I will certainly try to dominate the Eastern side from the Gallipoli peninsula, as I am particularly anxious to avoid, if possible, placing any troops on the Asiatic side; for not only do I fully realize the danger of placing there a more or less isolated force, but I know from personal observation that the country is big and difficult, and even a whole division would soon lose itself. You can, therefore, rely on my avoiding it if possible. You will have seen that arrangements have been made already in the direction you have indicated regarding threats on Bulair Lines. Also, before receiving your telegram, I had issued orders in practically identical terms regarding embarkation and disembarkation practice at Mudros Bay. It is probable that only the advanced Brigade would be able to take much advantage of this.

If I get in touch with local information later on I will telegraph an appreciation, but, as I said in a former telegram, at present this is not feasible, and it is impossible to say what troops may be in the vicinity of Constantinople when the Dardanelles have been forced. I cannot help thinking that when the Fleet arrives before Constantinople and threatens the bombardment of the city, opposition will collapse. I am not in a position to know if this would result in laying down of arms by Turkish Army, and at present I have no information to guide me in advising as to operations after the Gallipoli peninsula has been taken, and I have as yet no maps of the country. A man-lifting kite or a captive balloon would be of great use to the Navy. It would not only give great assistance in the spotting of long-range fire, but I would also be able to detect by its means the concealed batteries which are already troubling the Navy. I therefore strongly recommend the immediate despatch of one or the other.

Vice-Admiral Carden to Winston S. Churchill: telegram
(Copy, Churchill papers: 13/65)

4 March 1915
12.05 am
Secret and Personal

Gale moderated operations proceeding but aerial reconnaissance not yet possible to locate concealed guns.

Seaplanes have only been able to fly on one day since 19th owing to rough weather.

Your 77, fourteen days, but permission is requested to take 'QUEEN ELIZABETH' inside Straits when desirable.

She can now steam 18 knots with port engines, and large rudder power makes her sufficiently handy although starboard engines out of action.

Lieutenant-General Birdwood to Lord Kitchener: telegram
(Copy, Churchill papers: 2/88)

4 March 1915   Mudros
3.20 am

I have seen Admiral Carden and have discussed the situation with him. I have also carried out a personal reconnaissance as far up the Straits as is possible. As the numbers are constantly varying, it is practically impossible

w.c.3—ss

to determine the strength of the troops on either side of the Dardanelles. Troops are kept by the Turks on board transports at Constantinople and are ready to be brought down at any moment, while recently others have arrived from Adrianople. There are, however, probably 40,000 troops in the vicinity of the Dardanelles.

Acting under instructions he has received to force the passage as a purely naval operation, Admiral Carden intends if possible to do this.

In the event of it being impossible for the Fleet to silence the guns in hidden positions, alternatively, the Navy will either ignore the damage inflicted or co-operate with the Army in their destruction.

It depends on the urgency of the operations as to whether there will be time to wait for the latter alternative, as my force cannot be ready to disembark before 18th March at the earliest. If assistance of the troops is required, my proposals, with which Admiral Carden agrees, are that the Navy should make a strong demonstration against the Bulair lines accompanied by available transports with troops which are not required for immediate disembarkation. It is also probable that from about 16th March a demonstration will be made off Smyrna. A strong force would then be landed at Cape Helles point to work up north to a point from which the mainland batteries on the European side of the Narrows could be taken in reverse and also the concealed batteries dealt with elsewhere. I understand that this line forms a magnificent holding position and that it has been very heavily entrenched across the peninsula and is supported by howitzers and guns. After this line has been taken I fear it may be necessary to transfer a good part of my force to the Asiatic side to deal with the ground in the rear of Chanak and adjoining batteries, in whose vicinity we have information that there are guns. If, however, it can be satisfactorily done, this ground will be dealt with from the European side.

The action of the military forces will be, of course, dependent on the progress made by the Navy up to the 18th, but, in any case, troops will be moving in the right direction, and would probably keep a strong force entrenched in covered positions from Kephez Bay to Nagara, on the Asiatic side, to protect the Narrows. With the command thus secured of the lines across the Narrows, there may not be much further opposition until the Bulair lines are reached. I understand these are held in force and have been considerably strengthened, but, if the enemy holds them at all, I do not expect much difficulty there, with the co-operation which the Navy could give in assistance from each side. If Gallipoli is not held, it would seem a good place for concentration of my forces until further action, leaving behind a force to hold the Bulair lines, and, if necessary, to cover the Asiatic side as mentioned above.

With regard to further action I will telegraph again, but as communication to and from the mainland is impossible, any local information seems to be unattainable here. Such information as we have comes from Athens.

It is presumed that the Marines will bring 1st Line transport. I should be glad to hear of their organization.

Winston S. Churchill to Vice-Admiral Carden: telegram

(*Copy, Churchill papers: 13/65*)

4 March 1915   Admiralty
4.35 am

Secret and Personal

The following matters require your attention with a view to action when the time comes.

Should you succeed in entering the Sea of Marmora your first task is to destroy the Turco German Fleet wherever it is.

As soon as this is achieved you should send vessels to cut, by fire or landing parties according to circumstances, the Scutari Ismid railway line and the railway and road from Constantinople to Kuchuk Chekmeje.

Our policy is to cut off on the European shore as much of the Turkish Army as possible and to force them to capitulate later.

You are next to attack the Forts of the Bosphorus on which operation a memorandum prepared by Sir H. Jackson is being telegraphed to you in sections.

This is to be taken as a guide and not a rule.

When you see yourself within four days of entering the Sea of Marmora you are to make Askold[1] telegraph to the Russian Fleet at Sebastopol to come to blockade the Black Sea mouth of the Bosphorus and to attack with long range fire the outer forts.

You are to duplicate this telegram to us.

We want the Russians to block the exit and to increase the moral effect by opening fire simultaneously with your attack.

We are not counting upon them at this stage for any decisive operation.

---

[1] The *Askold* was a Russian light cruiser put at the disposal of the British Admiralty on the outbreak of war in August 1914, when she was in the Western Pacific. She took part in the search for the German cruiser *Emden* in the Indian Ocean, September 1914; was in the Suez Canal attached to the British naval force intended to protect Egypt from Turkish attack, November 1914; joined Vice-Admiral Carden's fleet at the Dardanelles, January 1915; and operated off the Bulgarian port of Dedeagatch after the outbreak of war with Bulgaria, October 1915. The ship's main function in 1915 was to ensure direct wireless communication with the Russian Black Sea Fleet.

When the above military necessities have been fully provided for you should deal with Constantinople.

The number of ships at your disposal will probably enable Constantinople to be summoned as soon as the Turco German Fleet has been destroyed without prejudice to the other warlike movements against railways and the Bosphorus just described.

We wish to obtain the peaceful surrender of the city and if you think it advisable and likely to prevent massacre or futile resistance you may at any time after you have entered the Sea of Marmora communicate with the American Ambassador or other neutral or Turkish Authorities accessible to you assuring them that prompt obedience and the orderly surrender of the City will save all private property from injury and that the utmost respect will be shown to all religious buildings especially mosques and objects venerated by Moslems.[1]

You will also concert with General Birdwood the necessary movements of troops.

You will report fully and regularly your views and intentions using your Chief of Staff for this purpose when you are too pressed.

It is of the utmost importance that we should be kept informed.

Antecedent to the above it is of course presumed that by the fire of ships in Saros Gulf you will as far as possible prevent all movements of troops guns and convoys across the Bulair Isthmus.

This appears to us to be of importance in the present phase.

Winston S. Churchill to Lord Kitchener

(*Copy, Churchill papers: 13/48*)

4 March 1915   Admiralty

My dear Kitchener,

I have now heard from Carden that he considers it will take him 14 days on which firing is practicable to enter the Sea of Marmora, counting from the 2nd of March. Of course bad weather would prolong, and a collapse of the Turkish resistance at the later forts would shorten this period. But it seems to me we ought now to fix a date for the military concentration so that the arrival of troops can be timed to fit in with the normal fruition of the naval operation. The transports for the 30,000 troops from Egypt, less those

[1] In 1899, in *The River War*, Churchill had censured Kitchener for ordering the destruction of the Mahdi's tomb, the holy place of the Dervishes at Khartoum. 'To destroy what was sacred and holy to them,' he wrote, 'was a wicked act. . . .' Were such conduct to be characteristic of the Government of the Sudan, he continued, 'then it would be better if Gordon had never given his life nor Kitchener won his victories'.

already taken to Lemnos, will all have arrived at Alexandria between the 8th and the 15th, that is to say the troops could be landed at Bulair or, alternatively, if practicable, taken through the Straits to Constantinople, about the 18th instant. By the same date the transports conveying the 8,000 men of the Naval Division from England could also reach the same points. In addition there are, I understand, in Lemnos 4,000 Australians and 2,000 Marines of the Royal Naval Division. Therefore I suggest for your consideration, and for the proper co-ordination of naval and military policy, that we fix in our own minds the 20th March as the date on which 40,000 British troops will certainly be available for land operations on Turkish soil. To make sure of this date it will perhaps be better to give all orders as for the 17th or 18th; we should then have a little in hand. I think the French should be given this date (20th) as their point, and should rendezvous at Lemnos not later than the 16th. We should also inform the Russians and the Greeks, and ask them what dates they can work to (assuming they are coming). It is necessary for me to know what your views and plans are in these matters.

I feel it my duty also to represent the strong feelings we have at the Admiralty that there should be placed at the head of this army so variously composed, a general officer of high rank and reputation, who has held important commands in war. I heard yesterday with very great pleasure you mentioned the name of Sir Ian Hamilton as the officer you had designated for the main command in this theatre. Certainly no choice could be more agreeable to the Admiralty and to the Navy; but I would venture to press upon you the desirability of this officer being on the spot as soon as possible, in order that he may concert with the Admiral the really critical and decisive operations which may be required at the very outset.

I wish to make it clear that the naval operations in the Dardanelles cannot be delayed for troop movements, as we must get into the Marmora as soon as possible in the normal course.

With regard to other British troops which it is understood you are holding in reserve, but about which no final decision has been taken, transport will be ready on the 15th for either the 29th Division or for the Yeomanry Division. It is not necessary for you to decide until about the 10th instant which you will send, and no doubt by then you will have heard from Birdwood. The need of one good division of regular infantry in an army composed of so many different elements and containing only British and Australian troops raised since the war, still appears to me to be grave and urgent.

Yours very truly
Winston S. Churchill

Sir George Buchanan to Sir Edward Grey: telegram

(*Copy, Cabinet Office papers: 22/1*)

4 March 1915   Petrograd
Secret

I read to Minister for Foreign Affairs this afternoon your telegram No. 298 of 2nd March, and his Excellency begged me to assure you that he had never doubted your sympathy, and that he was much touched with terms in which you had referred to Russian aspirations.

He thought, however, that the time had come for preparing public opinion in Great Britain and France for their approaching realisation. French Government were, equally with His Majesty's Government, fully acquainted with the views of Russian Government on Constantinople and the Straits, and the French Minister for Foreign Affairs expressed himself in entire sympathy with them except on one point which, as a matter of fact, Russian Government never raised. French Minister for Foreign Affairs had been under the impression that Russia intended to claim both shores of the Dardanelles. This was a mistake, as she had never intended to ask for the Asiatic shore, provided it was left in the possession of Turkey, and on the understanding that no fortifications were to be erected on it.

On my way to Ministry for Foreign Affairs with French Ambassador, latter had told me that in the audience in which he had presented General Pau yesterday to the Emperor,[1] His Majesty had in conversation himself said that there was one question—that of Constantinople—on which he must speak with precision. Passions of his subjects with regard to its possession were deeply stirred, and he had no right to impose on them the tremendous sacrifices entailed by the war without securing for them in return the realisation of a secular ambition. His decision was taken, and he must insist on a radical solution of the question of Constantinople and the Straits. He asked French Ambassador to call on Minister for Foreign Affairs the same afternoon and to repeat to him what he had said. Minister for Foreign Affairs had in the meanwhile received a [group omitted : ? message] from the Emperor informing him of above conversation and desiring him to come to Tsarskoe Selo to see His Majesty this morning.

This afternoon Minister for Foreign Affairs handed to me and French Ambassador *aide-mémoire*, of which translation follows, embodying result of his Excellency's conversation with Emperor and definitely recording Russian

---

[1] Nicholas, 1868–1918, Tsar, 1894–1917. Married, 1894, Princess Alix of Hesse, a grand-daughter of Queen Victoria. Imprisoned at Tobolsk, 1917–18. Murdered at Ekaterinburg, July 1918.

claims. His Excellency does not ask us publicly to announce our approval of these claims, but I gather that he would be grateful for an assurance that we would not raise any objections to them. [? Subsequently] public opinion might be gradually prepared for desired solution.

Aide-mémoire begins:—

'Course of latest events leads His Majesty the Emperor Nicholas to think that the question of Constantinople and the Straits must be definitely solved in accordance with traditional aspirations of Russia.

Any solution would be unsatisfactory and precarious if it did not incorporate henceforward in Russian Empire the city of Constantinople, western shore of the Bosphorus, of the Sea of Marmora, and of the Dardanelles, as well as Southern Thrace up to the Enos–Midia line.

Ipso facto and by strategic necessity, part of Asiatic shore included between the Bosphorus, River Sakharia, and a point to be fixed on the Gulf of Ismid, islands of the Sea of Marmora, islands of Imbros and Tenedos, ought to be incorporated in the empire.'

Special interests of France and of Great Britain in the region above described will be scrupulously respected.

Imperial Government likes to hope that above considerations will meet with sympathy of the two allied Governments. Said Governments are assured of meeting with, at the hands of Imperial Government, the same sympathy for realisation of desiderata which they may form in other regions of Ottoman Empire and elsewhere.

Sir Francis Bertie to Sir Edward Grey: telegram

(*Copy, Churchill papers: 26/4*)

4 March 1915   Paris
11.30 pm
Private and Secret

I have seen French Minister for Foreign Affairs this evening.

He says that Russian Government will not at any price accept co-operation of Greece in Constantinople expedition.

French Minister for Foreign Affairs thinks progress of Anglo-French fleet may be such as to appear before Constantinople without necessity of landing troops except a small body to hold the Bulair lines. There might consequently not be any occasion for military co-operation with Greece.

Greek Government have had several offers from Triple Entente for co-operation of Greece in the war. For one pretext or another Monsieur

Venizelos every time backed out of his assurances. French Minister for Foreign Affairs therefore considers that if the Greek Government offer co-operation in the Dardanelles expedition they should be told that co-opera-tion of Greece in the war must be entire and she must give active support to Serbia.

Admiralty to Vice-Admiral Carden: telegram

(*Copy, Churchill papers: 13/65*)

4 March 1915   Admiralty
8.45 pm

Admiral Jackson's plan of attack on Bosphorus Forts from South is as follows: —

Small squadrons or single ships where navigational difficulties exist to be used. No long range fire possible, so heavy volume at shorter ranges generally necessary.

Concealed batteries of howitzers and Field guns also minefields to be dealt with as occasions arise. They greatly increase the risk involved in the opera-tion. Efforts to be made to ascertain their position before entering Bos-phorus. Landing parties and minesweepers to be ready to assist squadrons when and where required. Ships not to anchor unless in dead water from all fire. . . .

Squared charts of the area are in hand.

Lord Kitchener to Lieutenant-General Birdwood: telegram

(*Copy, Churchill papers: 2/88*)

4 March 1915   War Office
11.30 pm

From the Admiral's estimate I understand that by 20th March he will probably have accomplished the forcing of the Dardanelles. It will, therefore, be possible by 18th March to concentrate at Lemnos the whole of your Australasian Contingent and in addition one division of French troops and 10,000 of the Naval Brigade, a total of approximately 65,000 men. If, how-ever, anything should occur to upset this calculation, I will let you know. We do not intend to issue orders for any more troops than the Brigade now there and the Naval Division, to start for Lemnos until 12th March, as it is evidently objectionable to keep troops in transports at Lemnos longer than is necessary. The date mentioned will give us time to judge the progress that has been made in clearing the passage and to obtain another and clearer estimate from the Admiral of the time when he will have passed the Straits. Unless the Navy are convinced that they cannot silence the guns in the Straits without military co-operation on a large scale, in which case further orders will be issued, there is no intention of using the troops enumerated above to take the Gallipoli peninsula. In such a case even more troops might be required to force the Turkish positions, and you might have to wait for further reinforcements from here. The numbers and composition of the additional force will be communicated to you after a decision has been taken, probably on 10th March. In the meantime, only small bodies of troops will be required for subsidiary operations while the Fleet are successfully silencing the forts, and, when needed by the Admiral, these should be supplied by you from the brigade now at Lemnos. If about 18th March it appears that the forts have been successfully silenced by the Fleet, and that the latter is about to proceed to Constantinople, it should be followed at close interval by the transports conveying the whole force for operations either at or near Constantinople or on the mainland on the European side in whichever place these may be found advisable. The above-mentioned reinforcements from England would, of course, follow and join the forces later. The situation which will be created in European Turkey by the passage of the Dardanelles by the Fleet is almost impossible to foretell. It will most probably only be necessary to leave a force sufficient to hold the Bulair Lines, as it is anticipated that the Turks will abandon the Gallipoli peninsula. Therefore the concentration of the troops at the entrance to the Dardanelles is not so much for operations on the Gallipoli peninsula as for operations subsequently to be undertaken in the neighbourhood of Constantinople. After sinking the Turkish Navy on their arrival at Constantinople, the first duty of the Fleet will be to open up the Bosphorus for the entrance of the Russian Fleet, which will be accompanied by a corps of Russian troops, probably numbering 40,000 men, and the operations on land will take place in co-operation with these forces.

Winston S. Churchill to Lord Kitchener

(*Copy, Churchill papers: 13/48*)

4 March 1915   Admiralty

My dear Kitchener,

By the 14th instant, transports will be at Alexandria sufficient to carry two Australasian infantry divisions as originally proposed by you, (less any portion carried meanwhile to Lemnos by transports locally acquired).

After this delivery of troops has been made, the ships can return by (say) the 24th, and can carry the additional 8,000 mounted troops as quickly as possible. The exact details will be furnished tomorrow.

The extra 8,000 mounted men is an addition to our arrangements, and requires a second trip; but you can count on 30,000 being transportable after the 14th (less those already carried). Will you please arrange your plans on this basis, and that the bulk of the mounted men are carried on the 2nd trip, and the residue, if any, on a third?

I am arranging with the French Navy direct about the French Division, and will report to you as soon as I know what they intend.

Yours very truly
Winston S. Churchill

Winston S. Churchill to Sir Edward Grey: not sent
(*Churchill papers: 13/48*)

4 March 1915   Admiralty

Mr Venizelos shd be told *now* that the Admiralty believe it in their power to force the Dardanelles without military assistance, destroying all the forts as they go. If so, Gallipoli Peninsula cannot be held by Turks, who wd be cut off & reduced at leisure. By the 20th inst 40,000 British Infantry will be available to go to C'nople, if the Straits have been forced, either by crossing the Bulair Isthmus, or going up the Dardanelles. A French Divn will be on the spot at the same time. M. Venizelos shd consider Greek military movements in relation to these facts.

WSC

Sir Edward Grey to Winston S. Churchill
(*Churchill papers: 13/48*)

4 March 1915   33 Eccleston Square

Dear Churchill,

It is much on my mind that sometime ago you spoke of the Dresden being in Chilean waters & of the possibility of sinking her if found there.

I hope you wont do anything of that sort in territorial waters: it will raise a storm especially just now that may do us incalculable injury.

Please, if there is any risk of this, instruct your ships to be careful.

Vy sincerely
E. Grey

Winston S. Churchill to Sir Edward Grey

(*Grey papers*)

4 March 1915   Admiralty

My dear Grey,

Dresden has violated the laws of neutrality by coaling twice in 3 months in Chilean waters, & by remaining 51 hours at Punta Arenas after the action at the Falklands. She is now believed to be hiding in an uninhabited inlet. If British cruisers find her there I certainly think that they shd sink her. Orders have been given to that effect; & I trust you will not allow weak chatter (of wh I have myself heard a ripple) to interfere with the course of events.[1] I do the best I can under many difficulties.

Yours always

W

Lord Fisher to Winston S. Churchill

(*Churchill papers: 13/56*)

4 March 1915   Admiralty

Dear Winston,

We have known all along that the German ships have all of them had aboard some 30 per cent addition to their regular crew, but now the 'Midshipman' tells us of their being divided into 3 watches so as to relieve the strain of war and how one third in action kept below under armour to fill up casualties.—We cant afford this.—So far luck has been on our side not requiring it, but without doubt—as far as we can—we should increase our complements of officers & men in the Grand Fleet. I have not said anything to Jellicoe or Jellicoe to me on this subject but we spoke of this together before the war began last July. Crease[2] tells me a long letter has come from Jellicoe but I dont know the substance of it. I dont ever cavil at anything he writes—his responsibility is very great. He *stands between us and Ruin*!

[1] 'I still think,' Grey wrote to Churchill on 4 March, 'we have much to gain by respecting Chilean territorial waters & an immense lot to lose by violating them.' (*Churchill papers: 13/48*) On 14 March the *Glasgow*, commanded by Captain Luce, found the *Dresden* in Cumberland Bay, on the Chilean coast. She and the cruiser *Kent* then bombarded the *Dresden*, which was set on fire, and finally blew herself up. The Chilean Government protested to Britain that the British warships had violated Chilean neutrality; the British Government expressed its regret, but Grey explained that it had had no other course of action, if the *Dresden* was to be destroyed.

[2] Thomas Evans Crease, 1875-1942. Entered Navy, 1889. Retired with rank of Commander, 1910. Naval Assistant and Secretary to Lord Fisher, both as First Sea Lord, 1914-15, and as Chairman of the Board of Invention and Research, 1915-16. Private Secretary to successive First Lords of the Admiralty, 1917-19. Captain, 1918.

There is no one else I know of his brains and his steady pulse and his phenomenal quick decision and determination.

I see reports of unwanted activity amongst the German armed merchant steamers in New York Harbour and their supposed conserted action with Eitel Frederick[1] and Patey[2] evidently thinks it on the cards that he may be 'von-spee-d' by a raid of German battle cruisers as part of a plan to set free all these New York German armed Liners to get abt the world and start us off again with a wholesale distribution of our fast cruisers! . . .

The more I consider the Dardanelles—the less I like it! No matter what happens, it is impossible to get out anything moving not even a dinghy! and why the hostile submarine has not appeared is a wonder.

Yrs

F

Winston S. Churchill to Sir Edward Grey
(Churchill papers: 13/45)

4 March 1915   Admiralty

Sir E. Grey,

The following infr. should now be sent to the G. D. Nicholas, if Ld K. approves:- 40,000 Br troops from England & Egypt will be able to disembark at Cple any time after the 18th inst if the *Dlles* are forced. A French Div of 18,000 will also probably be available there at the same time. These facts should be a guide to the Russian Military purpose, bearing in mind that bad weather may delay, & a Turkish collapse may shorten, the military operations.

WSC

Vice-Admiral Carden to Admiralty: telegram
(Copy, Churchill papers: 13/65)

5 March 1915   HMS Inflexible
4.30 am

Operations 4th March. 10 a.m. Demolition party landed at Kum Kali and Seddulbahr covered by one company of Royal Marine Brigade each side. The villages were shelled before landing and at 9 a.m. seaplanes had reported

---

[1] The *Prinz Eitel Friedrich*, a German armoured cruiser, had been active seizing and sinking unarmed merchant ships in the Pacific during 1914, and in the Atlantic from January to March 1915. She sought refuge in Newport News in the first week of April 1915, and was interned there for the rest of the war.

[2] George Edwin Patey, 1859–1935. Entered Navy, 1872. Rear-Admiral, 1910. Vice-Admiral commanding the Royal Australian Fleet, 1913–15, including the hunt for von Spee's squadron, and for the *Dresden*, 1914–15. Knighted, 1913. Commander-in-Chief, North American and West Indian Stations, March 1915–September 1916. Admiral, 1918.

no enemy's movements at entrance to Dardanelles. Both parties directly they landed were engaged by the enemy posted in the villages. The party at Seddulbahr having attacked could make no progress and were finally withdrawn, vacating at 1.30 p.m: they, however, discovered and destroyed four Nordenfeldts.[1] Party on Asiatic shore reached position under Fort No 4 where they encountered enemy in a well concealed position and were forced to retire. Covering fire from ships was only partially effective as enemy was not located though seaplanes reconnoitred frequently. Total casualties about 20.

PRINCE GEORGE shelled defences of Bashika.

SAPPHIRE silenced battery of field guns North of Dikili.

Winston S. Churchill to Vice-Admiral Carden: telegram
(*Draft, Admiralty papers: 137/109*)

5 March 1915   Admiralty
9.12 am
Personal & Secret

As soon as possible report to what point mine sweeping had progressed within the Straits up to evening of 4th March. Have you yet destroyed by shell fire Forts 8 & 9. Have any ships yet opened fire on the forts at the narrows.

[This is what I am anxious to know][2]

WSC

Lieutenant-General Birdwood to Lord Kitchener: telegram
(*Copy, Churchill papers: 2/88*)

5 March 1915   Mudros
12.55 pm

I am very doubtful if the Navy can force the passage unassisted. In any event the forcing of the passage must take a considerable time; the forts that have been taken up to the present have been visible and very easy, as the ships could stand off and shoot from anywhere, but inside the Straits the ships are bothered by unknown fire. The weather at present is very bad, only one out of several days being fine, and operations are much delayed in consequence. Before troops can be landed it is absolutely essential that the

---

[1] A Swedish machine-gun, in use in the 1880s; obsolete by 1914.
[2] Churchill deleted this final sentence before sending the telegram.

weather should be settled, for the landing sites are small and indifferent, and a small force only cannot be landed owing to the risk of being cut off by the weather.

I think Admiral Carden would have liked to see the troops landed at the Bulair Lines, but I am averse to doing this for the following reasons:—

1. I should be in no way enabled to carry out my rôle of assisting the Navy if necessary.

2. Owing to the conformation of the coast it would be necessary to land on the northern side of the lines, and these have been constructed expressly to meet a force from this direction.

3. If the Navy and my troops advance together from the south we can fully help each other, while if the troops work from north to south and the Navy south to north from opposite ends of the peninsula no co-operation is possible.

4. My rear would always be open to attack from any forces coming down from Thrace.

The coast of Besika Bay has also been fully entrenched and organized for defence. Moreover the crossing of Mendere river and the adjoining marshes would be a very difficult operation, while the right flank of an army advancing from there would be much exposed.

I therefore think the best line of action to be a cautious advance from Helles Point.

Sir Francis Elliot to Sir Edward Grey: telegram
(*Copy, Churchill papers: 26/4*)

5 March 1915   Athens
Private and Secret

Monsieur Venizelos asked French and Russian Ministers and me to meet him at this Legation this evening and made the following statement.

After describing the recent events as reported in my telegram he said he had to-day with approval of the Council of ex-Prime Ministers and consent of the Chief of the General Staff[1] proposed to the King to make the following offer to the Entente Powers. That Greece should place her fleet and one

[1] General Dousmanis. He remained as Chief of the General Staff until August 1916, when he was replaced by General Moschopoulos.

division of about 15,000 men, of whom 9,000 infantry, at their disposal for operations against Turkey.

The King had reserved his decision and until he had given it offer must not be considered as made. But Monsieur Venizelos declared at once and officially that Greece had no political aims with regard to Constantinople; she would not accept the city if offered to her; but he plainly avowed ambition of Greeks to be amongst the first to make sign of the cross at Saint Sophia.

Questioned as to declaring war against Austria and Germany as well as against Turkey he said that he wished to make the King's position as easy as possible and therefore he would not ask him to declare war against the first two, though he regarded war with them as a foregone conclusion.

For the same reason he would advise the King, if he agreed to his proposal, to keep his decision secret until it was known whether the Allies would accept the offer if made; if it appeared that they would reject it the King's Family need never know that His Majesty had agreed to make it.

If the Triple Entente refused offer, Monsieur Venizelos must resign as his position towards representatives of Germany &c., would be untenable. In that case Government would continue to be carried on by his party. If the King declined to adopt his policy whole Government would resign.

Monsieur Venizelos was hopeful of King's agreement and of the effect which would be produced upon other States by the example of Greece. Even Bulgaria he thought might be tempted to do likewise and would be welcome as an ally since the rest of the Greek Army would then be set free.

Only the one Division would be mobilised as well as enough reservists to form a new Division to fill vacant places.

In view of consideration stated in paragraph No. 5 an early reply is desirable.

Winston S. Churchill to Sir Edward Grey
(*Churchill papers: 26/2*)

5 March 1915   Admiralty

Sir Edward Grey,

The attitude of Italy is remarkable. If she cd be induced to join with us the Austrian Fleet wd be powerless & the Mediterranean as safe as an English lake.

Surely some gt effort shd be made to encourage Italy to come forward. From leaving an alliance to declaring war is only a step.

Odi quem laeseris.[1]

WSC[2]

Winston S. Churchill: memorandum

(Churchill papers: 21/38)

5 March 1915[3]   Admiralty

SEVEN PRACTICAL STEPS

1. Pass as a clause to the Defence of the Realm Act Amendment Bill the provisions in the Chancellor of the Exchequer's draft Bill, enabling the Government to close wholly or partly non-armament-producing works, subject to the legal exoneration of their owners in regard to outstanding contracts and a measure of compensation as an act of grace for loss of business.

2. Arrange that all future contracts with armament firms, or firms aided in any way in regard to the provision of labour or capital by the State, shall be on the 'Cost and Profit' basis, namely, cost of production as certified by the Government overseers, plus between 5 and 7 per cent. profit for management, goodwill, &c. Leave the existing contracts untouched.

3. Impose in the Budget a 'Tax on War Profits' as follows:—

Subtract the average income on which tax has been paid for the last three years from the income of this year. Take half the difference excess for the State, and leave half to the individual. This has the advantage of dealing with all classes who profit out of the war, including persons who make clothing, boots, saddlery, equipment of all kinds, with all their ramifications, as well as merely what are called 'armament firms.'

4. Attract workmen to the armament industries and industries necessary for the State by means of the payment of a special bonus for diligent and regular work and good timekeeping. This bonus to be additional to any wages hitherto arranged between employer and employed, or hereinafter to be arranged as the result of any industrial arbitration or agreement. Receipt of the bonus to be accompanied by a button of national service, and acceptance of the bonus to carry with it the waiving of all Trade Union conditions

[1] An abbreviation of a sentence of Tacitus (*Agricola*, 42): 'proprium humani ingenii est odisse quem laeseris': it is the peculiar quality of man to hate someone he has wronged. Presumably Churchill was implying that the Italians, having failed in 1914 to join their former allies of the Triple Alliance of 1887 (Germany and Austria-Hungary), would now be willing to go so far as to fight against them.

[2] Grey returned this letter to Churchill with the note: 'I will neglect no opportunity.'

[3] This memorandum was not circulated to the Cabinet until 12 March 1915.

hampering to production during the payment of the bonus and the period of the war.

5. Take power to billet national workers as if they were soldiers. Pay a subsistence allowance similar to that now paid in the Royal dockyards, to compensate workers who move from one part of the country to another for the expense of maintaining two establishments, and the disturbance.

6. Regulate the hours of public-house opening in all armament-producing centres, military and naval centres, and seaports used for the despatch of troops or for national purposes, to any extent that may be necessary to secure the efficiency of all labour employed.

7. Inaugurate with the political machinery of the Conservative, Liberal, and Labour parties a great educative campaign in all districts where it is required to impress upon workmen and employers the vital and perilous nature of the crisis through which we are passing, and the terrible consequences of defeat or the indefinite prolongation of the war. Form committees of workmen, employers, and other citizens to sustain public opinion and counteract anti-war propaganda under its various disguises. Use all the existing political machinery to that end.

WSC

Sir George Buchanan to Sir Edward Grey: telegram
(*Copy, Churchill papers: 13/45*)

5 March 1915   Petrograd
5.22 pm
Private and Secret

I have communicated the First Lord's message to the Grand Duke through the Minister for Foreign Affairs.

His Excellency told me orders have been given to the Russian fleet to proceed to the Bosphorus by way of Zunguldak and that he had induced Naval authorities to renounce their idea of occupying Burgas.

Winston S. Churchill: memorandum
(*Copy, Churchill papers: 13/58*)

5 March 1915   Admiralty
Confidential

A NOTE ON BLOCKADE

The international laws relating to blockade were framed without reference to the new conditions introduced into warfare by the presence of the submarine. However great the superiority of the stronger fleet, it is not practicable to draw blockading lines in close proximity to the enemy's coasts and harbours, as was always previously possible, because the submarines of the weaker fleet would sink the blockading vessels, although that fleet was unable or unwilling to put to sea. It therefore becomes necessary to draw the lines of blockade at a greater distance from the enemy's coasts and ports than was heretofore necessary, and this involves in certain cases the inclusion within the scope of the blockading lines not only of enemy, but of neutral ports. This prevents the use of the term 'blockade' according to its strict technical interpretation. But it does not in the least prevent an effective blockade in the natural and practical, as distinct from the legal and technical, sense. The British naval blockade of German North Sea ports is at present maintained by the cruiser cordon at the mouth of the English Channel and the flotillas at the Straits of Dover, and by the cruiser cordon and patrolling cruiser squadron from the north of Scotland to Iceland. These blockading lines are in every sense effective. No instance is known to the British Admiralty of any vessel, the stopping of which had been authorised by the Foreign Office, passing them unchallenged. It is not a case of a paper blockade, but of a blockade as real and as efficient as any that has ever been established, having regard to the new and unforeseen conditions of naval war. The means of carrying on an effective blockade of the enemy's ports ought not to be denied the stronger naval Power merely because neutral ships proceeding to neutral ports may be allowed to pass through the blockading lines after examination. Not to admit the legitimacy of such an operation is to deny the right of blockade as a practical measure under modern conditions to any belligerent. If belligerents were deprived of the right of maintaining an effective blockade by regular and humane methods, including all the customary safe guards of challenge, search, and trial, it is certain that other methods would be forced upon them. For instance, the sowing of the seas with contact mines, anchored or floating, would achieve in the fullest degree the objects which the British Admiralty have in view in regard to German trade. The stronger navy using its own swept channels could prevent the weaker belligerent from removing these mines without any special danger to its warships, and the deterrent effect of the losses to traders which would ensue would soon effectually prevent, not only enemy, but neutral trade. The British Admiralty have available very large quantities of mines, with large numbers of special vessels adapted for laying them. Hitherto they have laid no mines, except in the immediate approaches to military harbours or in certain areas carefully prescribed, and of which traders of all countries have received due notice. It is only in circumstances where neutral nations were not prepared to accord to the stronger belligerent navy, having regard to the conditions created by the submarine, any method of maintaining an effective blockade, that we should be driven to consider an alternative which strikes blindly at commerce, whether enemy or neutral, and endangers non-combatant life. All the time, however, we are ourselves subjected, so far as lies in the strength of the enemy, to indiscriminate attack by minelaying in the open sea, as well as to the deliberate sinking of merchantmen without challenge by submarine agency. It is for neutral nations to recognise that it is not practically possible, nor in neutral interests, to claim the maintenance of a situation which would deprive naval strength of all its rights while permitting naval weakness to indulge in every abuse.

WSC

Lieutenant-General Birdwood to Lord Kitchener: telegram

(*Copy, Churchill papers: 2/88*)

6 March 1915   Cairo

I have just returned to Cairo for a few days in order to make the necessary arrangements with Maxwell with regard to my corps, and shall shortly proceed again to Lemnos. I have already informed you that I consider the Admiral's forecast is too sanguine, and though we may have a better estimate by March 12th, I doubt his ability to force the passage unaided. I have in the meantime placed the brigade at Lemnos at the disposal of the Admiral for minor operations. I have no intention of wishing to rush blindly into Gallipoli peninsula, and quite realize that my movements must entirely depend on the progress made by the Navy. On this point I note I shall receive further orders; but if my anticipation is fulfilled and military co-operation is needed, I should propose to make my first and definite objective the line Kilid Bahr–Gabatepe. When this is attained, the Fleet would be enabled to get through to the Sea of Marmora. The Bulair Lines would then be reduced *en route* by bombardment from both sides, and for the time being my rôle would have been accomplished. Once the Fleet is through the Dardanelles, I agree that the Turks might evacuate the peninsula, and that my transports should therefore follow the Fleets, if such a course should be safe. I fear, however, that the transports would be liable to loss from guns, with which the Navy might not have been able to deal, elsewhere than in the forts.

Vice-Admiral Carden to Admiralty: telegram

(*Copy, Churchill papers: 13/65*)

6 March 1915

Operations 5th March. Attacked defences at Narrows commencing by indirect fire from QUEEN ELIZABETH who was supported by PRINCE

GEORGE and INFLEXIBLE in dealing with howitzers. Fire confined to forts 13, 16, 17. Twenty-nine rounds fired result considered satisfactory magazine in 16 blew up. Ships spotting inside Dardanelles IRRESISTIBLE, CANOPUS, CORNWALLIS, ALBION remainder under way. Owing to heavy fire from concealed guns this rendered spotting difficult but none of ships were hit. First seaplane sent to spot met with accident when at 3,000 ft. machine descended in vertical and spiral nose dives and totally wrecked, pilot Flight Lieut. Garnett[1] injured observer Lieut. Commander Williamson[2] who had been doing good work seriously injured, accident not due to enemy fire, engine salvaged. Second seaplane sent up returned owing to pilot Flight Lieut. Douglas[3] being wounded by bullet, not serious, in consequence seaplanes were not of any use. Casualties yesterday now reported as 19 killed, 3 missing, 23 wounded, fuller report not yet received. No movement (? troops) near Bulair line. SAPPHIRE fired on troops near Gulf of Andramyti and destroyed terrace station Tuzburna. She reports channel between Eleos Island and Moskoaivali is mined.

H. H. Asquith to Venetia Stanley
(*Montagu papers*)

6 March 1915   Walmer Castle

... Russia, despite all our representations & remonstrances, declines absolutely to allow Greece to take any part in the Dardanelles business, or the subsequent advance on Constantinople; and the French appear inclined to agree with her. On the other hand the Greeks are burning to be part of the force which enters Constantinople, and yet wish to avoid committing themselves to fighting against anybody but the Turks & possibly the Bulgarians. They won't raise a finger for Serbia, and even want all the time to keep on not unfriendly terms with Germany & Austria! We have of course told them that this is nonsense, that you can't make war on limited liability terms, & that therefore they must come in with us 'all in all or not at all'. . . .

---

[1] Hugh Stewart Garnett, 1891–   . Midshipman, Royal Navy, 1904–10. Entered Royal Naval Air Service, August 1914. Flight Lieutenant, October 1914. Sustained shock and minor injuries as a result of falling into the sea while flying near the Dardanelles on 5 March 1915. Flight Commander, June 1917.

[2] Hugh Alexander Williamson, 1885–   . Entered Royal Navy, 1904. Flight Commander Royal Naval Air Service, 1914; Lieutenant Commander, 1915; Squadron Commander 1916; Wing Commander, 1917; Chief Commander, 1918. Lieutenant-Colonel, Aeroplanes and Seaplanes, Royal Air Force. Served in Iraq Command, 1923–4. Group Captain, 1928.

[3] Norman Sholto Douglas, 1895–   . Entered Royal Naval Air Service, 6 August 1914, Flight Lieutenant, 1914. Wounded at the Dardanelles, March 1915. Squadron Commander 1918.

Sir Francis Elliot to Sir Edward Grey: telegram

(*Copy, Churchill papers: 26/4*)

6 March 1915   Athens

Urgent

The King having refused to agree to Monsieur Venizelos' proposals, the Cabinet has resigned.

Winston S. Churchill to Sir Edward Grey

(*Churchill papers: 26/4*)

6 March 1915   Admiralty

Sir E. Grey

Whatever happens I hope we shall stand by Venezelos. We must have Greece. The accession at this stage in the war of a new ally is a vital matter.

WSC

Winston S. Churchill to Sir Edward Grey: not sent

(*Churchill papers: 26/27*)

6 March 1915   Admiralty

My dear Grey,

I beseech you at this crisis not to make a mistake in falling below the level of events.

Half-hearted measures will ruin all—& a million men will die through the prolongation of the war.

You must be bold & violent. You have a right to be. Our fleet is forcing the Dardanelles. No armies can reach Constantinople but those wh we invite. Yet we seek nothing here, but the victory of the common cause. Tell the Russians that we will meet them in a generous and sympathetic spirit about Cple.

But no impediment must be placed in the way of Greek co-operation. We must have Greece & Bulgaria, if they will come.

I am *so* afraid of your losing Greece, & yet paying all the future into Russian hands. If Russia prevents Greece helping, I will do my utmost to oppose her having Cple.

She is a broken power but for our aid: & has no resource open but to turn traitor—& this she cannot do.

Yours ever

W

PS If you don't back up *this* Greece—the Greece of Venizelos—you will have another wh will cleave to Germany.

Vice-Admiral Carden to Winston S. Churchill: telegram

(*Copy, Churchill papers: 13/65*)

6 March 1915   HMS Inflexible
Secret and Personal

Mine sweepers have not advanced beyond line Suandere River–Kephez Bay. Any advance beyond this line brings minesweepers under fire from forts at the Narrows. When these have been dealt with ships will be in a position to make use of the channel which can then be swept in a few hours. The fact that a certain amount of dead water from howitzer fire has been found in shore and explosion of a mine off Suandere River close to Canopus has necessitated a thorough sweeping along both shores.

Mine sweepers can only work by night owing to fire from field guns. Battery 8 has been heavily shelled on every occasion on which it has opened fire; experience gained has shown that in order to render a fort innocuous, it is absolutely necessary to land and destroy each gun. With few exceptions the guns in forts at the entrance were found serviceable.

Fort 9 has not yet been engaged. It has not interfered with our operations.

The unexpected opposition yesterday to the landing party delayed main operations owing to necessity of extricating Royal Marine covering force from a dangerous position. It was found impossible to locate enemy who opened a heavy rifle fire isolating the advance party for some hours.

Seaplanes being unable to locate enemy from a safe height Flight Lieutenant Bromet[1] and Lieutenant Brown in Seaplane No. 172 attempted to do so from lower level without success seaplane was hit 28 times and badly damaged.

Flight Lieutenant Kershaw[2] and Petty Officer Merchant[3] afterwards made the attempt unsuccessfully, their machine number 07 being struck eight times.

[1] Geoffrey Rhodes Bromet, 1891–   . Sub-Lieutenant, Royal Navy, 1912. Flight Lieutenant, Royal Flying Corps (Naval Wing), 1914. Wing Commander, Royal Naval Air Service, 1917. Lieutenant-Colonel (Staff Officer), Royal Air Force, 1918; Squadron Leader, 1919. Retired, 1938. Re-employed, 1939. Air Officer Commanding 19 Group, Plymouth, 1941–3. British Senior Officer, Azores Force, 1943–5. Knighted, 1945. He married, 1965, as his second wife, Air Commandant Dame Jean Conan Doyle (daughter of Sir Arthur Conan Doyle and Director of the Women's Royal Air Force 1963–6).

[2] Ronald Hargrave Kershaw, 1894–1969. Private, London Balloon Company, Royal Engineers Territorials, 1913. Sub-Lieutenant, Royal Naval Reserve, 1913. Flight Lieutenant, Royal Naval Air Service, 1914; Squadron Commander, 1917. Captain, Royal Air Force, 1919.

[3] *Possibly* A. W. Merchant. Lieutenant (Observer Officer) and Honorary Captain, Royal Air Force, 1918. Retired, 1919.

Winston S. Churchill to the Grand Duke Nicholas: telegram

(*Copy, Churchill papers: 13/45*)

6 March 1915   Admiralty

Progress was good on the 5th and 3 principal forts at Kilid Bahr were damaged especially Fort Toprak with 2–35 cm guns.

We should like to know by what date Russian Fleet will be ready to co-operate and when Russian army corps will be ready to embark.

WSC

Winston S. Churchill to Sir Richard Peirse: telegram

(*Copy, Churchill papers: 2/88*)

6 March 1915   Admiralty

Secret. Friendly disposition towards the British and French subjects has recently been displayed by the Vali of Smyrna, who has openly deplored the war. You should get into touch with him by flag of truce or otherwise after destroying the forts. He should not be informed that we have no intention of landing, nor should any limit to your further operations be suggested, but he should be allowed to feel that we recognise his friendly attitude, and are well-disposed towards him and do not wish to harm the city. You should negotiate with him for the diversion of all small craft, barges, and steamers likely to be of the least use for landing troops elsewhere. All these vessels should be sent to Lemnos. Try and persuade him to collect as much rolling-stock as possible from both railways, and arrange for sweeping a good channel through the mines. No threat of bombarding the city should be made in any case, but if your wishes are met promise not to do so may be made. He should be invited to continue discharging his duties of maintaining order, and our desire to spare the vilayet of Smyrna the horrors of war should be emphasised. He should be told that the fall of Constantinople cannot be long delayed.

You can spend 50,000*l.* without further reference here if money is likely to be useful in dealing with him or other Turkish officials.

Our intention is not to get involved in military operations at Smyrna, but you may be able to acquire a very large measure of control by persuasion following the destruction of the forts and events in Dardanelles.

Your tact must guide you in this matter. Until further orders remain on the spot yourself. Act in the name of the Allies.

Full and frequent reports should be made.

Graeme Thomson to Winston S. Churchill

(*Copy, Churchill papers: 13/58*)

6 March 1915   Admiralty

TRANSPORT DIFFICULTIES

First Lord,

I wish to call attention to the fact that the transport work is now being conducted under serious difficulties.

The workmen—seamen, dock labourers, &c.—are rapidly becoming absolutely out of hand. The trades union leaders in most cases have no control over them whatsoever. The present labour situation on the Clyde and at Liverpool is merely the beginning. Unless effectual measures are taken we shall have strikes at every port in the United Kingdom, and supplies to the Army and the Fleet will be stopped. In the main, we have now to deal, not with the ordinary British workmen, but with what remains after our best men have been recruited for the Army and Navy. Wages are rising every day, and in order to get the crews to embark at all I frequently have to bribe them with still further rises.

Yesterday the crew of a transport deserted. The same thing happened the day before. The night before last I had to coerce the masters of two transports, who, I take it, feared torpedo attack, to sail by threat of instant dismissal if they disobeyed. The firemen go on board the transports drunk, making it impossible to get up a full head of steam, so greatly reducing the speed and endangering the lives of thousands of troops by making the vessels a target for submarines.

The root cause of the serious congestion at some of the docks is not a shortage of labour but the fact that the men can earn in two or three days what will keep them in drink for the rest of the week.

What is wanted, in addition to a proper control of the drink traffic, is a well-devised scheme promptly applied for bringing the seamen under naval, and other workmen in Government employ under military, discipline. It is already taking three times as long to get ships fitted and ready to sail as it did when war broke out. Expedition is a thing of the past, and it is obvious that this may at any moment have a disastrous effect on the naval and military operations.

The following practical instance of the effect of military discipline, even on those totally unused to it, may be of interest:—

We sent 250 dock labourers to Havre under capable civilian supervision. They all got drunk and out of hand in the first fortnight. We brought them back and enlisted a similar lot of men under military discipline. On the first pay day one got drunk and was given twelve months hard labour. There has been no trouble since, and the men are working splendidly.

Graeme Thomson

Sir John Jellicoe to Winston S. Churchill

(*Churchill papers: 13/48*)

6 March 1915   Iron Duke

My dear Mr Churchill

It is some little time since I wrote to you and I am therefore writing now, but I beg you will not feel called upon to reply unless you have something special to say. I hesitate to write for fear of drawing a reply and I know how every moment of your time must be fully occupied. Your recent short illness gives me an excuse.[1] I was so sorry to hear of it and hope you are now quite yourself again. While on this subject I must express my sincere gratitude for the great consideration you shewed me when I was laid up. I felt your kindness very much indeed. . . .

I have only two small anxieties. One is to get the ships refitted, and the men a little lean during refit, the other is to find them occupation & exercise. I am starting on training for a regatta as the best means of keeping the largest number physically fit, & occupied. Of course they do an immense amount of drill & practice, but the evenings are lengthening out now & occupation is necessary then. The health of the fleet is excellent so far & I am most anxious to keep it so and the men happy & contented while they are waiting for their chance. At Cromarty & Rosyth they can get ashore more for marching exercise. Here it so often blows too hard. Further the Rosyth squadrons have had their 'scraps' which keeps them happy.

I offer my sincere congratulations on the progress in the Dardanelles. The hardest part is of course yet to come, but progress so far is so encouraging that it seems as if we shall get through without nearly so much loss as one might have expected. I don't know the position on shore there or what force we have ready to occupy the peninsula. I know it pretty well as I was there in 1878, & constantly in the Bulair Lines, carrying despatches from Gallipoli to Xeros Bay. . . .[2]

---

[1] A reference to Churchill's influenza, which had first incapacitated him in February, and was to affect him again in April and May.

[2] In July 1877, when aged 17, Jellicoe joined the battleship *Agincourt*, which shortly afterwards sailed for the Aegean, under orders to prepare to force the Dardanelles during the Russo-Turkish war should Britain become involved and the Straits be closed. Jellicoe, who had charge of two steamboats and four cutters, was employed ashore as a despatch rider. He celebrated his eighteenth birthday at the Dardanelles.

I trust that Mrs Churchill is well and the children, and that the heavy strain is not telling on you. Lord Fisher tells me you get younger under the strain instead of older.

Yours very sincerely

J. R. Jellicoe

H. H. Asquith to Venetia Stanley

(*Montagu papers*)

6 March 1915   Walmer Castle

. . . In regard to things abroad, there have emerged two most infernal problems: I say 'emerged', because they have always been there latent & in the background. What I tell you about them is *most secret*. The first is that there are significant indications that, before very long, Italy may come in on the side of the allies. That seems natural enough, but what is strange is that Russia strongly objects. She thinks that Italy has kept out during the stress of the war, that she will demand an exorbitant territorial price, and that the Three Allies shd. continue to keep the thing entirely in their own hands. Both the French & ourselves I need hardly say take quite a different view.

The other question (and this is if possible *more* secret) is the future of Constantinople, & the Straits. It has become quite clear that Russia means to incorporate them in her own Empire. That is the secret of her intense & obstinate hostility to the idea of allowing the Greeks to take any share in the present operations & their consequences. When this becomes known (if it does) it is not unlikely that Greece, Bulgaria, & Roumania will all protest most vehemently. It is rather a matter of sentiment with Greece, but Bulgaria & still more Roumania—as the map shows you—will feel that they run a risk of having their exit from the Black Sea put permanently at the mercy of Russia. I really don't know how it will be viewed in France or in this country: it is of course a complete reversal of our old traditional policy. Personally I have always been & am in favour of Russia's claim, subject to proper conditions as to non-fortification of the Straits, and as to free commercial transit. With command of the Sea we could always block the entrance. It is monstrous that Russia shd have only 2 ports—Archangel & Vladivostock, both of wh. are ice-bound during the winter. . . .

Winston S. Churchill to Lord Kitchener

(*Kitchener papers*)

6 March 1915   Admiralty
Secret

My dear Kitchener,

The Admiralty Transport Department guarantee to carry on the 15th, 27,350 officers and men and 8,850 horses from Alexandria in one convoy, without drawing upon transports which have taken the advanced party of 4,900 men and 650 horses to Lemnos.

2. For this purpose it will be necessary to utilise a greater part of the 19 transports now carrying Australian drafts between Colombo and Suez. Neither these ships nor the men in them will therefore be available to reinforce India or to carry troops to Busra.

3. We have no knowledge of what transport is available in Bombay in case it is decided to reinforce Busra.

4. We believe that the troops in Busra and Kurna have no water transport with them, and consequently they cannot be evacuated until transports are sent from India.

5. I have asked Grey to obtain from Crewe the text of the telegram which he sent to the Viceroy yesterday. I agree strongly with your view that the Viceroy should be directed to send the necessary reinforcements to Busra, and that Duff[1] should be made to realise that he is professionally responsible for the reinforcements being adequate, and generally for the military conduct of the operations on the Tigris.

6. The Russian claims about Constantinople raise such large issues that a meeting of the War Council is to be held on Monday, to which very likely the Leaders of the Opposition will be invited. Pending this, I think it better not to ask any questions of the Grand Duke as to the despatch of an army corps and the Russian fleet.

7. An analysis of the forts mentioned in Carden's telegram shows that the progress is more important than I first supposed. Fort No. 16, whose magazine was blown up, contains two 14-inch guns, and is regarded as a very important factor in the defences.

Yours vy truly
Winston S. Churchill

[1] Beauchamp Duff, 1855–1918. Lieutenant, Royal Artillery, 1874. Major-General, 1903. Knighted, 1906. Lieutenant-General, 1906. Chief of Staff, India, 1906–9. Military Secretary, India Office, 1909–13. General, 1911. Commander-in-Chief, India, 1913–16.

Vice-Admiral Carden to Admiralty: telegram

(*Copy, Churchill papers: 13/65*)

7 March 1915   HMS Inflexible
10.25 am

Operations 6th March. QUEEN ELIZABETH supported by AGAMEM-NON and OCEAN continued indirect bombardment of fort No. 20 but owing to interference from howitzers which found her range at once and made accurate shooting, she was obliged to shift berth twice, finally to position twenty—twenty-one thousand yards from the fortress attacked. In consequence she only fired eight rounds. Howitzers could not be located and seaplanes, owing to engine trouble were unable to reach sufficient height for observing. Ships inside Straits VENGEANCE, ALBION, MAJESTIC, PRINCE GEORGE and SUFFREN fired on batteries 7 and 8 and were fired on by a number of concealed guns. Fort No. 13 also opened fire and was engaged and hit by 12 in. shells. QUEEN ELIZABETH and majority of the ships inside were hit but suffered no serious damage and no casualties.

H. H. Asquith to Venetia Stanley

(*Montagu papers*)

7 March 1915   Walmer Castle

. . . Winston wires that he cannot get away, wh. does not surprise me, as he is absorbed in his Dardanelles & in catching German ships. By the way one of the amusing parts of the Assyrian's diatribe was his violent invective against poor W, especially from the point of view of his possible candidature for the Indian Viceroyalty. . . .

I have been out for a little morning walk in the grounds with Clemmie & Goonie. We have brilliant sun & the Downs are more crowded than ever with every kind of vessel. Winston has again changed his mind & now says he will come to dinner. Clemmie says he is hopelessly undecided in small things. They are pounding away again to-day at the Dardanelles, having incidentally had a battering match with the forts of Smyrna. . . .

Winston S. Churchill to F. E. Smith

(*Copy, Churchill papers: 2/65*)

7 March 1915   Admiralty

. . . I wish you could manage to come over here in the near future for a few days. There are many things I want to talk to you about. I am sorry that you are away. In your absence Bonar Law is surrounded only by persons who wish to revive party bitterness at the earliest possible moment. Your influence here in politics would be invaluable and the services you could render to the country would be far greater than any you can render in the ungrateful sphere in which you move, but of course there is the difficulty of pulling out of the hunt.

I hope you have seen something of French and have got on friendly terms with him. I spoke very earnestly to him when he was here upon the subject of your position. Some of the smaller military people are very short-sighted. I know you do not let these passing irritations distress you.

All goes well at the Dardanelles. . . .

H. H. Asquith to Venetia Stanley
(Montagu papers)

7 March 1915   Walmer Castle
Midnight

. . . Winston appeared at about tea time, & was in his best form: he left immediately after dinner in one of his special trains. He agrees with me that there are now probably not more than 3 German submarines patrolling & 'blockading' our coasts. One of the funniest results of this last development is that we have a whole flotilla of our own submarines, huddled together in Dover Harbour, & afraid to go out, lest they should be rammed or sunk by British Merchant ships, which now go at once for every periscope that appears above the surface.

Vice-Admiral Carden to Admiralty: telegram
(Copy, Churchill papers, 13/65)

8 March 1915   HMS Inflexible
1.55 am

Operations 7th March. Four French Battleships entered Straits this morning to cover bombardment of defences of Narrows by AGAMEMNON and LORD NELSON. French ships engaged Battery No. 8 and concealed guns silenced former. AGAMEMNON and LORD NELSON engaged Forts at Narrows at 14,000 to 12,000 yards; Nos. 13 and 19 replied, both were silenced, after heavy bombardment, explosion occurred in both Forts. Bulair DUBLIN was fired at by 4″ guns between Maltata and Bulair no movements of troops reported. Eight floating mines seen to-day. Damage to allied ships

GAULOIS AGAMEMNON and LORD NELSON struck three times each
DUBLIN 3 or 4 times damage in every case not serious.

LORD NELSON started leak from hit 3 feet below water line, she also
had 3 wounded slightly. Sea too rough for seaplanes to fly.

Winston S. Churchill to Vice-Admiral Carden: telegram
(Copy, Churchill papers: 2/88)

8 March 1915
Secret and Personal   Admiralty

I am very much obliged to you for full and frequent reports you give of
daily progress. Your operations are producing profound political effects
throughout Europe, and it is necessary to time and concert nicely military
measures. It is, therefore, imperative that I should be exactly acquainted
with the situation each night, and anything you feel able to say about the
prospects will always be welcomed by me.

Sir Ian Hamilton to Winston S. Churchill
(Churchill papers: 26/2)

8 March 1915   Horse Guards
                                                    Whitehall

My dear Winston,

One line to say that I received on Saturday two rather interesting letters
from Commanding Officers; one the Officer Commanding the 48th Toronto
Highlanders,[1] the other, the Commander of the 2nd Gordon Highlanders.[2]

The special interst of the letters lay in this, that each one took an almost
identical view of the deadlock in which they were involved.

After describing the look of the country with its ditches, parapets and
barbed wire, one of them says that a single man behind such defences can
easily hold five in front of him; the other puts the thing differently; he says

[1] John Allister Currie, 1862–1931. Born in Canada, of Scottish parents. Entered journalism,
1880, as a junior reporter on the Toronto News. Left journalism, 1897, to become a mining
broker. Founder and managing director of the Imperial Steel and Wire Company. Member of
the Canadian Parliament, 1908–30. Lieutenant-Colonel, 1913. Commanded the 15th
Battalion, 3rd Canadian Brigade, at the Battles of Neuve Chapelle (March 1915) and St
Julien (April 1915), when they were attacked by poison gas, the first such attack of the war.
Suffering from the effects of gas, he returned to Canada in 1916, and devoted himself to
recruiting work.

[2] Henry Percy Uniacke, 1862–1915. Lieutenant, Gordon Highlanders, 1884; Major,
1903. Lieutenant-Colonel commanding the 2nd Battalion, Gordon Highlanders, 1911–14.
Severely wounded at Ypres, 30 October 1914. On sick leave, November 1914 to January
1915, he resumed command on his battalion of 26 January 1915. Killed in action at
Neuve Chapelle, 13 March 1915.

I suppose that ultimately we shall attack along a broad front, but in doing so I fear we shall inevitably lose in the proportion of five to one.

The coincidence lies in this, that they both talk of these highly elaborated defences as giving a five to one superiority to the defenders.

Under such circumstances what is to be done? Surely fight elsewhere in the meantime so as to gain as much territory and glory as possible, whilst the Germans are hardening their hearts to make a terrific onslaught upon defences which need no reinforcements to be able to hold them. Such at least is my reading of the situation.

Pardon my inflicting this screed on you. Don't acknowledge.

Yours ever
Ian Hamilton

Lord Fisher to Winston S. Churchill
(Churchill papers: 13/56)

8 March 1915   Admiralty

Dear Winston,

The 3 Monitors will leave Sheerness DIRECT for the Danube next Thursday (3 days time)—some maxims are wanted (*about which paper has been sent to you*) apparently they were taken from the Monitors to give to the Belgians. We MUST send these Monitors out properly equipped. It seems desirable to send some field guns and extra guffs of rifles in the accompanying transport as the Austrians have fitted out a transport to every rifleman &c. and field artillery presumably to work with their Monitors—I think every eventuality has been considered to make our 3 Monitors a success and there has been much hustling to start on Thursday. I agree with you their arrival in the Danube must be expedited to the utmost in view of Austrian activity with their new Monitors. *Six* tugs are going with them.[1]

Yours
F

Winston S. Churchill: minute
(Foreign Office papers: 371/2481)

8 March 1915   Admiralty

Nothing ought to stand in the way of the best possible military action. The Russian proposals about an armistice are much too weak. If the Fleet

[1] Churchill noted on this letter: 'The plan you have formed of conveying the 3 British monitors to the Danube cannot be pressed forward too quickly.'

enters the Marmara there should be a complete surrender of everything
Turkish in Europe to the allies.

Vice-Admiral Carden to Admiralty: telegram

(*Copy, Churchill papers: 13/65*)

9 March 1915

Operations on 8th March. Weather South wind some rain and mist. I
entered Dardanelles today in 'Queen Elizabeth' supported by Vengeance
Albion Irresistible Canopus and attacked fort 13. Owing to light failing
only 8 rounds fired with 3 hits. Howitzers which cannot be located shelled
the ships, projectiles fell close and hit Vengeance and Albion one each
without inflicting serious damage and no casualties. One seaplane up but
conditions became unsuitable for spotting. No movement of troops reported
from Bulair but works in some redoubts (?) shelled by Dublin. Request
reserve ammunition for Agamemnon and Lord Nelson may be hastened.
A resumé of the situation will be telegraphed tomorrow.

Winston S. Churchill to Sir John Jellicoe

(*Copy, Churchill papers: 13/48*)

9 March 1915   Admiralty

My dear Jellicoe,

The First Sea Lord is making extraordinary exertions to complete 6
Monitors by May 1st, 3–14″, 2–15″ and 1–12″. Allowing a fortnight to veer
and haul on, the attack on Borkum should take place on or about the
15th of May. I hope you have reflected on my long letter to you of
the [   ]. Besides the Monitors we shall have a bombarding squadron of
8 or 10 older battleships now being fitted with booms to carry double torpedo nets. Oil-ships converted into unsinkable transports will be ready to
carry 12,000 men. An aeroplane base of 60 machines will be established
immediately after the capture of the island, and we can shift whatever is
necessary of our destroyer and S/M flotillas to picket the enemy's coasts
instead of our own. Mining by the new mine-layers will play its part in
covering the operation. The Monitors settling down in shallow water after
the capture will provide an additional temporary defence. Our operations
will be covered by large numbers of our own S/M, and the enemy's S/M
will be warred against with nets and with destroyers with modified sweeps.
In 3 days the capture will be complete; in 6 the new base will be established.

If our present information lasts we shall probably know that the High Sea Fleet is divided between the Baltic & the North Sea. Anyhow I don't think that you would have to come down for the first day. The second day will be more likely to produce a movement in force by the enemy. If so, they would come into an area swarming with S/M and carefully prepared mine-traps. The Grand Fleet wd be in observation at a safe distance ready to act according to circumstances. Although personally I do not think the Germans will come out, yet I am sure the cannonade will draw all the blood their side. Every German ship will come through the canal & every German eye will be riveted on the violation of German territory. It seems to me that on the 5th, 6th or 7th day, when we have got the place & made ourselves secure, another operation of great importance will be easy, namely—the passing into the Baltic of a fast division composed (say) as follows:—Warspite, Queen Elizabeth, Tiger, Queen Mary, 6 Arethusa's, the 'M' flotilla, pro-ceded by 6 'E' boats. This force in the Baltic would dominate the situation, being strong enough to shelter any detachment or any fast vessels and too speedy to be brought to action by the German main fleet. The Russian Fleet in the Baltic (by then 4 super-Dreadnoughts) would immediately become a factor. We would declare a blockade of Northern German ports, cut off their supplies, and destroy their political influence in Scandinavia. Meanwhile the strength of the Grand Fleet wd not be compromised.

This Baltic operation is good in itself. There is a very good passage by Kempenfelt[1] on the use of heavy fast ships to contain a theatre where one cannot have a superiority. This was the principle which inspired our arrangements for holding the Meditn by battle-cruisers and was strongly affirmed both by Bridgeman[2] and Battenberg. But it is in relation to the situation which wd develop in the North Sea that its singular merit appears. Aerial reconnaissance quite apart from the good information will tell us daily which side of the canal the German fleet is. If they go through into the Baltic to attack our fast division, our Monitors will advance to attack Cuxhaven etc. If they come back to repel this assault, these forces in the Baltic will harry the Northern coasts of Germany right up to Kiel. I can of course only see the general conception of these operations; their working out and execution require professional attainments.

[1] Richard Kempenfelt, 1718–82. A British subject, the son of a Swede formerly in the service of James II. Rear-Admiral, 1780. He was responsible for radical alterations and improvements in the signalling system of the Royal Navy. Defeated the French at Ushant, 1781. Drowned with 800 sailors, tradesmen, women and children when the *Royal George* capsized, 1782.

[2] Francis Charles Bridgeman-Bridgeman, 1848–1929. Entered Navy, 1862. Rear-Admiral, 1903. Vice-Admiral, Commander-in-Chief, Home Fleet, 1907–9 and 1911. Knighted, 1908. Admiral, 1911. First Sea Lord, 1911–12.

Our affairs in the Dardanelles are prospering though we have not yet cracked the nut. They are involving profound political re-actions. Constantinople is only a means to an end, and that end is the marching against Austria of the five re-united Balkan states.

Similarly here in the North strategy and politics move together, and it shd be possible by a proper use of our fleets and armies in that combination which sea-power renders possible to bring both Holland and Denmark into the fighting line.

I beg you most earnestly to brood over these things with a view to the assertion of our naval strength in its highest and most aggressive form.

I am touched by the kindness of your letter. Barring a small dose of influenza I have been absolutely fit.

We are gradually and surely acquiring an absolute moral and physical mastery of the sea. The Grand Fleet is the power-house of the line and whether the enemy is provoked to battle or not, is deciding the fortunes of the war. I am most anxious to feed you up with light cruisers. I think it almost certain that Tyrwhitt's 4 could join you in time for an action, but as the new cruisers come to hand we shall push them up to you to form new squadrons for your battle and battle-cruiser fleets. After your exercises are over consider whether you could not come to the Forth in the 'Iron Duke' so that we could meet and talk things over.

With all good wishes and congratulations on your restoration to health.

Believe me

Winston S. Churchill to Sir Edward Grey
(Grey papers)

9 March 1915 Admiralty

Sir E. Grey,

Sir F. Elliot ought surely to say to the King that this was the moment when the assistance of Greece & particularly of the Greek flotillas wd have been especially valuable. This ought surely to be made known to the Greek people.

WSC

Lord Fisher to Winston S. Churchill
(Churchill papers: 13/56)

9 March 1915   Admiralty

Dear Winston,

As you rightly said[1] it is not too much for England to ask in return for her sacrifices—Alexandretta to the Persian Gulf and Palestine also.

Yours
F

I hope you've not got influenza!

H. H. Asquith to George V
(Royal Archives)

9 March 1915   10 Downing Street

Mr Asquith, with his humble duty to Your Majesty, has the honour to report that the Cabinet met this morning.

Mr Churchill reported that steady progress was being made in the bombardment & reduction of the Dardanelles forts.

He also reported that satisfactory progress was being made in the subsidiary operation at Smyrna, to which Lord Kitchener said he attached considerable importance, as its success would seriously hinder the movement of the Turkish troops in Asia Minor in the direction of Constantinople.

Sir E. Grey announced that a formal inquiry had reached him from M. Venizelos in regard to the use of Lemnos as a British naval base. This was expected, and indeed pre-arranged.

The Cabinet then proceeded to discuss the reply to be given to the Russian 'Aide Memoire' of the 4th March with respect to the future of Constantinople & the Straits. Lord Kitchener & Mr Churchill stated that neither on military nor on naval grounds did our interests require us to resist the Russian proposal. Attention was directed to the last paragraph in the 'Aide-Memoire', in which Russia assures the two Allied governments that she will meet with sympathy the 'realisation of desiderata which they may form in other regions of the Ottoman Empire and elsewhere'. Both Lord Kitchener & Mr Churchill were of opinion that, in response to this invitation, we should intimate to Russia that it was our desire to occupy & hold

[1] I can find no other record of Churchill's remarks to Fisher about British annexations in the Ottoman Empire; this subject was presumably raised in anticipation of the Cabinet meeting that day, and the War Council's meeting of 10 March, at both of which the question of annexations was discussed.

Alexandretta, the French receiving on their part Syria. It was strongly urged and generally agreed in the Cabinet that the special circumstances pointed to the desirability of a meeting of the three Foreign Ministers of the Allied Powers—preferably on board of a British man of war at or near Lemnos—to discuss orally & more or less informally the arrangements which must accompany the transfer to Russia of Constantinople & the adjacent territories which she claims. Sir E. Grey doubted whether such a meeting would lead to practical results, but agreed to endorse the suggestion, which M. Delcassé has already made, that it should, if possible, take place.

The decision was that, while accepting in principle the Russian proposal, Your Majesty's government should take note of the accompanying invitation to Great Britain & France, and announce that after consultation, whether at a meeting of the Foreign Secretaries or otherwise, the *desiderata* of Great Britain & France would be formulated. It was also agreed that Russia must assent to the creation of a free port at Constantinople, and to the free passage of the Straits for the commerce of all nations.

The Prime Minister stated that he thought it desirable to secure the concurrence of the Leaders of the Opposition in the decision of the Cabinet in regard to this important matter.

Lords Crewe & Kitchener announced that it had been arranged to reinforce General Barrett[1] in Mesopotamia by 1 Brigade from India & 1 Brigade from Egypt, bringing up his total forces to 22,000 men. . . .

Lieutenant-Colonel Hankey to Lord Esher

(*Esher papers*)

9 March 1915   2 Whitehall Gardens

My dear Lord Esher,

. . . the whole situation in the Balkans is in the melting pot. Very much depends upon whether the Fleet can get through, and as you know, I personally have always regarded this as a speculation, unless a biggish army was at hand to take the forts in reverse.

Yours ever

M. P. A. Hankey

---

[1] Arthur Arnold Barrett, 1857–1926. Entered Army, 1875. Adjutant-General, India, 1909–12. Lieutenant-General, 1911. Knighted, 1912. Commanded the forces in Mesopotamia, 1915–16. Commanded Northern Command, India, 1916–20.

Winston S. Churchill to Vice-Admiral Carden: telegram

(*Draft, Admiralty papers: 137/109*)

10 March 1915   Admiralty
Personal & Secret

It is important that your appreciation of the situation shd reach me as soon as possible. When can I expect it.

WSC

Vice-Admiral Carden to Admiralty: telegram

(*Copy, Churchill papers: 13/65*)

10 March 1915   HMS Inflexible
2.55 pm

Situation in Dardanelles.

After reduction of forts and destruction of guns at the entrance it was necessary to clear an area inside Dardanelles to enable ships entering and remaining more or less stationary to spot for 'QUEEN ELIZABETH' whilst firing from Gabatepe.

When it was found concealed howitzers could not be silenced it became clear that battleships inside Straits must be exposed to their fire and commencement was made with indirect fire by 'QUEEN ELIZABETH' the spotting ship remained as stationary as possible inside supported by three other ships to deal with the fire from guns which can be located.

The first days fire by 'QUEEN ELIZABETH' was promising though she was troubled by field guns being struck several times without however suffering serious injury.

The second day 'QUEEN ELIZABETH' was fired at by a heavy howitzer probably 6″ which caused her to shift berth twice until she finally moved out to 21,000 from target and this limited rounds fired to eight.

She was exposed to almost as severe fire as if she had been inside straits.

Direct bombardment by 'AGAMEMNON' 'LORD NELSON' was next tried Forts 13 and 19 being heavily shelled and finally silenced. Both ships were hit by heavy projectiles from these Forts.

'AGAMEMNON' holed through quarter deck and main deck also ships side of 'LORD NELSON' struck below water causing leak two bunkers flooded.

8th March 'QUEEN ELIZABETH' entered Straits for direct bombardment of forts 13 and 19 but light became very bad rendering fireing and spotting almost impossible though ship made her final run at 14,000 yards.

The risks run by the bombarding ship are not excessive from the Forts provided she does not close inside 14,000 yards or anchor but she is under fire from the howitzers.

The effect of indirect fire has not yet been confirmed as seaplanes have not been able to observe.

Both methods of attack may be employed simultaneously 'QUEEN ELIZABETH' bombarding from Gabatepe and 'LORD NELSON' or 'AGAMEMNON' from inside Straits with old battleships ready to close and take advantage of result of long range fire.

By this means the attack would be pushed more vigorously. The methodical reduction of the forts is not feasible without expenditure of ammunition out of all proportion to that available.

Ships inside Straits are constantly exposed to fire from concealed guns with which it has been found impossible to deal effectively their plunging fire is very destructive but up to the present its accuracy has been poor though that is improving.

To sum up situation we are for the present checked by absence of efficient air reconnaissance necessity of clearing mine fields and presence of large number of movable howitzers on both sides of Straits whose position up to the present we have not been able to locate.

In the meantime every effort will be made to clear mine fields by night with 2 battleships in support.

Two battleships by day watching shore on both sides of entrance and preventing enemy collecting in that locality or bringing guns.

Battleships will bombard defences of Bulair commencing 10th March.

Until it is considered advantageous to commence bombardment on large scale it is not advisable to send Battleships far inside by day as it only affords practice to the enemy's howitzers.

Our experience shows gun fire alone will not render forts innocuous most of the guns must be destroyed individually by demolition.

Meeting of the War Council: Secretary's notes
(*Copy, Cabinet Office papers: 22/1*)

Present: H. H. Asquith (in the Chair), Lord Haldane, Lord Crewe, Lewis Harcourt, Reginald McKenna, Winston S. Churchill, Lord Fisher, Sir Arthur Wilson, David Lloyd George, Sir Edward Grey, A. J. Balfour, Lord Lansdowne,[1] Andrew Bonar Law, Lord Kitchener, Sir James Wolfe Murray, Lieutenant-Colonel Hankey (Secretary)

10 March 1915   10 Downing Street

PROGRESS OF THE WAR

LORD KITCHENER said that the Russians were making good progress in the Caucasus. Otherwise there was little to report.

In Egypt some Turks were still reported at Bir Saba and Gaza.

There was no definite news as to the strength of the Turks in Mesopotamia. In order to secure the position there one brigade was being sent from Egypt and one brigade from India.

He then gave the following figures as to the forces sent to France:—

—	Officers	Other Ranks	Total	Guns
Original Expeditionary Force	5,807	157,000	162,807	543
Casualties	..	..	113,000	106
Present force in France ..	15,282	431,185	446,467	1,105 and 1,011 machine guns

The following was the approximate strength of the forces available against Constantinople:—

—	All Ranks	Guns	Horses	Remarks
Naval Brigade	11,000	6	1,266	
Australasian infantry	30,600	64	9,370	No transport at present available for these.
„ mounted troops ..	3,500	12	4,000	
XXIXth Division	18,000	56	5,400	
French Division	18,000	40	5,000	Provided they are at full strength, which is doubtful.
Russian Army Corps	47,600	120	10,750	
Grand total	128,710	298	35,786	

[1] Henry Charles Keith Petty-Fitzmaurice, 1845–1927. 5th Marquess of Lansdowne, 1856. Governor-General of Canada, 1883–8; Viceroy of India, 1888–93; Secretary of State for War, 1895–1901; Foreign Secretary, 1900–5. Minister without Portfolio, May 1915–December 1916. In 1917 he publicly advocated a negotiated peace with Germany. His second son, Lord Charles George Francis Mercer Nairne was killed in action in France, 30 October 1914.

He proposed to send General Peyton's[1] Territorial Mounted Division to Egypt as a reserve. In round numbers the grand total might be regarded as 120,000 men and 250 guns. He felt that the situation was now sufficiently secure to justify the despatch of the XXIXth Division. There were some signs of the beginning of a movement of German troops from East to West.

SIR EDWARD GREY said he hoped that no more troops than were absolutely necessary would be landed at Lemnos. In the present state of politics in Greece it might be very inconvenient. Up to now Turkey had not recognised the Greek annexation of Lemnos, and Greece had not proclaimed it as Greek territory. We had arranged for the withdrawal of Greek troops before our arrival at Port Mudros, and no difficulty had arisen. If, however, Turkey were now to recognise the Greek annexation of Lemnos, the position would be difficult. We must avoid being put into the position towards Greece that Germany occupied as regards Belgium.

LORD KITCHENER said that no troops would be landed. The water supply was insufficient at Lemnos for a large force.

MR. CHURCHILL said that our troops were sufficiently well placed in Egypt.

LORD FISHER said that in Egypt they would be within three days' steam of the Canal.

THE FIRST LORD said that the transport for the XXIXth Division would be ready on the 15th March, but the transport for General Peyton's Mounted Division would not be ready until later.

MR. BALFOUR asked the strength of the Turkish forces.

LORD KITCHENER said that, according to the best available information, there were supposed to be about 60,000 men in and about the Dardanelles, and possibly another 120,000 men for the defence of Constantinople.

MR. BALFOUR asked if the road across the Bulair isthmus was watched.

MR. CHURCHILL said a cruiser was always there, and nothing could pass.

LORD KITCHENER said that the normal communication between Constantinople and the Gallipoli Peninsula was by water. This route was still open.

---

[1] William Eliot Peyton, 1866–1931. Entered the Army as a Private, 1885. 2nd Lieutenant, 1887. Major-General, 1914. Commanded 2nd Mounted Division in Egypt, April–August 1915; at the later stages of the Suvla battle, Gallipoli, August 1915; and at the evacuation of the Peninsula, December 1915. At Scimitar Hill his Division lost nearly three-quarters of its officers and half its men. Commanded the Expedition against the Senussi west of Egypt, 1916. Knighted, 1917. Commanded the 40th Division, France and Flanders, 1918. Lieutenant-General, 1921. Military Secretary to the Secretary of State for War, 1922–6. Commander-in Chief, Scottish Command, 1926–30. General, 1927.

MR. CHURCHILL said there was not much news from the Dardanelles, as the bombardment had been interrupted by thick weather. On the afternoon of the 8th March the 'Queen Elizabeth' had entered the Straits and fired at Fort No. 13 (Rumilie Medjidieh Tabia); eight rounds had been fired from the 15-inch guns, three of which struck the fort. The light had then failed. On the 9th the weather had been too misty for long-range bombardment, and the only action had been the destruction by two battleships of the bridge over the Menderé River. Admiral Carden had promised to send an appreciation of the situation, but it had not yet been received. The only indication of his views was that he wanted to send the 'Inflexible' to Malta to change the guns in the fire-turret. These guns had been used a great deal, first in the Falkland Island battle, and then in the bombardment. This operation would take six days. It must be remembered that the 'Inflexible' had been sent to the Dardanelles for one purpose only, to engage the 'Goeben'. It was therefore evident that Admiral Carden did not expect to get through the Straits for a week or two. The forts must first be thoroughly broken up; there was no hurry; and some time might still be necessary, particularly if thick weather was encountered. He drew attention to the German report that none of the mines had yet been swept up. In regard to this Admiral Carden said that he could not undertake this until the batteries were smashed up. Once this was accomplished, the clearing of the minefields would, Admiral Carden said, only take a few hours. The Admiralty still believed that they could effect the passage of the Straits by naval means alone, but they were glad to know that military support was available, if required.

RUSSIA AND CONSTANTINOPLE

THE PRIME MINISTER said that the principal business for which this meeting had been called, and for which Lord Lansdowne and Mr. Bonar Law (whom he cordially welcomed) had been invited, was to consider the political, as well as the strategic, questions likely to arise after the fall of Constantinople.

SIR EDWARD GREY said that some months ago it had become clear that Russia wanted to know how she stood with Great Britain and France in regard to the questions of Constantinople and the Straits. The economic pressure on Russia had become great owing to the closing of the Straits on the intervention of Turkey in the war, as the Baltic entrances were closed by the German fleet; and Archangel and Vladivostok, both of them liable to be ice-bound, were the only available ports. We then gave a general assurance that a settlement of the question of the Straits in the Russian interest was necessary. The question had recently been raised again, and

M. Sazonoff had furnished an *aide-mémoire*[1] setting forth the Russian demands. In dealing with this question it had to be remembered that Germany was very desirous of concluding a separate peace with Russia and France; he had been informed by a neutral that Herr Jagow[2] had admitted this, and had said that Germany quite expected to settle with France and Russia on the basis of concessions, and would give an indemnity to Belgium, but that there would be no peace with England except on terms of a German victory. As regards France, he had no apprehensions. They were as anxious as we ourselves to see the business through to a final conclusion, and was as determined as we ourselves. When the question had first been discussed M. Sazonoff had expressed his personal opinion that Russia would be content with the possession of the Bosphorus and the neutralization of Constantinople. Now, however, they put forward a claim for Constantinople, the Straits, and Turkey in Europe up to the Enos–Midia line. In making this claim their principal idea was to obtain an outlet to the sea. Russia had already so much territory that the acquisition of German Poland or Galicia would not confer any great advantage, but one of her principal hopes from this war was to obtain an outlet to the sea. It had to be remembered that at one time Russia had absolutely vetoed Greek co-operation, though she had now somewhat modified this attitude, but she still was apprehensive of the effect of other Powers, such as Italy, Roumania, and Bulgaria, joining the Allies. She feared that Bulgaria, Greece, and Roumania might prejudice her claims for Constantinople, and, remembering our historical attitude towards this question, was suspicious that we might again check her aspirations. The urgency of the question was to remove Russian suspicions as to our attitude and to get rid of the Russian objections to the participation of other nations. It was therefore essential to the progress of the war that Russia should know where she stands, more especially as the occupation of Constantinople might be imminent.

THE PRIME MINISTER said that the Russian *aide-mémoire* referred to a *final* settlement, and not to an interim arrangement.

MR. BALFOUR said that he personally had no objection to an assurance being given to Russia for the realization of her aspirations as regards Constantinople and the Dardanelles, provided that the other Allies received similar assurances as regards their own wishes. The sentiments of the Russians, he said, were probably a good deal more moved by Constantinople than by Poland. If they obtained what they wanted now, they might slacken

[1] Sazonov's *aide-mémoire* was contained in Buchanan's telegram to Grey of 4 March 1915 (quoted on p. 631).

[2] Gottlieb von Jagow, 1863–1935. Entered the German Diplomatic Service as 3rd Secretary, Rome, 1895. Secretary of State for Foreign Affairs, 1913–16.

their efforts in the main theatre of war. We ought to consider what we wanted, for example, in the Persian Gulf and elsewhere.

MR. LLOYD GEORGE said that the Russians were so keen to obtain Constantinople that they would be generous in regard to concessions elsewhere. It was vital for us, if we made concessions, to say what we wanted in return.

LORD LANSDOWNE suggested that the matter depended to some extent on what each of the Allies had accomplished in the war. Supposing, for example, that the Allies in the West were very successful and crushed Germany, while the Russians in the East were to fail, ought we still to give an undertaking as regards Constantinople?

MR. BALFOUR replied that each of the Allies would have to do its share of the war, and that it would be invidious to differentiate between their efforts.

SIR EDWARD GREY said that, in any case, Russia might claim that the sacrifices she had made in East Prussia in the early days of the war had saved the Allies from defeat.

THE PRIME MINISTER said that, when Russian proposals were first put forward, the naval and military advisers were asked to consider them on their merits. They were asked if there was any objection on naval and military grounds to granting Russian claims? Their reply was that there were no objections. The naval authorities appeared to think that the establishment of Russia at Constantinople, and the granting of all she asks, would make it desirable for us to have an additional naval base in these waters, viz., Alexandretta, the probable terminus on the Mediterranean of the Baghdad Railway.

LORD KITCHENER agreed in the naval view. Alexandretta, he said, had a military, as well as a naval importance.

MR. BALFOUR thought it injurious to our interests to allow Russia to occupy a position on the flank of our route to India, but considered that this would have to be accepted.

SIR EDWARD GREY said that M. Sazonoff could now rely on French support to his proposals, as the French Government had agreed to them in principle, and wished to have a conference on the subject. He thought it probable that the Russians had communicated to the French their suspicion of the British attitude, and he (Sir E. Grey) had sent a reassuring telegram to our Ambassador in Petrograd, for communication to M. Sazonoff, to the effect that we had asked for the French views without making any comment. M. Sazonoff had expressed great satisfaction with this.

MR. BONAR LAW[1] suggested that we ought not to give Russia exactly what she wants immediately. He was in favour of taking up an attitude similar to that adopted by the French, that is to say, to tell Russia that she can count on the entire goodwill of the Government for a satisfactory settlement in regard to Constantinople on the conclusion of peace.

LORD LANSDOWNE agreed with Mr. Bonar Law. He suggested that, if Russia was granted all she wished for now, the result might be to choke off Italy and the Balkan States. This would be very unfortunate.

SIR EDWARD GREY pointed out that it would be still more disastrous if we conveyed the impression to Russia that we intended to join with the Balkan States and Italy in preventing her from obtaining Constantinople. He was inclined to suggest to Russia that they should offer Bessarabia to Roumania in the event of Russia herself obtaining Constantinople, as an inducement to join the Allies.

LORD KITCHENER did not think there was any chance that Bulgaria would fight Russia for Constantinople. Religious sentiment was too strong.

MR. BONAR LAW said that perhaps the best plan would be to say we would not oppose Russia, provided that we and France obtained what we wanted.

SIR EDWARD GREY agreed. Our acquiescence should be conditional on a successful termination to the war.

THE PRIME MINISTER read out the last sentence of the Russian *aide-mémoire*, as follows:—

'Imperial Government likes to hope that above consideration will meet with sympathy of the two Allied Governments. Said Governments are assured of meeting with, at the hands of Imperial Government, the same sympathy for realization of desiderata which they may form in other regions of Ottoman Empire and elsewhere.'

LORD LANSDOWNE asked if we were to formulate these desiderata now.

---

[1] Asquith had invited both Bonar Law and Lansdowne to the War Council meeting of 10 March 1915 to discuss the future of Constantinople, a question on which it was felt all party agreement ought to be secured. Thirteen years later, while reading the proofs of Lord Beaverbrook's book, *Politicians and the War*, Churchill set down his own recollection of why the Conservative leaders had been invited: 'The unexpected successful destruction of the Outer Forts at the Dardanelles, gave me a momentary ascendancy. I immediately recurred to the Coalition plan: & I persuaded the PM to invite the leaders of the opposition into council—ostensibly on the future destination of Cple, but really to broach the idea of bringing them into the circle. The conferences were not a success: for the good reasons given:—the Oppn leaders sat silent and hungry & Mr Asquith did not press forward. Not until he was forced by disaster wd he consent to treat Tories as equals.' (*Beaverbrook papers*)

MR. LLOYD GEORGE hoped we should do so.

SIR EDWARD GREY said that France would of course ask for Alsace and Lorraine, and perhaps for Syria. He proposed that we should agree to the Russian claims on some such terms as the following: 'Subject to the war being prosecuted to a victorious conclusion, so as to enable Great Britain and France to realize the desiderata referred to in the last sentence of the Russian *aide-mémoire.*'

MR. McKENNA expressed a preference for the French reply referred to above by Mr. Bonar Law.

MR. BONAR LAW and MR. BALFOUR both expressed a preference for Sir Edward Grey's form of words.

MR. LLOYD GEORGE pressed that our desiderata should be formulated at once.

MR. CHURCHILL agreed. After the war there might be mutual jealousies and heartburnings. He suggested it was very desirable to block in the general lines of the terms we required. As regards Alexandretta, we had already been hampered by French susceptibilities.

THE PRIME MINISTER read a telegram sent by the French Minister for Foreign Affairs to Russia, proposing a Conference at Paris on the question of the ultimate terms of peace.

MR. LLOYD GEORGE said that any interchange of views ought to be between the Foreign Ministers themselves, and not through the medium of Ambassadors. He suggested that they should meet either at Salonica or Lemnos or on board a British man-of-war in those waters, which could easily be reached from either country. He suggested also that a hint should be given to Italy, and perhaps to Greece and Bulgaria, that the fate of Asia Minor would probably be settled at the Conference. By this step we might perhaps bring in all the hesitating neutral States.

SIR EDWARD GREY said he did not want to prejudge this proposal or to negative it, but he would put some of the objections. It nearly always happened that allies quarrelled over the spoils, and this might happen in our case. It would be very difficult, and perhaps very risky, to discuss such delicate questions now as were involved. For example, we might have serious friction with France if we put in a claim for Alexandretta. It would also be very difficult for all the Foreign Ministers to absent themselves from their own countries for two or three weeks.

MR. LLOYD GEORGE said that the reason for friction in the division of the spoils was usually that the nations concerned did not discuss the matter beforehand. He felt considerable misgivings about the expediency of occupying Alexandretta. He suggested Palestine as an alternative owing to the prestige it would give us.

LORD KITCHENER said that Palestine would be of no value to us whatsoever. He saw no reason why the French should oppose our occupation of Alexandretta, provided it was put to them in the right way. Alexandretta was beyond the French sphere of influence in Syria.

MR. BALFOUR asked what was the military case in favour of an occupation of Alexandretta.

LORD KITCHENER said it was a question of communications. Troops could be sent rapidly by rail from Alexandretta to India and Mesopotamia.

MR. CHURCHILL said that the German Admiral Souchon, when on a visit to Alexandretta, had made a statement to the effect that Germany would have gone to war in order to secure Alexandretta alone, as it was the only good harbour between Smyrna and the Suez Canal.

LORD FISHER said that Alexandretta had a special importance as an outlet for the oil supplies of Mesopotamia and Persia.

MR. McKENNA said that the question hinged largely on that of the balance of naval power in the Mediterranean after the war. A naval base would be of no value without command of the sea. We ought, therefore, to consider what we are committing ourselves to. In 1912 the whole question of our naval policy in the Mediterranean had been reviewed, and we had deliberately come to the conclusion that we could not simultaneously retain command of the Mediterranean as well as of the North Sea. He suggested, therefore, that in return for concessions made to Russia at Constantinople and the Straits we should ask for compensation outside the Mediterranean.

LORD KITCHENER said it was essential we should retain command of the sea in the Mediterranean.

MR. CHURCHILL said that in 1912 we had been justified in reducing our peace strength in the Mediterranean owing to our concentration of naval force in the North Sea and our close friendship with France. After the war he hoped that our naval position would be very strong. If we succeeded in shattering German naval power we ought to be able to build a Mediterranean fleet against France and Russia.

MR. LLOYD GEORGE questioned whether it was worth while to press the question of Alexandretta up to the point of a quarrel with France.

LORD KITCHENER laid great stress on the importance of Alexandretta. With Russia in Constantinople, France in Syria, and Italy in Rhodes, our position in Egypt would be untenable if any other Power held Alexandretta.

MR. BALFOUR said he was somewhat loth to oppose on a point on which the Admiralty and War Office appeared to be in complete agreement. He wished, however, to point out that, from a military point of view, the natural line of communication with the Persian Gulf was maritime. If we come to depend on a line of railway communication from Alexandretta to Mesopotamia we should be in an embarrassing position in the event of its interruption in war.

SIR EDWARD GREY said that if we acquired any territory on land we should have to be prepared to defend it against someone. We ought to determine first whether we require a harbour, and, second, whether we want any more territory.

LORD KITCHENER said that we could not count on holding Egypt if Alexandretta were in the hands of some other Power.

MR. CHURCHILL asked if we were to give Constantinople to Russia, and Syria to France, and to receive nothing in return? He reminded the War Council that at the end of the war our naval and military strength ought to be very great indeed.

SIR EDWARD GREY asked what would be the fate of the German colonies?

LORD KITCHENER said it would be a mistake to acquire more of these than we could avoid, as it would more than anything else interfere with the future establishment of goodwill between Germany and ourselves after the war.

SIR EDWARD GREY agreed. He was strongly opposed to the acquisition of German colonies, but feared that South Africa and Australasia would never allow us to cede German South-West Africa and the Pacific colonies.

MR. HARCOURT agreed. He suggested that German East Africa might be acquired in order to settle the question of Indian emigration.

MR. CHURCHILL was strongly opposed to the acquisition of German East Africa. He also said that Egypt ought not to form part of the bargain. The question of Egypt had been decided long ago when it was bartered for Morocco. We ought not, as it were, to have to buy in over again.

MR. BALFOUR said that Lord Lansdowne and he had practically arranged the question of Egypt as part of the general settlement leading up to the *Entente cordiale* with France.

LORD LANSDOWNE agreed. He thought it possible that France had welcomed the Russian claim to Constantinople as a set-off against our occupation of Egypt.

MR. CHURCHILL asked what was to happen about the German fleet and the Kiel Canal? The destruction of the fleet and the removal of the Canal from German control were great objects of British policy. It was essential that we should not come out of this war leaving Germany the power to attack us again in a few years' time. He also pointed out the enormous strategic value of the Kiel Canal, which enabled Germany to transfer her fleet within a few hours from the Baltic to the North Sea and *vice versâ*. Ought we not, he asked, to demand the surrender or destruction of the German fleet?

MR. BONAR LAW said that, in his opinion, the first condition of peace was the elimination of the German fleet.

MR. BALFOUR drew a distinction between the destruction of the German fleet and the neutralization of the Kiel Canal, as the fleet could be rebuilt in a few years.

LORD LANSDOWNE pointed out that both these desiderata were as important to Russia as to ourselves.

LORD FISHER said that if, after the war, Germany started to build a new fleet, we ought to go and smash it at once.

LORD KITCHENER said that the question of armaments was entirely one of finance. The way to stop Germany from building a new fleet was to inflict an indemnity to be paid over a long term of years.

LORD HALDANE said he hoped that the possibility of some agreement for the restriction of armaments would not be abandoned.

THE PRIME MINISTER said that this discussion made him somewhat apprehensive. Russia had made a definite proposition with primary reference to the Ottoman Empire, which was the main subject of the present meeting. The discussion of this proposition had raised every subject which would arise at the end of the war. The conditions at the end of the war, however, could not be foreseen, and the present discussion ought to be limited to the Ottoman Empire. The question which really had to be decided immediately was the reply to be given to Russia. Personally, he advocated the adoption of Sir Edward Grey's formula. If the desiderata were to be formulated, they should be confined for the present to the Ottoman Empire.

SIR EDWARD GREY said that this practically confined the issue to the question of Alexandretta.

MR. HARCOURT said that he was not agreed at present as to the desirability of acquiring Alexandretta. He asked whether it was required as a harbour, or as the terminus of a railway from Mesopotamia. He suggested that Marmaris was a better harbour.

MR. BONAR LAW suggested that we should put off Russia with a statement that we should at the end of the war give them what they asked for, provided that we obtained what we wanted, without any attempt at present to define our desiderata.

LORD CREWE said that then Russia would be completely dealt with. Early in the war the Russians had said what they wanted with regard to Germany and Austria, and now they had stated their requirements from Turkey. If we did not block out what we want we might get left in the lurch. He added that he thought we ought to consider the expediency of leaving home territory to the Sultan of Turkey as the head of the Khalifate. The Mohammedans of India, for example, had in no way diminished their reverence for the Sultan by reason of the war.

LORD KITCHENER said that the location of the Khalifate was solely a question for the Mohammedan world.

SIR EDWARD GREY said he proposed to suggest to Russia to keep secret for the present the arrangement proposed as regards the future of Constantinople, otherwise the Balkan States might be alienated. There were three other stipulations which he considered necessary:—

1. Free passage of the Straits to the commerce of all nations.
2. Constantinople to be a free port for goods in transit.
3. Arabia and the holy places to remain in Mussulman hands.

THE PRIME MINISTER suggested also that a hint should be given to Russia that we are abandoning a traditional attitude and that a large section of public opinion in this country would be opposed to it. Also that Russia should be asked to interpose no obstacle to the intervention in the war on the side of the Allies of other nations.

Conclusions

1. *A reply to be sent to Russia in the sense that we should agree to the proposals put forward in the Russian aide-mémoire, subject to the war being prosecuted to a victorious conclusion, and to Great Britain realizing the desiderata referred to in the last sentence of the Russian aide-mémoire. These desiderata will be put forward by the British and French Governments as soon as there has been time to consider them. (A telegram in this sense was sent in March 1915.)*

2. *The War Office to prepare a memorandum setting forth the strategical advantages of Alexandretta.*

Winston S. Churchill to Sir Edward Grey

(Grey papers)

10 March 1915   Admiralty

Sir E. Grey,

Admiral Carden is asking for more destroyers to protect the Fleet from
submarine dangers. We have none to send him. The Greek flotillas wd have
been of inestimable value *now*. The Russian discouragements have vy likely
been a determining factor against fresh aid.

If you see an opportunity you shd bring this point home to the Russians.
They have put a spoke in our wheel.

WSC

Sir Henry Bax-Ironside to Sir Edward Grey: telegram

(Admiralty papers: 116/1336)

10 March 1915   Sofia

I discussed the political situation with Prime Minister[1] yesterday. He will
not be convinced as yet of possibility of forcing of Dardanelles, but our
persistent action is having a good effect on urban population, as is also
arrival of considerable numbers of refugees from Constantinople. It is
reported here that they are also going to Bucharest.

Confidential. King of the Bulgarians[2] is much upset at prospect of our
success.

[1] Vasil Radoslavov, 1854–1929. Leader of the Bulgarian Liberal Party. Minister-President
of Bulgaria, 1913–18. A leading architect of the German orientation of Bulgarian policy,
1915. In exile in Germany from 1918 to his death.

[2] Ferdinand Maximilian Karl Leopold Maria, 1861–1948. Born in Saxe-Coburg. Lieutenant, Austrian army, 1885. Elected Prince of Bulgaria, 1887. Proclaimed the Independence
of Bulgaria, 1908, and took the title of King (or Tsar). Commanded the Bulgarian Army
which defeated the Turks, 1912–13. Deeply resentful of Britain's role in preventing Bulgaria
from gaining the fruits of victory. Proclaimed the neutrality of Bulgaria, November 1914.
Allied to Germany, October 1915. Abdicated, 1918. In exile in Bavaria; ornithologist and
entomologist.

Winston S. Churchill to Lord Fisher

(*Fisher papers*)

10 March 1915   Admiralty

I.S.L.

V. A. Carden was told not to take the Q.E. into the Straits. Later he asked and received permission to do so. V.A. de Robeck contemplates the use of Q.E. firing from Gaba Tepe: I am sure he is fully alive to the special need of taking care of this ship. I see no objection to emphasizing this before the attack takes place, but it would not be right at this moment to make a rigid prohibition of her entering the Straits. Of course she will not attempt to pass through into the Marmora.

WSC

Sir Ian Hamilton to Winston S. Churchill

(*Churchill papers: 26/2*)

10 March 1915

My dear Winston,

... K has just seen me and told me he intends me to go to the Dardanelles. I have no instructions yet, or staff, but I mean to be off to Marseilles as soon as possible.

For this I feel myself everlastingly in your debt.[1]

Yours ever
Ian Hamilton

Lord Fisher to Winston S. Churchill

(*Churchill papers: 13/56*)

11 March 1915   Admiralty

First Lord

The only way of accounting for the 'Eitel Friedrich' being in an Atlantic United States Port is that she came through the Panama Canal but effete

[1] Churchill had not pressed for Hamilton's appointment as Commander-in-Chief of the Mediterranean Expeditionary Force; indeed, he had originally suggested Hunter-Weston. But when Kitchener had told him that Hamilton was likely to be chosen, he had given his approval. Hamilton had been his friend for nearly twenty years, and he had written of Hamilton's South African exploits in *Ian Hamilton's March*, published in 1900.

as events have proved our Consular Service to be in Chile & the Pacific Coast it is beyond the bounds of human idiotcy that our Consul General[1] would omit to tell us of this ship's arrival at both ends of the Canal—still it is suggested an immediate telegram be sent to him direct from Admiralty to enquire or it may be kept 24 hours at the Foreign Office.

F

Winston S. Churchill to Vice-Admiral Oliver
(Churchill papers: 13/56)

11 March 1915   Admiralty

What action will be taken to mark this ship down so that her career is ended.[2]

WSC

Sir Henry Jackson to Vice-Admiral Oliver
(Copy, Churchill papers: 13/54)

11 March 1915   Admiralty

Admiral Carden's report, No. 194 of 10th instant,[3] on the progress of operations in the Dardanelles shows he has made good progress, but that his operations are now greatly retarded by concealed batteries of howitzers, and that their effects are now as formidable as the heavy guns in the permanent batteries. He also states that demolition parties are essential to render the guns useless. The enemy's military forces have prevented this work from being effectually completed at the entrance, and they will be in even a better position to prevent it further up the Straits.

These points have all been foreseen, and a small military force supplied to deal with them, but the Vice-Admiral was instructed not to risk this force on shore in positions where they cannot be covered by ships' guns without further reference to the Admiralty.

The position has considerably changed recently; there are now ample

---

[1] Claude Coventry Mallet, 1860–1941. Served in various Consular posts in Central and South America, 1879–1907. Consul General, Panama and Costa Rica, 1908–14; promoted Minister, 1914–19. Knighted, 1911. Minister to Uruguay, 1919–25, and to the Argentine, 1919–20 and 1922. Ambassador to the Argentine, 1922–5.

[2] The British were unable to catch the *Prinz Eitel Friedrich* (see p. 636 *n.1*.)

[3] Carden's telegram of 10 March 1915 (printed in full on pp. 661–2).

military forces ready at short notice for co-operation with him, if necessary; and I suggest the time has arrived to make use of them.

To advance further with a rush over unswept minefields and in waters commanded at short range by heavy guns, howitzers, and torpedo tubes, must involve serious losses in ships and men, and *will not* achieve the object of making the Straits a safe waterway for the transports. The Gallipoli peninsula must be cleared of the enemy's artillery before this is achieved, and its occupation is a practical necessity before the Straits are safe for the passage of troops as far as the Sea of Marmora.

I suggest the Vice-Admiral be asked if he considers the time has now arrived to make use of military forces to occupy the Gallipoli peninsula, and clear away the enemy artillery on that side—an operation he would support with his squadrons.

With the peninsula in our possession the concealed batteries on the Asiatic side, which are less formidable, could be dealt with more easily from the heights on shore than by ships' guns afloat, and the troops should be of great assistance in the demolition of the fortress's guns.

HBJ

Winston S. Churchill to Vice-Admiral Carden: telegram

(*Copy, Churchill papers: 13/65*)

11 March 1915   Admiralty
1.35 pm
Secret and Personal

Your 194. Your original instructions laid stress on caution and deliberate methods and we approve highly the skill and patience with which you have advanced hitherto without loss.

The results to be gained are however great enough to justify loss of ships and men if success cannot be obtained without. The turning of the corner at Chanak may decide the whole operation and produce consequences of a decisive character upon the war, and we suggest for your consideration that a point has now been reached when it is necessary, choosing favourable weather conditions to overwhelm the forts at the Narrows at decisive range by the fire of the largest number of guns great and small that can be brought to bear upon them. Under cover of this fire the guns at the forts might be destroyed by landing parties and as much as possible of the minefield swept up. This operation might have to be repeated until all the forts at the Narrows had been destroyed and the approaches cleared of mines.

We do not wish to hurry you or urge you beyond your judgment, but we recognise clearly that at a certain period in your operations you will have to press hard for a decision and we desire to know whether you consider that point has now been reached. We shall support you in well conceived action for forcing a decision even if regrettable losses are entailed.

We wish to hear your views before you take any decisive departure from the present policy.

WSC

Lord Fisher to Winston S. Churchill
(*Admiralty Papers: 137/1089*)

11 March 1915   Admiralty

First Lord

From a reliable authority who cannot be quoted it is certain that Germany is shortly sending submarines in sections to Constantinople via Roumania and Bulgaria.

It is suggested that IMMEDIATE action be taken with Roumania and Bulgaria to prevent so unfriendly an act being permitted and every possible action taken to prevent quite easy concealment by stating the various portions of the submarines being machinery for civil purposes.

F

Lord Kitchener to Winston S. Churchill
(*Churchill papers: 13/48*)

11 March 1915   War Office

My dear Churchill

I am thanking the Grand Duke for enclosed.[1]

I wish his army would play up a bit they seem to do nothing but complain of the number of Germans in front of them.

Yours vy truly
K

[1] A telegram from the Grand Duke Nicholas, dated 11 March 1915, in which he reported that the Russian Black Sea Fleet had bombarded the Turkish port of Zonguldak, and had damaged dock installations there with a view to depriving the Anatolian railways of coal shipped from the port to Constantinople. He added that no occupation of Zonguldak was envisaged, and that the Russian Fleet would, from March 12, begin 'opérations démonstratives' at the mouth of the Bosphorus. (*Churchill papers: 13/48*)

Winston S. Churchill to H. H. Asquith

(*Copy, Churchill papers: 13/48*)

11 March 1915   Admiralty
Midnight

My dear Prime Minister,

The 1 S L & I attach the greatest importance to Ian Hamilton getting to
Lemnos at the earliest possible moment. The naval operations may at any
moment become intimately dependent on military assistance. In view of the
exertions we are making we think we are entitled to a good military opinion
as to the use of whatever forces may be available. The enclosed telegrams
will show you what the position is.

I trust you will be able to represent this to Kitchener.

Too much time has been lost already for nothing.

Yours ever
W

Lord Kitchener to Winston S. Churchill

(*Churchill papers: 13/48*)

12 March 1915   War Office

My dear Churchill

Hamilton cannot leave until we have thoroughly studied the situation with
which he may be confronted. I hope we will get him off Saturday night 'More
haste less speed'.

Yours very truly
Kitchener

Winston S. Churchill to the Grand Duke Nicholas: telegram

(*Copy, Churchill papers: 13/48*)

12 March 1915   Admiralty

Dardanelles operations have been hampered by fog wh prevents long range
firing enemys moveable howitzers cause difficulty but minesweeping is going
forward satisfactorily and the attack on the Narrows will be renewed at the
first opportunity.

We are vy glad the Russian Fleet will now watch the mouth of the Bosphorus to prevent the escape to a neutral port in the Black Sea of the Turkish

and German ships, and will be ready to begin the attack on the forts as soon
as we are successful at the Dardanelles.

Timely notice will be given.

WSC

Lord Fisher to Winston S. Churchill
(*Churchill papers: 13/56*)

12 March 1915   Admiralty

. . . W.R. Hall[1] came to me last night with this idea:—

The German best battleships rush the Dover Straits (dropping mines
behind them) and get to Dardanelles & gobble up all our ships and then
refuge at Constantinople! Colliers *en route* arrived at Carthagena if necessary
and Jellicoe PERFORCE *more than 24 hours behind all the way!* Afterwards they
(the Germans) gobble up the Russian Fleet in Black Sea & bombard as
convenient! Odessa! Varna! Constanza! &c &c.

Yours
F

Our submarines afraid to go out at Dover because our jolly merchant skippers
would ram them at sight! *Moral:—Carden to press on!* and Kitchener to occupy
the deserted Forts at extremity of Gallipoli and mount howitzers there!

Dont let us be fooled any more by the cunning Delcasse with *his continuous
evasions to Bertie!* Invite Bulgaria by telegram (direct from Sir E. Grey) to
take Kavalla and Salonica provided she *at once* attacks Turkey and tell Greece
'*Too late*'*!* and seize the Greek Fleet by a '*coup*' later on. They wd probably
join us now *if bribed!* All the kings are against all the peoples! Greece, Bulgaria,
Rumania! *What an opportunity for Democracy!*

[1] William Reginald Hall, 1870–1943. Entered Navy, 1883. Captain, Royal Navy, 1913.
Commanded the *Queen Mary*, 1913–14. Forced to give up his sea command after three
months of war because of uncertain health. Director of the Intelligence Division at the
Admiralty, 1914–18. Rear-Admiral, 1917. Knighted, 1918. Conservative MP, 1919–23;
1925–9. Conservative Party Principal Agent, 1924.

Lord Kitchener to Winston S. Churchill

(*Churchill papers: 13/48*)

12 March 1915   War Office
Most Secret

1st Lord

In answer to your question, unless it is found that our estimate of the Ottoman strength on the Gallipoli Peninsula is exaggerated and the position on the Kilid Bahr Plateau less strong than anticipated, no operations on a large scale should be attempted until the 29th Division has arrived and is ready to take part in what is likely to prove a difficult undertaking in which severe fighting must be anticipated.

K

Lieutenant-Colonel Hankey: diary

(*Hankey papers*)

12 March 1915

Sir Ian told me he is in an embarrassing position as Churchill wants him to try to rush Straits by a coup de main with such troops as are available in the Levant (30,000 Australasians and 10,000 Naval Division). Kitchener on the other hand wants him to go slow.

Lord Crewe to Lord Hardinge

(*Copy, Crewe papers*)

12 March 1915   India Office
Private

My dear Charlie,

... You will have had my secret telegram of the 10 March on the subject of the ultimate settlement as brought into the foreground by the attack on the Dardanelles. It cannot be denied that the acquisition by Russia of Constantinople, and perhaps even more the command of the Straits with the power to fortify them, will come as a severe shock to public opinion here, so complete a *volte-face* in policy does it represent. As the London crowd used to sing in our Cambridge days:[1]

'The Russians shall not 'ave Constantino – o – opal.' In fact the blessed

[1] Both Crewe and Hardinge were undergraduates at Trinity College, Cambridge, from 1876. During the Russo-Turkish war, which broke out in 1877, Britain was prepared to take military action to prevent Russia capturing Constantinople. As a young naval officer, Jellicoe participated in the British naval preparations at the Dardanelles (see *p.* 649, *n.*2).

word Jingo dates back to that very chant. But I may tell you, absolutely for yourself only, that we discussed the question with the leaders of the Opposition, and they agreed that this outcome is absolutely inevitable, and it is much better to assent graciously while making it clear that the assent is founded on the conditions (a) the joint prosecution of the war to a successful conclusion, and (b) the acquisition by the Allies of what the Russians themselves in their *Aide-Memoire* describe as '*desiderata* within the Ottoman Empire and elsewhere'. So we have to reflect what those *desiderata* are. We should first note that the change in the status of Egypt does not amount to very much and ought not to be treated as a solid acquisition. As regards the German Colonial Empire, it may be presumed that some of the Dominions will put in claims, notably the African Union for German South-West Africa; but generally speaking we are averse from the idea of making wide claims of our own to German Colonies. So we have to examine Asia, and as I telegraphed, the fighting departments consider it important to hold a strong position on the flank of our direct road to the East, and they regard Alexandretta as the most favourable place.[1] I can quite believe in its merits; but if its possession means holding the whole of the Euphrates valley, above Aleppo to Urfah, on to Baghdad, and thence to the Gulf, it is a large proposition in itself; which if Russia takes Armenia, Italy Adana, France Syria, and Greece wants Smyrna, the Turks remain with Anatolia and little else. This may be inevitable; and the counter argument is tremendously strong, that if another Power, say France, were to hold Alexandretta and control the railway thence to Baghdad, our possession of Mesopotamia would be seriously menaced in the event of trouble between ourselves and France or Russia or both. Kitchener is particularly strong on this point, though I do not understand that he would propose to hold the Alexandretta–Baghdad line by a strong permanent military force. Indeed we could not pretend to do so. . . .

Ever yours
Crewe

H. H. Asquith to Venetia Stanley

(*Montagu papers*)

12 March 1915   10 Downing Street

. . . I have just been reading the Admiralty secret report of the operations so far; they are making progress, but it is slow, and there are a large number of howitzers & concealed guns (not in the forts) on both shores wh. give them a good deal of trouble, and have made a lot of holes in the ships, tho'

[1] See map 11 on pages 1602-3.

so far the damage done is not serious. I think the Admiral is quite right to proceed very cautiously; Winston is rather for spurring him on. It is characteristic of W. that he has worked out since midnight & now sent me a time table, acc. to wh. Ian Hamilton by leaving Charing Cross at *5 this* afternoon can reach the Dardanelles by *Monday* (taking a 30 knot cruiser at Marseilles). It sounds almost incredible, doesn't it? . . .

Sir Ian Hamilton to Winston S. Churchill
(*Churchill papers: 26/2*)

12 March 1915   Horse Guards
1 pm

My dear Winston,

Just back from a three hours talk (!) at the W.O. Lord K. has decided I start *tomorrow* at 5 p.m. I fought hard for today but as the first idea was that I must wait a full fortnight, tomorrow is something substantial in gain of time.

I have got Jack Churchill's name duly registered by Colonel Callwell, Director of Military Operations, as one of my special service officers so the moment he comes back he has only to go to him and get his sailing orders. He is the only officer I am drawing from France as it is thought at the W.O. French may prove touchy at the idea of anyone going of their own free will from France to another theatre.

I must not in loyalty tell you too much of my W.O. conversation but I see I shall need some courage in stating my opinions as well as in attacking the enemy; also that the Cabinet will not be quite eye to eye whatever I may have to say!!

I am sending off a Staff Officer to see your people in order that I may know if it will still be all right about the train and the cruiser.

Yours ever
Ian Hamilton

John Churchill: diary
(*Copy, Churchill papers: 28/139*)

12 March 1915

For some time St. Omer has been a bore. To-day most people have moved off nearer the front and big things are expected soon. The C. in C. and C.G.S. [Sir William Robertson], have gone off to Hazebrouck. But here there is no news. About 12 Winston rang up on the telephone. Would I like to go else-where? Would I not? A letter is coming over asking the C. in C. to let me go and Sir Ian Hamilton will take me on his Staff. He leaves at once for the Dardanelles: I must be quick! At 2.30 the mail arrived—brought on by Sunny Marlborough and I obtain the letter. Then I seize a car, a rush to Hazebrouck to find Sir John French. I had to wait some time for he was out watching the operations which appear to be going well. At last he came in very pleased with all that was going on. The attack on Aubers was pro-gressing very well, and even the 2nd Cavalry Division had been ordered to saddle up and move, in case of there being an opportunity for a dash. My leave was granted at once. Sir John did not know Sir Ian was going to start. He asked about the 29th Division. Was it going to be sent also? He wanted it badly and said he did not think there would be much fighting at the Dardanelles. He said he wanted every man to help to push here and he grudged anybody going elsewhere. He said he thought the War would finish in five or six months! I went back to St. Omer and telephoned again. I have to leave at once and so after dinner I motored to Calais. There I found a destroyer the 'Saracen' and so off to London. The Channel was misty and we passed mine sweepers. We had to ask permission to enter Dover at the South Foreland. After some delay the boom was pulled aside and we entered the harbour.

Lord Kitchener to Sir Ian Hamilton

(*Copy, Churchill papers: 2/82*)

13 March 1915   War Office
Secret

Instructions for the General Officer Commanding-in-Chief the Mediterranean Expeditionary Force

1. The Fleet have undertaken to force the passage of the Dardanelles. The employment of military forces on any large scale for land operations at this juncture is only contemplated in the event of the Fleet failing to get through after every effort has been exhausted.

2. Before any serious undertaking is carried out in the Gallipoli Peninsula all the British military forces detailed for the expedition should be assembled, so that their full weight can be thrown in.

3. Having entered on the project of forcing the Straits, there can be no idea of abandoning the scheme. It will require time, patience, and methodical

plans of co-operation between the naval and military commanders. The essential point is to avoid a check which will jeopardise our chances of strategical and political success.

4. This does not preclude the probability of minor operations being engaged upon to clear areas occupied by Turks with guns annoying the Fleet or for the demolition of forts already silenced by the Fleet. But such minor operations should be as much as possible restricted to the forces necessary to achieve the object in view, and should as far as practicable not entail permanent occupation of positions on the Gallipoli Peninsula.

5. Owing to the lack of any definite information we must presume that the Gallipoli Peninsula is held in strength, and that the Kilid Bahr Plateau has been fortified and armed for a determined resistance. In fact, we must pre-suppose that the Turks have taken every measure for the defence of the plateau which is the key to the Western front at the Narrows, until some time as reconnaissance has proved otherwise.

6. Under present conditions it seems undesirable to land any permanent garrison or hold any lines on the Gallipoli Peninsula. Probably an entrenched force will be required to retain the Turkish forces in the Peninsula and prevent reinforcements arriving at Bulair, and this force would naturally be supported on both flanks by gun fire from the Fleet. Troops employed on the minor operations mentioned above (paragraph 4) should be withdrawn as soon as their mission is fulfilled.

7. In order not to reduce forces advancing on Constantinople, the security of the Dardanelles passage, once it has been forced, is a matter for the Fleet, except as in paragraph 6 with regard to Bulair.

The occupation of the Asiatic side by military forces is to be strongly deprecated.

8. When the advance through the Sea of Marmora is undertaken, and the Turkish fleet has been destroyed, the opening of the Bosphorus for the passage of Russian forces will be proceeded with. During this period, the employment of the British and French troops, which will probably have been brought up to the neighbourhood of Constantinople, should be conducted with caution. As soon as the Russian Corps has joined up with our troops, combined plans of operations against the Turkish Army (if it still remains in European Turkey) will be undertaken with a view to obtaining its defeat or surrender. Until this is achieved, landing in the town of Constantinople, which may entail street fighting, should be avoided.

9. As it is impossible now to foretell what action the Turkish military authorities may decide upon as regards holding their European territories, the plan of operations for the landing of the troops and their employment, must be left for subsequent decision. It is, however, important that as soon

as possible after the arrival of the Fleet at Constantinople, all communication from the West to the East across the Bosphorus, including telegraph cables, should be stopped. Assuming that the main portion of the Turkish Army is prepared to defend European Turkish territory, it may be necessary to land parties to hold entrenched positions on the East side of the Bosphorous, and thus assist the Fleet in preventing all communication across the Bosphorous.

10. Should the Turkish Army have retired to the East side of the Bosphorous, the occupation of Constantinople and the Western territories of Turkey may be proceeded with.

11. As, in certain contingencies, it may be important to be able to withdraw our troops from this theatre at an early date, the Allied troops working in conjunction with us should be placed in those positions which need to be garrisoned, and our troops might with advantage be employed principally in holding the railway line until a definite decision is come to as to future operations.

12. You should send all communications to the Secretary of State for War, and keep him fully informed of the operations and your anticipations as to future developments.

Kitchener

Winston S. Churchill to Captain Cameron:[1] *telegram*
(*Draft, Admiralty papers: 137/109*)

13 March 1915   Admiralty

In addition to Sir Ian Hamilton & his staff you shd embark as many seaplanes and aeroplanes, with their personnel, as can reach you before the time of sailings, and for which you have room. You must make arrangements to take as many officers as possible of the Staff, & also aeroplane officers. Apart from the General & the Senior Officers, you need not trouble about Cabins. Active service conditions must prevail, the officers sleeping on mattresses on deck or in hammocks. Make what arrangements are necessary for their food, but the point is to carry them to Lemnos, & nothing else matters except for the General. Any other officers for whom you have not room must follow by the 'Abda' carrying the aeroplanes which start 14th or 15th.

WSC

[1] John Ewen Cameron, 1874–1939. Entered Navy, 1887. Captain, HMS *Phaeton*, 1914–18. Rear-Admiral and Senior Officer, Yangtse river, 1925–7. Vice-Admiral, 1929.

Vice-Admiral Carden to Winston S. Churchill: telegram

(*Copy, Churchill papers: 13/54*)

13 March 1915   HMS Queen Elizabeth
2.50 am

Operations inside Dardanelles during daylight confined to destroying floating mines and preventing enemy moving guns. Sweeping operations last Night *not satisfactory owing to heavy fire, no casualties*.[1] Volunteer Officers and Men have been called to assist in each sweep; large number have responded. In Gulf of Zeros 'SUFFREN' 'GAULOIS' 'IRRESISTIBLE' 'DARTMOUTH' 'USK' and 'ARK ROYAL' operated against Bulair: shelled barracks and encampments; seaplanes reported two new works 1 mile East of Bulair village. No movements of troops observed.

Winston S. Churchill to Vice-Admiral Carden: telegram[2]

(*Copy, Churchill papers: 13/54*)

13 March 1915   Admiralty
Personal and Secret

Your 203[3] gives the impression of your being brought to a standstill both by night and day during 12th and makes me anxious to receive your reply to Admiralty telegram No 101.[4] I do not understand why minesweeping should be interfered with by fire which causes no casualties. Two or three hundred casualties would be a moderate price to pay for sweeping up as far as the Narrows. I highly approve your proposal to obtain volunteers from the Fleet for Mine Sweeping. This work has to be done whatever the loss of life and small craft and the sooner it is done the better.

Secondly, we have information that the Turkish Forts are short of ammunition and that the German Officers have made desponding reports and have appealed to Germany for more. Every conceivable effort is being made to supply ammunition. It is being seriously considered to send a German or an Austrian submarine but apparently they have not started yet. Above is absolutely secret.

[1] Words underlined by Churchill, who put an X in the margin, and wrote to Fisher: 'The sentence at X makes me squirm.' (*Churchill papers: 13/54*)
[2] Churchill sent this telegram to Fisher with the covering note: 'I propose to send the enclosed—wh is more fitted to a "Personal & Secret' than to an Admiralty order. Oliver agrees.' Fisher noted: 'Concur.' (*Churchill papers: 13/54*)
[3] The official number for Carden's immediately preceding telegram, of 13 March 1915.
[4] The official number for Churchill's 'Secret and Personal' telegram to Carden, sent from the Admiralty at 1.35 pm on 11 March (quoted on p. 677–8).

All this makes it clear that the operations should now be pressed forward methodically and resolutely by night and day the unavoidable losses being accepted. The enemy is harrassed and anxious now. Time is precious as the interference of submarines would be a very serious complication.

Thirdly, Sir Ian Hamilton leaves to-night to command the Army and will be with you on Tuesday 16th. Take him fully into your confidence and let there be the most cordial co-operation. But do not delay your own operations on this account.

The First Sea Lord has ordered QUEEN and IMPLACABLE to sail tonight to strengthen your Fleet and provide further reserves for casualties.

WSC

Winston S. Churchill: memorandum
(Churchill papers: 13/54)

13 March 1915   Admiralty

General Sir Ian Hamilton has been appointed to command the land forces, but, until they operate on shore, Adl Carden will be in charge of the operations at the Dardanelles & any communication from the Russian General Staff shd be made to him. The French Divn under General d'Amade will act under the orders of Gen Hamilton, & it is hoped that the Commander of the Russian Corps when it cooperates with our troops will also conform & receive general instructions from Sir Ian Hamilton who is a very senior & competent full General & an Aide de Camp General to His Majesty.[1]

Sir Arthur Wilson to Winston S. Churchill
(Copy, Churchill papers: 13/58)

13 March 1915   Admiralty

The opinion expressed by the Defence Committee in 1903, that the Russian occupation of Constantinople would not fundamentally alter the present strategic position in the Mediterranean, was arrived at under very different conditions from those that exist at the present time.

We had at that time a large fleet both in the Mediterranean and in the China Seas, which appeared to be sufficient to deal with any fleet the Russians then had, whether they were stationed in the Baltic or the Black

[1] This memorandum was drafted by Churchill after a discussion that same morning with Kitchener. 'These arrangements are quite satisfactory to the Admiralty,' Churchill noted at the bottom. The memorandum was sent to Fisher on 13 March by Commodore de Bartolome. 'I concur,' Fisher noted. *(Churchill papers: 13/54)*

Sea. The Russo-Japanese war had not then taken place, and attention had not been called to the enormous difficulty Russia afterwards experienced in bringing her ships in the Baltic to the support of her fleet in the Far East.

The position of the Russian ports has up to the present made it quite impossible for her to dispute the command of the sea with us, and she has consequently not attempted it, but as soon as the state of her finances admits of her creating a new fleet and making its headquarters in the Black Sea she may, if she likes, become a very formidable opponent to us indeed.

Whatever the position may have been in 1903, there is no doubt that under present conditions a hostile Russia in possession of Constantinople could make our communication through the Mediterranean with Egypt and India almost impossible.

A strong force of submarines established in the Dardanelles would be able to intercept and destroy a very large proportion of the ships attempting to pass between Crete and the coast of Africa, on the route to Alexandria or the Canal.

A fleet at Alexandria could not be kept supplied with fuel, nor reinforcements sent to Egypt, except through the Red Sea. No new fortified base that we could make would improve matters in this respect, and an island base could not be furnished with supplies except at great risk.

It may be assumed that when Turkey is driven out of Europe, the occupation of Constantinople by Russia is inevitable, as even if some small State were put in possession, the arrangement would only be a temporary one until Russia felt herself strong enough to turn it out. It is, therefore, best to consider our future policy under these conditions.

After the war, Russia—being relieved for a considerable time from any danger of aggression by Germany or Austria—will be able to devote herself to internal affairs, the development of her trade, and to strengthening her position in Asia.

Russia and Great Britain will be left face to face as the two dominant Powers in Asia. If they are antagonistic, Russia would be in the stronger position, as, although she could not pass through the Suez Canal or the Straits of Gibraltar, she could bring her whole military forces against India, which could only be reinforced and supplied by the long sea route.

The only way to avoid a competition in armaments far in excess of anything that we have undergone with Germany is to establish friendly relations and close co-operation with Russia in the affairs of Asia.

Winston S. Churchill to Sir Arthur Wilson

(*Copy, Churchill papers: 13/54*)

13 March 1915   Admiralty

Sir Arthur Wilson,

No consideration of the effect produced upon the strategical position which would be created after the war by the Russian possession of Constantinople and the Dardanelles is possible without dealing with the changes in naval matériel consequent upon the submarine. It is certain either that the submarine will dominate all narrow waters and render them impassable for heavy ships and for commerce, or that alterations will be made by bulges and bulkheads to the underwater structure of large ships, which will render them immune from the submarine. In the former case, we should have to recognise that the Mediterranean in time of war would, like the North Sea, become almost entirely a 'mare clausum'. We could not think of it as a sea road for transports to India. In the latter case, assuming we build transports, merchant vessels, and heavy ships which are immune from submarine attack, the control of the Mediterranean will rest with the superior sea power, and that control would not be affected to any vital degree by a Russian ownership of the Dardanelles.

WSC

H. H. Asquith to Venetia Stanley

(*Montagu papers*)

13 March 1915   Walmer Castle

. . . H Samuel had written an almost dithyrambic memorandum urging that in the carving up of the Turks' Asiatic dominions, we should take Palestine, into which the scattered Jews cd. in time swarm back from all the quarters of the globe, and in due course obtain Home Rule. (What an attractive community!) Curiously enough, the only other partisan of this proposal is Lloyd George, who, I need not say, does not care a damn for the Jews or their past or their future, but who thinks it would be an outrage to let the Christian Holy Places—Bethlehem, Mount of Olives, Jerusalem &c—pass into the possession or under the protectorate of 'Agnostic Atheistic France'! Isn't it singular that the same conclusions shd be capable of being come to by such different roads? Kitchener, who 'surveyed' Palestine when he was a young Engineer,[1] has a very poor opinion of the place, wh. even

---

[1] In 1874 Kitchener, aged 24, was attached to the Palestine Exploration Fund, and worked with it until 1878. In 1883 he did survey work in the Sinai Peninsula.

Samuel admits to be 'not larger than Wales, much of it barren mountain, & part of it waterless' &, what is more to the point, without a single decent harbour. So he (K) is all for Alexandretta, and leaving the Jews & the Holy Places to look after themselves.[1] . . .

Noel Buxton to Winston S. Churchill

(*Churchill papers: 26/1*)

13 March 1915   Kensington Palace Mansions

Dear Churchill,

I don't wish to trouble you but there is one important point that occurs to me in regard to operations in the Balkans.

It seems improbable that Turkish troops will have the initiative to turn against the German officers who have led them; so one may assume that the Bulgarian army will be a welcome ally in fighting them. For this purpose it will probably be necessary to promise Bulgaria both Monastir and Kavala, while Servia is promised Bosnia etc. and Greece the Smyrna country. If Bulgaria cannot be squared without Kavala the risk of chilling Greece is a smaller matter than the cost in men etc. of dealing with the Turkish army unaided.

The above terms embody your idea of 'an Entente map for fighters'. If Greece rejects the terms, she could be warned that Smyrna might be otherwise disposed of, just as Bulgaria, if she refused the offer to her, would run the risk of losing her rights.

Yours sincerely

N. Buxton

I have written in the same sense to Lloyd George.

[1] Three days later, on 16 March, E. S. Montagu (with Samuel and Lord Reading one of three Jewish members of the Government) protested against the idea of a Jewish home in Palestine. In a 'Confidential' memorandum he declared: 'There is no Jewish race now as a homogeneous whole. It is quite obvious that the Jews in Great Britain are as remote from the Jews in Morocco or the black Jews in Cochin as the Christian Englishman is from the Moor or the Hindoo.' He went on: 'How would the Jews occupy themselves? Agriculture is never attractive to ambitious people and the Jews in the main have long emerged into quicker, less pastoral pursuits. I cannot see any Jews I know tending olive trees or herding sheep. Literature! Are there any great or even remarkable Jewish literary men of to-day?' The idea of a Jewish national home was, he concluded, 'a rather presumptuous and almost blasphemous attempt to forestall Divine agency in the collection of the Jews which would be punished, if not by a new captivity in Babylon, by a new and unrivalled persecution of the Jews left behind. If only our peoples would cease to ask for special favours and cease to cry out together at the special disadvantages which result from asking special favours, if only they would take their place as non-conformists, Zionism would obviously die and Jews might find their way to esteem.' (*Lloyd George papers*)

Winston S. Churchill to Vice-Admiral Carden: telegram

(*Copy, Churchill papers: 13/65*)

14 March 1915   Admiralty
12.30 am

The Chief of Staff[1] of the Grand Duke Commander in Chief has telegraphed to the Admiralty for your information the instructions[2] which have been given to Admiral Eberhardt.[3] They are as follows:—

1st Period. During the operations of the Allied Fleet in the Dardanelles the Black Sea Fleet will confine itself to demonstrations purely naval.

2nd Period. When the Allied Fleet appears before the Princes Islands the Black Sea Fleet will undertake a serious attack against the fortifications of the Bosphorous. Headquarters are of opinion that it will be impossible for the Russian Squadron to force the passage to Constantinople without the assistance of the Allied Fleet.

3rd Period. The destruction of the Turkish Fleet and the junction of the Allied Fleet with ours will be followed by a landing previously arranged. These instructions however authorise Admiral Eberhardt to carry out any advice which Admiral Carden may desire to forward him.

Winston S. Churchill to the Grand Duke Nicholas: telegram

(*Churchill papers: 26/4*)

14 March 1915   Admiralty

The arrangements proposed for the action of the Russian Fleet are in every way satisfactory to us.

We have however not enough destroyers and small craft. All our flotillas are engaged in the Dardanelles operation or are occupied with submarines at home. The French flotillas are similarly occupied in the Adriatic. This is the moment when the assistance of the excellent Greek flotillas will be of the greatest service to us and a good protection against the intervention of German or Austrian submarines. Now that the political questions connected

---

[1] Nikolai Nikolaievich Yanushkevich, 1868–1918. Professor of Military Administration, Military Academy, 1910–13. Head of the Military Academy, 1913–14. Chief of the General Staff, 1914–15. Killed in the Caucasus in unexplained circumstances.

[2] The Grand Duke Nicholas had telegraphed these instructions in French to Churchill on 12 March. (*Churchill papers: 13/48*)

[3] Andrei Avgustovich Eberhardt, 1856–   . Commander, Russian Black Sea Fleet, 1911–16. In March 1916 he discussed with the Grand Duke Nicholas a combined naval and military attack on Trebizond, but was relieved of his command in June 1916, before this could be put into effect.

with Constantinople are satisfactorily adjusted I trust that the naval importance of assuring the immediate co-operation of the Greek fleet may be fully recognised and nothing done or said to discourage them from joining us.

The progress and even the success of the attack may be affected sensibly by their participation or abstention.

Vice-Admiral Carden to Admiralty: telegram

(*Copy, Churchill papers: 13/65*)

14 March 1915   HMS Queen Elizabeth
Noon

Fully concur with the view of Admiralty telegram 101.[1] It is considered stage is reached when vigorous sustained action necessary for success.

In my opinion military operations on large scale should be commenced immediately in order to ensure my communication line immediately Fleet enters Sea of Marmora.

The losses in passing through Narrows may be great therefore submit that further ships be held in readiness at short notice and additional ammunition be despatched as soon as possible.

Position with regard to minefields as follows.

In order to immediately follow up silencing efforts at the Narrows with close range bombardment, it is necessary to clear the minefields at Kephez. So as to economise ammunition the attempt being made to clear at night; this so far has been unsuccessful. A final attempt is to be made tonight, if it fails also, it will be necessary to destroy fixed and movable light guns defending minefields before continuing sweeping, destroying these guns will bring ships under fire of forts at the Narrows and will therefore entail silencing the latter which must now go on irrespective of air reconnaisances.

This accomplished, sweeping will be carried out working day and night but as minefield is extensive operations may occupy some time and expenditure of ammunition will be very great as the forts will require repeatedly silencing.

Request further half outfits may be sent at once for all ships except 'QUEEN ELIZABETH'.

[1] The official number for Churchill's 'Secret and Personal' telegram to Carden of 11 March (quoted on pp. 677–8).

Winston S. Churchill to Lord Kitchener

(*Copy, Churchill papers: 13/65*)

14 March 1915   Admiralty

My dear Kitchener,

Please see the enclosed from Carden. Fisher is very insistent, and I agree with him, in asking you to have the troops in Egypt which are available sent to rendezvous at Mudros Bay with the French who arrive on the 18th and the 16,000 men who are already there. We do not wish in any way to prejudice any decision which you may take as to the use of the troops after Hamilton has studied the situation with Carden and reported definitely to you. Mudros Harbour has been protected by a boom and nets against submarines, and can accommodate safely the whole transport fleet. We think it is only asking for a reasonable precaution that the forces now available should be concentrated there.

The naval operations of engaging the forts and sweeping the approaches to the Narrows will proceed steadily. They cannot be delayed, because of the increasing danger of submarines arriving, and of heavy howitzers being mounted.

We are sending the enclosed to Carden.

Yours very truly
Winston S. Churchill

Winston S. Churchill to Vice-Admiral Carden: telegram

(*Copy, Churchill papers: 13/65*)

14 March 1915   Admiralty
1.40 am
Secret and Urgent

You must concert any military operations on a large scale which you consider necessary with General Hamilton when he arrives on Tuesday night. Meanwhile we are asking War Office to send the rest of the Australian Divisions to Mudros Bay at once, thus giving with the French approximately 59,000 men available after 18th. This will be confirmed later. 29th Division, 18,000 additional cannot arrive till April 2nd.

Secondly, we understand that it is your intention to sweep a good clear passage through the mine fields to enable the Forts at the Narrows eventually to be attacked at close range, and to cover this operation whether against the forts or the light and movable armament, by whatever fire is necessary from the Battle Fleet, and that this task will probably take several days.

After this is completed we understand you intend to engage the forts at the Narrows at decisive range and put them effectually out of action.

You will then proceed again at your convenience with the attack on the forts beyond and any further sweeping operations which may be necessary. If this is your intention we cordially approve it. We wish it to be pressed forward without hurry but without loss of time. We do not gather that at this stage you contemplate any attempt to rush the passage without having previously cleared a channel through the mines and destroyed the primary armament of the forts. We wish to be consulted before any operation of such a nature is decided on and before undertaking it the parts to be played by the Army and Navy in close co-operation would required careful study and it might then be found that decisive Military action to take the Kilid Bahr plateau would be less costly than a Naval rush. You will be informed later about the ammunition aeroplanes and mine-sweepers.

WSC

Vice-Admiral Carden to Admiralty: telegram
(*Copy, Churchill papers: 13/65*)

14 March 1915   HMS Queen Elizabeth
4.55 pm

Sweeping operations on the night of 13th and 14th.
CORNWALLIS bombarded lights and batteries for one hour.
Sweepers attended by 5 picket boats and supported by AMETHYST and Destroyers then entered minefield. It has been found impossible to sweep against strong current it was necessary to get beyond minefield. To do this minesweepers and picket boats had to pass through an area lighted by two powerful searchlights and under fire of Forts 7, 8, 9 and 13 in addition to numerous light guns estimated about 20 to 30 each side. This passage was accomplished but on reaching point at which sweeping was to be commenced only two trawlers were able to get out their sweeps owing to damage to winches and gear in two vessels the whole working personnel were killed or wounded. Picket boats did excellent service in blowing up cables with explosive sweeps. A number of mines have been destroyed no vessel has been sunk but four trawlers and one picket boat out of action. AMETHYST did excellent work by drawing fire of many of the guns at a critical period, in consequence she suffered heavily.
Total casualties: Killed 27, wounded 43.
Conduct of all concerned in a very gallant enterprise was admirable. Defence of minefields against night sweeping is so well organised I am of

opinion that efficient sweeping by night is impossible. . . . Fleet sweepers will
be urgently required to preceed the Fleet in the Sea of Marmora. These
were asked for in my [telegram]¹ 19 [of] January 10th.

Sir Ian Hamilton to Winston S. Churchill

(*Churchill papers: 26/2*)

14 March 1915   In the train
5 p.m.

My dear Winston,

Just a tiny personal line to tell you we are all going strong and that the
fact of you and yours coming down to see us off has given us, morally, the
finest possible fillip.

Jack seems very cheery and fit and will be a great addition to our little
band of adventurers. I hope he will always mess with me when we get our
mess established and so I shall be able to keep a close eye upon him. I have
been reading all the papers in the train & I must say I don't see how these
concealed howitzers are to be tackled without storming the plateau. Only,
if we could smash up the search lights they would be no use at night. I feel
though it won't be easy to make up one's mind until we have had a thorough
aeroplane reconnaissance.

Deep salaams to Mrs Winston,

Yours ever
Ian Hamilton

Vice-Admiral Carden to Winston S. Churchill: telegram

(*Copy, Churchill papers: 13/65*)

15 March 1915
9.15 am
Secret and personal

Your 105,² I fully appreciate the situation and intend as stated in my 203
14th March³ to vigorously attack fortresses at the Narrows clearing minefields under cover of attack. Good visibility is essential and I will take first
favourable opportunity. . . . I am requesting C-in-C East Indies Squadron

¹ Not printed.
² Churchill's telegram to Carden of 13 March (quoted on pp. 687–8).
³ Carden's telegram to the Admiralty of 14 March (quoted on pp. 693–4).

to hold in readiness **TRIUMPH SWIFTSURE** to join me at short notice. Neither British or French mine sweepers can make headway against strong currents. When night sweeping operations were commenced it was hoped to knock out the searchlights and begin sweeping from above minefields in darkness. Large expenditure of ammunition from battleships, **AMETHYST** and destroyers failed however to extinguish a single light for more than a few minutes. My 203[3] described situation which then arose. The French method of minesweeping necessitates considerable preparation and their C.O.[4] did not consider it feasible to commence clearing the range of minefields under the conditions existing on the night of 12th. Being unable to make headway against current he withdrew after his vessels had been struck several times. Our minesweepers which were driven back in the night of 11th behaved splendidly on the 13th led by volunteer Officers who testified to the excellent behaviour of the crews. Casualties will always be faced when adequate military advantage can result. Almost one third of the minesweepers are already sunk or out of action for some time and there is much work before them after the Narrows are passed. . . . The steel plates protection provided at Malta has proved of good service. A minesweeping trawler which had her sweeps and winches wrecked before she reached the turning point besides many other hits and a heavy list suffered no casualties. Fleet sweepers urgently required. Meantime I am fitting some destroyers for this purpose with light sweeps.

Winston S. Churchill to Vice-Admiral Wemyss and Vice-Admiral Carden: telegram
(*Copy, Churchill papers: 13/65*)

15 March 1915   Admiralty
2.30 pm

. . . (1) Has the first French Convoy of their Division consisting of 5 or 6 ships arrived at Lemnos, where they were due last night. If so what troops have they on board.
(2) The British force at Lemnos consists of a Brigade of Australians and 11,000 Naval Division. Is there sufficient drinking water for these and French troops referred to above.

[4] Emile Paul Aimable Guépratte, 1856–1939. Entered the French Navy, 1871. Rear-Admiral commanding the French naval forces at the Dardanelles, February–October 1915. Vice-Admiral, October 1915. Knighted, 1915. Subsequently Préfet Maritime at Brest and Commander-in-Chief and Préfet Maritime in Algeria–Tunisia.

(3) To-morrow rest of French Division should arrive off Dardanelles. Admiral Carden will therefore have at his disposal on the spot 18,000 French and 16,000 British; and there will be at call at Alexandria remainder of Birdwood's force about 25,000.

(4) Under these circumstances consult with Admiral Carden whether it is advisable to concentrate the whole of Birdwood's force at Lemnos now, or would such a concentration create congestion and difficulties in your water supply.

(5) General Sir Ian Hamilton will arrive to take over command of the combined forces on the night of the 16th. . . .

Lord Fisher to Winston S. Churchill

(*Churchill papers: 13/56*)

15 March 1915   Admiralty

Dear Winston,

This is a copy[1] of what I handed to you on March 1st. I suggest your firing it off at the War Council as a whole & request the attendance of Lansdowne & Bonar Law as well as Balfour—a MEETING—TODAY! Delays now may have vital consequences. HOURS *now count* and the Opposition should be included in the making of *this* BIG DECISION!

Are we going on with Constantinople or are we not?

If NOT—then dont send half a dozen Battleships to the bottom which would be better applied at Cuxhaven or Borkum. If YES—then push the military co-operation with all speed & make the demonstration with all possible despatch at *both* extremities of the *Gallipoli Peninsula*—and telegraph at once for the Egyptian Transports to leave with all despatch.

Anyhow they are safer in Mudros protected by net defence than at Alexandria with it & subject also to being torpedoed en route when the Austrian submarines from the Adriatic arrive (WHICH THEY SURELY WILL! If not Germans also from England!) The German submarine off the coast of Spain was proved beyond doubt to my mind. Then we have Nos 51 and 52 *now on the scene.* these are the bigger ones! U34 *a big submarine* last night in the Channel from Heligoland may quite likely be en route to the Medn— Everything points to instant action by a collective vote & decision of the

[1] Julian Corbett's letter to Fisher of 1 March 1915 (quoted on pp. 604–5).

War Council with the Opposition joined in. *You fritter time interviewing in-dividuals!* How much more effective had the Admiralty plan been carried out of a Coast Advance than this costly frontal attack in France!)

F

Winston S. Churchill to Lord Fisher
(*Fisher papers*)

15 March 1915   Admiralty
Secret

My dear Fisher,

I don't think we want a War Council on this. It is after all only asking a lot of ignorant people to meddle in our business. I expect K will do what we want about the troops being concentrated at Mudros, if you & I see him together. But if not there is nothing for it but to wait for Hamilton's report wh shd reach us Wednesday. Meanwhile the naval operations are proceeding within safe & sure limits.

Yours ever
W

PS I am counting much on Hamilton

Sir Arthur Wilson to Winston S. Churchill

(*Churchill papers: 13/54*)

15 March 1915   Admiralty

First Lord,

It is impossible to foresee what form defence against submarines will take in the future, but it is hardly likely that ships can be made proof against torpedoes without at the same time greatly impairing their sea-going qualities, economy, and speed, so that merchant ships which would have to be used for transport and supply purposes would be greatly handicapped in their ordinary work if they had to carry out the necessary modifications.

Moreover, although bulges and additional watertight subdivisions might prevent a ship from being actually sunk by a torpedo, she would in any case be seriously damaged by the explosion, and would require docking before she could be considered again efficient.

I think some system of trapping by means of nets and explosive charges offers the best prospect of success as a means of destroying submarines, but it does not seem likely that any defensive measure likely to be devised in the near future will do more than slightly reduce the risk from submarine attack.

Of course the French submarines can equally interfere with our line of communication through the Mediterranean, but France alone cannot at the same time put an army on the Indian frontier.

Even if we could eliminate submarines altogether, the possession of Constantinople would still give a great strategic advantage to Russia.

Lieutenant-Colonel Hankey: diary

(*Hankey papers*)

15 March 1915

Spent almost whole day trying to devise for Churchill method of creating smoke blanket for covering sweeping operations in Dardanelles. Saw Lord Fisher in morning who showed me telegrams that minesweepers are losing heavily & unable to carry out operations owing to fire from light guns wh cannot be located.

Lieutenant-Colonel Hankey to Lord Esher

(*Copy: Hankey papers*)

15 March 1915

My dear Lord Esher,

. . . Although on general principles this operation is brilliantly conceived, and quite correct, I am not at all satisfied that it is being carried out in the best possible manner. Troops ought to have been there, or at any rate, within a day or two's reach, when the bombardment began. There ought to have been no blatant Press announcement at the outset, and the bombardment ought to have been announced merely as a demonstration. While the bombardment was commencing the transports ought to have appeared at some entirely different point of the Turkish Coast, such as Alexandretta, Haifa, or elsewhere. Then the troops ought to have come in as a bolt from the blue, immediately following the collapse of the outer forts, and closely supported by the Fleet, to have captured the plateau overlooking the forts of the Narrows by a coup-de-main. I urged this at the outset, but my suggestions fell on deaf ears. Now we have given the Turks time to assemble a vast force, to pour in field guns and howitzers, to entrench every landing place, and the operation has become a most formidable one. Please burn this.

Yours ever

M. P. A. Hankey

Lord Fisher to Sir John Jellicoe
(Jellicoe papers)

15 March 1915   Admiralty

. . . It was 'touch & go' yesterday whether I did not go off to Dardanelles this morning but it was decided otherwise. . . .[1]

I don't quite know who governs the country. There are a whole lot of Committees everywhere! . . .

Lord Fisher to Winston S. Churchill
(Churchill papers: 13/56)

16 March 1915   Admiralty
3. A.M.

Dear Winston,

'The advanced state of preparedness tomorrow morning' in Schillig Roads (where only 3 old German Battleships are absent) and von Pohl[2] 'longing to be at 'em' (with his 'plan of activity') finds no echo of expectancy in the British Admiralty! Since Jan. 24 we have been stagnant. Tyrwhitt's occupation (like Othello's) is gone! . . .

[1] At the Admiralty War Group on 14 March Fisher had offered to go out to the Dardanelles to take personal command of the Anglo-French naval forces. Churchill prevailed upon him to allow Vice-Admiral Carden to continue in his command.

[2] Hugo von Pohl, 1855–1916. Chief of the German Admiralty Staff, 1914–15. Commander-in-Chief of the German High Sea Fleet, 1915–16.

In the 'Forms of Prayer to be used at Sea' it is ordered in the last resort to pray. 'Let us pray'!

My original idea in getting Bartolomé (till you stole him!) was a brain of his calibre doing nothing else morning noon and night except imagining every inconceivable thing the enemy might do! and planning the counter stroke. Oliver certainly hasn't the time—he is buried in papers—he was 24 hours behind with your note on the submarine! and A.K.W. so d——d obstinate that it is only just now bursting on him that the submarine is not foolishness as he so lamentably thought as First Sea Lord (and Jellicoe writes to me stopped him building ——) followed by the fool Briggs!

Yours
F

Why should von Pohl make any signal when all his Fleet are collected round him—let us not trust in what has been previously our salvation! There's a 'time limit' to everything—even to stupidity! Let us imagine that von Pohl is wily! and makes no signals!

The decisive theatre remains and ever will be the North Sea—our attention is being distracted—Schleswig Holstein, the Baltic, Borkum are not living with us now!

Your big idea of 3 British armies in Holland in May obliterated by Bulair! and so to bed! (as Pepys would say!)

Vice-Admiral Carden to Winston S. Churchill: telegram
(Copy, Churchill papers: 13/65)

16 March 1915   HMS Queen Elizabeth
8.10 am

I will meet General Hamilton in consultation as soon as possible after he arrives. Your second[1] expresses my intentions exactly. Hope to commence operations, plans for which are practically complete on the 17th March but as good visibility and a wind which will prevent smoke interfering are essential, the start may have to be delayed. Meanwhile the area in which ships will have to manœuvre is being carefully searched for mines. As it was considered probable that the mines were attached to a jackstay across the Straits, picket boat on the night of 13th to 14th March towing explosives crept down the minefield and cut several cables; this has evidently caused a number of mines to trip their sinkers and drag to shallow water. Seaplanes at 2000 to 3000 feet have experimented in locating mines, these are clearly

---

[1] A reference to Churchill's telegram to Carden of 14 March 1915 (quoted on pp. 694–5).

visible at 18 ft depth and further trials are in progress. It is possible therefore that the shallow draft mines below the Narrows have been located which will facilitate the operations of sweeping. There is no intention to rush the passage without first clearing a channel.

Vice-Admiral Carden to Winston S. Churchill: telegram

(*Copy, Churchill papers: 13/65*)

16 March 1915
5.00 pm
Secret and Personal

Much regret obliged to go on the sick list.[1] Decision of Medical Officer[2] follows. De Robeck continues operations on lines indicated in Admiralty telegram 109 he is well in touch with all arrangements present and future and has been of greatest assistance in their preparation. I have fullest confidence in his judgment and determination.

Commodore Keyes is rendering all the assistance possible most valuable and energetic service. Hayes-Sadler[3] has always handled his division in action most ably suggest for consideration that he should be made Commodore under R. A. De Robeck.

Wemyss at Port Mudros is making all arrangements for military co-operation in a most satisfactory manner. He is prepared to act most loyally with De Robeck.[4]

[1] Carden was suffering from 'atonic indigestion' and was advised to be on the sick list for three or four weeks. He never returned to the Dardanelles or took up any further sea-going command.

[2] John Charles Rowan, 1869–1939. Qualified MB, Royal University of Ireland, 1893. Surgeon, African Steamship Company, 1894. Assistant Surgeon, Ebbw Vale Coal and Iron works, and Nantyglo & Blaina Collieries, 1895. Joined the Navy as a Surgeon, 1895; Fleet Surgeon, 1911. Retired, 1922, with the rank of Surgeon-Captain. Rowan's opinion was confirmed by two doctors from the hospital ship *Soudan*, Fleet Surgeon G. T. Collingwood, MVO, and Staff Surgeon J. K. Murphy, FRCS, MD, MA.

[3] Arthur Hayes-Sadler, 1863–1952. Entered Navy, 1877. Served as a Midshipman at the bombardment of Alexandria, 1882. Captain, 1904. Commanded HMS *Agamemnon* at the Dardanelles, 1915. Promoted Rear-Admiral, 19 July 1915; Vice-Admiral, 1919; Admiral, 1924.

[4] Wemyss, in command of the naval arrangements at Mudros, was senior to de Robeck, but agreed to serve under him as Second-in-Command. De Robeck was promoted Vice-Admiral, 17 March 1915.

H. H. Asquith to George V

(*Royal Archives*)

17 March 1915   10 Downing Street

... Mr Churchill reported that the bombardment of the Dardanelles was
being delayed by the difficulty of the sweeping operations, which are, however, becoming daily more effective. ...

Sir Arthur Paget to Lord Kitchener: telegram

(*Copy, Churchill papers: 26/4*)

17 March 1915   Sofia
Very Confidential

King of the Bulgarians received me in audience yesterday for more than
an hour. His Majesty's manner was most cordial and from conversation with
myself and later with Captain Glyn[1] I am convinced that operations in the
Dardanelles have made deep impression.

All possibility of Bulgaria attacking any Balkan state that might side with
the Entente is now over and there is some reason to think that shortly Bulgarian army will move against Turkey to co-operate in the Dardanelles
operations. No pains were spared to point out that unless Bulgaria moves
quickly and pledges herself to action now it may be too late. Present pro-
Austrian Ministry could not continue in office as a whole, should the King
decide to take action, and he is to see the Prime Minister to-day. Any
changes in the Government will be first intimation of definite action. Army
has been prepared and is ready, but could not be mobilised in less than
10 days. It is short of artillery ammunition, having not much more than 500
rounds per gun, and there is a large lack of horses.

From conversations I have had with many leading soldiers and Politicians,
fact of Greek inaction being Bulgaria's opportunity is fully understood. This
feeling grows stronger daily and when Bulgaria moves Roumania will at
once, either directly or through Italy, promise co-operation. In the circumstances I am convinced that no further bribing of this country at expense

---

[1] Ralph George Campbell Glyn, 1885–1960. Lieutenant, Rifle Brigade, 1904. Secretary
Unionist Reorganization Committee, 1911. Employed at the War Office, 1912–14. Captain,
on Missions to Serbia and Bulgaria, 1914–15. Liaison Intelligence Officer between the War
Office and GHQ France, May–August 1915. Served Gallipoli and Salonika, 1915–16;
France, 1917–18. Major, 1918. Conservative MP, 1918–22; 1924–53. Joint Parliamentary
Private Secretary to Ramsay MacDonald, 1931–7. Created Baronet, 1934. Created Baron
Glyn of Farnborough, 1953.

of Serbia is necessary, and in the past this policy has undoubtedly produced an impression of weakness. Since Bulgaria's action must through force of circumstances be confined to operations against Turkey all fear of her co-operating in main theatre, and thereby causing discord with both Roumania and Serbia, is at an end. All future excuses on account of the fear of Bulgarian action by either Roumania or Greece are now poor pretexts. Action by all in our favour is essential for them without any question of conditions being raised.

Secret

Bulgaria, while unable herself to operate in main theatre, would be prepared to assist in passage of troops of an Entente Power to main theatre. Such action in the opinion of many here would have as great an effect as taking of the Dardanelles, which would be considered as a necessary preliminary. Greek jealousy of Bulgaria must be reckoned with as smallest regrettable incident might assume alarming proportions. The presence of British troops to operate on left flank of Roumanians and so stiffen that army as Russian's left wing, would also produce a very calming effect on Balkans, through rendering possibility of trouble at a difficult moment most remote.

Unless Entente suffers a reverse, I shall be much surprised if Bulgaria does not give her assurances of co-operation within next fortnight.

Vice-Admiral de Robeck to Winston S. Churchill: telegram

(*Copy, Churchill papers: 13/65*)

17 March 1915
8.00 am

Good aerial record of minefields today 16th. Sweeps and picket boats with explosive creeps made good progress last night and destroyed several mines which operations on the night of 13th had displaced. Thorough search of area in which ships will operate proceeding tonight. Admiral Wemyss is arranging for General Hamilton and D'Amade to meet me at Tenedos evening of 17th. Weather permitting plan of attack arranged by Admiral Carden and approved in your 109 will be commenced 18th.

Winston S. Churchill to Vice-Admiral de Robeck: telegram

(*Copy, Churchill papers: 13/65*)

17 March 1915   Admiralty
Personal and Secret

In entrusting to you with great confidence the command of the Mediterranean Detached Fleet I presume you are in full accord with Admiralty
telegram 101 and Admiralty telegram 109 and Vice Admiral Carden's
answers thereto; and that you consider after separate and independent
judgment that the immediate operations proposed are wise and practicable.
If not, do not hesitate to say so. If so, execute them without delay and without further reference at the first favourable opportunity. Report fully from
day to day. Work in closest harmony with General Hamilton. Make any
proposals you think fit for the subordinate commands. Wemyss is your
second in command. All good fortune attend you.

Vice-Admiral de Robeck to Admiralty: telegram

(*Copy, Churchill papers: 13/65*)

18 March 1915
2.10 am

I have met and discussed the situation with General Hamilton and
D'Amade and Admiral Wemyss but pending results of our attack on the
Narrows no joint Naval and Military action can be decided on. General
Hamilton is making a personal reconnaissance of the North coast of Gallipoli
tomorrow 18th and later will view the South shore inside Dardanelles from
a battleship. Admiral Wemyss will be in charge of the Naval arrangements
in connection with the Military operations and in the event of my entering
the Sea of Marmora he will be in command of the ships that remain behind.
I suggest Captain Hayes Sadler be appointed Commodore for charge of the
older battleships.

Vice-Admiral de Robeck to Winston S. Churchill: telegram

(*Copy, Churchill papers: 13/65*)

18 March 1915   HMS Queen Elizabeth
10.20 am
Secret and Personal

Thank you for your telegram. I am in full agreement with telegrams
mentioned. Operations will proceed tomorrow weather permitting. My

view is that everything depends on our ability to clear the minefields for forcing the Narrows and this necessitates silencing the forts during the process of sweeping. Generals Hamilton and D'Amade and Admiral Wemyss have been on board today and interview entirely satisfactory.

H. H. Asquith to Venetia Stanley
(*Montagu papers*)

18 March 1915   10 Downing Street

. . . . K. also showed me a very interesting telegram from Ian Hamilton who got to the Dardanelles on Tues. night. The Admiralty have been very over-sanguine as to what they cd. do by ships alone. Every night the Turks under German direction repair their fortifications: both coasts bristle with howitzers & field guns (outside the forts) in concealed emplacements; and the channel is sown with complicated & constantly renewed minefields. The French General D'Amade (a good man who won fame in Morocco) arrived at the same time as IH: and together they are going to make a really thorough & I hope scientific survey of the whole situation. Carden (our Admiral) has fallen sick & gone back to Malta: perhaps a good thing, as de Robeck his successor is supposed to be a much better man. . . .

Lord Hardinge to Lord Crewe
(*Crewe papers*)

18 March 1915   Viceregal Lodge
                                                          Delhi

. . . The situation in Persia is undoubtedly serious[1] . . . that is why I am particularly anxious to hear of an early success in the Dardanelles, for I believe that the capture of the Dardanelles and the impending fall of Constantinople will have a strong effect in Persia and Afghanistan, and on the Mahomedans of this country. . . .

[1] Persia declared its neutrality in July 1914. But German influence worked continually against Britain. Between March and August 1915 the Germans prevailed upon the Persians to expel all British subjects from Kermanshah, Isfahan, Yezd and Kerman, leaving Britain in control only of the Persian Gulf. By the end of 1915 seven out of the seventeen branches of the British-owned Imperial Bank of Persia were under German control. But during 1916 the Russians began to counter German pressure in the north, while a British force under Sir Percy Cox began to restore British control over southern Persia.

Vice-Admiral de Robeck to Admiralty: telegram
(Copy, Churchill papers: 13/65)

19 March 1915   HMS Queen Elizabeth
9.00 am and noon

Attack on defences at Narrows commenced 10.45 a.m. QUEEN ELIZABETH INFLEXIBLE AGAMEMNON LORD NELSON first bombarded Forts 13 16 17 19 20. TRIUMPH PRINCE GEORGE fired at Batteries 7 8 and 8a. Heavy fire was opened on ships from howitzers and field guns. 12.22 p.m. SUFFREN GAULOIS CHARLEMAGNE BOUVET advanced up Dardanelles engaged forts at closer range. Forts 13 19 7 8 opened heavy fire. This was silenced by the ten Battleships inside the Straits, during this period all ships were hit several times. By 1.25 p.m. forts had ceased firing. VENGEANCE IRRESISTIBLE ALBION OCEAN SWIFTSURE and MAJESTIC were ordered to relieve the six old Battleships inside Straits. As the French Squadron were passing out BOUVET 1.54 p.m. was seen to be in distress large volume black smoke suddenly appeared on starboard quarter and before any assistance could be rendered she heeled over and sank in 36 fathoms North of Arenkiei village in under three minutes. Explosion BOUVET appeared to be an internal one 2.25 p.m. relief Battleships were passing up and 2.36 p.m. they were engaging forts who again opened fire. Attack on forts continued and Mine Sweepers were ordered in. 4.9 p.m. IRRESISTIBLE was seen to have a list to starboard. 4.14 p.m. INFLEXIBLE quitted the line and reported having struck a mine on the starboard side, she proceeded out of Dardanelles and is now at Tenedos. At 4.30 p.m. IRRESISTIBLE was listing heavily. H.M.S. WEAR alongside to take off her crew who were transferred to QUEEN ELIZABETH. At 5.50 ship was abandoned being under hot fire and sinking. She probably struck a mine manœuvring astern whilst engaging fort 8 both Engine Rooms being immediately flooded. At 6.5 OCEAN who had been covering rescue of IRRESISTIBLE also struck a mine. She took a heavy list and was abandoned when it was obvious she could not remain afloat both vessels sunk in deep water. R. A. Guépratte at 5.15 reported GAULOIS leaking badly her condition serious. She has had to be beached on Drepano Island—bows badly damaged by gunfire. . . .

All ships were manœuvred in area well below reported mine field. Mine Sweepers had swept area on several occasions and reported it clear and Seaplanes had not located any mines in it.[1]

[1] Twenty mines had been laid in Eren Keui Bay on the night of March 17, after the final British seaplane reconnaissance, by the Turkish ship *Nusret*. This was an area used—as the Turks had seen—by the allied ships after they had finishing firing and were leaving the Straits.

It therefore appears damage inflicted was due to drifting mines.

With the exception of ships lost and damaged Squadron is ready for immediate action but the plan of attack must be re-considered and means found to deal with floating mines many of which appear to be given whitened buoys and then attached to float; those floating are easily dealt with by picket boats. I much regret the heavy casualties in personnel and material. Only a few saved from BOUVET; practically whole crew OCEAN and IRRESISTIBLE were taken off by Destroyers under a heavy fire: much gallantry and fine seamanship was displayed by all Officers and men concerned.

Casualties not yet received.[1]

INFLEXIBLE sustained some being struck by a shell in the foretop. All times are local.[2]

John Churchill: diary

(*Copy, Churchill papers: 28/139*)

19 March 1915   Lemnos

. . . In England we considered, on the information given by Admiral Carden, that a 'rush' was possible. That the straits could be forced by the fleet perhaps without troops and that the battle for Constantinople might be fought a long way North of the Gallipoli peninsula. It is now certain that the fleet cannot get through without co-operation on land. A battle— probably a big one, will have to be fought to capture Bulair, and operations will have to be postponed until troops arrive and the force is properly organized. A base must be established as soon as possible. This island is no good. There is no water and no landing facilities. It seems probable we shall return to Alexandria from there commence what may well be an arduous campaign. Carden's telegrams are inexplicable. All the stories of forts being silenced are greatly exaggerated. Cape Helles and Kum Kale have been knocked out, but the enemy have mobile guns, and we were shelled yesterday at the very entrance to the Straits. Our mine sweepers are not strong enough and are too few. It is no good bombarding on Monday and then doing it again on Thursday. Every advantage must be made and maintained of each bombardment by troops on shore. The General has wired home and has presented the facts. We shall await an answer. I cannot believe that we shall turn from the difficulties now. . . .

[1] Six hundred sailors from the *Bouvet* were killed. There were fifty British deaths; thirty-three on *Inflexible*, fourteen on *Irresistible*, and one each on *Albion*, *Majestic* and *Ocean*.

[2] For a map of the naval attack of 18 March 1915, see map 7 on page 1598.

Sir Ian Hamilton to Lord Kitchener: telegram

(Copy, Hamilton papers)

19 March 1915   HMS Franconia

I am being most reluctantly driven to the conclusion that the Straits are not likely to be forced by battleships as at one time seemed probable and that, if my troops are to take part, it will not take the subsidiary form anticipated. The Army's part will be more than mere landings of parties to destroy Forts, it must be a deliberate and progressive military operation carried out at full strength so as to open a passage for the Navy.

Meeting of the War Council: extract from Secretary's notes

(Copy, Cabinet Office papers: 22/1)

Present: H. H. Asquith (in the Chair), Lord Haldane, Lord Crewe, Lewis Harcourt, Reginald McKenna, Winston S. Churchill, Lord Fisher, Sir Arthur Wilson, David Lloyd George, Sir Edward Grey, A. J. Balfour, Lord Kitchener, Sir James Wolfe Murray, Lieutenant-Colonel Hankey (Secretary)

19 March 1915   10 Downing Street

PROGRESS IN THE DARDANELLES

MR. CHURCHILL read a series of telegrams from Admiral Carden and Admiral de Robeck on the subject of the progress in the Dardanelles. The substances of this is contained in the press communiqué published in the morning papers of the 20th March. The most serious feature of these telegrams was the sinking of the 'Irresistible', 'Ocean', and 'Bouvet', the running ashore of the 'Gaulois', and the disablement of the 'Inflexible'. He also mentioned that the XXIXth Division was due to arrive at Alexandria on the 2nd April.

MR. LLOYD GEORGE asked if any success had been achieved to counterbalance the losses.

SIR ARTHUR WILSON said, so far as could be gathered from the telegrams, the forts had only been temporarily silenced.

MR. CHURCHILL said it would be impossible to form an opinion till further reports had been received. He said that, if the War Council agreed, he would instruct the Admiral to use his discretion in continuing the operations.

LORD KITCHENER read several telegrams he had received from Sir Ian Hamilton. He had arrived on the 18th March and at once held a conference on board the 'Queen Elizabeth' with the Admiral and with General d'Amade, the French general. He had also inspected the outer side of the Gallipoli Peninsula. He reported that large numbers of field guns and howitzers were available for the defence and that all the arrangements for defence appeared to have been made with German thoroughness. He said that Lemnos was not convenient as an advanced base. At the present moment there were at Lemnos a naval division, French division, and an Australian brigade. These troops had been embarked purely for transport purposes and would require a good deal of rearrangement before they could be disembarked for operations ashore. This could be more rapidly achieved by sending them to Egypt, where full facilities were available. He therefore proposed to send the British forces to Alexandria and the French to Port Said. A telegram on similar lines from General Maxwell in Egypt was read.

MR. CHURCHILL said we had information that the Turks were short of ammunition and mines.

THE PRIME MINISTER said there had been some rather ambiguous telegrams from Roumania and Bulgaria, which seemed to suggest that ammunition might have been smuggled through these countries from Germany.

SIR EDWARD GREY considered that this was not improbable. One always had to remember the possibility of the bribery of officials in these Balkan States.

(*Conclusion.*)
The First Lord was authorized to inform the Admiral that he could continue the operations against the Dardanelles if he thought fit.

ITALY

THE PRIME MINISTER read a telegram from the British Ambassador at Petrograd. The sense of this was that the French Ambassador had paid a visit to the Grand Duke's headquarters, and had been presented at a Conference attended also by the Emperor of Russia, the Grand Duke, and the Chief of Staff. The Emperor had expressed the view that, owing to the improvement in the situation in the last fortnight, the Russians ought soon to be in a position to take the offensive in the Carpathians and in Silesia. The Chief of Staff, however, had said that in his opinion the resumption of the offensive against Germany would have to be postponed for two or three months owing to the lack of ammunition and rifles, and the superiority of the German railways, which could move 450 trains a day to the frontier as compared with the Russian 90. The Grand Duke had laid great stress on the co-operation of Italy and Roumania, which he said was essential to the Russian offensive. The French Ambassador had been rather depressed by this discussion.

LORD KITCHENER said that the Emperor and the Chief of Staff had, in his opinion, been too optimistic. He fully agreed with the Grand Duke on the subject of Italian co-operation.

SIR EDWARD GREY said that he had proposed to our Allies to reply to the Italian Ambassador in the sense that their proposals were generally acceptable, except that their demands in regard to Dalmatia were rather too sweeping and did not give much chance to Serbia. He had already informed Italy that their proposals were generally regarded favourably.

LORD CREWE suggested that if the Grand Duke was so anxious to bring in Roumania, Russia ought to cede Bessarabia.

LORD KITCHENER said that for the first time the Italian military attaché had called on him, and had made representations for expediting the delivery of certain machine-guns on order at Messrs. Vickers. He had replied that he would see they received them, if they intended to use them. The military attaché had replied that, speaking unofficially, he felt sure that was the intention.

SIR EDWARD GREY said that, if no disaster occurred to Russia, and if Italy joined the Allies, it ought to be the beginning of the end.

LORD KITCHENER said it was very important that the date should be fixed as soon as possible. A good deal of time would be required for con-certing plans. We could not possibly discuss plans unless we had an absolute assurance that Italy would fight, as we might give away information.

(At this point there was some discussion of Italy's terms, and Sir Edward Grey explained them on a map. He added that they could hardly expect to receive them in full, but they might use the fact of their not getting them to wriggle out, if they thought the war was going badly for us.)

EFFECT OF THE DARDANELLES OPERATIONS

MR. BALFOUR suggested that the set-back in the Dardanelles would probably put back all these arrangements.

THE PRIME MINISTER said that it depended on the general results of the engagement, which were not yet known.

LORD FISHER said that it was impossible to explain away the sinking of four battleships. He had always said that a loss of twelve battleships must be expected before the Dardanelles could be forced by the navy alone. He still adhered to this view.

LORD KITCHENER said that a good deal depended upon whether the bombardment was continued.

MR. LLOYD GEORGE said he had told the Bulgarian Minister in the course of conversation that we expected to lose ships before getting through.

MR. McKENNA asked if the land forces would not be able to clear a passage.

MR. BALFOUR said he had heard Sir Ian Hamilton's telegrams with some misgiving.

LORD KITCHENER said that he had given Sir Ian Hamilton as many men as he could use on the ground.

THE PRIME MINISTER asked if Lord Kitchener approved the proposed change of base to Alexandria.

LORD KITCHENER replied in the affirmative.

THE PRIME MINISTER asked if any general plan and scheme of disembarkation had been worked out.

LORD KITCHENER said that the question had been examined in the War Office, but that they had not sufficient information to form a detailed scheme of disembarkation. This would have to be done by Sir Ian Hamilton and his Staff in concert with the Naval Commander-in-Chief.

THE PARTITION OF TURKEY IN ASIA

THE PRIME MINISTER said that the French Ambassador in Petrograd had laid claim to a very large part of Turkey in Asia as French desiderata in return for permitting a Russian occupation of Constantinople and the Straits. These desiderata included Cilicia, Syria, and Palestine. The Russians objected most strongly to the Christian Holy Places being in French hands.

SIR EDWARD GREY said that we had to make up our mind first on two great questions of principle:—

1. If we acquire fresh territory shall we make ourselves weaker or stronger?
2. Ought we not to take into account the very strong feeling in the Moslem world that Mohammedanism ought to have a political as well as a religious existence?

If the latter question were answered in the affirmative, Arabia, Syria, and Mesopotamia were the only possible territories for an Arab Empire. If we took this standpoint we could say to our Moslem subjects that, as Turkey had handed itself over to the Germans, we had set up a new and independent Moslem State.

LORD CREWE said that two different views were taken in the India Office. The Military Department, who were in general agreement with the Viceroy of India, considered that Turkey in Asia ought to be made as strong as possible. The Political Department, on the other hand, thought that Turkey should be sacrificed and Arabia made as strong as possible.

LORD KITCHENER objected to the Military Department's plan. The Turks, he said, would always be under pressure from their strong Russian neighbour, with the result that the Khalifate might be to a great extent under Russian domination, and Russian influence might indirectly assert itself over the Mohammedan part of the population of India. If, on the other hand, the Khalifate were transferred to Arabia, it would remain to a great extent under our influence.

LORD CREWE agreed with Lord Kitchener.

THE PRIME MINISTER read an extract from a memorandum by Sir Theodore Morison,[1] in which he stated the apprehension of some leading Moslems that they would become like the Jews—a people having a religion, but no country—and in which he expressed a hope that the Khalifate would obtain Syria and Mesopotamia.

LORD KITCHENER said that, if Mesopotamia was to be left undeveloped, it was all very well to leave it to the Arabs. But, if it was to be developed, we should only be creating trouble for ourselves by leaving to it them.

LORD HALDANE said there were two great questions of principle governing these questions:—

1. Whether we wished to acquire more territory at all.

2. Whether we intended to leave the Germans and Turks crushed up at the end of the war. In the interests of a lasting peace, he urged that this should not be aimed at. Napoleon had failed in the attempt to crush nations, and since 1870 Germany had failed to crush the nationality out of Alsace and Lorraine. All experience showed that a permanent peace could not be obtained except by general consent.

---

[1] Theodore Morison, 1863–1936. Writer on Indian subjects. Principal, Mohammedan College of Aligarh, 1899–1905. An additional member of Curzon's Legislative Council, India, 1903–4. Member of Council of India, London 1906–16. Knighted, 1910. Member of the Royal Commission on the Public Services of India, 1913–15. Political Staff, East African Force, 1916–18. Lieutenant-Colonel, War Office, 1918. Principal, Armstrong College, Newcastle-upon-Tyne, 1919–29.

MR. BALFOUR suggested that there was no comparison between our proposals and the Napoleonic plan of crushing nations. In Europe, he understood, there was a general consensus that divisions of territory should be by nationality. But in Asia we had to deal with countries which had been misgoverned by the Turks.

LORD KITCHENER said that India would expect some return for her effort and losses in Mesopotamia.

LORD CREWE said that all shades of opinion in the India Office agreed that the Basra Vilayet must form part of the British Empire. Some, however, thought that we ought to be content with a protectorate over the Baghdad Vilayet, which would be in a position somewhat similar to the Soudan.

LORD KITCHENER asked what object was to be gained by raising such difficulties for the future?

MR. CHURCHILL said that in this question of the partition of Turkey in Asia the main difficulty was likely to be between England and France, leaving out the question of the Christian Holy Places, in which Russia also was concerned. He suggested that the best plan would be to postpone our conversations with France on the subject. Consideration of the question was really premature. We should say to France outright that we had not made up our mind. We had been obliged to settle with Russia, because the question was urgent, but there was not the same urgency with France. Either France and we ourselves should both agree to a self-denying policy in regard to the acquisition of territory, or we should discuss the matter in detail, which would at present be inconvenient.

LORD CREWE said he would have preferred to postpone the whole question, if Russia had not suggested that we should formulate our desiderata.

SIR EDWARD GREY said that at present it was a question of making up our own mind, and not of discussing the matter with France.

MR. LLOYD GEORGE said that the Lord Chancellor's idea made the same appeal to him. We ought not to rule out the possibility of giving Germany a bone of some sort. She would always be a very powerful nation, and it might eventually even be desirable to have her in a position to prevent Russia becoming too predominant.

LORD CREWE agreed, but said it would be very dangerous to put the Germans back on the Baghdad Railway.

MR. CHURCHILL said that the whole question depended on whether we intended to divide Turkey. Surely, he suggested, we did not intend to leave this inefficient and out-of-date nation, which had long misruled one of the most fertile countries the world, still in possession! Turkey had long shown herself to be inefficient as a governing Power, and it was time for us to make a clean sweep.

THE PRIME MINISTER said that he had great sympathy with Sir Edward Grey's first proposition that we have already as much territory as we are able to hold, but the fact was we were not free agents. Russia intended to take a good slice of Turkey. France, Italy, and Greece each demanded a piece. If, for one reason or another, because we didn't want more territory, or because we didn't feel equal to the responsibility, we were to leave the other nations to scramble for Turkey without taking anything ourselves, we should not be doing our duty.

MR. McKENNA suggested that, in the meantime, we should put forward a suggestion that none of us take anything.

SIR EDWARD GREY suggested that our reply about our desiderata should be, in the sense, that our first requirement was the preservation of a Moslem political entity, and that we are pledged to the maintenance of the Moslem Holy Places. The first thing we had to consider was as to what that entity should include. We might base our first reply by taking up this line.

LORD CREWE said that we must have a political capital for the Mohammedan State, and that this could not be at Mecca, as no one except Mohammedans could go there.

Conclusion.

A reply to be sent to Petrograd in the sense proposed by Sir Edward Grey, viz., that, after the Straits had been forced, and Constantinople had passed into the hands of the Allies, our first desideratum would be the establishment of a Moslem entity. It would have to include Arabia, and the question would arise as to what was to go with it. In the meantime, it would be premature to discuss the partition of Turkey.

Lieutenant-Colonel Hankey to David Lloyd George
(*Lloyd George papers*)

19 March 1915

Dear Mr Lloyd George,

I have written to the Prime Minister urging the appointment of a joint Committee to work out the attack on the Dardanelles in detail, to estimate how many men, how many years, how much time, how many boats, how many pills, how much food and drink, how much transport &c are required and how they are to be got ashore and where.

Whether your more ambitious plan can be brought off or not we shall have to attack the Dardanelles, and we cannot afford another fiasco due to inadequate staff preparation.

I hope you will back me up in this if you get a chance. We don't want Lord K. and the First Lord on the Ctee but just technical people. They can overhaul the Report afterwards, but have no time for the detail. Mr Balfour would be a good chairman.

Yours very sincerely
M P A Hankey

P.S. The plan this time must be worked out with the precision of our War Book.[1]

MPAH

Lord Fisher to Winston S. Churchill

(*Churchill papers: 13/56*)

20 March 1915   Admiralty

Dear Winston,

I count up 28 Destroyers & Torpedo boats at Dardanelles and in view of the very narrow entrance of the Dardanelles and restricted area of operations this is infinitely a bigger proportion than we have at home—but all the same we ought to press the French to send more Destroyers and more light cruisers. It's ridiculous what little the French do! and what good their keeping a force on the Syrian Coast? I have only one anxiety the German and Austrian submarines—*when they appear the game will be up*! That's why I wish to press on the military co-operation and get a base at Cape Helles anyhow. It will be 3 weeks before the military can do anything according to present arrangements.

Yours
F

I forgot to suggest to you last night to agree to d'Eyncourt's proposal to order some more fast Fleet Sweepers which can be finished in 4 to 5 months

---

1 The 'War Book' had been drawn up before in the Committee of Imperial Defence in 1914, and contained the details of action to be taken by all Government Departments on the outbreak of war with Germany. Its efficient working in August 1914 had done much to enhance Hankey's reputation as an organizer and planner.

—to relieve strain on Destroyers for convoy duties and aid in hunting submarines.

Dardanelles   16 English Destroyers
                    6 Torpedo boats
                    6 French Destroyers
                   ——
                    28

Winston S. Churchill to Lord Fisher

(*Fisher papers*)

20 March 1915   Admiralty

My dear Fisher,

I do not think you have any need to be anxious about our strength at home. Nothing has changed since you & A.K.W. were anxious that a 13.5 ship shd go to D'Iles—except that the Warspite is nearly ready: & will be ready before the German fleet concentrates again.

Irresistible has hardly lost anybody. I doubt if all told we have 150 casualties.

Remember we cannot man the monitors & the new ships without laying up most of the old battleships. As long as the crews are saved there is no cause for serious regret.

You & A.K.W. were splendid yesterday.

This is a vy hard war to win.

Yours always
W

Admiralty to Vice-Admiral de Robeck: telegram

(*Copy, Churchill papers: 13/65*)

20 March 1915

We regret the losses you have suffered in your resolute attack. Convey to all ranks and ratings Their Lordships' approbation of their conduct in action and seamanlike skill and prudence with which His Majesty's ships were handled. Convey to the French squadron the Admiralty's appreciation of their loyal and effective support, and our sorrow for the losses they have sustained.

QUEEN and IMPLACABLE should join you very soon; and LONDON and PRINCE OF WALES sail to-night.

Please telegraph any information as to damage done to forts, and also full casualties and ammunition expended.

It appears important not to let the forts be repaired or to encourage enemy by an apparent suspension of the operations. Ample supplies of 15" ammunition are available for indirect fire of QUEEN ELIZABETH across the peninsula.

Lord Esher: diary

(Esher papers)

20 March 1915

. . . General Kaulbars[1] is at G.H.Q.; he says that the Russians do not wish the Balkan States to come in; he thinks that they will be more trouble than their military value warrants. Russia will be quite satisfied if the end of the War yields them Constantinople.

Winston is very excited and 'jumpy' about the Dardanelles; he says he will be ruined if the attack fails.

Sir Ian Hamilton to Vice-Admiral de Robeck: telegram

(Copy, Churchill papers: 13/65)

20 March 1915   Lemnos

From every point of view consider change of military to Alexandria and Port Said advisable. I can bring you military help from there quickly and in better shape than from here where there are no facilities. Propose therefore to transfer base and troops to Alexandria and Port Said, leaving 4000 Australian infantry at Lemnos at your disposal. I hope that you will agree. Presume you wish to retain marines now in Cawdor Castle and Braemar Castle at Tenedos otherwise they might accompany remainder of Naval Division to Port Said.

Vice-Admiral de Robeck to Sir Ian Hamilton: telegram

(Copy, Churchill papers: 13/65)

20 March 1915

As a military measure I concur with your proposal to make Egypt the head quarters, but submit political result of withdrawl of troops from

---

[1] Baron Nikolai Vassilievich Kaulbars, 1844–   . Commanded the 3rd Manchurian Army at the Battle of Mukden, 1905. Commander-in-Chief of the Odessa Military District.

Mudros at the moment requires the gravest consideration. If Governments of Balkan States take it to mean failure or abandonment of attack on the Dardanelles result might be far reaching. To prevent wrong interpretation being placed on the movements of the troops I suggest their departure be delayed until our attack is renewed in a few days time. Meantime feint of landing on a large scale on several points of the coast of Gallipoli might tend to draw off field guns from the general action when they are likely to seriously hamper our sweeping operations.

Vice-Admiral de Robeck to Admiralty: telegram
(*Copy, Churchill papers: 13/65*)

21 March 1915

The firing of the fleet appears very accurate but it is difficult to estimate actual damage sustained by the forts, seaplanes which were over Chanak during 18th could not report with certainty whether any guns were actually damaged. The forts will be reconnoitred again at earliest opportunity. For 'Queen Elizabeth' to fire by indirect laying from Gabatepe it is essential she should have a seaplane up to spot. Strong southerly gales and low visibility have prevented flying since 18th. It is hoped to continue this form of attack directly weather moderates. From experience gained on 18th I consider Forts at the Narrows and the batteries guarding mine fields can be dominated after a few days engagement sufficient to enable minesweepers to clear Kephez mine fields. Howitzer and field gun fire must be faced as it is impossible for the ships to deal with it. Our first consideration must be organizing strong military mine sweeping force with which to clear first the area in which squadron will manœuvre to cover the minesweepers operating in the Kephez mine fields. Until preparations for this thoroughly completed I do not propose engaging the forts by direct attack. Following telegrams were exchanged between General Hamilton and myself 20th March.[1] I will confer with General Hamilton as soon as possible.

[1] The preceding two telegrams.

Winston S. Churchill to Vice-Admiral de Robeck

(*Copy, Churchill papers*)

21 March 1915

It appears that several war correspondents have established themselves at Dardanelles; amongst them Ward Price[1] and Stevens.[2] Their accounts, for the most part, have been discreet and loyal, but it is necessary to establish at once an effective censorship, and every communication, either by letter or telegram, should be censored. A suitable officer for censor would be Major the Hon G. Peel,[3] who is now acting as Provost Marshal, RND; but if he is not available you can choose another. As a general rule no objection is seen to descriptive accounts of matters necessarily known to the enemy, but details of damage to ships and descriptions of mine-sweeping operations &c, and future plans are being sent freely by telegram now, and can be freely read en route. Such communications must be strictly censored. Every person permitted to telegraph as a correspondent must be definitely recognised and regulated. Fleet should not be approached by any unauthorised person. Tenedos is conquered Turkish territory, and you have full powers over it and should exercise your authority.

General Hamilton's views should be ascertained.

Correspondents of good standing can be of considerable use if handled by good officers. Three correspondents and a photographer to represent the whole press are being sent out from England, and if convenient may be accommodated on board. Military zone must be cleared of all unauthorised correspondents on their arrival. Individual cases, if hardship is involved, might perhaps be considered.

Complete control over the cables should be established forthwith, and traffic of small boats may be regulated in any way you may think suitable.

These matters can quite well be dealt with by some competent staff officer, who, in case of difficulty, should apply to Admiralty. Do not bother yourself too much with them.

[1] George Ward Price, 1886–1961. *Daily Mail* War Correspondent with the Turkish Army during the 1st Balkan War, 1912. Paris Correspondent of the *Daily Mail*, 1912–14. Representative of the Newspaper Proprietors Association at Gallipoli, 1915; Salonika, 1916; and on the Italian front, 1917–18. *Daily Mail* Foreign Correspondent, 1918–39. Director of Associated Newspapers from 1926 until his death. Present when Hitler entered Vienna, and when German troops entered the Sudetenland, 1938. *Daily Mail* War Correspondent, North African Campaign, 1942, and in Korea, 1950.

[2] G. T. Stevens, War Correspondent of the *Daily Telegraph*, Gallipoli, Salonika and Serbia.

[3] Arthur George Villiers Peel, 1868–1956. 2nd son of the 1st Viscount Peel, and grandson of Sir Robert Peel. Temporary Major, Royal Marines, 1915. Provost-Marshal, Royal Naval Division, Gallipoli, 1915. Head of the War Trade Department, Egypt, 1917. Conservative MP, 1917–18. Author of several works on economics and tariff reform.

John Churchill: diary
(*Copy, Churchill papers: 28/139*)

21 March 1915   Lemnos

Birdwood turned up at last and I expect we shall soon be off to Alexandria. De Robeck does not approve of our going away, but I do not see how we can land here. It would take a very long time, probably over a fortnight to land. There are no facilities. And the re-embarkment would take longer. We must go back and get everything properly organized. All idea of rushing the Peninsula must be abandoned. There is a plan of making a double landing near the southern end of the promontory, under cover of the guns of the fleet. . . .

H. H. Asquith to Venetia Stanley
(*Montagu papers*)

21 March 1915   Walmer Castle

. . . The Assyrian . . . is a good deal exercised by the hypnotic ascendency wh. he thinks A.J.B is gaining over Ll.G. as well as Winston. He regards A.J.B. as secretly but genuinely hostile to me, and as a dangerous confidant, when these impulsive rhetoricians pour all their grievances against K. & the rest of their colleagues into his ears. Winston it appears has even gone so far as to suggest (not to me) that he A.J.B. shd be put in charge of the Foreign Office when Grey goes next week for his fishing holiday!

Winston S. Churchill to Vice-Admiral de Robeck
(*Copy, Churchill papers: 2/88*)

22 March 1915   Admiralty

Secret and Personal. Reports from various sources as to alleged transit of German artillerymen, arms, and ammunition through Roumania to strengthen the Dardanelles, and any rumours as to appearances of submarines in the Mediterranean or Adriatic, are being transmitted to you as a matter of routine. It should, however, be understood that this information is merely passed on by the Admiralty, and that reports of this nature are frequently discovered later to be unreliable. It is asserted by the Roumanian Government that all possible steps have been effective. Similar assurances have been given by the Bulgarian Government, and it is not improbable that their assurances are true as they may possible feel it incumbent on them to occupy the Enos-Midia line.

Submarines—It is known that the German Government on the 12th instant had serious intention of sending a German or Austrian vessel. It would appear from this nearly certain that nothing had left Germany before the 12th. There is no later information to the effect that the difficulties which have long stood in the way of sending submarines have been removed, except yesterday's report from the Consul at Corfu.[1] No possible precaution, however, should be omitted.

Turkish Ammunition—It is known that the forts on the 12th instant were short, and that steps were being taken to obtain replenishments from Germany. It is not considered that these steps have as yet been successful. Is any estimate possible of the amount of ammunition expended by the forts in the recent operations?

Vice-Admiral de Robeck to Admiralty: telegram
(Copy, Churchill papers: 13/65)

23 March 1915   HMS. Queen Elizabeth
5.35 am

At meeting to-day with Generals Hamilton and Birdwood the former told me army will not be in a position to undertake any military operations before 14th April. In order to maintain our communication when the Fleet penetrates into the Sea of Marmora it is necessary to destroy all guns of positions guarding the Straits. These are numerous and only small percentage can be rendered useless by gun fire. The landing of demolishing party on the 26th February evidently surprised enemy. From our experience on the 4th March it seems in future destruction of guns will have to be carried out in face of strenuous and well prepared opposition. I do not think it a practicable operation to land a force adequate to undertake this service inside Dardanelles. General Hamilton concurs in this opinion. If the guns are not destroyed any success of Fleet may be nullified by the Straits closing up after the ships have passed through and, as loss of material will possibly be heavy, ships may not be available to keep Dardanelles open.

[1] George Raymond, 1852–1930. Consul for the Ionian Islands, residing in Corfu 1907–24.

The mine menace will continue until the Sea of Marmora is reached being much greater than was anticipated. It must be carefully and thoroughly dealt with both as regards mines and from floating mines. This will take time to accomplish but our arrangements will be ready by the time Army can act. It appears better to prepare a decisive effort about the middle of April rather than risk a great deal for what may possibly be only a partial solution.

Winston S. Churchill to Vice-Admiral de Robeck: telegram, not sent[1]
(Draft, Churchill papers: 13/53)

23 March 1915   Admiralty

Your 818[2] involves abandonment of the original plan for naval forcing of Dardanelles and apparently requires employment of the whole military force available wh cannot be ready before Ap. 14. The danger of submarines arriving in the interval is serious, & might be fatal to the whole operation. But if the delay were faced and if the whole army were available on Ap. 14 the storming of the Kilid Bahr plateau by the army supported by the fire of the Fleet wd seem to be the right & obvious step. The gate of the Narrows wd be opened & kept open by an army holding the Kilid Bahr plateau. The forts on the European side of the Narrows wd be captured those on the asiatic side wd be dominated. From all the information at our disposal here it seems that this costly operation by the army would if successful be decisive. And there wd be no need for the Fleet to be risked, nor for landing operations from inside the Straits—except of a minor character to demolish the forts. Secondly.

It is clear that the army shd at once prepare to attack the Kilid Bahr plateau at the earliest date which unhappily cannot be before April 14. This is for War Office to settle. But the question now to be decided by Admiralty is whether the time has come to abandon the naval plan of forcing the Dardanelles without the need of a large army. It may be necessary to take the action of the 18th as a decision to admit that the task is beyond our powers & if you think this you shd not fail to say so.

But before deciding certain facts must be weighed first the delay and the consequent danger of submarines coming & ruining all.

---

[1] Fisher had threatened to resign if this telegram were sent. Churchill modified it, and the redrafted version (printed on p. 728) was sent on 24 March, although Fisher continued to protest.

[2] The preceding telegram, sent by de Robeck at 5.35 a.m. that morning.

second

the heavy losses at least 5000 wh the Army wd suffer

third

the possibilities of a check in the land operations far more serious than the loss of a few old surplus ships.

These must be balanced against the risks and hopes of a purely naval undertaking. Here you must not ignore the supreme moral effect of a British fleet entering the Sea of Marmora provided it is strong enough to destroy the Turco-German vessels. The Gallipoli peninsula wd be completely cut off if our ships were on both sides of the Bulair isthmus.

It seems vy probable to us here that as soon as it is apparent that the fortresses at the narrows are not going to stop the fleet a general evacuation of the peninsula will take place: but anyhow all troops upon it wd be doomed to starvation or surrender.

Besides this there is the political effect of the arrival of the Fleet upon Constantinople which is incalculable & may well be absolutely decisive on Turkish resistance everywhere.

Assuming that the minimum good results follow the successful passage of the fleet into the Marmora, viz that the Turkish army on Gallipoli continues to hold out and with forts & field guns closes up the Straits, & that no revolution occurs at Constantinople—then the army wd have to storm the Kilid Bahr plateau and secure a permanent reopening of the Straits. It wd be possible with the ships left behind at the entrance, & with those in Egypt to give the necessary naval support to the military operations. So that at the worst we shd only have to do after you had got through, what we shall have to do if the view of your telegram 818 is accepted. While on the other hand the chances that your getting through would decide all favourably to us are extremely good. Further once through the Dardanelles the current wd be with you in any further attack on the forts & the mining danger wd be over. Therefore danger to your line of communications is not incurable.

Thirdly as to the actual business of getting through It is presumed the plan would be to silence the forts at the Narrows, then while keeping them silenced to sweep the minefield. Then to go in to 2 or 3000 yards range & ultimately even to 500 yards and from there damage them seriously & dismount their principal guns, then bringing up fresh ships to silence the Nagara forts and sweep up another area, & then having mastered the larger guns and dealt with the torpedo tubes to bring up all your sweepers and push steadily on till you reach the Marmora. The whole operation taking perhaps 4 or 5 days continual fighting. Do you think this possible with a loss of 7 or 8 old ships. And if so when wd you be ready to begin.

Fourthly

I wish to hear from you further before sending any official reply to your 818. You may discuss this telegram with General Hamilton if he is with you and then telegraph full. Admiralty will then give their decision.

Meanwhile all your preparations for sweeping shd go forward.

H. H. Asquith to Venetia Stanley

(*Montagu papers*)

23 March 1915　　　　　　　　　　　　　　　10 Downing Street

... We had a longish Cabinet this morning. The news from the Dardanelles is not very good: there are more mines & concealed guns than they ever counted upon: and the Admiral seems to be rather in a funk. Ian Hamilton has not yet sent his report, but the soldiers cannot be ready for any big concerted operation before about 14th April. I agree with Winston & K that the Navy ought to make another big push, so soon as the weather clears. If they wait & wait, until the army is fully prepared, they may fall into a spell of bad weather, & (what is worse) find that submarines, Austrian or German, have arrived on the scene.

All this was rather kept back from the Cabinet, who spent their time in discussing how cheaply we can purchase the immediate intervention of that most voracious, slippery, & perfidious Power—Italy. She opens her mouth very wide, particularly on the Dalmatian coast, and we must not allow her to block the Serbs' access to the Sea. But short of that, she is worth purchasing: tho' I shall always think that on a great scene she has played the meanest and pettiest of parts. ...

Lord Kitchener to Sir Ian Hamilton: telegram

(*Draft, Churchill papers: 26/3*)

23 March 1915　　　　　　　　　　　　　　　10 Downing Street

I am informed you consider the 14th April as about date for commencing military operations if fleet have not forced the Dardanelles by then. I think you had better know at once that I consider any such postponement as far too long, & shd like to know how soon you cd [get] on shore.

Lord Kitchener to Sir Ian Hamilton: telegram
(*Draft, Churchill papers: 26/3*)

23 March 1915   10 Downing Street
Secret

Undoubtedly silenced guns should be destroyed and the forts demolished
and for this purpose the admiral should call upon the army authorities to
provide landing parties of considerable force whenever necessary for the
purpose—It is important to keep up the bombardment and all attempts to
pass the narrows by ships. Once ships are through the Gallipoli military
position ceases to be of importance.

Sir Ian Hamilton to Lord Kitchener: telegram
(*Copy, Churchill papers: 2/88*)

23 March 1915
8.10 pm

I have now conferred with Admiral and we are equally convinced that
to enable the Fleet effectively to force the passage of the Dardanelles the
co-operation of the whole military force will be necessary. The strength of
the enemy on the Gallipoli Peninsula is estimated at about 40,000, with a
reserve of 30,000 somewhere west of Rodosto. The unsettled weather prevailing in March introduces a dangerous incalculable factor into the operation of landing a large force in the face of certain opposition, but the weather
next month should be more settled and I am sanguine of the success then
of a simple straightforward scheme based on your broad principles.

I have already worked out the main features of my scheme and I can
communicate them if you think it safe to do so.

Practically the whole of my force will be required to effect what I have
planned, and on the thoroughness with which I can make the preliminary
arrangements, of which the proper allocation of troops, &c., to transports
is not the least important, the success of my plans will largely depend. This is
one of the principal reasons why I attach importance to the thorough
organization of the expedition at a convenient base like Alexandria.

The Turks will be kept busy meanwhile by Admiral.

Sir John French to Winston S. Churchill
(*Churchill papers: 1/117*)

24 March 1915

Head Quarters
British Army

My dear Winston

We have to thank you heartily for our excellent entertainments last night.[1] The channel was like a mill pond—the night beautiful—& the officers of the 'Attentive' most kind to us. I think our meeting was a great success & fully justified all you said as to the advisability and the use of it. I was sorry to see K looking so tired and worried but he cheeed up tremendously during the evening and I venture to think our friendly and intimate talk did him good—if this is so it is (like so many other good things) all *your* doing! Well my dear friend you were very anxious I know but your great heart will bear you thro' and your work will end *in success*. I feel it instinctively.

Let us see you soon again.

Yours alway
JF

Winston S. Churchill to Vice-Admiral de Robeck: telegram[2]
(*Copy, Churchill papers: 13/65*)

24 March 1915
Personal and Secret

Admiralty

It is clear that the army should at once prepare to attack the Kilid Bahr plateau at the earliest opportunity, and Lord Kitchener hopes that April 14 can be ante-dated. This is a matter for the War Office. But the question now to be decided by Admiralty is whether the time has come to abandon the naval plan of forcing the Dardanelles without the aid of a large army. It may be necessary to accept the check of the 18th as decisive and to admit that the task is beyond our powers, and if you think this you should not fail

[1] On the afternoon of 23 March Sir John French crossed to Dover on board HMS *Attentive*. Churchill had arranged the crossing. French met Kitchener on board, and they talked together about ammunition supplies. French recorded in his diary: 'K. . . . spoke of the operations in the Dardanelles—said he thought W.C. was too impulsive and headstrong and that he had driven Carden off his head. He (K.) was not hopeful of success! This is always the way with K. Absolute pessimism always!' (Diary extract quoted in Gerald French, *The Life of Field-Marshal Sir John French*, London 1931, p. 288)

[2] Fisher noted on the final draft of this telegram before it was coded: 'Although the telegram goes from you personally, the fact of my remaining at the Admiralty sanctions my connection with it, so if it goes I do not see how I can remain.' The telegram was sent to de Robeck at 7.35 pm; Fisher, however, did not resign.

to say so. But before deciding, certain facts must be weighed; first the delay
and the consequent danger of submarines coming and ruining all; second the
heavy losses at least 5,000 which the army would suffer; third the possibilities
of a check in the land operations far more serious than the loss of a few old
surplus ships; fourth the fact that even when the Kilid Bahr plateau has been
taken by the army and the Kilid Bahr group of forts rendered untenable, the
Asiatic forts will be still effective and most of the mine danger which is now
your principal difficulty will menace you in the long reaches above the
Narrows.

These must be balanced against the risks and hopes of a purely naval undertaking. You must not underrate the supreme moral effect of a British fleet
with sufficient fuel and ammunition entering the Sea of Marmora provided
it is strong enough to destroy the Turco-German vessels. The Gallipoli
Peninsula would be completely cut off if our ships were on both sides of the
Bulair Isthmus. It seems very probable that as soon as it is apparent that the
fortresses at the Narrows are not going to stop the Fleet a general evacuation
of the peninsula will take place; but anyhow all troops remaining upon it
would be doomed to starvation or surrender. Besides this there is the political
effect of the arrival of the Fleet before Constantinople which is incalculable
and may well be absolutely decisive.

Assuming that only the minimum good results follow the successful passage
of the Fleet into the Marmora, namely, that the Turkish army on Gallipoli
continues to hold out and with forts and field guns closes up the Straits, and
that no revolution occurs at Constantinople, then perhaps in the last resort
the army would have to storm Kilid Bahr plateau and secure a permanent
re-opening of the Straits. It would be possible with the ships left behind
at the entrance, and with those in Egypt, to give the necessary support to
the military operations, so that at the worst the army would only have to do,
after you had got through, what they will have to do anyhow if your telegram 256 is accepted. While on the other hand the probability is that your
getting through would decide everything in our favour. Further, once
through the Dardanelles, the current would be with you in any return attack
on the forts, and the mining danger would be practically over. Therefore
danger to your line of communications is not serious or incurable.

What has happened since the 21st to make you alter your intention of
renewing the attack as soon as the weather is favourable? We have never
contemplated a reckless rush over minefields and past undamaged primary
guns. But the original Admiralty instructions and telegram 109 prescribed a
careful and deliberate method of advance, and I should like to know what
are the reasons which in your opinion render this no longer possible, in spite
of your new aircraft and improved method of minesweeping. We know the

forts are short of ammunition. It is probable they have not got many mines. You should be able to feel your way while at the same time pressing hard.

I cannot understand why as a preliminary step forts like 7 and 8 should not be demolished by heavy gun fire, first at long range and afterwards at short range, now that you have good aeroplane observation.

I wish to hear further from you before any official reply is sent to your 256. You may discuss this telegram with General Hamilton if he is with you, and then telegraph fully. Admiralty will then give their decision.

You must of course understand that this telegram is not an executive order but is sent because it is most important that there should be no misunderstandings at this juncture.

WSC

Lord Fisher to Sir John Jellicoe
(Jellicoe papers)

24 March 1915   Admiralty

You MUST write frequently to Winston. He LOVES it and he HATES you for writing to me. . . .

Things are not promising in the Dardanelles but it does not do to mope or repine!

I AM AN OPTIMIST. . . .

Lord Fisher to Winston S. Churchill
(Churchill papers: 13/56)

24 March 1915   Admiralty

Dear Winston,

I understand Mr Balfour is now all in favour of Alexandretta and the Euphrates waterway. De Robeck really better than Carden so Providence is with us. But let not our eyes be too much off the main theatre—read enclosed[1] carefully drawn up so well by Hope—and obviously we have been near some big event though A.K.W. and Oliver wont have it! but why was plan so suddenly cancelled? Which of us is trying to unravel this? *Our eyes elsewhere!* You will observe something to happen at *Memel* suddenly. . . .

I hope Sir Iron Bax-side[2] has prevented ammunition and submarines passing through to Constantinople. The Foreign Office stick to their fools! . . .

---

[1] A wireless message from the German Admiralty to the German High Sea Fleet, intercepted by the British and decoded; Fisher interpreted it as implying naval preparations for a sortie of the High Sea Fleet.

[2] Fisher's nickname for Sir Bax Ironside, British Minister to Bulgaria.

Winston S. Churchill to Lord Fisher, Vice-Admiral Oliver and Sir Arthur Wilson

(Churchill papers: 13/54)

24 March 1915   Admiralty
Very Secret

The First Lord wishes to record his opinion that a long series of indications in the intercepts point to a general offensive movement by the German High Sea Fleet at no distant date; & that the chance of a large part of our forces in the Medn create a strategic situation less unfavourable to Germany than will exist at any later time.

Every precaution shd therefore be taken during April to keep the grand Fleet in the highest condition of strength & readiness: and light cruiser reconnaissance shd be pushed in towards Heligoland at irregular but not infrequent intervals, in order that we may not rely entirely upon the intercepts.

WSC

H. H. Asquith to Venetia Stanley

(Montagu papers)

24 March 1915   10 Downing Street

. . . Winston is coming over to see me: perhaps about the Dardanelles. I will tell you later what he says. Your posts are rather mysterious, but you ought to get this early in the morning.

11.30 p.m Winston came to talk about the Dardanelles. The weather is infamous there, & the Naval experts seem to be suffering from a fit of nerves. They are now disposed to wait till the troops can assist them in force, which ought to be not later [than] about April 10th. Winston thinks & I agree with him, that the ships, as soon as the weather clears, & the aeroplanes can detect the condition of the forts & the positions of the concealed guns ought to make another push: & I hope this will be done.

Lord Fisher to Winston S. Churchill

(Churchill papers: 13/56)

24 March 1915   Admiralty

Dear Winston,

It's the right thing without any doubt whatever to send Bartolomé & THE SOONER THE BETTER![1] Dont delay for 'Phaeton' the French will have a

---

[1] Nothing came of this proposal to send Commodore de Bartolomé to the Dardanelles.

fast vessel at Marseilles or Toulon—He might find Pound[1] useful—he is very clever—he is a very first rate Torpedo officer also. Full of resource—*Everyone says he is A1.* (All my swans get stolen!) but I wouldn't force him on Bartolomé—a nice companion.

You are very wrong to worry and excite yourself! do try and remember that *we are the lost ten tribes of Israel!* We are sure to win! I know I am an optimist! *—always have been!* THANK GOD! A vituperative woman once called me a 'Sun-Dial'!

'There he stands amongst the flowers
Counting only sunny hours
Heeding neither rain nor mist
The Brazen-faced old optimist'!
ask Bartolomé!

Yours
F

Send no more telegrams! Let it alone!
D—n the submarines! You can't have everything! It's von Pohl just now! I dont believe we shall get intercepts. I see signs!
Where are your outpost submarines accompanied by Destroyers with good wireless? Minelayers with steam up to block return of von Pohl!
Are your Destroyers & Light Cruisers massed ready for INSTANT action?—where???

Winston S. Churchill: memorandum

(Churchill papers: 13/56)

24 March 1915   Admiralty

I

Capture of Borkum

1. The attack on Borkum[2] shd take place as soon as the weather is favourable after May 15th. By that date the following shd be ready:—

   a) 6 heavy monitors (& possibly several light monitors.)

---

[1] Alfred Dudley Pickman Rogers Pound, 1877–1943. Entered Navy, 1891. Torpedo Lieutenant, 1902. Captain, 1914. Second Naval Assistant to Lord Fisher, December 1914–May 1915. Flag Captain, HMS *Colossus*, 1915–17. Took part in the Battle of Jutland. Served on the Admiralty Staff, 1917–19. Director of Plans Division, Admiralty, 1922. Commanded the Battle Cruiser Squadron, 1929–32. Knighted, 1933. Second Sea Lord, 1932–5. Commander-in-Chief, Mediterranean, 1936–9. Admiral of the Fleet, 1939. First Sea Lord and Chief of the Naval Staff, 1939–43. He declined a peerage in 1943, on account of his lack of means.

[2] See map 13 on pages 1606–7.

b) a bombarding sqn fitted with double torpedo nets (10 ships)

c) oil-tankers converted into unsinkable transports, sufficient to carry 12,000 men.

d) specially constructed boats (ISL's design) to land the troops.

e) a complete aviation park, specially organized for landing on an island, comprising 60 aeroplanes & seaplanes.

f) 4 mine-laying vessels of adequate speed.

g) steamers capable of laying at least 5 miles of anti-submarine net.

h) Trawlers & Drifters capable of laying at least 40 miles of S/M indicator net.

i) smoke-making flotilla

j) a sqn of dummy ships.

2. The operation shd be covered by 14 E class S/Ms, & 20 C or B boats (total 34) with the M (13) & 6 (20) flotillas of destroyers, together with the Beagles (14) & Tribals (12) total 59, supported by 6 light cruisers, the whole of this covering force to be under Commodore T.

The Grand Fleet will not be required to advance beyond the intersection of the 5th meridian on the 55th parallel.

3. *First day of attack.* At earliest daylight the covering flotillas will be in their stations, & fire will be opened on the batteries by the bombarding sqn. & the monitors, from the best positions. An anti S/M net will be laid across the mouth of the Randzel Gap. Other lengths of net will be disposed to seaward of the bombarding sqn, wh will also be protected by the trawlers & drifters with their indicator nets as may be best devised. Two seaplane-carrying ships will attend for aerial observation of the artillery. During the day the special service sqn of dummy ships will cruise behind a line of indicator nets about 10 miles to the N. of Borkum, thus attracting the enemy S/Ms & at the same time giving the enemy the impression that our main fleet is close at hand, & that therefore counter-attacks by small detachments will not suffice.

4. *Second day of attack.* If all has gone well on the first day, & the enemy's guns are well held, the transports conveying the landing force will start in time to arrive when darkness falls on the 2nd day. Meanwhile the bombardment will continue, & the cover as on the previous day. During the night of the 2nd day, the troops will be landed either on the islands of Juist & Memert, or on Borkum itself, according to the views of the military & the progress of the bombardment. A small temporary air base will be established on Memert during the dark hours, & reconnaissance to ascertain the dispositions of the German High Sea Fleet pushed out at dawn on

5. *the third day of the attack.* During this day, & the next if necessary, the bombardment will be continued, & the troops will make & press their attack on Borkum, using the smoke flotilla if convenient to cover their landing and

their advance. A relief bombarding sqn will be available, & the bombardment & the attack will both be maintained continuously in concert until the
surrender of the garrison.

6. As soon as this is achieved & the island is in our possession, (say the 5th
day of the attack), the main flying base will be landed, & a permanent
aeroplane patrol at 8,000 ft established to attack all Zeppelins or hostile aircraft, & take what steps are necessary to establish an effective mastery of
the air.

7. Also on this day the depot ships of the S/Ms & destroyers, their oilers,
& the store ships of the troops, will berth themselves in the Randzel Gap.
Nets & minefields will be laid to make this a secure S/M-proof anchorage.
The monitors will dispose themselves to serve as forts until the shore-defences
can be repaired. The bombarding sqn will return. The movements of the
special service sqn must be determined by the loss it has suffered & whether
its character has been detected. All the S/M & destroyer flotillas employed
on covering duties as specified in para (2) will be based on Borkum, & these
with the monitors & an elaborate system of minefields, all carefully concerted, will be the whole defence of the island. It is an essential principle that
the freedom of the Fleet must not be in any degree compromised by the need
of defending Borkum.

8. It is unlikely that the German fleet will attempt to interfere directly with
the attack on Borkum. To do so, they wd have to enter an area dominated
by S/Ms more numerous than have ever been employed in war, & to face
mining dangers of all kinds with the certainty of bringing themselves within
striking distance of the British Grand Fleet.

The island of Borkum belongs to whoever has the command of the sea, &
the only true strategic action open to the German fleet is to ignore the
Borkum operation, avoid the submarine-infested area, & proceed direct to
attack Sir J. Jellicoe's fleet. If they win the main battle, the fate of the
Borkum attack is incidentally decided. If they do not feel strong enough to
come out and offer general battle, they wd be right to remain in harbour. If
they come out to seek a general battle, our Fleet will have choice of position
& time.

It is much more probable than the Germans will use their flotillas & light
cruisers to dispute the capture of Borkum. Most of their S/Ms will be at sea
on commerce destruction, & cannot be recalled in time. 5 or 6 is probably
the most that wd be available, & with a good arrangement of nets & trawlers,
& with a large & active force of destroyers, it shd be possible to baffle these
& destroy some of them. The area in wh our own S/Ms can operate will of
course be accurately defined.

But the destroyer force of the enemy cd be used energetically by night or day, & it is vital that our flotillas should be in great & superior force. To this end one flotilla from the Grand Fleet & 20 destroyers from the Coast Patrol, & all the Scouts, must be held in readiness to reinforce the 59 heavy boats already detailed. Nothing cd be more satisfactory to us than that destroyer fighting on a great scale shd develop & be pertinaciously maintained. The superior gun power of the British boats shd bear down everything before it, & break up this force wh otherwise wd be so dangerous to our Grand Fleet in general battle.

Any enemy cruisers or battle cruisers wh intervened must of course be dealt with by the battle cruiser & cruiser sqns of the G. Fleet. The intervention of German battle cruisers in the Br mine & S/M area is however vy unlikely, & wd be most unwise from their point of view.

After the capture of B has been completed, the Br garrison wd be reduced to the number necessary for its defence. The forts will be repaired & their guns remounted. Most of them will be found not to be permanently damaged. If our Intelligence can be trusted sufficiently, a certain amount of ammunn to fit the Borkum guns shd be made now. The aeroplane station will organize attacks on the German aircraft station in the vicinity & retain the command of the air. It will also supply regular daily reports of the disposn of the German Fleet. The islands of Juist & Memert might be occupied if convenient by outposts. If any large force of Germans is moved on to them, these men can certainly be cut off by monitors & small craft operating in the creeks, & captured or destroyed whenever their numbers make it worth while to do so.

The extensive sands between Borkum, Juist, Memert & the mainland at low water are it is believed vy favourable to the operations of armoured motorcars with maxims. This shd be verified, & experiments made with armoured cars on sandy beaches. A defence of this character wd be most effective against any but the most serious attacks, & a serious attack in great force is most dangerous—almost impossible—to launch in the short time available between the tides. Further acquaintance with these sands wd possibly open out a great rôle for armoured cars.

II

The Closing of the River Mouths

If the German High Sea Fleet does not challenge the Grand Sea Fleet to battle at the time of the capture of Borkum, it is hardly likely that they will do so later. We may also assume that flotilla fighting of a vy serious character has occurred & that we have secured the predominance. We are now assumedly in the first week of June, when more Monitors will be available,

& others will be liberated by the completion of the Borkum defences. We have therefore the means of employing our monitors our C class S/Ms, our destroyer flotillas & our light cruisers, aided by our aircraft, in a steady advance towards the Jade & Elbe estuaries. The aircraft will always report upon the state of readiness of the German High Sea Fleet, & which side of the Canal they are. If they come out, they will have to face the S/M & mining dangers. The Monitors do not fear the S/Ms, & the torpedo station at Heligoland can therefore be bombarded at long range without difficulty. The enemy's destroyers & light cruisers will be kept overawed by our similar vessels. The Dockyard at Wilhelmshaven will be rendered unsafe by continual aircraft raids on an ever increasing scale. The relation of the Grand Fleet to these operations is that of a distant & occasional support.

It is not possible to forecast in detail the character of these operations which are essentially governed by manoevre & fighting and by the decisions obtained from day to day in conflict. But there is every reason to believe that except for their S/Ms the Germans will lie closer at home every day, & in these operations we shall not require to employ heavy ships except on rare occasions. The object is to close up the mouth of the Jade the Weser & the Elbe, first by lines of mines & secondly by lines of anti-S/M nets, & so protect these minefields from disturbance by monitors & destroyers wh are themselves not afraid of S/Ms.

III

The Entry of the Baltic

The possession by the British of the Island of Borkum not only enables the close flotilla watch of the German debouches to be maintained & the operations described above to be carried forward, but it menaces with military force the whole German coastline of the North Sea. This will entail the movement to the German seaboard of very large numbers of troops wh can ill be spared from elsewhere, & the feverish occupation & fortification of many islands wh we have no desire or need to take. It also affords a great measure of protection to Denmark, because of the danger of being cut off to which a German Army invading Jutland wd be exposed. We are therefore in a position to address ourselves to the Danes.

As soon as the S/M base has been established & all the B & C boats come into play for oversea purposes, the E boats, 14 in number, can go through the Sound to Copenhagen. Once established there they wd prevent the bombardment of the Danish capital by a German fleet. We shd then invite Denmark to join the Allies. Until or unless she does so, the entry into the Baltic by ships other than S/Ms is vy difficult. But with a friendly Denmark

& strong flotillas of S/Ms well established inside the Baltic & capable of operating off Kiel to cover the passage of the Bælts, the operation, tho' requiring a fine piece of war seamanship, can be carried out.

The force to operate in the Baltic shd be strong enough to beat the German Battle Cruiser Sqn, & fast enough to escape the German Battle Fleet. It must in no circumstances compromise the supremacy of the Grand Fleet. The following force fulfils the above conditions: *Warspite—Q. Elizth, Q. Mary— Princess Royal*; 6 Arethusas; the M Destroyers (relieved at Borkum by a patrol flotilla); & the E class S/Ms. It must be remembered that we shd at every stage know on which side of the Canal the German High Sea Fleet was placed, & consequently can choose our moment for the passage of the Bælts when we know no serious naval force can be brought against us.

Once in the Baltic, the above force wd dominate the situation. The 4 Russian Dreadnoughts & the rest of the Russian Fleet, wh now count for nothing, wd immediately become a weighty factor. A blockade of all German Baltic ports cd be proclaimed, & the whole N. German coast threatened by the Russian armies, entailing further immense dissipation of German military forces. If & while the German fleet remains on the North Sea side of the Canal, serious military operation can be launched against her Northern Coast.

If the German Fleet comes through the Canal into the Baltic, it will find nothing to strike at, for it cannot catch our squadrons; & wd have to run the gauntlet of our S/Ms out & home; & immediately our Monitors in the North Sea will advance up the river mouths to bombard Wilhelmshaven & Cuxhaven, & to consolidate the wiring & mining-in of the North Sea rivers. Thus the position of the Germans between these two alternative dangers wd be most unfavourable. The only escape from it is by a Fleet action after breaking out through mines & S/Ms into the North Sea.

IV

The decisive military stroke.

It is not proposed to enter into military details but the landing of a British army of invasion, not less than 500,000 strong, at Emden, to establish itself on the 30-mile broad neck of the East Friesland Peninsula, & to invest Wilhelmshaven in conjunction with the sea-attack, wd be an operation of the highest advantage; & from this broad base an advance cd be made subsequently either through Hanover on Berlin, or into Westphalia. The effect of such a movement, & indeed of the whole Borkum operation, upon Holland may well at any moment be decisive in determining that country to join the Allies.

As regards the early stages of this concerted scheme these thoughts are definitely outlined, but after the Borkum operation has been described the intention is to shew the general direction of a war policy & not to go into detail.

WSC

Winston S. Churchill to Lord Kitchener

(*Kitchener papers*)

24 March 1915   Admiralty
Private

My dear Kitchener,

For the last seven months, indeed since the earliest days of the war, I have kept a squadron of armoured cars at Dunkirk in connection with the naval aeroplanes there. About three weeks ago at the same time that I relieved Sampson's aeroplanes prior to sending them to the Dardanelles, I also relieved the armoured car squadron by Westminster's squadron from home. I had no intention that they should go into your domain at all until they were officially applied for by the War Office. But Westminster has a great many friends high up in the Army, and it appears that when the Neuve Chapelle fighting was about to begin, they were requested to come and take part in it by one of the divisional commanders, with the sanction of Sir Douglas Haig. They naturally lost no time in complying with the invitation; and on four successive days were sharply engaged. The cars mounting the 3-pdr. gun did very useful work by running up close to a fortified house defended by Germans and firing 75 shell into it. All the cars were covered with bullet splashes and several of the men were hit, but none were killed or wounded.

When I went to see French the other day, I found Westminster had been invited by Douglas Haig, with the approval of G.H.Q., to attach himself to the Army, and as I felt that, after our conversations on the subject, you would regard this as irregular, I gave directions for his immediate return to Dunkirk with his squadron, and made it clear that they are not to enter the area of the British Army unless urgently and directly summoned for some emergency.

I write you this to show you how careful I have been to avoid doing anything you might not like, and also to let you know of the somewhat irregular participation of this squadron in the battle of Neuve Chapelle. I hope, however, that you will now consider whether you cannot allow this squadron to join the Army. In your letter to me of the 19th inst., you told me you were proposing to ask for two squadrons; but I shall be quite content for the present if you can allow this one to serve. I know that Sir Douglas Haig would be glad to have it with his Corps; and if they are found to be useful, the value of these cars can be tested.

Yours vy truly
Winston S. Churchill

Margot Asquith to David Lloyd George
(Lloyd George papers)

24 March 1915   10 Downing Street

... DO warn Winston (DON'T give me away) to be careful of what he tells Arthur Balfour. I cd feel at lunch yesterday & when he came to tea 2 evenings ago alone with me that Arthur is really au fond *hostile*—VERY hostile. You & Winston don't know A.J.B. as well as I do. That cool grace, easy mind & intellectual courtesy takes the eye off like the 3 card trick. He is a bitter party opponent. ... As you know, Arthur & I have been REAL friends outside all political social ostracism since I was 17 years old.

Winston S. Churchill to Sir Edward Grey
(Admiralty papers: 116/1336)

25 March 1915   Admiralty

Sir E. Grey,

Please see X[1] wh causes me the utmost concern.

The facts shd surely be investigated in the most stringent manner with the Roumanian & Bulgarian Governments; & we shd say plainly that the forwarding of any war material to Turkey at this juncture wd be regarded as a grave step, & if this is discovered later when the allies enter Cple the impression produced upon the Allied Governments will be vy painful, etc.

They are playing a double game. But now is the time to stop the war material. This is vital.

WSC

[1] A report from Constantinople printed in the *Morning Post* on 25 March, alleging that 'During the last fortnight about 150 mines, any amount of ammunition, guns &c. have been coming through Roumania from Germany', and that such war materials had gone by rail through Bulgaria.

Lord Kitchener to Winston S. Churchill

(*Churchill papers: 2/58*)

25 March 1915   War Office

My dear Churchill

As Fitzgerald explained, we are pushing on preparations for land operations. In the meantime I hope the Navy will continue to engage the forts as vigorously as possible and thus induce the Turks to expend their ammunition.

Yours very truly

Kitchener

Vice-Admiral de Robeck to Admiralty: telegram

(*Churchill papers: 13/65*)

25 March 1915   HMS Queen Elizabeth

I understand date given me by General Hamilton may be advanced by a few days.

In preparing the decisive effort in conjunction with Army referred to in last paragraph of that telegram, it is proposed to resume a vigorous offensive as soon as weather permits, having following objects:—

Firstly, completely clearing the area in which Squadron must manœuvre in order to cover the minesweeping vessels operating in Kephez minefield.

Secondly, with assistance of aeroplanes systematic reconnoitring both shores in order to locate and destroy gunfire of Howitzers and other concealed guns and carry out indirect attack on Chanak Forts by 'QUEEN ELIZABETH' with aeroplanes spotting.

In Gulf of Xeros French Squadron will endeavour to attack Gallipoli and camps near Bulair with their aircraft, British seaplanes if available attacking Turkish supply depots at Maitos and vessels above Chanak some of which are said to be loaded with mines.

Aerodrome at Tenedos complete.

Officer commanding aeroplanes considers it satisfactory.

Owing to bad weather it has not been possible to land machines yet.

Winston S. Churchill to Lord Fisher
(*Churchill papers: 13/56*)

25 March 1915   Admiralty
Secret

My dear Fisher,

The Prime Minister seemed disappointed last night that we had not sent de Robeck a definite order to go on with his attack at the first opportunity, and he expressed his agreement with the telegram to that effect wh I drafted yesterday morning. I explained that the gale was rendering all operations impracticable & that nothing wd be lost by a full interchange of views, such as wd be effected by my 'Personal & Secret' of yesterday afternoon.

Mr Balfour also pointed out to me that de Robeck show that he anticipates getting through if he tries and that his anxiety now is for his communications after he has got through. This anxiety I am convinced is not well grounded. The arrival of 4 or 5 ships in the Marmora decides the issue.

My own feeling is that de Robeck shd try to clear the Kephez minefield and to smash the forts at the narrows, according to our plans, that any question of going further cd only arise after very marked success had been achieved in the above task.

This is not a vy great extension of what he proposes in this telegram, just received: but it means that we have not abandoned our undertaking, or set definite limits to our sea efforts, & that we shall press on methodically but resolutely with it, and hold ourselves free & ready to profit by any success that may be reaped.

Meanwhile the Army will go ahead with their preparations to begin at the earliest moment.

I hope we shall be together in this.

Yours ever
W

PS There is no need for any action till we hear further.

H. H. Asquith to Venetia Stanley
(*Montagu papers*)

25 March 1915   10 Downing Street
a.m.

. . . Massingham[1] told Margot yesterday a 'horrible tale', which he swears can be proved true on the best authority. It is that Winston is 'intriguing

[1] Henry William Massingham, 1860–1924. Editor of the *Daily Chronicle*, 1895–9, resigning because of the unpopularity of his opposition to the South African War. Editor of the *Nation*, 1907–23. In 1909 he wrote an introduction to an edition of Churchill's speeches, *Liberalism and the Social Problem*. Supported Lord Lansdowne's advocacy of a negotiated peace, 1917. Joined the Labour Party, 1923.

hard' to supplant E. Grey at the Foreign Office & to put A.J.B in his place. I gave you the other day a milder version of the same story, which the suspicious mind of the Assyrian had treasured up. There is no doubt that Winston is at the moment a complete victim to B's superficial charm; he has him at the Admiralty night & day, and I am afraid tells him a lot of things which he ought to keep to himself, or at any rate to his colleagues. Since I began the last sentence, Ll. George has been here . . . I asked him what he thought of the Massingham story, & rather to my surprise he said he believed it was substantially true. He thinks that Winston has for the time at any rate allowed himself to be 'swallowed whole' by A.J.B., on whom he, L. G., after working with him for a week or two, is now disposed to be very severe. It is a pity isn't it? that Winston hasn't a better sense of proportion, and also a larger endowment of the instinct of loyalty. As you know, like you, I am really fond of him: but I regard his future with many misgivings. Your little Indian plan for him commands I am afraid no favour in any quarter: the mere mention of it makes the Assyrian foam at the mouth, and is received with less demonstrative but equally emphatic disapproval by the 2 or 3 others to whom I have casually hinted at it. He will never get to the top in English politics, with all his wonderful gifts; to speak with the tongue of men & angels, and to spend laborious days & nights in administration, is no good, if a man does not inspire trust. . . .

Winston S. Churchill to Vice-Admiral Oliver

(*Churchill papers: 13/54*)

25 March 1915   Admiralty

1. Why cannot submarines be used to sweep up the lines of moored mines in the Kephez minefield?

The position of these mines can be accurately located by aeroplanes. Suppose a couple of destroyers make a dash past the first line of mines at night and lay above them a long cable buoyed so as to be at the right distance below the surface, leading the ends of this cable back on to our side of the minefield, and then let a couple of submarines get hold of the ends and, showing only their periscopes and thus being immune from fire, haul steadily. If the mines are moored by vertical attachments the whole lot must be gathered together in a bunch and torn from their moorings or exploded. Meanwhile we run no risks at all except the two destroyers which have to lay the cable above the line of mines. If, on the other hand, the mines are not moored by vertical attachments but are simply strung on to a jackstay, then the submarine could herself dive deep underneath the minefield and, with the current in her favour, tow a kite trailing numbers of explosive creeps some of which are bound to cut the jackstay. There must also be some breaches in the line of mines. If not, one can easily be made by sending an old ship through to explode one, and this breach can be located by aeroplanes and if necessary buoyed. Through this breach the submarine can go with only her periscope showing, and once a cable or rope is laid above the line of mines the current is in our favour and by slowly hauling a great many mines must come away.

If it is objected that a strong enough cable could not be carried up above the first line of mines (which is all I am thinking about now), it should be possible to carry an anchor with a pulley wheel attached to it, through which a comparatively light cable could be passed, and this could be pulled on quite slowly from below the minefield until a stronger one had been hauled up above the line of mines.

Here is another way. Why should not a submarine, working at her leisure with only her periscope showing, tow a good long string of explosive charges through a gap previously marked in the minefield (like the German submarines come through the gaps in our minefields) and lay them above the line of moored mines buoyed to the proper depth so that they will certainly drift down with the current and get entangled with the mines? Then when she is sure of this and has got back again to a safe distance, let these be exploded by an electric battery and they will blow up with them the whole line of mines. In this way it should certainly be possible to make quite easily a wide breach through the lines of moored mines, taking one line at a time. I cannot conceive that naval ingenuity will not be equal to such a simple problem.

2. As to drifting mines. Clearly without a moment's delay measures must be taken to make sure that an efficient arrangement of movable nets which can be towed up and anchored obliquely so as to fend off driving mines should be made. There ought to be 4 or 5 lengths of this, each 400 or 500 yards long and capable of being moved about like the nets closing the Eastern Entrance of Dover Harbour, but in this case we are not trying to stop a torpedo but only a floating mine drifting placidly with the moderate current. Therefore ordinary rope nets properly weighted and buoyed will do perfectly well. All that is required is to tow them obliquely into action ahead of the area where the ships are operating by destroyers, which must if necessary sacrifice themselves for this purpose, and then to drop the anchors which will hold them. A study of the current also would show where a net should be fastened further down which would collect in a sort of pocket mines which had been fended off higher up by the obliquely fixed nets. Nothing is easier than to provide protection which only needs to keep in position for a few

days against these weakly drifting mines which have done us so much injury. Fishing nets rushed up by destroyers or trawlers and laid under fire above the minefields would be effective, provided that they are at the right angle and have a slight belly or curl at their downstream end. Afterwards the ground gained could be made good by a more stronger arrangement.

WSC

Vice-Admiral Oliver to Winston S. Churchill
(*Churchill papers: 13/54*)

25 March 1915   Admiralty

Submitted,

1. I think it would be simpler to do it altogether by Destroyers, as we know that Destroyers can tow and manage sweeps.

The Admiral has fitted some of his Destroyers for rapid sweeping with gear made at Malta.

A sweeping wire between two Destroyers is in effect what you propose. The kites which the sweep wire reeves through perform the function of the buoys to keep the long cable the right distance below the surface. Buoys were tried in the early days of mine-sweeping and given up in favour of kites.

I am doubtful if a submerged submarine could steer or keep her depth properly with a rope bearing a considerable strain attached to her, but I will ask the Commodore S.[1] when he returns.

The explosive creep is the best way to sever a wire jackstay or a cable along the bottom conveying current to mines.

It is the result of a good deal of experience and experiment in the past and I had explosive creeps sent out to the Mediterranean early in February and drew attention to them in the Operation Orders.

2. Nets will not tow; a long length of net will bring the towing vessel to a standstill, or if she is too powerful to be brought up, the net will part. They can be easily shot, however. A Lieutenant R.N.R. with a lot of net experience is being sent out overland with two Volunteer Drifter Skippers who are very anxious to go: they will be able to show the bluejackets and officers all the professional tips for shooting and managing nets to catch drifting mines.

H. F. Oliver

[1] Sydney Stewart Hall, 1872–1955. Entered Navy, 1885. Commanded the Submarine Service, first 1906–10, and again, in succession to Roger Keyes, 1915–18. Rear-Admiral, 1919. Vice-Admiral, 1925. Admiral, 1929.

H. H. Asquith to Venetia Stanley

(Montagu papers)

25 March 1915   10 Downing Street
pm

Winston & the 'natural man' (whom he very well represents) are anxious that if, when the war ends, Russia has got Constantinople, & Italy Dalmatia, & France Syria, we should be able to appropriate some equivalent share of the spoils—Mesopotamia, with or without Alexandretta, a 'sphere' in Persia, some German colonies &c.

I believe that, at the moment, Grey & I are the *only* two men who doubt & distrust any such settlement. We both think that in the real interest of our own future, the best thing would be if, at the end of the War, we could say that (apart from regularising the status of Egypt & Cyprus, & perhaps picking up a few Pacific islands for Australia & New Zealand) we have taken & gained nothing. And that not from a merely moral & sentimental point of view (which, however, with our record of *perfide Albion*, & the universal cormorant counts for something) but from purely material considerations. Taking on Mesopotamia, for instance—with or without Alexandretta[1] (I suppose you haven't got a map, but I cd. explain this in 2 minutes) means spending millions in irrigation & development with no immediate or early return; keeping up quite a large army white & coloured in an unfamiliar country; tackling every kind of tangled administrative question, worse than we have ever had in India, with a hornet's nest of Arab tribes; and, even if that were all set right, having a perpetual menace on our flank in Kurdistan, just like Afghanistan & the Pathan tribes who overshadow the Punjab. . . .

The great thing for the moment is to bring in Italy, voracious as she is: and to attain this, if possible, Grey is postponing his holiday until Wed in next week. . . .

I have just heard that McKenna is coming to see me. I loathe the whole scheme of the Universe, at times: here to-day, for instance, I have had in person or in writing E. [Grey, [Ll George, Kitchener, now McKenna, & inevitably sooner or later Winston. . . .

---

[1] On 16 March 1915 Kitchener had written a long memorandum, 'Alexandretta and Mesopotamia', in which he strongly advocated the annexation of both, in order to counter Russian post-war influence in the Mediterranean, to protect the Persian oil fields, and to establish a firm territorial base for British interests in the Persian Gulf. He asserted that with proper irrigation Mesopotamia could 'become again one of the most fertile and highly productive areas in the world' and would also serve as 'an almost ideal field of colonization for the surplus population of India'. His memorandum was printed for the War Council on 18 March. *(Cabinet papers: 42/2)*

John Churchill to Winston S. Churchill
(*Churchill papers: 1/117*)

25 March 1915   HMS Franconia
                                               Nearing Alexandria

Dear Winston,

We hope to land tomorrow. Most of the R.N.D. have preceeded us and the French div follow. This delay is very irksome, but it was absolutely necessary. Lemnos was unpractical and would have increased the delay. There was no water for so large a force and no facilities for landing horses or transport. Some Australians effected a landing, & have been left there. The R.N.D. had to land somewhere to reorganize. They seem to have been shoved on board the transports in army formation. They must sort themselves out and arrange their transports and stores.

The plans of embarcation ought to have been worked out carefully. They should have known that their departure would be sudden. I hope that they have everything. I believe their transport is rather sketchy—but we shall see.

The French div is in the same plight. They are rather a scratch lot. Zouaves Senegalese and Foreign Legion! They must sort themselves out. The 29th div are awaited impatiently—I trust that they will be quite ready.

We are up against a very tough proposition. Since the 18th many people have altered their views. The sailors are now inclined to acknowledge that they cannot get through without the co-operation of troops. Long range fire on forts is no good unless infantry occupy the fort afterwards and maintain themselves there. Stronger mine sweepers are necessary against the current. The aeroplane spotting is very bad & at present does not help very much. Half the targets are concealed and the ships have the greatest difficulty in locating and firing at the mobile guns. The spotters have little experience. Samson's arrival is not awaited with any great enthusiasm. Some of the experienced army airmen 'spotters' are prayed for.

De Robeck behaved very well during the 18th. He never showed any anxiety and remained most calm and cheerful until the evening. When it was all over he is reported to have said 'I suppose I am done for'. The Admiralty message was gratefully received and created a very good effect. Saving the men from the Ocean [and] Irresistible was a wonderful feat. One destroyer came out with 650 men! De R. is very popular in the fleet, and there is some fear that he may be superseded. Hamilton considers him a very sound pusher & they are entirely in agreement. H. asked me to write privately to you to say that everyone had confidence in him in spite of the 18th. I said I thought it was unnecessary. Should you receive a cable via Eastern Co in

W. Office code signed by me and making any reference to the operations, you will know that the message is inspired. We call this expedition the last 'Crusade' and shall expect a papal cross for it!!

Yours

Jack

Vice-Admiral de Robeck to Admiralty: telegram

(Copy, Churchill papers: 13/65)

26 March 1915
1.10 pm

I do not hold check on the 18th March decisive but having met General Hamilton on the 22nd March and heard his proposals I now consider a combined operation essential to obtain great results and object of campaign.

Therefore my considered opinion is that the Fleet should prepare way and act as indicated in my telegram 268.[1]

To attack Narrows now with Fleet would be a mistake as it would jeopardise the execution of a better and bigger scheme.

Regarding other points raised, General Hamilton is in Egypt: copy of your telegram 140[2] has been sent to him in 'DORIS'.

Full appreciation of the situation in the Dardanelles is being prepared and will be telegraphed.

Winston S. Churchill to Sir Edward Grey and Lord Kitchener

(Admiralty papers: 116/1350)

Admiralty

26 March 1915
Secret

Sir Edward Grey
Lord Kitchener

Please see attached[3] which I had not seen when I spoke in Cabinet this morning.

In this matter, should it come to anything, time is vital. The success of the German coup would depend on swallowing Holland or nearly all of it before anyone was alive to the danger; so that they might have another skin to sell instead of another army to fight.

[1] De Robeck's telegram to Churchill of 25 March (quoted on p. 740).
[2] Churchill's telegram to de Robeck of 24 March (quoted on pp. 728–30).
[3] A report from the Admiralty Convoy Officer in Rotterdam, Ernest Maxse, suggesting that a German invasion of Holland was imminent.

It appears to me that F.O. should without delay speak to the French and thereafter to the Dutch on the basis of British military help, and that W.O. shd have all its plans ready for the eventuality. We want to be able to tell Holland that if she is attacked or goes to war, we will put immediately (say) half Sir John French's army plus whatever Ld. Kitchener can assign from England at her disposal, & that they can arrive at certain points by certain dates. This means the French must agree to send some of Joffre's reserve army to fill our places on the northern flank. It seems to me that this contingency might be talked over between Ld. Kitchener and General Joffre at their approaching meeting.

The vital point to realise is this—that if the Germans can overrun Holland very quickly they will have gained a great advantage; whereas if they are held up at or near the frontiers, they will be ruined.

There is no need for action now—only the most minute preparations. The blow may come very quickly if it comes at all.

I am having the naval aspect thoroughly studied.

WSC

Lord Fisher: minute
(*Admiralty papers: 116/1350*)

26 March 1915   Admiralty

The following points emerge from a first glance at the Dutch situation:—

1. The English Troops will land at Hook of Holland as the Germans can so easily cut the railway from Flushing & isolate it.

2. That subject to Dutch advice—Terschelling will be our Submarine & Destroyer base as being the nearest suitable position to the German Frontier out of range of German guns.

3. That our 3 Monitors (proposed to be stopped at Malta) would be of inestimable value in the Zuyder Zee.

4. That directly Bethell's men return from leave his squadron should go to the Swin to practise gunnery ready for bombarding Zeebrugge &c—

5. That the Grand Fleet will come from Scapa Flow to a rendezvous convenient for intercepting German High Sea Fleet.

6. That even now at the 11th hour it would be a wise project for the British army (re-inforced) to advance along the Belgian coast to the Dutch Frontier and so close Antwerp.

7. That the Germans can over-run all Holland up to the inundations in a few hours by means of the enormous mass of motors they possess and of

which Mr Deterding[1] told me a little time ago as being massed along the Dutch frontier with large stores of Petrol at defended depôts.

Lord Fisher to Winston S. Churchill
(*Churchill papers: 13/56*)

27 March 1915   Admiralty
3 A.M.!!! Early enough!

Dear Winston,

I do hope you will stay in bed! or you will come an awful smash! (however you are as obstinate as A.K.W. & Oliver!)

On further reflection and studying the book of word's procured from W. R. Hall last night & War Office reports I have nothing to add to the précis I sent you *last night at 8. p.m.* which is really the Bovril of the situation as regards our action to be taken re Holland! It is awful our having at this juncture to send Destroyers and submarines to the Dardanelles and we want *Inflexible & Queen Elizabeth* in the North Sea. . . .

There's no doubt the moment is most opportune for Germany to seize Holland when they *now* have nearly a million of German soldiers to dispose of and it is an immense asset the acquiring of such a big whack of fresh territory untouched by war and full of war resources and more rich territory to bargain when peace comes! As you say the sinking of the Dutch ship with charges has been deliberately planned & will be a success but the 300,000 Dutch soldiers will be tough I think.

Deterding tells me they are all fighters who have had fighting experience in Sumatra where there is always fighting going on.

Yours
F

Of course I am going on 'thinking' & last night I gave Crease & Pound & Hope the problems. They are a good '*Tria juncta in uno*'.

[1] Henri Wilhelm August Deterding, 1866–1939. Director-General of the Royal Dutch Petroleum Company; a Director of the Shell Transport and Trading Company Limited. A Dutch citizen, he received an honorary knighthood in 1921.

Lieutenant-Colonel Hankey to Winston S. Churchill

(*Admiralty papers: 116/1350*)

27 March 1915
Very secret

First Lord

With reference to our short conversation last night on the question of the menacing attitude of Germany towards Holland, I enclose a copy of a Report and Proceedings of a Sub-Committee of the Committee of Imperial Defence on the military needs of the Empire, 1909, in which the question of the employment of the British Army in Holland was discussed *inter alia*. I have put in markers to show the portions of the Report and Proceedings in which this question is discussed. Appendix 9 containing a Memorandum by the General Staff is the most important portion, and there is a map at the end.

There is not much reference to the possibility of naval co-operation, although on page 6 Admiral Slade is reported as referring to the question of river flotillas.

I have not had time to examine the question in detail, and it is rather one for the War Staff, but at first sight my impressions would be in favour of the following immediate action, if Germany violates Dutch territory:—

(1) The blocking and extensive mining of the Scheldt.
(2) The despatch of monitors and other light draught vessels to aid the Dutch in the rivers. ?Should the Monitors on the way to the Dardanelles be recalled?
(3) The seizure of a Dutch island e.g. Terschelling as an aeroplane base, and its military occupation.

The Dutch will probably retire at once behind their inundations. It is very desirable that they should hold Hadzand, N. Beverland, S. Beverland, and Walcheren, but their army is so small that I doubt their ability to do so. We ought to consider the removal or destruction of all stores of petroleum, rubber, wool &c.

MPAH

H. H. Asquith to George V

(*Royal Archives*)

27 March 1915   10 Downing Street

. . . Lord Kitchener informed the Cabinet that the Naval Division had already arrived at Alexandria, and that the 29th Division and the French contingent, would be landed there today; Mr Churchill added that the 'London', 'Prince of Wales', go 1 a.m. and 'Illustrious' were now on their way to reinforce the fleet at the Dardanelles. . . .

H. H. Asquith to Venetia Stanley
(Montagu papers)

27 March 1915   Walmer Castle

There was no news in the F.O. telegrams this morning, except that Russia still vetoes the Italian demand to the Dalmatian coast. She will allow her the bit from Zara to Sebenico (alas! you have no map) but insists on the rest going to Serbia or being neutralised. On the merits, Russia is quite right, but it is so important to bring in Italy at once, greedy & slippery as she is, that we ought not to be too precise in haggling over this or that. As I told you yesterday, Roumania is now a certainty—at any rate after the 1st May. If in addition we cd. rope in both Italy & Bulgaria (Austria being now almost in extremis) we ought to be within sight of the end of the war. . . .

Vice-Admiral de Robeck to Winston S. Churchill: telegram
(Churchill papers: 13/65)

27 March 1915
1.30 am
Secret

I do not consider check on 18th was decisive and am still of opinion that a portion of Fleet would succeed in entering Sea of Marmora. Nothing has occurred since 21st to alter my intention to press enemy hard until I am in a position to deliver a decisive attack. On 21st I was prepared to go forward irrespective of the Army as I fully realised that this matter must be carried through to a successful issue regardless of cost and also because in view of the military opinion expressed in your 70[1] and which if persisted in would in no wise assist the Navy in their task I did not anticipate the possibility of Military co-operation in the forcing of the Straits though I have always been of opinion that decisive result would be best obtained by a combined operation rather than by either a Naval or Military force acting alone.

On 22nd having conferred with General and heard his proposals I learned that the co-operation of the Army and Navy was considered by him a sound

---

[1] Churchill's telegram to de Robeck of 24 March 1915 (quoted on pp. 728–30).

operation of war and that he was fully prepared to work with the Navy in the forcing of the Dardanelles but that he could not act before the 14th April. The plan discussed with General Hamilton and now in the course of preparation pending your approval of my 256 will effect in my opinion decisive and overwhelming results.

The original approved plan for forcing the Dardanelles by ships was drawn up on the assumption that gunfire alone was capable of destroying forts. This assumption has been conclusively proved to be wrong when applied to the attacking of open forts by high velocity guns; for instance Fort 8 has been frequently bombarded at distant and close ranges, the damage caused is possibly one gun disabled. Shells which hit either expended their destructive power uselessly on the parapet or destroyed some unimportant building in the background of the fort; to obtain direct hits on each gun has been found impracticable even at ranges of 700 to 800 yards as was attempted in the case of forts 3 and 6. One gun in fort 4 was found loaded and fit for service on 26th February although the fort had been heavily bombarded for two days at long range and at short range.

The utmost that can be expected of ships is to dominate the forts to such an extent that gun crews cannot fight the guns; any more permanent disablement could only be carried out with an excessive expenditure of ammunition at point blank range, the report of operations carried out against Tsing Tau recently received strengthens this opinion. Conclusions drawn from the attack on the cupola forts at Antwerp by heavy howitzers are quite misleading when applied to the case described above. To engage forts 7 and 8 at close range entails ships coming under fire of forts at the Narrows, these have therefore to be silenced with consequent heavy expenditure of ammunition which cannot be spared.

Further, wear of the old guns is causing me some anxiety; on the 18th there were several premature bursts of common shell and guns were out of action from time to time. It would be the worst policy to carry out bombardment which could not be brought to a decisive result. To destroy forts therefore it is necessary to land demolishing parties. To cover these parties at the Narrows is a task General Hamilton is not prepared to undertake and I fully concur in his view. To carry the demolition out by surprise is impracticable. The mine menace being even greater than anticipated the number of torpedo tubes, by all reports, having been added to, combined with the fact that they cannot be destroyed, materially increases the difficulties of clearing passage for the Fleet which has to be carried out while the forts are kept silenced by gunfire.

The result of Naval action alone might in my opinion be a brilliant success or quite indecisive. Success depends largely on the effect that the appearance of the Fleet off Constantinople would produce on the Turkish army which appears to control the situation in Turkey at present and which is itself dominated by the Germans, but if the Turkish army is undismayed by the advent of the Fleet into the Sea of Marmora and the Straits are closed behind it the length of time which ships can operate as indicated in your 86 and 88 and maintain themselves in that Sea depends almost entirely on the number of Colliers and ammunition which can accompany the Fleet and as the passage will be contested the percentage of large unprotected ships which can be expected to get through is small.

The passage of supply ships for the Fleet through the Dardanelles with the forts still intact is a problem to which I can see no practical solution. In such a case it would be vital for the Army to occupy the Peninsula which would open the Strait as guns on Asiatic side can be dominated from the European shore sufficiently to permit ships to pass through. The landing of an army of the size contemplated in the face of strenuous opposition is in my opinion an operation requiring the assistance of all Naval forces available. A landing at Bulair would not necessarily cause Turks to abandon Peninsula and there could be no two opinions that a Fleet intact outside the Dardanelles can do this better than the remains of a Fleet inside with little ammunition. With Gallipoli Peninsula held by our Army and Squadron through Dardanelles our succ ss would be assured. The delay possibly of a fortnight will allow co-operation which would really prove factor that will reduce length of time necessary to complete the campaign in Sea of Marmora and occupy Constantinople.

Winston S. Churchill to Vice-Admiral de Robeck: telegram

(*Copy, Churchill papers: 13/65*)

27 March 1915   Admiralty
11.40 am
Secret and Personal

I had hoped that it would have been possible to achieve the result according to original plan without involving the Army but the reasons you give make it clear that a combined operation is now indispensable.

Time also has passed, the troops are available & the date is not distant.

All your proposals will therefore be approved by Admiralty telegram.

I intend you to retain the command irrespective of Admiral Carden's recovery.

GOLIATH has been ordered to join you & the 3 cruisers in Egypt will come to Lemnos on the eve of the attack.

8 more BEAGLES & 3 of our best submarines have started.

W.C.3—3C

Lord Fisher: memorandum
(*Churchill papers: 13/56*)

27 March 1915   Admiralty
Secret

With reference to the Private and Personal telegram sent this forenoon (March 27th) by the First Lord to Vice-Admiral de Robeck (copy enclosed), stating that an official telegram from the Admiralty would be sent him approving his proposed action as conveyed in his private telegram to the First Lord (copy enclosed), my decided opinion is that before any such action the Admiralty should have before them the report to the War Office of Sir Ian Hamilton as to his proposed future action, together with the remarks thereon of the War Office as to the likelihood of the proposed military operations (in co-operation with the Fleet) being so favourable as to ustify the very considerable Naval losses that may ensue.

Such justifiable losses for so great a political prize as Constantinople might possibly at the same time jeopardise our desired large margin of superiority over the German Navy in the decisive theatre—observing that the despatch of submarines and destroyers from England to-day to the Dardanelles, together with those detained there on passage home, is a serious diminution of our required force in home waters; and that also, in all directions, such as aircraft, nets, monitors, repair ship and light cruisers, our home resources are being heavily drawn upon by the Dardanelles operations, but perhaps most especially in the amount of ammunition and wear of the big guns.

It is only right, therefore, that at this critical stage, before the final plunge is taken and now that Sir Ian Hamilton has himself carefully surveyed the whole scene of operations and been in close consultation on the spot with Vice-Admiral de Robeck and his Officers, that we should be very fully informed by him of his considered opinion of all the probabilities of the military operations he had in prospect; and we ought to know also whether the War Office concur.

There have been signs of activity in the German High Sea Fleet, notably since the appointment of the new Commander-in-Chief, von Pohl, that indicate more vigorous action than has hitherto occurred, and quite likely our large detachment of the British naval force to the Dardanelles may lead to the German fleet undertaking, in conjunction with the seizure of Holland by the German Army, some big sea operation. The sudden hostile German attitude towards Holland, together with the submarine attack on five Dutch ships in the last few days, opens up possibilities of our requiring all our margin of Naval Force to operate on the Dutch Coast and in the North Sea.

We cannot lessen the strength of Sir John Jellicoe's command, some of whose much wanted light cruisers and destroyers we have been reluctantly compelled to withdraw for other services, so that his Fleet is not so well equipped as could be wished in these respects. Therefore there should be a very strong assurance of success in the Dardanelles project to justify the risks we run by this depletion of our strength in the decisive theatre of the war.

Vice-Admiral de Robeck is very explicit in pointing out that our bombardment has not disabled more than one of the Turkish guns; nor will our passage through the Narrows be effective unless the military operations give us the possession of the whole of the Gallipoli Peninsula. Also, he expresses his anxiety as to any further considerable use of the big guns of the old ships.

We have also to consider the arrival of hostile submarines when the troops may yet be in the transports and the Fleet not yet past the Narrows!

It must be added that the battle-cruiser Inflexible has been badly damaged at the Dardanelles, necessitating her being convoyed to Malta for repair, and that the Queen Elizabeth is dependent on one engine, so is a cause of anxiety until repaired. And we have lost two battleships, and the battleships Lord Nelson and Agamemnon are requiring repair. We have sixteen battleships now at the Dardanelles.

The appointment of Herr Kuhlmann[1] as the new German Minister at the Hague is of itself a most significant and sinister act, and, taken in conjunction with the expressed desire of the German Military Staff for the termination of Dutch neutrality, makes very probable some big German operation requiring all our force in the decisive theatre.

Winston S. Churchill to Vice-Admiral de Robeck: telegram

(*Copy, Churchill papers: 13/65*)

27 March 1915   Admiralty
5.40 pm
Secret & Personal

What will the Fleet do if the Army is checked? Suppose for instance that the Army is brought to a standstill against the Kilid Bahr Plateau, do you intend to push through separately leaving only sufficient ships to support the Army, or do you consider that your decisive attack can only be delivered if the Army have already succeeded?

---

[1] Richard von Kühlmann, 1873–1949. Entered the Berlin Foreign Office, 1893. Counsellor of the German Embassy in London, 1908–14. On missions to Turkey and Scandinavia, 1915–1917. Secretary of State for Foreign Affairs, 1917–18. An advocate of a negotiated peace, he tried to arrange for negotiations with Sir William Tyrrell in Holland in the summer of 1918, and was dismissed by the Kaiser.

Secondly, my desire is to sustain you in all action necessary for our success & therefore it is important I should know exactly what you have in mind.

Do not be vexed by these enquiries.

The only thing is to win.

Winston S. Churchill to Lord Fisher
(*Churchill papers: 13/56*)

28 March 1915   Admiralty

Your Memm of 27th.

I agree with you that we shd receive a full statement of the W.O. views on the action to be taken by the army at the Dlles. I will ask Kitchener about it when he returns on Tues. Meanwhile there is nothing to be done. Preparations are going forward out there, & the utmost vigilance shd be exercised at home.

I see no reason for anxiety here; tho' as a measure of added precaution you might, indeed I think you shd, send the remaining two Duncans available up to join Bradford; & expedite at the first safe moment the despatch of Warspite to Scapa, whether her 6″ director is finished or not.

It will be necessary when the time comes to launch the decisive attack at the D'lles——

We cannot go back now.

WSC

Vice-Admiral de Robeck to Winston S. Churchill
(*Churchill papers: 13/65*)

28 March 1915

I now think it possible there may be minefields above the Narrows of which we know very little.

Also the Germans may sink obstacles in the channel and may place submerged hulks and pontoons. I refer particularly to the very large pontoons now in the Golden Horn which carried the old road bridge between Stambul and Pera.

Of course there will be still the howitzers which are so difficult to locate from the sea.

In my opinion Gallipoli Peninsula will have to be taken and held by land force before Dardanelles can be passed with certainty by capital ships fitted to deal with Goeben and by the colliers and other vessels without which the utility of capital ships is very limited.

Lord Fisher to Winston S. Churchill

(*Churchill papers*)

28 March 1915   Admiral

Secret

First Lord

I noticed some indications in the 'secret papers' (after seeing you last night) that something big may be brewing after March 29th, and it may well be very serious when taken in conjunction with the recent very sudden and quite unexpected hostile German attitude towards Holland. Then there is the appointment of Kuhlmann to the Hague as German Minister; also the reported intention of the German General Staff to press for an immediate termination of Dutch neutrality; then the deliberate and apparently pre-meditated seizure of five Dutch ships in the last few days, and, above all, the sinking of the Dutch ship 'MEDEA' when laden only with oranges and her Dutch nationality proved by her papers to be undoubted; and also, as you have so clearly pointed out in your own paper (read by Lord Kitchener and Sir E. Grey last evening),[1] all favours your view that immense benefit will accrue to Germany by Holland being forced out of her neutrality at this special moment, when Germany has a great number of troops available—and can strike at once and gets five-sixths of Holland and also Antwerp and the Scheldt.

All this naturally re-acts on the Dardanelles business. We have, or shall have, sixteen Destroyers there that are very badly wanted indeed at home; the three Monitors have gone: the 'RELIANCE' (new repair ship); so also the 'ADAMANT' and three submarines, besides the Australian new submarine detained out there; also all sorts of home resources largely drawn on—e.g., Samson and his aircraft; nets; mine sweepers, etc, etc; and finally, the chief anxiety of all—the large expenditure of big gun ammunition, and, as pointed out by de Robeck, the serious anxiety as to the continuing efficiency of the big guns in the old ships. They will be certainly all worn out. The 'INFLEX-IBLE' *hors de combat* and about to be towed to Malta. The 'ELIZABETH' with only one engine (and so always a cause of anxiety, the 'OCEAN' and 'IRRESISTIBLE' sunk and 'LORD NELSON' and 'AGAMEMNON' requiring repair.

If the Germans decide (as well they may)—influenced largely no doubt by our having so large a force away from the decisive theatre—on some big thing at home, there is (you must admit) much cause for anxiety, especially

---

[1] This refers to a meeting held on 27 March between Churchill, Fisher, Kitchener and Grey, primarily to discuss the danger of a German invasion of Holland.

with the German and Austrian submarine menace to the yet unlanded troops and our Dardanelles fleet.

What is Ian Hamilton's report as to probable success? Admiral de Robeck does not look forward to disabling the Turkish guns.

Is the capture of the Gallipoli Peninsula going to be a siege? We should have the military opinion on this.

Is Ian Hamilton assured of the sufficiency of his force?

We know Admiral de Robeck to be a brave man, and he talks assuredly; but his assurance is really based on military co-operation and especially on the demolition of all the guns, thus assuring him of his safe communication with the sea and the safe passage of his storeships, colliers and ammunition supplies.

I prepared a formal Memorandum on the whole subject last night, which I attach.

P.S.

I am not blind to the political necessity of going forward with the task, but before going further forward let the whole situation be so fully examined that success is assured while safety in the decisive theatre is not compromised.

Lord Fisher to Winston S. Churchill

(*Churchill papers: 13/56*)

29 March 1915   Admiralty

Dear Winston,

The reason the enclosed two papers are typed—one written at 11.P.M. last night & the other at 3 A.M. this morning—I had put things that would only teaze you and no compensating good so I scratched them out & I was too tired to rewrite them.

The slowness of brain of many in high places appals me.

Your paper on Holland about the very best you ever wrote—it produced no effect whatever.

I am having a day out but will be at Admiralty this evening.

Yours

F

The 'Adamant' and the 3 submarines of 'E' Class will reach the Dardanelles on *April 12th*.

Vice-Admiral de Robeck to Winston S. Churchill: telegram

(Copy, Churchill papers: 13/65)

29 March 1915

There is only one idea here & that is to win.

The additional reinforcements will place us in strong position for attack & co-operation with Army & should prove adequate.

Directly the Army is landed in the Gallipoli Peninsula the Fleet commences its attack on the Narrows. To make this attack decisive, the co-operation of the Army is necessary in order to utterly destroy the forts of Kilid Bahr.

No matter where the Army effects its landing, the extreme objective of both Services must be above the forts & the intention is to attack them simultaneously with all our forces; until the passage through the Narrows is secure it would be militarily unsound to operate with the Fleet in the Sea of Marmora. If the Army is checked in its advance on Kilid Bahr, the question as to whether the Navy should or should not force the Narrows, leaving the forts intact, will depend entirely on whether the Fleet could assist Army in their advance to the Narrows best from below Chanak with communications intact, or from above cut off from its base. So many Military considerations enter into the question that it is impossible to lay down anything definite, but if the forcing of the Narrows by ships alone is found to be expedient the Fleet will do so.

There has been really no delay; training the personnel of mine sweeping vessels & mine net craft was necessary & has been proceeding during recent bad weather under lee of Tenedos Island & is still proceeding.

As the Fleet will be engaged besides being occupied by covering landing Army & sweeping operations, few officers can be spared from the ships to assist in these important duties, I am therefore asking officially by mail for Officers who I know are well qualified for these services, & if approved, I request they may be sent at once via Marseilles or Toulon with all despatch.

Winston S. Churchill to Lord Fisher, Vice-Admiral Oliver and Sir Arthur Wilson

(Churchill papers: 13/54)

29 March 1915   Admiralty

Most Secret & Urgent

There are many indications of an impending movement—possibly tomorrow.[1] If we wait till we are certain what is going to happen we shall be too late

---

[1] A reference to intercepted German naval wireless messages, which on several occasions had suggested, and were to suggest, an imminent naval sortie by the German High Sea Fleet into the North Sea (see also pp. 731, 901).

to act, because too far away. We ought *now*—on the chance—to send Commodore T [Tyrwhitt] with 3 Light cruisers, 4 to 6 sms, & the M's & L's to cruise out of aerial reconnaissance range about 50 miles N.E. of Terschelling. He can stay there 3 days comfortably, & if meanwhile any movement is [seen] he can attack the enemy's ships with the torpedoes by sms by day or with destroyers by night as convenient.

But nót to act now—is to throw away the torpedo opportunity as we have done on every previous occasion.

WSC

Lieutenant-Colonel Hankey: diary
(Hankey papers)

29 March 1915

. . . [Fisher] kept me alone in his study for an hour, explaining his difficulties with Churchill, who insists on sending telegrams to the Admirals marked 'private' but dealing with public matters with which the Board alone ought to deal. Fisher again threatens to resign, but I dissuaded him. . . .

H. H. Asquith to Venetia Stanley
(Montagu papers)

29 March 1915   10 Downing Street

. . . McKenna came to see me just before lunch, with a tragic history of intrigue. The idea is that Northcliffe (for some unknown reason) has been engineering a campaign to supplant me by Ll.G! McK is of course quite certain that Ll.G, & perhaps Winston are 'in it'. Which I don't believe. However, he (McK) has a certain amount of evidence as to Ll.G to go upon. I can't write it down, wh. makes me the more irritated that we couldn't have had our drive & talk this afternoon. For, as you know well, yours is my best & most trusted opinion.

I lunched with the Assyrian, tête à tête, and his loyalty is a certain & invaluable asset. Of course he is rather anti-McK, whom he suspects as a mischief maker.

I asked him what wd happen if the so-called 'intrigue' were to come off, & I was supposed to go. He replied without a moment's hesitation that the *whole* Cabinet, including Ll.G. & Winston, would go with me, & make any alternative impossible. . . .

H. H. Asquith to Venetia Stanley

(*Montagu papers*)

30 March 1915   10 Downing Street

. . . I had a small conclave here this morning—K, Winston, myself, & Hankey—to go over carefully & quietly the situation, actual & prospective, at the Dardanelles. There are risks, & it will in any event be an expensive operation, but I am sure we are right to go through with it.

This is the really critical month of the war; an actual equilibrium, with perhaps a slight turn in favour of the allies: the possible belligerents (Italy, Greece, Bulgaria, Roumania) all hanging in the balance; everyone anxious about their own & their opponents' supplies of ammunition: and so much depending upon whether the coin turns up Heads or Tails at the Dardanelles.

If all (or most) of these doubtful hazards go well for us, the war ought to be over in 3 months. But we have had little, & ought not to count on more, of the favours of fortune: so all one can do is to possess one's soul in patience. . . .

Sir Ian Hamilton to Vice-Admiral de Robeck: telegram

(*Copy, Churchill papers: 2/74*)

30 March 1915

Copy of number 140[1] from Admiralty received. I had already communicated outline of our plan to Lord Kitchener and am pushing on preparations as fast as possible. War Office still seems to cherish hope that you may break through without landing troops. Therefore, as regards yourself I think wisest procedure will be to push on systematically though not recklessly in attack on Forts. It is always possible that opposition may suddenly crumple up. If you should succeed be sure to leave light cruisers enough to see me through my military attack in the event of that being after all necessary. If you do not succeed then I think we quite understand one another.

[1] Churchill's 'personal and secret' telegram to de Robeck of 24 March 1915 (quoted on pp. 728–30).

Maurice Bonham Carter to Winston S. Churchill

(*Admiralty papers: 137/110*)

30 March 1915   10 Downing Street

Dear Mr. Churchill,

The Prime Minister has decided to appoint a small departmental Committee to consider the nature of British desiderata in Asia Minor in the event of a successful conclusion of the War, with especial reference to the memoranda on the subject which have lately been drawn up by the Foreign Office, India Office, War Office, Admiralty, and the Defence Committee. The Committee will be composed of representatives of the offices named, together with the Board of Trade. Sir Maurice de Bunsen[1] will act as Chairman.

The Prime Minister would be much obliged if you would nominate a representative of your Department.[2] It is advisable, in his opinion, that the Committee should be a small one, and therefore one member from each Department appears to be sufficient.

Yours sincerely
M. Bonham Carter

H. H. Asquith to Venetia Stanley

(*Montagu papers*)

30 March 1915   10 Downing Street
6.00 pm

. . . I told you I was going to have an interview à trois with Ll. G. & McK. So they came here at 3.30 and we had an hour together. It was as you may imagine at moments 'rather' exciting. L.G. began on a very stormy note, accusing McK of having inspired Donald[3] to write the article in the Chronicle wh. was headed 'Intrigue agst the P.M', and in one sentence of which (only

---

[1] Maurice William Ernest de Bunsen, 1852–1932. Entered the Diplomatic Service, 1877. Secretary of Embassy at Constantinople, 1897–1902. Knighted, 1905. Ambassador, Vienna, 1913–14. Created Baronet, 1919.

[2] Churchill nominated Sir Henry Jackson to serve on the Committee. The other members were G. R. Clerk (Foreign Office) Major-General Callwell (War Office), Sir Thomas Holderness (India Office), Sir Hubert Llewellyn Smith (Board of Trade) and Sir Mark Sykes, MP, with Lieutenant-Colonel Hankey as Secretary. The Committee's secret report was circulated to the senior Ministers on 8 July 1915. It examined five schemes for the territorial future of Turkey. Under each scheme, Russia would annex Constantinople and control the Gallipoli Peninsula, while Britain would have a dominant influence in Mesopotamia.

[3] Robert Donald, 1861–1933. Editor, *Daily Chronicle*, 1902–18. Chairman, Empire Press Union, 1915–26. A Director, Department of Information, 1917. A strong advocate of dropping leaflets over enemy territory. Knighted, 1924. A friend of the first Labour Prime Minister, Ramsay MacDonald, for whom he undertook publicity work.

one) his name was mentioned. McK as hotly denied that he had ever said or suggested to Donald that Ll. G. was in the 'plot', while admitting that he had had a talk with him on the subject of the attacks in the Tory press. Ll. G. proceeded to accuse McK of always seeing imaginary plots: e.g. in this very matter, and Winston's supposed campaign against Grey. To wh. McK rejoined that the person he really suspected was A.J.B, with whom we all agreed Winston was much too intimate. . . .

H. H. Asquith to Venetia Stanley
(Montagu papers)

30 March 1915   10 Downing Street
11.30 pm

. . . I had a most characteristic letter from Winston, just before dinner. He said he had refused Ll. G's invitation to come to our interview this afternoon: because (as he said) 'I feel that my case is safe in your hands'. That bears out what you said in your most darling letter—that (whatever happens) W. is really loyal to me. I am sure, & have never doubted, that he is. So that silly 'plot' is done with.

Lord Fisher to Winston S. Churchill
(Churchill papers: 13/56)

31 March 1915   Admiralty

I concur in your proposal to remit this question [Borkum] for careful study by Sir A. K. Wilson with whom I have on many occasions discussed it in general terms. (*The whole problem depends on the efficiency of our arguments for protection against submarines—an effective means of protection is not yet in sight*). This operation would necessarily await the trend of events in the Dardanelles— we must know what forces remain before embarking on a new undertaking.

We are now committed to the Dardanelles at all costs so must anyhow wait till middle of May by which time events in Holland may quite change the position and indicate Terschelling as our base.[1]

H. H. Asquith to George V
(Royal Archives)

31 March 1915   10 Downing Street

. . . Mr Churchill reported that sweeping operations were being continued at the Dardanelles. . . .

[1] On 1 April Churchill sent Fisher's letter to Sir Arthur Wilson with the note: 'I agree with First Sea Lord. I shall be greatly obliged if you will "implement" this project on the assumption that we are not crippled by losses at the Dardanelles.' (*Churchill papers: 13/56*)

April 1915

Lord Fisher to Winston S. Churchill

(Churchill papers: 13/57)

2 April 1915   Admiralty

Dear Winston,

I hope this finds you—as it leaves me—quite well!

I thought I had a throat coming on but drastic measures have cured it (I harangued about 20 meetings yesterday on various admiralty topics.)

I told Crease last night he could find the Borkum papers in a sealed envelope addressed to you in my drawer. I had intended giving them to you myself last evening. No doubt you will speak yourself to A.K. Wilson & not simply hurl them at his head! As usual he is quite sure to loyally dissect every detail and work it all out and let us hope that the Dardanelles will be past & over by the desired date to your honour & glory and that those d—d Greeks will be jolly well sold by the Bulgarians being first in & so getting *Salonica & Kavalla & Macedonia generally* as their reward! I EARNESTLY HOPE THIS MAY RESULT! Had the Greeks come in all would have been well without doubt! (Did you see that a Bulgarian General[1] strongly urged an alternative disembarking place for our troops! *Does Kitchener know?*)

We cant send another rope yarn even to de Robeck! WE HAVE GONE TO THE VERY LIMIT! and so they must not hustle and should be distinctly & most emphatically told that no further re-inforcement of the Fleet can be looked for! *A failure or check in the Dardanelles would be nothing—a failure in the North Sea would be* RUIN! but I dont wish to be pessimistic! & let us hope that Gal-

---

[1] Not traced, but the Bulgarian Prime Minister, Vasil Radoslavov favoured neutrality. On 2 April *The Times* reported a speech he had delivered in Sofia on 28 March, stressing that Bulgaria would observe 'the strictest neutrality' and would not yield 'to any pressure, nor even to vague promises, from whatever sources they may emanate because the Government is bound to safeguard the real interests of Bulgarian....' Every Bulgarian Government, he had continued, 'must be on its guard against temptations which, however, attractive, whether they come from the East or the West'.

lipoli aint going to be Plevna or that de Robeck will be 'Duckworthed'! I shall be at Admiralty at 11.

Yours
F

There's an excellent article by Spenser Wilkinson[1] in last night's Westminster Gazette.[2] I know the Morning Post has kicked him out! he used to be the Chief Leader writer!

Winston S. Churchill to Lord Fisher

(*Admiralty papers: 137/1089*)

3 April 1915   Admiralty
1.S.L

It is clear that the favourable turn to our affairs in S.E. Europe arose from the initial success of our attack on the Dardanelles, was checked by the repulse of the 18th, & can only be restored by the general success of the operations. It is thus necessary to fight a battle, (a thing wh has often happened before in war) & abide the consequences whatever they may be.

WSC

Sir Edward Grey to Sir Francis Bertie and Sir George Buchanan: telegram[3]

(*Copy, Admiralty papers: 137/1089*)

3 April 1915   Foreign Office

The attack by the Allied forces on the Dardanelles will be pressed to a decision. Our Naval and Military authorities consider that the undertaking presents good prospects of success, but it is of the highest importance to make sure of success in view of the effect which the result of these operations is bound to have.

[1] Henry Spenser Wilkinson, 1853–1937. Naval and military historian. Leader writer and writer on military affairs for the *Morning Post*, 1895–1914. Chichele Professor of Military History at Oxford, 1909–23.

[2] On 1 April, in an article entitled 'Stocktaking' in the *Westminster Gazette*, Spenser Wilkinson wrote approvingly that the 'strategical conscience' of the navy was not in the head of the Admiralty Board, but 'in the 1st Sea Lord's pocket'. The Admiralty, he continued, 'will listen to its strategical conscience, which says "Do not divide your fleet" '. The danger lay, he wrote, in the Grand Fleet 'weakening itself by detachment'; for that, he believed, was the moment when the German High Sea Fleet would attack.

[3] Churchill noted on this telegram, for Lord Fisher and Vice-Admiral Oliver: 'This telegram was drafted by PM in response to Admiralty representations.'

It is therefore very desirable that Greece or Bulgaria or preferably both, should at once define their position and enter the war on the side of the allies.

The Admiralty attach the utmost importance to the co-operation of the Greek fleet and flotillas, particularly the latter. Ample number of small craft will greatly increase the feasibility of passing an allied fleet into the Sea of Marmora.

His Majesty's Government therefore hope that the Government to which you are accredited will agree to our informing the Greek Minister for Foreign Affairs[1] that we should welcome Greek assistance if Greek Government were ready to offer it. We could remind Greek Government at the same time that, unless such co-operation is offered now, there will be little or no opportunity left for Greece to advance claims for compensation in the Smyrna region at the end of the war.

John Churchill to Winston S. Churchill

(Churchill papers: 1/117)

3 April 1915   GHQ
Secret   Mediterranean Expeditionary Force

Dear Winston,

Things are shaping themselves. The task of unloading so many ships is almost finished and re-embarking begins on the 5th. The delay has been very irksome, but it was absolutely necessary. The ships were packed anyhow and a reshuffle was essential. It would have been fatal to have attempted anything, without having units completely self contained, and ready to disembark under any circumstances.

My letter has to go through the ordinary post, but I can give some aspects of the situation. My friend [Sir Ian Hamilton] is very well. He is very determined and takes 'must' as his motto, while considering all the difficulties to be overcome. The lieutenants B., H.W. & D'A[2] are rather gloomy, and see only the difficult side of the question. They talk of impossibilities and have put their views on papers. D'A is helpful and fully prepared to do whatever is asked to the best of his ability, but the enthusiasm shown by H.W. in London & B, when he thought he was to command, has partly evaporated.

[1] George Zographos 1863–1920. Greek Minister of Foreign Affairs 7 July–15 August 1909 and 28 February–6 July 1915. Regional Governor of Epirus 1913–14. Joint Governor of the National Bank of Greece, 1914 and 1915–17.

[2] Generals Birdwood, Hunter-Weston and D'Amade, who commanded respectively the Australian and New Zealand (Anzac) forces, the 29th Division, and the French forces at the Dardanelles.

They all have alternative plans which do not meet the immediate case. My friend considers the main object at the moment is to enable the RN to get through as soon as possible. Once that is done the whole situation must be reviewed and further orders will be given from home. He is confident that the others will be allright 'on the day', and their forebodings have not affected the plans and orders in any essential. Write to me now & then. The staff have all turned up. They were all selected by the W.O. and no one here was consulted as to the choice, which seems odd. The Australians have a most magnificent appearance and I am told the 29th is one of the very best div's ever sent abroad.

Best love. Next time I hope to write good news about guns going off!!

Yours
Jack S C

Winston S. Churchill to David Lloyd George
(Lloyd George papers)

3 April 1915   Admiralty

My dear David,

Kitchener has been fumbling and peddling over these rifles[1]—vitally needed—for the last 3 or 4 months.

If you approve I will buy them, & carry them away, & give them to him. Let me have an answer by return. Strong measures are needed.

Yours ever
W

David Lloyd George to Winston S. Churchill
(Admiralty papers: 116/1681)

4 April 1915   Treasury Chambers

My dear Winston,

Certainly get them any how & at any price. Do you wish me to make arrangements about cash or will Dawson see to that?

Yours
D. Lloyd George

Von Donop could have had the Krag Jorgensens[2] also if he had been smart about it.

[1] The short Springfield rifle, which since 1904 had been the standard rifle of the United States army.
[2] The Krag-Jörgensen was the standard rifle of the United States army up to 1904, when it was replaced by the short Springfield.

Vice-Admiral de Robeck to Admiralty: telegram

(*Copy, Churchill papers: 13/65*)

4 April 1915

Covering force will be landed in pulling boats, from transports and ships, towed in towards landing place(s), transports not approaching until footing has been gained; details of covering force which cannot be landed in first trip will approach landing place(s) in destroyers and mine sweeping vessels, &c.

General Hamilton has not informed me yet whether the covering force will land at night and attempt a surprise or by day and obtain maximum assistance from gun fire of Fleet; our preparations cover both contingencies. Main body will be landed chiefly in lighters; 44 of these are available all horse boats from Egypt being brought in transports; to tow these are 18 tugs together with picket boats of Fleet and some trawlers. Picket boats have all had thorough overhaul since the 18th and ships boats have been fitted with brows. Floating pier head has been constructed; once pier has been built French mine sweeping vessels will be able to land men themselves direct. Everything is being done to ensure a rapid landing which will continue day and night.

Personnel. All tugs, lighters, and transport boats are being provided with service ratings. For first two, crews from OCEAN, IRRESISTIBLE, have been taken, remainder will be found by battleships. Supply of Officers is chief difficulty. Beach and transport parties are being detailed and all arrangements that can be undertaken before the return of General Hamilton are being pushed on. Captain Mitchell[1] has gone with General Hamilton to Egypt to complete certain details with which he has been occupied for several weeks. Progress to date has I consider been good and directly General Hamilton returns the final orders will be given. Rear Admiral Wemyss who is in general charge of the landing has made arrangements for a regular service of supply ships to run between Mudros and the army.

With regard to progress of mine sweeping preparations 17 British trawlers all available have had service or volunteer crews placed in them; Naval Officers are in command of each. 8 BEAGLE class destroyers have been fitted with 9 foot kites and $2\frac{1}{2}$ inches sweeps (as fast as possible?). 8 BEAGLES will

---

[1] Francis Herbert Mitchell, 1876–1946. Entered Navy, 1891. Captain, 1913. Served at Gallipoli on the Naval Staff, 1915. Naval Adviser to the C-in-C of British Forces in Egypt, 1916. Commanded HMS *Exmouth*, 1916–17 and HMS *Bellerophon*, 1918–19. Commanded the Naval Gunnery School, Portsmouth, 1920–3. Rear-Admiral in the 2nd Battle Squadron, Atlantic Fleet, 1925–6. Vice-Admiral and Admiral Superintendent, Malta Dockyard, 1928–31. Admiral, 1933.

be similarly fitted at Malta these will be used as fast sweeping boats. 6 RIVER Class have been fitted with light sweeps for use as mine-seekers. Picket boats are prepared with explosive creeps. Net parties organised. All are practiced daily and sweep inside Dardanelles to keep clear area in which ships will manœuvre primarily.

Lord Fisher to Sir John Jellicoe
(*Jellicoe papers*)

4 April 1915   Admiralty
BURN

My dear Jellicoe,
   I have time for little else now but increasing anxiety over the Dardanelles situation. I know so very little of de Robeck and Ian Hamilton that I am not able to rely on their judgment, and Keyes is very shallow and has not shined so far! No good purpose would be served by my resigning. My opinions are known. But the politicians took the bit between their teeth and decided it was a Cabinet and not an 'expert' question, and Kitchener unwittingly led on by thinking it was going to be a purely naval operation, which Carden undoubtedly said but I never agreed to, and so here we are! . . .
   It's no use being downhearted! Sir E. Grey has gone trout-fishing and the Prime Minister gone to the country!

                                                                  Yours
                                                                     F

David Lloyd George to Winston S. Churchill
(*Churchill papers: 2/68*)

5 April 1915   11 Downing Street

My dear Winston
   I am sorry that in our conversation this afternoon I got angry & said what I ought not to have allowed myself to say.[1]
   I was very rattled altogether after a most disappointing interview with K. That is my only excuse but it is an inadequate one at best. I am altogether disappointed at the way we are facing—or rather not facing our difficulties.
   Pray accept my apology

                                                        Yours sincerely
                                                        D. Lloyd George

[1] The cause and course of the dispute between Churchill and Lloyd George on 5 April is described in Frances Stevenson's diary for 8 April (quoted on pp. 776–7).

W.C.3 — 3D

Winston S. Churchill to David Lloyd George

(*Lloyd George papers*)

5 April 1915   Admiralty

My dear David,

It was *I* who was churlish & difficult.

It is vy kind indeed of you to write as you do.

I admire & value intensely the contribution of energy courage & resolve wh you are making to the progress of our affairs at their crisis. I share your anxieties, & am not at all removed in thought from your main policy.

Yours always
W

Lord Fisher to Winston S. Churchill

(*Churchill papers: 13/57*)

5 April 1915   Admiralty

Dear Winston,

A.K.W. spoke to me last night of the rich 'Kettle of fish' there'd be if those 21 fast armed German ships escaped from New York—! Our 'Glasgow' class as he truly says no use in big Atlantic Seas and heavy gales to catch these huge ships built for these seas and gales—and he says a Battle Cruiser the only thing we possess to catch them but we cant spare one! We must just chance it. From Maginess[1] report the 'Inflexible' is far worse than 'Lion' so will be quite 3 months hors-de-combat! The war may be over by then if Holland comes in! I dont think you are sufficiently impressed by Cambon's warning as to Holland! *We ought to have every detail organized to move in a moment to Texel!* You are just simply eaten up with the Dardanelles and cant think of anything else!

D—n the Dardanelles! they'll be our grave! A.K.W. says *Texel* not *Terschelling*—that ought to be settled—Kitchener ought to have some good troops told off—transports ready—Every one told off—! We shall be as usual 'Too late'!

We could have had the Greeks & everyone else at the right time but we are 'too late' ALWAYS! This war might be described as '*Procrastinations—vacillations—Antwerps*' (That's copyright!)

Yrs
F

[1] Edmond John Maginess, 1857–1938. Naval constructor. Chief Constructor, Pembroke Dock, 1912–15. Constructive Manager, Chatham, 1915–18. Deputy Director of Dockyards at the Admiralty.

Winston S. Churchill to Sir John Jellicoe: not sent
(*Draft, Churchill papers: 13/50*)

5 April 1915   Admiralty
Secret and Persona

My dear Jellicoe,

Our main attack on the Dardanelles should take place about the middle of this month. If this is successful the 'Queen Elizabeth' will be able to return home at once, although, as some of the blades have been removed from one of her reversing turbines, there is a loss of one-eighth power going astern. The 'Warspite' is ready now and only awaits a favourable moon to join you. 'Albemarle' and 'Russell' are similarly situated and should go North about the 8th or 9th to join Bradford. They are certainly doing no good isolated where they are. I have always done my best to strengthen your Fleet in every way and have taken a great deal of trouble during the last three months to secure you the 'Australia', to collect as many powerful armoured cruisers as possible for you, and to equip you with light cruisers of both 'Town' and 'Arethusa' classes. Your position is now a very strong one, far stronger than at the beginning of the war, and so I think you are rather hard on the Admiralty in your letter of the 21st March.

At the beginning of this letter you assume that the 'Lutzow' and 4 of the 'König' class are already armed with 15″ guns, and before you reach the end of it you treat this as a fact on which calculations are to be based. There is no foundation at all for such an assumption. I have had the matter re-examined by the Committee which formerly dealt with the suggestion that 14″ guns were being put in these vessels, and their report will be forwarded to you officially. When due consideration is given to the evidence on both sides, to the immense structural alterations involved in the substitution of 15″ for 12″ guns, to the time required in dockyard hands to effect structural changes of this kind, and to what we know of the movements of most of these ships since the war began, it will be seen that the assumption you wish to treat as a fact is not one which can be reasonably entertained. Neither is there any sign of any marked acceleration of German shipbuilding. We know in fact that the 'Regensburg' was considerably behind her expected date, and other vessels, so far as we can check them, seem to be conforming to the normal. Our own experience of warship building deliveries is that the construction of great ships, and particularly of their gun mountings, cannot be pressed forward beyond a certain minimum of time. You are so well informed on these matters that I do not enlarge on them. It does not therefore seem to me right for you to assume that you will have to meet 6 ships armed with 15″ guns before a single vessel similarly armed has joined you, especially in view of the fact that the 'Warspite', to which you omit all reference, will be with you in a few days. That you should wish to have the 'Queen Elizabeth' and, indeed, every other new vessel of all classes attached to the Grand Fleet is natural [but it should be possible for you to give expression to this desire without using a number of arguments which cannot possibly carry conviction to persons who have the means of making themselves acquainted with the facts].[1]

I am so great an admirer of the skill and care with which you handle the immense Fleet now under your command and of the efficiency of your work in every branch, that I cannot help feeling sorry when I see the Admiralty records filling up with a long series of letters of complaint full of pessimism and alarms for which there is no warrant in the circumstances. Of course, every endeavour will be made to add to our fighting strength at sea as quickly as possible, and 'Valiant', 'Barham', 'Canada', and 'Malaya' are all being pushed forward with the utmost speed.

I consider, and have several times mentioned to you the fact, that while the operations in the Mediterranean are still undetermined and the Germans know we have a number of ships absent there, you should so far as possible keep your Fleet rested, ready and at its highest strength. When 'Warspite' become efficient and 'Queen Elizabeth' and 'Inflexible' join you, and when perhaps a large number of the ships now employed in the Dardanelles have returned to home waters, refits might proceed more rapidly than hitherto. But during this month I have a feeling that great events might easily take place and I grudge the departure of any capital unit of the first class. I say this not because of any doubt of the sufficiency of your margin, but on the broad principle of having everything possible in the line on the great occasion.

I am sorry I could not meet your wishes about Heath.[2] It is plainly his duty to stay where he is. Tottenham,[3] though personally I do not think him very agreeable, is a man of character, determination, and professional ability, and fully deserves a Cruiser Squadron in the Grand Fleet. I have had to ask you on other papers for your opinion in regard to Warrender.[4]

[1] None of this letter was sent; and the passage in square brackets was deleted by Churchill from his original draft.
[2] Herbert Leopold Heath, 1861–1954. Entered Navy, 1874. Captain, 1902. Naval Attaché, Berlin, 1908–10. Admiral Superintendent, Portsmouth Dockyard, 1912–15. Rear-Admiral Commanding the 7th and 2nd Cruiser Squadrons, and 3rd Battle Squadron at Jutland, 1916. Knighted, 1917. Vice-Admiral, 1917. 2nd Sea Lord, 1918–19. Admiral, 1919. Commander-in-Chief, Coast of Scotland, 1919–22.
[3] Henry Loftus Tottenham, 1860–1950. Entered Navy, 1873. Fought at Tel-el-Kebir with the Naval Brigade, 1882. Rear-Admiral with the Home Fleet, 1912–14. Commanded the 7th Cruiser Squadron, Grand Fleet, 1914–15. Vice-Admiral, 1915. Admiral, 1918.
[4] It was not until December 1915 that Jellicoe finally decided that Warrender's growing deafness made him unsuitable to continue in his command of the 2nd Battle Cruiser Squadron, which he had commanded since 1912.

He is an old friend of mine and I should greatly grieve to cause him pain, but the interests of the service must prevail and, if it is found that his increasing deafness is a serious bar to his efficiency, a change must be made.

H. H. Asquith to Venetia Stanley

(*Montagu papers*)

5 April 1915   10 Downing Street

. . . The delay in the Dardanelles is very unfortunate: visible progress, and still more a theatrical coup, in that quarter would have goaded all the laggard States including Greece & Bulgaria into the arena. Meanwhile the Bulgarians, by way of a little fun, have been raiding the Greek & Serbian frontiers.

Winston S. Churchill to Lord Kitchener

(*Copy, Churchill papers: 13/50*)

6 April 1915   Admiralty

My dear Kitchener,

On the 16th of February the Admiralty wrote an official letter to the W.O. asking for information about the anticipated deliveries of trotyl & picric acid month by month to the end of December next as compared with naval & military requirements. An early reply was asked for on the 1st & 18th of March, & again on the 2nd of April. Up to the present no answer has been given us.

I am afraid I must ask you for this information without wh it is impossible to arrange about the ammunition of the Fleet, the supply of mines, bombs, explosive sweeps etc. [I cannot possibly accept the responsibility while remaining in ignorance on a vital matter like this.

It adds enormously to the labour of official work when reasonable & necessary inquiries by one department are not taken any notice of by the others.

I will have to ask at the Cabinet tomorrow for a decision whether I shd be informed of the exact state of supplies of army ammunition & explosives.

I am vy sorry indeed to trouble you personally; but it is really not my fault.][1]

[1] The passages in square brackets were deleted by Churchill before he sent the letter.

Informal Meeting of the War Council: Secretary's Notes

(*Copy, Cabinet Office papers: 22/1*)

Present: H. H. Asquith (*in the Chair*), Winston S. Churchill, Lord Kitchener, Lieutenant-Colonel Hankey (*Secretary*)

6 April 1915   10 Downing Street

LORD KITCHENER read certain telegraphic correspondence with Sir Ian Hamilton, the Commander-in-Chief of the Dardanelles Expeditionary Force, and stated that no complete plan for the attack of the Straits had as yet been received.

MR. CHURCHILL read the full written report from Admiral de Robeck regarding the attack on the 18th March. The First Lord urged that the attack should be pressed home vigorously.

LORD KITCHENER agreed that the attack would have to be made.

LIEUTENANT-COLONEL HANKEY said that the difficulty would be to land the troops at all, owing to the opposition of howitzers in the ravines which intersect the Gallipoli Peninsula.

MR. CHURCHILL did not agree. He anticipated no difficulty in effecting a landing.

After some further discussion the meeting adjourned.

Winston S. Churchill to Vice-Admiral de Robeck: telegram

(*Copy, Churchill papers: 13/65*)

6 April 1915   Admiralty
Personal and Secret

I shall be glad if you will let me know what arrangements you are making—
(1) for net protection of ships against floating mines.
(2) for mine-bumpers. Three pairs of lighters with nets on frames attached to them are being prepared at Malta. You should ask A.S. Malta when they will arrive. Have you any other appliances for this purpose which you think it practicable to use?
(3) Have you considered the possible use of smoke screens to cover landings, or blanket off particular portions of the defence either from inside or outside the Straits?
Malta has been ordered to prepare a smoke making flotilla and you should ask for particulars and progress.
(4) We are told there is practically no water on Gallipoli Peninsula. If so this

would restrict numbers of Turkish garrison. Have you any information on this subject.

(5) Has any information been obtained of dispositions of enemy troops on either bank by aerial reconnaissance? Lord Kitchener wishes to know.

H. H. Asquith to Venetia Stanley
(*Montagu papers*)

7 April 1915   Foreign Office

. . . Hankey has just been in: very anxious about the Dardanelles, which he says Robertson (Chief of French's staff) describes as the stiffest operation anyone cd. undertake. Now that things look better with Italy & Roumania, Hankey strongly urges postponement—lest a check there shd. set back the whole situation. There is a great deal of force in this: . . . I am disposed to say that, before any landing is attempted, we shd. get from Sir I. Hamilton on the spot a considered review of the prospects. It is one of the cases in which military & diplomatic considerations are completely intertwined. . . .

Winston S. Churchill to Lord Kitchener
(*Kitchener papers*)

7 April 1915   Admiralty

My dear Kitchener,

I am distressed to have got into a dispute with you this morning.[1] It was far from my intention to do so, & I am vy sorry I allowed myself to become angry and hope you will dismiss from your mind anything wh I may have said unjustly.

Yours vy truly
Winston S. Churchill

This is a vy anxious time & we all have our worries.

Winston S. Churchill to David Lloyd George
(*Lloyd George papers*)

7 April 1915   Admiralty

My dear Chancellor of the Exchequer,

The proof of the Admiralty paper on excessive drinking was sent you before I had seen it; & I do not feel that I cd myself accept responsibility for

---

[1] In Cabinet. No records were taken of Cabinet discussions before 1918, and I can find no evidence of the subject of the dispute.

this document. I have no doubt the facts are accurate, but I do not feel convinced that they represent fairly the general labour situation. Naval officers & officials are prone to dwell on the weaknesses they notice in working men, & this is also true of employers. I could not without much more enquiry agree to the circulation of this paper outside Cabinet circles; nor do I think it ought to be published, or made the foundation of a prohibition campaign. I enclose you a note by Hopwood, which it seems to me you shd also take into consideration. I fear that if your energies are dissipated in a great prohibition campaign, the comparatively small practical measures which wd deal with the local evils, & the misbehaviour of minorities in particular places, will be overlooked. Certainly the Admiralty wd have instituted some very effective curtailment of hours & other measures against drinking in the military ports under the Defence of the Realm Act, if we had not thought it better to remit the matter to you for general treatment. I beg you to think of this. I am also hopeful about enlisting men into guilds or unions of Government workers. I think the most hopeful line is to restrict the quantities of alcohol in particular beverages. After all the French are drinking their wines & the Germans their beer; & we have never been a drunken & inefficient nation as the Russians were.

Yours vy sincerely
Winston S. Churchill

Frances Stevenson:[1] *diary*

(*Countess Lloyd-George papers*)

8 April 1915

. . . C[2] was discussing the drink question with Churchill, & Samuel & Montagu were also present. Churchill put on the grand air, and announced that he was not going to be influenced by the King, and refused to give up his liquor—he thought the whole thing absurd. C was annoyed, but went on to explain a point that had been brought up. The next minute Churchill interrupted again. 'I don't see . . .' he was beginning, but C broke in sharply:—

'You will see the point,' he rapped out, 'when you begin to understand the conversation is not a monologue!'

Churchill went very red, but did not reply, & C soon felt rather ashamed

---

[1] Frances Louise Stevenson, 1888–　　. Schoolteacher. Private Secretary to Lloyd George, 1913–43. She married Lloyd George in 1943. Countess Lloyd-George of Dwyfor, 1945.

[2] 'C' is an abbreviation for 'Chancellor', Frances Stevenson's way of referring to Lloyd George in her diary. At other points in her diary he is referred to as 'D' for 'David'.

of having taken him up so sharply, especially in front of the other two minions.

Vice-Admiral de Robeck to Winston S. Churchill: telegram

(*Copy, Churchill papers: 13/65*)

8 April 1915
3.15 am
Personal and secret

I do not anticipate difficulties in protecting ships against mines floating on the surface; picket boats can, and did on the 18th March, deal with these effectually they will also keep special watch for mines with slight negative buoyancy suspended from floats.

Mines drifting below surface are the chief dangers and against these I must rely upon the tunny nets and indicator nets with reduced mesh, these will be laid across Straits above area in which ships will manœuvre to attack Forts in the Narrows and defences of Kephez minefield. Malta is despatching an additional two miles of tunny nets which have a depth of 30 ft. There will be enough nets to completely span Straits. To silence the numerous guns a large number of ships must come into action using broadside fire and with 9 or 10 large ships operating in such confined waters it is in my opinion essential their manœuvring powers should be in no way hampered and that there should not be any risk of fouling propellers by gear shot away or carried away as would be the case in a formation effectively protected. In three cases out of 4 on 18th March vessels were struck by mines abaft the beam.

2nd, when fleet advances through Narrows, ships fitted with mine bumpers and net defences against torpedoes will lead. Difficulty has been experienced in extemporising effective protection, on lines suggested in Admiralty telegram 161 without docking ships, this is the objection to other devices which have been suggested. When the lighters being prepared by Malta arrive they will be tried but I do not anticipate being able to use any such protection in the first phases of attack as liberty to manœuvre is essential.

3rd, Smoke-screens will be used if they can be usefully employed but they may be double-edged weapons. They might be invaluable under certain conditions and I am glad to have them available.

4th. From intelligence furnished to the military by Greek inhabitants there is a plentiful supply of water in the peninsula, good springs are found in Seddul Bahr, Krithia, and farms in the vicinity and a Greek states that in Maidos during the last war Turks found a plenty of water (? plentiful supply of water in the) middle of summer for 50,000 troops, 2,000 horses besides 10,000 inhabitants in those towns. Our seaplanes report water in the Suandere and Avuzlar streams.

5th. during daylight Turks remain hidden. Our aerial reconnaissances have been unable to detect even small bodies of troops. Very few camps have been seen. The enemy chiefly occupy the villages. Ships at night using search lights have failed to discover any body of troops who are extremely well concealed. Deserters' estimates of numbers vary between 50,000 and 100,000 on both sides of the Straits.

Winston S. Churchill to Lord Kitchener

(*Copy, Churchill papers: 2/88*)

8 April 1915   Admiralty
Secret

My dear Kitchener,

If the military attack is checked at the Killid Bahr position, sites can be found for the 15-inch howitzer which will enable the forts at the Narrows to be bombarded with all the accuracy of fire attainable only in a shore gun. We think therefore it is a necessary precaution at this stage to get the gun on the way, and one which if we are checked may materially assist the Fleet passing the Narrows. All the arrangements have been made for ship and train. Admiral Bacon anticipates no difficulty whatever in getting the gun ashore, and in conveying it to a firing position. The fourth gun is now practically ready at Sheerness and will be over in France to replace this gun before French can want it.

In these circumstances the First Sea Lord and I wish most strongly that the despatch of the gun should go forward with the utmost speed as has been arranged.

I should be glad also if you would send the following to Sir John French from First Lord:—

We regard the immediate despatch of the gun as an imperative precaution at this juncture. We can replace it within a week by the fourth gun now finishing proof at Shoebury. We do not wish Admiral Bacon to go to the Dardanelles with the gun: his services are urgently required for a naval command here, and we shall be very grateful if you can spare him from the field army.

Yours sincerely
Winston S. Churchill

A. J. Balfour to Winston S. Churchill

(*Churchill papers: 13/50*)

8 April 1915   4 Carlton Gardens

My dear Winston,

In reference to our conversation of last night, I have looked up the account of the Gallipoli water supply in a 'Report on the Defences of Constantinople', prepared in 1909 by the General Staff. From this it appears that your informant was in error. Besides the Gallipoli Source there are apparently a large number of perennial springs at different points in the Peninsula; and I also gather that, at this time of year, immediately after the rainy season, water is to be found in the streams. It is clear, therefore, that we can build no hopes upon this particular kind of deficiency in the supplies of the Turkish garrison.

As you know, I cannot help being very anxious about the fate of any military attempt upon the Peninsula. Nobody was so keen as myself upon forcing the Straits as long as there seemed a reasonable prospect of doing it by means of the fleet alone—even though the operation might cost us a few antiquated battleships. But a military attack upon a position so inherently difficult, and so carefully prepared, is a different proposition: and, if it fails, we shall not only have to suffer considerably in men, and still more in prestige, but we may upset our whole diplomacy in the Near East, which, at the present moment, seems to promise so favourably.

If you can get your submarines through, we shall evidently be able to blockade the 70,000 Turks now massed in the Peninsula. They will not be able to get supplies by sea: and the only road can be absolutely denied them by ships in the Gulf of Xeros. If, and when, an arrangement could be come to with Bulgaria, quite a small force would lock up the whole of the Turkish garrison until they surrender from starvation or panic; and in the meanwhile, without at all abandoning our scheme, it would, I should have thought, be worth considering whether we should not delay its completion till we have destroyed the Turkish Army in Syria. Compare Napoleon in 1805![1]

These are but stray reflections, to which too much attention should not be paid: but I thought you ought to know at once that no hope can be built upon the deficiency of the Gallipoli water-supply.

Yours very sincerely
Arthur James Balfour

[1] In 1805 Napoleon defeated the Austrians at Ulm (20 October) before defeating the Russians at Austerlitz (2 December).

Winston S. Churchill to A. J. Balfour

(*Copy, Churchill papers: 13/50*)

8 April 1915   Admiralty
Secret

My dear Mr Balfour,

I telegraphed two days ago to the Admiral to check Sir A. Wilson's statement to me abt the scarcity of water. I enclose the telegram recd this morning—please let me have it back.

I have always kept in mind the possibility of a postponement of a few days in the attack if the Italian decision is hanging in the balance. It certainly looks hopeful now that Italy will be decided by the 14th, & shd greatly regret delaying the attack beyond the first favourable day after that. But I spoke to the PM this morning on this point, & if another week is needed for Italian purposes, it must be conceded.

Never forget meanwhile the approaching fatal danger of German S/Ms.

You must not be unduly apprehensive of the military operation. The soldiers think they can do it, & it was their influence that persuaded the Adl to delay the renewal of his attack till their preparations were completed. The military attack is in addition to, & not in substitution for, or derogation from, the naval attack. Both attacks mutually aid each other; & either by succeeding wd be decisive.

It seems vy difficult to believe that with the naval artillery support wh can be brought to bear upon the flank & rear of every position from both sides of the Peninsula the army will not be able to advance comfortably at least as far as the Suandere River, & maintain themselves there indefinitely. This in itself cd be a success, & wd greatly aid the naval attack upon the narrows. A 15″ howitzer will be there by the 20th to bombard the forts from a stable platform.

No other operation in this part of the world cd ever cloak the defeat of abandoning the effort against the Dlles. I think there is nothing for it but to go through with the business, & I do not at all regret that this shd be so. No one can count with certainty upon the issue of a battle. But here we have the chances in our favour, & play for vital gains with non-vital stakes.

yrs vy sincerely
WSC

Fisher: memorandum

(*Churchill papers: 13/57*)

8 April 1915   Admiralty
Secret

The probability that Italy will join the Allies within a few days raises a question of great importance as regards the Dardanelles attack. If the attack is a failure before Italy has definitely declared war, the repulse of our attempt might have a most prejudicial effect upon her conduct. If she does come in, we probably get the whole of the Balkans in too, and the results need no discussion.

The question is—Is it worth while to risk the attack at this moment? Is it not better to wait a few days, or to divert the attack elsewhere?

If it is practically certain that Italy will come in within a few days, and that she has now decided upon her attitude, I should suggest that the attack be postponed. If, on the other hand, she is waiting for the result of the attack before deciding, there is another operation which we might undertake, which our sea command enables us to do—attack Turkey elsewhere. The place I should suggest is Haifa, to be followed by the capture of Damascus. She is still entirely unprepared for a blow in that part, though she is said to have been making ready at Haifa and Beirut. But as we have openly announced that we are going to take the Dardanelles with our Army, and as our preparations at Mudros and elsewhere can have left little doubt that we are going to do so, it is there that the Turks have now made their main defence, and nothing would be so utterly disconcerting to them as the attack, with our 80,000 odd men in a wholly different region. Hindenburg's[1] strategic railway victories would not compare with it. The success of it would be beyond doubt. Italy's decision would then be placed beyond all shadow of doubt, and the Dardanelles could be dealt with after the Turkish Syrian army had been starved or destroyed. A rising in Syria could be engineered to enable our troops to withdraw, which they would do ostensibly for Egypt but really for the Dardanelles, the resistance at which place would be proportionately weaker.

The effect of this surprise blow would be prodigious in Europe; and it is suggested that these two alternative courses deserve the immediate consideration of the War Council.

[1] Paul von Benckendorff und Hindenburg, 1847–1934. 2nd Lieutenant, 1866. Fought in the Austro-Prussian and Franco-Prussian wars, 1866, 1870–1. Retired from the Army with the rank of General, 1911. Recalled, 1914. Commander-in-Chief, 7th Army, 1914. In August 1914 he moved German troops rapidly by rail from Gumbinnen, where they had been defeated by the Russians, to Tannenburg, where they were victorious. Marshal and Commander-in-Chief of all German Forces in the East, 1915. Chief of the General Staff, 1916–18. President of the Reich, 1925–34.

Winston S. Churchill to Lord Fisher
(*Churchill papers: 13/57*)

8 April 1915   Admiralty

1.S.L.

'And thus the native hue of resolution
'Is sicklied o'er by the pale cast of thought,
'And enterprises of great pith & moment
'With this regard their currents turn awry
'And lose the name of action'

'We are defeated at sea because our Admirals have learned—where I know
not—that war can be made without running risks'[1]

WSC

Sir Frederick Hamilton, Rear-Admiral Tudor and Captain Lambert to Lord Fisher
(*Fisher papers*)

8 April 1915   Admiralty

First Sea Lord

We wish to ask you to reassure us on certain points connected with the
conduct of the war.

We will start from ground on which there is common agreement, viz:
That the Grand Fleet should always be in such a position, and of such
strength, that it can be at all times ready to meet the entire fleet of the
enemy with confident assurance as to the result.

Is it quite certain that we are not putting that assurance in jeopardy?

There can be no doubt that the ideal method of deciding general questions
of the larger strategy is by having one person whose decisions, based on
ample advice, are final.

That person, subject to the high points of policy which can only be
decided by the Cabinet, is, and should be, the *First Sea Lord*.

If, however, he has not the final voice, the result must be that the policy
becomes one of compromises, which is obviously unsound, and likely to lead
to mistake, and possibly to disaster.

To go into particulars.

The attack on the Dardanelles is probably, from the point of view of high
policy, quite correct.

---

[1] The first quotation is from Shakespeare's *Hamlet* (Act III, Scene 1); the second is a
comment said to have been made by Napoleon after the battle of Trafalgar (1805).

On that point we have not sufficient acquaintance with the political situation to enable us to form an opinion, but what we are quite certain of is that it is a very expensive policy, and is likely, before we have done with it, to cost us several ships and an enormous expenditure of ammunition.

We have already lost, or more or less demobilized, ten battleships (including 'Inflexible'). It is true that they are mostly old ones, and on the other hand, we have added, or shall shortly add, seven.

The Germans have lost none and have added six.

As to the future, it is not known, so far as we are aware, what the Germans are going to do. But we do know that we are postponing battleship completion for the sake of arming a number of small craft, whose actual proposed use we are not familiar with, though obviously it must be for something totally unconnected with the bed-rock policy of maintaining the crushing superiority of the Grand Fleet.

Another matter which is delaying Battleship completion is the construction under the Admiralty of 15 'Howitzers' for purposes quite unconnected with any Fleet requirement.

Are you satisfied with the rate of progress of Battleship completion in the light of attached statement?

Is the prospect of obtaining supplies of ammunition sufficiently good to ensure there being enough available for the use of the Grand Fleet in the light of the expenditure involved by operations in the Dardanelles?

These are matters about which we are uneasy, and we ask you to assure us that the whole policy has your concurrence, and that you are satisfied with it.

If not, and you think there would be any value in the support of the Board (which still exists, at all events in name), we shall consider it our duty to give it to you.

FTH
CFL
FCTT

Lord Fisher to Sir Frederick Hamilton, Rear-Admiral Tudor and Captain Lambert

(*Copy, Fisher papers*)

8 April 1915   Admiralty
Secret

I have read your remarks with great attention and I desire to say that I am entirely in agreement with the fundamental principle which you seek to uphold, viz: that the Grand Fleet should always be in such strength that it can at all times be ready to meet the entire Fleet of the enemy with confident assurance as to the result.

The Dardanelles operation is undoubtedly one the political result of which, if successful, will be worth some sacrifice in matériel and personnel: it will certainly shorten the period of the war by bringing in fresh Allies in the Eastern theatre and will break the back of the German–Turkish alliance, besides opening up the Black Sea.

It was with hesitation that I consented to this undertaking, in view of the necessarily limited force of ships which could be devoted to it, of the shortage of shell and cordite, and of the factor of uncertainty which must always obtain when ships attack land fortifications and mined areas under their protection.

But, as you state, these high points of policy must be decided by the Cabinet; and in this case the real advantages to be gained caused me eventually to consent to their view, subject to strict limitation of the Naval forces to be employed, so that our position in the decisive theatre—the North Sea—should not be jeopardized in any one arm.

I am of opinion at the present time that our supremacy is secure in Home Waters and that the forces detached are not such as to prejudice a decisive result should the High Sea Fleet come out to battle. But at the same time I consider that we have reached the absolute limit, and that we must stand or fall by the issue, for we can send out no more help of any kind. I have expressed this view very clearly to the First Lord, and should there at a later period be any disposition on the part of the Cabinet to overrule me on this point, I shall request my Naval colleagues to give their support in upholding my view.

I agree with you as to the desirability for proceeding now with the completion of the battleships in hand. The 'Warspite' sails to-day to join the Grand Fleet, and I understand that 'Barham', 'Valiant', and 'Malaya' are being pushed to the utmost extent, and also 'Canada', and that the remaining 15-inch land howitzers are not now being permitted to stand in the way. The 'Royal Sovereigns' building by contract should also be pressed on, but those in our own Dockyards cannot be concentrated upon to the same extent because of the primary claim of the refits and repairs of the active fleet.

I am satisfied with the position at present and in the near future, but shall of course be more satisfied when we get the battleships back from the Dardanelles.

The supply of cordite is very far from satisfactory. We cannot, however, stop the Dardanelles operations on this account and must accept the temporary reduction of the reserve of two outfits which it entails, exercising the greatest economy in expenditure of 15-inch and other critical calibres. But all extraneous sources of expenditure must be cut off at once.

H. H. Asquith to George V
(Royal Archives)

8 April 1915   10 Downing Street

. . . Sir I Hamilton was to leave Alexandria that day (the 7th). The fleet at the Dardanelles has been reinforced by 5 battleships, and a large addition of small craft. The mine sweepers are now much more efficient and are manned by naval ratings. . . .

Lord Hardinge to Lord Crewe
(Crewe papers)

8 April 1915   Viceroy's Camp
Private   India

My dear Crewe,
  . . . What you say in your letter of March 12th upon the future acquisition by Russia of Constantinople and the Straits is very true. It is the complete reversal of all the principles of our diplomacy for the last fifty years or more, and yet I see no means of avoiding it, although I fear it will be very unpalatable to the Moslems in this country. Russia has a very just claim to take steps to put outside the bounds of possibility the recurrence of a situation by which her exits to the open sea from the Baltic and Black Sea are closed to her, and I do not see how such security can be obtained except by her possession of Constantinople and the Straits. I trust however that guarantees will be given that the Straits are to be regarded as an international fairway for trade and not as the gates of a 'mare clausum'.

Although the matter is one that is outside my proper sphere, there are two points in connection with the future settlement of Turkey which I hope will be observed. In the first place we are all agreed, I think, that Turkey will have to quit Europe, but there are at least ten million pure Turks in Turkey, and these should be consolidated in a state in Asia Minor of a respectable size, and I look forward, even after the addition of Van and Erzerum to Russia and the creation of an autonomous province of Armenia, to seeing a Turkish State established in Anatolia of a respectable size under suitable guarantees stretching from the Black Sea to the Mediterranean, and roughly comprised between two lines drawn from Trebizond to Adana and from Ismidt to Brussa and Smyrna. I hope there will be no question of allowing the Greeks to get to Smyrna or the Italians to Adalia. If we can show our Indian Moslems that we have done something to prevent the Turkish Empire being wiped out our position with them will become exceedingly strong, and I should like to see a Turkey in Asia purified and rejuvenated under our control and protection.

I share Kitchener's view of the importance of Alexandretta to us on account of our position in Mesopotamia, but as I have already said in one of my telegrams, it would be necessary to hold the hinterland as well as far as Aleppo, and it would be to our advantage so long as we have control of the sea that the Baghdad Railway from Alexandretta to Baghdad should never be built. . . .

Ever yours
Hardinge of P

Sir John French to Winston S. Churchill
(*Churchill papers: 26/2*)

9 April 1915   Head-Quarters
                                                    British Army

My dear Winston,

I was very sorry to have bad accounts of your health but much hope you are better now. You are very anxious of course but I am in hopes you will get relief in a very few days by the success of the joint Dardanelles operation. It was a wrench to part with Bacon & the 15″ Gun, but if it will be of assistance to you I am content.

We are steadily preparing here for great events. Ammunition is of course what we most need! We are beginning to pick it up better now and I am very hopeful as to the future.

Some Belgian Officers who have escaped from Lille tell us that Germans who had started *Shops* & *Businesshouses* there have closed them & gone back to Germany since our successful attack at Neuve Chapelle, and the German Officers there have sent their wives & families away. They are in a very 'jumpy' & disturbed condition all along our line.

I hope by the time we begin *real work* again you will be less engaged & able to have a look in—altho' I shall *watch* you very carefully!!

Goodbye for the present My Dear Friend. I am sure your Great Heart
is holding you up in this time of anxiety.

I feel you are going to 'do' it.

Yrs always
JF

Winston S. Churchill to Vice-Admiral de Robeck: telegram
(Copy, Churchill papers: 2/88)

10 April 1915   Admiralty
Most Secret and Personal

Possibility that a submarine may be sent out by the Germans to the
Dardanelles should be constantly borne in mind in making your arrangements. 'U 33' is said to have left Germany on the 27th March westward for
an unknown destination, and we have not identified her in home waters
up to now.

This from a trustworthy agent.

Take steps to deal with her if necessary.

Winston S. Churchill to Vice-Admiral de Robeck: telegram
(Copy, Churchill papers: 2/88)

10 April 1915   Admiralty
Most Secret and Personal

It is well to be prepared for submarines, but 'U 33' has now been located
in home waters.

Lord Fisher to Winston S. Churchill
(Copy, Fisher papers)

10 April 1915   Admiralty

First Lord.

The 'Inflexible' was left at the Dardanelles solely on account of the
'Goeben' but contrary to Admiralty intentions Admiral de Robeck hoisted
his flag in her and took her into close action when she certainly should have
been kept out of danger as much as the 'Queen Elizabeth'—so it seems
desirable to send a telegram to Admiral de Robeck that on no account

whatever is the 'Queen Elizabeth' to be risked as was the 'Inflexible' and she should be kept solely for long range firing from the Northern side of the Gallipoli Peninsula and not risked inside the Straits.[1]

F

Vice-Admiral de Robeck to Winston S. Churchill: telegram
(Copy, Churchill papers: 13/65)

11 April 1915
2.00 am
Most secret

General Hamilton arrived morning of 10th. and communicated his plan of operations confidentially to me which is as follows:—

A main landing at Cape Helles and Morto Bay with the Krithia Ridge as the objective covering force from which advance will be made against the Kilid Bahr plateau. Simultaneously a feint will be made near Gabatepe which will probably develop into landing and a seizure of a covering position on foot of hill of Saribair whence enemy can be prevented from reinforcing the Kilid Bahr plateau from the North. At the same time there will be demonstrations in North Xeros and a heavy bombardment of Bulair Line so as to keep the enemy busy everywhere and attempt to mystify him as to real point of attack.

I am completing arrangements for meeting his requirements and this will fully occupy the whole resources of the Fleet; directly the army is established the combined attack on the defences of the Narrows will take place, Navy and Army advancing side by side.

I will inform you fully of the details of the Naval co-operation when complete. Navy will be ready to act when the Army is assembled. The date of the actual commencement must then be governed entirely by the weather.

Winston S. Churchill to David Lloyd George
(Lloyd George papers)

11 April 1915   Admiralty
Secret

My dear David,

Please see attached paper. Von Donop's letter, blocking decisively the only two available sources of American rifle supply, is curious, & indeed to

---

[1] Churchill replied that same day to Fisher's request about the Queen Elizabeth: 'it would not be right at this moment to make a rigid prohibition of her entering the straits. Of course she will not attempt to pass through into the Marmora.' (Fisher papers)

me inexplicable. The Cabinet, with Grey's assent, have again & again authorized the purchase of the Krags, & I cannot conceive any F.O. ground against either Krags or Springfields. The US government can at any moment veto the transaction.

Subject to a satisfactory answer from Dawson to my telegram to him, I think he shd be told to buy the Springfields, although they are exactly double the normal US Govt price. They are clinking weapons.

It is of course possible that von Donop objects to *our* purchasing Krags because he was trying to get them himself (?) & that it is only to the Springfields that diplomatic objections are entertained. With your agreement I shall go ahead.

Yours ever,
W

H. H. Asquith to Winston S. Churchill
(Churchill papers: 26/2)

11 April 1915   Walmer Castle
Secret

My dear Winston,

We have confidentially told both the French & the Russian Govts that active offensive operations will not be resumed at the Dardanelles while the Italian negotiation is trembling in the balance. I hope it may come to a good end in the course of a few days. But meanwhile it is of the utmost importance that neither the naval or military people on the spot shd [upset] the situation.

Yrs always
HHA

Winston S. Churchill to H. H. Asquith
(Copy, Churchill papers: 26/2)

11 April 1915   Admiralty

My dear Prime Minister,

I venture to give you my views about Bulgaria. Russian methods as proposed wd be 'kill or cure'. This is not the moment to force the issue. The accession of Italy & Roumania, or any success at the Dardanelles, will influence Bulgaria decisively in our favour. At present she has a free choice. Alienate her now, & she may not only go wrong herself but keep the others out. Therefore I am dead against indulging justifiable Russian indignation against her.

Greece on the other hand has no choice of sides open, & can & shd be forced, as roughly as necessary, to come in. If she won't come in, there again we shall have the means of influencing Bulgaria by a frank abandonment of Greek claims to Cavalla, or if necessary to Salonica.

The operations at the Dardanelles will probably be delayed a few days from various causes, & when they begin the first phase, though delicate, is not the decisive one. At the point to which these operations have now reached, military considerations & favourable weather shd rule. Kitchener & I wd deprecate any check on non-military grounds to the normal development of what must certainly be a task extending over some considerable time. There is no question of an immediate decisive attack, with consequent risk of flagrant failure, occurring at present. Therefore I hope matters there may be allowed to take a purely military course.

John Churchill to Winston S. Churchill
(*Churchill papers: 1/117*)

11 April 1915   Mediterranean Expeditionary Force
                                                    Lemnos

Dear Winston

We are back again in Mudros Bay and things are at last moving rapidly. Every two or three hours a great transport arrives full of troops and this time they have been properly embarked and are ready to disembark in proper order. I had a long talk to Keyes yesterday. He and De R are very pleased at their treatment by the Admiralty. Particularly the latter, who fully expected to be superseded. He has always been rather against you & your policy etc. but since all the things he has asked for, have been given, he has become an ardent admirer. They all appear to be in the best of spirits but no longer talk of it as being an easy job. The Queen E. goes tomorrow on a steam trial. They are awfully relieved at having got their engines right. They lived in daily terror of being sent away. The bay here, nearly as large as Kalloni at Mitylene—presents an extraordinary sight. It is already nearly full and by the time all the transports are up—every available corner will be filled with great ships.

Better water reports are coming in about the Peninsula. Last night it rained a good deal, which all helps. The weather is not yet settled, and yesterday it blew half a gale all day. This of course is rather disconcerting—but we believe that by the time the flag falls the real summer will have set in and these winds will be at an end.

My friend gets on very well with the sailors and has formed a very high opinion of De R. Keyes tells me that on the 18th it would have been possible to have got through, but that the Admiral knew if he did so, he might never get out again until troops landed. He thought he might save himself from being superseded by going through, but was prepared to go under rather than do a spectacular thing which might have necessitated another fleet coming here to cover the troops landing. When he retired on the 18th he fully believed it was his last day in command. Wemyss is working very hard and behaving most loyally to De R. Keyes says I should note the name of Capt. Godfray[1] R.M.A. in the Queen E. and send it to you, if anything happens to him. He has done wonderfully well throughout.

Best love
JSC

Lord Fisher to Vice-Admiral Oliver and Winston S. Churchill

(*Copy, Fisher papers*)

11 April 1915   Admiralty

COS

First Lord

Admiral de Robeck showed an ominous want of judgment in arranging for an old second class cruiser like the 'Talbot' to tow the 'Inflexible' from Cape Malea to Malta—every Midshipman knows what the Malta Channel and mouth of the Adriatic is at this time of the year.

The 'Inflexible' would undoubtedly have foundered had not the Admiralty overruled Admiral de Robeck.

It was a disastrous want of judgment Admiral de Robeck hoisting his flag in 'Inflexible' (against known Admiralty intentions) and taking her into close action.

There may be a third lack of judgment as regards 'Queen Elizabeth' so I press for my telegram, proposed yesterday, being sent at once.

Admiral de Robeck ought also to be warned against using Lord Nelson and Agamemnon in preference to the older ships and I think he ought to be warned that the instant return of 'Queen Elizabeth', 'Lord Nelson', 'Agamemnon' and Light Cruisers, Torpedo Destroyers and Submarines may be imminent.

F

---

[1] Alfred Denis Bertram Godfray, 1882–1950. 2nd Lieutenant, Royal Marine Artillery, 1900. Captain 1911; Major, 1917. Retired 1920.

Winston S. Churchill to Lord Fisher

(*Copy, Churchill papers: 13/57*)

11 April 1915   Admiralty
Private

My dear Fisher,

A telegram has been sent (enclosed) abt 'Q. Elizabeth'. Personally I think it superfluous, but since you wish it I concur.

I do not consider that at this critical moment it wd be right to harass the Adl by imposing any restrictions on his use of 'Agamemnon' & 'Ld Nelson'.

There is no reason for withdrawing yr confidence from him because of the 'Inflexible'. He had already ordered 'Canopus' to go the whole way with her, when you vy prudently telegraphed. Anyhow—I am told by the experts— that either 'Talbot' or 'Canopus' cd equally carry away any available hawsers.

It appears to me indispensable to send the Adl Capt Phillimore[1] & the officers he requires for the vital & critical operation of landing the troops. See his last telegram. I am sure you will agree that this authorization shd go first thing tomorrow. It ought to have gone tonight; but I do not wish to act without you even in the smallest matter.

Seriously my friend you are not a little unfair in trying to spite this operation by sidewinds & small points when you have accepted it in principle. It is hard on me that you shd keep on like this—every day something fresh: & it is not worthy of you or the great business we have in hand together.

You know how deeply anxious I am to work with you. Had the Dlles been excluded, our cooperation wd have been impossible. It is not right now to make small difficulties or add to the burden wh in these times we have to bear.

Excuse frankness—but friends have this right, & to colleagues it is a duty.

Yours always
W

---

[1] Richard Fortescue Phillimore, 1864–1940. Entered Navy, 1878. Captain, 1904. Commanded *Inflexible* at the battle of the Falkland Islands, December 1914, and during bombardment at Dardanelles, February–March 1915. Rear-Admiral, 1915. Principal beach master, Gallipoli, April 1915. Commanded First Battle Cruiser Squadron, 1916–18. Knighted, 1918. Admiral Commanding Aircraft, Atlantic Fleet, 1919. Vice-Admiral, 1920. Commanded Reserve Fleet, 1920–2. Admiral, 1924.

Lord Fisher to Winston S. Churchill

(*Copy, Churchill papers: 13/57*)

12 April 1915   Admiralty

Before the Dawn! Yet, It's light enough now at 4.30 AM to see a submarine! I tried just now to see how far off I could see the stem of a lamp post!—

My dear Winston,

It's intensely exasperating to have lost the 'Kronprinz Wilhelm' when we so very accurately knew her exact course on her rendezvous—*thrice repeated to us!* and such a mass of vessels as we had all round her! I suppose also we have lost the 'Macedonia' her supply ship[1]—and that exceeding ugly little man King Hall[2] seems to be doing his level best to lose both the 'Konigsberg'[3] and her relief ship in the Mozambique Channel!

But this stupendous coming week knocks out such mosquito bites as these! It seems to me that the positions are all well chosen for all our different activities, and Jellicoe fully alive to wireless silence. I've been poring for hours and hours over the chart with 'vain imaginings' but it all comes in the end to what that old Greek gentleman said before Salamis that no matter what you plan and what your superiority may be the result is entirely dependent upon 'Providence and—*a good Admiral*'! (Like the Fish shop— our '*Admirals are cheap today!*') (I hope we shall see to it that '*Kings are cheap*' at the end of the war! The Kings of Greece, Bulgaria and Roumania will I hope disappear and the King of Italy also and perhaps one more thrown in!!) I have been telegraphing at 4 AM to ask if the 15 inch howitzer has sailed—no reply as yet.

Yrs

F

P.S. The 'Great Fisher Bank' is quite a likely spot for the Battle to be joined! Supposing we intervene between von Pohl and his base and cut him off from the Skagerrak also!

---

[1] The *Kronprinz Wilhelm*, a German armoured cruiser, and her supply ship, the *Macedonia*, had been active sinking and capturing allied merchant ships in the Atlantic in March 1915. The *Macedonia* had in fact been captured on 28 March. The *Kronprinz Wilhelm* had sought refuge in a United States port, Newport News, on 11 April; she was interned there for the rest of the war.

[2] Herbert Goodenough King-Hall, 1862–1936. Entered Navy, 1875. Captain, 1900. Assistant Director of Naval Intelligence, 1906–8. Director of Naval Mobilization, 1909–11. Rear-Admiral, 1909. Commanded the Cape of Good Hope station, 1912–16. Vice-Admiral, 1915. Knighted, 1916. Admiral, 1918. Commanded Orkneys and Shetlands, 1918–19.

[3] The German light cruiser *Königsberg* had been blockaded in the Rufigi River delta since November 1914. She was destroyed on 11 July 1915 by the British monitors *Severn* and *Mersey* (see also p. 9 *n.1*.)

Lord Fisher to Winston S. Churchill
(*Churchill papers: 13/57*)

12 April 1915   Admiralty

Dear Winston,

I did not get your upbraiding letter till after I had written to you about 'Inflexible' being repaired at Gibraltar which still seems desirable.

Never in all my whole life have I ever before so sacrificed my convictions as I have done to please you! THAT'S A FACT! Whoever told you that the 'Talbot' was as good as a Battleship to tow 'Inflexible' must have been hypnotized by you—nor is it correct that de Robeck had given orders before the Admiralty telegram—off my own bat I suggested the immediate despatch of 'Lord Nelson' & 'Agamemnon' (hoping they would shield 'Elizabeth' & 'Inflexible'!). de Robeck will hoist his flag in the Lord Nelson you may be sure—instead of the 'Vengeance' his former Flagship—For the work in hand the 'Vengeance' quite as good for close action— Nevertheless I say no more— The outside world is quite certain that I have pushed you and not you me! So far as I know the Prime Minister is the solitary person who knows to the contrary—I have not said one word to a soul on the subject except to Crease & Wilson & Oliver & Bartolome and you may be sure those 4 never open their mouths!

Indirectly I've worked up Kitchener from the very beginning via Fitzgerald—I think it's going to be a success but I want to lose the oldest ships, and to be chary of our invaluable officers & men, for use in the decisive theatre.

                                                                    Yrs
                                                                    F

Winston S. Churchill to Lord Fisher
(*Fisher papers*)

12 April 1915   Admiralty
Private

My dear Fisher,

I was so grateful to you for your letter.

I am sure we are going to *win*. Anyhow it's already revolutionised the Balkans.

Now your first condition has been satisfied. An army to help. Therefore there shd be whole hearted agreement.

Never mind the 'Kronprinz'. Look what she sets free.

The Gt. Fisher Bank is the lair of the Grand Fleet. Please God they come this time.

                                                                Yours always
                                                                W

Harold Laski[1] to Winston S. Churchill

(*Churchill papers: 2/65*)

12 April 1915   McGill University
                                                 Montreal

Dear Mr Churchill,

My good friend Mr Norman Hapgood[2] who is the editor of 'Harpers' Weekly' and probably the first journalist in America, is sailing for England next Saturday. He stays with Sir Horace Plunkett[3] in Ireland for a few days and then goes to London. He is tremendously anxious to see you and busy though I know you are I venture to trespass on the many kindnesses you have shown me to ask you to do so if you possibly can. He is a big man in the United States; he has much influence at places like Harvard and not least of all, he is a close personal friend of President Wilson.[4] I imagine that if you could see him his writing would effect a great deal.

I wish you would have your various navy speeches reprinted as a small pamphlet: there is a great demand for them over here and no means of giving it satisfaction. The result is that the Canadian newspapers envision a government in which the main constituents are Mr Lloyd and Mr George. It would be helpful to make them realise that there are others!

With my many thanks in anticipation.[5]

                                                 I am, Yours very truly
                                                 Harold Laski

[1] Harold Joseph Laski, 1893–1950. Political Philosopher and historian; the son of Nathan Laski, an influential member of the Jewish community in North-West Manchester, Churchill's former constituency. Lecturer in History, McGill University, Montreal, 1914–16; Harvard University, 1916–20. Professor of Political Science, London, 1926–50. Member of Executive Committee of Labour Party, 1936–49.

[2] Norman Hapgood, 1868–1937. Journalist and author. Editor, *Collier's*, 1903–12. Editor, *Harper's Weekly*, 1912–19. Editor, *Hearst's International Magazine*, 1925–7. United States Minister to Denmark, 1919.

[3] Horace Curzon Plunkett, 1854–1932. Engaged in cattle-ranching, Wyoming, 1879–89. Promoted Agricultural co-operation in Ireland from 1889. Conservative MP, 1892–1900. President, Irish Agricultural Organisation Society, 1894–9 and 1907. Vice-President, Department of Agriculture and Technical Instruction for Ireland, 1899–1907. Knighted, 1903. Chairman of the Irish Convention, 1917–18. Senator, Irish Free State, 1922–3.

[4] Thomas Woodrow Wilson, 1856–1924. President of the United States, 1912–21. In December 1916 he sought to persuade the belligerents to negotiate peace, but in April 1917, following repeated German sinkings of US ships, he obtained a declaration from Congress that a state of war existed with Germany.

[5] Churchill noted on this letter: 'No. I cannot see him.' Nor were his wartime navy speeches ever printed in pamphlet or book form in the United States. His Navy Estimates speech of 15 February 1915 had, however, been issued as a twenty-page pamphlet by the Liberal Publications Department in London. In 1913 the American Association for International Conciliation had issued his Naval Estimates speech of 26 March 1913 in a thirteen-page pamphlet, the text having been taken from the report of the speech in *The Times*.

Lord Kitchener to Winston S. Churchill
(Churchill papers: 13/50)

14 April 1915   War Office

My dear Churchill,

When the Italians come in what are you going to do about the naval command in the Adriatic—I hear the Italian navy object to coming under a French admiral. I have no doubt you have thought it out.

I believe there might be some difficulty about the French navy going under an Italian admiral but as they would have a preponderating force it seems the correct solution.

Yours very truly
Kitchener

Winston S. Churchill to Lord Kitchener
(Kitchener papers)

14 April 1915   Admiralty
Secret

My dear Kitchener,

The Italians stipulate expressly for French & British naval co-operation. The Austrian Fleet wd have a good fighting chance against them single-handed.

We have from the beginning of the war assigned the control of Med^n to the French, & the concentration of a great fleet for the Dardanelles is only an episode. The moment it is over, the ships must come back to the decisive theatre, where there is important work for them to do.

A British sqn will remain in Egyptian waters.

Yrs sincerely
WSC

Lord Kitchener to Winston S. Churchill
(Churchill papers: 13/50)

14 April 1915   War Office
Secret

My dear Churchill,

Surely the Italian fleet in the Adriatic would be vastly superior to the Austrian—I should have thought a British squadron would have been required there. I hope it may not be necessary to hand over the Mediterranean entirely to French and Italian command in naval matters, as I fear it would have a very bad effect on British prestige in the near East if this were done.

Yours very truly
Kitchener

Winston S. Churchill to Lord Kitchener

(Copy, Churchill papers: 13/50)

14 April 1915   Admiralty

My dear Kitchener,

Italy should have the command in the Adriatic and England & France should each place a squadron under the direction of the Italian Commander in Chief[1] so that the margin of superiority over Austria is unmistakeable. If the French gave up the control in the Adriatic I think they would require to have the local command at the Dardanelles after the active naval operations are over and the naval role has ceased to be the primary one. I should agree to this provided that 6 or 8 of the best French Dreadnoughts came round to Brest & were available for the decisive theatre. Ultimately I seek to create a force strong enough to enter the Baltic; and this would be an important step on the road.

We should thus have in the Mediterranean two triple fleets

(1) Italian-Anglo-French in the Adriatic and an Italian C in C: and

(2) An Anglo-French-Russian fleet in Turkish waters under a French admiral.

The French wd also have the general direction of the naval war in the Medn & the Admiralty in all other theatres. I presume that an English Genl will continue to direct the land operations in Turkey; & civil administration of Cple is to be conducted by the 3 Powers jointly during the war.

If you agree yourself I will discuss the subject with the French Minister of Marine.

Winston S. Churchill to Lord Kitchener

(Churchill papers: 13/50)

14 April 1915   Admiralty

If Italy joins us, the Italian Commander in Chief, the Duke of the Abruzzi, shd have the supreme command in the Adriatic. The Italian fleet shd be

---

[1] Luigi Amadeo Giuseppe Maria Ferdinando Francesco, 1873–1933. Duke of Abruzzi, Prince of Savoy. Arctic and African explorer. Commander-in-Chief of the Italian Navy; 1915–17.

reinforced by a British Squadron. The French sqn shd consist of 4 battle-ships, of wh at least two shd be Dantons, & the rest Patries, & the British sqn of two Ld Nelsons & perhaps 'Swiftsure' & 'Triumph', or two others. The French shd provide with their battleships a destroyer flotilla, & we wd provide a light cruiser sqn.

Until the Dardanelles & Bosphorus operations are over, we cannot pro-vide any ships for the Adriatic. In the meanwhile the French shd provide not only their own above-mentioned sqn, but an additional force equal to ours.

As soon as the Dardanelles & Bosphorus operations are completed, & the role of the Navy in that theatre ceases to be primary, we shd accord to the French the command in Turkish waters, wh they greatly desire. We wd leave a sqn of 4 battleships, with some smaller vessels, under their orders, & wd advise the Russians also to come under the general direction of the French. We shd keep a sqn in Egyptian waters. The French wd keep their sqn in Syrian waters. The general direction of the naval war throughout the Meditn wd rest as originally arranged with the French C in C.

All the rest of our ships engaged in the Dlles operations wd return to the decisive theatres in the N. Sea & the Channel, & in pursuance of this principle we shd request the French to transfer their 4 Dreadnoughts & 4 Dantons from the Mediterranean to the Atlantic, based on Brest.

I think it probable that these arrangements will commend themselves to the French. The First Sea Lord concurs in them, & I propose to discuss them with the French Minister of Marine at an early date.

WSC

Lord Charles Beresford to H. H. Asquith

(*Asquith papers*)

15 April 1915   1 Great Cumberland Place

. . . The War Staff, since its creation, has not had sufficient time to make out proper plans of campaign. . . .

We appear, however, still to be drifting without a clearly cut and dried plan of campaign, more particularly in respect of operations against Con-stantinople, and also as to the continual attack on our Mercantile Marine by the enemy's submarines. . . .

In the attack on the Dardanelles, the war organisation appears very defective. It was surely premature and unwise to use the Fleet until any army was ready to land, or had landed. . . . We have only arrived at partial com-mand of the sea by unprecedented and Providential luck, aided by the astounding and unlooked for incompetence of the German Naval War Staff. On our side we have to spend money like water, no one can estimate how many millions, in order to reach that position of security which the country was led to believe existed. . . .

16 April 1915   Admiralty

. . . The principal object of this letter seems to be to draw attention to the great cleverness and foresight of Lord Charles Beresford in the past—and inferentially to the disadvantages under which the country is labouring by not utilising these qualities now. . . .

The substance of the letter is such drivel as to be unworthy of serious attention, and I suggest that it does not receive any. . . .

16 April 1915   Admiralty

My dear Prime Minister,

In the middle of a great war we cannot waste time with this old clown.

I enclose you a minute by the First Sea Lord; but I deprecate any further attention being paid to the matter.

Yours vy sincerely
Winston S Churchill

15 April 1915   Admiralty

My dear Grey,

I really do not think that likes & dislikes ought to hamper action in this most important matter.

When I authorised Dawson to embark on these negotiations, the F.O. & W.O. had reached a complete break down, & the Legation reported that 'nothing wd move the scruples of the President'.

Therefore whatever happens now, we cannot be worse off than we were.

On the other hand the advantage of getting these rifles is immeasurable. The gravest interests of the country are affected.

I cd not send the addition you propose to any telegram to Dawson. The Legation has no right to stand aside, if their action can help to settle the issue in our favour. The mere fact of their standing aside wd probably recreate the deadlock. They ought not to let their amour propre stand in the way of national interests but shd work loyally & heartily to secure the result by any legitimate means.

Frankly—your suggested addition has an air of detachment about it wh makes me vy unhappy.

Yours ever
W

Robert Donald to Winston S. Churchill
(Churchill papers: 13/51)

16 April 1915   The Daily Chronicle

Dear Churchill,

The American correspondents greatly appreciated your frank & friendly talk with them yesterday. While fully respecting your confidence they will retain a more sympathetic understanding of the part which the Navy is playing & of the great work which it has done.

It was very good of you to give them so much time.

Believe me

Yrs very truly
Robert Donald

John Churchill: diary
(Copy, Churchill papers: 28/139)

16 April 1915

Bad news came in this morning. One of the transports with the 29th Division Brigade Artillery signalled 'Torpedoed—S.O.S.' Ships were sent out to rescue. Later messages came in that she had not been hit. It appears that a Turkish torpedo boat from Smyrna came up to her without colours and when quite close hoisted the Turkish flag and gave the Captain[1]

---

[1] J. McMath, a merchant navy master. The *Manitou* had left the United Kingdom on 20 March 1915, carrying 60 officers, 1,000 men and 640 horses.

10 minutes. Everyone took to the boats and in the process—whether there was panic or not is not yet certain—nearly 100 men were drowned! While this was going on the 'Osiris' turned up and the torpedo boat went off in chase. The 'Osiris' had the legs of her and back came the boat to find the 'Manitou' under weigh again. She fired 3 torpedoes and missed! Having nothing left she bolted. Later in the afternoon she was caught and ran herself ashore on one of the islands. I believe this is the first time men have been drowned off a transport since the war began. Nearly a million and a quarter men have been transported over sea and this is the first mishap.

One of the Naval Captains went on board an Australian transport to-day and discussed details of the landing. He showed the gun positions near the beach. 'Oh!' said the Australians. 'We hope the ships will not interfere with them. You know they are our pigeons!' The aircraft have located a strong line of defences guarding the Narrows and running down the middle of the Peninsula from Maidos past Erveden, round Achi Baba to De Tott's battery. A camp of 10,000 men has been seen at Erveden. Their news is not very reassuring. Guns appear to bristle on every ridge. The submarines did not try yesterday but will attempt to go up to-morrow. Two submarines will enter the channel—one 'A' awash the other sunk 'B'. 'A' will sink and proceed up the channel, while 'B' will come up and turn round and retire. It is hoped the Turks will think that only one boat is there and that it is going home. The 'Queen E.' left to-night to have a few shots at some ships at Maidos. She will fire over the peninsula from the bay of Saros. . . .

H. H. Asquith to Venetia Stanley

(*Montagu papers*)

16 April 1915   10 Downing Street

. . . As soon as the Cabinet met, K who was evidently a good deal per-turbed, went off at score, abusing Ll. G. for having disclosed at the Munitions Committee the figures wh. he (K) had confidentially communicated to the Cabinet of the Armies now in the field & actually or prospectively at home. He declared that he could be no longer responsible for the War Office under such conditions, tendered his resignation, rose from his chair, & was about to leave the room. Ll. G. & Winston were both (the former having quite a presentable case) aggressive and tactless, and the situation was for the moment of the worst—particularly as Grey—a good deal to Ll. G's chagrin —strongly championed Kitchener. . . . Ll. G (who of course is not quite au fond a gentleman) let slip in the course of the altercation some most injurious & wounding innuendoes wh. K will be more than human to forget. . . .

W.C.3 — 3F

H. H. Asquith to Venetia Stanley
(*Montagu papers*)

16 April 1915   Walmer Castle
Midnight

    ... The man who comes out of it best is Kitchener—clumsy & tactless in expression as he often is: as Crewe says, one who has been all his life accustomed either to take or to give orders, and who therefore finds it difficult to accommodate himself to the give & take of Cabinet discussion & comradeship. He was really moved to-day, though I am sure he wd. not have persisted in resignations, and showed in the end a largeness of mind & temper wh. I greatly admire. On the other hand, the people who ought to have known better showed themselves at their worst. Winston was pretty bad, but he is impulsive & borne along on the flood of his too copious tongue, and in the end was frankly regretful & made amends. The two who came out really worst were Ll. G, who almost got down to the level of a petty police court advocate, & McKenna, who played the part of a wrecker, pure & simple. It will take me a long time to forget & forgive their attitude. ....

Vice-Admiral de Robeck to Winston S. Churchill: telegram
(*Copy, Churchill papers: 13/65*)

16 April 1915
Secret and personal

    Colonel Napier[1] and Mr. Fitzmaurice met General Hamilton and myself this morning. They expressed their opinion that Bulgaria would probably join the Allies against Turkey at an early date, and they suggested postponement of our operations until Bulgaria was ready. Hamilton quite against postponement in absence of definite guarantee; I entirely concurred. Admiral Eberhardt is evidently unwilling to undertake the transport of a large body of troops to Turkey and in view of the activity of GOEBEN and BRESLAU I agree with him. It would however be a very different matter to transport a smaller force and land them in a friendly harbour such as Bourgas. I am informed that this project is being seriously discussed. To assist our operations here by preventing the despatch of further reinforce-

[1] Henry Dundas Napier, 1864–1941. Entered Army, 1884. Lieutenant-Colonel, 1903. Military Attaché, St Petersburg, 1903–7; Belgrade and Sofia, 1908–11. Retired from the Army, 1912. Temporary Military Attaché, Sofia, 18 August 1914–18 October 1915, when Britain declared war on Bulgaria. Captured by a German submarine in the Adriatic, 1915. Prisoner of war in Austria, 1915–18. Military Representative, Sofia, 1918.

ments by Turkey to the Dardanelles Russia should act at once. If the above is impossible please send following telegram to Admiral Eberhardt: 'To prevent the despatch of reinforcements from Constantinople to Dardanelles I request that you will make a great show of embarking troops in transports and spread report that they are to go immediately to Turkey.'

Winston S. Churchill to Vice-Admiral de Robeck: telegram
(*Copy, Churchill papers: 13/65*)

17 April 1915   Admiralty
Secret

The best way to bring Bulgaria in on our side is to make a successful attack on Dardanelles.

Your decision & Hamilton's not to postpone operations is approved.

Secondly—Russians have several times proposed to land troops at Bourgas, but we have always protested against any violation of Bulgarian neutrality even to force the hand of the Bulgarian Government.

Your telegram to Admiral Eberhardt has therefore been sent.

David Lloyd George to Winston S. Churchill
(*Churchill papers: 21/37*)

17 April 1915   Treasury Chambers

My Dear Winston,

Noel Buxton tells me the Bulgarian Minister is in despair after his talk with Grey. He said Grey gave him the impression that the Cabinet would not consent under any circumstances to Cavalla being given to Bulgaria. That certainly is not my reading of the Cabinet decision. I wish you could urge Grey to give the Bulgarian Minister a more helpful reply. We owe nothing to the Greek King. He is essentially as hostile as he dare be & he will play with us until his help, if it ever comes, will be on a level with Portugal's. Venizelos is our friend & to give Cavalla to Greece is to ruin him for ever.

I forgot yesterday to remind K that Joffre had already published authentic figures not only of his armies at the front but of his reserves. What a traitor to his Country & his Army thus to imperil their safety!!

Ever yours
D Lloyd George

H. H. Asquith to Venetia Stanley
(Montagu papers)

17 April 1915   Walmer Castle

... Kitchener arrived quite unexpectedly at tea time having motored over from his place at Broome. ... He had a few not very important bits of business to discuss, but reported a most untoward affair—the torpedoing by a Turkish Destroyer somewhere near Smyrna of one of our transports, wh. was carrying 1000 troops from Egypt to the Dardanelles: whether they were lost or saved he didn't yet know. It is almost inconceivable that the Naval people shd be so intolerably careless as either not to know that the Turks had such a vessel there, (they have been bombarding Smyrna off & on for weeks) or, if they did know, not to provide proper protective escort for the transports. No transport has yet been sunk in the whole war. Doesn't it shake one's confidence in them, coming on the top of so many mishaps & miscalculations & incomplete successes? ...

John Churchill: diary
(Copy, Churchill papers: 28/139)

17 April 1915

The 'Queen E.' did not go after all as of course news came in that the boats at Maidos have gone. The 'Manitou' came in during the morning. There does not appear to have been any panic. One of the davits carried away and sixty men were killed and drowned. It has raised many points as to who should do what in such a case. The general opinion is that the Captain might have attempted to get away, but it is very easy to criticise after the event. Bad news has come in about the submarine. She is aground about 8 miles at the channel and a Turkish torpedo boat is along-side her. This report comes from an aeroplane. There are no details yet. By a coincidence the officer in the aeroplane[1] is the brother of the commander of the Submarine![2]

[1] Charles G. Brodie, 1884–1964. Entered Navy, 1900. Lieutenant, 1904. Commanded the Submarine C.3, 1912. Served as a Lieutenant-Commander on de Robeck's staff, 1915; he was not the pilot of the plane but a passenger. Commander, 1916; Captain 1922; Rear-Admiral, 1934.

[2] Theodore S. Brodie, 1884–1915. Entered Navy, 1900; Lieutenant, 1905. Commanded the submarine D.8, 1911. Lieutenant-Commander, commanding the submarine E.15 at the Dardanelles, 1915. On 17 April 1915, his submarine having run aground on the Asiatic Shore of the Dardanelles, he was killed by Turkish shellfire while in the conning tower.

H. G. Selfridge[1] to Winston S. Churchill
(*Churchill papers: 26/2*)

17 April 1915

Selfridge & Co Ltd
London

Dear Mr. Churchill,

I discovered, much to my joy yesterday, in a book I have, describing the Krupp Works, a bird's eye view of these same Works, and of course it is officially correct because it is a part of the book which was issued by the Krupp Company itself to its friends at the time of its one hundredth anniversary. I have had this coloured picture of theirs photographed and send the photograph to you.

It has always seemed to me that a successful air raid on Essen would, perhaps, do more to make the Germans realize that they were likely to be beaten than any similar effort that we could make. At any rate please receive this photograph with my Compliments.

I believe the area is about 160 acres, or at least it was, but it may have been enlarged recently. The chief hammers, forges, etc., however, are no doubt to be found near the bottoms of the big chimneys.

The entire book, which is a beautiful publication of several hundred pages written in German, is at your disposal, if you care to see it.

With kind regards and with all certainty of final success,

Yours very sincerely
H. Gordon Selfridge

Winston S. Churchill to John Churchill: telegram
(*Draft, Churchill papers: 13/65*)

19 April 1915

Admiralty

Private and Personal

Deeply interested by your two letters of 3rd, and 11th. I consider prime responsibility rests with Navy to spare Army as much as possible our friend ought not to be underrated; supreme moral and political effects of the apparition of a strong British fleet in the Sea of Marmora even if Gallipoli

[1] Harry Gordon Selfridge, 1857–1947. Born in the United States. Joined the Marshall Field store, Chicago, 1877; became a partner, 1889; left, on not being made senior partner, 1902, having raised the profits of the store from $370,000 to $1,500,000. Came to England, 1900. Laid the foundation stone of Selfridges, Oxford Street, 1908; the store opened in 1909. Acted as purchasing agent for the French Government, 1914–18. Sold over three million pounds worth of War Bonds in nine days, December 1917. The first public demonstration of Television took place in Selfridges, 1925.

Peninsula is still defended by enemy Kitchener considers it would be decisive. Also I am sure that forts will be quelled if we go on steadily for two or three days hard action. We know they are running short of ammunition particularly for the 14-inch guns.

The vital thing is not to break off because of losses but to persevere. This is the hour in the world's history for a fine feat of arms and the result of victory will amply justify the means. I wish I were with you. It would be easier than waiting here. All my thoughts are with you, give every good wish to all my friends and particularly your revered Chief. I rejoice he and de Robeck and Keyes get on so well together. They may put full confidence in the loyalty of those at home.

WSC

Major-General Braithwaite[1] to Lieutenant-Colonel Fitzgerald

(*Kitchener papers*)

Private
20 April 1915   Lemnos

My dear Fitz,

Sir Ian received a message this morning in a cable sent by 'Winston' to a third party. As in order to reply to it he would have to express views on the situation which he does not feel justified in doing, he has sent the following message:

'Sir Ian wishes you were here as in old times and knows you will understand his silence so long as he is working with the fleet.'

He asked me to let you know this as he has closed his letter to Lord Kitchener and, knowing how rumours get about, Sir Ian is anxious that the S of S should be in possession of the facts.

Excuse scrawl to catch the post.

All ready now—or practically so—& anxious to 'have a go'.

Yours
Walter Braithwaite

Very pleasant to find in Roger Keyes—the Chief of Staff of the Fleet— a very old friend with whom it is a great pleasure to work.

WB

[1] Walter Pipon Braithwaite, 1865–1945. Entered Army, 1886. Director of Staff Duties at the War Office, 1914–15. Chief-of-Staff to Sir Ian Hamilton at the Dardanelles, 1915. Major-General, 1915. Knighted, 1918. Lieutenant-General, 1919. Commander, Western Command, India, 1920–3; Scottish Command, 1923–6; Eastern Command, 1926–7. Adjutant-General, 1927–31.

Lord Fisher to Sir John Jellicoe
(*Jellicoe papers*)

20 April 1915   Admiralty

. . . The First Lord is off this afternoon to France for three or four days. This is supposed to be a dead secret but I expect all the world knows and wonders!

The Dardanelles will now soon begin. It is a huge gamble, but all the politicians both sides have shoved us into it or rather Winston has shoved all of them! If a success it undoubtedly will be an immense coup to have got Constantinople. . . .

Lord Fisher to Sir John Jellicoe
(*Jellicoe papers*)

21 April 1915   Admiralty
Private

My dear Jellicoe,
. . . You MUST have aeroplanes and undoubtedly they can (*if you have a sufficient number*) defend you against the Zeppelins. You should write direct to First Lord and ask for them at once, before they are all sent to the Dardanelles, where they are now going by dozens!

Yours
F

Lord Fisher to Sir John Jellicoe
(*Jellicoe papers*)

22 April 1915   Admiralty

My dear Jellicoe,
. . . Let us hope for the best, *and the unexpected always happens in war.* The German General in command may make a mess of it, or the Turkish ammunition may fail. The Germans have sent their best Generals and Admirals there. SECRET. We have got hold of communications to them! But yet they may fail. *Even Homer nodded!*

F

Captain Richmond: diary

(*Richmond papers*)

22 April 1915

... there is really no settled policy. Old Fisher is useless & will not express an opinion if he can help it. Winston is ignorant: & Oliver's advice is not taken. . . . It is quite useless to advise: I only get snubbed when [I] put forward my opinions. . . .

James Masterton-Smith to Sir Edward Grey

(*Churchill papers: 13/51*)

22 April 1915   Admiralty
Secret

Sir Edward Grey,

The First Lord asks me to say that he has received a message from Mons. Cambon, through the French Naval Attaché, suggesting that the naval conversations the First Lord had with Mons. Augagneur at Boulogne last Tuesday night regarding Italian co-operation should be continued at Paris. As the question of military co-operation will have to be discussed at Paris, the First Lord's view is that it would be convenient if the naval conversations were continued at the same time; and, if you agree, he would propose to reply in this sense through the French Naval Attaché. The First Lord's idea is that he would go to Paris himself accompanied by one or two Admiralty officers.

As Mons. Cambon would like to have a reply tonight, the First Lord wishes me to send this note to you direct.[1]

J E Masterton-Smith

Winston S. Churchill to the Comte de Saint Seine

(*Copy, Churchill papers: 13/51*)

22 April 1915   Admiralty

My dear Comte de Saint Seine,

I shall be quite ready to come to Paris with some of the Admiralty officers to join in the discussions *à trois* about Franco-British-Italian Naval co-operation whenever it is found convenient.

Please convey this to your Ambassador.

Yours sincerely
Winston S Churchill

[1] Grey returned this letter to the Admiralty with the note: 'I quite agree.'

H. A. Gwynne to H. H. Asquith

(Copy, Bonar Law papers)

22 April 1915

Morning Post
346 Strand, W.C.

. . . When I had the honour of writing to you on October 16, 1914 regarding the Antwerp expedition, I pointed out to you that I did not consider the First Lord of the Admiralty a man who should be in charge of the Fleet during this war. I considered that the Antwerp expedition thoroughly justified this opinion, and the recurrence of the same lack of study, the same desire to rush on without due preparation, and the same ignorance of strategic and tactical principles in the Dardanelles expedition confirms this opinion. What I ventured to prophesy in October has come to pass in March, and it is for the Government over which you preside to consider whether the First Lord of the Admiralty should continue to hold that office. I would like to point out that I have no personal animosity whatever against the First Lord of the Admiralty; indeed I have a great admiration for his political talents and his perseverance and energy . . .[1]

Major-General Callwell to H. A. Gwynne

(Gwynne papers)

23 April 1915

War Office

My dear Gwynne,

I agree in the main with your Dardanelles article,[2] but you rather overlook the real object of the operations. We want to smash Austria and to enable Russia to turn on the real enemy, Germany. We want those 1,000,000

---

[1] This extract is from a fifteen-page letter on the Dardanelles expedition, a copy of which was sent by Gwynne to Bonar Law.

[2] On 23 April the Morning Post's leading editorial was entitled 'The Dardanelles Blunder'. The 'chief enemy', the editorial declared, was Germany, 'and in war a blow at the heart is of infinitely more value than a blow at a limb; a minor operation is of infinitely less value than a major operation'. But the editorial warned that minor operations 'have a trick of developing into major operations. As they develop they clamour for more and more guns than are thought necessary at the outset, and the thing expands into something very big and very costly'. According to the editorial, Churchill, 'against the opinion of his naval colleagues', had represented to the Cabinet 'that it was possible for the Navy alone' to force its way through the Narrows: 'The experiment was made, and, as we know, it ended disastrously.' The article concluded that 'our constitutional theory has no place for a civilian Minister who usurps the functions of his Board, takes the wheel out of the sailor's hand, and launches ships upon a naval operation. . . . We have seen at Antwerp, in the case of Cradock's squadron, and in this disaster of the Dardanelles, how a nation is punished which persists in allowing its politicians to conduct naval operations'.

Russian troops who are wasting their time defeating Austrians, to go into Silesia and either take 500,000 Germans from Belgium and France or else push on to Berlin and finish the business.

If the Dardanelles affair succeeds—possibly even if it fails—our operations there bring in Italy and Roumania, worth a million men, who will end up in Austria with Russian assistance by July. If that is accomplished we shall beat the Germans down before Christmas, but I do not believe that we shall do it otherwise. 80,000 British and French troops cannot make any great difference in France at present, but they can increase the Allied forces by fully 1,000,000 in the Near East. That in short is the story. But the whole business has as you show in your article been shamefully bungled by Winston.

Yours ever
Chas E. Callwell

Winston S. Churchill to Admiral de Robeck
(Copy, Churchill papers: 29/1)

23 April 1915   Admiralty
Secret and Personal

British Ambassador at Petrograd reports as follows:— 'Following information from sure source reaches me from Minister for Foreign Affairs. Telegram to Ministry of War, Vienna, from Austrian Military Attache, Constantinople,[1] giving details of operations in Dardanelles, contains statement that in consequence of expenditure of large quantity of ammunition Turks have now not enough to repulse two similar attacks. Sender of telegram urged that Roumanian Government should be pressed to allow free passage for munitions of war.'

This agrees with our information, and importance of forcing forts to fire as often and as long as possible, in order to exhaust their ammunition, will doubtless have occurred to you. I have consulted Lord Fisher before sending this telegram, but, of course, you are free to act as you think fit, so I mark this telegram personal, as intention of all we say is merely to be helpful and a guide, and not a hard and fast instruction.

---

[1] Josef Pomiankowski, 1866–1929. Austro–Hungarian Military Attaché in Belgrade, 1901–1907; in Constantinople, 1907–18. Major, 1902; Major-General, 1914. Joined the Polish Army, 1919. Head of the Polish Military Mission to Sweden, 1919–22. Head of the Polish Military Purchasing Commission, Paris, 1922. In 1928 he published an account of his eleven years in Turkey entitled *Der Zusammenbruch des Ottomanischen Reiches*.

Frederick Guest to Winston S. Churchill

(*Churchill papers: 26/2*)

24 April 1915   Head-Quarters
                                                British Army

Dear Winston

This morning I referred to your proposal to visit us and the Chief said that he thought 'better not'—I did not press it as the atmosphere was a little electrical. As you can imagine there have been some rather intense moments during the last 36 hours[1]—

The efforts to retrieve the lost ground will I fear chiefly fall to our lot at any rate during the initial stages. What a blessing it is that the general refused to relieve the 9th & 20th French Corps a month ago. As it is now, the lately arrived divisions give us a very comfortable reserve.

Asphixiating gas had something to do with the stampede—one can only guess how much or how little. It is certainly a very serious weapon for trench warfare.

What I expect now is another push in the district of St Eloi. The salient looks very quaint at this moment! POTIGE and the Summer house is now the centre of the semicircle.

Later. At lunch the Chief referred to your proposed visit and seemed rather anxious lest you should be hurt. I assured him that you quite understood and that I had written you fully—etc.—There is no doubt that he has been subjected to a very great strain since the 22nd and I know you will make allowances. It is really appalling how rapidly things happen in a panic. In one night they advanced over a front of 9000 yds and at the furthest point gained 6000 yds—bringing them within sight of where we passed north of YPRES the other day—about 2000 to 3000 yds north of the town. Since I saw you last you will have read the P.M.'s statement re 'Munitions'[2]—It is unfortunate that it is in flat contradiction to the General's published statement on that subject. The Army who know the truth are furious— All I am anxious about is that there should be no misunderstanding between the

---

[1] The second battle of Ypres opened on 22 April, with a successful German poison gas attack. But despite their initial advantage, the Germans failed to capture Ypres. The battle continued until 25 May, when the front line was stabilized three and a half miles to the east of Ypres. In a month of severe fighting, the British lost 737 officers and 26,000 men. German losses were somewhat less.

[2] Speaking at Newcastle on 20 April 1915 Asquith had asserted that there was no shortage of ammunition for the British forces in France. His assertion was based upon a letter which Kitchener had sent him six days earlier, reporting that Sir John French was confident that with his existing supply of ammunition he would have as much as his troops could use in the attack to come.

General and the P.M. Dont you think the P.M. might send him a line of explanation?[1]

I am glad you enjoyed your last visit.

Good bye for the present

Yrs
Freddie

I made enquiries re motor machine guns referred to by Eye Witness on 23rd—I find that they were not the naval section. It appears that each army has got a section of its own.

Latest news.

French have retaken LIZERNE and the village of STREENSTAATE all except one house.

This presumably means the bridgehead.

Winston S. Churchill: Cabinet memorandum
(*Churchill papers: 13/58*)

24 April 1915   Admiralty

I have heard that unfavourable comment has been made on the alleged 'failure of the Admiralty to foresee the dangers to which ships operating in the Dardanelles would be exposed from floating mines'.

I therefore append an extract from the original orders issued from the Admiralty to Admiral Carden.

*   *   *

Vessels covering the mine-sweepers will be exposed to attack by drifting mines especially when at anchor. Torpedo nets will be some protection against pairs of mines, connected by lines, coming alongside when the connecting rope takes across the stem.

It may be advisable to prepare buoys to be paid ahead of vessels anchoring in the Dardanelles to catch drifting mines and also to make use of fishing nets between buoys to intercept mines. Concrete blocks could be used as moorings for the buoys.

Drift nets have been found efficacious in the North Sea as a means of clearing away moored mines. They are allowed to drift with the tide, and foul the mines and break them adrift.

---

[1] Sir John French soon wanted more than 'a line of explanation'. Early in May he sent his two ADCs, Frederick Guest and Brindsley Fitzgerald, to London to inform political leaders and the Press that he had not received sufficient ammunition.

Nets might be laid at night by shallow-draught vessels or picket boats above the minefields to drift down with the current.

There may be considerable difficulty in dealing with observation mines owing to the depths at which they may be moored.

The cables will probably have to be crept for with explosive grapnels, but it may be possible also to sweep with mine-sweeping vessels to a sufficient depth.[1]

Lord Fisher to Winston S. Churchill

(Churchill papers: 13/57)

25 April 1915   Admiralty

Dear Winston,

Sir Michael Seymour[2] lunched with me yesterday—He has been staying with his son[3] on board the 'Centurion' in the Grand Fleet—He SPON-TANEOUSLY said to me that in all his experience he had never known an Admiral so implicitly trusted and loved by all under him as Jellicoe! and Dreyer[4] said the same AND ADDED he could not imagine a higher state of efficiency than now in the Grand Fleet! *So there really is some Balm in Gilead!*[5]

Yrs
F

---

[1] In an early draft of *The World Crisis* Churchill admitted: 'The mine-sweeping force as originally provided by the Admiralty was inadequate. The minesweepers were too slow and could not make sufficient headway against the currents, and their personnel was not sufficiently trained to stand the severe ordeal to which they were subjected.' (*Churchill papers: 8/84*) Churchill deleted these sentences before the volume went to the printer.

[2] Michael Culme-Seymour, 1836–1920. Entered Navy, 1850. Served with the Naval Brigade in the Crimean War, 1854–5, and at the capture of Canton, 1857. Commander-in-Chief, Pacific station, 1885–87; Channel squadron, 1890–9; Mediterranean station, 1893–96, and Portsmouth, 1897–1900. Succeeded his father as 3rd Baronet, 1880. Admiral, 1893. Vice-Admiral of the United Kingdom, 1901–20.

[3] Michael Culme-Seymour, 1867–1925. Lieutenant, 1889. Captain, 1905. Rear-Admiral, at Battle of Jutland, 1916. Commanded Black Sea and Caspian Squadron, 1919. Succeeded his father as 4th Baronet, 1920. Commander-in-Chief, North America and West Indies station, 1923–24. Second Sea Lord and Chief of Naval Personnel, 1924–25.

[4] Frederick Charles Dreyer, 1878–1956. Entered Navy, 1891. Jellicoe's Flag Commander, 1910–12. Appointed to War Staff, 1912. Captain, 1913. Flag Captain to Jellicoe on HMS *Iron Duke*, 1915–16. Assistant Director, Anti-Submarine Division, Admiralty Naval Staff, 1916–17. Director, Naval Ordnance, 1917–18. Director, Naval Artillery and Torpedo, Admiralty Naval Staff, 1918–19. Commodore and Chief of Staff to Jellicoe, 1919–20. Director, Gunnery Division, Admiralty Naval Staff, 1920–2. Rear-Admiral, 1923. Assistant Chief of Naval Staff, 1924–7. Commanded the Battle Cruiser Squadron, 1927–9. Deputy Chief of Naval Staff, 1930–3. Knighted, 1932. Admiral, 1932. Commander-in-Chief, China Station, 1933–6.

[5] 'Is there no balm in Gilead; is there no physician there? Why then is not the health of the daughter of my people recovered?' *Jeremiah 8, 22*.

I'm QUITE sick about our submarines and mines and not shooting at Zeppelins (who never can go higher than 2000 yards) and light cruisers bound to bring them down & we always know exactly where they are!

Really yesterday had it not been for the Dardanelles forcing me to stick to you through thick & thin I would have gone out of the Admiralty yesterday never to return and sent you a post card to get Sturdee up *at once* in my place—

You would *then* be quite happy!!! and I have a room ready at the Hotel de Paris at Monte Carlo—I got a letter yesterday from a charming American *Millionairess* to say so.

Winston S. Churchill: obituary notice of Rupert Brooke

(*The Times*)

26 April 1915

Rupert Brooke is dead. A telegram from the Admiral at Lemnos tells us that this life has closed at the moment when it seemed to have reached its springtime. A voice had become audible, a note had been struck, more true, more thrilling, more able to do justice to the nobility of our youth in arms engaged in this present war, than any other—more able to express their thoughts of self-surrender, and with a power to carry comfort to those who watch them so intently from afar. The voice has been swiftly stilled. Only the echoes and the memory remain; but they will linger.

During the last few months of his life, months of preparation in gallant comradeship and open air, the poet-soldier told with all the simple force of genius the sorrow of youth about to die, and the sure triumphant consolations of a sincere and valiant spirit. He expected to die; he was willing to die for the dear England whose beauty and majesty he knew; and he advanced towards the brink in perfect serenity, with absolute conviction of the rightness of his country's cause and a heart devoid of hate for fellow-men.

The thoughts to which he gave expression in the very few incomparable war sonnets which he has left behind will be shared by many thousands of young men moving resolutely and blithely forward into this, the hardest, the cruellest, and the least-rewarded of all the wars that men have fought. They are a whole history and revelation of Rupert Brooke himself. Joyous, fearless, versatile, deeply instructed, with classic symmetry of mind and body, ruled by high undoubting purpose, he was all that one would wish England's noblest sons to be in days when no sacrifice but the most previous is acceptable, and the most precious is that which is most freely proffered.

26 April 1915   10 Downing Street

Dearest Winston,

I must write one word to tell you how beautiful I thought your tribute
to our beloved Rupert in to-day's Times.

All those who loved him must be grateful to you for it.

I feel heart-broken. He was the most radiantly perfect human being I
have ever known—so flawless that one sometimes wondered whether he
quite belonged to this ragged scheme of things—whether he hadn't strayed
here out of some faery land.

He obviously belonged to the 'predestined'—so obviously that one could
not but hope that even Fate might shrink from so cruel a platitude as his
destruction.

He never had a doubt about his death himself. Not only did he often
speak to me of it in those last days at Blandford—& Avonmouth—but in
2 of the letters I have had from him since he started, he refers once indirectly
—& once quite directly to it (telling me not to mind too much).

He had so much left to give the world.

Poor Eddie—my heart aches for him—his whole life pivoted on Rupert.

Goodbye dear Winston—bless you.

Yrs ever
Violet

26 April 1915   Admiralty

Should you find it useful in pursuance of your plans at any time to use
10 or 15 empty Transports for the purpose of finding a way through minefields or screening ships from torpedoes or blanketing off torpedo tubes dont
hesitate to take anything you want from the Transports available without
further reference on the score of expense or authority.

F
WSC

Sir Ian Hamilton to Lord Kitchener: telegram

(*Copy, Crewe papers*)

26 April 1915
1.00 pm

Thanks to the magnificent co-operation of the Royal Navy, we succeeded in landing 29,000 men in 6 landings[1] in the face of determined opposition from Infantry and Artillery, entrenched behind successive lines of wire entanglements which ran in all directions and were sometimes 50 yards wide. We are far from out of the wood yet. We are held up all day in the amphitheatre just west of Seddel Bahr, but just at sunset a fine attack by the 29th Division south-east along the heights from Tekke Burnu has succeeded, I hope, in relieving this pressure.

The Australians made very good progress in their landing at Kaba Tebe and between 3.30 and 8.30 a.m. actually succeeded in getting 8,000 men ashore. They pressed on with excessive boldness but the country was everywhere entrenched and wired, and owing to their Artillery not being ashore they were not able to reply to the enemy's howitzers and were brought to a standstill on the lower slopes of Sari Bair.

Three battalions and a battery were landed at Kum Kale by the French, who advanced with great gallantry against Yeni Shahr, this being a necessity in order to relieve us from fire from the Asiatic shore.

I regret to say that Brigadier-General Napier[2] has been killed and our losses are heavy, but I am as yet unable to estimate them.

If things go well during the night, the 29th Division will advance tomorrow against Achi Baba while the Australians keep any enemy reinforcements from going south across the narrow part of the Peninsula between Kaba Tebe and Maidos.

Winston S. Churchill to Lord Kitchener: not sent

(*Copy, Churchill papers: 13/45*)

26 April 1915   Admiralty

My dear Kitchener,

I hope you will not cut Hamilton too fine. A loyal man like that will go on with what he has got & never say a word till he cracks up. The easy good fortunes of a beginning may depart again.

[1] See map 8 on page 1599.
[2] Henry Edward Napier, 1861–1915. Entered Army, 1882. Colonel, 1911. Officer commanding No. 11 District, Irish Command, 1914–15. Brigadier-General commanding units of the 88th Brigade, V Beach landing, Gallipoli, 25 April 1915.

I sh'd feel vy much happier if you c'd manage to have another 20,000 in the offing—even if they were never landed. It would be a great insurance; & surely at a pinch you c'd spare them from Egypt for a fortnight. Do not brush this aside with confident scorn. The things that have to be done are vy difficult and a sincere opinion deserves to be considered.

Do consider this. Don't run short of stuffing behind your attack—even if you never need it. My feeling is you are running it vy fine.

Don't be vexed with me for bringing this up. It costs so little to have a shot in the locker.

Don't wait till he asks you. It is sure to be too late then.

Yours sincerely
Winston S Churchill

Winston S. Churchill to Lieutenant-Colonel Fitzgerald: not sent
(*Copy: Churchill papers: 13/45*)

26 April 1915   Admiralty
Most Secret

My dear Fitzgerald,

I hope K will not cut Hamilton too fine. I have a feeling that there ought to be another 20,000 men in it. They could get there in a week from Egypt. A valiant & successful attack like this may go well for a time: but there must be *stuffing* behind & inside it. So far all is well, but watch carefully that these two or three precious days that decide things are not lost.

I think there ought to be more men: at any rate more *near* the spot.

Remember every minute of this is history: and every attack requires backing.

Yours sincerely
Winston S Churchill

Sir Ian Hamilton to Lord Kitchener
(*Copy, Crewe papers*)

27 April 1915
Secret

I was over sanguine in anticipating an advance to-day to the attack of Achi Baba. Sedd-el-Bahr was still in the hands of the enemy this morning and the Australian and New Zealand Army Corps at Sari Bair and the

French detachment at Kum Kale were put to it to maintain their position against very determined counter-attacks. Sedd-el-Bahr was a dreadful place to carry by open assault, being a labyrinth of rocks, galleries, ruined houses and wire entanglements and held by sharp shooters and machine guns. In fact, with the devoted help of the Navy, it has taken a day's hard fighting before we have been able thoroughly to make good our footing on the peninsula. Achi Baba hill, which lies only a cannon shot distant, will be attacked to-morrow by the 29th Division with part of the French Division.

Some of our battalions have lost a quarter of their effectives but all are in excellent spirits. The French have taken 500 prisoners.

John Churchill to Winston S. Churchill
(*Churchill papers: 1/117*)

27 April 1915   HMS Queen Elizabeth

My dear,

The landing beaches were numbered S, V, W, X, Y, Z, and were as follows:—

    S. East pt of Morto Bay just under De Tott's Battery.
        (Covering party—S. Wales Borderers).
    V. Between Seddel Bahr & C. Helles.
        (Covering party—Munsters & Dublins in 'Wooden Horse').
    W. Between C. Helles & Tekke Burnu.
        (Covering party—Lancashire Fusiliers).
    X. Just North of Tekke Burnu.
        (Covering party—29th Division).
    Y. Two miles North of X.
        (Covering party—KOSB's. & marines).
    Z. 2½ miles North of Kaba Tepe.
        (Covering party—Australians).

The French to land one regiment at Kum Kale.

The RND to land at NW Corner of Bay of Xeros.

The general idea was: The *RND* to land the night before the main operations, light fires on their beach and demonstrate as much as possible. Then re-embark the following day. The *French* to demonstrate on the Asiatic side and so keep howitzer battery occupied and prevent them from shelling Morto Bay and transports. *Birdwood* to land before dawn at Z without artillery preparation—this was his choice. The *29th Division* to land on S,V,W,X, and Y at dawn under cover of the ships.

The 'Queen E' left Imbros about 4 a.m. and passed near Y beach at 5. No firing had taken place, but Y party were already busy landing. We turned

N towards Gaba Tepe. It was growing lighter every moment and behind us we could see a large fleet lying off Cape Helles, while ahead another great fleet of ships loomed up off Gaba Tepe. At 5.5 the guns at Cape Helles opened fire from the ships. The sun had risen but was not yet over the hills. It was quite clear with a northerly breeze and a calm sea. Nothing could have been better for the operations as far as weather was concerned. At 5.15 we were nearly opposite Z beach, and heavy musketry could be heard from the shore. As it grew lighter, I could see rows of tows lying along the beach. Birdwood had evidently effected his landing. At 5.30 the captive balloon rose from its ship and the sun came over the hills. Visibility became difficult. Cape Helles was only just in sight, but heavy firing could be heard and the flashes clearly seen. Heavy musketry continued on Z and at 5.45 we learnt that 4,000 men were on shore. The enemy were bursting shrapnel over the beach and some fell near the 'Bacchante'. A seaplane rose from the 'Ark Royal' at 6 and passed over the peninsula. Birdwood signalled that he was making good progress. At 6.30 we turned and steamed south to look how the others fared.

As you pass along the coast, the contours and outlines change so rapidly that it is difficult to realise exact localities. Y, X, and W covering ships were all firing 12″ and 6″ guns and the 'Old Castle' ridge behind Seddel Bahr was being blanketted with shell. Half-way between Gaba Tepe and C. Helles the spectacle was wonderful. Ahead of us and behind us lay enormous fleets of ships of all sorts. All the men-of-war were in action. It sounded like a continuous royal salute from the whole fleet at Spithead. But in addition we had the roar of the shells as they burst on the ridges. News reached us here that the Y party had all landed and were scaling the cliffs without opposition. At 7.12 we came opposite Cape Tekke Burnu. Here also the X party seemed to have landed safely. The sun was in our eyes and it was difficult to see. Little figures could be seen running about on the top of the cliff. They seemed to have made some headway inland, but were evidently under fire. At 7.20 Y party flashed to the ships 'cease firing, we want to advance'. Things seemed to be going well. Here was the weather—the one thing that even optimists feared—perfect, and 3 beaches out of six successfully accomplished. We steamed on, slowly turning to port. Cape Helles came in to view. Clearly W party had also landed and made good considerable ground. I could see that the ruin of the Helles lighthouse was occupied by our men. Infantry were lying down all along the top of the cliff. A mass of wire entanglements could be seen in front of them. Some little figures ran about and crouched. They also were under fire. All ships continued to fire rapidly. We were moving all the time and round C. Helles, Seddel Bahr came into view. In the little bay between these two points we could see the 'Wooden Horse', otherwise the 'River Clyde'. It soon became clear that all was not well here. The boat had done well and was piled up on the shore. The lighters formed a pier from her bows to the beach, but she was still full of men. Under a little ridge, where the sand joined the mainland, crouched a couple of hundred men. Evidently they had landed and could not make any progress. As I watched 2 or 3 men tried to get back into the ship. At once the beach and water all round them sprang into the air, and the rat, tat, tat, of a couple of maxims broke out. Inland 20 yards beyond the men more wire could be seen. The situation was clear. It was an amphi-theatre. The 'Wooden Horse' and her advanced party were in the centre of the stage. The semi-circular 'house' was 'full'. Any man who moved on the stage received the 'applause' of everyone from the stalls, 20 yards in front of that beastly wire, from the 'stage boxes' which contained maxims on each flank, and from the 'dress circle and gallery', who occupied various trenches all up the steep slope. At 7.45 the French fleet, a little south of us, opened fire on the Asiatic shore. They fired rapidly and soon Kum Kale and Yeni Shehr were enveloped in smoke.

At 8 we could see little figures from W party extending on the cliff tops to their right. If only they could have gone another $\frac{1}{2}$ mile, they would have worried the 'gallery' of the amphi-theatre. But again there was more wire and heavy rifle fire. The little figures suddenly fell flat and remained taking what cover they could. We went on a little more to the east so as to have the sun behind us. We passed the 'Albion', who was making beautiful shooting at the rim of the amphi-theatre. You must realise that the little bay looked very small, and it is in fact only $\frac{1}{2}$ mile from Seddel Bahr to the next point westwards. Something had to be done to help the poor 'Wooden Horse'. She had promised to give us a 'star turn' and was in a bad way, with Achilles looking at her from his tomb exactly opposite! And so at 8.20 the 'Queen E' fired a 15″ into Seddel Bahr. I was on the searchlight bridge at the time and was taken by surprise. My cap went one way and my note book another. My pipe fell to the floor and after a gulp or two, I looked at the village in front. About 150 yards of houses seemed to suddenly rise in the air in a great cloud of smoke and dust. It was two or three minutes before the debris settled. A shrapnel burst near our bows and we fired again. We closed in near the shore and must have been well within rifle shot, but I saw no sign of any bullets directed at us. We were now well into the straits. What a situation! In front of me the great 15″ shells were blowing the last village in Europe to hell, and behind the French melinite was blasting great holes in Asia! I looked round and counted 67 ships lying round the entrance of the straits. There must have been another 40 off Gaba Tepe, while far away off Imbros the Naval Division and the remainder of the French were collecting. I could now see the tows of the S landing party lying under De Tott's battery. No news came from them and their position did not seem enviable. S and V both gave cause for anxiety. V were completely held up and it might be necessary to re-embark. S were few in number and a long way off and very much 'en l'air'.

At 9 o'clock Birdwood signalled that he had 8,000 men on shore at Gaba. We began firing salvos of six 6″ guns at Seddel Bahr and the amphi-theatre. The noise on board and the explosions on shore were terrific. Behind us the French re-doubled their fire. At 9.20 the French tows could be seen landing at Kum Kale. They had been ordered to do this at 6 a.m., but here, as in France, their punctuality is not their strong point. However, as the howitzers from the Asiatic side had not opened fire, their lateness did not matter. At 9.30 more news came in. The S party had occupied 141 and De Tott's battery and were digging themselves in. X beach were doing well and Birdwood had made good progress. At 10 the fire into the amphi-theatre had increased. The audience were having their money's worth. But they would not go and the maxims could still be heard whenever anyone tried to leave the 'Wooden Horse'. The situation continued unchanged. Seddel Bahr had been blown to bits, but still the beach party could not advance. At 1.30 General D'Amade reported that he had made good progress towards Yeni-Shehr, and had taken 400 prisoners. Y beach now complained that they were held up by a battery firing from the plain south of Achi Baba. The 15″ were turned on and the complaints ceased.

The W party could be seen again working to their right. They only had a little way to go to reach point 138, but a heavy fire held them up. At 3 o'clock I saw the Worcesters advance along the top of the cliffs. Suddenly the leading company began to run. The men bent double and were evidently under fire. They reached wire and fell down to take cover. Then two little figures rose and calmly began to cut the wire. Two more joined them and soon they were through. It was a wonderful sight and we all watched with baited breath, expecting every moment to see them fall. But they got through and were followed by the remainder of the company. A few figures fell in the wire and remained there, but another company ran up and through with their bayonets fixed. At 3.15 hill 138 was occupied. At 3.40 Hunter Weston reported that a battery of his guns were landing on W. We remained watching the V position, which was unchanged. At 6.30 a few men crawled to the foot of the old Seddel Bahr fort on the sea front. The Worcesters made a determined attempt to get further to the right, but failed, and at 7 I could see some of them running back. At 7.20 visibility became impossible, but a ripling fire continued.

And so the first day ended leaving us very anxious. Z seemed to have made good progress. Y said they were happy. W and X had joined hands and were well established and S were firmly fixed at De Tott's battery. There remained only V and we hoped that morning would find them in a better position. Late at night Hunter Weston came on board and gave a glowing account of the capture of several points which we knew his men had not reached. But his optimism was an improvement on his former attitude. Later again, a destroyer came from Z. Birdwood was in difficulties. The Australians and New Zealanders begun very well and had made good progress, but they had not attempted to dig themselves in. A few shrapnel burst over them and they had retired and were much shaken. There was even a question of their re-embarking at once! But the C-in-C said no. They were ordered to dig and hold on at any price. They had had 2,500 casualties. The 29th Division lost one brigadier killed and two wounded, also 2 brigade majors killed, including Frankland,[1] who was caught with you in the train in S. Africa. The 'Queen E' fired 370 rounds of 6" during the day.

The dawn of morning found us back at Gaba Tepe, ready to help the Australians. They were holding a little triangle near the shore, and I could see them clinging on to the scrubby ridges. At 6.10 the 15" began, and there is no doubt that the moral effect on the Turks made a great difference. After a few rounds their shrapnel ceased and the Australians signalled 'thanks, now we can land our supplies'. At 7.20 bad news came in. S was still isolated but comfortable. V position was unchanged. W and X were joined but had not joined V and Y announced that they were in desperate straits. At 9 o'clock we went off to Y beach and found the men—some 2,000—climbing down the cliff and re-embarking under cover from several battleships. They had had 400 casualties, or 25%, but how they got into such a state is not yet quite clear. W and X now signalled that they could not advance without further troops. We returned to Cape Helles and at 1.30 General D'Amade came on board. He received orders to reinforce Hunter Weston. This he promised to do at once by landing a brigade at 3 o'clock. The situation along the end of the promontory appeared to be unchanged. Back we went to Gaba Tepe and at 1.50 found the Australians to be in a better position. The Turks had made a considerable counter-attack, but had been repulsed. The Australians were finding their feet and the situation was much improved. The 'Queen E' kept up a considerable fire with her 15". The balloon spotting was good, but we received no information at all from the aeroplanes. At 4.30 we returned to Helles to find the French had not began to disembark. As we approached the point I was gazing at the back of the old castle of Seddel Bahr, when

---

[1] Thomas Hugh Colville Frankland, 1879–1915. 2nd Lieutenant, Royal Dublin Fusiliers, 1899; captured with Churchill in the armoured train ambushed by the Boers, and imprisoned with him in Pretoria. Brigade-Major, 86th Brigade, 1915; killed during the W beach landing, 25 April 1915.

suddenly I saw little men standing round it in the open! There could be no doubt, only English soldiers would stand about like that. Clearly the ridge behind Seddel Bahr was ours. And if so—then V beach was relieved from pressure. The line must be complete and W, V, S could join hands! Sir Ian came up from tea and as he passed asked whether there was anything new. I told what I could see and that I believed the coast line was all ours. He was very excited and doubtful of any such good fortune. But the position was soon clear. A few minutes later the whole plateau above Helles and Seddel Bahr came into view. It was covered with men standing up and walking about, in spots where three hours ago I had seen skirmishers crawling under fire. The amphi-theatre had been taken and the whole of Seddel Bahr was in our hands. The whole situation was greatly relieved and the danger of the landing had been overcome. It was a great relief to everyone. The whole position had been one of great danger, but now the coast was held and guns were disembarking. It would take a great deal to shift that 29th Division and the Turks had evidently retired. We remained off Helles during the night. At 6.30 a.m. on Tuesday a message flashed from Gaba Tepe saying that a submarine had been seen! As you may imagine this news created a disturbance. The 'Queen E' ran to ground among the transports and tried to make a noise like a cruiser. But a few minutes after a signal came that the submarine was only an overturned boat. We came out of our hiding place and steamed up to Gaba Tepe at 8.45. The Australians had had a good night and were well maintained. They were firing heavily and the enemy were firing many shrapnel at the beach. But most of their shell fell into the water and did no harm. The ground rises rapidly from the beach and is very steep—but progress had been made and I could see some guns busily working several hundred feet up the slope of the hill. The fire sounded very hot and the battery was firing continuously. The 'Queen E' opened fire with her 15″ and the situation seemed to change at once. The firing died down a little and the enemy's shrapnel ceased. The effect of the 15″ gun was enormous. At 10 o'clock the balloon announced that a man-of-war was lying in the Narrows. Soon after a couple of big shells fell close to us. We were ordered under armour and I spent an hour in the 6″ battery. We continued to fire 15″ at the Narrows and 6″ at the shore. The enemy's ship bolted but was not hit. At 12 o'clock two transports were reported in the narrows. The 'Queen E' fired three rounds over the peninsula and at 12.5 the balloon reported that one of the transports had bolted and that the forecastle of the other could only be seen! She was an 8,000 ton ship and our third shot went right through her. The range was 15,500! At 12.45 we returned to Helles and found to my delight that the front line of the 29th Division had dug themselves in. The French had only managed to put 2 battalions ashore! Hunter

Weston was anxious to attack and move forward a little. A tremendous fire was turned on the Krithia plain south of Achi Baba. The 'Implacable' signalled that she had spotted some troops in mass. She fired a 12″ shrapnel and when the smoke cleared away there only remained one riderless horse! At 4 o'clock we heard that 6″ guns were shelling the transports at Gaba. Back we went again and our approach silenced the guns! We returned again to Helles and found a further advance had taken place without much opposition. The whole situation was excellent and everybody was now fully satisfied. Such was the fighting during three days as I saw it from the 'Queen E'. My story is very disjointed and a great many important facts have not yet come to hand. We were moving all the time and tried to lend a hand with the big guns whenever needed. Z beach had an exciting time landing. The Turks formed up on the beach. The destroyers went close in and the men charged as they landed. There were considerable losses, but the Australians did very well and drove the enemy up the hill. They landed 4,000 men in the first half-hour! This I think is a record in the face of an enemy. They were very foolish on the first day and did not dig themselves in. The shell fire upset them very much and there might have been a bad accident. But now they have found their legs and are allright. Their fire control is bad. Yesterday they were firing fast all day and only had 350 casualties. I am afraid they wasted ammunition, but they will improve. The situation at Y beach has not yet been cleared up. They lost heavily, but had they held on a little longer they would have had a splendid target of the Turks retiring from X and W. However, they felt lonely and they lost a lot of officers and the retirement was made. X had an easy time. The landing party at W found themselves in an amphi-theatre very similar to the V position. The Lancashire Fusiliers landed under heavy fire and charged up the ridge. They went through the wire and the Turks fled. They were enfiladed by maxims but nothing could stop them. The flank platoons were annihilated, but they swept everything before them. I have already described V. The South Wales Borderers had a bad time landing at S. Maxims were turned on to some of the boats and several were sunk with everybody in them. But about 700 landed safely and held on. The fire from the ships was terrific, but spotting was difficult and not well done. I don't know that the aeroplanes helped very much in this. The Navy have never had such a time. They dug great chunks out of the hills with their lyddite. Things are going very well, and I hope ships will be in the Sea of Marmora in a fortnight. I think de Robeck will have a try to get through as soon as possible. I enclose a map showing the positions of the beaches and our track along the coast.

Yours
Jack S. C.

Josiah Wedgwood to Winston S. Churchill
(*Churchill papers: 21/43*)

27 April 1915[1]   HMS River Clyde
                                                    Off Tenedos

Dear Churchill,

This ought to be a most interesting letter if it is ever finished for we are on the wreck ship.

As usual I have fallen in pleasant places. Seeing that cars were not likely to be of use here for a time I trained my squadron for working the maxims on their flat feet.

As soon as Hamilton arrived I reported to him (as provided in my blessed Sailing Orders), & soon got fixed up to arm this ship, commanded by Comdr. Unwin,[2] the inventor of the Wreck ship idea. We made casemates for our guns, & have also got 18 Motor Cycles aboard so that we can run our guns (or other peoples Ammn) up to Krithia if all goes well. We are attached to the 29th division under Hunter Weston.

Today, this afternoon, unless the wind again puts us off, 2400 Munsters & Dublins & Hampshires come on board, & conceal themselves in the holds of the Wooden Horse (We are in sight of the windy plains of Troy). In the ships sides great ports are cut. As soon as the crash comes & we grind ashore, these dragons teeth spring armed from the ports & race along a balcony to the stern of the vessel, there they pass forward along a steam hopper & thence over a draw-bridge to dry land.

You may ask why we have not got dozens of wreck ships instead of only one. The answer is that it is an experiment, & only a First Lord makes experiments on a lordly scale. But you can imagine *our* joy at being on the experiment.

Of course we may get sunk going in, but bar that it seems to me much the least risky way of landing troops, & you get a serviceable jetty for landing alongside for other guns & stores.

I must finish this page for the first instalment. So six of your Maxim's rush the heights $\frac{3}{4}$ m. inland with the troops; then the bikes come to Sedel Bahr

---

[1] This letter, begun on 24 April 1915, was sent on 27 April.

[2] Edward Unwin, 1864–1950. Lieutenant, Royal Navy, 1895. Commander, retired, 1909. Recalled, 1914. Served on the staff of Rear-Admiral Wemyss at Mudros, in preparations for the Dardanelles campaign, March 1915. Commanded the *River Clyde* at the 'V' Beach landing, 25 April 1915. Awarded the Victoria Cross as a result of the landing. Commanded the lighters at the Suvla Bay landing, 6 August 1915, and promoted Captain for his part in the operation. Principal Naval Transport Officer, Egypt and Eastern Mediterranean, 1917–19. Resigned from the Navy to become a yachtsman, 1920.

& prepare while I report to the Genl. for further orders. This is better than heckling McKenna.

Only Francis Maclaren has left us & gone on board the 'Doris', alas!

26 April 1915   Sedel Bahr

We ran ashore on 'V' beach at 6.30, being shelled on the way by 6″ guns from the Asiatic side. The hopper ran aground in the wrong place. The fire from the shore was heavy, & the original plan could not be worked to.

Five tows of 5 boats each with some 30–40 men in each came onto 'V' beach simultaneously with ourselves, & in 10 minutes there were some 400 dead & wounded on the beach & in the waters. Not more than 10% got safe to shore & took shelter under the sand edge. Some of the Munster Fusiliers tried to land from the 'River Clyde' about 7, a.m., after some sort of a connection had been made with a spit of rock. Very few of them got safe to land, & Genl Napier & his Brigade Major[1] were killed on the lighter. Thereafter the wounded cried out all day & for 36 hours;—in every boat, lighter, hopper & all along the shore. It was horrible & all within 200 yards of our guns trying to find & shoot the shooters. If the 'River Clyde' had not been on that beach with our 11 Maxims on board not one of the 400 still living on the shore could have survived.

That night we landed the rest of the Munsters & the Hampshires (some 1000 in all). The losses then were small. For 3 hours I stood on the end of the spit of what had been rock in 2 feet of water helping the heavily laden men to jump ashore on to submerged dead bodies & trying to persuade the wounded over whom they had to walk that we should soon get them aboard. This is what went on monotonously 'Give me your rifle'; '& your shovel'; 'your left hand'; 'jump wide'; 'it's all right, only kits'; 'keep clear of that man's legs, can't you'. And all the time the gangway along one boat worked to & fro on wounded men; & wounded men were brought to the end of the spit & could not be got aboard because the other stream was more important & never ending, & there they slowly sank & died.

There was hard fighting all that night ashore; our ship was riddled & we could see nothing & not help. But the casualties there were small. So far we had had little help from the fleet but on Monday morning, all our men (say 3000 reduced to 2000) being ashore, the 'Queen Eliz.' & others made the semicircle of hills, & village & fort a lyddite ruin & our Munsters, Dublins & Hampshires, helped on the left by some who had landed at 'W' beach,

[1] John Henry Dives Costeker, 1879–1915. Entered Army, 1898. Staff Captain, Irish Command, 1914. Brigade Major, 4 September 1914 until his death on 25 April 1915.

won the hills. So we now hold 1 mile from the beach all round, the village, castle & crest. I have just come down from the picket line where we have been standing to arms & shooting all night long,—my 3rd sleepless night. The French have landed 3000 & relieved us.

Our guns & men have won golden opinions from the military. Apparently we covered their attack yesterday very well; besides saving them on Sunday. And now let me tell you of the deeds of heroism I witnessed. It is pleasanter, & I could not have believed them possible.

Midshipman Drury[1] of the 'Clyde' swam to the hopper, was wounded in the head, got a line off the hopper & got somehow back to the ship with it. *Cmdr. Unwin*, maddened by the failure of his landing plan, stood up alone on the hopper & hauled surrounded by dead & wounded. He was slightly wounded. He went in again & rowed to the wounded on the rock jetty & loaded them in to the boat under fire. One of our men, *J. H. Russell*, seeing him wounded & unable to lift the men out of the water, went overboard swam to him. He was shot thro' the stomach & with Unwin lay in the water as though dead for a while, got somehow into the boat in a lull, & were pulled back to the ship by a line.

The wounded were still crying & drowning on that awful spit. Lieut. Tidsdale[2] (?) R.N.D. took a boat, one of the 'Clyde's' sailors & one of my men, *Rumming*. They got four men aboard before Tidsdale (?) & the sailor were shot & wounded. Hiding behind the side of the boat they walked & swam it back. I saw one of the wounded stretch out his hand & stroke Rumming's as he hung on to the side, the most pathetic thing I have ever seen. Rumming volunteered again to go ashore with me in the dark & stood (on the dead) for another 3 hours on that horrible spit under occasional fire. I have officially recommended both him & J. H. Russell for the V.C., but I don't know *who* ought really to do that or what course such a recommendation takes.

---

[1] George Leslie Drewry, 1894–1918. Merchant seaman. Castaway for 14 days during a voyage to Cape Horn. Joined the Peninsular and Oriental Steam Navigation Company as an officer, 1912. Joined Royal Naval Reserve, July 1913. Called up for active service as a midshipman, 3 August 1914. For his bravery at the V beach landing he was awarded the Victoria Cross. Lieutenant, Royal Naval Reserve, 1916. Fatally injured while on patrol in command of a trawler in the North Sea, 2 August 1918.

[2] Arthur Walderne St Clair Tisdall, 1890–1915. Educated at Bedford School and Trinity College, Cambridge. Enlisted as an Able Seaman, RNVR, August 1914. Attached to the RND as an interpreter at Antwerp, October 1914. 2nd Lieutenant, October 1914. Sailed for the Dardanelles, February 1915. Twice wounded at 'V' beach, 25 April 1915. Killed in action, 6 May 1915. His collected poems from 1909 to 1912 and his letters from Gallipoli were published in 1916 as *Verses, Letters and Remembrances of Arthur Walderne St Clair Tisdall*. All the verse he wrote after 1912, together with his diary, were lost at Gallipoli.

In the evening my *sublieut. Parkes, C.P.O. J. Little,* & *P.O.'s Barton, Tailyour, Cecil Murray* went out to help the detachments of wounded on the beach.[1] They went westward to the furthest boat's crew, about a mile; landed two wounded from one sinking boat; found in the furthest boat 7 wounded, 9 dead, (the shells will keep going over my head, & bursting 50 yards further & I have to stop at the end of each pair of lines to lie down. I will indicate by a **X** in future.) & two Maxims; & that boat they rowed back to the ship. **X** The Turks were not shooting, but they passed them within 50 yards like cats in **X** the dark.

Then **X** yesterday the Munsters, without officers, could not face the last bit of the charge on the Old Castle hill. They were dead tired, not afraid. Col. Wylie,[2] intelligence officer being on board the 'Clyde',[3] ran ashore & without cap or rifle **X** dashed up to them & led them on & fell at the crest with a bullet thro' his head.

Just 100 yards from me by the beach lie, each two yards from the other, facing the enemy, 5 heroic Munsters. Right at the beginning on Sunday, after ⅘ths of their comrades had fallen, these 5 ran forward to cut the wire entanglement, a hopeless thing to attempt; but what courage it must have required.

You may be very well satisfied with your 3rd Squadron of 'Armoured Cars'. As soon as they & we are rested, we are going forward on foot with the 29th Division.

[1] Of those mentioned in the previous three paragraphs, Midshipman George L. Drewry, RNR, and Lieutenant Tisdall, were both awarded the Victoria Cross for their part in the landing. Petty Officer J. H. Russell, RNAS, and Petty Officer Rummings, RNAS, were both specially mentioned by Vice-Admiral Wemyss for 'extraordinarily gallant conduct'; Russell was later killed in action, at Passchendaele in 1917. J. Little was killed in action at the Dardanelles in June 1915; J. F. St C. Barton was killed in action in France in 1918.

[2] Charles Hotham Montagu Doughty-Wylie, 1868–1915. Entered Army, 1889. Severely wounded in the South African war, 1900. Major, 1907. British Consul, Addis Ababa, 1909–12 and 1913–14. Director, British Red Cross, Turkey, 1912–13. Lieutenant-Colonel, 1915. Killed at V Beach, Gallipoli, 26 April 1915; he was awarded a posthumous Victoria Cross.

[3] The *River Clyde* lay aground at V Beach until 1919, when she was sold by the Royal Navy to a Spanish shipping company and renamed *Angela*. In 1929 she was sold again, to another Spanish company, and renamed *Maruja y Aurora*. She plied as a collier on the Spanish coast until 1966, when she was broken up—sixty-one years after having been launched at Port Glasgow.

Will you please send a copy of this letter to my daughter, Helen Wedgwood,[1] Clough Hall, Newnham College, Cambridge.

I am going to lie down & sleep, the first sleep for 3 eternal days & nights.

Yours

Josiah C. Wedgwood

H. H. Asquith to George V
(Cabinet papers: 37/127)

27 April 1915   10 Downing Street

Mr Asquith, with his humble duty to Your Majesty, has the honour to report that the Cabinet met yesterday.

Lord Kitchener & Mr Churchill described the latest phases of the operations in France & the Dardanelles. . . .

Sir E. Grey reported that the agreement of Alliance between Italy & the Entente Powers had been signed on behalf of all the parties immediately before the meeting of the Cabinet.

The importance of bringing in Bulgaria, and the danger of an anti-Bulgarian movement on the part of Greece & Serbia, were again discussed. . . .

Lord Fisher to Winston S. Churchill
(Churchill papers: 13/57)

27 April 1915   Admiralty

Dear Winston.

. . . Fitzgerald told me last night that Ian Hamilton *had carte blanche to send for more troops from Egypt. All the same I hope you sent your telegram.*

In haste from

F

---

[1] Helen Bowen Wedgwood, 1895–   . Josiah Wedgwood's eldest daughter. Educated at Newnham College, Cambridge. In 1920 she married Michael Stewart Pease (who died in 1960). She became a Justice of the Peace, 1925.

Winston S. Churchill to John Churchill: telegram

(*Copy, Churchill papers: 13/65*)

27 April 1915   Admiralty
Private & Secret

[I refrain from rejoicing till results are further defined but][1] I hope your
friend will ask in good time for more men if he wants them. There must
be another 20,000 available at a pinch in Egypt. I am sure he would be
supported if he asked through the regular channels. I only refer to this by
way of precaution. Show this only to your friend.

Vice-Admiral de Robeck to Winston S. Churchill

(*Churchill papers: 13/51*)

28 April 1915   H.M.S. Queen E.

Dear Mr Churchill,
    As the General has a King's Messenger leaving at once, I send just a short
line this evening & pray excuse a long letter from a very tired person?
Nothing could have exceeded the good co-operation between the services &
the landing of the troops established a record in every way; the taking of the
Cape Helles defences & Seddel-Bahr was one of the most gallant & desperate
efforts ever undertaken by troops & must live for all time! The Australians
rushed the beach North of Kaba Tepe in the most wonderful way & rushed
up the ridges & evidently exhausted themselves in their efforts, afterwards
being very heavily shrapnelled all day, they got rather rattled, but are now
doing splendidly; though still want room & are very tired! At the Cape
Helles end today the troops did not make the progress that was hoped,
mainly owing to the men wanting a rest & the Turks are showing wonderful
courage & make any number of counter attacks, their losses are reported as
being very heavy, as also are ours & if we can only hold on to what we have
got, we shall do all right, though more troops will be required to make a
great success! As regards the Fleet our efforts for the present must be devoted
to assisting the army & securing their position, the expenditure of ammunition is heavy, but it was absolutely necessary owing to the Army having very
few guns on shore at present & the ground where the Australians are making
it impossible to get them into action! Still by all reports from prisoners it

---

[1] Churchill deleted the words in square brackets before sending this telegram.

has not been thrown away & the Turks have suffered. Today during a counter attack by the enemy the 'Q.E.' got a 15" shrapnel right into a large body & it looked to wipe them clean out, Turks, rifles, & bayonets going in all directions & it must have its effect on the enemy's troops. 'Q.E.' also got a transport off Maidos yesterday, third round range 15,600, indirect fire, with the assistance of the balloon; the steamer was seen to sink in a few minutes after being hit! The other ships have all done splendidly & the devotion of officers & men of the boats crews & beach party when landing the troops was magnificent, I hear wonderful accounts & when collected will be forwarded. Between Cape Helles & Seddel Bahr we ran the S.S. 'River Clyde' ashore with two thousand men on board & she was our salvation as the covering party in the boats got almost entirely 'wiped out' & the steamer proved herself a fort, as the troops could not advance from the beach— The trenches & wire defences being of the most exceptional order & the machine guns could not be located & for the whole day no advance could be made! Lieut Unwin & a RNR midshipman behaved like heroes aboard her from all accounts. From the W/T reports I think both A.E.2 & E.14 are now safely through the Dardanelles & expect that they will soon exert a great effect on the operations.[1]

Poor Brodie in E15 no doubt got carried over by the current on to Kephez point & the picket boat attack in order to destroy her was truly a worthy piece of courageous effort & I was with all the Fleet delighted at Robinson's[2] promotion, he has *no* fear!

The aircraft have done a great amount of good works, especially for the military & best of all for our work is the balloon & only wish we had more of them. The fleet are all ready to have another attack on the Chanak defences & only await the right moment. We are sweeping up a good many mines still, whether they have been laid or have drifted out of the mine field after our explosive creeps have parted their moorings is hard to say. I

[1] While in the Sea of Marmara the British submarine E.14 sank a Turkish transport ship (29 April), sank a troopship (10 May) and forced a small steamer to go aground (13 May); she returned through the Dardanelles to the Aegean on 18 May. The Australian submarine AE2 was sunk on 30 April while trying to enter the Sea of Marmara; most of her crew were captured.

[2] Eric Gascoigne Robinson, 1882–1965. Entered Navy, 1897. Wounded during the Boxer rising, China, 1900. Lieutenant-Commander, 1914. Commanded a picket boat at the Dardanelles; he disabled the E.15 submarine which had run aground off Kephez Point—within a few hundred yards of a Turkish fort; promoted Commander for this action. Wounded at the Suvla Bay landing, and invalided home. Awarded the Victoria Cross for his bravery at Gallipoli. Commanded a Flotilla in the Caspian Sea, 1919. Captain, 1920. Commanded Torpedo Schoolship, Devonport, 1926–8. Deputy Superintendent, Devonport Dockyard, 1932. Rear-Admiral, 1933.

have made Captain Heneage[1] take entire charge of the sweeping arrangements, it was too big an undertaking for a Commander & H. is an expert in that line. It has been a delightful pleasure to deal with Sir I. Hamilton & both services are pulling splendidly together, we realize we have a difficult undertaking; but we *must win!*

Thank you for all your support & believe me when I say I appreciate it from the bottom of my heart, even if I dont say so!

Believe me, yrs sincerely
J M de Robeck

Lord Kitchener to Winston S. Churchill
(*Churchill papers: 13/51*)

28 April 1915   War Office

My dear Churchill,

Canada is making considerable fuss about our not being able to supply them with transports for a division ready to embark as soon as ships are available— Could you hurry this up as we want the division badly—

Yours very truly
Kitchener

Winston S. Churchill to Lord Kitchener
(*Copy, Churchill papers: 13/51*)

28 April 1915   Admiralty

My dear Kitchener

Please see enclosed wh answers your letter to me of this afternoon.

Yours sincly
WSC

---

[1] Algernon Walker-Heneage, 1871–1952. Entered Navy, 1886. Captain, commanding First Squadron of Minelayers, 1914. In charge of minesweeping arrangements, Dardanelles, 1915. Commodore commanding Small Vessels, Eastern Mediterranean, 1915–16. Commanded Allied barrage in Straits of Otranto, 1917. Senior British Naval Officer in Italy, 1917–18. Rear-Admiral, 1918. Assumed surname Walker-Heneage-Vivian, 1921. Retired, 1920. Admiral, 1927.

Graeme Thomson to Winston S. Churchill
(*Churchill papers: 13/51*)

28 April 1915　　　　　　　　　　　　　　　　　　Admiralty

First Lord,

The Admiralty has never been asked to provide Transports for the Canadian reinforcements or divisions until the receipt of a telegram from War Office at about 5.30 p.m. to-day. Arrangements have so far been made by the Canadian Government.

As has already been communicated verbally to the War Office, I am not in a position to give an estimate of any value of the time required to carry the division and reinforcements until I have been able to communicate with Shipping Firms.

I am prosecuting enquiries in England, Canada and United States of America, but in the meantime my own opinion is that we could embark 10,000 men (without horses or artillery) in about 10 days time. I understand this is the most urgent requirement.

I am quite unable to furnish any estimate of the time required before we can embark the remainder until replies are received to telegrams already despatched.

Director of Transports

Sir Edward Grey to Winston S. Churchill
(*Admiralty papers: 116/1681*)

29 April 1915　　　　　　　　　　　　　　　　　Foreign Office

Dear Churchill,

My opinion and experience of this affair is that De la Force[1] has from the beginning ruined any chance of getting these rifles & that the chance has long ago disappeared.

It is now proposed to induce United States officials as well as Brazilian Embassy in the United States to give an appearance that De la Force represents neutral buyers.

This is untrue & a sheer fraud & the result may be a scandal that will jeopardize the export of ammunition from the United States. To bring

---

[1] Captain William de la Force, an arms dealer whom Churchill was using in an attempt to purchase Brazilian rifles. Churchill had instructed de la Force not to disclose that he was acting on behalf of the British Admiralty. Churchill ignored Grey's injunction, and the negotiations continued; but on 9 May 1915 the Brazilians finally refused to sell the rifles.

United States officials into this matter is disastrous & will cause the greatest resentment in the United States.

The whole business seems to me to have become most dangerous & I think it essential in the public interest that the legation at Rio should keep out of it & stand aside.

Y sincerely

E. Grey

John Churchill to Winston S. Churchill

(Churchill papers: 1/117)

29 April 1915   HMS Queen Elizabeth

The messenger has not left and so I can add a little.[1]

I have just been ashore at Z beach and seen the Australians. Their landing was marvellous. Sir Ian landed and we walked along some of their trenches. They started for the shore in the dark and intended to land near Gaba Tepe point. The current took them down the coast about half a mile and they landed opposite a series of very steep ridges. They had been told to keep silent and as they approached the shore, Turks could be seen running along the beach fixing their bayonets. The naval beachmaster told me that not a man made a sound. Then firing began: men were hit frequently and several boats had holes knocked in them. Still no one said a word. The boats reached the sand and the fire became hotter. The men leaped out silently and threw their kits down. Then they broke into a yell and went straight up a place which an hour ago I found difficult to climb. At the top they found a Turkish trench beautifully dug and into this they fell, driving the Turks on to the further ridge. This they also took and held, until the shrapnel became too hot. It is a wonderful story, and if you were to see the place you would wonder how they managed to do it. Providence landed them at a spot which is dead ground for the Turkish guns! Had they landed ½ a mile further south, as was intended, I think they would have been shelled out of existence. The spot at which they are is rough steep scrubby gullies and is very difficult to move over. Yesterday they found 5 men in our uniforms among their supports. They were Turks and were shot at once. A sniper was found in the middle of their camp sitting in some dense scrub with 30 days food and water and 1,000 rounds of ammunition. I think he must have been their regular look out man.

This morning Sir Ian went to V beach. I did not go with him, but I hear

---

[1] To his letter of 27 April 1915 (quoted on pp. 818–24).

that it is a terrible place. It is as I described it to you, an amphi-theatre. The Turks had dug a series of great caves and from them they could shoot anyone on the beach, while guns could not touch them. Four hundred and fifty of our men have already been buried there! It was a death trap. And the fact that the Dublins and Munster Fusiliers were finally able to fight their way up reflects great credit on the man who led them—a Col. Doughty Wylie of G.H.Q., who was killed at the top.

Yesterday Hunter Weston advanced considerably and we spent the day in protecting his left flank. Some of our shooting had a great effect, particularly one 15″ shrapnel which completely annihilated a counter-attack. I have described it in a letter to Goonie which she will show you. To-day there has been a general halt, and little has been going on, although there were lots of bullets flying overhead when we landed at Z, and several nasty looking splashes in the water when we left the destroyer in a launch. The 29th Division have done magnificently and are tired out. They were told to rest and dig in to-day. The R.N.D's. are supporting and landing on both beaches W and Z. The Indian brigade should be fit in a day or two and I think things are quite satisfactory. I wish you were here—you would adore it. It is ten times more interesting than France.

Yours
Jack S. C.

By the way the wire on shore is terrible stuff—very thick and closely barbed. It is fixed to iron stanchions instead of wooden posts. It is mostly at the spots indicated in Sir Ian's secret orders!!

A letter found on a Turk shows that the Austrians told the Turks to expect our attack on the 21st. It is the very day which was originally fixed!!

Vice-Admiral de Robeck to Admiralty: telegram
(Copy, Churchill papers: 13/65)

29 April 1915

Position now quite satisfactory on shore. More troops and stores have been landed, weather today again perfect. Wounded nearly all embarked and sent to Egypt. Ships bombarding batteries as necessary. TRIUMPH set on fire MAIDOS which has been burning for four hours. ALBION was rather badly hit yesterday 28th below water near collision bulkhead; she will continue with squadron after repairing at Mudros.

Vice-Admiral de Robeck to Admiralty: telegram
(*Copy, Churchill papers: 13/65*)

30 April 1915

GOLIATH has left for Egypt. The situation though now satisfactory on shore does not permit of the withdrawal of the Naval support in the least degree. ALBION is temporarily out of action. Success in present operations depends on efficient co-operation. This is worked out to the last man. Any withdrawal of more ships at this moment would dangerously emperil position. There is already a shortage of Officers and men for beach and transport work; ships cannot be further depleted of personnel. I trust their Lordships will leave it to me to inform them the moment ships can be spared.

Frederick Guest to Winston S. Churchill
(*Churchill papers: 26/2*)

30 April 1915   Head-Quarters
                                                                  British Army
Dear Winston,

It was good to hear your voice this morning, and I am so thankful that things are going well. You have been very patient during an anxious time but your courage has been rewarded.

I want you to pause a minute and consider the few following lines—the two outstanding features of this war have shown themselves to be the *submarine* & the *aeroplane*. I wont ask you to think still more how to defeat the former as I expect you think of little else already—But I do urge you to *think* more yourself & *make others think* more of the *aeroplane*.

The aeroplane is the key of the whole problem of this war as far as the land operations are concerned.

The side that watches the enemy & keeps his own movements secret will with absolute certainty win and win easily.

There is an absolutely absurd idea that we have obtained the mastery of the air. We have not even got it over our own little section of 31 miles.

It is true that our airmen do wonderfully brilliant things and have shown courage beyond praise but we have not stopt the enemy from overlooking us practically when ever he really wants to do so. I have seen a great many instances of this during the war but this last week has provided two more.

1. During this weeks fighting I visited a good many of the troops engaged, especially the Cavalry who were in support on the west of the canal. Many

officers who had been there 3 or 4 days told me that the enemy held almost undisputed control of the air—you can imagine with what effect.

2. Yesterday Dunkirk was bombarded—*why with such accuracy*. We think we have located the gun at FESSEI one mile east of DIXMUDE.

The previous day they only reached Rosendaal, 2000 yds short but the Taubes were busy spotting & recording & now they have got the range! A week more of this treatment and the town will be evacuated unless I am much mistaken. But for this aeroplane spotting they would never have hit the place more than once in six months. Certainly not any more than we hit CHANAK at 23,000. Aeroplanes and antiaircraft guns are more important than men or howitzers.

Our anti aircraft guns are beneath contempt— Your own aerodrome at ————[1] is defended by an obsolete 3 pounder, upside down, with a percussion fuze! The enemy force our men to fly at nearly 8000 ft. such is the accuracy of their weapons. Do try and get the W.O. to concentrate on this problem.

Sufficient machines for almost continuous patrolling apart from those necessary for raiding or reconnaisance. And many many more and better antiaircraft guns. This is the golden key to our problem and it will save thousands of lives.

No one can get people thinking better than you can—so have a try—

Yours
Freddie

Winston S. Churchill to Sir Edward Grey
(*Draft, Churchill papers: 13/51*)

30 April 1915   Admiralty

My dear Grey

The Gk telms show that the *Dlles* medicine is working with its normal efficacy. In a couple of days all the artillery of the Dlles army will be landed, & in action. The Southern force will assault Achi Baba. The Sari Bair force ought to make progress against the Turkish communictns. I think you wd be wise to await the result of these operations before relieving this recreant Govt. & unfriendly King from their profound disquietude.

We have won the 1st coup twice over now, but we have never won 2 coups running yet. Bulgaria, not Greece, ought to be our objective now. The distress of the Gk Govt is evident from the telems attached.

[1] The name of the aerodrome is left blank in the original letter.

Their help cannot arrive in time, unless we have a check, when it will certainly be withheld.

Yours ever

W

Captain Glyn to Winston S. Churchill

(Churchill papers: 2/65)

30 April 1915   War Office

Dear Mr Churchill,

. . . I have been longing to have the chance of telling you of various aspects of both Russian & Balkan affairs but you have as usual, Sir, been more than fully occupied. Having been out there one leaves one's heart where the only real movement to smash Germany via Austria now finds its beginning—the Dardanelles. . . .

Yours very sincerely

Ralph Glyn